PETER HENNESSY

Having It So Good

Britain in the Fifties

ALLEN LANE
an imprint of
PENGUIN BOOKS

ALLEN LANE

Published by the Penguin Group
Penguin Books Ltd, 80 Strand, London WC2R ORL, England
Penguin Group (USA) Inc., 375 Hudson Street, New York, New York 10014, USA
Penguin Group (Canada), 90 Eglinton Avenue East, Suite 700, Toronto, Ontario, Canada M4P 2Y3
(a division of Pearson Penguin Canada Inc.)
Penguin Ireland, 25 St Stephen's Green, Dublin 2, Ireland (a division of Penguin Books Ltd)
Penguin Group (Australia), 250 Camberwell Road,
Camberwell, Victoria 3124, Australia (a division of Pearson Australia Group Pty Ltd)
Penguin Books India Pvt Ltd, 11 Community Centre,
Panchsheel Park, New Delhi – 110 017, India
Penguin Group (NZ), 67 Apollo Drive, Mairangi Bay, Auckland 1310, New Zealand
(a division of Pearson New Zealand Ltd)
Penguin Books (South Africa) (Pty) Ltd, 24 Sturdee Avenue,
Rosebank, Johannesburg 2196, South Africa

Penguin Books Ltd, Registered Offices: 80 Strand, London WC2R ORL, England

www.penguin.com

First published 2006
1

Set in Linotype Sabon
Typeset by Palimpsest Book Production Limited, Grangemouth, Stirlingshire
Printed in Great Britain by Clays Ltd, St Ives plc

A CIP catalogue record for this book is available from the British Library

ISBN-13: 978-0-713-99571-8
ISBN-10: 0-713-99571-8

For Chelly Halsey, Richard Hoggart,
the late Anthony Sampson
and the late Michael Young
with gratitude for making me think about
the years encompassed herein.

Contents

Illustrations

Acknowledgements

In writing on Britain in the Fifties I have benefited from a host of companions – written, visual, sonic and oral from the decade itself and professionals, such as my friend and indispensably meticulous editor Stuart Proffitt and his team at Penguin. The Department of History at Queen Mary, as always, has provided my ideal home for trying out thoughts and pooling information with staff and students alike. In recent years my research students have run their own Mile End Group which has been the most stimulating forum I have ever encountered in which to discuss postwar Britain with both Queen Mary regulars and a stream of outside participants and contributors. Warm thanks are also due to the staff of the National Archives and the record sections of Whitehall departments, particularly the Cabinet Office, for their constant help with the discovery and release of documents. The book has been strongly influenced, too, by the television series *What Has Become of Us?* prepared by Rob and Gill Shepherd for Channel 4 in 1993–4. Working with them was a special pleasure.

I should also like to express gratitude and acknowledgement to the Trustees of the Harold Macmillan Book Trust for permission to quote from the Macmillan diaries and thanks also to the staff of the Bodleian Library, Oxford, where the unpublished entries are preserved. One of my students, Matt Lyus, deserves special mention as my expert word-processor. He has fingers nimble on the keyboard and a mind well primed on the details of the road from 1945. I am immensely grateful, too, to Trevor Horwood (my ace copy-editor) and to Sam Johnson (of Penguin) and Chris Walley (of *The Times*) for marvellous help with picture research.

Walthamstow and Mile End, July 2006

Prelude

'... *the chances of war brought to England, either as soldiers or as refugees, hundreds and thousands of foreigners who would not normally have come here, and forced them into intimate contact with ordinary people ... Those of them who had the gift of observation will have seen for themselves that the real England is not the England of the guide-books. Blackpool is more typical than Ascot ...*'

George Orwell, 1943–4.[1]

'*England was stuck in the Thirties until the Sixties.*'   Jonathan Miller, 1999.[2]

If I were asked to recall the formative childhood decade of my British life, I would arouse my memory with a film, and a very obscure one at that. *Holiday* was made in Blackpool by British Transport Films, the cine arm of the British Transport Commission which, in a ramshackle and cash-strapped fashion, held together the railways, waterways and lorries the Attlee government had brought into public ownership in the late 1940s.

For me, *Holiday* mixes the prosaic and the magical. Its executive producer was Edgar Anstey, a titan of the film documentary movement[3] who would go on to win an Oscar for his craft in the mid-1960s. The colour photography was by David Watkin and the music from Chris Barber's Traditional Jazz Band, one of the stars of the Blackpool summer season of 1956, when the picture was shot, as Britain was moving towards its disastrous war in the Middle East at the peak of the Suez crisis.

A mere seventeen minutes long, *Holiday* opens with its title in spangly, jaunty letters reminiscent of the graphics used to promote the 1951 Festival of Britain.[4] A whistle sounds. Unseen, a steam train rattles, brakes and squeaks to a halt. The first shot is of holidaymakers alighting in the sunshine in great numbers and lugging suitcases along platforms 11 and 12 of Blackpool station (plentiful trains and great surges of passengers demanded many berths in those days). The men are dressed in jackets over open-necked shirts, the women are in flouncy summer dresses and their children wear smaller versions of the same. But for the post-nationalization BR red-and-cream liveried rolling stock, it could still be the 1930s.

The voiceovers in *Holiday* are brief, allowing the pictures and the jazz to carry it. The opening burst of commentary has a touch of the Jonathan Miller 1930s fusing with the 1950s about it. Delivered in standard BBC English, it declares that

Journey's end is also a beginning. Sun and breeze bring a first reviving whiff and promise of the world of *Holiday*. Office and kitchen, school and factory and mill have escaped to the seaside of Lancashire.

Mum and Dad, Lass and Lad – they come back here for as long as we can remember. What excitements this year? What romance? What thrills await us now?

By now, the holidaymakers are streaming past the station's redbrick Victorian façade. It was in the 1870s that industrial Lancashire and Yorkshire really took to the seaside.[5] By the 1930s, 7 million visitors came to Blackpool every summer.[6]

Suddenly there is a roll of drums and *Holiday* hurls itself into thrill backed up by traditional jazz – two divers fling themselves from a great height into Blackpool's huge open-air swimming baths – you can almost smell the chlorine. Chris Barber's Band strike up and the film swiftly cuts to wind-blown, smiling, exuberant young women, jumpered and pearled, atop the seafront big-dipper.

The music shifts again, to the distinctive voice of Ottilie Patterson, Chris Barber's wife, singing 'I Wish That I Could Shimmy Like My Sister Kate' and the camera spies on open-air dancers before moving to the crowds walking the promenade. Most are tidy and groomed, the women in slacks or skirts and just the occasional cowboy hat or Teddy Boy hairstyle among the younger men. There is a lad in an RAF uniform, part of the National Service generation required to man the late imperial garrisons in Malaya and the new Cold War frontlines in Germany. The older men are in suits; their ladies tote huge handbags. There are no black or brown faces. Commonwealth immigration was underway but the extended families from the Empire had yet to take their holidays on this strip of the mother country's edge.

The seafront offers still more evocations of the 'long 1930s'. Nearly all the stars of that Blackpool season came from the music hall/variety tradition or the apogee of Britain's radio days. The diminutive yet 'big hearted' Arthur Askey is top of the bill in 'Love and Kisses'. On the hoardings are Morecambe and Wise, Tommy Cooper, Ruby Murray (a singer later immortalized in rhyming slang for curry) as well as the Barber Band. The camera lingers intrigued over the freak shows ('Why did they let it live!' a hoarding grimly inquires); sticky pink and white rock shot through with BLACKPOOL; whelks in close-up; hot dogs and onions; Yates' famous wine lodge with its 'Champagne on Draught'. (Nearly twenty years later, while reporting from a Conservative Party conference, I took Rhodes Boyson there. Rhodes was never exactly a shrinking violet, but seemed slightly ill at ease. The reason, as he explained in his broad East Lancashire tones, was that his temperance parents had held up the Blackpool Yates' Wine Lodge as the ultimate temple of Mammon![7])

From bustle to tranquillity, the scene shifts to a quiet stretch of the Fylde coast down towards the Ribble estuary. Dunes, marram grass aplenty and the shore empty but for a homemade sand yacht sweeping and turning to the captivating sounds of Monty Sunshine's clarinet leading the Barber Band into 'When Love Comes to Call'. Back to the heart of Blackpool as the jazz strikes up 'Everybody Loves My Baby' and we are in the middle of a poolside beauty competition. The girls are plumpish (an alluring quality in the Fifties), in one-piece swimsuits and highheels, carrying before them a heart-shaped card with their competition number on it. There's not a bikini in sight. Men and women in the watching crowd are quite formally dressed and often behatted. Where the men are bare-headed, Brylcreem glistens in the sunshine. (This was the era of Denis Compton, the 'Brylcreem Boy' and cavalier batsman for Middlesex and England, whose agent bagged one of the first modern money-making deals linking a sportsman with a personal consumer good.[8]) The winner, looking remarkably like Marilyn Monroe, sheds a fetching tear in the sunshine as a sleek-haired middle-aged worthy drapes the coveted sash across her bosom.

The voiceover informs us that it is now the 'height and heat of the day'. Scenes of lunchtime pints and flirting adolescents while Monty Sunshine improvises on his clarinet. Only an occasional pair of jeans is seen among the dresses and flannel trousers, for 1956 was just a little before the full-scale denim revolution.

All ages are holidaying together. Grans and grandads seated in the seafront shelters write on picture postcards while their grandchildren look on. Boys with homemade go-carts wait for new arrivals outside the railway station to carry luggage to the boarding houses for a bob or two. The boarding houses are refilling as families come back for 'dinner' (such establishments habitually offered two, sometimes three, meals a day before bed and breakfast became the norm).

'Once more the sap rises,' intones the narrator, '. . . and the signal sounds for afternoon,' cueing in 'Whistlin' Rufus' from Chris Barber. Families walk from boarding house to beach. There's a little boy in short trousers, cap and sandals. (It could have been me except that, at that time, I'd have been in Herne Bay or Sandown, Isle of Wight.) The beach is quickly packed as are the shallows. The children's swimsuits (elasticated, chunky-ruched for the girls, tight fitting woollen trunks for the boys) rounded off for the non-swimmers by plastic inflatable rings. Dads with rolled-up trousers and milk-bottle legs supervise their paddling offspring.

Deckchairs abound, with hardly a gap between them; masses of polka-dots on skirts; black plastic sunglasses with white rims. One hot and bored girl is plainly resisting the tentative foreplay of a young man. Another nuzzles happily on her bloke's shoulder as they lie on a towel.

Swoop up to the top of Blackpool Tower. A young boy, his father behind him grinning and sporting an RAF handlebar moustache, trains a telescope activated by a sixpence in the slot on the discontented couple on the beach, the girl looking moodier than ever. A Brownie box camera snaps the foreshore between the Tower and one of the huge piers. Trams rumble below.

Now it's sunset. A summer haze mixes with the Blackpool coal smoke (the Clean Air Act of 1956 has yet to change the habits of the grate). The Tower is in silhouette. Thoughts of young and old turn towards the evening. Ottilie Patterson asks 'Ain't We Going To Have A Time Tonight?'

Suddenly it's dark, summer is over and the famous Blackpool illuminations blaze out from fixed roadside latticework and mobile gaudy trams alike. On the tram, a young man and a young woman cuddle up, gaberdine mac to gaberdine mac. Two small children, perhaps brother and sister, are captivated by it all from their top-deck seat on the tram. They chatter away and point, she in a red bonnet he in his Cub cap. (This, again, could have been me!) Fireworks illuminate the sky as, between the bursts, the director, John Taylor, reprises David Watkin's sequences of shots – the diving; the big dipper; the sand yacht.

Holiday is a snapshot, a warm vignette of a settled moment in national life flecked with gold, or so it can easily seem to eyes such as mine which first glimpsed the world in 1947. Yet danger lurks among the sentiments it stimulates. Richard Hoggart, a matchless evoker of the smell, the feel and the language of mid-century Britain, has warned about the dangerous relationship between memory and nostalgia: 'Nostalgia is sticky memory, unable to let memory stand free; emotion has overflowed.'[9]

That society, in which anyone over thirty had personal memories of slump and war, had a sense of the fragility of life and the caprice of events and, by 1956, an appreciation of how the world might end in a nuclear cataclysm that could trump any previous shared catastrophe. Prosperity might be growing, with full employment seemingly assured and a health service still seen as a talisman of national progress, but the 'never again' impulse – and all the manifestations of a 'better yesterday', to borrow Ralf Dahrendorf's phrase[10] – might prove shallowly rooted.

There was anxiety mixed with pleasure and yet, in many ways, it was, as *Holiday* depicted, a relatively golden time, a more innocent age before the jets from Manchester Ringway took the place of the holiday steam specials and the Blackpool sands lost pride of place to those of Torremolinos. From the Suez summer and autumn of 1956, illusion after illusion was reluctantly and sometimes painfully shattered for the settled people on that *Holiday* beach and those who governed them. Even by 1960 Anstey's film might have already struck the discerning viewer as an evocation of a world we were losing. Some of that world's more socially rigid aspects we were well rid of; other solidarities less so or not at all. But dull to live through it was not. It was, as Jonathan Miller expressed it, 'all part of the ice-break and . . . it was nice to be in the floe'.[11]

Overture

'Let's be frank about it; most of our people have never had it so good. Go around the country, go to the industrial towns, go to the farms, and you will see a state of prosperity such as we have never had in my lifetime – nor indeed ever in the history of this country. What is beginning to worry some of us is, "Is it too good to be true?" or perhaps I should say, "Is it too good to last?"'

Harold Macmillan, speech at Bedford football ground, 20 July 1957.[1]

'With regard to the general result of the Election, naturally my colleagues and I . . . are more than satisfied. But we realise the heavy work that lies ahead, both at home and abroad. The people at home have become accustomed to a very high and stable economic situation. The slightest change in the barometer, although it might be due to factors quite outside our control, would correspondingly depress them. Abroad, although hopeful, they are a little more realistic.

'The most encouraging feature of the Election, however, from Your Majesty's point of view, is the strong impression that I have formed that Your Majesty's subjects do not wish to allow themselves to be divided into warring classes or tribes filled with hereditary animosity against each other. There was a very significant breakdown of this structure of society which, in spite of its many material advantages, was one of the chief spiritual disadvantages of the first industrial revolution. It will be curious if the second industrial revolution, through the wide spread of amenities of life to almost every home in the country, succeeds in destroying this unfortunate product of the first. At any rate, anything that makes Your Majesty's subjects more conscious of their unity and of their duty to each other seems to me to be a real gain.'

Harold Macmillan to the Queen, 10 October 1959, the day after winning the general election of 8 October with a majority of 100 seats[2]

'One of the difficulties of being an Englishman in 1950 is the persistent delusion that it is after the deluge. It is not. The deluge is still with us . . . Britain has commitments far greater than she could possibly fulfil . . . Insistence on its traditional rights by a

power in decline leads perilously quickly to war ... The peace of the world depends therefore on the Englishman being able to reconcile himself to a continuous diminution in the consequence of his country. This can only be done if he can learn to separate his personal prestige from the prestige of his nation state.' Peter Laslett, 1950[3]

'Gradually we discovered that life had three components. There was "now", which is what we thought we understood, there was "during the war", which was, it seemed, a very important topic of conversation and there was "before the war", which had golden connotations of great times, quality (of goods) and something lost. It took time ... to realise that not everything that happened "before" was preferable to what was happening "now" and in the better years to come.'

Howard Mallinson recalling an early-1950s childhood in 2001[4]

This is the second volume of a general history of Britain since 1945. The first, *Never Again*, was written in the late 1980s and early 1990s about the 1940s and the tail-end of the Attlee governments of 1945–51. A general title for *Never Again*, *Having It So Good* and the volumes on the Sixties, Seventies and Eighties that will follow might be 'The Road from 1945' or 'The Long Postwar: From Victory in Europe Day 1945 to the Fall of the Berlin Wall in 1989'.

Taken together the first two studies embrace what I see as 'The Short Postwar' which was the period from the triumphant, if exhausting, outcome of 1939–45 to the early months of 1960 which saw a significant reappraisal of Britain's place in the world and a growing recognition of Britain's incapacity to sustain the level of influence its political class still craved in the bipolar age of American and Soviet superpowerdom. This book's hinge is the traumatic Suez crisis of the summer and autumn of 1956, when a combined Anglo-French invasion of Egypt was halted in unconcealably humiliating circumstances by American pressure, stimulating a determined effort to restore the US–UK special relationship and a succession of mainly private but genuinely agonizing reappraisals within Whitehall.

To a remarkable degree, the memory of the United Kingdom's superb collective performance between 1939 and 1945 (especially the year of 'standing alone' against the dictatorships between the fall of France in June 1940 and Hitler's attack on the Soviet Union in June 1941) sustained the country through the vicissitudes of successive economic crises and waning global power in the Forties and Fifties. These were, in Mark Connelly's words, the images and memories which stood up 'like a rock in a sea of mediocrity'[5] well into the 1960s for a country which had taken 'the applause of the world' as the only combatant nation fighting the Second World War from its first day till its last.[6] As a child they were my images and memories too and they still shape and colour my approach as a historian and author.

In a sense, the 'Road from 1945' volumes are (and will be) the story of my generation, my age. My clear memory dates back to 1951 (when I was four). So, unlike in the pages of *Never Again*, I am a conscious figure in the chapters that follow, especially after the Suez affair, since which time I have read at least one newspaper every day. And, like everyone else in 'my age', I can be transported back in a moment to the 1950s by coal smoke on a damp wind, a glimpse of an old lady in a grey pakamac, a snatch of Perry Como singing 'Magic Moments'[7] or even the sight of a bottle of Babycham.

But between Perry Como and, as it were, the defiant strains of 'Land of Hope and Glory', *Having It So Good* seeks to reconstruct the making of the society Macmillan sought to describe for the Queen in the glowing moment of his and the Conservative Party's triumph in autumn 1959. His letter touched on both the pleasures of domestic economic consumption that surpassed any previously enjoyed by her subjects and what the new Prime Minister saw as increasing national realism about the Cold War and Britain's position as a global power. One of the pleasures of writing this volume has been the meta-phorical company of Harold Macmillan, a politician who thought, breathed, acted and, above all, wrote historically (in his diary especially) as he went.

Macmillan was an eloquent exponent of centrist politics – the pursuit of a middle way. And since the mid-1970s there has been a vigorous argument among historians about whether a 'postwar consensus' was indeed achieved which embraced the essentials of politics, political economy and the role of the state as the knitter of a safety net for society as a whole.[8] There was a high and noisy level of partisanship about some aspects of Labour's 1945 pro-gramme. Michael Young, drafter of the Labour manifesto *Let Us Face the Future*,[9] characterized its core as 'Beveridge plus Keynes plus socialism'[10] – welfare, full employment and nationalization. And there certainly was not a consensus on public ownership, the nationalization of iron and steel in par-ticular. But on the welfare/full-employment front there existed an usually high level of agreement between the two main political parties.

For example both Denis Healey on the Labour side and Quintin Hogg (later Lord Hailsham) for the Conservatives reckoned general agreement covered 80 per cent of the policy spectrum in the late 1940s and early 1950s and, in Healey's words fifty years later, 'most of the remaining 20 per cent had to do with nationalisation'.[11] In Chapter 1 I outline my own view that there *was* a high level of agreement in the early postwar years around a set of politics which, taken together, amounted to a British 'New Deal'. Though nobody else at the time or since has borrowed that label from Franklin Roosevelt's America and attached it, suitably modified, to the Britain of Attlee, Churchill, Eden and Macmillan, it is a theme that will run throughout the book.

My approach mixes the thematic and the chronological. I examine several moments of especially revealing crisis, including some that went largely unreported at the time such as the proposal to float the pound in early 1952 which, unknown to Parliament, split the Cabinet. The easing of official secrecy since preparing *Never Again* has also enabled me to revisit certain nuclear and intelligence aspects of the late 1940s in a detail not available to me when writing in the late 1980s.

The book opens with an examination of the society in which political life sought to operate as Mr Attlee's Britain gave way to Mr Churchill's. The powerful and worrying theme of British people living in the shadow of nuclear weapons features strongly, just as it did in the mind of Winston Churchill. Another important aspect of Churchill's last premiership, though a pleasurable one in this instance, was the Coronation of Queen Elizabeth II in 1953 and the widespread but not quite universal celebration of what a later generation would call 'national identity' that accompanied it.

Evident throughout is the attempt by every set of Cabinet ministers and their advisers to maintain a British influence in world affairs beyond a level which the country's population, economic performance and military capability could, at face value, be expected to sustain. In this context, there is a danger that shared historical memory will recall the Eden premiership for only one event: the Suez crisis. Shattering and lastingly repercussive though Suez was and remains,* there was much more to his twenty-one months in office, as will be examined in Chapter 8.

Macmillan, though in personal terms the greatest single beneficiary of Eden's demise, was scarred by the experience of Suez. Its significance and memory was in the air at almost every meeting of Cabinet Committee and secret review team between November 1956 and early 1960, when the Prime Minister began to nudge his colleagues towards a more realistic and less imperialistic approach to their country's place in the world. Late-Fifties Britain,

---

* Just as the book was going to press, the Cabinet Office released a scattering of Suez-related documents as we shall see in Chapter 9.

too, saw the beginnings of a cluster of social and attitudinal changes, only partly influenced by Suez – the succession of social 'dam bursts' that provide Chapter 11 with its title.

One member of 'my age', Bob Morris, who observed many a social shift as a senior civil servant in the Home Office, described early-Fifties Britain as 'a right, tight, screwed-down society walled in in every way'.[12] It certainly appears that way in retrospect as, to a significant degree, it did to many in the last years of the decade when the respectable and the traditional were subjected to a rising clamour of criticism and challenge which often baffled the generation in authority, not least the Prime Minister himself.

Finally, as Macmillan and his top Whitehall advisers did, I attempt an audit of Britain's wealth, power and influence as the decades turned. But the thinking and arguments of the powerful in their private offices and their committee rooms is only part of the story. I come from a British historical tradition that is uneasy with high politics absorbed neat. It is vital to try to convey the smell, feel and sound of an age – especially if one has lived through it oneself – and it is with the grain of early-Fifties society that the book begins.

I

The British New Deal and the Essentials of Life

'We all turned up in cars from various corners of the Kingdom and I realised that, whatever our differences, we had common membership of that tiny proportion of the human race who learnt to fly an aeroplane before driving a car. My most vivid impression from that reunion was that here were five grammar school boys who, admittedly after common moulding as RAF pilots, went off to various careers in industry, commerce and education, and to various levels of income and status, and to quite different party-political loyalties, yet remained essentially solidaristic as Englishmen who had been made patriotic collectivists by war.'

A. H. (Chelly) Halsey writing in 1996 about the 1973 reunion of the RAF group with whom he trained in 1944–5.[1]

'I was born during the War. To talk of "the War" nowadays is to define oneself as a child of the forties as surely as printing one's birth certificate, but at least until recently you could be confident of sharing a common language; the Falklands and the Gulf have forced us not to take so much for granted. It was "the War" that provided the basic grammar for my parents' lives ... The period of the War was invoked with mathematical regularity through our childhood and their memories wound up and regulated our emotional clock.'   Richard Eyre, 1993.[2]

'The leading problem of modern British history is the explanation of economic decline.'   Martin Wiener, 1981.[3]

'The great press baron, Lord Northcliffe, used to tell his journalists that four subjects could be relied upon for abiding public interest: crime, love, money and food. Only the last of these is fundamental and universal. Crime is a minority interest even in the worst regulated societies. It is possible to imagine an economy without money and reproduction without love but not life without food ... It is what matters most to most people for most of the time.'   Felipe Fernández-Armesto, 2001.[4]

6

This chapter and the next are about the state of Britain in the early 1950s – the configurations of society, the patterns of consumption and the condition of the economy which underpinned them. It is a story of easement tinged with anxiety, a paradox which, in a way, captures Britain in the Fifties as a whole. Woven into the mix are two of the historical debates which, in the last quarter of the twentieth century, came together to make much of the political weather – consensus and relative economic decline.

It would have needed a clairvoyant with a strong streak of pessimism in his or her make-up in the early 1950s to have foreseen this conjunction. One must, therefore, begin with the political and social climate of the time which derived from recent experiences and current preoccupations. For, in the early Fifties, the shadows of the world war past (1939–45), the limited war present (Korea) and the possibility of absolute war[5] future (terminal) were ever present.* The first was the remarkable shared experience a mere six years or so in the past, which still conditions the debate about the period to a high degree. Ross McKibbin, the leading historian of class and culture in England (his geographical delineation) from the end of the Great War to the installation of Churchill's peacetime government, saw a remarkable paradox between great political change and palpable social and institutional continuity:

Anyone who visited England in 1939 and then in 1950 would have been astonished at the political transformation. The extraordinary hegemony of the Conservative Party had been overthrown quite unexpectedly and in its stead a Labour government had carried through a programme of social welfare and nationalization which would have seemed impossible in 1939. But the visitor would have found the institutions of civil society almost wholly recognizable and the old 'ideological apparatus of the state' largely intact. Outside the realm of social services or nationalized industries the visitor would have not observed a social democracy.[6]

It is difficult to describe what a working 'social democracy' fully imple-mented and moving into maturity would look like. But McKibbin has a point when he argues that: 'The Attlee government operated deeply, but on a narrow front. As an instance, it abolished the voluntary hospitals but left intact an independent education sector which guaranteed those who attended it a privileged access to both public and private markets without equal in any com-parable country, and which enormously reinforced social stratification; and it

---

* The singular shadow of the bomb will be examined in Chapter 3.

encouraged the development of a system of secondary education in which Labour's working-class supporters were definitely not favoured.'[7]

In September 1940 during the London Blitz, in the very first phase of that transforming shared experience which, taken as a whole, propelled Mr Attlee and his party to power inside five years, George Orwell had examined exactly this phenomenon – the enduring features of England. As for McKibbin, the dominant nation within the Union was his social prism. Even at a potentially revolutionary moment, his celebrated essay, 'The Lion and the Unicorn', saw England as a 'family with the wrong members in control'.[8] Perhaps McKibbin and Orwell in their different ways were right to treat the arrival of Attlee, Bevin and a scattering of Labour figures in senior ministerial positions with the formation of the Churchill coalition in May 1940 as the first partial take-over by the 'right' family members, and the construction of Attlee's majority government in July 1945 as but the completion of the change of personnel at the top of the family hierarchy.

But the front across which the politics and the social and political economies advanced between 1940 and 1950 was very wide compared with what had gone before (including the 'New Liberal' reforms and the impact of the Great War combined). New norms and expectations had been created of a kind and to a degree that, even when the 'wrong' members of the family regained control in October 1951, they could not revert to the old ways even if they had wished to. Add to this the fuses lit beneath the enduring old social orders by, for example, the 1944 Education Act and the real possibility of a genuine mass-consumption society once rationing and postwar shortages were eased or removed altogether, and one can see even in that peculiar mixture of advance and ossification described by McKibbin at mid-century the essentials of a permanently transformed society in food, dress, style, manners and social attitudes.

Shortages, of food in particular, the 'kitchen front' as it was called in the war, is where the re-creation of early-Fifties life must begin. In the context of early postwar Britain, food was, in both senses, on everybody's lips. It escapes, therefore, many of the problems that often beset social historians in their analytical (as opposed to descriptive) mode, especially when probing the deeper underlying factors at work in society. As Raymond Aron put it in the mid-1950s, '[s]ocieties are not at the mercy of causes they know nothing of, they are swept along by human passions.'[9]

From the moment the government began to piece together a serious siege economy in early 1940 to the summer of 1954 when the last commodities were derationed, food brought real life and public administration together in a continuous symbiosis that was central to every one of King George VI's and Queen Elizabeth's subjects. And, once the war was over and with it the unarguable need for stomachs (and wardrobes too) to be placed under conditions of siege, in the late 1940s and early 1950s food was the roughage of politics in its rawest form. As we shall see in Chapter 4, it was a powerful factor in changing the government during the autumn of 1951.

The movement of goods, not just on and off the ration, but variations in the quantities rationed out, attracted a level of public attention comparable to the fortunes of the leading soccer teams. And some consumption benchmarks, such as the final ending of the sweet ration in February 1953 (it had experienced a phantom finish in April 1949 only to be reimposed in August the same year because of runaway demand[10]) will, I suspect, be remembered by readers over sixty almost as vividly as the Stanley Matthews Cup Final, the Coronation and the scaling of Mount Everest in the same year. A selection of other rationed items is shown in the table below.[11] All but two – preserves and bread – were still on ration at the time of the autumn 1951 general election.

COMMODITY	ON RATION	OFF RATION
Bacon	January 1940	July 1954
Ham	January 1940	October 1952
Meat	March 1940	July 1954
Butter	January 1940	May 1954
Margarine	July 1940	May 1954
Cooking Fat	November 1941	May 1954
Cheese	May 1941	May 1954
Sugar	January 1940	September 1953
Sweets	July 1942	February 1953
Chocolate	July 1942	February 1953
Preserves	March 1941	December 1948
Tea	July 1940	October 1952
Bread	July 1946	July 1948

This table tells only part of the story. The meat ration reached its lowest ever level in 1951, nearly six years after the war had ended and deep into the period when, in Ina Zweiniger-Bargielowska's words, 'wartime acquiescence in civilian sacrifice [had been] replaced by post-war discontent'.[12] Dr Zweiniger-Bargielowska, who is regarded by many as the leading analyst of the economics and politics of mid-twentieth-century austerity and consumption, noted that:

Labour explained the drastic cut in the ration [from 87 per cent to 69 per cent of the 1934–8 level[13]], which was due to the breakdown of negotiations of a new contract with Britain's major supplier, Argentina, as part of the government's anti-inflationary policy in the context of world shortages ... not surprisingly, it provided ammunition for the Conservative opposition to government purchasing ... *Popular Pictorial* showed a photograph of 'your weekly meat ration [which] is not bigger than a matchbox'.[14]

Devilling among the data is necessary and revealing and Christopher Driver's table of the growth in individual consumption between 1950 and 1960, reproduced below, is central to any reconstruction of British life in the Fifties.[15]

CONSUMPTION (OUNCES PER PERSON PER WEEK)	1950	1960
Liquid milk (pints)	4.78	4.84
Other milk (equiv. pints)	0.43	0.31
Cheese	2.54	3.04
Butter	4.56	5.68
Margarine	3.94	3.66
Lard and compound cooking fat	3.11	2.63
Eggs (number)	3.46	4.36
Preserves (inc. syrup, treacle)	6.30	3.21
Sugar	10.13	17.76
Beef and veal	8.06	8.74
Mutton and lamb	5.43	6.63
Pork	0.30	2.02
Bacon and ham (inc. cooked)	4.52	5.32
Poultry	0.35	1.68
Sausages	4.01	3.52
Other meat products	7.82	7.98
Fish, fresh and processed	6.18	4.69

Canned fish	0.44	0.95
Frozen fish and fish products	n.k.	0.29
Fresh green vegetables	13.81	15.34
Other fresh vegetables	11.38	9.13
Tomatoes, fresh	4.78	4.75
Frozen vegetables	n.k.	0.63
Canned vegetables	4.55	6.21
Potatoes (excl. processed)	62.04	56.14
Fruit, fresh	14.41	18.16
Canned fruit	3.68	6.84
Flour	7.25	6.76
White bread	50.91	36.63
Brown bread (inc. wholewheat and wholemeal)	2.55	3.35
Other bread	4.29	5.49
Buns, biscuits, cakes	10.37	11.98
Breakfast cereals	1.40	1.80
Tea	2.16	2.80
Coffee (inc. instant)	0.21	0.39
Soups	1.31	2.10

As Driver himself put it, when 'interpreting the table, it is important to realise that even though rationing was still in force in 1950, the national diet was already in measurable respects (that is, 10 per cent in protein and 4 per cent in energy value) better than it had been in 1939'.[16] The Driver table charts a real rise in the culture of contentment and in certain health-bringing foods such as fresh vegetables and fresh fruit. Yet it also, to the eyes of subsequent analysts, contains within it a surge in the rise of fats generally (from 329.2 grams per person a week in 1950 to an all-time high of 339.4 grams a week by 1960[17]) which included the highly saturated ones that came in the 1970s especially to be linked with the rise of cardiovascular diseases.[18] The politics of food had a great potency for a decade. Dr Zweiniger-Bargielowska marshals considerable evidence to support her claim that: 'Disaffection with austerity, particularly among women, undermined the popularity of the Labour government elected with a landslide majority in 1945, while the Conservatives' critique of austerity was instrumental to the Conservative electoral recovery and the party's victories in the general elections of 1951 and 1955.'[19]

Yet voting in the 1950s was a heavily class-based phenomenon[20] and, in

Driver's words, '*post bellum triste* was a typically middle-class affliction. Most manual workers, and, above all, their wives, had never enjoyed abundance, let alone luxury, and the monotonous but nutritious diet of the industrial canteens that had grown up during the war represented a marked improvement whose effects began to show in the health of the population, even though – or rather because – there was little to be had from the sweetshop on the corner. It was the higher socioeconomic groups that had watched their servants disappear into those factories and canteens, never to return, and had spent the war years learning how to shop and cook and keep their families tolerably fed.'[21]

Elizabeth David, whose cookery books helped to extend the national palate in continental directions during the Fifties, reinforced this wonderfully well when she wrote in her 1951 *French Country Cooking* that: 'Rationing, the disappearance of servants, and the bad and expensive meals served in restaurants, have led English women to take a far greater interest in food than was formerly considered polite . . .' She coupled this judgement with a plea for food and its preparation to become the centrepiece of the housewifely life: 'Some sensible person once remarked that you spend the whole of your life either in your bed or your shoes. Having done the best you can by shoes and bed, devote all the time and resources at your disposal to the building up of a fine kitchen. It will be, as it should be, the most comforting and comfortable room in the house.'[22]

With rationing ended in the summer of 1954, Hitler and successive Ministers of Food in Whitehall could no longer be blamed for shortages. This changed both the politics and the stimulators of consumption. As Driver put it:

From 1954 onwards, people were free to eat as much as they wanted of anything they could pay for. This restored freedom, coupled with a decisive increase in real disposable income, put the onus for any inadequacy of supply and choice, in food as in other consumables, on to the market mechanisms which are controlled by capitalists small and (increasingly) great. It is therefore no coincidence that from this point onwards, advertising campaigns, cookery literature, immigration, foreign travel and the ebbs and flows of fashion could make their effects felt quickly and directly.[23]

This is a transformation that I and my postwar generation can still taste fifty years later. Add to this the coming of commercial television in September 1955 and you have the ingredients of a new and increasingly widespread British lifestyle which far surpassed the 'better 1930s' which was what the UK initially experienced once the interwar retail revolution (halted and, in some cases, reversed by the imposition of rationing) resumed as the last goods came off coupon.[24]*

The taste buds and nostrils of the country were soon to experience a slow and cumulatively significant set of changes, but not quite yet. As Christopher Driver noted, 'by 1955, the British diet had completed its post-war recovery and the contemporary food scene was beginning to take shape. But ... only beginning. In the mid-1950s, the predominant styles of cooking, and the staple foodstuffs on which they were based, were British to the last chip, whether the meal was being eaten at home or away ...'[25]

When it came to harbingers of change, the Italians were often in the vanguard, initially from a district in the Emilian Apennines. Even before the Great War, as the 1911 census indicated, there were 500 Italian café or restaurant owners in the UK backed up by 1,400 bakers and confectioners, 900 chefs and 1,600 waiters.[26] In the 1920s and 1930s many a British high street had an Italian café with a distinctive frontage, its name in plain but chic metal, whose menu did not just rely on its homemade ice cream to beat the dominant British fare of meat-and-two-veg served by the domestic competitor down the road.[27]

For the postwar years, two Italian names have instant evocative power – Charles Forte (who had a home in Britain) and Achille Gaggia (who did not). Forte, starting with a milk bar in Upper Regent Street not far from the BBC's Broadcasting House, 'combated the postwar gloom and the dreariness of dirty mackintoshes by painting his milk bars in red-and-white stripes and dressing his counter girls in a red-and-white (freely adapted) "Puritan" costume',[28] a neat adaptation to British conditions by the man the social historian Harry Hopkins dubbed 'the most notably successful caterer of the period'.[29]

By the mid-1950s, the Italian trattoria was well established in London and several other cities such as Edinburgh and Plymouth (where the trade press indicated that Gennoni's restaurant was serving up half a hundredweight of spaghetti a week[30]). Just five years beyond the scope of this volume in 1965,

* When Brits of 'my age' recall Fifties' childhoods it's interesting how it's the first half of the decade which we can conjure up. For example, Russell Twisk, then Editor of *The Listener*, and I did so in October 1986 and the two of us characterized our winter Sunday lunchtimes ('Sunday dinner') in identical terms – roast and two veg; rhubarb crumble and custard; the windows all steamed up (no ventilation) and everyone listening to the *Billy Cotton Band Show* on the wireless.

the largest pasta factory in Europe opened in St Albans, thirty miles north of London (a former Roman town, as Christopher Driver noted).[31]

But it is not the motorway service stations or the hotels of what eventually became the vast TrusthouseForte empire that has excited the attention of British sociologists when contemplating the Italian connection. That distinction goes to a bar owner from Milan. Achille Gaggia achieved his breakthrough in 1938 when he 'invented a piston system for forcing hot water at high pressure through finely ground coffee contained in a filtered holder'.[32] Raymond Postgate, socialist, economic historian, novelist, clubman and gourmet, who, with his fellow member of the Savile Stephen Potter created the Good Food Club in 1950 (out of which came the *Good Food Guide*), paid the greatest tribute to Gaggia when he wrote: 'There is a machine called the Espresso which makes it quite difficult to make really bad coffee.'[33] This was a top-flight accolade in a country where the choice was usually between drab and dreggy powdered varieties and the liquid Camp coffee essence.

Although he had patented his coffee machine in 1938, thanks to the war Gaggia could not market it until 1946: all gilt and hiss with his name emblazoned on the front (as it still is). Espresso bars sprang up across Italy and quickly spread to Britain, exerting an Italianizing effect perhaps equalled only by the Vespa and Lambretta scooters which, a little later, brought a particular style to British roads in the 1950s and a rash of not always so agreeably stylish 'mods' atop them at seaside Bank Holiday gatherings a few years later.

Driver, like Postgate a truly discriminating connoisseur, pays the espresso machine the highest compliment in his masterly *The British at Table*. 'The Gaggia,' he writes, 'delivered, for the first time in England since coffee houses of a much earlier period, drinkable coffee in a public place – places, moreover, whose Festival of Britain colours, false ceilings, potted plants, and engaging flimsiness encouraged the young to believe that austerity had been banished at last.'[34]*

Social critics and those worried by the latest manifestations of adolescence waxed frequently and long about the culture of the 'coffee bar' or the 'milk bar' (which preceded it in the terminology of consumption), especially when Italian style met one aspect of American mass culture blended within a very British setting. Richard Hoggart wrote perhaps the most influential book about British popular culture, *The Uses of Literacy*, between 1952 and 1956 while teaching at Hull University.[35] Its reach and celebrity surprised both the

---

* For those not Gaggiaized in Fifties conditions, the coffee can be sniffed vicariously in the 1959 film *Expresso Bongo*, one of Cliff Richard's more toe-curling vehicles.

author and his publisher, Chatto. It was the decision of Allen Lane of Penguin, creator of the paperback revolution, while sitting in the sun in the Balearics in 1957 reading Hoggart's account of working-class life in Leeds, to buy it and publish it as a Pelican the following year.[36] It led swiftly to Hoggart's elevated position in the field of British cultural history, sustained almost from that day to this.

In one of the most celebrated passages of the book, Hoggart laments the contamination of the traditional by taking as its symbol the milk bars which

indicate at once, in the nastiness of their modernistic knick-knacks, their glaring show-iness, an aesthetic breakdown so complete that, in comparison with them, the layout of the living-rooms in some of the poor homes from which the customers came seems to speak of a tradition as balanced and civilized as an eighteenth-century town house. I am not thinking of those milk-bars which are really quick-service cafes ... I have in mind rather the kind of milk-bar – there is one in almost every northern town, with more than, say, fifteen thousand inhabitants – which has become the regular evening rendezvous of some of the young men. Girls go to some, but most of the customers are boys aged between fifteen and twenty, with drape-suits, picture ties and an American slouch.[37]

It was the jukebox, an evolution of the American nickelodeon, which pulled the adolescents in, according to Hoggart: 'Compared even with the pub around the corner, this is all a peculiarly thin and pallid form of dissipation, a sort of spiritual dry-rot amid the odour of boiled milk.'[38]

American influence on the tight-knit British Isles, whether manifested in a milk bar or the increasing domination of Hollywood in British cinemas (later described by Conservative politician Chris Patten as 'the Californian tide of glamour, sex and violence' washing over us[39]), left few neutral in the early postwar years when it was still working its way through. Some, like Hoggart, treated it as a kind of cultural imperialism – a matter of Coca-Colonization,[40] turning us into an 'American-lite' society. Others, such as the theatrical director Richard Eyre, though a left-winger like Hoggart, saw it as a cultural liberation. Eyre has written vividly of just such a sensation as he passed through Sherborne (his public school, for which he did not feel affec-tion) at much the same time as Hoggart was eviscerating the northern milk bars full of young men who 'waggle one shoulder' in time to the jukebox 'or stare, as desperately as Humphrey Bogart, across the tubular chairs'.[41] For Eyre, by contrast, isolated in the epicentre of Englishness, my brain was willingly, indeed eagerly, colonised by American culture – Marvel comics, rock and roll, jazz, fiction, movies, TV, even the theatre. Like many of my generation in the late fifties, I was a cultural Fifth Columnist for most of my formative years. It wasn't just that American culture was something *other*, something not British, it was simply better than anything we had.[42]

Eyre makes no mention of the near all-conquering American invention of 1904 – the hamburger (the first franchised McDonald's opened in Illinois in April 1955[43]). Oddly enough, it didn't acquire perhaps the place it deserved in the battleground for the British palate until the eve of the BSE-related anxiety of the 1990s.

Hoggart claimed an enduring ascendancy for home cooking rather than café or works canteen meals (let alone anything fancily foreign) in the early 1950s: 'A husband will complain that the food there "has no body" and the wife has to "pack something up," which usually means a pile of sandwiches with "something tasty" in them, and she prepares a big hot meal for them in the evening.'[44] Here lies one of Hoggart's most vivid themes: '"Something tasty" is the key-phrase in feeding: something solid, preferably meaty, and with a well-defined flavour. The tastiness is increased by a liberal use of sauces and pickles, notably tomato sauce and piccalilli.'[45]

One can only sense an affluence-borne decline when listening to Hoggart's litany of now largely lost 'range of favourite savouries, often by-products – black puddings, pig's feet, liver, cowheel, tripe, polony [a type of cooked sausage], ... chitterlings ...; and the fishmongers' savouries – shrimps, roe, kippers and mussels'.[46] The fish finger, introduced into the UK by Birds Eye in 1955, convenient and ubiquitous virtually ever since ('part of the British family way of life', it has been claimed[47]), could never beat that Hoggartian fare, however garnished.

Yet with the immigrations of the 1950s, Indian, Chinese and Middle Eastern flavours began increasingly to fill the desire for 'something tasty'. In the 1930s the Empire Marketing Board had urged the consumers of the home island to eat and drink imperially.[48] But this was different. For me it was the reverse effect of the British Empire, rather than American Coca-Colonization, that altered the standard fare and the collective palate of the home nation for ever. It originated with immigrants from Hong Kong, the New Territories in particular, and began its cumulative sweep down the high streets of the UK from about 1955 on, when the Chinese restaurant broke out of the dockland hinterlands of Liverpool, Cardiff and Limehouse to which locations it had largely been confined hitherto.[49]*

The Chinese wave was supplemented by successive culinary breakers rolling in from the former Empire – Indian, Greek and Turkish (both chiefly from Cyprus) and, rather later, Malaysian cooking. Perhaps surprisingly, the first wave of postwar immigration – that emanating from the Caribbean – did not manifest itself prominently in the domain of the restaurant or takeaway, though the markets close by West Indian districts in London were soon enlivened by yams and red snapper fish.[50] Bundle together the cafés, the markets and the fish shops, the Gaggia machine and the Italian restaurants, and there was an impact on the British palate from the mid-1950s not experienced 'since the medieval world discovered the spice routes'.[51]

The first time I heard a family conversation about the new blush of affluence was also in 1955 and it had to do with that other necessity alongside food – clothing. It took place one Saturday evening when my sister Kathleen was home from Exeter University and my sister Terry back from nursing training in south London. The youngest of my three sisters, Maureen, had bought that day a pair of two-toned, coffee and cream high-heeled shoes. It was Kathleen, I think, who said how remarkable it was that there had suddenly become available an extended range of affordable clothing and footwear that reduced the difference in appearance between all but the seriously wealthy and the rest of us.

Recalling this conversation in the spring of 2003, over lunch just after scattering our father's ashes in Kew Gardens (Dad had the reverse of good taste in clothes but he liked a nice bloom), Kathleen said, 'When I went to university in 1953 most of us were still knitting our own jumpers.' Maureen added, 'Then you were suddenly allowed to have yards of material.'[52]

The economy of appearance had changed profoundly on 1 June 1941, Whit Sunday, when the wartime coalition government imposed clothes rationing. Twenty coupons was the initial allocation for the remainder of that year – very tight when you converted them into garments (a lady's coat needed 14 coupons, a woollen dress 11, a blouse 5). And it got worse – 60 coupons for the whole of 1942; down to 40 in 1943; up to 48 in 1944.[53]

In 1942 the Board of Trade commissioned a group of top designers, including Hardy Amies, to create a range of basic outfits for women (coat, suit, afternoon dress and a cotton overall dress). These were then mass produced

---

* For me, the perfect symbol of this transformation was the Chinese restaurant in Brecon town centre which my family encountered in the early 1990s housed in an old provisions shop whose highly evocative frontage had been left intact, proclaiming the lost world of 'Home and Colonial' to each passer-by.

as 'utility fashions' alongside a 'make-do-and-mend' campaign.[54] Such clothing, plus the headscarves which adorned shopper and war worker alike, forms part of the collective imagery of the remembered war sixty years on, as does the combination of 'severe, square-shouldered suit worn with heavy, wedge shoes and shoulder bags . . .'[55]

Fashion design was essentially frozen by wartime rationing and utility.[56] This tightest of regimes had one significant, if delayed effect, however, which gradually became apparent after clothing finally came off the ration in September 1948 (though the Board of Trade persisted with its 'utility' guidelines to manufacturers until 1952[57]). The ready-to-wear approach to clothing manufacture which expanded rapidly in the 1950s 'owed not a little to the war-time and post-war activities' of the designers and firms, as what Jane Ashelford calls the legacy of the 'applied democracy'[58] of war and early postwar clothing combined with the rapid growth of advertising media to propel 'fashion . . . to change faster than ever before and the rise of the ready-to-wear market meant that everyone had a chance of wearing it'.[59]

The name most associated with the postwar clothing transformation is Sir Simon Marks of Marks and Spencer. 'Marks and Sparks', as the company became universally known, drove both the overt and concealed parts of the revolution – overwear and underwear alike. As Israel Sieff, Marks's brother-in-law, wrote in his memoirs: 'After the war, Simon deduced, women would want light, comfortable clothes, the cheapest of which would not be greatly different to look at from the most expensive. Shop girls were going to expect to look like duchesses – as they had in the WRNS [Women's Royal Naval Service] or the ATS [Auxiliary Territorial Service] – and feel just as comfortable.'[60]

M&S's head of design, Hans Schneider, brought a particular feel to the company's early 1950s push for shopgirl and duchess alike. Marcus Sieff, Israel's son and a future M&S chairman, relates how the newspapers picked up this phenomenon, citing Laurence Thompson writing in the News Chronicle in 1955 in a J. B. Priestley-like fashion: 'Before the Welfare State there were broadly two classes of consumers, the middle class who had the money, and the working class who hadn't. Now there is only one class and I am told . . . that many a debutante wears a Marks and Spencer nylon slip beneath her Dior dress as if she were just a Gateshead factory girl.'[61] Note the word 'just'. Even when dealing with perhaps the one area (underwear) where social equality *had* been achieved, Thompson lets his own slip show.

Between 1948 and 1958, M&S's profits quadrupled, leading one social historian to declare that Britain had achieved 'the revolution', but 'according to Marks, not Marx'.[62] The social historian Harry Hopkins also noticed that children's clothes were also transformed with 'notable improvement in colour, fabric and design in these years'.[63] (I have to admit this passed me by.)

In the mid-1990s I talked to Marty Wilde, of 'Teenager In Love' fame, in his recording studio in Knebworth about the moment when the first stirrings of affluence pushed purchasing power to places it had never previously reached and the teenager with cash burst upon the scene. Marty said: 'You were brought up with three colours – grey, brown and black. They were all the colours I associate with the war. Almost everything was grey. It wasn't until the Fifties that all colours started to come in clothes, colours of cars . . . T-shirts – it was the age of the T-shirt. We had a sense of freedom. Fantastic hairstyles as well were coming in . . .'[64]

The mid-Fifties 'Teddy Boy' phenomenon is what folk memory retains, but, more prosaically, the non-youthful/disaffected male also started to clothe his frame in a different way in the early 1950s. Harry Hopkins has traced both the shift in the style of the male drapers and the contents of their racks in a new era of takeovers and chain shops: 'The bold black-and-white sign-boards of the "Fifty Shilling Tailors" changed discreetly, first to a non-committal "F.S.T", then, with much internal and external restyling, to "John Collier" shops, with a facsimile signature as their "personalising" emblem. For here, too, one could now dispense with . . . the image of "cheapness" . . .'[65]

With one in two suits fashioned by a big multiple tailor, stigma disappeared along with the standard blue or brown serge suits of the 'demob' style, the new lines supplemented by 'slacks' of several colours which usurped the '"grey flannel bags" of Old England'.[66]

Sitting in his Whitehall ministerial suite in September 1952, the determinedly old Savile Row Harold Macmillan tried, in his diary, to make sense of the consumer changes swirling around in Oxford Street half a mile to the north. Macmillan, writing (quite naturally for him) in a grandly Whiggish style, was convinced that 'the "proletariat" [had] now come into its own, and [was] determined to maintain its standard of "panem and circenses" [bread and circuses] at all costs'.[67]

It was all too baffling for a politician who, to the end, had an ambiguous relationship (as we will see) to the affluence with which his name will always be associated (not least in the title of this book). 'One of the embarrassing legacies of war,' he wrote, rather mixing up his tenses along with the war and postwar years,

is the change in the pattern of spending. Since necessities, like food, are short and many luxuries, like music-halls and circuses impossible in the black-out, with clothing, dancing, travel, holidays etc rationed or impracticable, all the inflationary wages of the people are spent on the few available luxuries or pleasures. Roughly, those are tobacco, alcohol – and (for the war) books.[68]

Being a publisher/politician, Macmillan added ruefully, 'Now television, cinemas, dancing etc. are taking the place of books.'[69]

Macmillan's job at the time was to lead the Churchill government's huge push to build 300,000 houses a year. This he achieved by the end of 1953 to great political acclaim and, eventually, to huge personal benefit (for his 'people's houses' were the infrastructure that substantially paved his way to the premiership), but at considerable cost to both the balance of the shaky UK economy and the Churchill government's other social programmes (see Chapter 4).

Macmillan was brilliant at bringing a mixture of Disraeli (the condition of the people housed in not just two but several nations) and Hitler (the damage wrought to the cities and the halt the war imposed upon slum clearance) to his aid at the Cabinet table.[70] Macmillan wrote his own Cabinet memoranda rather than leaving the drafting to his officials. His papers for his colleagues were a peculiar mixture of *Daily Mirror* tabloid punchiness (strong words, short paragraphs) and economic and social history which, between them, leave an unusually vivid picture of the shortcomings of the nation's shelter.

Macmillan liked to hit his colleagues with the unexpected. For example, he opened his October 1952 Cabinet paper on the 'Reconstruction of Blitzed City Centres' thus:

It's 'Tommy this, an' Tommy that,' an' 'chuck 'im out, the brute'; But it's 'Saviour of 'is country,' when the guns begin to shoot! (R. Kipling)

as a preamble to 'the story of the blitzed cities', which was 'a moral as well as a material problem'.[71]

The following January Disraeli and Hitler were wheeled in behind Kipling as Macmillan surveyed the condition of the country's 'Houses – Old and New', turning to the 'slums and near slums':

They are no doubt partly the inheritance of years when the public conscience was insufficiently aroused over these matters [Macmillan delighted in quoting Disraeli to his party on the need to 'be conservative to conserve all that is good and radical to uproot all that is bad'[72]]; but they are largely the result of war. For the war caused

a.) total destruction of 225,000 houses;

b.) severe damage to 550,000 more houses.

This led, owing to shortage of accommodation, to

c.) stopping of slum clearance for 13 years.

If there had been no war, the progress of 'slum clearance' – at 1938 rates – would have got rid of 1 million such houses by now.[73]

The dash to clear the narrow Victorian terraced streets of Britain's cities and towns and the tilting of publicly funded housing 90 degrees upwards into tower blocks (which largely postdates Macmillan's time as Housing Minister[74]) in the name of modernity, efficiency and social justice will be examined later in the book. Macmillan's push for the magical 300,000 new homes a year was overwhelmingly a *state* enterprise – a partnership between central and local government. As he told the Cabinet in November 1952:[75]

The number under construction at the 30th September, 1952 was 275,263 made up as follows: –

Local Authorities and Housing Associations	219,206
New Towns	8,829
Government Departments	10,854
	238,889 (Total for letting)
Private Enterprise	36,374
	275,263

The building of these dwellings brought a glow to Macmillan right to the end of his days. Running the Ministry of Housing and Local Government, he recalled deep in old age, 'was like cricket, you could see the runs, the houses were built'.[76]

But of all the men seated around Churchill's Cabinet table (and in 1951–2 they were all men), I suspect that it was Macmillan above all who understood most fully the wider significance of the re-made relationship of the citizen and the state since Hitler had so abruptly stopped the prewar slum clearance programme and much else. As a Tory reformer who believed in enhanced state intervention, Macmillan had discerned in a 1938 volume, *The Middle Way*, the outlines of a 'principle I am seeking to illustrate [which] is that the individual has the right to demand that the economic life of society should be so organised to guarantee the basic essentials of life in return for the minimum surrender of his time and liberty; but that society, on the other hand, cannot extend this principle to extreme lengths without infringing the right of the individual to live his life in his own way'.[77]

To an historically remarkable degree, between 1939 and 1951 the state *had* undertaken such a range of functions which, to my mind, represented not so much a new 'principle', to use Macmillan's word, as a British 'New Deal' between state and citizen. The existing concept that comes nearest to describing this extraordinary phenomenon (which, as I pointed out at the end of *Never Again*, had already made the Britain of 1951 so different and a far better 'place in which to be born, to grow up, to live, love, work and even to die' compared to 'the UK of 1931 or *any* previous decade'[78]) has been developed by the historians of welfare, and by two in particular: Anne Digby, who coined the phrase 'classic welfare state' in her 1989 study of *British Welfare Policy*,[79] and Rodney Lowe, whose masterly *The Welfare State in Britain since 1945* was first published in 1993 and updated in 1999. The works, which were intended to coincide respectively with the 50th anniversaries of the Beveridge Report and the vesting day of the National Health Service (though he was a year out in both cases[80]), have made him its leading cartographer and analyst just as Nick Timmins's *The Five Giants* makes him its leading biographer.[81]

First, what were the boundaries of this 'classic welfare state' which held until the mid-1970s (as Lowe and I see it):

- *Full employment*. Without this, as Beveridge himself had warned, the whole linked enterprise would be unsustainable in terms of both consumption and the tax revenue needed to finance the extended state services and benefits.
- *Social security*. The acceptance of a state responsibility to provide for *all* citizens at times of unemployment, disability or loss of income for whatever reason – in other words the 'universalist' principle which distinguished the

'classic welfare state' from what provision had existed before its construction and what would remain in place after its partial dismantling.

- *Health care.* A National Health Service, taxpayer funded and free at the point of delivery (apart from fluctuating partial charges after 1951 for certain items such as prescriptions) for all, irrespective of personal wealth or lack of it.
- *Education.* Free secondary schooling for all. Scholarships for the initially small number, but later rising for all deemed capable, as demonstrated through examinations, of a place in higher education.
- *Housing.* An expanded and sustained provision of state built and subsidized social housing both for reasons of social justice and to improve the mobility of the labour force.
- *Personal social service.* Gap-filling provision to assist the special needs of the very young, the very old, the physically and mentally handicapped and 'problem families'.

Within this configuration lie at least two points of Michael Young's trio – Beveridge, plus Keynes, plus socialism – which pumped at the heart of Labour's programme in 1945. The 'socialist' outrider – public ownership – was not part of the consensual terrain of the postwar settlement (though, as we shall see, the incoming Conservative government did very little to dismantle or seriously alter the nationalized industries).

Several interlocking forces and factors were involved in the construction and shaping of the 'classic welfare state'. They make the period from 5 July 1948 (when the last big elements fell into place with the National Health Service, National Insurance and National Assistance all beginning on the same 'appointed day' chosen quite deliberately as the third anniversary of the country going to the polls in the 1945 general election) to 1975–6 so distinctive in the history of the United Kingdom.

The impulses which created it were given a powerful fillip by the Second World War and the damage, privation and destruction it inflicted upon George VI's kingdom. But they were far deeper in origins than that (in developing the welfare reforms of the Liberal governments of 1906–14) and went way beyond making good the damage wrought by the war. As Harold Macmillan understood, the new thinking went far further, too, than underpinning the essentials of life such as food, clothing and shelter. The notion of a collective roof over *everyone's* head, which bound together the classic welfare model and made it fit for the purpose of slaying Beveridge's 'Five Giants' ('WANT,

DISEASE, IGNORANCE, SQUALOR and IDLENESS,' all written in bold, black capitals in his 1942 Report[82]), was the single most distinctive feature of the first thirty years of British life and experience after the Second World War.

Driving this British New Deal was a fusion of philosophies of social justice and national efficiency. And the heart of the 'deal' was this: there would be an end to avoidable injustices, inequalities and privations in return for a mitigation of old, deep-rooted class, social and industrial antagonisms which both pulled down Britain's economic performance and weakened the fibre of its society. This was a great prize in itself, but the British New Deal would also create an indispensable base for underpinning the new settlement *and* a platform for further advance.

It was hugely ambitious, and as a scheme (which is how Beveridge saw it) for integrating the country's government, economics and society quite without predecessor or successor. All its instruments were in place by the time Mr Churchill replaced Mr Attlee in No. 10 in October 1951. Attlee and Churchill, however, were essentially practical politicians rather than theorists or integrators; not for them any explicit political expressions of the notions being expounded in the late 1940s and early 1950s at the London School of Economics by T. H. Marshall, mentor to several of the most eloquent intellectual guardians of the 'classic welfare state' such as Chelly Halsey.[83] Marshall saw the work of the years between 1940 and 1948 as completing the cycle of British rights acquired over centuries (civil in the period 1650–1832; political between 1832 and 1918; social thereafter) in a manner that might transcend society's fissures of class and status.[84]

There were occasional fleeting moments when the premiers who presided over the making of the British New Deal reflected it in their political language. Attlee, for example, went on the wireless in the summer of 1948 to remind the unofficial strikers in the London docks that new rights implied new duties and a clear break with the past:

This strike is not a strike against capitalists or employers. It's a strike against your mates. A strike against the housewife. A strike against the ordinary common people who have difficulties enough now to manage on their shilling's worth of meat and other rationed commodities. Why should you men strike? You're well paid compared with the old days. You have a guaranteed minimum wage of £4 8s 6d a week whether you work or not. You no longer have to go to the Labour Exchange and stand in the queue. Whose only obligation is to attend at the proper call times, and, if there is no work, to sign on and get your money.

... We will not allow these subversive influences [by which he meant members of the Communist Party of Great Britain in the dock labour force] to wreck this tremendous social experiment which obliterated from the dockside the curse of casual labour and casual earnings.[85]

Churchill had a number of cherished catch-phrases he liked to apply to the concepts of welfare and social insurance, most notably on the need for social security to bring 'the magic of averages nearer to the rescue of the millions' as 'an essential part of any postwar scheme of national betterment', as he put it in a War Cabinet paper not long after the publication of the Beveridge Report.[86] And in his speech to the Conservative Party conference in Blackpool in the autumn of 1946, as the 'classic welfare state' was being shaped by a succession of bills passing through Parliament, Churchill, in his own very special mix of the homely and the grandiloquent, told the activists of the party which had lost power the previous year due in no small part to their perceived passivity in the face of economic and social distress in the interwar years, that, 'We do not seek to pull down improvidently the structures of society, but to erect balustrades on the stairway of life, which will prevent helpless and foolish people from falling into the abyss.' Yet he was determined both to recognize the significance and magnitude of the latest attempt at 'national betterment' and to remind his listeners how engaged he had been on this noble enterprise since early in the century, first as a Liberal and then as a Tory:

It is 38 years since I introduced the first Unemployment Insurance Scheme [as Liberal President of the Board of Trade], and 22 years ago since, as Conservative Chancellor of the Exchequer, I shaped and carried the Widows' Pension and reduction of the Old Age Pensions from 70 to 65. We are now moving forward into another vast scheme of national insurance, which arose, even in the stress of war, from a Parliament with a great Conservative Majority.[87]

In the late 1940s and early 1950s, leading political figures of both major parties *competed* to be seen as the progenitors of the 'classic welfare state'.

In the space between the Attlees and the Churchills and the Marshalls and the Halseys, there existed a group of people formed by the experience of slump and war who did have an acute sense of the British New Deal. Noel

Annan was their collective biographer. 'Our Age', he called them, lifting the phrase his friend and mentor, Maurice Bowra, used to describe 'anyone who came of age and went to university in the thirty years between 1919, the end of the Great War, and 1949, or, say, 1951, the last year in which those who had served in the armed forces during the Second World War returned to study. To him they were all one generation.'[88]

In *Our Age*, which he wrote in the late 1980s more than a little scarred by the consequences of the failure of the postwar settlement to heal, mend and propagate a more productive and just society, Annan has a mightily eloquent passage about those young men and women who treated the Labour government of 1945 as 'the great landmark of their times that had introduced an irreversible revolution into British life, greater than the Liberal governments after 1906'.[89] 'Our Age,' wrote Annan, 'believed that the welfare services and supplementary benefits would lift hundreds and thousands out of the anguish of extreme poverty and calm the anxieties of millions more.'[90] (There is a strong echo here of Nye Bevan's use of the word 'serenity', which for him was better and richer, as his friend and biographer, Michael Foot, put it, than the word 'security' as the encapsulation of the essential purpose of the welfare state.[91])

In Annan's depiction of their collective *mentalité*, this crucial generation, who were to become the managers and operators of the New Deal institutions from the expanded universities to the NHS, the Keynesian-dominated Treasury and the Bank of England to the nationalized industries, really did integrate consciously the theory and the implementation, fully understanding that the whole ambitious enterprise was meant to be far more than the sum of its parts:

Full employment meant more than a Keynesian statistic to Our Age. It embodied all their hopes for a more decent life for the working class ... Our Age was the first generation to recognize the importance of trade unions and to sympathize with their aims. The war and full employment had returned bargaining power to them. Our Age believed that they were the key to ending the appalling relations between management and labour.[92]

And those members of 'Our Age' who took the 'reconstruction competitions' to gain entry to the higher civil service on returning from ships, squadrons and battalions, such as Ian Bancroft of Balliol College Oxford and the Rifle Brigade in north-west Europe, 1944–5 (who entered the Treasury in 1947 and became Head of the Home Civil Service thirty years later), were a generation of civil servants who 'began their official lives believing that everything was achievable'.[93]

It was a friend of both Noel Annan and Ian Bancroft, Kenneth Berrill of the LSE and the Royal Electrical and Mechanical Engineers – unlike them, a professional economist who would rise to head the Government Economic Service in the Treasury and, later, the Central Policy Review Staff in the Cab-inet Office – who, having lived through a succession of economic and currency crises between 1947 and 1976, identified the most obvious and persistent factor that sapped the foundations of the British New Deal throughout the period of the 'classic welfare state' and beyond: 'After the war, not having been defeated, not having been occupied, we hadn't that tough approach to the postwar problems which I think France [and] Germany ... had ... We had won the war and we voted ourselves a nice peace.'[94]

The generation for whom 'everything was achievable' eventually, none the less had to confront a parlous economic position (in 1951 as well as 1945) that had to be coped with before the possibly benign but certainly long-delayed benefits of the new settlement worked their way through into the human factors of production and, ultimately, into the trade figures and productivity levels.

With Britain still at the heart of an empire expressed not just in terms of vast swathes of territory overseas but also in an imperial trading system based on tariffs and the running of the world's second reserve currency (after the US dollar), it was not easy for the early postwar generation generally to appre-ciate just how precariously based were the country's industries and services and its wherewithal to feed and supply a nation of around 50 million people, nearly a third of whose wealth had been burnt up by the war. Add to this Ken Berrill's notion of a 'nice peace' and the installation of a 'classic welfare state' and you have a set of illusions which deserve some – if not all – of the treat-ment they retrospectively received when Corelli Barnett completed what he came to call his 'Pride and Fall Sequence'.[95]

As Alan Milward, the great comparator of post-1945 reconstructions across a range of western European countries, has hinted, 'set of inflexibilities' might be a more accurate notion – inflexibilities imposed on widely shared percep-tions of both the failings of the interwar years and the successes of the years of wartime struggle on both the home and the military fronts.

Of Attlee's first government, Milward wrote that it

had been elected by an overwhelmingly popular majority with a clear mandate to sustain full employment and a higher level of social welfare. Seen from the viewpoint of 1945 the economic and social conditions of the 1930s had been made utterly unacceptable by the war. Any economic policy which did not seem to offer the possibility of permanent escape from those conditions was also unacceptable.[96]

Milward warns, too, against recent historiography being too glibly read back into the widely shared political, economic and social mentalities of VE Day and after:

In recent years there has been a tendency to see the performance of the British economy and the condition of the majority of the British population during the 1930s in a more favourable light. But that is hardly the point; a mass of social and economic criticism before the war, followed by the powerfully forged sense of positive national purpose during the war, meant that the 1930s were now seen as wasted years. To ensure that there should be no further wasted years had become a historical imperative brooking no question, a first, necessary, inflexible priority of all economic policy.[97]

Though Milward does not use the term, this was another essential aspect of the British New Deal. His analysis of its rigidities is also the beginning of the explanation of its eventual – but, by no means, inevitable – demise, though a sustained UK growth rate across the so-called 'thirty golden years' of shared west-European economic expansion from 1945 to roughly 1975[98] comparable to that of France and Italy, let alone Germany, *might* have preserved more of the essentials of the British New Deal through the sterling crises and oil shocks of the 1970s.

On a most basic level, however, the earliest postwar years in real terms (as opposed to expectations) were not the palmiest on which to impose Milward's imperatives as part of what Attlee called 'this tremendous social experiment'.[99] Questions about the UK's relative economic decline are some of the most protracted, complicated and developed of all those posed by both the historians whose task is to reconstruct the elements of modern British history and those politicians who seek to fashion the explanations they favour into bullets to fire at their opponents. There are those, too, who maintain that the whole enterprise is a delusive distraction, that 'declinism' is almost a disease of the mind, that decline simply did not happen, that post-1945 growth rates were higher than at any previous period in the life of the British Isles and that the lives of those who lived upon them were dramatically richer and better in consequence.[100]

The British debate is particularly fascinating because it is intertwined with the most dramatic of all postwar retreats from imperial superpowerdom (apart from that of the Soviet imperium which 'died in the saddle' within a few short years in the late 1980s and early 1990s). Living standards did indeed improve in a sustained fashion during the postwar years but affluence at home was repeatedly punctuated by sterling crises and spending and defence reviews. For some observers, this is a key explanation of declinism as *mentalité*: that the 'elite' in both government circles – the penumbra of commentators in the serious press and those whose mornings began with reading their output – conflate the reductions in British power and prestige with the getting, spending and consuming of the British majority whose serenity is not bound up to the same degree with the UK's supposed position in the world.

I am sure that David Landes, the leading American economic historian of the early postwar years (who has an exceptional feel for the factors of production in post-1945 western Europe, including Britain), is right to stress that change is a thing of 'the realms of both the spirit and the flesh',[101] and that 'nothing rouses [the historian's] suspicions faster than the monistic explanation – what we might call "the analytical fix"'.[102] The warning I would add to Landes' is the constant need to recreate the moods and explanations of those in the Cabinet Room and the back rooms of the Treasury and the Foreign Office, particularly at times when events obliged them to concentrate on the deeper factors lurking behind the immediate crises on their agendas.

To illustrate this, I have eavesdropped on the Cabinet Room at some late Forties and early Fifties moments when economic crises knocked on the door of No. 10. In particular I have listened to a quartet of leading political figures (two each in Attlee's and Churchill's Cabinets) with an ear attuned to the later debate about the UK's relative economic performance.

First, exhibit one, Herbert Morrison, Lord President of the Council, in a paper to the Cabinet on 'The Economic Situation' dated 21 July 1949 in the middle of the severe currency crisis which was to lead to the devaluation of the pound from an exchange rate of $4.03 to $2.80 nearly two months later on 18 September 1949. Morrison had been the Attlee Cabinet's economic overlord until the currency crisis of the late summer and early autumn of 1947, when Stafford Cripps replaced Hugh Dalton as Chancellor of the Exchequer and became indisputably the number one economic minister.[103] Morrison none the less continued to be a major player in Attlee's Cabinet and its Economic Policy Committee and, as Lord President, remained overlord of the government's information policy. The preamble to his paper was, as so often with politicians in office in a government which regards itself as reforming, hugely

self-serving. Its theme was that the measures needed for a permanent transformation are in place but will take some time yet to blunt and overcome the
accumulated failings of others in the past. 'In view of the success which we
have achieved in working out our socialist plans,' Morrison told his colleagues,
'it is right, I submit, to watch carefully that any necessary economic adjustment does not injure their progress, at any rate in essentials. At the same time
we have always appreciated that it would take a considerable period to bring
the inadequate production of the old inherited system up to a sufficient level,
and that there would be setbacks on the way, especially through American
recession and other factors outside our control'.[104]

Morrison went on to warn the Cabinet against reacting to the current crisis
in a way that would both jeopardize the government's social goals and push
them 'into an economic and political blind alley from which there is no tolerable way out, and which may lead to political crisis and defeat for the
Government and the principles for which we stand'.[105]

This was the prelude to a commendable burst of realism and contemporary
historical context-setting:

The economic system must be safeguarded from breaking under a load it is not yet
ready to bear. It is also vital that the Government should govern. Everyone, including
our own people and those with whom we are closely associated such as the other countries of the Commonwealth and the Americans, as well as our opponents in the 'cold
war', should know that the Government clearly recognise the situation, and are tackling
it with firm grip and decision. The temptation to defer action until it is publicly seen
to be dictated to us by events should be resisted if we are to retain and maintain
confidence. If there is one thing the British will not easily forgive it is a 'mess'.

Morrison's subsequent suggestions on 'how the working out of our essential plans can be safeguarded while making adequate provision for relieving
the strain on the economic machine'[106] did not, to borrow a phrase later
beloved of Roy Jenkins (then a young Labour backbencher), quite 'rise to the
level of events'.[107] The gist of his recommendations was a tighter control of
public expenditure and public sector manpower plus a possible new Cabinet
Committee to oversee this with a drive 'to reawaken the nation to the seriousness of the economic problem while making clear the new directions in which
effort is needed, and confirming confidence in the Government's leadership'.
Above all, Morrison wanted 'to avoid harsh and panic measures such as were
forced on it in 1931 ...'.[108] when the MacDonald government of which he
was a member broke up amid the economic crisis of August that year and the

party split (still a vivid scar on the psyche of those who sat round Attlee's Cabinet table).

To his credit, Morrison recognized the problem of what political scientists would call 'overload'[109] upon a governing system devoted to the absorption of a *new* range of economic and welfare programmes, the maintenance of an *old* great power reach and responsibilities *and* the fighting of the Cold War (whose novelty the Cabinet paper recognized by placing the phrase within inverted commas). But a tightening of public money and manpower, a tweaking of the machinery of government and a burst of public exhortation was not much of a policy for tackling such a combination.

The next figure on whom we might intrude is Roy Jenkins' hero, Hugh Gaitskell,[110] then Chancellor of the Exchequer, as he tried to bring his colleagues on the Cabinet's Economic Policy Committee in closer line with realities during the crisis-ridden summer of 1951 a few months before Labour lost office to the Conservatives. Gaitskell's 'Economic Policy' paper of 22 June 1951 was devoted to the 'new circumstances' they faced which, in summary, were a dramatically worsening balance of payments position, renewed inflationary pressures and the difficulties being experienced in implementing the hugely expanded defence programme occasioned by the outbreak of the Korean War a year earlier and the general rearmament triggered by the resulting fear of a possible Third World War and the need to put military substance behind fledgling NATO structures.

The devaluation of the pound in September 1949, as intended, had made British goods more competitive in world markets and produced a set of excellent trade figures in 1950 as R. A. Butler, Gaitskell's successor, showed to the incoming Conservative Cabinet that following year. Between January and June 1950, the British economy had achieved a payments surplus of £42m. In July–December 1950 this had surged to £179m. But for the first six months of 1951, a deficit of exports over imports had appeared of £122m.[111]

Gaitskell's paper was eloquent about the extra strain resulting from Korea-related rearmament, especially on what Morrison called 'the economic machine', since the summer two years earlier when Morrison's analysis was put to the Cabinet – and all this against a worsening political backdrop since Bevan and Harold Wilson had resigned from the Cabinet in April 1951 over the level of rearmament and the introduction of limited health service charges. Gaitskell, understandably, did not infuse a formal Cabinet Committee paper with such intra-party political judgements but he was eloquent enough about it within the pages of his private diary during the summer of 1951:

Relations with the Bevanites continue to be very bad. They are apparently becoming more and more intransigent and extreme. They hope to capture the Party Conference and have, I am told, been forming themselves into a kind of shadow Government. They no doubt have a considerable following in the constituency parties; partly because it is difficult for the Government to put the case against them.[112]

What was the economic case that Gaitskell might have wished to make to explain the pressures and setbacks of 1951 and to what extent are they revealing of the wider economic and industrial problems of mid-twentieth-century Britain?

Exhibit two, therefore, is his Economic Policy Committee paper showing the impossibility and incompatibility of the five 'chief objectives' as Gaitskell summarized them:

(i)   To carry out the Defence Programme as smoothly and swiftly as possible [interesting and significant that this should be placed number one, showing both the profound impact of Korea-induced Cold War anxieties *and* the centrality of the planned quadrupling of defence spending over a three-year period[113]].

(ii) To maintain a level of exports sufficient to pay for our imports, excluding purchases for stockpiling.

(iii) To maintain as much as we can of our home investment programme.

(iv) Within the limits set by these aims, to maintain the highest possible standard of living for our people.

(v)   To keep inflation in check because it will endanger our balance of payments and give rise to acute social friction at home.[114]

The incompatibility and impossibility judgement is mine, not Gaitskell's, but his memorandum sings it out in a rather desperate refrain. Britain's was still very much a command/siege economy six years after the ending of the Second World War. Gaitskell reminded his fellow ministers that achieving the five objectives 'depends very much on getting enough raw materials – which largely govern the rate of increase of production; and on keeping in check import prices, which through changes in the terms of trade are now imposing a heavy burden on us in addition to rearmament'.[115]

The Americans were themselves stockpiling on a grand scale as part of their rearmament, which worsened the raw material position globally, while at home the 'execution of the Defence Programme is meeting difficulties in labour and material shortages'. The rise in import prices, warned Gaitskell, would push the sterling area into a dollar crisis once more and, as 'sterling is one of the two great international currencies of the world, . . . stability in international trade must in general be very advantageous to us, since as a nation we can only exist through a large volume of trade'.[116] Internally, inflation looked as if it might rise to 10 per cent over the year, creating an upward spiral; the trade unions were most unlikely to restore the voluntary wage restraint policy Cripps had persuaded them to adopt in 1949 (it lasted until the autumn of 1950[117]) and increasing government subsidies on food to keep the cost of living down was beyond the Exchequer's means. What could Gaitskell offer his colleagues? In his own words, 'no more than the outline of a policy' – abroad an attempt to get the Americans 'to agree on an effective policy for stabilising commodity prices in the world markets'; at home 'we should adopt a stricter credit policy [and] extend price control'.[118] And Gaitskell's was the finest-trained economist's mind to occupy the Chancellor's room since 1945.

For exhibit three we turn to the feline mind of his successor, R. A. Butler (whose university disciplines were history and international law[119]). In a celebrated page of his memoirs, the famously ironic 'Rab' recalled that Churchill appointed him to the Exchequer in 1951, instead of the more *laissez-faire*-inclined Oliver Lyttelton, while lying in bed at Hyde Park Gate, with the words, 'I have thought much about this offer and in the end Anthony [Eden] and I agreed that you would be best at handling the Commons. In this crisis of our Island life, when the cottage homes could so easily be engulfed in penury and want, we must not allow class or party feeling to be needlessly inflamed . . . It is no great matter that you are not an economist. [As Chancellor] I wasn't either.'[120]

Equally famous is Butler's description of how 'I started my Treasury life by responding to an invitation to meet Edward Bridges and William Armstrong at the Athenaeum Club. The first was head of the Treasury . . . the second, destined to head the civil service himself in later years, was to be my Private Secretary.'[121] (What Butler did not know was that when Gaitskell had come in that morning to say farewell to the Treasury, he 'found a letter waiting for me from Edward Bridges which contained, to my surprise, a very warm message from Churchill. This may of course be interpreted as a kind of first move towards a Coalition; or, on the other hand, it may be simply Winston's impulsiveness.'[122])

It had plainly been a long morning for all concerned on Monday 29 October 1951 because when Butler and the pair of Treasury men arrived at the Athenaeum,

[w]e sat at a table in the window and ate what remained of the Club food after the bishops had had their run; for we were somewhat late, and the bishops attack the sideboards early. Both my singularly able advisers stressed the critical state of the economy and promised me a memorandum within a few days. Their story was of blood draining from the system and a collapse greater than had been foretold in 1931. I returned home in sombre anticipation of what was to be dished up to me . . .[123]

Butler didn't have long to wait. Two days later Bridges exposed him for two hours to all the Treasury top brass. Also present was Robert Hall, the head of the Cabinet Office's Economic Section, who recorded the scene in his diary, which, in its own way, picked up, through Butler, Churchill's consensual determination that neither class nor party feeling should 'be needlessly inflamed':

The Chancellor, like Cripps, looks much less attractive in pictures than in the flesh. He was almost pathetically anxious to stand well with his officials but showed enough firmness when it was necessary: and enough ability to follow most of the arguments . . . We ran right through all the recommendations and it was rather sad to see how difficult it will be for the Tories to do what is needed without breaking most of their election pledges . . . It is a weakness, though it should be a strength of the Tories that they want to placate their opponents while Labour on the whole wants to appear to treat theirs as badly as possible. One might almost say that Labour would like to conceal pro-Capitalist measures under a cloak of anti-Capitalism and the Tories to conceal anti-Labour measures under a cloak of benevolence.[124]

Butler came to rate Hall very highly, describing him in his memoirs as 'our strong, silent man who came to have more and more influence'.[125] Later that day the outcome of the tyro Chancellor's first meeting of minds with his top Treasury echelon had been converted into exhibit three – the first paper to be taken by the Churchill Cabinet.

The combined effect of the Athenaeum lunch and his meeting with senior officials persuaded Butler of the need to chill the bones of Churchill and his colleagues. This he did by concentrating on the balance of payments, 'The Deteriorating Position and Outlook' being the key theme, and by opening with a piece of contemporary history:

We are in a balance of payments crisis, worse than 1949, and in many ways worse even than 1947. Confidence in sterling is impaired, as witness the large discounts on forward sterling in New York, and speculation against it is considerable, increasing the deficits and the drain on our gold and dollar reserves.[126]

So much for the beneficial effect of the devaluation just over two years earlier. The new rate was now under severe pressure. What of the export-led boom it was meant to engineer? As we have seen, the shining promise of 1950s performance was tarnished by a deficit of £122m for the first half of 1951. The Treasury's forecast for the second half was far worse – a deficit of £350m – such were the combined effects of the UK rearmament on its export industries and the impact of the Korean War on the price of imports.

'Currently,' Butler explained, '(i.e. in the present half-year) we are running an external *deficit* at a rate of £700 million a year, compared with an annual rate of *surplus* of some £350 million in the corresponding period a year ago – a deterioration of more than £1,000 million per annum.' The symbiotic relationship between trade performance and the UK's gold and dollar reserves was rammed home next. Current indicators 'would bring them down to under £900 million by 31st December, compared with their peak £1,381 million on 31st June – a loss of nearly £500 million in six months. The present drain on the reserves themselves is greater than at any time since the war.'[127] On top of all this, Butler said, had come the loss of oil from the Anglo-Iranian (later known as BP) refinery at Abadan following its nationalization by the Mossadegh government in Tehran.

Butler completed the analysis part of his 'Analysis and Remedies' paper by concluding:

This very serious deterioration in our position, coming as it does at the inception and not during the full impact of the rearmament programme, threatens the whole position of sterling and of the United Kingdom and sterling area [essentially the British Empire and Commonwealth – minus Canada which was in the dollar zone – plus the Republic of Ireland]. It is a clear indication not only that there are serious underlying weaknesses in our position, but also that foreign confidence in our ability to deal with these weaknesses is greatly impaired.

Hence the new Chancellor's recommendation that 'the first and most important object' of the new government's policy should be the putting right of the UK's economic position and the restoration of confidence in the pound.[128]

Robert Hall was right: for a government coming in on a cry, as Churchill put it during the campaign, that election day, 25 October, would be 'a day of liberation from fears as well as from follies',[129] a tightening, through state intervention, of existing austerity was hardly consistent with setting the people free from socialist policies. But this is exactly what Butler felt obliged to place before the Cabinet and, as he put it later: 'The first move was to cut imports, and cut them good and hard', with £350m 'knocked off' external expenditure in November 1951 with a further £150m off in January and another £100m in March 1952.[130] Rationed as well as unrationed food was hit, though a degree of 'special consideration should be given to housing', reflecting the manifesto pledge, Churchill's wishes and Macmillan's clout. Overriding priority would be granted to coal and steel output, the engineering industry and exports. On monetary matters, Butler broke with Labour's 'cheap money' policy, restoring a degree of flexibility not seen since before the war and announcing a rise in Bank rate (as the Bank of England base rate was then called) from 2 to 2.5 per cent when he made his statement to the House of Commons on 7 November. Hall's diary entry for the following day was intriguing:

The speech yesterday was a great success – I had a few words with EB [Edward Bridges] just after and he was obviously delighted, a most unusual compliment . . . It's a great thing to have got so far safely, told Ministers the worst and got them to tell the country and adopt some remedies. The crisis is so like several we have had in the past that I don't think anyone minds much. There is a run on tinned meat. Bank Rate went off calmly enough and the stock exchange actually improved.[131]

Much to decode there: the degree to which Butler's Cabinet paper and Commons statement were shaped by the Treasury and a recognition that the country had become used to a kind of permanent economic crisis since 1945 whose eruptions usually meant a temporary and immediate tightening in their food consumption.

Butler's Cabinet paper, though pointing to 'serious underlying weaknesses', did not anatomize these apart, implicitly, from the levels of overseas spending and defence costs. Hall's diary and Butler's 'Analysis and Remedies' paper were, to a remarkable degree, an unconscious echo of Keynes's paper on the unsupportability of the costs of the British Empire and Britain's other overseas responsibilities which he prepared for the War Cabinet as the European war came to a close in 1945 (of which I made much in Never Again[132]). With characteristic linguistic verve, Keynes noted the lack of effective Treasury control on military spending overseas: 'When we had thrown the Germans out of Africa, and the Middle East was no longer in danger, our expenditure in those parts remained much as before. The Major-Generals in Cairo look like becoming chronic [fixtures] . . . the prima facie evidence of the global statistics is that unless it is advisable and practicable to bring this expenditure under [drastic control at an early date (and perhaps it is not), our ability to pursue an independent financial policy in the early post-war years will be fatally impaired.'[133]

So it proved. Despite imperial withdrawal from the Indian subcontinent, the handing over of military responsibility for the defence of Greece and Turkey to the USA, two punishing sterling crises in 1947 and 1949, the worsening Cold War and continuing imperial commitments, the unquestioned appetite of Attlee and his senior ministers that Britain should remain a great power meant, as Bernard Alford has calculated, that the UK's 'continuing commitment to defence on a world scale' resulted in defence spending in 1951 (because of the Korea-related surge) accounting 'for 20 per cent of total public expenditure or 7.6 per cent of GDP [gross domestic product]'.[134]

Whether the problem of both the major-generals abroad and their Whitehall ministers at home could have or would have remained, in Keynes's words, so 'chronic' had not the dollar lifeline in the shape of the American loan and, later, substantial Marshall Aid been forthcoming from the USA is a serious question. Almost certainly without it, substantial adjustments would have had to be made to the external expenditure Keynes saw as so threatening to the UK's financial independence. In 1951, Keynes (who died during Easter 1946) was no longer there to give the Treasury tough remedies to sell to the Cabinet. But Robert Hall, in some ways Keynes's successor as the leading economic mind in Whitehall, was, and he had no doubt on this score, recognizing in his diary in July 1951 that: 'We have had [from the USA] an average of over a billion dollars a year one way and another since 1946 and of course under Lend/Lease [during the Second World War] we had a great deal more. In fact our whole economic life has been propped up in this way.'[135]

It is utterly naïve to read *forward* from Keynes's 1945 paper to the War Cabinet and *back* from early twenty-first-century Britain (albeit at the time of writing under a Prime Minister who has presided over more War Cabinets than any other premier since 1945) and conclude that the accumulated responsibilities of at least a couple of centuries of empire and great powerdom could be shed substantially, swiftly or easily in the years after 1945, even if the Cold War had not rapidly developed into a severe and protracted anxiety. And, as international historian Paul Kennedy has put it:

It's very difficult psychologically and culturally to be in the first . . . or second generation of the decision-makers who confront relative decline and feel that they have to do something about it. And it seems to me perfectly natural, knowing how human beings behave, that they tend to deny it and say: 'Well look, all it needs is a patch-up job or a little bit of change here, not a major transformation.'[136]

Alongside Butler's first paper to the Churchill Cabinet, we must examine exhibit four, its Siamese twin – the memorandum on 'British Overseas Obligations' presented to the same body by the Foreign Secretary, Sir Anthony Eden, in June 1952. Before dissecting it, we must bear in mind not only Kennedy's humane appreciation of how difficult it is to contemplate harsh reality in the first or second generation of those in straitened circumstances but also Napoleon's exhortation to recall how the world looked when one was twenty (1917 in Eden's case) if we wish to understand it.

His paper began impressively enough with an air of toughness and self-awareness, apart from its caveat which I have put in italics. Its object, the Foreign Secretary told his colleagues, was to consider the extent to which 'the United Kingdom is committed overseas and to examine where *if anywhere* our responsibilities can be reduced so as to bring them more into line with our available resources'.[37] Significantly, Eden placed before a rather Paul Kennedy-like analysis about the relationship between a nation's economic performance and its global reach, his view of the 'fundamental factors' which 'determined' British foreign policy:

(a) The United Kingdom has world responsibilities inherited from several hundred years as a great Power.
(b) The United Kingdom is not a self-sufficient economic unit.
(c) No world security system exists, and the United Kingdom with the rest of the non-Communist world, is faced with an external threat.

Next came Eden's pre-echo of Kennedy's 'imperial overstretch' and post-echo of Keynes's 'chronic' major-generals:

The essence of a sound foreign policy is to ensure that a country's strength is equal to its obligations. If this is not the case, then either the obligations must be reduced to the level at which resources are available to maintain them, or a greater share of the country's resources must be devoted to their support. It is becoming clear that vigorous maintenance of the presently-accepted policies of Her Majesty's Government at home and abroad is placing a burden on the country's economy which is beyond the resources of the country to meet. A position has already been reached where there is no reserve and therefore no margin for unforeseen additional obligations.[138]

The paper plunges straight into an abyss at this point by making plain what is unthinkable and, therefore, off the agenda despite the presence of great burdens and the absence of the money to pay for them, illustrating perfectly the point made by Kennedy-as-psychotherapist. Their 'first task', Eden told the Cabinet,

must be to determine how far the external obligations of the country can be reduced or shared with others, or transferred to other shoulders, without impairing too seriously the world position of the United Kingdom and sacrificing the vital advantages which flow from it. But if, after careful review, it is shown that the total effort required is still beyond the capacity of existing national resources, a choice of the utmost difficulty lies before the British people, for they must either give up, for a time, some of the advantages which a high standard of living confers upon them, or, by relaxing their grip in the outside world, see their country sink to the level of a second-class Power, with injury to their essential interests and way of life of which they can have little conception. Faced with this choice, the British people might be rallied to a greater productive effort which would enable a greater volume of external commitments to be borne.[139]

Quite apart from its depiction of 'the British people' as a fine, loyal, if unthinking body of people devoted to the idea of their country cutting a significant figure in the world, the linkages between global reach and wealth are asserted as givens. (Five years later, once Macmillan had succeeded Eden as Prime Minister, he commissioned the first ever cost–benefit analysis of the British Empire, which came to a rather different conclusion, as we shall see.)

Eden, understandably enough, went on to explain how the Cold War meant it would be difficult to engineer 'a complete abandonment of a major commitment . . . in the present state of world tension', for 'unless arrangements have been made for the burden to be transferred to friendly shoulders, the Russians would be only too ready to fill any vacuum created by a British withdrawal . . .' But it is the notion of Britain's 'prestige' being linked by hoops of steel to its 'status as a World Power' which dominates the pages of Eden's memorandum and drives out any possibility of significant new thinking that might engender the slightest chance of British ambitions being reconciled to the capacity of the UK economy to sustain them. This is the paradox which proved to be such an aider and abetter of the country's relative economic decline – fear of collapse into second-rater status led to a sustained allocation of an excessive amount of the UK's productive resources to relatively unproductive purposes, which weakened still further the ability of the British economy to construct the sinews of great powerdom.

There is no trace at all in Eden's key paragraphs of this self-reinforcing and malign vortex at work. Instead the choice is presented as an ethereal if not quite divine mission, the alternative to which is a collapse into the unknown. Withdrawal from 'a major commitment', Eden told the Cabinet,

would affect the international status of the United Kingdom. By reducing the value of the United Kingdom as a partner and ally, it would undermine the cohesion of the Commonwealth and the special relationship of the United Kingdom with the United States and its European partners and other allies. Their attitude towards us will depend largely upon our status as a World Power and upon their belief that we are ready and willing to support them. It is evident that in so far as we reduce our commitments and our power declines, our claim to the leadership of the Commonwealth, to a position of influence in Europe, and to a special relationship with the United States will be, *pro tanto*, diminished.

The economy did intrude at this point, but, according to Eden's analysis, its vitality, too, was inseparable from being a major power as 'the British world position brings with it concurrent and beneficial results of an economic and financial nature. The abandonment of our position in any area of the world may well have similar concurrent and adverse effects on our economic and trading interests.' Notice Eden's use of the word 'any' here and the implicit acceptance that imperial preference in trade and a world role for sterling and the City of London were natural boosters of British power.

The peroration which follows has an air of defiance and desperation in equal measure, most interesting in a politician who, just over four years later, would lead his country into a war with Egypt because, for him, a line had to be drawn on further British humiliation and decline:

Finally, there is the general effect of loss of prestige. It is impossible to assess in concrete terms the consequences to ourselves and the Commonwealth of our drastically and unilaterally reducing our responsibilities; the effects of a failure of will and relaxation of grip in our overseas commitments are incalculable. But once the prestige of a country has started to slide there is no knowing where it will stop.[140]

Eden's patriotism could never be doubted, but his sense of reality could. That passage reminds me of two things. First, the Permanent Secretary of the Foreign Office in Edwardian times, Sir Thomas Sanderson, who wrote (privately, naturally) in 1907 that reading the newspapers left an impression of the British Empire as a 'huge giant sprawling over the globe, with gouty fingers and toes stretching in every direction, which cannot be approached without eliciting a scream'.[141] Eden's section on the Falkland Island Dependencies in the South Atlantic (the island of South Georgia and other, tinier outcrops), for example, is pure Sanderson:

A very minor commitment which we could endeavour to dispose of to the United States is the Falkland Islands Dependencies. I do not, however, advise such action, for public admission of our inability to maintain these traditional possessions would cause a loss of prestige wholly out of proportion to the saving in money obtained. It might precipitate a scramble by the numerous claimants to various parts of British territory.[142]

Such desperate clinging to the notion of 'prestige', its inviolability and indivisibility, also reminds one of Peter Laslett's warning in 1950 that: 'The peace of the world depends ... on the Englishman being able to reconcile himself to a continuous diminution in the consequence of his country. This can only be done if he can learn to separate his personal prestige from the prestige of his nation state.'[143] Eden plainly could not – then or later. The chief conclusion that Eden placed before the Cabinet in June 1952 was that the UK should try 'gradually and inconspicuously' to 'transfer the real burdens', in the Middle East and South-East Asia especially, 'from our own to American shoulders ...'[144]

This 1952 version of Sanderson's 'gouty giant' is a vivid revelation of the geopolitical paralysis which gripped Whitehall's policy-makers until the shock of Suez stimulated a percussive series of reviews and reappraisals examined later in this volume. Decline adds to the sense of precariousness which, in turn, freezes the nerve to do anything about it for fear of prestige loss and further, uncontrollable slippage. Substantial and sustained overseas and defence commitments plus the cost of investing at home in the social and welfare programmes at the heart of the British New Deal had much to do with the UK's relative underperformance economically and help explain why Britain's 'Thirty Golden Years' were not so gilded as those of its western European neighbours, Germany, France, Italy and Benelux in particular.

Here the figures do tell a story; explaining which factors lay behind that story is the problem. A preoccupation with growth progressively gripped the British political class in the late 1950s and early 1960s. This was partly in response to the publication of influential 'Penguin Specials' such as Andrew Shonfield's 1958 study *British Economic Policy since the War*, which seriously questioned the value to the British economy of the sterling area[145] whose weakening or, worse still, dissolution so worried Eden in his 1952 paper. (No surprise here: 'This would be regarded in other countries as a heavy blow to the influence and prestige of the United Kingdom; it would undermine the cohesion of the Commonwealth; and would thus further weaken British authority in world affairs.'[146]) Shonfield had no doubt in the late 1950s that '[a]t the root of Britain's economic troubles are the political objectives of a great power.'[147]

By the time Michael Shanks's landmark volume *The Stagnant Society* appeared in 1961,[148] the original six nations within the Common Market of the European Economic Community were already benefiting from the second tranche of European integration that started on 1 January 1958 (the first being the Coal and Steel Community which began operating in 1952) and were opening up a still wider growth gap between themselves and the UK, which had declined to join them in phases one and two. For the politically literate and the economically numerate, such figures became the common currency of political exchange. Take a look at the average annual percentage rates of growth per-capita GDP at constant prices shown in the table below.[149]

COUNTRY	1959–1960	1960–1970
Belgium	2.0[a]	4.1
France	3.5	4.6
Germany (West)	6.6	3.5
Italy	4.9[b]	4.6
Japan	6.8[c]	9.4
Netherlands	3.3	4.1
UK	2.3	2.3
USA	1.2	3.0

Notes: ECSC/EEC nations are in italics; [a]figures for 1953–60; [b]figures for 1951–60; [c]figures for 1952–60.

Measurement matters. Herbert Morrison, the creator of the *Economic Surveys*, the annual expression of the Attlee government's rudimentary and generally ineffectual planning machinery,[150] used to stress the need for 'statistical floodlighting'.[151] There has been no shortage of this in postwar Britain. Harold Wilson as Prime Minister was similarly obsessed,[152] and, under his first administrations in the 1960s, there was a substantial influx of professional economists and statisticians into Whitehall.[153] But bathing British industries and services in the light of a Whitehall arc lamp was one thing; understanding the causes of what was thereby illuminated quite another. There were some in Whitehall who always appreciated this. Douglas Allen (who became Lord Croham on retirement from the civil service in 1977) was the first university-trained economist and statistician to fill the seat of Permanent Secretary to the Treasury (which he did from 1968 to 1974).

Allen was by nature a sceptic who did not shrink from telling ministers what he thought they needed to know rather than what they wished to hear. For example, he was (and remained so later) convinced as a young official in the Central Economic Planning Staff that the unsustainable Korean War-related rearmament instituted by the Attlee government so damaged the late-1940s export drive that the best chance of a postwar British economic miracle was lost for good.[154] And he thought that there were limits to what his fellow economists could do. For example, as Permanent Secretary to the Department of Economic Affairs, Labour's growth ministry in the mid-to-late 1960s, Allen believed that ministers' insistence on picking a growth rate target substantially higher than the 2.5 to 3 per cent usually achieved by the British economy without understanding what underlay that level of performance was 'farcical' and self-defeating.[155]*

Lord Croham is one of a small band of trained economists in the UK who has also held one of the great public positions where finance and administration meet. Their twin professions can give them a special bite as analysts. Another in a later generation is Mervyn King.

In the summer of 2003, King and I conducted a small exercise on the 'relative decline theme'. A friend of mine since our shared Harvard days as Kennedy Scholars over thirty years earlier, Mervyn King had just become Governor of the Bank of England. Mervyn was a rarity in the history of the gubernatorial office in being both a top-flight scholar and a central banker. Not only is he an economic theoretician of distinction, he has a passion for history. Over lunch to celebrate his new office, I asked him to write down on the back of the menu the factors that might be – but should not be – over-

---

* I remember one typically jovial-cum-sceptical lunch with him in the mid-1970s, by which time he had left the Treasury to become Head of the Home Civil Service, when the conversation went like this:

'Have you noticed, Douglas, that since all those economists and statisticians started pouring into Whitehall ten years ago, the pace of our relative economic decline has quickened?'

'Yes, Peter, but there's one consolation. Ours will become the best-measured decline in world economic history!' [156]

looked in any attempt to investigate the vicissitudes of Britain's economic performance in the years since 1945.[157]

Mervyn King's 'lunchtime list' was in the spirit of David Landes, not least because it included the cultural elements which have increasingly gained a place in the debate about Great Britain's relative economic decline. These were the factors the Governor wrote out spontaneously and without prior warning over his lunch table as those I should consider in the search for UK-specific explanations on several levels:

· Productivity growth
· Labour market/restrictive practices
· Tax system and attitudes towards it
· Macroeconomic policy, rise of inflation, intellectual failings of the economics profession
· Education and management
· Nobel prizes v. R and D.
· Inflation; composition of the retail prices index

As befitted a senior vice-president of Aston Villa Football Club, Mervyn enjoined me not to forget to use sport, soccer in particular, as an illustration of the indispensability of international competition as a spur to domestic performance – how English soccer, the national side having disdained to appear in the World Cup until 1950, when they were beaten 1–0 in Brazil by what the immortal Tom Finney of Preston North End and England called 'a team of no-hopers from the United States'[158] and failed to proceed beyond the first round, took decades to adjust to the best in the world, and then only after overseas players began to enrich the League in the 1990s. (The Hungarians' destruction of England 6–3 at Wembley in 1953 had left Finney 'thinking we were light years behind' the best of the continentals.[159])

At the outset of any search for home-grown causes of Britain's relative economic underperformance, an immediate danger lurks of an excessive and narrowly national (even nationalistic) concentration on the UK and its singularities. Another is to use as scapegoats groups or factors which, sometimes unconsciously, fall conveniently in line with one's own views about politics, society and political economy.

A great cast of possibilities is thrown up by Mervyn King's list of factors (especially in terms of productivity, labour relations and the quality of management), depending on one's place on the intellectual/political spectrum

– excessive trade union power since 1906; too many nationalized industries between the late 1940s and the late 1980s; a lack of entrepreneurship since the 1880s; too many wars (hot and cold) since 1914; the distraction of imperialism and the survival of the Great Power impulse long after the Empire's demise; a generally feeble political class divided into parties obsessed by crude notions of capital versus labour; a supine and unprofessional civil service; an enduring aristocratic landed-cum-financial tradition which never really gave way to an industrial-managerial spirit; a determinedly non-vocational educational system at all levels. And finally, often capping the lot and infecting most of the other factors, a ruinous capacity to let social class get in the way of progress, with said class fixation mutating to the point of genius and reinventing itself in different forms generation upon generation.[160]

But, before plunging into the maelstrom of rival laments and explanations, what of the wider picture? Economic historians have long focused on the notion of 'catch up' – that countries which pioneer breakthroughs such as a scientific revolution which transforms technological and industrial possibilities granting great competitive advantage cannot expect that hard-won bonus to last. Rivals learn from innovators' mistakes and often swiftly outperform them. They talk, too, of 'convergence clubs' of relatively advanced nations whose human, technological and physical capital means that they are likely to move forward together, jockeying for relative position within fairly narrow parameters.

This was very much a feature of postwar western European experience in which the UK's economic performance was couched. As Alan Milward has pointed out, it is misleading to date the postwar western European boom from around 1950; the reconstruction period of 1945–50 was not only the platform on which it was built, it was integral to it not least because the European Recovery Programme (as Marshall Aid was officially known) 'permitted the sustained high levels of investment in 1947 and 1948'[161] which, but for the wider dollar lifeline, would have been choked off by struggling governments (or embryo government in the case of the Western Zones in Germany). As Milward puts it:

With few exceptions analyses of Western Europe's greatest and largest economic boom suggest that it was a phenomenon of the 1950s which gradually petered out in the 1960s. The most frequently given starting date for this astonishing period of increasing output and incomes is 1950 itself. There is no justification for this. The trend of growth of national income was unbroken, if diminishing, between 1945 and 1960 and by any possible statistical definition Western Europe's greatest boom began with the end of the war and proceeded without interruption until 1967. There is only a separate 'reconstruction period' in the sense . . . [of] . . . the period of time taken to create a satisfactory international basis for the *continuation* of the boom.[162]

The key question about the UK at this time for economic historians – and for any investigator of the phenomenon of relative decline in its mid-twentieth-century phase – is why the 'sustained growth of manufactured exports and levels of productivity' elements of the transition from reconstruction to sustained boom were those 'for which Britain's own reconstruction had left the economy particularly ill-equipped'.[163] Some believe that to treat this as a core question of great importance (as I do) is to perpetuate a distortion present even in the early 1950s. The mere fact that output was no longer measured in terms of British-owned goods and services (gross *national* product) but as gross *domestic* product (i.e. *all* the goods and services produced annually in the UK from both British- and foreign-owned companies) should illustrate the folly, even before a renewed globalization had begun to rip, of treating a country's wealth as somehow different if it has not been generated solely from the efforts of born-and-bred Britons. Andrew Gamble, one of the most accomplished synthesizers of the great British decline debate, captured the intellectual and econometric problems here perfectly. As the twentieth century turned, he wrote:

[so long] as there are national governments . . . the lure of thinking in terms of national economic spaces, how such territorially defined populations and economies perform against one another, and how policy might improve performance is bound to be strong. But on a longer view the discourse of decline seems likely to fade away.[164]

This represents a big claim for a debate that began to bite into the British psyche almost from the moment the exhibits were taken away from Joseph Paxton's Crystal Palace in Hyde Park after the Great Exhibition of 1851, when Britain had 41 per cent of the world's trade in manufactures (by the end of the 1950s this was down to 14.5 per cent).[165] For Gamble, the great decline debate is likely eventually to go the way of the British Empire because

[m]any of the narratives underpinning it have collapsed. The era of protectionism and developmental states [those with a strong central apparatus intended to steer their economies] is over, and Britain's Empire is becoming a distant memory. Within a single market and single-currency Europe, national economic decline would have no meaning. But even if Britain were to withdraw from the European Union or the European Union were to fall apart, decline will not be the dominant framework of interpretation in the

twenty-first century in the way that it has been in the twentieth. The re-emergence of a unified global economy and the redistribution of state functions between different levels within the international state system profoundly changes the concerns of domestic politics and the way in which these are expressed.[166]

Gamble may well be right when he judges that twenty-first-century historians 'are likely to see decline, in part, as a specific episode in British history determined by the particular circumstances of Britain's loss of hegemony and the slow adjustment of the British political class to this change, and in part as a set of discourses which constructed decline as a problem and urged political action to remedy it'.[167]

Taking a truly *longue durée* approach, one might extend the Gamble analysis-cum-prediction and argue that the UK's relative economic decline should be seen as a particularly protracted fluctuation within the cycles of ups, downs, recoveries and rises that take place within a 'convergence club' which, since the United States and Germany joined it and reawoke a peculiarly British angst from the last quarter of the nineteenth century, has seen more and more advancing nations first knock on its door and then gain entry. For all these longer views and speculations, it remains true that the condition of the national UK political economy, and its place within the sterling area and a system of imperial tariffs, meant these questions were lively, serious and relevant and that no accurate reconstruction of mid-twentieth-century Britain is complete without a treatment of them.

So why, in Milward's words, was the British economy so 'particularly ill-equipped' to make the early 1950s transition from the 'reconstruction' boom to the sustained wider western European one based upon the remarkable 'growth of manufactured exports and levels of productivity'?[168] At such moments, the mix of explanations can be powerfully laced, if the politically partisan or highly ideologically charged are involved, with huge doses of scapegoating. In 1958, Shonfield saw the 'central failure of postwar Britain' as 'inadequate investment' crippled by political choices which allowed the maintenance of a big defence budget and the sustenance of a reserve currency to produce one balance of payments crisis after another, the remedy for which was domestic deflation to prop up the pound at the expense of production.[169] In the early 1960s Michael Shanks wanted more and better planning, exposure to competition by joining the Common Market and a rebuilding of Britain's trade union movement which, with some justification, he saw as 'a decaying empire', rather like eighteenth-century Spain in which, as 'the grasp and vigour of the centre slackens, in the outer provinces rebel leaders – called "wildcats" in this context – operate with greater and greater impunity, and shop stewards like guerrilla princelings establish their own little autonomous empires'.[170]

For Landes too, writing nearly twenty years on from that crucial 1950–51 fulcrum in his masterly *The Unbound Prometheus*, it was the weight of its history bearing upon an old country which led Britain to

misread completely the needs and opportunities of the post war economy. Her face was resolutely turned backwards; her efforts, directed towards the restoration of the *status quo ante* [the Second World War]: the primacy of the pound sterling, the special commercial ties of the Empire and Commonwealth, the protection of British workers from painful competition.[171]

Landes (in a view from Harvard which strongly stressed the spiritual rather than the measurable, which in turn led him to place great emphasis on entrepreneurship) brutally dissected the different legacy of attitudes the 1940s bequeathed the *status quo* nation par excellence (the UK) and the fresh-starters, most of whom formed the nascent European communities of 1952 and 1958:

European businessmen of the fifties were learning to look on change as normal, even good, where they had once feared it and worked to dampen its effects. The European governments that had, as a result of the depression of the thirties, assumed with some reluctance the obligation to maintain employment, now accepted the much more far-reaching obligation to sustain and foster growth ... the people of Europe came to look at expansion and improvement as normal, even indispensable.[172]

By contrast, the 'record of British negotiations in the forties and fifties is a litany of timorous clichés covering the rejection of promising but hazardous opportunities'. This, said Landes succumbing fully to preaching mode, 'is the sin of anachronism – for a nation, there is none more deadly ...'[173]

There is plentiful evidence for the anachronistic impulse, not least in the short, if monstrously eventful, twenty years following the Ottawa Agreement of 1932 when, in response to the collapse of the gold standard in 1931, a national coalition government set aside the free trade synonymous with the UK's political economy since Peel's time and cocooned the British economy in the warm but eventually delusory security blanket of an Empire- and Commonwealth-wide tariff-based trading arrangement (imperial preference) with a currency system (the sterling area) to protect it still further from the chill winds of a depression-wracked and increasingly autarkic world.

As a result of Ottawa, the proportion of British trade with the Empire and Commonwealth rose to new heights. When war broke out in 1939, almost half the UK's exports went to the Empire (29 per cent to the five dominions: Australia, New Zealand, Canada, South Africa and the Irish Free State; 19 per cent to India and the colonies; a further 15 per cent to Latin America and the scattering of other countries usually treated as part of the 'informal' British Empire).[174] These were 'soft' markets. Trading in them did little to sharpen the competitive edge of British industry.[175]

The consequences of this were becoming increasingly evident during the years when Morrison, Gaitskell and Butler were drafting their respective analyses and remedies and Eden was telling the Cabinet why no serious adjustment could be made anywhere in the UK's overseas obligations for fear of an adverse balance of payments in that most evanescent but to him so powerful commodity known as 'prestige'. For while 'British exports stagnated in 1949 in uncompetitive and undemanding markets ... intra-Western European trade continued to grow powerfully, creating an expanding market for high-value exports ... Furthermore, British manufactured exports were finding their main market in economies where in the next decade they would be most at the mercy of import-substitution policies imposed by governments seeking more rapid development.'[176]

Here lies the link with the Landes analysis of a timorous, risk-averse, backward-looking political class that could not contemplate joining the first steps at European economic integration represented by the outline for a European Coal and Steel Community (ECSC) brought to London in May 1950 by the extraordinary genius behind France's postwar planning apparatus, Jean Monnet.[177] As Alan Milward put it,

deep anxiety about Britain's international position in the 1930s, the protectionism which arose from that, the inability to find any certain way in which the high standard of living which trade and industrialization had created in Britain could be enhanced in the future, the conviction that no risks could be taken with exports, the war effort, the defeat of Germany and the influence that had in preventing government from coming to terms with the longer view of history in which that enormous event was only a temporary aberration – all these things kept Britain out of the ECSC.[178]

Yet it was precisely within the integrating western European market, whether a participant's national economic strategy was noticeably based on state planning like France or that of a social market such as the new West Germany, that the intangibles Landes attempted to anatomize were at work, producing, in contrast to the UK, a virtuous circle whose arcs were delineated by high-quality, high-value goods circulating powerfully amid rising productivity rates as the consumer boom built on itself and stimulated in turn a boom in manu-facturing exports to the rest of the world.[179]

To be sure, Britain could not slough off its external debts as the defeated Germany and Italy had; and its empire and world role were far more distended than France's (neither was France trying to run a big world reserve currency). But the 1932 solutions to the threats of an unforgiving world looked increas-ingly tatty as the pattern of world trade shifted away from the old imperial arrangements. Instead, the Bretton Woods monetary system, the liberalizing effects of the tariff-cutting rounds of GATT (the General Agreement on Tariffs and Trade, the institution established in 1947 to pursue freer trade alongside the International Monetary Fund and the World Bank created after the Bret-ton Woods conference of 1944) *and* the remarkable economic dynamic of non-UK western Europe increasingly made the pace and surpassed any of the expectations even the most fervent integrators could have entertained for it in 1951.[180]

These were the immediate if almost wholly unappreciated problems which confronted the men in the Cabinet committee rooms and atop the Whitehall ministries as they tried to fire up an economy now required to finance a Brit-ish New Deal at home, a hefty residual empire abroad and find enough troops and weapons to increase the chances that Stalin's Red Army would remain east of the River Elbe. What of the deeper-set and more enduring problems, among which, for example, must be included those on Mervyn King's lunch-time list?

It is significant that Professor King placed productivity at the top as the key indicator of relative performance – output per worker per hour – as this is a revealing factor which applies to any national economic unit irrespective of the size of its workforce. And here, I think, we find a phenomenon at work (or, rather, not working properly) that is crucial to any explanation of the UK's relative underperformance. For as Sir Alec Cairncross, a man better placed than perhaps any other to observe the wider picture across the postwar period from 1945 to 1968, when he retired as Head of the Government Economic Service,[181] put it, 'in relation to the investment that *was* undertaken [in postwar Britain], the response in additional output was disappointing in comparison with the response elsewhere'.[182]

Relatively poor productivity was recognized by the Attlee government as a fundamental problem, and managers and trade unionists were despatched to the USA by Sir Stafford Cripps in the late 1940s as members of the Anglo-American Council on Productivity (part of the Marshall Aid programme[183]). These emissaries may have seen the results of a productivity rate twice the UK's, but they seem to have found precious few ways of narrowing that gap once back in their British factories. The need for a high level of standardization in successful mass-production was a common theme among the returning seekers-after-efficiency.[184] And here several anatomists of decline have pointed to the observations of the British economic historian Hrothgar (later known as Sir John) Habbakuk. Habbakuk, in his influential comparison of British and American technological development in the nineteenth century which he published in 1962,[185] noticed that from the outset, the USA's catch-up trajectory built in labour-saving features (a vigorous approach to time and motion, heavy investment in new employment and a determined pursuit of economies of scale) suitable to a vast but relatively thinly populated economic unit without the craft/skills base enjoyed by both the maker of the first industrial revolution (the UK) and its great European pursuer (Germany).[186]

The persuasiveness of this analysis is enhanced when seen as an important factor in why Britain failed to dominate the 'second industrial revoluation' of the late nineteenth century (based on electricity, large mass-production lines, sophisticated synthetic organic chemistry and the internal combustion engine) as a newly unified UK had created and led the first industrial revolution in the eighteenth century (based on coal, steam-power and a craft/apprentice system with a high premium of relatively small clusters of noticeably skilled workers).[187]

The argument is further strengthened when we observe how stubbornly UK labour productivity remained stuck at around half the American level for the bulk of the postwar years[188] and the persistent if 'unsuccessful attempt to apply American mass production techniques'[189] even after the UK gained access to the huge European market which might, at last, have fed back into ever-more competitive production lines in Britain. Some analysts point to the relatively improved UK productivity levels of the 1980s and 1990s, after allowing for the curbing of union power in the Thatcher years, as partly reflecting how 'technological trends had moved back in Britain's favour'.[190]

And here we come to at least three of Governor King's other factors – education and management; pure scientific prowess as opposed to applied science and technology ('Nobel Prizes v. R and D'); and the condition of the labour market and the social underpinnings of the society in which it operates.

The most persuasive analysts of the economic take-offs which have produced the world's advanced industrial societies tend to stress two aspects of the initial concatenation of circumstances that produced it, in the British Isles in particular. The first is the precarious shift in the balance of forces in a society needed for the first trigger – or what Ernest Gellner calls the relationships between the wielders of the 'plough' and the 'sword' and the creators and disseminators of the 'book'.[191] That without a fortuitous initial detonator, a 'cognitive transformation', where knowledge can be acquired and applied that is free of tribal or religious restrictions protected by the efforts of the specialists in violence and the guardians of belief and orthodoxy at the service of the old regimes, no scientific revolution is possible. Only such a revolution can provide the corpus of scientific analysis, the second indispensable trigger for an economic, technological and industrial revolution that sustains itself with ever greater output and reach, transforming landscapes, living patterns and societies as it goes. The final trigger – the one needed to prevent a serious faltering in this dynamic, interlocking process that might bring about a collapse back into old ways with the bookmen succumbing once more to the ploughmen and swordsmen who prevailed in the old, pre-industrial agricultural societies – is the installation of a set of political and social arrangements which create what Gellner calls a 'social bribery fund',[192] the state benefits and subsidies sufficient to buy off both the hankerers after the old and those suffering the transition pains of the new.

This summary hardly does justice to a very sophisticated argument, but the inner cores of successful and sustainable advanced societies, if you accept the essentials of this analysis, as I do, are twofold: the scientific revolution must proceed apace with its knowledge successfully converted into productive output; and the maintenance of such societies, not least their educational and general welfare bases, must be overseen and, if necessary, guaranteed by a larger, more sophisticated and more intrusive state.

Ernest Gellner was a philosopher, social anthropologist and historian whose very mixture of the polymathic has, I think, prevented him from having the influence he deserved on the historiography of western Europe. For his wider-angled look at the essences of the advanced industrial societies which developed in their different ways within the multiplicity of political units between the Atlantic and the Urals has much to offer to those attempting to comprehend the factors at work in mid-twentieth-century Britain, for all its singularities.

For example, could it not be argued that one of the spectres haunting the

Cabinet Room when late 1940s and early 1950s sets of ministers sat down to grapple, in bafflement and gloom, with a lumpy, sluggish economy, a rocky currency and a depressing balance of payments position was the relative failure of the UK of fifty to sixty years *earlier* to match the human capital investment many of its larger competitors were making, whether it be in the technical high schools of Germany or the 'Land Grant' higher education institutions in the USA? Late-Victorian and Edwardian attempts to produce a British equivalent, in Imperial College, London to the Massachusetts Institute of Technology or the already legendary technical universities of Wilhelmine Germany were sufficiently prominent neither in quantity nor in prestige compared to the stranglehold that the classical humanities and the pure sciences jointly exerted across the tiny British university system as a whole.[193] (There were no business schools in the UK until the 1960s; the first in the USA, the Wharton, part of the University of Pennsylvania, opened its doors in 1881.[194])

With the apex of the educational system so little infused with the attitudes required by a scientific and advanced industrial society, little wonder that the best endowed schools reflected this while the less well-endowed were obsessed with the religious questions that bedevilled elementary schooling until the Butler Act of 1944 reached a satisfactory settlement.[195] It was hardly surprising, therefore, that these factors, together with a crafts-based apprentice system suitable for the first industrial revolution, left Britain poorly placed to triumph in the second. Add to this the serious seepage of resources, physical and human, in the two world wars and it is no surprise that a memorandum on the economic position from the Lord President or the Chancellor, let alone a paper from the Foreign Secretary on the difficulties of sustaining the UK's global position, were not occasions for universal rejoicing in Mr Attlee's or Mr Churchill's Whitehall.

The lingering scars of the first industrial revolution, whose healing was so much a motive force of the British New Deal, might have appeared to be on the mend during and just after the first Labour government in power with a majority was installed and its place as an estate of the realm established by the repeal of the punitive post-General Strike Trades Disputes Act 1927 as an early Cabinet priority. There was a powerful human factor, too, in the presence of Ernest Bevin, the incarnation of Labourism, at the Cabinet table. And many of the welfare changes of 1945–8 were dedicated to improving the lot of the three-quarters of the population who were then manual working people or members of their families (a proportion much as it had been before the

Great War).[196] In this sense, the trade unions and their representatives had come of age, but as with other elements of the New Deal there were paralysis-inducing rigidities about enhanced union power, especially in the lack of mobility within the labour force which was a far more important constraint than the power of monopoly trade unions within the public monopolies of the nationalized industries that so preoccupied Conservative ministers in the 1980s.

With good reason, the secret papers prepared by Whitehall in 1960 for the Cabinet, at Macmillan's request, on the questions confronting the UK as it inched towards its first application to join the EEC were candid about the reforms the British economy would need, including improved labour mobility, if it were to withstand and then prosper from the increased competition membership would bring – changes which could involve 'social hardship', ministers were warned.[197] The incoming Churchill government in 1951 made a serious pitch, led by the Old Man himself, to achieve not just a *modus vivendi* with the trade unions but also a high degree of social peace, as we shall see in Chapter 4.

Place the British New Deal measures in the context of both Gellner's 'social bribery fund' and his notion of the indispensability of the state taking a sustained and permanent role if the notion of modern nationhood is largely to be built around the maintenance and 'the consequences of an ever-growing, ever-progressing society',[198] and you see in the Britain of the late 1940s and early 1950s what he called the 'package-deal quality of the provision of services'. This required 'something approaching half the national income [to pass] through the hands of political authorities . . . [as the] . . . infrastructure is large and lumpy, and it can only be erected and maintained by the collectivity'.[199] This notion does not fit post-1979 Britain but it does that of a United Kingdom nestling, perhaps a touch too comfortably, within the folds of the postwar settlement.

Advanced countries vary in how they measure the proportion of their wealth and resources which pass annually through their public and private spheres. The British figures show a consistently high level of public expenditure even if one runs on the figures beyond Mrs Thatcher's first two administrations (see table).[200]

Such a 'large and lumpy' infrastructure of state provision requires 'a large and lumpy' tax-take to match, which brings us to another of Governor King's

PROPORTION OF GDP (AT MARKET PRICES) TAKEN IN TAXES, SOCIAL
SECURITY CONTRIBUTIONS, ETC.

YEAR	%
1948	35.2
1958	29.7
1968	34.8
1978	33.5
1988	36.7

lunchtime preoccupations – or rather two of them, because it carries within it the danger of an inflationary spiral, particularly under the conditions of reasonably full employment which held until the mid-1970s and a 'lumpy' labour market which held for about a decade longer.

The taxation watersheds are some forty years apart – from the 1941 budget when personal taxation surged – to the 1980s budgets when it was progressively reduced. In 1941, as A. J. P. Taylor noted in his celebrated *English History, 1914–1945*, '[f]inance took on a startlingly new shape' as the Chancellor, Kingsley Wood, took advice from Keynes and the modern school of economists, using the latest national income assessment techniques.[201]

Of Wood, Taylor wrote:

He did not try to balance his budget, though this time the British people paid for 55 per cent of the war in taxes – a much better figure than in the first war. Wood's main concern was to close 'the inflationary gap' between what the government was spending and what it received in taxes . . . Half the gap was raising income tax to 10s in the pound [i.e., to 50 per cent] and by reducing the allowances, thus bringing most industrial workers into the class of income-tax payers for the first time [though part of this came in the form of 'tax credits' to be repaid after the war].[202]

The economic historian W. D. Rubinstein, very much a man of the *laissez-faire* right who has come round to the view that income tax should be abolished,[203] chooses two characteristic (for him) examples of what tax did to people in Mr Baldwin's Britain compared to Mr Attlee's:

A bachelor earning £10,000 had retained £6,222 after income tax and surtax in 1937, but only £3,501 in 1948, despite the fact that inflation had nearly halved the value of the pound. The maximum rate of death duties on a millionaire estate passing for probate reached 75 per cent in 1946–9, whereas it had been taxed at only 50 per cent in the period 1930–9 and only 65 per cent during the war.[204]

'It was in this period,' adds Professor Rubinstein, bringing a touch of Evelyn Waugh and *Brideshead Revisited*[205] to twentieth-century British economic history, 'that the wealthy, especially those who had inherited landed wealth, appeared to be a doomed species, scheduled for extinction. The war and post-war era probably witnessed the end of "Society" in its traditional sense, with its "network of country houses" and widespread servant-keeping.'[206]

Not for Rubinstein or Waugh the notion of a progressive state infrastructure, redistributive taxation to fund a 'social wage' in terms of personal, social and public services as a badge of an advanced society practising the politics of decency. But even for those ministers at the consensual heart of the British New Deal such as Herbert Morrison and Rab Butler, there was an acute recognition that personal taxation had reached a ceiling of manageability.

In his paper for the Cabinet during the devaluation summer of 1949, Morrison noted that 39 per cent of 'national income' would be absorbed via central taxation and local rates for public spending purposes during the current financial year:

The incentive to effort for workers as well as professional and technical people and employers is seriously affected by this burden, which, in turn, reacts on our costs, and on our capacity to earn dollars . . . it seems difficult to believe that revenue can be maintained even at present levels without pressing on the limits of the taxpayer's endurance.[207]

Morrison, seen by some historians as the most sensitive figure in Attlee's Cabinet in terms of what the entity we would now call 'Middle Britain' would or would not take, warned his colleagues that '[s]ooner rather than later the taxpayer will rebel verbally and at the ballot box'.[208] Butler said much the same thing to an economic Cabinet committee in the last days of 1951, arguing that 'taxation has reached, if not exceeded, the limits which can be imposed in peace-time'.[209] As economic historian Martin Daunton has noted: 'By 1950, there was general acceptance both in the civil service and the Labour government that a long-term review of the tax system was needed to moderate the competing needs of social justice and equality on the one hand and efficiency and incentives on the other.'[210]

What about those economists in Whitehall, members of that economics profession which failed to grasp the problem of the rise of inflation, which so exercised their eminent successor, Mervyn King, over the Governor's lunch table in the summer of 2003? The influential ones, such as Robert Hall, were at the ear of Labour and Conservative ministers alike in mid-century Britain. Keynes's defenders have a strong point when, like his most recent biographer, Robert Skidelsky, they argue that had he lived, that supplest of minds would have turned to 'attack' the problems thrown up by full employment and inflation and the stagflation which followed the tarnishing of the 'Thirty Golden Years'. His classic *General Theory of Employment, Interest and Money*[211] had been published in 1936 and reflected the underuse of physical and human capital after the crisis of 1929–31, utterly different conditions from the long, western European postwar boom and the circumstances after 1973 which brought about its demise. As Skidelsky noted laconically of his subject: 'But he was no longer there, and his book was.'[212]

Douglas Allen told me in a conversation during the early phase of the creaking, grinding and vexing adjustments which began to be made in both policy and analysis in the mid-1970s that, having been surprised by the long and sustained recovery plus relative boom period after the war, the economics profession swung from excessive pessimism to excessive optimism in their expectation that the old 1930s problems had been vanquished for ever. In the summer of 2003 I asked Lord Croham, as he had by then become, to elaborate further on what he had meant in recalling the attitudes of his fellow Whitehall economists in the early postwar years. He said:

It is true that the prewar generation of Treasury people, some of whom were just surviving in the 1950s, still couldn't accept budget deficits [as a way of sustaining full employment along Keynesian lines] and didn't understand the arguments. Way on into the 1950s when Robert Hall and all the young economists around him believed that full employment was the key, they didn't think that money mattered at all. Once they were installed [in Whitehall], there was very little worry about inflation. I wasn't quite such an ardent Keynesian. I'd been brought up with [Lionel] Robbins and [Friedrich von] Hayek [at the London School of Economics].[213]

For some economic historians, at the time and since, such distinctions as the differences of approach between Morrison and Butler or Hall and Allen are but rows about the disposition of the deckchairs aboard the vast and falsely glittering ocean liner of capitalism. Professor John Saville, who left the Communist Party of Great Britain with his friend and fellow scholar, Edward Thompson, over the Soviet suppression of the Hungarian uprising in 1956, has not changed his view of the Attlee and Churchill governments and the postwar settlement since living through them. Writing in 2003, Professor Saville was as exercised as ever by what he calls 'the conservative iniquities of British labourism' in the years when the electorate gave Mr Attlee his 146-seat majority:

The modest improvements in social welfare, with the National Health Service the most advanced, were the least that could be expected to be introduced and full employment, common to all the advanced industrial countries, was the most significant part of the general increase of living standards.[214]

Any reader of *Never Again* or this volume will not be surprised that I do not see the British New Deal as a development easily engineered and installed.

John Saville has a point, however, about full employment. It certainly was a common policy aspiration of all three mainstream British political parties after 1944, but did not those politicians in power in the recovery and relative boom years benefit from its achievement even though their efforts had little to do with its existence and sustenance? Did not that mysterious and little-comprehended post-1945 boom have more to do with catch-up, the wider application of new technologies at a time when technological advance was still labour-intensive as opposed to labour shedding (hence the extra bonus enjoyed by Italy and France, which had, unlike Britain, a considerable agricultural workforce that was increasingly drawn into the factories and the cities – the West Germans enjoyed this *and* yet another dividend, too, in the stream of often highly skilled refugees from the East – until the Berlin Wall went up in 1961)? It is certainly true that the moment full employment became difficult to sustain in the early to mid-1970s, not only Britain's but all Western governments showed themselves baffled and relatively powerless to do more than tinker with its consequences.

John Saville, however, makes an even more interesting point in his paean of non-praise for those postwar years. 'Far too many of the conservative structures of our society,' he writes, 'were left untouched and the six years of Labour rule were followed easily and without any spectacular changes by thirteen years of Conservative governments.'[215] Before turning to the durability and the mutations of British social structures and habits in the mid-twentieth century in Chapter 2, we need to linger on one aspect of the structural conservatism detected by Saville, because it relates powerfully to the construction and course of the British New Deal and the great decline debate – the failure to modernize the state's capacities at the same time as loading Whitehall with new, substantial and, in many cases, intentionally permanent tasks.

Hitler had given Whitehall a test-bed on which to develop an interventionist state which, in wartime conditions, could recruit virtually whomsoever it liked from outside to supplement its largely non-interventionist regular civil servants for the purposes of mobilizing both the home and fighting fronts and of drawing every last fighting ounce from the nation's human and physical capital. Yet this benign legacy from a malign tyrant – for without Hitler there would have been no 1940s goad to spur the UK's 1930s administrative system into sharpening itself and its capacities – was wilfully and deliberately thrown away after the Second World War. Nearly all the gifted outsiders, many brimming with specific professional skills (as distinct from the all-rounder abilities of the Whitehall generalists) were allowed to return to their firms, their professions and their university departments.[216] Both skill sets are needed at the top in peace as in war. In early 1946 Sir Edward Bridges, as Head of the Civil Service, summoned his fellow permanent secretaries to a pair of meetings to ponder exactly this question. Attlee had put the question of reform to Bridges after one of the more business-minded of the 1945 intake of Labour MPs, Geoffrey Cooper, had asked the Prime Minister if the current 'executive instrument' was capable of implementing the cataract of bills then passing through Parliament to create a National Health Service, an extensive welfare state and a clutch of nationalized industries.[217]

In setting the scene for their meetings, the hugely respected and influential Bridges wrote to his colleagues outlining his own thoughts:

Speaking for myself, I have been disposed to think of the change-over from war to peace, as it affects the civil service, largely in terms of what happened at the end of the last war. In that war, too, large numbers of business men, industrialists and others came into the civil service, and at the end of it, when the war problems came to an end, they packed up and went back to their businesses.

It is true that in this war we have made far better use of the industrialists and others who have come to our assistance, and we have greatly regretted the loss of their help when the time came for them to go. But have others – like myself – been working on the general expectation that civil service problems in a year or so resume more or less the same general pattern which they took before the war?[218]

Almost without exception, they had.

The most striking exception was the young Oliver Franks, about to return to his philosophy books in Oxford (he had been recruited as a Temporary Principal in 1939 from the University of Glasgow into the new Ministry of Supply and had risen to become its Permanent Secretary). Many years later he told me how in March 1946, at the first of Bridges' two meetings, he had said 'in a rather brash way' that he 'thought there was considerable need for change and ... that the role of the civil service in the war and from now on would be ... more managerial and less purely administrative'.[219]

The minutes of that crucial – and ultimately barren – Saturday morning meeting at the Treasury on 2 March 1946 record Franks' powerful but unheeded call for a rejigging of the state to cope with the British New Deal. Intriguingly, Geoffrey Cooper in his letter to Attlee had reminded the Prime Minister that on setting out on *his* New Deal in 1933, F. D. Roosevelt had commissioned an investigation into whether the administrative systems were up to the task. 'Is there not a parallel here for our country at the present time?' Cooper had inquired of Attlee.[220]

Without alluding to New Deal Washington, Oliver Franks plainly thought there was. In the reported speech of the minutes he said:

The real difficulty was that in recent years the functions of the civil service had changed from being purely regulative (functions for which the education and training of the civil servant were ideally suited) and had become more and more those of management. Instead of analysing the problems of others, the civil servant now had to tackle those problems himself. This called for somewhat different qualities, of which the most important were nerve and ability to push a thing through to its conclusion. The old distinction between administration and execution no longer held good. The civil servant would thus have to acquire some of the qualities of the businessman. But the introduction of businessmen into the service was not itself a solution. Public administration was on a far larger scale than any business, and this was a fact seldom appreciated by people outside the field of public administration.[221]

As an analysis, that could not be faulted in 1946 and it identified a classic instance of what Mancur Olson called 'institutional sclerosis'.[222] The gap identified by Franks underlay the Fulton Report of 1968 and Ted Heath's 'new style of government' in the early 1970s,[223] the Thatcher reforms of the 1980s associated with the names of her successive efficiency advisers, Sir Derek Rayner in particular,[224] and Tony Blair's preoccupation with the delivery capabilities of the civil service in the late 1990s and early 2000s.[225]

David Marquand widened the analysis of this lack of capacity at the centre to design and run and update the new functions and institutions that came out of the Second World War and the recovery/reconstruction period which followed in noting the British failure to build a 'developmental state',[226] as the French did in those years with an impressive degree of deliberation and verve. Not for Whitehall a postwar equivalent of the Ecole Nationale d'Administration (founded in 1945) to swiftly train a cadre of young technocrats to replace the discredited senior officials who had worked for Vichy.[227] And the Central Economic Planning Staff was in no way comparable to Monnet's Commissariat au Plan with its drive to push through growth and modernization in the key industries (particularly in the fuel and power sectors) in post-liberation France.[228]

Lord Plowden, who headed the Central Economic Planning Staff, told me many years later 'it's cloud cuckoo land to think that one *could* have created a Monnet system in this country' given the nature of ministerial responsibility (which meant he had nothing like the scope of Monnet for independence of operation) and Plowden's determination to work with 'the Civil Service machine. Otherwise, I was quite sure, we would have no influence whatever after quite a short time.'[229] As Eric Hobsbawm has often stated, it is very striking that planning was Labour's 'big idea' in the late 1940s and yet the outcome, a mix of exhortation and diminishing physical controls left over from the war, was so feeble.[230]

Even more difficult, had they wished to do it (which they did not), would have been a boost to entrepreneurialism and competition, albeit overlaid with a social safety net for those bruised by the scourings of advancing capitalism which was the West German way once Dr Ludwig Erhard had gained sway in the economic arguments that took place in Bonn during the early days of the new state after 1949.[231] The Labour government did set up a Monopolies and Mergers Commission in 1948 but this had a low priority and had published only two reports by the time the Attlee administration fell in 1951.[232] As President of the Board of Trade and Chancellor of the Exchequer, Stafford Cripps was managerially minded and was the moving spirit behind the creation of the British Institute of Management.[233] But, if this was to have a beneficial effect, it was to be slow, cumulative and long term.

It could be, too, in the human terms that Landes emphasizes, that the UK lacked sufficient men and women of what Lloyd George would have called the 'push and go' type – the kind of people, many of whom were just being born in the late 1940s, who, in the words of Dick Olver (who rose to be number two in BP and later chairman of British Aerospace), 'were unwilling to lose' in the competition for global advantage.[234]

So, with a huge legacy of protectionism and cartelization in the 1930s, the heroic but exhausting (in terms of plant and people) early 1940s behind them, Britain failed to produce the equivalent of either a Monnet or an Erhard and it ignored Franks on the need for a new state machine. Instead, it pressed for a better yesterday with a domestic new deal. In its way it was a remarkable act of collective faith. But would putting right the shortcomings of the inter-war years by mobilizing the lessons of the shared exertions of wartime produce that benign, self-renewing symbiosis of economic growth and greater social justice?

2

Society, Pleasure and the Imponderables

'Sociology, like history, is a department of knowledge which requires that facts should be counted and weighed, but which, if it omits to make allowance for the imponderables, is unlikely to weigh or even count them right.' R. H. Tawney, 1950.[1]

'... the objects deployed in the construction of a world are not some homogenous assembly of similar grains, differing only in – what? Colour, shape, hardness? ... On the contrary, the constituent elements form a system whose parts are in intimate and intricate relation with each other. Separation of all separables is not the heart of wisdom, but of folly.' Ernest Gellner, circa 1994–5.[2]

'The wider family of the past has, according to many sociologists, shrunk in modern times to a smaller body ... Kindred were bound together throughout their lives in a comprehensive system of mutual rights and duties ... But as a result of the social changes set in motion by the Industrial Revolution, relatives have, we are told, become separated from each other ... We were surprised to discover that the wider family, far from having disappeared, was very much alive in the middle of London ... all the more so when it transpired that the absence of relatives seemed to be as significant on the estate as their presence in the borough.'

Michael Young and Peter Willmott on the Bethnal Green of 1953–5.[3]

'It is widely believed, both in Britain and abroad, that the British are obsessed with class in the way that other nations are obsessed with food or race or sex or drugs or alcohol.' David Cannadine, 1998.[4]

So obsessed are they, that class can infuse in Britons a remarkable range of emotions from laughter to rage. On laughter, just think how high a proportion of British humour is based on class distinction, sometimes of the more subtle kind, of nuance, no more than a raised eyebrow or a look of disdain; often on the crude signs of manner, appearance, dress, speech and deportment. A dropped 'h' alone will do. On rage, pay heed to one of the most saintly and scholarly figures of the twentieth century, R. H. Tawney.

Tawney came from a family of high-minded educators in India, and passed through a traditional grooming at Rugby and Balliol as the nineteenth century turned. Then a strain of altruistic Christian socialism began to express itself in a life split between the university and the fledgling Workers' Educational Association. Intellect, powers of observation and conviction were toughened up when, back in England wounded in 1916, he described unforgettably in an article in the *Nation* 'the people with whom I really am at home, the England that's not an island or an empire, but a wet populous dyke stretching from Flanders to the Somme'.[5]

But the Tawney on whom this volume needs to eavesdrop is not the sergeant of the Manchester Regiment. The Tawney who concerns us is the LSE professor of thirty years later, revered by his students who, when needed, would beat out the brush fires on his hairy tweeds as fast-burning volatile tobacco spilt from his pipe when he paused and puffed during lectures.[6]

This is Tawney updating in 1950 an article he had first written in 1935 on 'Christianity and the Social Revolution'. He is talking of the need to banish differences of class and parental income from education. But, he continues, 'The vice which paralyses the effort to offer a better life to the young is largely that which poisons other parts of our national life. It is the homage paid to the idea of social class, and to the degrading distinctions which the worship of class creates and perpetuates.'[7]

Rightly, Tawney treats the great British fixation with class as 'a complicated phenomenon': 'In England it has two main roots. The first consists of the decaying remnants of the social stratification of pre-capitalist society. The second consists of the newer type of economic inequalities created by capitalism. The latter provides the cruel and brutal reality. The former invests it with a sentimental and pseudo-historical glamour.'

This, Tawney argued, when the 'decorous drapery' had been pulled aside, resulted in an assumption that 'common persons', by which is meant about four-fifths of the nation, 'have not the same right to a good life as a privileged minority ... [which] ... is noxious to the individual soul, for it is the parent of insolence – never so insolent as when blandly un-selfconscious – and of servility. It is noxious to society, for it destroys the possibility of a common culture, and makes the struggle of classes a national institution.'[8]

It is with the latest nuances, practices and noxiousness within that 'national institution' in 1951 that we must start this section as Mr Attlee's attempts to improve the lot of Tawney's 'four-fifths' (actually, just under three-quarters by then) passed into the hands of Churchill and his ministers.

In 1921 the British working classes (as defined on an occupational basis by the government's Registrar-General) made up 78.29 per cent of the population (Tawney's four-fifths). By 1931 it was slightly down to 78.07. By 1951 it had fallen to 72.19 per cent. But with population growth this still amounted to over 36 million people, much as it had twenty years earlier.[9] In other words, the working classes remained, by a substantial margin, the bulk of the British people, and, as we have seen, it was to an improvement in their lives and life chances that much of the Attleean settlement and the British New Deal was directed.

Even before the 1944 Education Act began to accumulate its effects, several ladders of upward mobility into a skilled lower middle class had been put in place by the shift in the scientific and technological basis of British industry. This applied especially to the new industries such as vehicle and aircraft manufacture in the Midlands and the south-east which drew in migrants from the north-east, the north-west, Scotland and Wales as the old staple industries of the industrial revolution declined and unemployment in those areas rocketed. As Ross McKibbin noted, the Second World War accelerated and extended existing processes in this as in so many other areas of national life:

Many fewer men worked in the staple industries in the 1950s than in 1918; many more in the newer metal trades, in motorized transport, in building and engineering. There were fewer skilled workers; more semi-skilled and unskilled. Migration of labour in the interwar years meant that a considerably larger part of the industrial working class lived and worked in the Midlands and the South-East and a correspondingly smaller part in the North. The working class had also done comparatively well out of the Second World War. It had gained in wealth, in social esteem and political power; it had gained by a mild redistribution of income (which operated within the working class as well) and by the abolition of large-scale unemployment. In terms of standard of living, the second was probably more important.[10]

As for the initial making of the world's first great proletariat on the back of the world's first sustained industrial revolution, there lay a paradox at its heart which Michael Young and Peter Willmott detected in the early 1950s when they immersed themselves in the working-class streets and family lives of Bethnal Green. On one level, the shift in the late eighteenth century from an ordered, stable, agriculture-based social hierarchy into a vast, crowded yet anonymous increasingly urbanized class system was marked, both in Britain and, later, in other industrializing nations, by relationships which were more fluid and more random.[11]

One of Marx's central understandings was how technological develop-ments change class relationships; they do not invent them. The unpredictable and unprecedented upheaval of the first industrial revolution and the production processes which drew thousands of families from the land between 1750 and 1880 (by which time more British people lived in cities or large towns than in the countryside, making early Victorian Britain the world's first urban-dominated society[12]) produced trauma, fluidity, squalor, dystopia and prolonged adjustments which were still working their way through in 1951. And yet, a deep-set pattern of urban family life and kinship developed whose persistence and stability so surprised Young and Willmott (though it was about to change dramatically with dispersals to 'overspill' estates, the throwing up of high-rise flats and immigration flows from the new Commonwealth nations, so called to distinguish them from the old dominions to whom independence came sooner).

An anthropological approach to the making of industrial societies of the kind developed by Ernest Gellner does fit, however, with some of the most persuasive historical studies of the nature of British class society between the mid-nineteenth and the mid-twentieth centuries. Gellner's analysis was shaped by his search for an explanation of how and why the first swathe of European industrialized societies became so swiftly and so powerfully suffused with nationalism, a trait which marked British society very strongly as the twentieth century gave way to the twenty-first – not least in the aggregate emotional deficit the UK felt towards an integrating European Union. Though rarely cited in the endless 'great European debate' within Britain, at least some of the roots of British resistance lay in the transition from a farming to an industrial society 200 years earlier. For agrarian society, in Gellner's analysis,

with its relatively stable specializations, its persisting regional, kin, professional and rank groupings, has a clearly marked social structure. Its elements are ordered, and not distributed at random. Its sub-cultures underscore and fortify these structural differentiations, and they do not by setting up or accentuating cultural difference within it in any way hamper the functioning of the society at large.[13]

For those coming off the land, industrial society represented a range of instant and dramatic differences from their previous experiences and, eventually, had profound consequences for the nature and reach of the state.

Its territorial and work units are *ad hoc*: membership is fluid, has a great turnover, and does not generally engage or commit the loyalty and identity of its members. In brief, the old structures are dissipated and largely replaced by an internally random and fluid totality, within which there is not much (certainly when compared with the preceding agrarian society) by way of genuine sub-structures. There is very little in the way of an effective, binding organization at any level between the individual and the total community.[14]

Here Gellner injected the nation-state in its powerful late-nineteenth-century manifestation as the force which counters the disturbing effects of spiralling industrialization and prevents industrial society from disintegration, if not explosion. 'This total and ultimate political community [the state] thereby acquires a wholly new and very considerable importance ... The *nation* is now supremely important, thanks both to the erosion of the sub-groupings and the vastly increased importance of a shared, literary-dependent culture. The state, inevitably, is charged with the maintenance and supervision of an enormous social infrastructure ... The educational system becomes a very crucial part of it ...'[15]

This analysis fits the telescoped British experience between 1850 and 1950 quite well. It took a long time – until the creation of the 'classic welfare state' in the late 1940s, in fact – for a fully fledged Gellnerian 'social infrastructure', including its educational component, to be put in place. But specifically British qualifications to his overall picture are required about the absence of binding factors between the human capital of an industrial nation until state level is reached.

For one of the most intriguing, significant and far from predictable developments of mid-nineteenth-century Britain was the growth of what Harold Perkin called a 'viable class society', one in which there was a widely shared if not always articulated 'belief that class conflict is not a war to the death but a limited contest for power and income between opponents who recognize each other's right to exist ...'[16] According to Perkin, the emerging middle classes accepted this in relation to the aris-tocracy during the 1830s with the passage of the Great Reform Act that recognized them as an estate of the realm. It took rather longer for the working class to do the same for those above them in the hierarchy – not until the Chartist demonstration on Kennington Common had passed off peacefully in 1848. To a remarkable degree, the emerging trade union movement adapted to the existing party structure as the political arbiter of the ground rules between capital and labour in the second half of the nineteenth century.

Perkin's model consists of a pre-industrial wide and vertical hierarchy of a society being replaced by a pyramidal structure of horizontal classes, upper at its tiny peak, middle beneath it atop a very large working-class base. Each layer had considerable solidarities within itself and genuine antagonisms between itself and the others, but ones almost invariably moderated and managed to the extent that few wished to push differences to a revolutionary point at which the pyramid would implode, requiring a new society to be built from its fragments. Of course there were perilous moments and the trade unions, as the century turned, narrowly decided to abandon the Liberal Party as the vehicle of working-class advance, seeking instead through the Labour Representation Committee, and, shortly after, the Labour Party, to send bespoke representatives of working people's interests into the House of Commons. This level of solidarity and mutual organization within the Labour movement, as it became known, modifies the Gellner picture of sub-structures with very little to bind them.

Only in the 1940s, with Labour's arrival in the War Cabinet Room (Ernest Bevin especially) and, later, with the formation of the Attlee government, did the viability of Perkin's layered society become fully manifest, an important element in the stand-off between capital and labour, and the political expressions thereof, which underpinned the British New Deal and contributed to the economic rigidities which threatened its longer-term durability. It explains, too, the constitutional conservatism of all concerned. Even the laconic Attlee verged on the effusive about this in advance of Labour's 'high tide' (as Hugh Dalton called it[17]), writing in a 1943 memorandum for the War Cabinet entitled 'The Application of Democratic Principles of Government' that: 'There is one particular condition which is necessary for the successful working of any form of democracy, but more particularly that of the Westminster Model, that is the willingness of the minority to accept the will of the majority in the hope that they too will in due course become the majority.'[18]

The postwar consensus was perhaps at its most complete in the widely shared belief across the political parties and within Whitehall about the virtues of the British constitution in the 1940s and 1950s. These, too, were the years, when a 'decent' (that great 1940s word) social infrastructure was finally put into place just as the shared experience of a total war whose front line was as much in Bow as in Benghazi knitted together a tight little nationalism, and a shared culture to match built partly on what Gellner called an 'old and well established self-image'.[19] This, as we shall see, was to cause particular problems not just in relation to an integrating Europe in the 1950s and 1960s, but to the domestic integration of the Queen's overseas subjects when the sons and daughters of the extended Empire began to arrive on the boat trains at Waterloo, and, later, long-haul flights to Heathrow, in considerable numbers.

Education as the means of transmitting shared values and senses of identity became increasingly important as a stabilizer within advanced industrial nation-states.[20] In Britain this, historically, had either not existed at all, or, when compulsory education swept across the land from 1870, it immediately and profoundly took on the class and status characteristics of the nation within which it was imposed, and, to make matters worse, it was shot through with those religious differences which mattered so much to Victorian and Edwardian society. For later generations, attuned to regarding education if not as a bringer of equality, as a none the less important and indispensable 'social escalator'[21] and a vital creator of the human capital any advanced or advancing nation needs to sustain itself, it is difficult, perhaps, to appreciate the degree to which education before the late 1940s added to and even reinforced social inequality. Yet, it is both naïve and misleading to treat the question as merely a matter of dropping down sufficient ladders of educational opportunity for matters to be put right in an incremental fashion as successive generations of the gifted clamber up (which, I must admit, is how I saw it as a grammar-school boy in the early 1960s).

It is certainly true that God or Nature (depending on one's position in the spectrum of faith/disbelief) does not distribute intellectual curiosity according to the socioeconomic status of the loins that deliver us into this world. But, as Michael Young's magnificent satirical warning *The Rise of the Meritocracy* showed, an unmoderated meritocracy, while righting some of the wrongs of past centuries, can bring with it new inequalities of even greater rigidity as the professional and meritocratic classes surge ahead of the less gifted, who are left both permanently disadvantaged and disdained by those who rose solely on their merits and are, therefore, wholly without guilt or a trace of *noblesse oblige* towards those who, for whatever reason, have been left trailing in the meritocratic wake of the high flyers.

So, even the most apparently democratic of republics of the intellect carry dangers in their most avowedly progressive practices – a recognition which led to great pressures within British politics and the state system as from the mid-1950s the single, inclusive, comprehensive ideal was pitted against the tripartite notion of meritocracy as laid down by the 1944 Education Act whereby all would have secondary schooling but there would be divisions post-11 into grammar, technical and secondary modern institutions. This became the great educational battleground of the 1950s and, especially, the 1960s. It looked for a time that the comprehensive notion had clambered probably permanently atop the commanding height in the late 1960s and early 1970s. But selection once more had its day under both Conservative and Labour governments from the mid-to-late 1980s. Virtually the last of Michael Young's appearances in print[22] was, at the time of the 2001 general election, devoted to railing against Tony Blair's misunderstanding of his satire and his warning when the Prime Minister opened the campaign in his Sedgefield constituency by proclaiming the notion of meritocracy as New Labour's core theme.[23]

But this is to jump mightily ahead. I have written in *Never Again* about the making of the Butler Act and its early implementation under Labour's doughty Ellen Wilkinson.[24] Since it was published, Michael Barber (later to become David Blunkett's adviser on reform at the Department of Education and Skills, and, later still, head of Tony Blair's Delivery Unit) wrote a very good short history of *The Making of the 1944 Education Act*,[25] bringing out the special combination of conservatism and consolidation that had enabled R. A. Butler to steer it past not just the Churches (the religious question had vitiated many previous reform attempts), but also a sceptical Winston Churchill and the unenlightened or uninterested on his own party's backbenches, while lacing it with the possibility of substantial innovation, not least in 'continuing education' of a technical kind for 16- to 18-year-olds.[26]

The 1944 legislation was the first of the great legal makers of the classic welfare state to reach the statute book and the only one to be closely associated with a Conservative politician. Barber's analysis of it is particularly interesting retrospectively as he was one of a very few close to Tony Blair (David Miliband and Andrew Adonis being the others) who had a genuine feel both for the late 1940s settlement and the continuities and the shifts from it in the Blair/Brown remaking of welfare provision in the late 1990s and early 2000s.

Shortly before moving into Whitehall, Professor Barber published his *Learning Game* in which he depicted and regretted the battle lines which were dug and entrenched during the period covered by this volume as the effects of the Butler Act worked their way through the nation:

On the political right were those who believed that the goal of education should be diversity ... Hence the right's defence of the grammar and secondary modern system and its opposition to comprehensive schools . . . An inevitable consequence of diversity, it argued, is inequality which regrettably we will simply have to live with . . .

On the political left, by contrast, the argument was that the overarching goal of education should be equality. If the consequence of the pursuit of equality was uniformity, then so be it. Hence the left's support for comprehensive education, its opposition to religious schools and its repeated demands for the abolition of private schools.[27]

Barber argued that the growth of diversity within British society since the early post-Butler days meant that 'the stale conflicts of the post-war era'[28] had to be transcended both to reflect Britain's more kaleidoscopic society *and* to find ways of combining the maximum amounts of diversity and equality. And he was a key player in Labour's assaults on monopoly providers in the shape of local education authorities, the deliverers of the Butler Act whose philosophy was a national system of education locally administered.

In the early autumn of 2003, as I was starting to write this chapter, Michael Barber and I pooled thoughts on the current remaking of the early postwar New Deal in which his Delivery Unit, by now housed alongside Gordon Brown's public spending team in the Treasury, was a key instrument. Earlier in the year I had heard him define the early-twenty-first-century battleground as between 'the enabling state' and the 'minimalist state'. And here, class intruded into the analysis, albeit in a different way, as it did when Attlee and his ministers concentrated on the life chances of the 75 per cent (by 1991 the figure for manual workers was down to 38 per cent of the UK labour force[29]). Now it was the professional middle classes who were making the weather in terms of the political economy of welfare.

The 'big choices', Michael Barber told me, lie here for governments of the centre left 'if they want services that are inclusive (so that the wealthy want them, too, and will pay tax for them). This is the challenge of delivery which becomes very acute in an impatient, cynical world. The long-term strategy must have short-term results.' This, he explained, was 'central' to the Blair government's 'political project'.

The conversation, ranging back from the Blair years to the Attlee era, continued with my asking, 'So it's a new deal with the middle classes?'

'Yes. Absolutely,' replied Barber. 'We have to avoid poor services for poor people. Once people who can afford to live in gated communities do so, they won't pay for the police . . . The crucial element of the deal is quality public services in return for 40 per cent of GDP rather than 30 per cent. You also want "new deal" public services not just for the middle classes but to promote equity and social cohesion. And this is solidly in the social democratic tradition.'[30]

So, welfare in the shape of public services – Gellner's 'enormous social infrastructure (the cost of which characteristically comes close to one half of the total income of the society)' in which the 'educational system becomes a very crucial part of it'[31] – remains central to the British centre left, as it has since the time of Asquith and Lloyd George. But now, if the poorer elements are to be provided for above a subsistence level ranging from the meagre to the adequate, the middle classes must be appeased. This is an exact reversal over 130 years from the late-Victorian days when Joseph Chamberlain could ask, at a time when the labouring masses were on the rise in power and political reach, 'What ransom will property pay for the security it enjoys?'[32]

But, in the early 1950s, at a pivotal moment between the Joe Chamberlain and Michael Barber arguments, was 'property' (i.e. the middle-class taxpayer) as well as the population as a whole getting a better deal thanks to the settlement of the Butler Act? The clutter and noise from the grammar school/comprehensive debate has tended to drown out other, more basic but equally important themes such as the sheer investment in plant (schools) and people (teachers) that the short postwar witnessed. Here, rightly, Barber detected 'impressive' progress: 'In 1938 education expenditure was 3 per cent of gross national product; by 1961 it was 4.5 per cent ... The number of teachers increased from 175,275 in 1946 to 448,034 in 1977; the number of university students [I shall examine higher education shortly] from 38,000 in 1944 to 139,000 in 1964.'[33]

Yet key elements of the 1944 Act – like most statutes, a licence to reform, not a guarantor of progressive advance – were never implemented. Its clauses had shied away from prescribing what should be taught, but it did intend to boost technical education. And here, the County Colleges, to which 15–18-year-olds in work were intended to go on day-release to supplement their apprenticeships or equivalents with a rolling programme of technical education, were central to the purposes of the Butler Act. But they never materialized under successive Labour and Conservative governments.

It was interesting, and significant, that sixty years after the Bill was being drafted within the Board of Education, when I asked a former Conservative Secretary of State for Education to tell me, off the top of her head, what the 1944 Act meant to her and to the country, the lost County Colleges featured so prominently. The ex-Secretary of State was Gillian Shephard, and this is how she answered without a pause when asked for her word associations with 1944:

'Rab. Tripartite (failed). Churches. Keystone policy on which much is still based. In a way never bettered. Who else knows of any other Education Act? Revolutionary – but in a very quiet way.

'If it had been implemented fully, including the County Colleges, we wouldn't have had the perpetuation of class-based attitudes towards education which we still have. We would be like Germany.'[34]

There is much of interest here. It was Michael Barber, on the other side of the political divide, who brought out the shared, one might almost say consensual, criticism of the aftermath of 'Rab' when he commented on Correlli Barnett's view that, in the end, religion and the need to get a settlement with the Churches became a greater shaper of the Education Bill than its efforts to tackle 'Britain's lamentable failings in technical education'.[35]

Barber believes this judgement is excessively harsh on Butler as

the religious settlement was not, as Barnett imagines, an *alternative* to an education reform which would have improved technical education, it was a *precondition* of it. Indeed, having settled the religious question, the Act did provide for compulsory part-time attendance of 15–18-year-olds at county colleges.

The failure lay not with the Act, but with its implementation. In this respect Barnett's critique is highly pertinent. A more industrially minded culture would not have allowed the politicians to drop this part of the Act off the bottom of the list of priorities. The most that can legitimately be said in criticism of the Act is that it did little to challenge the inadequacies of the prevailing culture.[36]

The more one looks at the technical educational question – the point on which the Shephard, Barber and Barnett analyses converge – the more convincing is the argument that here lies the greatest of the opportunities offered by the Butler Act but forsaken by successor administrations.

In his tally of the economic failings of the Attlee government, Bernard Alford concentrates not on those phantom County Colleges but on the existing technical schools, whose number was not increased in the postwar years, hobbling the third, and, perhaps, most needed of the legs of Butler's tripartite system. In 1946 and 1950, Alford noted (revealingly), the breakdown of the secondary school population in England and Wales was as follows:

1946

Total: 1,269,000
Secondary moderns: 719,000 (56.7%)
Grammar schools: 488,000 (38.5%)
Technical schools: 60,000 (4.7%)

1950

Total: 1,670,000
Secondary moderns: 1,095,000 (65.6%)
Grammar schools: 503,000 (30.1%)
Technical schools: 72,000 (4.3%)

Alford concluded that technical education had 'made virtually no headway and the indications are that the greater part of the potential number who would have benefited from a technical school were funnelled into the secondary modern sector', and that this, given the emphasis of not just the Butler Act but also the Percy Committee on Higher Technological Education of 1945 and the Barlow Report on Scientific Manpower of 1946 (both of which recommended the expansion of science and technology courses at university level), represented 'a record of failure'.[37]

Why did the technical schools never achieve their place in the educational sun despite the few that existed pre-1939 being popular with many employers and with parents? Perhaps partly because Labour politicians, who, on the face of it, should have been their champions, were, in fact, often ambiguous about technical schools. For example Chuter Ede, Butler's deputy and a former teacher, believed they confined their largely working-class intake to vocational subjects, thereby ghettoizing them. As Ross McKibbin has noted, 'Ede ... struck from the 1944 Act specific reference to technical schools in favour of a clause obliging local education authorities to offer secondary education of "sufficient variety".'[38]

A more powerful factor, I suspect, was a combination of dearth and expense. Very few technical schools existed in the 1930s (only 2.6 per cent of boys and 1.4 per cent of girls leaving the elementary schools went into them) and they 'were expensive to build and equip, and since they had to be re-equipped regularly, their recurrent costs were high. Furthermore, staff–pupil ratios were, and had to be, lower than in other schools.' As a result, between 1944 and 1965, when the Wilson government strove to make comprehensive education the norm, the 'technical schools did not disappear but their numbers fell and they educated a decreasing proportion of schoolchildren', resulting in Butler's tripartite scheme being essentially 'a quasi-bilateral' system consisting of grammar schools and secondary moderns.[39]

What of Gillian Shephard's related points on class and status? The secondary moderns never came near to achieving parity of esteem with grammar schools and which one a child went to depended a great deal on where he or she lived as well as his or her performance in the 11+ examination. The average percentage of each age group in England and Wales going to a grammar school settled down around 25 per cent but it could be as high as 40 per cent (Westmorland) or as low as 10 per cent (Sunderland).[40]

For a working-class child getting to a grammar was one thing; thriving there could be quite another. The effects of the 1944 Act, when subjected to the key test of social mobility (so important to questions of both social justice and the efficient use of the nation's human intellectual/capital resources), produce some depressing and paradoxical results. I am with Gillian Shephard in believing that, over the long term, the Butler Act was quietly revolutionary in widening and deepening the professional base of the UK, helping improve the position of women within it and, after a time lag of nearly twenty years, obliging the Macmillan government and its successors to ensure an increasing proportion of 18-year-old school leavers went on to some kind of higher education.

But, initially – bearing in mind Michael Barber's stressing of the need to weave middle-class consent into the fabric of a general advance – there was a very great deal indeed in the Butler settlement for them. The slump of the 1930s saw a *worsening* of the proportion of working-class children in grammar schools as economic hardship left fewer working-class families able to let their children take up the few scholarship places available to them. As a consequence, there were more places for middle-class children (whose parents' occupations largely escaped the unemployment so associated with these years) to take up, including those in a position to pay for their own fees.[41] This partly explains why many in the interwar Labour generation of local councillors were so keen on getting more grammar schools built in working-class areas. As McKibbin puts it: 'The conquest of the grammar school, not its abolition, was thus their aspiration.'[42]

Though this began to happen in the 1940s, in comparison to the 1930s (an especially bad decade for them) the *relative* position of working-class children 'actually deteriorated after 1944 . . . the relative beneficiaries of the 1944 Act were the sons and the daughters of professionals and businessmen. The proportion of their children competitively successful rose everywhere; and often more than doubled. Denied the right to buy places at grammar school by the 1944 Act, they won them instead by examination and at no cost.' McKibbin has calculated that by 1950 around 60 per cent of the children of professionals and businessmen could expect to win grammar-school places compared with 10 per cent of children from the 75 per cent of the population who lived in working-class homes.[43] The position was made worse by the relative difficulties experienced by working-class children in staying the course (lack of privacy and a quiet room at home for homework; relative scarcity in the grammar schools of their local peer group). As a result they were 'more likely to end up in the school's C-stream; premature leaving and under performance as much characterised working-class children in grammar schools as non-entry itself'.[44] This, naturally, had a knock-on effect several fences down what George Steiner once called the 'Grand National Course' of the British educational system[45] when grammar-school upper-sixth formers arrived at the Becher's Brook of university entrance.

Hitler had given a double boost to British universities. Firstly, in the 1930s, there took place a 'German-Jewish migration ... [which] ... was to enrich profoundly the country's academic life'.[46] This was an extraordinary intellectual bonus, and some of the figures who comprised it transformed the nature of their discipline, such as Otto Frisch and Rudolf Peierls at Birmingham, who discovered just how much enriched uranium a viable atomic bomb would require, or Karl Popper at LSE, who changed most people's notions about the philosophy of science.[47] Secondly, though the Attlee government simply could not afford the British equivalent of the American GI Bill of Rights of 1944, whereby a huge number of men in uniform went straight from the barrack room to the seminar room (around 2.2 million by 1956 when the scheme ended[48]), some in the King's Armed Forces whose intellect was matched by their guile were able to claim the war had interrupted their path to college and the government found both their fees and living grants. Chelly Halsey did just this when, during his last days in the RAF in 1945, he 'overcame any moral scruples about the complete non-existence in my own case, indeed my rejection, of the idea of a university education' and put himself down for the entrance exam to LSE.[49] Without war and conscription, other grammar-school boys from the 1930s and 1940s would not have put a foot near the higher rungs of the education ladder.

Even Hitler could only boost Britain's university population a little in terms of the proportion of the age group forming its entry cohort. The absolute figure had dropped during the years of war (understandably enough) from 50,000 in 1939 (1.7 per cent of the age group) to 38,000 in 1945, but by 1950 there were 90,000 full-time students as all, not just demobilized service-men and women, became eligible for free tuition and maintenance grants (although the latter were subject to a means test).[50] Nevertheless, for most, a university place continued to be a rarity and a prize, especially if that place was within the mellow stone walls of an ancient university.

In her autobiography Joan Bakewell has a vivid description of 'the single most significant event of my life', the autumn of 1951 when 'the narrow self-contained world of my home [in Manchester] and school [Stockport High School for Girls]' gave way to Newnham College Cambridge and the Econom-ics Tripos.[51] Joan Rowlands, as she was then, was the first member of her family and only the second girl from her school to get to Cambridge, and she describes what it was like to be among one of the first 'sprinklings' of those who 'had arrived courtesy of the 1944 Education Act' which left them 'expect-ing to work hard. As a college scout put it to Jonathan Miller: "Once they were all gentlemen on this staircase. Now there are more of them 'up on their brains'!"'[52]

Miller's college was St John's. By the time I turned up there in 1966, also courtesy of the 1944 Education Act, the college prided itself on recruiting grammar-school boys. This, by the standards of those days, justified its claim to be one of the most democratic and widely socially based of the colleges by the Cam, yet even there the prospect of women being admitted was never seriously considered. When Joan Rowlands arrived at the Newnham porter's lodge in 1951, the Butler Act had only just begun to work its quiet way through the capillaries of the education system. For a while, the relative position of women actually worsened – the postwar expansion in numbers was largely male; the proportion of women in British universities in 1950 was lower than it had been in 1920. 'As a system of recruitment university entrance thus dis-criminated in two ways: against girls of all social classes and against working-class boys.'[53]

The proportion of the 18–21 age group becoming full-time university stu-dents in the UK crept up from 3.2 per cent in 1954 to 4.2 per cent by 1959.[54] Those who made it could, according to their parents' means, expect the state to pick up much of the tab. Scarcity and privilege, in this sense, marched hand-in-hand. The middle class did very well out of it and, as in the years I rode the government-cranked education escalator between 1959 and 1969 through grammar school and university, it was all free. My generation was the best provided-for in the history of British education – if one could get round that Grand National course with its ever higher jumps of competitive examinations. The state gave us a three-year bounty which we would repay over forty years of professional contribution to the country. It was human investment with a purpose.

Yet higher education in the 1950s was classically a 'positional good' in Fred Hirsch's definition of one that is 'scarce in ... [a] ... socially imposed sense' and 'subject to ... crowding through more extensive use'.[55] Hirsch's brilliant piece of analysis, *Social Limits to Growth*, did not appear until 1977. But it mapped those items of consumption which – because they are physically finite (country cottages with marvellous views; prime stretches of nearly empty beach) or rationed, for one reason or another, with the effect of preserving a high status value (a university place in 1951) – are best treated as separate from a straightforward physical good which can be produced in ever greater quantities without devaluing its inherent utility. People of the generation older than mine are lamenting the loss of 'positional goods' when they talk of the effect of more cars on improved roads swamping the Lake District or Snowdonia during holiday periods or package tours ruining the special qualities of certain parts of Mediterranean or Aegean littorals. On Fred Hirsch's terrain, class, status, income and consumption all meet with a vengeance. And, to a high but not ubiquitous degree, the divides in the way the 1950s British pursued their culture, their leisure and their pleasure reflected this.

Though the County Colleges lay pinned to the face of the 1944 Education Act and Britain's twenty-six universities[56] caught but a tiny fraction of the population in the early 1950s, there was one form of compulsory tertiary education nearly all males over the age of eighteen had no choice but to undertake. National Service, in Trevor Royle's words,[57] was, 'like the steam train, the Teddy Boy and *Mrs Dale's Diary*, ... simply a part of the fabric of everyday life' in the 1950s.[58] A combination of the early Cold War and the difficulty of garrisoning a still vast but increasingly restless territorial empire led the Attlee Cabinet to cut against the traditional grain of a nation that, historically, had disliked and disdained in peacetime both a large standing army and compulsory military recruitment. For the government there was no other way of meeting its defence requirements.[59] In 1947 it legislated to replace Second World War conscription with a peacetime call-up for all males aged between eighteen and twenty-six. In the autumn of 1948 ministers decided to extend the period of service from a year to eighteen months,[60] partly because the services told ministers they could not both train and make use of rookie soldiers, sailors and airmen within a year.[61] The outbreak of the Korean War in 1950 caused the government to stretch this to two years with a further three and a half on the reserve list (down from the four years prescribed by the 1948 Act[62]). By 1951, half of the British Army's manpower consisted of National Servicemen.[63]

Bevin treated compulsory military service as a kind of side deal of the New Deal, a reasonable thing for the government to ask of the nation's young men in return for the social benefits of the welfare state.[64] This mini deal, which lasted until 7 May 1963 when National Serviceman 23819209 Private Fred Turner of the Army Catering Corps returned to civilian life,[65] affected a huge number of young Brits during the short postwar. For conscientious objectors, only a tiny proportion of the eligible males, never more than 0.4 per cent,[66] there was provision which involved alternative non-military forms of service or a posting to a non-combatant regiment such as the Royal Pioneer Corps.[67] Some occupations qualified for exemption or indefinite deferment (which, in practice, meant the same thing). Piety and affliction could also keep you out of uniform:

Exemption from National Service was granted without qualification to British subjects in government posts abroad, to mental defectives, to the blind, and to clergymen. As long as they stayed in their jobs, indefinite deferment amounting to exemption was also granted to coalminers, oil shale underground workers, merchant seamen and seagoing fishermen, agricultural workers in essential food production, graduate science teachers, and police cadets. Deferment was readily given if the youth was an apprentice completing indentures, or a student engaged on a course. Proof of exceptional domestic hardship could also result in deferment.[68]

Exemption and deferment aside, on 'Enlistment Thursdays' vast rivers of young men would flow through the stations of the big cities on the way 'to Inverness for Fort George, to Darlington for the branch line to Richmond and Catterick, to Preston for Fulwood Barracks, to Worcester for Norton Camp [or] to Brookwood in Hampshire for North Firth Barracks'.[69]

Put them all together for the period from May 1945 to when Fred Turner was demobbed from the Catering Corps in 1963 and the picture looks like this:

UK MILITARY CALL-UP 1945–63

Total: 2,301,000[70]

Divided between the Royal Navy, Royal Marines, the Royal Air Force and the Army in the proportion of 1 sailor/marine to 12 airmen and 33 soldiers.[71]

The Army took 1,132,872.[72]

In each of the eighteen years between 1945 and 1963 some conscripts saw action.[73]

395 National Servicemen were killed in action.[74]

Cumulatively, this had a marked impact on British society.[*]

Uniforms in the street and at railway stations were commonplace. Not until nearly a decade after the last call-up did the British armed forces end the practice of wearing uniforms while on the move in public (a precaution prompted by the recrudescence of the Troubles in Northern Ireland but one largely negated in the hirsute 1970s by the severity of military barbers).

There was a rough equality about the first stages of what sociologists would call the military socialization of the new recruit. Everyone had to register on his eighteenth birthday with the Ministry of Labour and National Service. In a fortnight or so, attendance at a medical was required on pain of up to two years in prison or a £100 fine if you failed to turn up.[75] The medics were skilled at detecting sharp practices. Probably apocryphal stories abound of lads turning up with severe hangovers or substituting cow's urine for their own or feigning mental instability.[76] Peter O'Toole and his fellow drama students used to give classes on how to increase your chances of fooling the doctors using a touch of acting, an excess of alcohol, a starvation diet and sleep deprivation as preparation for the medical.[77]

Once accepted, basic training was a great, if short-lived, equalizer of young British males whatever their social origins. It was designed to be 'intentionally brutal' for eight to twelve weeks.[78] A very high proportion of the recollections vividly describe the official rites of passage once in the barracks after letters,

[*] I reached the age of eighteen five years after the last National Serviceman was called up (though my father and I gave the penultimate recruit a lift one wet Friday night in Shropshire, while en route from Gloucestershire to Liverpool), but even now, I sometimes detect the traces of a special kind of faintly subversive humour laced with vulgarity that characterized the National Service generation which, I suspect, I picked up from the boyfriends of my elder sisters.

telling of safe arrival, have been posted, closely followed by a parcel containing the civilian clothes in which they arrived on the lorries that brought them from the railheads. The endless drills, the lack of privacy, the inventive verbal abuse of the corporals and sergeants, the throwing together of all sorts and conditions of people, most of whom had neither been away from home for any length of time (unless they were public schoolboys) nor subjected to sustained abuse.

Perhaps the most vivid account I have read of a National Service first night is Alan Bennett's, an occasion made all the more poignant and excruciating as he was, at that stage in his life, a sensitive and devout Anglican in the habit of saying his prayers on his knees before going to bed:

Saying prayers was much on my mind on this particular day as the sickly tableau of my kneeling down in my barrack-room bed to the derision of my fellow-conscripts has been one of several highly coloured scenes with which I have been tormenting myself in the months leading up to my conscription. To me at eighteen, such ostentatious piety constitutes a real spiritual hurdle and one that God, I feel, will be expecting me to take . . .

I lie there in my bed that night as the blizzard of obscenity that has been going on all day gradually dwindles and my comrades fall asleep; I wonder if I were to get up in the dark and say my prayers whether anyone would notice. Next moment it is morning and all hell breaks loose again. Morning prayers are out of the question.

Bennett felt he had let his maker down.[79]

Once within the grip of the National Service Acts your future was in the lap not so much of the gods of war but, in the case of the Army, of a set of acronyms behind which lived a range of people and systems. Your interview with the Personnel Selection Officer (PSO) led, without your knowledge, to your being placed in one of five Summed Selection Groups (SSGs) based on the level of education received before call-up and performance during basic training.[80] If you were deemed to have officer potential, a 'Wosby' (War Office Selection Board) could whip you out of squaddieland to the less abusive and vastly more comfortable milieu of Eaton Hall in Cheshire or the Mons Barracks in Aldershot.[81]

The Army's equivalent of the 11+ involved more than IQ test plus exam and recruits could nominate themselves for consideration when in front of the PSO.[82] Trevor Royle has summed up the late 1940s and early 1950s requirements for conversion into an officer and gentleman as the possession of a good education, social confidence, some previous military training [in a combined cadet force at school] and a certain conceit: most of these qualities, the Army generally agreed, were to be found in the products of a public or grammar school education. Not without reason, National Servicemen came to believe that it was pointless putting themselves forward unless they had those qualifications; although it has to be said, too, that many public schoolboys and university graduates refused to be considered as potential officers on a point of principle, because they disagreed with the whole system.[83]

For a gifted few, there was blessed relief from Eaton Hall or Mons if they showed a special aptitude for languages, Russian especially (all those Red Army captains and submarine commanders from Murmansk to be interviewed if World War III came and any fell into British hands before Armageddon). In the grim-to-bliss league, those on the Russian course at Cambridge (who could dress like undergraduates and live in college provided they cleared each exam hurdle) took the palm – a life immortalized in Michael Frayn's novel *The Russian Interpreter*. (Frayn and Alan Bennett were in Cambridge together once Bennett had escaped the horrors of Pontefract Barracks.)[84]

At the bottom of the table, those graduates who did their National Service as 'schoolies' in the Royal Army Education Corps had a demanding time trying to compensate for the failings of pre-Butler Act provision. In 1949, it was admitted within the War Office that '[t]he quality of intake now reaching the Army, whilst failing to provide its high grade requirements, is producing an embarrassing number of men whose ability and capacity for learning is so limited that they are capable of performing only the most simple administrative and general duties.'[85] And, early on, it was not just the semi or truly illiterate incoming National Servicemen who were put in the care of the 'graduates and well-qualified school leavers' who filled the sergeant-instructor rank of the Education Corps: 'quite a few sergeants of war-substantive rank had been either threatened with demotion or reduced to corporals on account of their lack of formal education, and were anxious to regain their stripes, pay and privileges'.[86]

One of the best National Service jokes captures this to perfection:

Regular Sergeant to raw National Service recruits: 'You 'orrible lot reassemble heeyah at two hay clock. This afternoon you have got hadult educashun. You've got a lecture on Keats.'

Pause

'I bet half of you ignorant bastards don't even know what a Keat is!'

(There is an alternative ending told me by my old history master from

Marling School, Eric Pankhurst, himself a National Serviceman before going up to Oxford, involving 'Kipling' and 'how to kipple'.[87])*

National Service jokes survived into the satire boom, Roy Kinnear doing a particularly good impression of a squaddie suggesting they should have their own political party on the very first *That Was the Week that Was* broadcast on 24 November 1962.[88] And every Sunday lunchtime the BBC Light Programme broadcast two-, three- or four-way *Family Favourites* in concert with the British Forces Broadcasting Service. The voices of Jean Metcalfe and Cliff Michelmore were a national phenomenon as they read out the formulaic requests: 'here's Anne Shelton singing "Lay Down Your Arms and Surrender to Mine" for Sapper X in Singapore reminding him that month Y in year Z [the demob date] is not very far away'.

But the real political residue, once the last bit of coal had been painted white and toecap heated, dubbined and polished, related to another and inevitably enduring social theme of the postwar – what was then called juvenile delinquency and would now be called youth crime. As memories of *The Army Game* (a late-1950s TV sitcom set in an army barracks which rested on the shared knowledge of military life and its absurdities) faded and recorded crime rose, it became a regular cry that what testosterone-soaked late adolescents needed was a return to National Service discipline rather than the 'having it so good' version of youth culture which became the surrogate shared experience. A more progressive version of this was a notion of national voluntary service in the community rather than on the parade ground.

The regular military, seeking an ever more skilled professional armed force, were not keen to become an adjunct of the welfare state or the penal system or a kind of moral rearmament in uniform.[89] National Service never returned, although an ex-Scots Guardsman called Willie Whitelaw introduced a 'short-sharp-shock' regime for young offenders modelled on the military glasshouse when he was Home Secretary in the early 1980s. The short-lived experiment did not succeed.[90]

Of all the social arithmetic historians attend to for their analyses, crime

---

* One of the best surviving officer-class National Service jokes is of two debutantes discussing the fate of an acquaintance of theirs:

Deb 1: 'I hear Henry's got a Commission in the East Africa Rifles.'
Deb 2: 'Oh really. Are they black?'
Deb 1: 'Only their privates.'
Deb 2: 'Oh how *very* contemporary!'

figures are the most skimmed and unreliable. Terence Morris, who has devoted his professional life to their study, declares bluntly that

of all social statistics, those relating to crime are probably among the most inaccurate. Births, marriages and deaths are reported not only because they are important events, but also because those reporting them may have something to lose and frequently something to gain by doing so, such as Child Benefit, tax rebates or insurance payments. Criminal statistics derive from two sources: the reporting of events by members of the public and direct observation of actions by the police. Of the two, the former predominates and this is a primary source of difficulty. For not everyone has the motivation to report an offence; it may be too trivial, it may be inconvenient or embarrassing or it may involve a conflict of loyalties.[91]

Even allowing for all the caveats about unreliability, the first decade after the Second World War, like the decade that preceded it, saw Britain almost certainly at its most lawful and orderly ever. The war that separated them provided a blip – the blackout being a boon for the criminal, whether bent on burglary or violence against the person. The growing anxiety about juvenile delinquency in the late 1940s and early 1950s also partly stemmed from the delayed consequences of fatherless homes during the six years of war.

In fact, recorded offences fell between 1951 and 1955[92] (though the 1951 figures represented a noticeable rise on those for 1935 when, of those aged over seventeen, the number convicted in courts of all kinds of serious offences was 148 per 100,000; by 1951 it had risen to 259[93]). Violent crimes against the person (murder and rape excepted) averaged just under 2,000 a year between 1930 and 1939. Prisons were actually closed down in the 1930s through lack of custom (though this was particularly due to a rise in non-custodial sentences).[94]

Given the debates about both the beneficial effects of National Service and the malign impact of economic deprivation, it is perhaps telling that British crime figures began to rise significantly only after 1955 (at which time National Service was still putting large numbers in uniform), when the postwar consumer society really began to take off. The crime figures for 'indictable offences known to the police' in England and Wales (see table; Scotland had its own crime jurisdiction and legal system) for the long postwar illustrate, for example, the wartime surge and show the 1955–60 period as taking the dubious honours for the largest percentage increase over a five-year period (one among several 'social dams'[95] that burst around then).

YEAR	TOTAL OFFENCES	VARIATION OVER PRECEDING 5 YEARS	RATE PER MILLION	VARIATION OVER PRECEDING 5 YEARS
1945	478,394	+56.8%	12,705.3	+30.7%
1950	461,435	−3.6%	12,097.3	−4.8%
1955	438,085	−5.1%	11,234.7	−4.8%
1960	743,713	+69.8%	18,474.1	+64.4%
1965	1,133,882	+52.5%	28,258.7	+53.0%
1970	1,555,995	+37.2%	38,030.9	+34.6%
1975	2,105,031	+35.3%	50,350.1	+32.4%
1980	2,520,600	+19.7%	58,811.9	+16.8%
1985	3,426,400	+35.9%	78,204.7	+33.0%

Source: Terence Morris, *Crime and Criminal Justice since 1945* (Blackwell, 1989), p. 91.

The early 1950s may have represented relative tranquillity in terms of the crime statistics, but it did not feel like that. Teddy Boys, urban youth dressed in the manner of Edwardian dandies plus a great deal of hair cream on show and knives and coshes concealed (accoutrements to which the average upper-class early-twentieth-century beau was a stranger), caused a good deal of fear on the night-time and weekend streets, and among those in authority.[96] The cultural imperialism of the United States added to this in 1956 when Bill Haley and the Comets brought rock-and-roll to the UK and the Teds, in cinemas showing *Rock Around the Clock*, not only jived in the aisles of the picture palaces but began to tear up the seats as well.[97] (The imperative title of Haley's follow-up hit, 'Rip It Up', was sometimes taken rather too literally.) Churchill's Cabinet in 1954 became so exercised by American 'horror comics' (very tame by comparison to what the electronic children of fifty years later could encounter in their computer games) that they circulated exhibits among themselves.[98]

It was George Orwell, writing in 1944 in his *The English People*, who captured through the eyes of his imaginary 'intelligent foreign observer' the law-abiding gentleness of the Brits by having his visitor wander the streets of London, taking a look at the 'old prints in the bookshop windows'. In doing so, Orwell surmised, it would occur to him that if these things are representative, then England must have changed a great deal. It is not much more than a hundred years since the distinguishing mark of English life was its brutality. The common people, to judge by the prints, spent their time in an almost unending round of fighting, whoring, drunkenness and bull-baiting. Moreover, even the physical type seems to have changed. Where are they gone, the hulking draymen and low-browed prize-fighters . . . What had these people in common with the gentle-mannered, undemonstrative, law-abiding English of today?[99]

Yet the same Orwell, writing four years earlier in *The Lion and the Unicorn*, was only too well aware of the continuing 'brutality' of the UK penal system (and not just the imperial adaptations of it that he had experienced in Burma[100]).

Since Orwell drew his incomparable picture of the enduring characteristics of deep England, the law had been reformed by the Attlee government's Criminal Justice Act of 1948. Corporal punishment, unless one was a member of the prison population, ceased to be a sanction available to judges and magistrates when sentencing. The House of Commons, during the passage of the 1948 Act, had voted for the suspension of the death penalty for a trial period. The House of Lords threw it out.[101] When power shifted from Attlee's Cabinet to Churchill's, Sir Ernest Gowers was heading a Royal Commission on the subject.[102] Orwell's 1940–41 picture, however, still had both resonance and explanatory power a decade later when he noted that

the gentleness of English civilization is mixed up with barbarities and anachronisms. Our criminal law is as out of date as the muskets in the tower . . . [and overseen by] . . . that typically English figure, the hanging judge, some gouty old bully with his mind rooted in the nineteenth century, handing out savage sentences. In England people are still hanged by the neck and flogged with the cat o' ninetails. Both of these punishments are obscene as well as cruel, but there has never been any genuinely popular outcry against them. People accept them . . . almost as they accept the weather. They are part of 'the law,' which is assumed to be unalterable.[103]

It took the Gowers Report of 1953 and a spate of disturbing capital cases between 1953 (when 19-year-old Derek Bentley was hanged even though his 16-year-old accomplice, Christopher Craig, fired the shot which killed a policeman in Croydon) and 1955 (when Ruth Ellis was last woman on the gallows),[104] before parliamentary opinion shifted sufficiently to set in train a process which, within a further decade, was to remove the rope from British jails after Labour returned to power in the mid-1960s. Public opinion, however, continued to remain in favour of capital punishment.[105]

For all their acceptance of the law, its cruelties and its follies, there was one illegal activity in which literally millions indulged every year – gambling – as Orwell fully appreciated.[106] This was linked not only to horse racing but also to several popular working-class sports such as greyhound racing, angling, crown-green bowls, boxing, pigeon racing and rugby league.[107] As Ross McKibbin put it:

A large and sophisticated industry was constructed to meet the demands of the small bettor. A press with a huge circulation told him (more rarely her) what he needed to know to make an informed bet; an army of tipsters was at hand to assist him further; and, above all, in most pubs and clubs, in nearly every factory or workshop and on the streets of every working-class community there was a bookmaker with whom he could make that bet. There was only one problem: it was illegal.[108]

There were legalized islands in this sea of bustling criminality: punters could back a horse legally at the racecourse and the rich could avoid the stigma of criminality if they opened credit facilities with a legal bookmaker off course.[109] The football pools (coupons containing lists of Football League matches on which home wins, away wins and draws could be forecast) flourished mightily in a grey area. John Moores, when he pioneered Littlewoods Pools in Liverpool in the 1920s (using part of his resulting fortune to buy Everton Football Club), was soon prosecuted under the wonderfully titled Ready Money Betting Act. The prosecution failed. By 1950 it was estimated that nearly half the population had, at one time or another, made a bet using a football coupon.[110] Out of a population of just over 50 million, between 10 and 15 million people were regular bettors if all forms of betting were aggregated.[111] The laws against gambling were plainly both unenforceable and largely ignored.

The British love of sport was enhanced by gambling, but sport was an addiction which rested on a wider base than taking a punt. If inventing sports had its own system of Nobel Prizes, the UK would be the world's most garlanded nation. As Orwell noted,

The English were the inventors of several of the world's most popular games, and have spread them more widely than any other product of their culture. The word 'football' is mispronounced by scores of millions who have never heard of Shakespeare or Magna Carta. The English themselves are not outstandingly good at all games, but they enjoy playing them, and to an extent that strikes foreigners as childish they enjoy reading about them and betting on them. During the between-war years the football pools did more than any other one thing to make life bearable for the unemployed. Professional footballers, boxers, jockeys and even cricketers enjoy a popularity that no scientist or artist could hope to rival.[112]

The names, for my generation, of Denis Compton or Len Hutton at the wicket, Frank Tyson or Freddie Trueman hurling themselves towards it (or Jim Laker and Tony Lock doing a peculiar dance on the way to it) or Stanley Matthews dribbling or Tom Finney centring a football *are* utterly evocative, letting, as Joan Bakewell put it in her memoirs, 'the mind spin away', and comparable, as arousers of memory, 'to chasing after a scent on the wind and the snatches of an old song'.[113]

Sport is immensely important to any serious attempt to reconstruct a nation's collective life in any period since the mid-to-late nineteenth century, when it became organized with rules plus bodies to oversee them.[114] What one might call the 'shallow play' of a country is very indicative of the rival pulls of the individual and the collective (even within team games), the private and the public and, inevitably, the fissures of class and status that exist (and, in the case of Northern Ireland, of religion too). In that sense it is also highly revealing of the 'deep plays' at work in a society.[115]

Mid-twentieth-century Britain was something of a golden patch. For me, it appears that there really was an unplanned full enjoyment policy which ran alongside full employment. '"Working-class" sports were the main beneficiaries of these conditions: for the first time in a generation they catered for a class in full employment.'[116] The gilded memory of late 1940s and early 1950s sport glisters all the more brightly because international soccer and the Football League and Test and County cricket virtually closed down for the duration of the war. There was a huge, pent-up demand awaiting satisfaction once it was over.

It is difficult, for example, from the perspective of the early twenty-first century to appreciate just how powerful a grip cricket exerted on the collective sporting *mentalité* of the English in the early postwar years. Though governed by a very small number of very narrowly recruited (in the social sense) figures around the MCC, this particular passion transcended the class divide like no other major spectator sport (except perhaps Rugby Union in South Wales). As Ross McKibbin put it, writing of the period 1918–51:

In so far as cricket was played and followed throughout the country by all social classes and by both men and women, it was the most 'national' of all sports [McKibbin is dealing exclusively with England, not Scotland, Wales or Northern Ireland]. It was administered by the upper and upper middle classes, was the predominant sport in both independent and grammar schools, and was, even more than rugby, a socially useful sport which men did not hesitate to use for the advancement of their careers; but the majority of professional cricketers were of working-class origin and, although never as important to working men as football, nor played by as many, cricket was closely followed by them, particularly by skilled working men.[117]

Cricket had a remarkable breadth of appeal. It could captivate the numerate and the nerdy with its comparative statistics. It could appeal to those with a special empathy for the places and occasions where aesthetics of the visual and the athletic meet, such as a county match at a beautiful ground such as Worcester, set beside the River Severn and overlooked by the Cathedral.

The incomparable John Arlott, a poet both through the wireless speaker and on the page (he combined both talents in a poem called 'Cricket at Worcester, 1938'[118]), became the natural accompaniment to the Fifties game, his warm Hampshire burr and measured words, rich in nuance and metaphor, a part of any Test-match afternoon from the England v. Australia series in Coronation year right through to the end of the Seventies. Arlott described 'that remarkable immediate post-war atmosphere [which has] never been reproduced' with its cricket-hungry and hugely attentive crowds turning up for the Test matches (especially those against Australia) in record numbers.[119]

It was, however, the most lyrical cricket-driven pen ever, that of the *Manchester Guardian*'s Neville Cardus, which explained the special nature of the game's wide appeal. Here he is writing of the 1930s, for Cardus the golden age when technique and grace in the era of Jack Hobbs of England and Don Bradman of Australia had neared perfection. (It was the abrupt ending of this shimmering epoch, of cricketing years taken away by Hitler in the case of the Hutton, Compton, Washbrook generation, 'just at the time when talent matures to more than talent',[120] that added particular poignancy to what had gone before and a real keenness of anticipation to the first seasons of postwar restoration.)

Tell the average English sportsman that cricket is in its way an affair of art and the chances are he will regard you, eyebrows raised, with some suspicion. He has come to abhor the word, especially when it is written (or pronounced) with a capital A. None the less, his reactions to the game, the manner in which he talks about it, appreciates it, make convincing proof that he is never so much the artist as when he is at a cricket match, looking on from the popular side or from the pavilion. Go among the shilling crowd any fine day at the Oval and what do you hear? Little technical jargon, little talk of off-breaks and the position of the left funny-bone in the late cut. Instead you will hear many delighted cries of 'Beautiful stroke – beautiful.'

Now that same word 'beautiful' is one which average Englishmen are not in the habit of using; it is, indeed, a word they commonly distrust quite as much as they distrust the word 'art'. The truth is we are as a people prone to be ashamed of living the life aesthetic; we see and feel beauty even in our games, but we rarely confess to it. Yet that 'Beautiful!' which a glorious cover drive by Hobbs will bring warmly from our tongues tells the truth; Hobbs is for us an artist.[121]

Cardus, who could also do for music what he did for cricket within the pages of the *Manchester Guardian*, is one of the most intriguing and revealing writers when it comes to feeling the wider textures of the fabric of mid-twentieth-century Britain. Note his sense of the disdain of 'ordinary' people for 'the life aesthetic' and his feel for the linguistic distaste for the use of posh, pretentious language (a national divide to which we will return shortly).

Cardus's use of cricket as a metaphor for wider aspects of our culture, the webs of significance that we spin for ourselves,[122] even reached the deeply consensual approach his fellow countrymen and women took to the British constitution, the rules of the game by which they were governed. In his 'A Game of the English Summer', Cardus declared that the

laws of cricket tell of the English love of compromise between a particular freedom and a general orderliness, or legality . . . Law and order are represented at cricket by the umpires in their magisterial coats [they were long, white and unadorned by any sponsor's logo in those days] . . . And in England umpires are seldom mobbed or treated with the contumely which is the lot of the football referee. If everything else in this nation of ours were lost but cricket – her Constitution and the laws of England or Lord Halsbury – it would be possible to reconstruct from the theory and the practice of cricket all the external Englishness which has gone to the establishment of that Constitution and the laws aforesaid.[123]

Shallow play as very deep play here.

Cardus was especially good at social 'anthropological nuancemanship'.[124] His linking of the spirit of an age to a particular sporting individual was faultless. For the early postwar years, Denis Compton of Middlesex and England, the 'master batsman who allowed no bowler to enslave him',[125] was his chosen instrument. Compton's most golden season was the one which followed the chilled and gruelling winter of 1947. With consumption tighter than ever, Cardus drew a picture of 'worn, dowdy' crowds turning out across the land to savour Compton's 'genius' at the crease: 'There were no rations in an innings by Compton. Men, women, boys and girls cheered him to his century running all his runs with him.'[126] What was it that held them?

After taking guard at the beginning of an innings, he would twiddle his bat as he surveyed the fieldsmen and their placings. As with all truly great batsmen, his bat looked as though it possessed sensitiveness, as though it were tactile, and as though some current of his own nervous system were running from him, via his fingers, into the blade. He moved to the ball on light fantastic toe. Now and again he would skip out of his crease as the bowler was more than halfway through his run. If he found that the ball, when pitching, was too short for a forward stroke, he would skip back to his crease and perform a neat late-cut through slips, which, having expected to see him drive to the off, had stood up and relaxed.[127]

This was the artistic spectacle that appealed to all sensibilities whatever the background of the spectator or the language in which they expressed the resultant pleasure.

Great, possibly absurd and undeniably unprovable claims were made for the social and political impact of cricket not only in England but also both in the bonding of the territorial Empire, and, later, in the largely peaceful severing of those bonds. In one of the most famous lines he ever penned, G. M. Trevelyan declared without caveat that, 'If the French *noblesse* had been capable of playing cricket with their peasants, their chateaux would never have been burnt.'(This claim might not have sounded that eccentric during Trevelyan's heyday of influence in the interwar years as there 'had been much talk in the 1930s, not all of it in jest, about the unfortunate circumstance that the Germans did not play cricket'.)[128] In the Empire, Harold Perkin has argued, beating the home country at the sports it had invented and exported along with dominion, colony or protectorate status 'became for the expatriates and white settlers a sort of rite of passage, a test of manhood, almost a proof of fitness for home rule. Every cricketing or rugby-playing dominion looks back on its first Test victory over England as its coming of age, and Australia's famous winning of "the Ashes of English cricket" in 1882 was only the first of such colonial victories.'[129]

For the non-white subjects of the King, the 1950 West Indies touring team was a revelation. Though captained by a white man, John Goddard, it displayed to the watchers of the imperial game the prowess of two spin-bowlers of immense guile – 'Those two little pals of mine, Sonny Ramadhin and Alf Valentine,' as the contemporary calypso had it – and the three 'W's of great batting skill, Frank Worrall, Everton Weekes and Clyde Walcott.[130] After noting that no other empire ended in a fashion whereby 'the successor states played games against the imperial power' so happily ('Would the Franks, Vizigoths or Huns have played football with the Romans – except with their heads?'), Perkin went on to judge that '[l]osing at organized sports and games prepared the British psychologically just as winning prepared the colonists for decolonisation and for mutual respect and independence on both sides . . .'[131]

For English cricket, Compton, a paid professional rather than an unpaid amateur (in a game that institutionalized and ritualized this distinction at its highest levels until the early 1960s),[132] was, with Len Hutton (the first professional to captain England), a talismanic figure. Theirs are the names associated above all with the reclaiming of the Ashes after nineteen years on the fourth day of the fifth and final Test against Australia at the Oval in 1953 – Compton because his was the boundary that sealed the eight-wicket victory.[133] History needs to capture, too, the degree to which Compton was the first of the modern sporting celebrities in commercial terms thanks to his fine head of black hair, just crying out for application of the Brylcreem it advertised, as well as those supple muscles and strong, yet sensitive, batsman's nerves.

Though plagued by worsening knee trouble in the 1950s, Compton remained, for Cardus, 'an artist-batsman, beyond the powers of assessment of the scoreboard'. He was frequently recognized in public in the days when television was still in tiny, wooden boxes in very few homes (certainly between its postwar restoration in June 1946 and the Coronation seven years later). 'Round about 1947–48,' Cardus recalled, 'I sometimes took Kathleen Ferrier [a beautiful and matchless contralto from Blackburn in Lancashire who died of cancer in 1953] to dinner at the "Ivy Restaurant" [in London's theatreland]. Not many of the people at the tables knew who she was. But once, when Denis was my guest, one diner after another came to him asking for his autograph . . . His face was known to thousands never present at a cricket match. His portrait was to be seen on hoardings everywhere, advertising a haircream – and on the field of play, at any rate, Denis's hair was unruly beyond the pacifying power of any cream, oil or unguent whatsoever.'[134] Compton has his place in virtually every Fifties nostalgia book, sleek, black-tied and dinner-jacketed alongside the white pot of Brylcreem with its distinctive shape and logo and strap-line: 'BRYLCREEM keeps your hair *right* in the picture'.[135] As if this cornucopia of cricketing and physiognomical prowess were not enough, Compton played on the wing for Arsenal as well, and won an FA Cup winner's medal with them in 1950. (He played on the wing for England in a wartime international.)[136]

As a drawer of crowds and a generator of revenue, professional association football was the dominant British sport throughout the twentieth century. It was the world sport, too. In mid-century, as earlier, football's 'primacy at home, tacitly conceded by all, was earned by the extent of its popularity among the 75 per cent of the population who were wage-earners. The English industrial working class was neither politically nor culturally homogeneous, but love of football united them almost more than anything else.'[137] The professionals were almost entirely drawn from the 75 per cent – the English, Scottish, Welsh and Northern Irish working classes – and they were paid a maximum wage which equated with that of a skilled artisan (which is exactly how the League club chairmen saw them and treated them).

Sir Tom Finney, the famous and much-loved 'Preston plumber', retired in April 1960, the year before the maximum wage was abolished leaving the road open to star wages as well as star status, which Finney, one of the two artist-genius wingers of postwar English football – the other being the equally gentlemanly Sir Stanley Matthews – undoubtedly possessed. 'At my peak,' he wrote forty-three years after walking off the pitch at the end of his last First Division match, against Luton Town on 30 April 1960,

in a structure governed by the maximum wage, my income from playing a year with Preston North End struggled to reach £1,200. When I first signed as a professional [in 1939] it was for shillings – ten bob a match to be precise. That's 50p. So when you read of players now being paid up to £100,000 a week for doing the same job you might think I would be envious but you would be wrong. I would never criticise players for the amounts they are paid . . . The whole deal was so wrong in the forties and fifties . . . I would have loved to earn more, but I also believe that football treated Tom Finney well.[138]

In the late 1950s, Finney earned £20 a week from Preston North End in season and £17 a week during the summer. When he turned out for England he received £50. Every five years he qualified for a benefit from his club of £500.[139]

A similar financial fate was the lot of Finney's legendary England team-mate, Stanley Matthews, perhaps the most naturally gifted player ever to wear the national shirt. His reward was immortality, not cash. The Blackpool v. Bolton Wanderers FA Cup final of 2 May 1953 will always be remembered as 'The Matthews Final'. Blackpool's Matthews was thirty-eight and played the full ninety minutes on the right wing (no substitutes were allowed then). With thirty minutes to play, Blackpool were losing 3–1. Matthews passed to Stan Mortenson, the centre forward, who scored. Mortenson got another from a free kick. With a minute left, a magical run from Matthews followed by a per-fect cross enabled Bill Perry to score. Blackpool won 4–3.

Today Matthews and Finney would be multimillionaires, thanks to a player whose career overlapped theirs. He noticed that income from a benefit match was taxable only if your club had organized it; the cannier cricketers got out-siders to organize their benefits and so avoided the taxman. A shrewd, bearded (rare in those days) and energetic young player at Brentford, Jimmy Hill saw how 'Denis Compton [qualified] for a double helping from both Arsenal and Middlesex [and that he] was taxed on his football earnings and not on the manna from heavenly Lord's.'[140] It was Hill, as chairman of the Professional Footballers' Association in the late 1950s and early 1960s, who, with the help of the Ministry of Labour, finally shifted the monstrously resistant club chair-men off the maximum wage, both giving a huge boost to the players' pockets and creating a new stratum of celebritocracy as their golden lifestyles, espe-cially when tarnished by personal peccadillos, became almost as important to the media and the public as the gifted feet that had initially propelled such young men to stardom.[141]

Hill is quite an evoker of the days when huge, largely standing crowds, a high proportion of whom had no protection from the weather, turned out in great numbers across the land in dirty, uncomfortable stadiums that reeked of that great postwar perfume sometimes labelled as 'piss-and-chips'. The badly drained pitches quickly became mudbaths after the early autumn rains. This is Hill on Finney rising above it all during a Brentford–Preston match one soaking Saturday afternoon in the early 1950s when

Griffin Park [Brentford's home ground] was looking more like the River Thames than a football pitch. Saturday morning came and the rain had not let up, but despite the inclement weather the magic of Finney had enticed a vast crowd of over 25,000 people . . .

Three-quarters of an hour before kick-off, the referee announced that he would take the ball [then a thing of dense leather strips connected by heavy stitching with great water-absorbing properties] out and bounce it around the penalty-spot; if it bounced, the game would go ahead . . . They nearly lost it sinking into the mud . . . For reasons known only to himself, the referee said the game would proceed. There was about a yard or so of decent grass fringing the pitch, that was all.

By half-time Brentford were three goals down, all of them having been constructed by Finney. The Master didn't deign to use the muddy parts of the pitch but stayed fixed in his wing position until one of his colleagues managed to get the ball to him. Tom conjured up all three first-half goals dribbling his way down to the corner flag, turning sharp left, bamboozling further opponents on his way in towards the near post, and picking the precise moment to lay on three perfect goal scoring opportunities.[142]

Preston eventually won 4–2. 'I shall never forget,' Hill wrote, 'the majestic performance of Tom Finney in overcoming conditions which would have sent many superstars I have known scuttling home to their mummies. I'd have given him his gong there and then.'[143] Finney rose through the honours system with comparable grace and modesty, receiving his OBE in 1961, his CBE in 1992 and his knighthood in 1998.[144] The citation could have been – but wasn't – written by Jimmy Greaves, who called Tom Finney 'The first gentleman of football', his natural gracefulness matched only by his aversion to fouling opponents.[145]

But the Fifties footballing memory that surpasses all others is a tragic one – the Munich air disaster of 6 February 1958, when several of the 'Busby Babes', the pearl of a team being nurtured at Manchester United, perished after the BEA Ambassador aircraft carrying them home from a victorious European Cup quarter-final in Belgrade failed to clear the runway in a snowy Bavaria. Many of my age can remember what we were doing when we heard the news (I can recall the exact car with which I was playing at home in Finchley). Busby himself nearly died. Seven members of the squad, three club staff and eight travelling journalists did. The brilliant Duncan Edwards, the pillar around whom the England sides of the Sixties would have been constructed, died in a Munich hospital fifteen days later. In its grief, Manchester United stamped its image on the footballing world for ever.

Some sports peaked in the fleeting, flavourful early postwar years. Horse racing kept a sustained hold on a very wide public throughout the postwar years, partly, though not wholly, as it provided the freshly raw material for the nation's gamblers. And the early 1950s saw it reach a special level of recognition when the newly knighted Sir Gordon Richards, an outstanding jockey since the mid-1920s, won his first Derby at his twenty-eighth attempt (riding Pinza) in Coronation year. (The Queen, as was her mother, is a devotee of the turf.) The soldier/scholar Bernard Ferguson (later Lord Ballantrae) wrote a wonderful little poem which performed a far better class analysis of gambling and horse racing than any Marxist could have managed. He called it 'The Higher Motive' and it ran like this:

> The lower classes are such fools
> They waste their money on the pools.
> I bet, of course, but that's misleading
> One must encourage bloodstock breeding.[146]

Dog racing, the sport of no king except the London Pearly, enjoyed a remarkable popularity in the late 1940s with a total of 50 million attending the country's seventy-seven tracks in the first year of peace. But the severe winter of early 1947 began a decline from which it never fully recovered. By 1960 attendances were down to 16 million.[147]

Speedway, stripped-down motorbikes skidding round cinder tracks, did count a crowned head – King George VI no less – among its fans,[148] but, like dog racing, its following was overwhelmingly working class and it, too, peaked in the early postwar, when 6 million turned out in 1946 and by '1951 most towns had at least one track'. (It also had quite a following amongst women.[149]) In most big towns the dog and speedway tracks (often one and the same) were supplemented by another working-class favourite, the boxing hall, although the spread of affluence and the dispersal of inner-city communities to outlying estates 'destroyed the culture of the small halls where most of the registered professional boxers had once fought'.[150]

One sport usually overlooked by historians saw something of a working-class takeover in the first decade after the war – rock climbing. To say it had been the preserve of the athletic, the outdoor-minded and the well connected before the Second World War would be an exaggeration. In the north-west of England, for example, the Fell and Rock and the Wayfarers' clubs attracted members of the skilled working class and the middle class, like my own parents, with the Lake District and Snowdonia within an easy motorbike ride of Liverpool or Manchester. But the postwar years saw a definite change. This was the era of Joe Brown and Don Whillans, two extraordinary technicians who took climbing to new extremities when they began to attack the great grim cliff of Clogwyn du'r Arddu on Snowdon's flank above Llanberis. Brown, on leave from National Service in the Army (his weekday job in civilian life was as an all-round builder and plumber), first took up the challenge in Easter 1948 in a partnership that was to make both him and Whillans famous:

An aura of mystery surrounded this cliff. While we [the Valkyrie Club, a small group of hardened climbers from Derbyshire and the Manchester towns] had information [on] about a dozen climbs, it was spoken of with bated breath and one seldom met anyone who had climbed there. Those who had were looked upon as gods. There was no question that 'Cloggy' – as it is affectionately known – was the most continuously steep and near impregnable rock face in Snowdonia, perhaps in the country . . . As we approached the spur where the cliff lay hidden, slowly, one by one, a concertina of blank vertical walls looked through the mist. It was the most dramatic sight that I have ever seen.[151]

In a nice touch, Brown named the first new route he pioneered up 'Cloggy' Vember, after the daughter of Mrs Williams who ran the Half-Way House café on the main track and close to the mountain railway to the summit of Snowdon: 'During the period of strict rationing after the war they helped us with items of food and an occasional bucket of coal to keep the fire burning in a derelict house that the Valkyrie sometimes used near the railway . . . Mrs Williams and Vember had remarkable eyesight. They would keep a watch for us coming up the track . . . and tea or a light snack . . . would be ready when we tramped into the café.'[152] So 'Vember' the route became.

Brown's name is now synonymous with Llanberis where he lives and his famous climbing shop is open on the main street. His account of his 'first sight of Wales' over Christmas 1947 is intriguing, not least because of its sensitivities to class and voice. After travelling on a night train which deposited him and his companions at Bangor at two in the morning, they made their way in foul weather along the old eighteenth-century military road, more prosaically the A5, up to Ogwen:

Four days of sleet and snow chilled us to the marrow. Camping in such weather, clothes could never be dried and no one got a proper wash till he returned home. All the routes on Idwal Slabs were climbed before the party was stopped by the Holly Tree Wall. This piece of rock was much steeper. It was snowing and we were wearing gym shoes. Nearby a party of Oxford types stretched out in Javelin Gully was having a difference of opinion about the merits of climbing in gym shoes in the prevailing conditions. In a high voice the leader was ordering one of his companions to get off the rope because he was wearing gym shoes. The conversation between them was most unfriendly. We wondered if this sort of conduct was normal in climbing relationships because it was the opposite to our behaviour with each other.[153]

'Two ropes, two nations' as Disraeli might have put it had he been a climbing man (which he most certainly was not). For despite all the relative mixing and newish social solidarities of the shared wartime experience, an accent, an inflexion of voice, a manner of behaviour, even a snatch of conversation overheard in rough conditions on an exposed rock face could be enough to indicate a social and behavioural chasm between fellow countrymen. The branding of the British on the tongue, as writer and novelist Wyndham Lewis put it,[154] was a deep-set and tenacious element in social life throughout the short and long postwar.

Listen to a pair of respected novelist/observers separated by fifty years. First George Orwell in *The English People*. After quoting Wyndham Lewis on tongue branding by language and accent,[155] Orwell went on to claim that

the English language ... suffers when the educated classes lose touch with the manual workers. As things are at present [1944], nearly every Englishman, whatever his origins, feels the working-class manner of speech, and even working-class idioms to be inferior. Cockney, the most widespread dialect, is the most despised of all. Any word or usage that is supposedly Cockney is looked on as vulgar, even when, as is sometimes the case, it is merely an archaism. An example is *ain't*, which is now abandoned in favour of the much weaker form *aren't*. But *ain't* was good enough English eighty years ago and Queen Victoria would have said *ain't*.[156]

Next, John Le Carré, writing in his mid-1990s novel *The Tailor of Panama* of the moment the cockney tailor-in-exile Harry Pendel encounters the Old Etonian SIS officer Andrew Osnard in his bespoke shop in Panama City:

Both men, as Englishmen, were branded on the tongue. To an Osnard, Pendel's origins were as unmistakable as his aspirations to escape them. His voice for all its mellowness had never lost the stain of Leman Street in the East End of London. If he got his vowels right, cadence and hiatus let him down. And even if everything was right, he could be a mite ambitious with his vocabulary. To a Pendel, on the other hand, Osnard had the slur of the rude and privileged who ignored Uncle Benny's [tailoring] bills.[157]

Orwell had expected that 'the class labels' might fall away from English tongues if a new, shared national accent (definitely not that of the received English of the BBC radio announcer) developed when one strain ('a modification of Cockney, perhaps, or one of the northern accents') became both dominant and socially acceptable. This could be seen as an uncanny forecast of the spread of 'Estuary English' as the conglomerate south-eastern accent was dubbed in the 1980s.[158]*

The 'looking down' upon regional or class accents became both satirized and slightly fetishized in the mid-1950s when novelist Nancy Mitford, the eldest of the remarkable sextet of daughters sired by the deeply eccentric Lord Redesdale, wrote an article in *Encounter* magazine on varieties of speech and language. Her distinctions between 'U' (or upper class usages) and 'Non-U' (everyone else's) turned into a kind of national obsession.[159] 'People', Harry Hopkins noted, '... exhibited such an avidity for the information that, for instance, the Upper Class possessed "false teeth", whereas the rest had "dentures", that ... the expressions "U" and "non-U" went into the language.'[160] So it was that false teeth had their own shiny place in the pantheon of material which went into the making of national humour.

It should have been treated – but was not by the status-obsessed – as both an elaborate joke *and* as essentially inaccurate. Mitford's great friend and regular correspondent, Evelyn Waugh, himself a brilliant and ruthless decoder of social origins as revealed by speech, dress or manner, went to the heart of the nonsense when he told her that:

I wish in your Upper-class Usage you had touched on a point that has long intrigued me. Almost everyone I know has some personal antipathy which they condemn as middle class quite irrationally. My mother-in-law believes it middle-class to decant claret. Lord Beauchamp thought it m.c. not to decant champagne (into jugs). Your 'note-paper' is another example. I always say 'luncheon' but you will find 'lunch' used in every generation for the last 80 years [by?[161]] unimpeachable sources. There are very illiterate people like Perry Brownlow [Lord Brownlow, friend of the Duke and Duchess of Windsor] who regard all correct grammar as a middle-class affectation. Ronnie Knox [Monsignor and the leading English Catholic intellectual of his day] blanches if one says 'docile' with a long 'o'. I correct my children if they say 'bike' for 'bicycle'. I think everyone has certain fixed ideas that have no relation to observed usage.[162]

* Most of us postwar upwardly mobiles, children of the Butler Act, either became bilingual in the local accent *and* BBC Home Service (as I did) or oscillated uneasily between the two like Alan Bennett when he 'tried to lose my northern accent at one period, I suppose, when the provincial voice was still looked down on. Then it came back and now I don't know where I am, sometimes saying my "a"s long, sometimes short, though it's the "u"s that are a continuing thread – words like butcher, study, sugar, and names like "Cutbush" always lying in ambush' (Alan Bennett, *Telling Tales* (BBC Books, 2001), pp. 94–5.

Like Mitford, however, Waugh understood the overwhelming potency of the tongue branding of class. 'The curious thing is that, as you say,' he told her, 'an upper class voice is always unmistakable though it may have every deviation of accent and vocabulary.'[163]

It is perhaps surprising that a combination of expanding education provision, the use of an ever-more professionalized and technology-based industrial culture *and* the shared Second World War experiences that fostered what McKibbin called a 'redistribution of esteem' had had such a limited effect on the factors that signalled class and cultural divisions within the British population.[164] Usually, spreading affluence and an easing of working hours are seen as the twin engines of leisure growth and of a less brutal and stratified society generally. The Second World War, as the publisher/politician Harold Macmillan indicated, which involved tight restrictions on consumption and a high level of coercion and danger, also saw a surge in book reading as it did in concert going. The society hostess Lady Colefax enthused to the aesthete connoisseur Bernard Berenson in 1945:

The war has proved my pet thesis –! In spite of our dear Kenneth [Clark], Eddy Sackville-West, the intelligentzia – the enthusiasm of the English for music has proved up to the hilt – hitherto the music was too expensive and either by day when the workers could not go or by night when they were too tired or it was too dear – All through the war there have been concerts in the lunch hours in factories . . . all . . . received with touching enthusiasm.[165]

And the paperback revolution meant that a light and conveniently sized book (a 1935 innovation by Allen Lane of Penguin) could be carried easily by a soldier wherever he found himself, whether it be a thriller or a serious-minded piece of political analysis inside the covers of a Penguin Special (the series started in 1937[166]). As Gellner and others have shown, the spread of literacy is indispensable to the sustenance and development of an advanced industrial society with a politics and a culture worthy of it.

Separated by forty years, two of the most influential thinkers of the centre left saw within the spread of literacy and learning immense possibilities of social and political liberation, and personal and collective enrichment. R. H. Tawney, in a remarkable essay penned for the *Times Educational Supplement* in February 1917 while home from the Western Front and recovering from his Somme-inflicted wounds, called for a 'reconstruction of education in a generous, humane and liberal spirit [that] would be the noblest memorial to those who have fallen, because, though many of them were but little "educated", it would be the most formal and public recognition of the world of the spirit for which they fell'.[167]

Tawney was in no doubt that the learning most of his fellows carried with them into 'the unspeakable agonies of the Somme'[168] reflected an educational system which had been

created in the image of our plutocratic, class-conscious selves, and still faithfully reflects them. Worshipping money and social position, we have established for the children of the well-to-do an education lavish even to excess, and have provided for those of four-fifths of the nation the beggarly rudiments thought suitable for helots who would be unserviceable without a minimum of instruction and undocile helots if spoiled by more. The result has been a system of public education neither venerable, like a college, nor popular, like a public house, but merely indispensable, like a pillar-box.[169]

Nothing approaching Tawney's prescription was adopted until the 1944 Education Act brought 'secondary education for all'.

Forty years after Tawney wrote his plea for 'A National College of All Souls', an education system worthy of the fallen, the Tawney-like Richard Hoggart (himself powerfully influenced by the adult learning world of the Workers' Educational Association that Tawney had helped create) devoted some of the most important sections of his *The Uses of Literacy* (which greatly shaped my generation) to an audit of the shining moment created by the working through of the Butler Act, the spread of affluence and the carving out of leisure time from working-class lives previously over-dominated by work. Hoggart focused on the cognitive and cultural market in which the WEA had to operate in mid-1950s Britain and was disturbed by what he saw:

The personal and social needs for self-acquired education seem by no means obvious and pressing today. The productions of the popular publicists [by which he meant chiefly the written media of newspapers, magazines and romance-thriller writing] are much more powerfully offered now than they were when liberal adult education for working-class people began just over fifty years ago. The difficulty now lies less in the material lack of working people than in their being over-provided with one kind of material. The economic barriers to knowledge have been largely removed, but there is still a struggle – to ignore the myriad voices of the trivial and synthetic sirens.[170]

Hoggart had an acute sense that, even before independent television began to infiltrate the nation's cultural antennae,[171] a great postwar opportunity to build upon the autodidactic legacy of 1939–45 was being lost.

Hoggart noted that in early postwar Britain, more books had been published than in any other country and 'we all know of the success since the thirties of the Penguin and Pelican series. There has been a very great increase in the number of books issued from public libraries ... During a Gallup Poll in 1950, 55 per cent of those interviewed said they were currently reading a book; this proportion was higher than that found in, for instance, the USA or Sweden. There have been increases in the sales of several of the decent periodicals.'[172] For example, sales of the immensely decent BBC weekly *The Listener* peaked at 151,350 in 1949, which Hoggart had in mind when he talked to me of reading *The Listener* and listening to the BBC Third Programme in the early postwar years as being akin to an 'act of faith'.[173]

Hoggart was eloquent on the 'shiny barbarism' that accompanied even the earliest phase of having-it-so-good mass consumption produced by better wages, an end to rationing and the rise of advertising whose appeal, he sensed, would increasingly overwhelm the best competition the serious book or radio programme might pit against it in the struggle for working-class leisure time.[174] He thought the working-class activists of the political left in the Labour Party and the trade union movement were thinking so much in terms of the material advancement of their people that they failed to appreciate the degree to which 'material improvements can be used so as to incline the body of working-class people to accept a mean form of materialism as a social philosophy'. He warned that if 'the active minority continue to allow themselves too exclusively to think of immediate political and economic objectives, the pass will be sold, culturally, behind their backs'.[175]

Hoggart was especially good at reconstructing the ambiguities and anxieties of the intellectually curious younger members of the working class, not least because of the high degree of autobiography that informed his writing on the theme. Hoggart was a scholarship boy in Leeds even before the Butler Act put down its educational ladders, but he spoke for many a later Butler boy and girl in his chapter dealing with those made 'uprooted and anxious' by the meritocratic propulsion involved in the 'physical uprooting from their class through the medium of the scholarship system. A great many', he wrote, 'seem to me to be affected in this way, though only a very small proportion badly ...'[176]

For Hoggart, this uprooting gave those on the rise a sense of not acquiring new and surrogate roots for those left behind,

a sense of no longer really belonging to any group. We all know that many do find a new poise in their new situations. There are 'declassed' experts and specialists who go into their own spheres after the long scholarship climb has led them to a PhD. There are brilliant individuals who become fine administrators and officials, and find themselves thoroughly at home. There are some, not necessarily so gifted, who reach a kind of poise which is not yet a passivity nor even a failure in awareness, who are at ease in their new group without any ostentatious adoption of the protective clothing of that group, and who have an easy relationship with their working-class relatives, based not on a form of patronage but on a just respect.[177]

Whether they adapted easily or not, Hoggart was very insightful of the world of '[a]lmost every working-class boy who gets through the process of further education by scholarships [finding] himself chafing against his environment during adolescence. He is at the friction-point of two cultures ...'[178] Many never quite lose this, whatever the economic and professional rewards of the 'brains ... the currency by which he has bought his way'.[179] Though the scholarship boy becomes bilingual (one accent for home; another for grammar school[180]), he never completely decouples himself from the class of his birth,

and it is interesting to see how this occasionally obstructs (particularly today [mid-1950s], when ex-working-class boys move in all the managing areas of society) – in the touch of insecurity, which often appears as an undue concern to establish 'presence' in an otherwise quite professional professor, in the intermittent rough homeliness of an important executive and committee-man, in the tendency to vertigo which betrays a lurking sense of uncertainty in a successful journalist.[181]

These observations apply to working-class *men* bashing their way upwards in the 1950s in still small but growing numbers, through the once nearly impenetrable ceilings of profession and status – a phenomenon detectable in all subsequent phases of professional upward mobility, male and female. It is tough in a hundred and one ways for pioneering generations 'up on their brains'.

What of the potentially shared cognitive and cultural particles that accrued in daily and weekly tranches in early-Fifties Britain – the media that carried word, sound or image pictures of the home country and the world? (Hoggart, like Matthew Arnold, wished them to reflect the best thought, written or said by mankind.) Here Hitler really had done the high-minded an unintended favour that could not have been anticipated in 1939. For, as Colin Seymour-Ure noted: 'Wars make us hungry for news. Despite newsprint rationing, fewer pages without any reduction in price, sales rose during the war. They continued to do so among all kinds of paper until about the early 1950s . . . Most papers did not mind, however, for the government restrictions kept their paper and printing costs low and enabled them to make good profits from the big demand for advertising space.'[182]

As Seymour-Ure's figures showing newspaper circulation demonstrate, virtually every variety of newspaper did well both during the war and in the first decade of peace (see table),[183] especially as newsprint rationing lasted until 1955[184] (beyond all other rationed goods if foreign exchange is excluded[185]). But, once independent television got into its stride, the struggle for advertising space became intense and the newspapers began to suffer noticeably from 1957 on.[186]

YEAR	NATIONAL MORNING	NATIONAL SUNDAY	PROVINCIAL MORNING	PROVINCIAL EVENING	PROVINCIAL SUNDAY	LONDON EVENING	WEEKLY AND BI-WEEKLY
1939	10.53	15.48	2.16	4.99	0.48[a]	1.71	8.56
1945	12.53	19.76	2.38	5.39	n.a.	2.38	7.37
1947	15.63	26.60	2.87	6.41	1.66	3.48	11.30
1949	16.45	29.32	3.03	6.79	n.a.	3.80	13.32
1951	16.62	30.59	2.94	6.84	1.00	3.75	13.69
1953	16.07	30.20	2.80	7.13	1.07	3.29	13.68
1955	16.22	30.22	2.35	7.06	1.14	2.98	16.21
1957	16.71	29.08	2.30	6.85	1.16	2.85	16.03
1959	16.11	26.84	2.56	6.39	1.05	2.51	16.79
1961	15.69	23.33	1.89	6.61	2.09	2.25	14.73

Notes: Figures are millions of copies. [a]1937 figure.

It is extraordinary to recall how slim the early postwar national newspapers were and that all but two (the *Daily Mirror* and the *Daily Sketch*) were broadsheet rather than tabloid. They varied from four to eight pages in length, apart from *The Times* which usually came out in ten (nine of news and a front page consisting solely of advertisements, a practice that continued until 1966[187]). The size of newspaper and magazine sales, like the number of books published per year, meant in Ross McKibbin's nice formulation that '[t]he English were a people of the book. Even more were they a people of the press . . . During the war, when patterns of newspaper reading were often disrupted, 77 per cent of the population saw a morning newspaper "every day or most days", 87 per cent saw a Sunday paper "last Sunday". In 1950, five papers had readerships of 10 million or more; another four had readerships of 5 million or more.'[188]

A glance at the 1950 breakdowns shows that the quality daily and Sunday papers had a comparatively limited reach into a national population of only 50 million, but notice the appeal of the centre left, serious minded but presentationally brilliant *Picture Post* selling over 8.5 million copies every week (see table).[189]

READERSHIP IN MILLIONS OF TEN MOST POPULAR NEWSPAPERS AND PERIODICALS IN 1950

Radio Times	20.470	*Daily Mirror*	10.140
News of the World	17.630	*Sunday Express*	9.530
People	13.020	*Picture Post* (weekly)	8.680
Sunday Pictorial	12.180	*Daily Mail*	6.200
Daily Express	11.630	*John Bull* (weekly)	5.060

PERCENTAGE OF TOTAL READERSHIP HELD BY NATIONAL DAILIES

	1931–2	1950
Daily Express	18.67	31.4
Daily Herald	11.82	12.2
Daily Mail	26.64	16.7
News Chronicle	13.05	9.3
Daily Mirror	8.97	27.4
Daily Sketch	8.15	n/a
Daily Telegraph	3.84	6.9
Morning Post	1.98	n/a
The Times	3.11	1.9

(table continued overleaf)

PERCENTAGE OF TOTAL READERSHIP HELD BY SUNDAY NEWSPAPERS

	1931–2	1950
News of the World	24.32	47.6
People	22.55	35.2
Sunday Pictorial	18.87	32.9
Sunday Express	12.49	25.8
Sunday Chronicle	10.87	6.3
Sunday Dispatch	12.22	16.8
Empire News	10.17	10.3
Sunday Graphic	8.55	6.7
Sunday Times	3.55	4.5
Observer	2.86	4.3

When it came to competition-by-medium for news and interpretation, the newspapers' only rivals in the early 1950s were the radio and the newsreels shown weekly in the cinemas, which reached vast numbers of people. In 1950, 10 per cent of the *world's* cinema attendance accumulated in England alone.[190] Their tone was jauntily conservative, upbeat and patriotic with a very distinctive style of voiceover, the sound of which can return a certain generation instantly to the days of Pathé News and Movietone.*

In the days when television consisted of a single channel, reached a tiny audience (a mere 344,000 in 1950, though this had spurted to 1,449,000 by the end of 1952[191]) and then only for around thirty hours a week (fifty by September 1955, when independent television first set out its commercial stall to challenge the BBC[192]), cinema newsreels had a certain immediacy and bite, even though their content changed but once a week.

Yet these were still wireless days *par excellence*; the radio trumped even cinemagoing in the early postwar years and, unlike cinema, it embraced all sexes, ages and classes.[193] In terms of the careful dissemination of information, the *Nine o'Clock News* on the BBC Home Service continued to grip the nation as it had

---

* It was a genre that laid itself wide open to parody. In the mid-1980s I would occasionally present *What The Papers Say* for Granada Television. One of its readers had a very creamy voice which reeked of newsreel where, in fact, as a young man, he had made his reputation. One day, to universal nostalgia and amusement, he enlivened a rehearsal read-through with a perfect pastiche of the genre:

'And here's brave Private Tommy Atkins. He's lost both his hands but he can still give . . . THE THUMBS-UP!'

during the Second World War, when half the population listened to it.[194] This astonishing figure fell after 1945, but the dignity and detachment of voice and presentation meant that 'the overwhelming majority of listeners thought the radio news were more reliable than the press'.[195] For a radio generation boy like myself, the sound of Big Ben striking (which still opens the *Ten o'Clock News* on the Home Service's lineal successor, BBC Radio 4) remains evocative of that pre-television era, as do snatches of long-gone signature tunes. Fifties Saturday afternoons, for example, are inseparable in my memory from the Central Band of the Royal Air Force playing-in Eamon Andrews and *Sports Report* on the Light Programme to the sound of 'Out Of The Blue'. Andrews' pleasing Dublin voice, too, is indistinguishable from such gems as 'Accrington Stanley 3, Port Vale 2'.

Marches, in that early shadow of the war, feature prominently in the aural memory of my age group. *In Town Tonight*, which gave me in Finchley my first notions of what was chic in the West End a mere five miles to the south, opened to 'The Knightsbridge March', part of Eric Coates' London Suite. Even the school radio quiz programme *Top of the Form* began with 'Marching Strings' from Ray Martin and his Orchestra, while *Radio Newsreel* each weekday evening roared imperially with the Central Band of the Royal Air Force's 'Imperial Echoes' (ironically enough, it was through this programme that I kept up with the Suez crisis when home from school on autumn evenings in 1956). For the postwar 'baby-bulge', as we were called before the 'baby-boomer' Americanism usurped local usage, the following radio themes probably still exert a certain power to evoke:

Paul Temple (detective thriller): 'Coronation Scot' by Vivian Ellis played by the Queen's Hall Light Orchestra.

Victor Sylvester (strict tempo dance band leader): 'You're Dancing On My Heart' by Bryan Mercer played by Victor's own dance orchestra.

Music While You Work (a hangover from the war which lasted until the 1960s): 'Calling All Workers' by Eric Coates played by the Band of the Grenadier Guards.

Say It With Music: the eponymous theme tune by Irving Berlin from Jack Payne and his Orchestra.

Mrs Dale's Diary (the serial story of a suburban GP's wife): Marie Goosens trilling madly on the strings of her harp to a tune especially composed for the title character who was forever being 'worried about Jim' (her husband).

The Archers (the first real British 'soap'): the tales of 'everyday . . . country folk' in Ambridge endure, but its signature tune, 'Barwick Green' by A. Wood, was belted out in the 1950s with a touch of drama by the New Concert Orchestra; today it's played on a harmonica.

When British popular culture began its profounder changes in the mid-1950s on the back of television and rock-and-roll, it is Don Lang and his Frantic Five playing-in the *Six-Five Special* nearly every Saturday evening for two years (1957–8) that has particular resonance, not least for me, as the opening credits showed an Edinburgh–Aberdeen express racing along the Forth Bridge pulled by a streamlined A4 Pacific steam locomotive (the top of the range for little old trainspotting me at the time).

The phenomenon that linked a modified version of the trainspotting impulse (tabulation/comparison/chit-chat of a faintly obsessional kind) and popular culture will, for my age group, be associated with yet another television theme, 'Hit and Miss', played by the John Barry Seven Plus Four, with which the immensely smooth David Jacobs opened *Juke Box Jury* on BBC Television (another Saturday-evening show).[196]

It is surprising, in retrospect, to recall how long the jukebox/hit-parade phenomenon took to leap the Atlantic, not least because (to many young English women) the swing/bebop generation came across the water in large and hunky uniformed quantities in 1942–4. Hit parades and jukeboxes were mid-1930s breakthroughs in the USA, but the combination that so irritated Richard Hoggart did not reach the UK until the early 1950s, when it fused with the products of Achille Gaggia.[197] British 'big band' music never recovered from this development, but crooning balladeers continued to flourish. From the very first 'Top 12', published by *New Musical Express* on 14 November 1952, the solo singer was dominant – until 25 November 1955 when Bill Haley and the Comets hurled 'Rock Around The Clock' into the number 1 slot.

As I write these words, I'm listening to Disc 1 of HMV/EMI's *The Greatest Fifties Collection*,[198] and it drips with croon, the first three tracks being Perry Como's 'Magic Moments', Tony Bennett's 'Chicago' (more a belt than a croon, this one) and Dean Martin's 'Return To Me'. The very first British number 1, Al Martino's 'Here In My Heart', held its position for nine weeks and was, therefore, also the first British Christmas number 1.

In the first year of the British *NME* chart (see table),[199] the solo singers (usually, but not always, American) were occasionally challenged by 'novelty' numbers such as Lita Roza's 'How Much Is That Doggie In The Window?' or faintly poignant orchestral schmaltz such as Mantovani's 'Moulin Rouge', but for the most part it was ballads all the way.

DATE (1952–53)	TITLE/ARTIST/LABEL	WEEKS AT NO. I
14 Nov.	'Here In My Heart', Al Martino, Capitol	9
16 Jan.	'You Belong To Me', Jo Stafford, Columbia	1
23 Jan.	'Comes A-Long A-Love', Kay Starr, Capitol	1
30 Jan.	'Outside Of Heaven', Eddie Fisher, HMV	1
6 Feb.	'Don't Let The Stars Get In Your Eyes', Perry Como, HMV	5
13 Mar.	'She Wears Red Feathers', Guy Mitchell, Columbia	4
10 Apr.	'Broken Wings', Stargazers, Decca	1
17 Apr.	'How Much Is That Doggie In The Window?', Lita Roza, Decca	1
24 Apr.	'I Believe', Frankie Laine, Philips	9
26 Jun.	'I'm Walking Behind You', Eddie Fisher, HMV	1
3 Jul.	'I Believe', Frankie Laine, Philips	6
14 Aug.	'Moulin Rouge', Mantovani & His Orchestra, Decca	1
21 Aug.	'I Believe', Frankie Laine, Philips	3
11 Sep.	'Look At That Girl', Guy Mitchell, Philips	6
23 Oct.	'Hey Joe', Frankie Laine, Philips	2
6 Nov.	'Answer Me', David Whitfield, Decca	1
13 Nov.	'Answer Me', Frankie Laine, Philips	8

Note: David Whitfield's 'Answer Me' made a brief rally to become joint No. 1 with Frankie Laine's rendition on 11 December 1953. The Laine version was the 1953 Christmas number 1.

New Musical Express may have had the idea of, at last, emulating American hit-parade practice, but to hear those records on a proper chart programme one had to forsake the BBC Light Programme, as the Forces Programme was renamed in 1945, for the commercial station Radio Luxembourg. Technical progress was partly responsible for this – and not just Luxembourg's powerful transmitters, capable of breaking the BBC's UK monopoly, which brought advertising power into our homes. (Remember

Horace Batchelor of Keynsham – 'spelt K-E-Y-N-S-H-A-M' as he intoned every week – with his Horace Batchelor 'method' for increasing your chances of winning the football pools?) Before the war, the big wireless in its wooden case with its array of glowing valves behind was rivalled only by the coal fire in the hearth as the focus of the room in which families spent the bulk of their non-working lives. Cheap and smaller Bakelite sets (still valve laden – the transistor was some way off) began to spread from the late war years, bringing radio into bedroom reach. Thanks to these wartime 'utility' sets, by 1945 10.8 million BBC radio licences were purchased through the General Post Office network, a figure which represented a sizeable majority of all households.[200]

But for us kids, the little white plastic 'crystal set' with its headphones was the way to plug ourselves into Radio Luxembourg's charts while in bed. It broke the domestic monopoly of the big family set, which, for example, my father would commandeer for Wagner on the Third Programme of a Sunday afternoon. In 1953 the complete 'Ring' brought a special glow to the valves[201] – valves which just a while before had brought us ventriloquist(!) Peter Brough educating his dummy Archie Andrews on the lunchtime Light Programme. The editorial on the new Third Programme in the *Evening Star* (the London evening newspaper in the autumn of 1946) perceptively commented that: 'True, the demand for good music and plays is higher now than ever before. But Wagner and Greek Tragedy digest easier with light seasoning.'[202]

Television was about to take off on a trajectory to living-room dominance which it has never since lost. This was masked to a large extent even as late as 1951 as the shades of its founder, John Reith, were still heavy over the BBC even though he had resigned from the Corporation in 1938. It was the intensely religious Reith who told John Freeman in an extraordinary and rightly celebrated interview on BBC Television's *Face to Face* series in October 1960 (FREEMAN: How much do you yourself listen in and look at television? REITH: None at all[203]) that he was 'perhaps more conscious of that [religion – Scottish, Protestant, Free Church] than anything else'.[204] It was Reith's refusal to allow BBC Radio to broadcast dance music on the Sabbath that enabled the continental commercial stations, Radio Luxembourg and Radio Normandie, to begin their assault on the British eardrum.[205]

William Haley, Director-General of the BBC from 1944 to 1952 (when he became editor of *The Times*), was a much more rounded figure than Reith, though just as high minded in his way – he was the 'founding father' of the Third Programme, which he wished to be truly open-ended and not to succumb to the 'carpentering' involved in the construction of schedules for the Light and Home Services. ('The people in charge of it [the Third] all shall have a completely blank open space of up to five hours every night, night after night. And if they want five nights to do something in, then have five nights.'[206])

Haley had a powerful sense of how BBC radio should relate to early postwar British society. His was an adaptation of Reith's view that it was the duty of the BBC to '[g]ive the public slightly better than it now thinks it likes',[207] or, as Reith put it to Haley over lunch at Broadcasting House in April 1951, to 'seek to use broadcasting to raise public taste and not to lower it'.[208] Haley's version of the Reithian ideal was to be delivered by the medium of wireless, not television, and it would be divided like the British class system (my analogy, not Haley's, though he would probably have thought it apt) into three main sections with upward mobility actively encouraged. As he recalled,

I have always believed ... that every civilised nation, culturally and educationally, is a pyramid with a lamentably broad base and a lamentably narrow tip. And ... I devised these three programmes with the idea that we would have a Light Programme which would cover the lower third of the pyramid. We would have a Home Service which would take more than the middle third, take everything up to the tip. And then we'd have a Third Programme. Now it has been said that this was stratifying or segregating listeners into classes. Well, it was in a way, but that was only the start; it was not meant to be a static pyramid. And my conception was of a BBC through the years – many years – which would slowly move listeners from one stratum of this pyramid to the next ... Unfortunately it never really worked out . . .[209]

As a perceptive and sympathetic *New Statesman* profile of Haley in February 1954 put it, in the early postwar BBC

was to be found a satisfaction for all his most cherished beliefs in the efficacy of self-education, in the dissemination of culture, in the pervasive influence of honest reporting – in short, of liberalism. He invented the plan of the Light, Home and Third programmes, believing with all the conviction of his nineteenth-century faith in 'improvement' that listeners' appetites whetted by brief, sugar-coated extracts from the classics on the Light would move on to the fuller diet of the Home and thence to the full feast of beauty, wisdom and culture the BBC was waiting to provide on the Third. In fact, the reverse has taken place. The number of listeners to the Third has consistently fallen, while the audience of the Light has no less consistently swelled.[210]

The Beveridge inquiry into broadcasting was told in 1949 that 'while the average winter evening audiences for the Light Programme and the Home Service were 5½ million and 3¼ million people respectively, the Third was "in the neighbourhood of 90,000"'.[211] Colin Seymour-Ure has penned as lapidary a summary of the generally agreed views of Haley's BBC career as could be imagined: 'Sir William Haley . . . was a self-made man whose career started as a telephonist on *The Times*, and he had much of Reith's commitment to the enlightening and educative value of broadcasting. But he failed to appreciate the potential of television.'[212] Though that is certainly true, it could be argued in Haley's defence that television between 1946 (restoration-of-service day) and Haley's departure for *The Times* in 1952 could not, of itself, have been treated as a great instrument for cultural and cognitive transmission.

The BBC radio and TV licence figures tell part of the story (see table),[213] but, as we shall see in Chapter 5, it was the allure of the Coronation and the BBC's drive to extend the reach of television across the new Queen's kingdom that gave the medium its very special lift-off by Royal Appointment.

YEAR	LICENCES ISSUED	
	RADIO	TELEVISION
1947	10,713,000	15,000
1948	11,082,000	45,000
1950	11,819,000	344,000
1952	11,244,000	1,449,000

Reach was one thing, visibility, duration and content, too, limited television's potential as those wireless-age politicians, Attlee and Churchill, swapped jobs. Peter Lewis caught this view well in his evocation of the Fifties:

In 1950 you would have taken it for a tall, rather ungainly cocktail cabinet. It stood in the corner with a pair of double doors veneered in walnut or mahogany, which were kept closed like eyelids. The little grey screen inside was not much more than a letter box giving out onto the outside world, nine or ten inches across . . . It was called *the* television as in 'Have you got the television?'

. . . BBC transmitters opened at 3 p.m. on weekdays and 5 p.m. on Sundays. They closed down religiously from 6 p.m. to 7 p.m. to make sure the children were put to bed at a proper hour. They closed for the night at 10.30 p.m. . . . Even in between there were frequent 'interludes' when the screen was occupied with soothing images – a windmill turning, horse ploughs ploughing . . . a potter's wheel revolving hypnotically . . .

The programmes themselves were also of a blandness that is hard to recapture. There was about them a strong flavour of evening classes run by a well-endowed Workers' Educational Institute: cookery lessons from the TV chef, the goatee-bearded Philip Harben; gardening hints from the TV gardener, the venerable Fred Streeter; 'Music for You' – nothing too demandingly classical – conducted in a black tie and introduced with an ingratiating few words by Eric Robinson; and, for nursery tea, the dancing, or rather jerking, puppets, Muffin the Mule, Andy Pandy and the Flowerpot Men.[214]

Of politics on television there was hardly a trace apart from *In The News* (which began in 1950), 'made up of disputatious conversationalists' such as Michael Foot and Bob Boothby.[215] The 14-day rule – a convention, not a law – prevented discussion (on radio or television) of any issue likely to arise in the Houses of Parliament in the coming fortnight and no Bill could be discussed until it had passed through all its parliamentary stages.[216] Television 'kept clear' of the 1950 general election 'while the all-pervasive BBC radio gave it no coverage – except for 20-minute talks by five Conservative, five Labour and three Liberal spokesmen'.[217] Things changed very slowly. The 1951 general election saw the first televised party election broadcasts. Party politicals started in 1953. The following year R. A. Butler gave the first Budget Day broadcast by a Chancellor and the Conservative Party conference that autumn was the first to be televised.[218] Deference infused interviewers' every syllable. Not until the aftermath of the Suez crisis was the 14-day rule abandoned.[219]

One aspect of early-Fifties cultural transmission where deference was remarkably *not* the order of the day was humour, or one extraordinary and path-breaking strand of it which, perhaps even more surprisingly, became a BBC classic – *The Goon Show*. From its inception in May 1951 it was like no other. It transcended the best of the music hall/variety tradition, some of which transferred exceptionally well to radio with a range that embraced Charlie Chester and Frankie Howerd. Unlike the two Maxes – Miller and Wall

– there was nothing 'blue' (as that generation of taste-custodians would have put it) and hence, unlike the Maxes, access to the microphone was easy. Theirs is an extraordinary range of sound, language and metaphor that I associate with the earphones of my crystal set in the 1950s. There should be a plaque over the fruit shop in Shepherd's Bush where 'up three flights of stairs' lay the 'office containing teapots, typewriters, electronic devices, encyclopaedias, and books ranging from *The Dialogues of Plato* ... and *The Tragedy of the Caesars*, to *Birds of Our Country* [where] the extraordinary hallucinations of *The Goon Show* [were] hammered into script form every week by Spike Milligan and Larry Stephens'.[220] For that cluttered room changed the DNA of British humour, its only rival being Tony Hancock's *Hancock's Half Hour* which began on radio later in the decade in 1954 before moving to TV two years later.[221]

The Goons, like the satirists of *Beyond the Fringe* a decade on and *Monty Python* nearly twenty years later,[222] fed off a rich residue of Britain's accumulated imperial past. It cried out to be sent up in the early 1950s above the Shepherd's Bush fruiterer if not in a Cabinet Room treated to doses of Anthony Eden's fixation with prestige. Peter Sellers, who with Harry Secombe, Milligan and Michael Bentine comprised the early *Goons* cast, could do a wonderfully fruity British ruling voice riper even than Eden's, most memorably when playing the smoothly dastardly Hercules Gritpype Thynne. The first voice of Empire with which I was familiar was Sellers' as the ex-Indian Army major, Dennis Bloodnok, and his constant raging against trapped wind ('Damn those curried eggs!'). My initial encounter with the universally life-diminishing British 'jobsworth', as the breed would now be known, was with William, who in my mind's eye is always 'old mate' from his whining 'You can't park 'ere, mate'.

From the Prince of Wales down, my generation can embarrass others (if never itself) by silly Goon voices (Eccles and Bluebottle or Minnie Bannister in particular) which we would 'put on' indiscriminately at home or in the school playground to deliver standard Goon catchphrases such as 'He's fallen in the wa-ter' or 'I'm deaded'. Herein, I think, lay, and perhaps still lies, the key to radio humour: much more so than television comedy it can be a private relationship between listener and performer. For radio, or 'listening in' as we called it then, I think falls into that category Orwell called in *The Lion and the Unicorn* 'the *privateness* of English life'.[223]

I did not share the family appetite for gardening but I recognized early on the importance both of the 'extra room' notion of a backyard of lawn and flower and, slightly more distant, the centrality of the vegetable allotment not just to an Orwellian England (in the benign, not the *Nineteen Eighty-Four* sense) but also to families on low income. Allotment life, as I remember it from the north London of the mid-Fifties, was a classic example of the mix of the private and the communal that Orwell explored. My father's was on a patch belonging to Finchley Borough Council between the red-brick railway arches of the viaduct that carried the Northern Line branch from Finchley Central to Mill Hill East over the Brent Brook and the beautifully tended playing fields of Christ's College, Finchley. The soil was tough and rested thinly on heavy, yellow London clay. But to my untutored eye, the yield was good. Dad grew some grotesquely large vegetables which won him prizes at the annual horticultural show held in a hall on Hendon Lane. His solitary bouts of digging – he liked to be alone and in the open air, but he didn't mind me being there (not that the urge to emulate him ever struck me) – would be broken up with veg-infused chats with his allotment neighbours, some of whom had made almost a second home out of their garden sheds. What I liked best was the smell of woodsmoke and compost that hung over the place of a late summer evening.

Naturally, at the age of seven I was a stranger to the finer points of the Allotment Act 1922 whose significance Richard Hoggart was committing to paper some 150 miles to the north in Hull, as the pages of what became *The Uses of Literacy* grew in unknowing harmony with Dad's shallots. Hoggart dropped the allotment theme into his observation on how the regular jobs of working people were 'often undemanding and undiscriminating' but 'by their integrity and devotion to a craft' they could turn themselves into devoted specialists. He noted

the persistence of the desire to grow things, in window-boxes and on patches of sour soil in back-yards, which are often well-tended; and on allotments – behind hoardings in the main street or on the edge of the permanent way [the railway], or on strips of three hundred square yards let at a nominal rent under the provisions of the 1922 Allotment Act ('Every citizen who is able and willing to cultivate an allotment garden is legally entitled to be provided with one').[224]

During the war there had been 'a popular and informative' programme on the Home Service called *Radio Allotment* in which Tony Hay, the Royal Parks gardener, passed on tips to those digging for victory on the home front.[225] Further afield, one of the most touching aspects of British allotmentry was its extension into the prisoner-of-war camps deep in Nazi Europe. The Royal

Horticultural Society joined up with the International Red Cross and in a very British operation during 1943 got 979 parcels of seeds into 72 POW camps holding some 141,000 detainees.[226]

Rationing ensured that necessity combined with individual horticultural craftsmanship deep into the peace. And by the time rationing finished, gardening was well established as one of those traditional pursuits-cum-pleasures on which the developing electronic media seized as a relatively cheap way of making a big-audience programme.

Better known to the public, for example, than any of the genteel plant societies (though there was a postwar flowering of these with the National Begonia Society of 1948 and the British National Carnation Society founded a year later [227]) was the first well-known television gardener, Percy Thrower. Fred Streeter (what reassuring names they all had) had shown the way with his early-postwar radio programme, *In Your Garden*, with rural wisdom imparted on practical matters in a rich countryman's voice. And *Gardener's Question Time* (of which my father was a devotee) started on the Home Service in 1947 and brightens up early Sunday afternoons on Radio 4 to this day. But the 'cult of the television personality gardener' took off in 1955 when Thrower joined with Roland Smith, head gardener to the Earl of Bradford, on the weekly *Gardening Club*, which eventually became *Gardener's World*.[228]

Thrower unwittingly acquired a place in the history of the British Royal Family during a February 1960 *Gardening Club* session (like much else, broadcast live in those days) when 'the face of the usually unflappable' presenter 'went the colour of one of his prize tomatoes' as he had to interrupt a disquisition on soft fruits, delivered in his homely Shropshire accent, to cue in an announcement of the engagement of the Queen's sister, Princess Margaret, to the fashionable photographer Anthony Armstrong-Jones. 'It only came,' Thrower recalled, 'at a moment when I was showing viewers how to plant a gooseberry bush. When we came back on air, I congratulated the Princess on her engagement but I think I rather spoiled it by adding, "And now back to the gooseberries."'[229] Quite the reverse. The inimitable Percy behaved in exactly the way the English, at least, saw themselves – a country where pomp and domesticity existed side-by-side, exactly as Walter Bagehot had described in his evocation nearly a hundred years before in *The English Constitution* of the importance of having a '*family* on the throne . . . [as it] brings down the pride of sovereignty to the level of petty life'.[230]

The other Fifties' name that fuses the practical individual pursuit with shared collective memory is that of Barry Bucknell, who was to DIY what Percy

Thrower was to the flowerbed and the allotment. (The two of them were bringers of a mid-twentieth-century version of Samuel Smiles' 'self help' but without his nineteenth-century preachiness.) Bucknell drilled his way into the nation's living rooms a little while after Thrower had popped up in its back gardens. Nineteen fifty-seven was the year DIY took off (though the magazine *Practical Householder* was first published in October 1955[231]). By one indicator – correspondence – Bucknell even outstripped Thrower once *Do It Yourself* opened on BBC Television in late 1957.* Barry Bucknell, a tad defter than Bill Hennessy when up a ladder, was an instant hit. As the television historians Hilary Kingsley and Geoff Tibballs put it, 'From the first edition – a festive show in which Bucknell demonstrated how to make a stand for a Christmas tree as well as giving some tips on tree-lights – his popularity soared to the point where he received more mail than anybody else on television, up to 35,000 letters a week! He needed to employ ten secretaries.'[232]

It was exactly these Thrower/Bucknell-style developments, plus his observation of greater equality within more 'companionate' marriages in both Bethnal Green and the new London County Council estates in Loughton, Essex, that led Michael Young to set up the Consumers' Association and its famous magazine, *Which?*, in 1957 to enable (as he hoped) working-class families to make more informed choices as the accoutrements of their new-style home lives developed. That *Which?* became largely an instrument of the middle classes pained Young somewhat.[233]

What of the wider ecology in which the domestic micro-ecologies of countless individual gardens rested? It is the *absence* of an environmental movement in the early 1950s that is so surprising. It took the great London smog of December 1952 to cause the government to move in the direction of cleaner air, not sustained pressure from activist groups. Home and hearth are inseparable in both the language and the image of the Britain that existed from the moment coal changed the face of the land and the economy in the eighteenth century right through to the 1960s. Not for the rare travelling Brit the clean, impersonal efficiencies of continental neighbours. The environmental historian B. W. Clapp quotes Edward Gibbon writing in his memoirs that he 'had now exchanged my elegant apartment in Magdalen College [Oxford] . . . for a small chamber ill-contrived and ill-furnished [in Lausanne, Switzerland],

___

* A magazine of the same name had set up the previous March in competition to *Practical Householder*. – causing one of my sisters to tell Dad, to his mild irritation, to 'do it yourself, practical householder' when the latest bit fell off our big house in Lyndhurst Gardens N3, which Finchley Borough Council had requisitioned for large and impecunious families such as ours after it fell vacant during the war.

which on the approach of winter instead of a companionable fire must be warmed by the dull invisible heat of a stove'.[234]

Clapp has described how those homes about to be Bucknellated and those gardens under progressive Throwerization were enveloped in a fall-out partly of their own making:

The design of domestic grates did not change substantially until concern about the evils of smoke became widespread in the 1950s. In 1948, 98 per cent of living rooms still had an open fire, or a fire combined with a back-boiler or a stove. Coal-fired cooking stoves were still being installed in many new houses between the wars, and a quarter of homes were still cooking by coal in the early 1950s. At first sight it would seem that the war against smoke on the home front was being lost as the twentieth century wore on.[235]*

Before turning to the blowing-back of coal-based air pollution from the mid-1950s, we must examine a less obvious contamination that the war and early postwar brought to the UK's ecology which is probably irreversible. Even to the trained eye of a remarkable British social observer, it took over forty years for this change to register fully. It applies to rural England – deep England in particular – not to urban Britain. Chelly Halsey described it as a 'sense of tension between change and changelessness in English society which over-laps with my tension between town and country' – the result of the London Midland and Scottish Railway lifting the Halsey family from Kentish Town to rural Rutland and, later, Northamptonshire in the early 1930s.

The London townscape has been transformed in my lifetime – invaded, that is, by the international architecture of le Corbusier and modern brutalism. New towns appear and old industrial development falls into decay. But underneath lies the never-defeated countryside, the English temper refuses to give up its rural nostalgia.

Yet even so, I now realise, subtle rural change is equally part of our history. In 1995 I visited Iona, where nothing much has happened since Columba built an abbey in the

* My age can smell and feel that room. The morning ritual from early autumn to late spring of lay-ing chopped wood, paper doused in paraffin ('firelighter' white solid-fuel blocks a little later), bits of coal on top and the mixed smell of the paraffin, briefly the wood smoke and then the coal smoke was what one woke up to. As the day wore on this was superseded by the constant emissions of buses and trains alike, and the whiff of tobacco smoke, Old Holborn especially, in those days of roll-your-own. Of everywhere I lived the coal-smoke-in-the-morning phenomenon was true until I went up to Cambridge in October 1966 and had the bizarre and utterly unnatural sensation each morning of electric underfloor heating plus a storage heater in the then newly completed Cripps building of St John's College Cambridge. Upstairs was my friend John Browne, who, when in charge of BP, was to change the face of British and world energy policy – not that we gave our warm feet much consideration in 1966–7.

6th and the Benedictines rebuilt it in the 14th century. But there has been no pesticide revolution. At first I was mystified by déjà vu before a meadow until I realised that I was surveying an array of species and colours that had passed from my memory of childhood in Northamptonshire before World War II.[236]

For it was siege-economy wartime and food-scarce early postwar Britain that opened the stopcocks on a cascade of production-boosting, bug and weed-killing chemicals that flooded and changed the face of the landscape of the Halsey memory. Up against government-sponsored programmes and agribusiness, the meadow had no chance. And it did not stop there. Those creatures the ladies who founded the Fur and Feather Group (later the Royal Society for the Protection of Birds and now a million members – of both genders – strong) had in mind also suffered grievously from the chemical revolution (the ladies' chief enemy in 1879 had been the fashion trade). Birds and flowers are key indicators of the health of the countryside, as the social historian and naturalist Brian O'Leary expresses it.[237]

Buttressing Halsey's memory in Iona, Graham Harvey, the historian of the countryside, has noted that classic English farming practice based on the four-course rotation pioneered in Norfolk during the eighteenth century lasted almost unchanged until the Second World War. As a result, '[a]part from the effect of urban expansion, almost every hedge, wood heath and fen on the large-scale Ordnance Survey maps of the 1870s appeared on Luftwaffe aerial photographs taken in 1940.'[238] Postwar agricultural policy, notably the Agriculture Act 1947 designed to maximize domestic food production, subsidized the use of organochlorine insecticides like DDT and the weed-killing dust, MC PA.[239] Not until the marine biologist Rachel Carson published her widely read *Silent Spring* in America in the early 1960s[240] did the process of intellectual and political rollback begin with what Brian O'Leary calls the 'heavy nasties' among the pesticides and insecticides eventually being banned. In the 1950s and 1960s, he writes, 'it was the impact of those chemicals on the "top of the food chain" predators that was most noticeable'. By the late 1950s, for example, 'sparrowhawks had disappeared from south eastern England and the cause was traced to the organochlorine pesticides Dieldrin, Aldrin, DDT and their metabolites which built up in the food chain, and affected the birds . . .'[241] At the very top of the food chain, peregrines feasted on pigeons that fed on the crops affected by pesticides and the 'concentration of the pesticide residues in the bodies of the peregrines led to thinning eggshells, infertile eggs, and even inability to lay'.[242]

People dying in the nation's capital from a freezing, livid murk that penetrated into houses and public buildings day after day provided both more tangible and more visible evidence than the peregrines and sparrowhawks having a bad time in East Anglia. The Great London Smog of 1952 led directly to the clean-air legislation of the mid-1950s. Britain in the steam age really was a land of mists and fogs. Those with memories of the 1940s and 1950s are right to peer back if not exactly through a permanent 'pea-souper' as the thickest of the 'smogs' (a linguistic, if not a chemical, fusion of 'smoke' and 'fog' in common use since Edwardian times) were called, but through a common haze in the autumn and winter months for city and large-town dwellers. For as peace returned in 1945, 'the home consumption of coal rose and thin fog still hung over London for between 40 and 60 days a year'.[243] For some, this was the magical attraction of London. When Monet travelled from France at the end of the nineteenth century this is what he had come to paint – especially the waterfronts of the Embankment and the Houses of Parliament: 'Then, in London, above all what I love is the fog ... It is the fog that gives it its magnificent breadth. Those massive regular blocks became grandiose within that mysterious cloak.'[244]*

For my generation of Londoners it did have a certain sort of pungent magic. We can still sniff the smell of sulphur dioxide that swirled through every street from late September to early April. And we all have stories of walking to school with but ten yards visible ahead and the cars and buses creeping by (the trolley buses I remember as being the weirdest for, propelled by electricity, they were virtually silent when barely moving). One weekday evening in 1957 my father took me after school to hear Francis Jackson, Organist at York Minster, give an early-evening concert in the Festival Hall on the South Bank during what I remember as one of the very last pea-soupers. (There was a bad one in 1962 but I was living in the Cotswolds by then.[245]) The Northern Line carried us from Finchley Central to Waterloo or we would never have made it. The utter murk outside and the River Thames flowing oleaginously alongside seemed to add to the effect, enhancing in a strange way the Bach being played within and certainly adding to the sense of adventure.

But, for all its opacity, the Francis Jackson evening simply did not compare to the smog that had entered the nation's folk-memory five years earlier. For

* The murk regularly penetrated those magnificent Westminster and Whitehall buildings so beloved of Monet. As late as the early Fifties, for example, that grandest of departments, the Foreign Office, would take on a special, evocative air when '[o]ccasional wisps of fog were granted admission to the heart of the building to remind us of the vanity of efforts to spread light in the world', as the then young diplomat, Douglas Hurd, recalled in his memoirs.

'on the night of 8 December 1952 the audience with balcony seats in the Royal Festival Hall could not see the stage'.[246] It got everywhere – creeping filthily in and leaving 'an oily greasy film' in home, school, hospital and public building. What exactly was 'it', this 'fluid ink', as Carlyle called it in the nineteenth century?[247] A cocktail of pollutants which, when the smog set in on 5 December on top of the cold spell that had chilled London for two weeks already, reached ten times the quantity normal for that time of the year:

If more than one part per million of sulphur dioxide is present in air (2860 micrograms per cubic metre), breathing may be affected. Much higher levels were found ... Concentrations of smoke at 4.46 micrograms per cubic metre were well above what was needed for a severe fog. A normal winter concentration of smoke in a residential/commercial area of inner London would have been 0.5 micrograms. Smoke is not simply carbon dust, but contains tar and soot. Not surprisingly, an oily greasy film reappeared in London houses during the fog within an hour of being wiped away.[248]

The sick and the elderly with bronchial problems could not escape whether they were at home in bed, in an ambulance with its bell ringing as it made its slow way to hospital or even in the hospital itself. What excited Monet and gave Conan Doyle some of his best London backdrops against which Holmes and Watson and assorted villainy could plot and operate, propelled them, far from easefully, from this world to the great smokeless zone (incense excepted) in the sky.

Until then the worst London smog in popular memory was that of 1948, when deaths from bronchitis doubled and mortality generally in the capital rose by 30 per cent. December 1952 turned out to be four times as lethal. It merited comparison with some interesting earlier catastrophes: 'while it [the 1952 smog] lasted its effects were more severe than those of the cholera epidemic of 1866, in that deaths exceeded the norm by a larger margin. Only the influenza epidemic of 1918 among modern outbreaks of disease increased the death rate more sharply.'[249] As a result the Ministry of Health set up the Beaver Committee to inquire into air pollution and the Clean Air Act was passed in 1956. 'Few reports into a social evil have led to such swift action ... Within ten years of the Clear Air Act, industry had reduced its smoke emissions by 74 per cent, so that it was domestic smoke that did most to pollute the air.'[250] We took longer, until the 1970s, to become a central-heating rather than a home-and-hearth nation.

Part of the dramatic reduction of industry-generated smoke came from the disappearance of a coal-fired phenomenon to which some of us were even more attached than the grate in our front room – the steam locomotive. It takes a great effort now to recall just how many steam locomotives still ran on British rails in the early 1950s, even for a 'platform soul', as Nicholas Whittaker christened us in his hilariously poignant *Platform Souls: The Trainspotter as Twentieth-Century Hero*.[251] Sir Hugh Beaver, the inquirer into smog, reckoned that in 1952 there were still between 40,000 and 50,000 hand-fired boilers in use in British industry.[252] In January 1955, when the British Transport Commission published *A Plan for the Modernisation and Re-equipment of British Railways*,[253] there were 18,426 steam locomotives in service, just 1,000 fewer than in the full last year of peace, 1938.[254] And these characterful creators of smoke, smut and sulphur, as poetic as they were polluting, were not included in Beaver's figures. The last of them was not withdrawn until the summer of 1968.*

The attempt, as Enoch Powell put it in the House of Commons debate on the 1955 Modernization Plan, to find 'in our present railway system, as a sculpture is concealed in a block of marble, the railway system of the future which does pay and which corresponds to the economic needs of the country'[255] has been expertly analysed by a former student of mine, Chas Loft.[256] As I write in the early twenty-first century we are still waiting. In a prosaic way, there has probably been more fantasy (quite apart from the romance of the steam enthusiasts) about Britain's railway system than anything except its royal family and its secret services. One of the treasures Chas Loft unearthed when researching his PhD was this gem of an editorial from *The Economist* magazine stimulated by the Modernization Plan:

From the grime and muddle of 1955, from a very recent piece of politicking which everybody would like to forget, the public is invited to lift its eyes towards 1974. Look; there is an electric or diesel (or, just possibly, atomic) train pulling silently, briskly competitive, smog-free, out of the glistening chromium of the new King's Cross. This is the stuff to give a government which likes to seem forward-looking.[257]

---

* Steam infused, as well as enthused, my childhood. For example, the first film I saw (in 1955) which terrified me, the Ealing Comedy *The Lady Killers*, was shot in and around King's Cross Station and, without steam-hauled goods trains in the cutting between the tunnels just to the north of the terminal, would simply not have been effective. Even Alec Guinness (the voice of the 1950s for me) as the ghastly 'Professor' who masterminded the robbery at King's Cross while sheltering with his criminal gang (all posing as chamber musicians) with the perfect Edwardian old lady, Mrs Wilberforce, in a house atop the tunnel, would not have been so effective without the smoke and the noise – his own demise occurring when a signal crashes down on his head and he joins his final victim as the goods train beneath, released by the signal, trundles away with the bodies in a northerly direction.

This was the period when great hopes were entertained by those advanced nations which could, or soon would, build civil atomic power stations that nuclear-generated electricity would, despite high initial capital costs, beat fossil fuels both in terms of cost-per-unit *and* in the cleanliness stakes. This turned out to be one of the brightest false dawns of the 'long postwar'.[258]

Another factor that intrigues me is a dawn-that-never-was – the place of women in society. This featured remarkably little in the early postwar years apart from the pursuit of equal pay and the ending of marriage bars (which required women to resign) within the public service and teaching professions.[259] Class was an immensely more potent issue than gender even as a 25-year-old woman inherited the crown on the death of George VI in February 1952.[260] It is extraordinary, for example, to recall that Sir William Beveridge declared in his 1942 report that the most important work women could undertake for the foreseeable future was to 'ensure the continuation of the British race'.[261] As Jane Lewis has noted:

Beveridge's picture of married women as housewives fitted the 1930s much better than his wartime world, or as it transpired, the post-war world. But his conviction that adult women would normally be economically dependent on their husbands became embodied in the post-war social security legislation which in turn had a prescriptive effect. The Beveridge model for married women's entitlements to social security was not revised until the middle of the 1970s.[262]

The other profound change involving huge numbers of people – the decline in active religious practice if not belief itself – was more predictable, and there were some who had had a sense of it ever since the men came home from the trenches in 1918–19. Monsignor Ronald Knox was eloquent about the real significance of what was later described as the phenomenon of 'believing without belonging' – the argument that a fall in the outward signs of belief (most notably church attendance) did not necessarily indicate a loss of inner faith.[263] For the historian, the social arithmetic of belief is one of the most vexing areas. Attendance figures are rarely reliable[264] and in any case how do you measure belief? This is firmly in Tawney's realm of the imponderables.

Knox, writing in 1930, had a profound sense of this:

The hearts of our fellow-men are not open to scrutiny. I do entertain the uneasy feeling that the symptoms of our time are being widely misread. There is no evidence that people are more religious; there *is* evidence that people are fonder of talking about religion, and of talking about it in public.[265]

Knox, intriguingly, linked the question of faith to the great decline debate. Of the alleged 'reawakening' of public interest in religion in 1920s Britain, he said,

It would be encouraging if we could regard this as a healthy sign. But is it not rather our experience that, while men are in health, their health is the last subject which pre-occupies them; that it is only when symptoms of age or decay begin to set in that they air their maladies for public inspection? The same reflection applies to the body politic: in the piping times of Victorian prosperity people did not talk about trade or employ-ment – it would have been almost vulgar: nor did people exercise their minds over the continuance of our world-hegemony; they took it for granted. It is when the public mind becomes less easy on such topics that they are freely ventilated.

For Knox it was 'difficult not to conclude that a society talks about religion more freely and more publicly when religion is beginning to die out. Like the enfeebled pulse or the dwindling exports, the empty pew begins, for the first time, to arrest our attention.'[266]

Knox was concerned by attendance and adherence to organized religion and its doctrinal discipline. Here the admittedly shaky statistics point to a steady decline among the UK's Christian churches throughout the twentieth century. Peter Brierley has calculated that Sunday attendance fell from 19 per cent of the population in 1903 'to 15 per cent in 1951 to 11 per cent in 1979 to 10 per cent in 1989 to an estimated 8 per cent in 2000', represent-ing 'a decline of 0.6 per cent compound per annum' throughout the twentieth century.[267]

Membership figures over the period 1910–60, perhaps no more reliable than the attendance data, show that the only serious growth to have taken place was among Knox's (and my) co-religionists. And the substantial Roman Catholic surge is largely explained by immigration from Ireland, especially during and just after the war. The religious impact of immigration from the Indian subcontinent begins to show up in the 1960 figure for other religions (see table).[268]

It is interesting how small a proportion of the Christian total (not much more than a third by 1960) was provided by the active members of the state church in England – the Anglicans. The strong Presbyterian figure reflects the established, as well as the spiritual, status of the Church of Scotland north of the border.

RELIGIOUS MEMBERSHIP IN THE UK

	1910	1920	1930	1940	1950	1960
Anglican	3,876,000	3,820,000	4,172,000	3,908,000	3,441,000	3,341,000
Roman Catholic	1,699,000	1,795,000	1,909,000	1,998,000	2,223,000	2,626,000
Presbyterian	1,820,000	1,867,000	1,879,000	1,877,000	1,860,000	1,868,000
Methodist	868,000	826,000	868,000	830,000	772,000	766,000
Baptist	418,000	405,000	406,000	382,000	337,000	318,000
Others[a]	708,000	755,000	845,000	816,000	801,000	848,000
Total Christian	9,389,000	9,468,000	10,079,000	9,811,000	9,434,000	9,767,000
Total Christian as % of population	32%	30%	29%	27%	24%	24%
Other religions	179,000	194,000	209,000	244,000	270,000	421,000
Total number	9,568,000	9,662,000	10,288,000	10,055,000	9,704,000	10,188,000
Total % of population	33%	30%	29%	27%	25%	25%

Note: [a]Independent, Orthodox, Pentecostal, New and other Churches.

The spiritual roofing above the nation continued to matter in the early 1950s, and not only on symbolic occasions such as the Coronation of Queen Elizabeth II in 1953. It was, to quite remarkable extent, built in by statute to the life of the state schools recognized under the terms of the 1944 Education Act. Michael Ramsey, a future Archbishop of Canterbury, saw this in especially interesting terms – as a device for reconciling the split between 'religion and humanism', the once-fused cultures, in Ramsey's analysis, of 'the humanism of the Graeco-Roman world, and the Biblical religion of the Jews'. Through the 1944 Act, Ramsey told a group of schoolteachers in his Durham bishopric during the early 1950s, 'the state acknowledges the link by requiring in every State School in the country a daily act of worship and a regular period of Biblical instruction'.[269]

But Ramsey knew full well that starting the day with a hymn, a thought and a prayer was one thing, but the great machine for cognitive and cultural improvement which, for all its imperfections, the post-1944 system was both in absolute terms and compared to what had gone before, ensured that the 'sciences and the humanities stand in the curriculum in their own right'.[270] This was true, too, in the state-subsidized Catholic schools, wherein, I think, lies a good part of the story of what Dennis Sewell has called the rise of the UK's most important 'stealth minority' to a position whereby at the end of the twentieth century, 'not only did baptized Catholics account for 1 in 8 of the population in England and Wales', they also 're-engineered themselves' in a manner 'undetectable by conventional social radar' into positions of great influence across public and professional life.[271]

Observers such as Sewell and McKibbin agree that for Britain's Catholics, the Sixties rather than the Fifties saw the real change with the shifts in secular attitudes to matters both sexual and of conscience (which had a powerful effect generally, not just on Catholic youth) and the effect of the reforms associated with the Second Vatican Council. A fizzing fuse had been lit twenty years earlier when Parliament passed the 1944 Education Act. The compromise deal struck between the Catholic hierarchy and Rab Butler rested on a high level of state funding for Catholic schools without state interference in what was taught (this was thirty years before any notions of a core curriculum). It paved the way for successive generations of Catholics to receive, for the first time, a fully fledged and often excellent secondary education whatever the socioeconomic status of their parents (and only a very few Catholics from the old recusant families had both money and status in early postwar Britain).

This resulted in the progressive growth of a substantial Catholic professional middle class whose numbers and importance would dwarf the old pattern of a small, highly educated Catholic elite shaped by the traditions of the old recusancy, with the bulk of the rest rarely getting beyond the school-leaving age. Out of this cultural mix came the Catholic lapsings of the Sixties and after, and a good deal of intense questioning of the received orthodoxies by those who continued to practise.

How could it be otherwise when, very sensibly, most state church schools, Protestant and Catholic, kept the Ramsey separation in place? And a high-quality secondary education, whether arts or science based, usually produces, at its best, a care with evidence, a scepticism about received wisdom (which is not the same thing at all as cynicism) and a high degree of tolerance for diversity and dissent (which is not the same as permissiveness or relativism). Such necessary scepticism was bound to spread to matters religious as well as secular.

These developments brought a high degree of anxiety to 1960s and 1970s Catholics who, like Knox in the late 1920s, could certainly tell the difference between inner-directed, individualistic beliefs and the doctrine of centuries as practised by a great global church. Yet the real sufferers from the rise of secularism in twentieth-century Britain were that cluster of smaller, often intensely indigenous, Protestant faiths that comprised the great dissenting nonconformist tradition which had made the Liberal Party what it was in its mid- to late-nineteenth-century apogee and, during the early twentieth, put so much of the high-minded decency into the Labour Party and the wider Labour movement.

As McKibbin has expressed so pithily in his (partial) autopsy of them, the 'Free Churches coped less well with secular forces than any other major religion; they were worst affected by both world wars and recovered from them with least success. Unlike the Church of England, the Free Churches had no national endowment: their structure depended on the willingness and ability of the congregations to pay for them.'[272] And these congregations were most numerous in exactly those areas where economics moved against them – the industrial heartlands reliant on the old staple industries and agriculture. 'The neglected bethels of South Wales,' writes McKibbin elegiacally, 'and the crumbling chapels of Co. Durham were poignant souvenirs of these regional catastrophes.'[273] A crucial part of that 'moral machinery' which, as Edward Thompson showed, had gone into the making of the English and Welsh working class,[274] was in rapid decline – though a secular version of it was powerfully represented in the Labour Party, not least at the top in the persons of two of its premiers, Harold Wilson (Congregationalist)[275] and Jim Callaghan (Baptist).[276] Clem Attlee subscribed to 'the ethics of Christianity. Can't believe the mumbo-jumbo,' as he characteristically put it to his official biographer, Kenneth Harris.[277] Churchill, like his nineteenth-century predecessor in Downing Street, Lord Melbourne, gave the impression of supporting the Church of England from the outside as a flying buttress does a cathedral. But he did not believe in the after-life. 'I believe that death is the end,' he told his friend Violet Bonham Carter, '. . . when it comes to dying I shall not complain. I shall not miaow.'[278]

The norms of personal and sexual morality were heavily influenced by Christianity as interpreted by the Churches in mid-twentieth-century Britain even if the consciences of those tempted by the sins of the flesh concerned rarely visited a pew. Physical sexual behaviour is easier to measure than the spiritual activities and impulses by which it may – or may not – be shaped or constrained, but I would still classify it as one of the imponderables despite the amount of social arithmetic applied to it. Unlike sport (even the most solitary of sporting pursuits such as angling, which was very popular in the late Forties and early Fifties[279]), 'horizontal refreshment', as Field Marshal Montgomery liked to describe sexual intercourse,[280] is not susceptible to accurate qualitative or quantitative description in terms of its active expression.

Attitudes towards sex, as opposed to sexual activity itself, are more easily divined. Most social historians of the early postwar when discussing sex and the nation turn to Geoffrey Gorer's *Exploring English Character*, published in 1955 but based on a vast national questionnaire sponsored by the *People* Sunday newspaper in 1951 (over 11,000 completed it, filling in details of their views about family life, religion, friends and neighbours as well as sex and marriage).[281] Given the long-term decline of religious attendance (the Catholics apart) and fears that the disruptions, anxieties and opportunities of the Second World War might have seriously sundered the bonds of aggregate national morality, Gorer's findings were revealing of attitudes which would have brought considerable comfort to the guardians of public morality, ecclesiastical or otherwise.

Gorer found that 52 per cent of the population in 1951 were against any sexual experience for young men before marriage. Inequality between the genders reared its head here too. The equivalent figure for young women was 63 per cent. The reasons given, as Gorer broke them down, are interesting (see table).[282] 'Religion' was not perhaps as strong a factor as one might have expected, though if it is fused with 'morality' – mumbo-jumbo plus ethics, as Mr Attlee might have put it, though I doubt that he read the *People* in No. 10, let alone was tempted to fill in Gorer's questionnaire – the combined figure is quite high.

REASON FOR ABSTINENCE	YOUNG MEN (%)	YOUNG WOMEN (%)
Marriage should be a new experience	13	12
Man wants virgin wife	0	9
Man should be pure because he wants wife to be	6	1
Against morality	7	6
Against religion	4	4
Not necessary – Nature teaches	4	5
People should have self-control	2	2
Unfair to girl	2	1
Degrades girl	2	8
Danger of pregnancy	2	6
Danger of VD	2	1
Danger to health of future children	0	1
People wouldn't marry if they could get it without doing so	2	1
Leads to promiscuity after marriage	1	1
Husband may bring up later	0	1
Danger of invidious comparisons	0	1

Gorer did not inquire about the impact of the war, but this might account for the relative permissiveness of the 25–34 age group in 1951 when compared with those both older and younger than themselves (though this difference should not be exaggerated):

The very young tend to be more severe in their ethical judgements than their elders, though nearly a quarter of under 18's have not made up their minds; the height of permissiveness is reached by the people aged between 25 and 34, but it is only a small difference; people between the ages of 18 and 24 are just as severe in their moral notions as people 20 years older.[283]

Class generally made no difference to the replies to Gorer's questions about sex, with one exception:

[A] far higher proportion of the lower working class are in favour of sexual experience before marriage than of any other group. It is only in this group that there is an absolute majority in favour of pre-marital experience for men; and a third are in favour of it for women too.[284]

It is intriguing how many in Gorer's 'vox pop' section on sex attribute the breakdown of their marriage to their failure to thrive between the sheets because of prior sexual inexperience, leading Gorer to conclude 'that ignorance, particularly on the part of the men, is a major hazard in English marriages'.[285]

Marital breakdown associated with the separations and stresses of war was noticeable and easy to gauge. The Attlee government was sufficiently alarmed that it invested public money in the establishment of a National Marriage Guidance Council. The figure of 60,000 divorces in 1946–7 turned out to be 'freakish' and despite the extension of legal aid to divorce in 1950, the average annual rate for the years after 1945 was much lower. It was, however, generally much higher than pre-1939, partly because the passage of A. P. Herbert's Private Member's Bill on Matrimonial Causes in 1937 had extended the grounds for divorce to desertion, cruelty, insanity and drunkenness and the postwar figures reflected this.[286] Before the war there were under 10,000 divorces a year in England and Wales. 'After wartime excitements,' as David Coleman noted, 'the total in the 1950s had risen to about 40,000 per year but was declining.' (The 1960s saw the most significant change, though that must wait until the next volume, and by 1971 divorces in England and Wales were running at about twice the rate for the 1950s.)[287]

The deeper, most hidden and more enduring effects of the Second World War are the true Tawney 'imponderables'. Scholars such as Pat Thane have emphasized the importance of this missing dimension of early postwar social and medical history,[288] but it was recognized as early as 1946 by a psychiatrist who had treated disturbed members of the armed forces, Dr T. F. Main of the Cassel Hospital.[289] As he told a conference of the Royal Medico-Psychological Association in Birmingham on 10 October 1946,

In recent months most of us have seen patients who have been in the Services and who now present features of psychiatric illness. Many of them are in the ordinary run of our experience, and we have no difficulties – other than the usual ones – of understanding the origins and patterns of their present distress. By and large, the ordinary clinical breakdowns occurring in the Services were of a kind familiar to us before the war, while during the war we became familiar with most of the disturbances of behaviour and feeling produced by specific stresses of service life . . .

The large and compelling problem of their treatment and effective rehabilitation should not blind us to another newer problem – that of ex-servicemen who made satisfactory adjustments to civilian life before the war, and to service life during the war, but who are now in severe difficulties under the stresses presented to them by their return to civilian life.[290]

Main told his fellow psychologists that most of those so affected had simply not expected to 'become ill-at-ease in familiar surroundings, phobic, depressed or irritable, asocial, confused, retarded, aggressive, antisocial or restless'. All this, he judged, damaged their 'social, domestic or industrial' lives 'in serious and subtle ways'.[291] Too subtle, one suspects, for social history to pick it up properly, let alone quantify it.

Not least because of the succession of narrow escapes, from the crisis summer of 1940, through the Battle of the Atlantic two years later and the massive eventual accumulation of 5 to 1 force against (roughly speaking) that it took to defeat the Axis powers,[292] the Britain of the early 1950s, for all the shortages and everyday rubbing points, did have a collective sense of deliverance. A combination of tradition and modernity had seen the British people through the fighting Forties with their institutions intact and the everyday decencies of public and private life preserved. What Tawney called 'the vulgar irrelevances of class and income'[293] still distorted relationships and life chances, but there was a sense of progress. Behind the dreariness of many of the externals of life, '[c]lothes and shops still drab, still weary, after the second great bloodletting of the century', as Melvyn Bragg put it in his novel *Crossing the Lines*, set in the Fifties,[294] there was a bubbling if not a piping prospect (to borrow Knox's word) about future possibilities in a settled but far from static society. There was no sense that what Margaret Drabble called the 'social hope' of those early postwar years would, fifty years on, be mourned as having suffered a 'progressive death' (*the* great regret of her generation, as Drabble put it at a *New Statesman* lunch in November 2000[295]).

It could even be argued that the blight of class in a status-sensitive nation and the need to avoid excessive polarization between them – to change the country without wrecking it, that vital development of the second half of the nineteenth century – were as much responsible for the political and social accommodations of the British New Deal as the shocks inflicted by the Kaiser and Hitler had been. And lest the returning Conservatives be tempted by excessive triumphalism with a majority as low as seventeen, as Tawney reminded the readers of *Socialist Commentary* in June 1952, a Labour government would 'in due course, be again returned to power', meaning that the Churchill government would 'in part undo' the policies of 1945–51 but they would be most unlikely to 'dissipate' the Attleean 'estate' in full.[296] Tawney, who died in 1962, was not to know that he would not live to see a Labour restoration or that his friend and protégé, Hugh Gaitskell,[297] would speak at his funeral but himself die within a year and never make it to No. 10.[298]

Yet early-Fifties society was strangely preoccupied with the future for all the grain of tradition shaping attitudes and assumptions. A still new possibility, more deadly than any of the anticipated class confrontations of the nineteenth or even the total wars of the first half of the twentieth century, was sensed and feared. It was the scholar/theologian in Durham, Michael Ramsey, who expressed the paradox of the Fifties, the combination of easement and fear, with special force in a lecture on 'Faith and Society'. It was, he said, a marvellous thing that '[t]he Welfare State has appeared to cut the ground from beneath the feet of the Christian sociologist. In the days of gross injustices in wages, and of neglect of provision for the workers' health and security and housing, Churchmen were concerned with a Christianized politics and economics as a corollary of the Incarnation.'[299]

Yet a malaise, a crisis even, was growing at the heart of the Church's social teaching and political thinking because '[a]t the same time the security of the Welfare State is crossed by the radical insecurity of a world that might suddenly be blown to bits ... all these attempts at a Christian politics for an atomic age are dulled ... [by this thought] ... and it hardly matters whether we leave it one at a time or all together now.'[300]

The saintly figure in the Bishop's Palace in Bishop Auckland and the worldly but vastly eminent old man in No. 10 Downing Street shared their nightmares as they and their country lived and slept under the shadow of the bomb.

3

The Shadow of the Bomb

'I think it unlikely that the Soviet Government, if they meant to begin a general war, would embroil themselves in Yugoslavia. This is the only part of the Western front which is strongly defended by fighting men in mountainous regions. There is very little to be got out of it any way. On the other hand all the capitals of Western Europe, outside the Iron Curtain, are at their mercy . . . How silly for the Russians to get tied up in the mountains of Bosnia when they could march into Paris, Brussels, the Hague and Copenhagen.' Winston Churchill to Anthony Eden, November 1951.[1]

'I'd seen our defences in front of me and I wasn't so scared now. If I had known how the Chinese dealt with this kind of barricade I might not have been so relaxed, but ignorance is bliss so I was happy, relatively speaking. As I peered into the gloom another comforting thought occurred to me: the Chinese couldn't see as well as we did. I based this on the fact that every Oriental that I had ever seen in the movies wore very thick-lensed glasses. But standing alone with my thoughts, I began to wonder exactly what I was doing defending capitalism in a country I had never heard of against the red menace for four shillings per day. The people who had the real capital were not here and so far the system that I was defending for them had treated me like shit.'
Michael Caine recalling in 1992 his time as a National Serviceman in Korea during 1952.[2]

'It was a bad time . . . because we lived under that black shadow of the mushroom clouds . . . we were all living in a kind of nervous hysteria.'
Eric Hobsbawm recalling the 1950s in 2002.[3]

'We have no direct knowledge, from our own trials, of the effects of a hydrogen bomb explosion. But, from our experience with normal nuclear explosions, fairly accurate assessments can be made of the blast and, to a somewhat less extent, of heat effects . . . The type of atomic bomb used at Nagasaki was equivalent to about 20,000 tons of

*T.N.T. but it is quite feasible to construct a hydrogen bomb, for delivery by air, which
is equivalent in power to ten million tons of T.N.T.'*

The Strath Report, March 1955.[4]

The Strath Report on the effects of a hydrogen bomb attack on the United
Kingdom was placed in Churchill's hands in the very last days of his peacetime premiership. Although it could not be read by the uninitiated until March
2002 when it was declassified at the request of myself and my students at
Queen Mary, it became for Britain's Cold War state what the Beveridge
Report was to its welfare state – the primer against which developments were
judged and tested for two or three decades. Fear of what the H-bomb –
between 1,000 and 1,500 times more powerful than the atomic bombs that
ended the Second World War[5] – could do to both his beloved Britain in particular and the world in general, came to obsess Churchill and was one of
the reasons he clung on to office for so long in the 1950s, pursuing what
turned out to be an illusory summit meeting with the Americans and the
Russians that might ease the Cold War before it roared into a nuclear
exchange and utter destruction.[6]

This last throw of Churchillian global statesmanship, to be examined fully
in Chapter 7, created by the perhaps fleeting opportunity occasioned by Stalin's death in March 1953 and the injection of material into Whitehall's inner
politico-military circles gleaned from successive American thermonuclear tests
in the Pacific, was eighteen months away when the Grand Old Man re-entered
Downing Street after the election of October 1951. His Cold War anxieties
were, however, acute from the very start of his last premiership. Only in its
second part did they ameliorate: in September 1953 he referred, in a letter to
Lord Woolton appointing him Minister of Materials on the demise of his
experiment with Cabinet 'overlords' (of whom Woolton had been one),[7] to the
'war emergency' which had existed when the said overlords were appointed in
1951 having now 'receded'[8] following the Korean armistice of July 1953.[9]

Churchill was an avid consumer of intelligence material throughout his
ministerial life, from his days as First Lord of the Admiralty before and during the Great War until his last moments in Downing Street in April 1955.
Christopher Andrew, the official historian of the Security Service, MI5, dates
his love affair with the clandestine even earlier: 'Churchill had greater faith
in, and fascination for, secret intelligence than any of his predecessors.
During his early adventures at the outposts of empire he had acquired a
fascination for cloaks and daggers which never left him.'[10]

From the moment he resumed the premiership, Churchill was aware of the huge number of divisions (175 was the aggregate figure which featured in the late 1940s assessments[11]) the Joint Intelligence Committee believed the Soviet Union and its allies could put up against what Churchill called the 'skinny front of the Western Powers'[12] before any real military flesh had been put upon the infant bones of NATO, then a mere two years old. Churchill, like his intelligence analysts, was acutely aware that, as a 1950 JIC report put it, 'it must be clear to the Soviet leaders that the North Atlantic Treaty Powers cannot muster sufficient land forces to oppose the Soviet Army on level terms in any of the possible theatres of conflict'.[13] And shortly before Attlee relinquished office, he was briefed on the possibility that the Soviet Union might now be in a position to assemble an atomic bomb in the UK using components smuggled in via their embassy's diplomatic baggage or concealed in a Soviet freighter.[14]

Churchill himself was briefed by the Cabinet Secretary, Sir Norman Brook, on the bomb-in-a-boat in March 1952, though not about the planners' anxiety over a possible 'suicide' mission from Russia in the form of a crude atomic bomb in a civilian aircraft to be crashed into a key British target.[15] Breaking the convention that premiers do not see the papers of their predecessors, Brook attached his July 1951 brief for Attlee explaining that, in the meantime, 'I have taken no further initiative to raise the matter since I myself believe that this is a risk against which we cannot at present take, in normal times, any effective precautions.'[16]

Shortly before the responsibility of preparing for East–West conflict, overt or covert, passed from Attlee to Churchill, the Cabinet Office and the Chiefs of Staff drew upon the lessons of Churchill's 1940–45 premiership to prepare a drill for the prime ministerial assumption of 'supreme control' in the event of a Third World War on which Attlee or Churchill would sit atop a streamlined War Cabinet. The officials plainly thought it an advantage to have seasoned veterans of the second conflict leading the major political parties as, '[w]hen war experience has passed away . . . it will be necessary to prepare a more elaborate memorandum.'[17] Attlee accepted the idea that, like Churchill in 1940, in the event of war the Prime Minister would become Minister of Defence as well, the difference being that in 1951, unlike 1940, a real as opposed to what we would now call a virtual MOD existed and, therefore, as Attlee put it, 'on the outbreak of war the Prime Minister would have to assume, not merely the additional title "Minister of Defence", but all the functions of a peace-time Minister of Defence'.[18]

This represented one of the latest refinements to the Cold War state apparatus over whose construction Attlee and Brook had presided. But exactly how 'refined' was the machinery put in place lest Stalin's Red Army made a thrust for the Rhine or a ghastly clandestine attack was mounted using his recently acquired weapon of mass destruction? In short, not very. And it took the first severe confrontation of the Cold War, the Berlin crisis in 1948, to stimulate such preparations as had been made by the autumn of 1951.

When writing my *Never Again* in the late 1980s and early 1990s, I had very little declassified material with which to reconstruct the first marque of Britain's Cold War secret state and, therefore, the war planning and intelligence aspects of Mr Attlee's engine room were correspondingly thin in that volume.[19] The archive, though still incomplete, is far richer today, and I can now fill in some of the detail not available for consideration in *Never Again*, paying particular attention to the nuclear aspects of Churchill's last premiership as he was the first British Prime Minister who had to grapple so personally with this truly chilling aspect of the job, being the first to have such a weapon at his personal disposal. Equally, the British people had to assimilate the awesome new possibility of a nuclear attack on their island.

What Churchill inherited by the way of cold/hot war apparatus, planning and machinery of government was, in a way, a considerable tribute to him for it bore in almost every aspect the imprint of the transformation of the state he himself had wrought in 1940–41 – the glorious and perilous year in which Britain stood alone. On one level this is surprising, because the very first paper Attlee prepared in August 1945 as Prime Minister for the initial meeting of the small number of political colleagues on his Atomic Energy Cabinet Committee, GEN 75, is suffused with the belief that the two nuclear weapons dropped on Japan by the Americans earlier that month had changed virtually everything in terms of home, imperial and civil defence.

His memorandum, simply titled 'The Atomic Bomb', is a mere three pages long and combines typical Attleean terseness and directness:

It must be recognised that the emergence of this weapon has rendered much of our post-war planning out of date ... For instance a redistribution of industry planned on account of the experience of bombing attacks during the war is quite futile in the face of the atomic bomb. Nothing can alter the fact that the geographical situation of Britain offers to a Continental Power such targets as London and other great cities. Dispersal of munition works and airfields cannot alter the facts of geography ... Again it would appear that the provision of bomb-proof basements in factories and offices and the retention of A.R.P. [Air Raid Precautions] and Fire Services is just futile waste.[20]

Attlee identified a civil defence dilemma here which was never resolved by any of the politicians who followed him as Britain's premier during the Cold War. He went on to emphasize another problem not resolved until the early 1970s when British forces finally withdrew from east of Suez:

All considerations of strategic bases in the Mediterranean or the East Indies are obsolete. The vulnerability of the heart of the Empire is the one fact that matters. Unless its safety can be secured, it is no use bothering about things on the periphery.[21]

The old soldier in No. 10 (he was known as Major Attlee, his Great War rank, in the 1920s and 1930s) told his colleagues that, though it 'is difficult for people to adjust their minds to an entirely new situation', they had 'to realise that even the modern conception of war to which in my lifetime we have become accustomed is now completely out of date'. Safety now rested on deterrence (though Attlee did not use that word):

We recognise or some of us did before this [i.e. the Second World] war that bombing could only be answered by counter bombing. We were right. Berlin and Magdeburg were the answer to London and Coventry. Both derive from Guernica [which was bombed by the German Air Force on 27 April 1937 during the Spanish Civil War]. The answer to an atomic bomb on London is an atomic bomb on another great city.[22]

Attlee was always a reluctant cold warrior. He infuriated his Chiefs of Staff as late as the last months of 1946 and the first days of 1947 by refusing to accept 'a strategy of despair'[23] whereby 'we are persuaded that the USSR is irrevocably committed to a policy of world domination and that there is no possibility of her alteration . . .'[24] It was the bomb, however, which caused him his greatest anxiety then in his first days as premier.

In August 1945 he saw international control of the weapon as the best hope; in January 1947 he presided over the decision that Britain should make its own bomb. Referring to the joint US/UK/Canadian Manhattan Project which had produced the Hiroshima and Nagasaki weapons, Attlee told his GEN 75 team:

Scientists agree that we cannot stop the march of discovery. We can assume that any attempt to keep this as a secret in the hands of the U.S.A. and the U.K. is useless. Scientists in other countries are certain in time to hit upon the secret . . . The most we may have is a few years' start. The question is what use are we to make of that few years' start.[25]

Attlee did not know at this time the extent of Soviet penetration of the Manhattan Project. The following month Igor Gouzenko, a cypher clerk in the Russian Embassy in Ottawa, would walk out with 'more than a hundred classified documents under his shirt'[26] which began the exposure of major Soviet spy rings in North America, including the atomic ones. The progressive unravelling of these networks once the so-called VENONA Soviet military intelligence traffic between New York and Moscow began to be broken and decoded in the last months of 1946[27] showed those on the inner intelligence loops in Washington and Whitehall what a bonanza of atomic-related scientific and technical intelligence was available to the Russian bomb-builders virtually from the outset of the Manhattan Project.[28] A 'few years' start' turned out to be an accurate prediction. In August 1949 the Russians tested their first atomic device in Kazakhstan.[29]

For his atomic group Attlee raised the possibility of nuclear pre-emption:

We might presumably on the strength of our knowledge and of the advanced stage reached in technical development in the U.S.A. seek to set up an Anglo-American hegemony in the world using our power to enforce a world wide rigid inspection of all laboratories and plants . . . I do not think this is desirable or practicable. We should not be able to penetrate the curtain that conceals the vast area of Russia. To attempt this would be to invite a world war leading to the destruction of civilization in a dozen years or so . . . The only cause which seems to me to be feasible and to offer a reasonable hope of staving off imminent disaster for the world is joint action by the U.S.A., U.K. and Russia based upon stark reality . . . We should declare that this invention has made it essential to end wars. The new World Order must start now. The work of the San Francisco Conference [out of which emerged the United Nations] must be carried much further.[30]

Attlee concluded his paper in what was for him a remarkably millenarian fashion: 'No government has ever been placed in such a position as is ours today. The Governments of the U.K. and the U.S.A. are responsible as never before for the future of the human race . . . The time is short . . . I believe that only a bold course can save civilization.'[31]

Within eighteen months that potential joint-rescuer of the human race, the USA, had cut off virtually all atomic collaboration with its transatlantic wartime ally under the terms of the 1946 McMahon Act, the hopes of international control of the bomb had diminished almost to the point of disappearance and Attlee and yet another inner nuclear group of ministers in GEN 163,[32] his one-off bomb-decision-taking Cabinet committee, were about to make sure that Britain had a weapon with which to annihilate the capital of any power that set its nuclear-bomb sights on London.

The British bomb, though not tested until 3 October 1952 off Australia,[33] was the first serious piece of Cold War state capacity to be put in place. On returning to office Churchill was struck by Attlee's concealing its costs from Parliament (that work upon it was underway had been admitted in May 1948 as part of a terse and guarded reply to a planted parliamentary question with no additional detail, financial or otherwise divulged[34]).

Churchill's chief adviser on atomic energy was Lord Cherwell, the famous 'Prof' Lindemann of the second war who was now Paymaster General. Churchill greatly admired what he called the Prof's 'beautiful brain', though he was mystified by his capacity, as a convinced vegetarian, to live largely on the whites of eggs, and, on returning to power, put him in the Cabinet and installed him next door on the top floor of 11 Downing Street.[35] Cherwell had prepared a lengthy brief for his patron and friend during the first month of the new government's life 'about the position which has grown up within the last five years' on the British atomic bomb.[36]

Cherwell told Churchill that since 1946 when 'the [Attlee] Government decided to make fissionable material for research and for bombs on a scale demanded by the C.O.S. [Chiefs of Staff] . . . nearly £m. 100 has been spent on this'.[37] This briefing, intended to prod Churchill into a swift decision to let the planned test off the Australian coast proceed, also stimulated him to dictate one of his classic, terse, Second World War-style minutes to Sir Edward Bridges, the Permanent Secretary to the Treasury who had been Secretary of the War Cabinet throughout his wartime premiership:

How was it that the 100 millions for atomic research and manufacture was provided without Parliament being informed? How was this very large sum accounted for? Pray let me have a one-page note on the position and on the sequence of events.[38]

Bridges' brief on 'Atomic Energy Expenditure' reached Churchill four days later showing that the latest accumulated figure was £104,642,000 if the revised estimate for the financial year 1951–2 was included.[39]

Adhering to the convention covering the privacy of a previous administration's discussions, Bridges' reply gave no hint about the ministerial groups Attlee had used to reach the bomb decision, but it revealed that some parliamentarians had been told more (it could hardly have been less) than Attlee's

Minister of Defence, A. V. Alexander, had given away in his sparse Parliamentary answer in May 1948:

Details of expenditure on works services, including atomic energy projects, are given to the [House of Commons] Public Accounts Committee in a secret supplement to the annual Appropriation Account . . .

A global figure for atomic energy expenditure, actual or estimated, has been given in secret to N.A.T.O. for the years 1949–1954 . . .

In June 1951 the [Labour] Minister of Defence [Manny Shinwell] told the Chairman of the [House of Commons] Select Committee on Estimates that senior official witnesses might have discretion to give the Estimates Committee orally and in confidence unpublished information about defence matters on the understanding that it would not be quoted. This discretion was not to extend to particularly secret subjects: but it enabled the Estimates Committee to be given in confidence the 1951–52 figure for total atomic energy expenditure as then estimated.[40]

For the vast bulk of MPs and the interested general public, however, a very high level of bomb-related secrecy had been maintained.

'The short answer' to Churchill's question on how the nuclear public money had been spent without Parliament's knowledge, Bridges explained, 'is that expenditure on atomic energy is provided as part of the general expenditure on the Ministry of Supply Vote ['Votes' is the old term for specific public spending items approved by the House of Commons]: and that this Vote does not show how much of the expenditure on research is for atomic energy, how much is for aircraft and how much is for guided missiles, etc.'[41] Bridges appended a fascinating and detailed breakdown for Churchill of the pattern of spending on the bomb since 1946–7 explaining how the atomic element was concealed in the current Ministry of Supply Vote figures for 1951–2 (Annexes A and B – reproduced below).[42]

One subhead involved deliberate deception – 'B4 Loan for Production of Uranium' (the raw material for the warhead) is listed as £1m when the actual amount spent was £2.5m.

Bridges' explanatory minute to Churchill stresses the absence of precise information rather than the presence of an intentionally misleading statistic:

Since 1945 the Government has deliberately restricted the information in [parliamentary] Estimates about defence and in particular about research and development. This policy, which was re-affirmed by Ministers, following reviews by the Joint Intelligence Committee and the Chiefs of Staff in 1947, 1948, 1949 and 1950, applied to atomic

ANNEX A
TOTAL (NET) EXPENDITURE ON
ATOMIC ENERGY

	£
1946/47	4,782,000
1947/48	11,090,000
1948/49	17,026,000
1949/50	16,827,000
1950/51	23,214,000
1951/52	31,703,000 (a)

(a) Revised Estimate. Original Estimate was £26,982,000

ANNEX B
MINISTRY OF SUPPLY
ESTIMATE 1951/2 (a)

(1) Ministry of Supply Subhead			(2) Total of Subhead	(3) Amount included in (2) devoted to Atomic Energy
			£	£
Subhead A		Salaries and Wages (H.Q.)	6,750,000	100,000
	B1	Research & Development: Salaries and Wages at Research Estab.	17,500,000	5,387,000
	B2	Research & Development: Stores, etc.	13,000,000	9,407,000
	B3	Research & Development: Work by Industry, etc.	45,000,000	1,050,000
	B4	Loan for Production of Uranium	1,000,000	2,500,000
	C	Royal Ordnance Factories	30,000,000	150,000
	E1	Armaments	28,000,000	85,000
	E4	Mechanical Transport	55,000,000	30,000
	F1	Clothing & Textiles	38,000,000	40,000
	G2	Radiac Production	4,800,000	10,000
	H1	Salaries & Wages, Inspection	6,800,000	350,000
	K1	Capital Expenditure: Land and Buildings	1,300,000	94,000
	L1–3	Works Services	24,450,000	10,631,000
	M1	Capital Expenditure on plant, etc.	11,000,000	4,560,000
	N1	Fuel, Water, etc.	3,250,000	1,405,000
	N2	Travel & Subsistence	1,350,000	212,000
	N5	Miscellaneous	400,000	1,000
				36,038,000
	Z	Appropriations in Aid		4,336,000
				31,703,000

(a) As revised December 1951.

The figures in column 3 are not, of course, shown in the Estimate.

{Neither do they sum to the figure shown – P.H.]

1. Winston Churchill speaks for Lady Violet Bonham Carter, the Liberal candidate, in Huddersfield Town Hall during the 1951 general election campaign: 'I find comfort in the broad harmony of thought which prevails between the modern Tory democracy and the doctrines of the famous Liberal leaders of the past.'

2. The Chancellor who nearly floated: R. A. Butler and his wife Sydney leave their Smith Square home for the House of Commons on Budget Day, 11 March 1952.

3. Fighting the jungle and the communists in Malaya, 1953: a soldier of the Royal West Kent Regiment burns off a leech with a cigarette.

4. Peace dividend: prisoners-of-war, home from North Korea, disembark at Southampton, 16 September 1953.

5. The newly crowned Sovereign: the Bishop of Durham, Michael Ramsey (*left*) controls his eyebrows and the Queen her mirth, Westminster Abbey, 2 June 1953.

6. Land of smoke and glory: 'The Elizabethan' at speed on its inaugural non-stop run from King's Cross to Edinburgh pulled by Gresley A4 Pacific *Walter K Wigham*, 29 June 1953.

7. On top of the world: the conquerors of Mount Everest, Edmund Hillary and Tenzing Norgay, arrive in London, 3 July 1953. Expedition leader John Hunt waves a patriotic ice-axe.

8. Mau Mau suspects rounded up in the Great Rift Valley, Kenya, 1952.

9. Ebullient summiteer and seething sherpa: Sir Winston Churchill and Sir Anthony Eden on the Southampton quayside after returning from New York on the *Queen Elizabeth*, 5 July 1954.

10. The Wizard of Wembley: Stanley Matthews strikes the pass enabling Bill Perry to score Blackpool's fourth and winning goal against Bolton Wanderers in the last minute of the match on Cup Final Day, 2 May 1953.

11. Tom Finney, awash but elegant: Chelsea v. Preston North End, Stamford Bridge, March 1956.

12. Striding into immortality: Roger Bannister reaches the tape in 3 minutes 59.4 seconds, Iffley Road, Oxford, 6 May 1954.

13. Three greyhounds and a lion: Chris Brasher, Christopher Chataway and Roger Bannister in Downing Street, 1 June 1954.

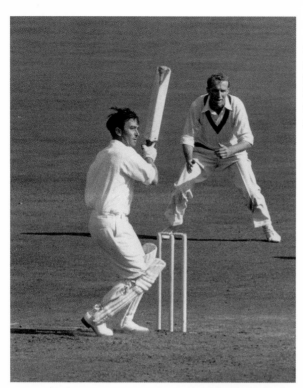

14. Denis Compton steering England towards the Ashes in the fifth and final test at the Oval, August 1953.

15. Grit meets granite: Joe Brown (*right*) took rock-climbing to new heights.

energy equally with other defence research and development: indeed successive [annual] Defence White Papers have given a single total for all defence research development and production with the express purpose of concealing the expenditure on atomic energy.[43]

Churchill, as was his practice, referred Bridges' briefing to Cherwell for comment.

Cherwell, a great man for secrecy, concurred with the existing line as established by Attlee and his ministers but coupled it with an absurd and crudely partisan slur on the patriotism of individuals whom he knew well enough from their days in the wartime coalition: 'Concealment was certainly very necessary at the inception of atomic energy work. And frankly I am agreeably surprised that the Socialist Government was sufficiently imaginative and patriotic to risk the Parliamentary criticism to which this might expose them.'[44] Cherwell said he was 'pleased that it should be possible to wrap up such expenditure in the Estimates so well' but '[n]ow that most of our great atomic buildings are in being or in course of construction, no doubt the Russians have a pretty good idea of the scale of our effort in this field, so that there would seem to be less reason to conceal the broad facts of our expenditure on atomic energy.'[45]

The internal Whitehall argument about how much detail to give Parliament and the public and, by extension, the Russians about UK nuclear expenditure ran on throughout the Churchill administration and was to become bound up in the wider H-bomb discussions of 1954. It was, in fact, the question of how much the bomb would cost which most exercised Churchill on his return to No. 10, even before he demanded to be told how Mr Attlee had hidden the £100m. To the amazement of Cherwell, Churchill proposed in the third week of his peacetime premiership that Britain did not actually need to *make* its own atomic bombs and that President Truman should be asked to give the UK a portion of America's nuclear arsenal when the two of them met in Washington during the coming January.

Cherwell had advised Churchill on the bomb throughout its Second World War genesis and the US–UK collaboration that eventually produced the Hiroshima and Nagasaki weapons, and Churchill's proposal left him speechless, to say the least. He replied to Churchill's two-paragraph minute of 15 November 1951 with a determined, almost passionate ten-pager of his own. For Cherwell was determined that Britain should have its atomic test and its own nuclear weapon as swiftly as possible. And Churchill plainly had not appreciated what had happened since Congress passed the McMahon Act in 1946, cutting off very nearly all atomic collaboration with the British.

What had Churchill written that had driven the Prof to near distraction? 'I have never wished,' Churchill told him in his 15 November minute, 'since our decision during the war that England should start the manufacture of atomic bombs. Research, however, must be energetically pursued. We should have the art rather than the article. A large sum of money will have to be provided for this.'[46]

This was the most extraordinary statement from a man widely regarded as the greatest geopolitician-strategist-statesman of the age, framer and declaimer of the famous Fulton, Missouri 'Iron Curtain' speech but five years or so earlier.[47] By the 1950s he was a figure of 'unique status' across the world, and not merely its English-speaking parts.[48] Even allowing for his passion for the US–UK 'special relationship' (a phrase he coined in the Fulton speech[49]), the notion that the political incarnation of Britain's special role in the world should turn to another power for the ultimate weapon of the age is (or would have been if the intention had leaked or the idea come off) very surprising.

'When we go to Washington in January,' he told an incredulous (one imagines) Cherwell, 'we can, I have no doubt, arrange to be allocated a reasonable share of what they have made so largely on our initiative and substantial scientific contribution.'[50] Great though that initial British input had been,[51] it is most unlikely that the members of the Truman administration would regard themselves as having been merely the wealthy and technically gifted production engineers of a British idea on the road to the making of the atomic bombs dropped on Japan.

No one was more sensitive than Churchill to the anxieties of the Cold War, yet he told Cherwell: 'As to your experiments [i.e. the bomb test] surely the question is not urgent.' He was confident that 'when we produce the Treaty we made in the war and demand that it shall be published we shall get very decent treatment from Truman and his military advisers'.[52]

Here was another extraordinary piece of misunderstanding. The Quebec Agreement Churchill had struck with Roosevelt in 1943 covering prior consultation before the bomb was used and any civil nuclear power programme introduced was just that – an agreement, not a treaty, and a secret one at that. Congress had passed the McMahon Act in ignorance both of Quebec and the Hyde Park aide-memoire concluded between Roosevelt and Churchill in 1944 which extended the Quebec collaboration into peacetime.[53]

It took Cherwell six days to produce his very direct rebuttal of all Churchill's points, exposing them as wishful thinking of a high order:

Prime Minister

Atomic Energy

Your minute of 15.11.51

I am afraid this reply has got very long but I hope you will read it. It is vital you should be informed about the position which has grown up within the last five years.[54]

Cherwell knew better than anyone about Churchill's aversion to long memos. So, in case his boss didn't read it, he reduced its gist to the single page the old man preferred. We know, in fact, that Churchill read the whole memo because of the annotations he made on its pages.

The first of these was a '?' alongside the opening point of Cherwell's summary which told him bluntly: 'The wartime agreements have been superseded. We should gain nothing by referring to them now.'[55] This was followed by

2. The McMahon Act (1946) forbids Americans to disclose any atomic secrets to foreigners. A recent amendment allows certain exchanges of scientific information but nothing about the bomb.

and

3. In 1946 the Government decided to make fissionable material for research and for bombs on a scale demanded by the C.O.S. and nearly £m100 has been spent on this.

Churchill has ringed the '£m100' which, as noted earlier, triggered his interest in the methods of its concealment.

4. A [Churchill scribbled something illegible over the 'A', which has been scratched out. It looks like 'one single'] bomb will soon be ready. The Socialist Government foolishly asked the Americans whether we could test it in Nevada. The Americans refused but offered to test it and tell us the results. All here agree we should test it ourselves in Australia. We shall get important data which could not be obtained in Nevada even if we did the test there ourselves.

5. It is vital to authorise finally the Australian test, for which our preparations are well

under way. We must not miss the Australian season. Nor must we risk being jock-eyed into a test in Nevada when we should reveal our secrets without our getting any in return.

The memo concluded:

6. A decision is wanted now.[56]

In terms of nuclear decision-taking Churchill already stood alone in 1951 – and he still does. For under the terms of that same Quebec Agreement whose status and vitality so vexed him on returning to power, he took with Harry Truman the joint decision that an atomic weapon should be used in anger, the only British premier to do so,* when he gave his consent to the atomic attack on Japan on 1 July 1945 without consulting his caretaker War Cabinet.[57] (The wartime coalition had been dissolved and the general election was four days away.)

Part of Cherwell's task just over six years later was to make plain to Church-ill that the British Prime Minister no longer had the power to veto an American President's action if he wished to use nuclear weapons. And it was with a section on 'Relations with America' that Cherwell began the main text of his November 1951 'Atomic Energy' brief. He began by explaining how Attlee had travelled to Washington in November 1945 and had agreed with Truman and the Canadian Prime Minister, Mackenzie King, that their tripar-tite nuclear collaboration should continue:

Detailed agreements were drafted, but were rejected by the Americans under the influence of Byrnes [James Byrnes, the somewhat anti-British Secretary of State replaced by General George Marshall in 1947]. Soon after, Congress passed the so-called McMahon Act which forbade the handing over of fissionable material or even the disclosure of confidential atomic information to any foreigner – literally on pain of death. This made impossible the full cooperation on which had been agreed.[58]

---

* Although at least one, Jim Callaghan, has done so in hypothetical circumstances. If, when Prime Minister, he had been wiped out by a Soviet-launched nuclear bolt from the blue the Commander and Executive Officer of the Royal Navy Polaris submarine on patrol carried his instructions to retaliate in the vessel's safe. (Peter Hennessy, *Muddling Through: Power, Politics and the Quality of Government in Postwar Britain*, Gollancz, 1996, p. 129. Lord Callaghan divulged this in an interview with me for the 1988 BBC Radio 3 documentary on the British nuclear weapon, *A Bloody Union Jack on Top of It*.)

Cherwell explained that the 'wartime agreements' were later divulged to the US Atomic Energy Commission and the Joint Congressional Committee which monitored it whereupon 'Attlee made a fresh effort, and a two-year agreement (known as the modus vivendi) for a very limited amount of interchange of information and cooperation was concluded with the approval of the Congressional Committee.' The committee 'refused to include the obligation to consult us about using the bomb. On the other hand, we became free to develop industrial applications, work on which, according to the original Quebec agreement, we could only do with the President's consent.' (Churchill marked this last part with an 'x' in the margin.)[59]

At this point Cherwell gave a telescoped account of the negotiations for an agreement that would have given Britain more but which were ruined by the growing anxieties in Washington about Britain's security. Decoded Soviet intelligence traffic was stimulating an investigation which would soon expose Donald Maclean, the British diplomat who had helped draft the 1948 'modus vivendi',[60] and Klaus Fuchs, a senior scientist who had worked in the team sent to Los Alamos in New Mexico as part of the British contribution to the Manhattan Project and was still working on the theoretical side of the UK nuclear weapons programme at Harwell.[61] (He was convicted of espionage and sentenced to fourteen years' imprisonment on 1 March 1950.) 'We are still limping along on the remains of the modus vivendi,' Cherwell explained.[62]

Churchill, in effect, heckled his most intimate atomic adviser when he read the next paragraph. 'Since the wartime agreements have been shown by Truman to the Congressional Committee,' Cherwell judged, 'I should be greatly surprised if he were very seriously disturbed by the threat of publication.' 'I want them published,' Churchill has written beside this. 'So far as I can make out,' Cherwell continued, 'the reason why he did not want them published was that they would be exploited against the Democrats by his political opponents.' 'Doubtful,' interjects the Prime Minister.

Cherwell records that during the summer of 1951 the McMahon Act had been amended slightly to permit exchanges with friendly nations whose security is of high quality 'on the purely scientific and industrial aspects of atomic energy but specifically excluding all data on the design and fabrication of atomic weapons'. But the Prof's analysis of the significance of this brings about another burst of Churchillian barracking:

This is a step forward and I believe it may help us, especially if we can obtain information about the results of the American trials – knowledge of which is clearly vital to
our strategic and military plans as also to our Civil Defence preparations. But in view
of the ferocious penalties of the original McMahon Act it would be quite inconceivable
that the Americans should give us any information about bomb design, still less an
allocation of bombs.

Churchill drew a ring round the word 'inconceivable' and wrote 'no' in the
margin. He underlined 'still less an allocation of bombs' and placed 'xxll'
beside the words.

Cherwell, as if anticipating his boss's irritable dissent, concluded the 'Relations with America' section with the sentence: 'Whether we like it or not this
seems to be the present position.'[63]

The second section of the brief, 'Production in the U.K.', has no trace of
Cherwellian sneering at 'the Socialist Government' or its alleged lack of patriotism. He is an Attlee man through-and-through here and uses arguments
worthy of Ernest Bevin to rebut Churchill's 'art rather than the article' argument. Reprising the 1947 decision to go it alone, Cherwell declared:

I entirely concur with the late Government's decision for the following reasons: –

1.) If we are unable to make the bombs ourselves and have to rely entirely on the
American army for this vital weapon we shall sink to the rank of a second class
nation, only permitted to supply auxiliary troops like the native levies who were
allowed small arms but no artillery.

2.) It would be quite useless to hope to go into production after war started. It would
take years to build the [plutonium] piles and many months after that before they
began to produce the detonating fissionable material. Unless a war lasts a very long
time, 5 years, nations will have to fight it with the atomic bomb production capacity and stock which they possess at the beginning. [Churchill placed a bracket
around '5 years']

3.) It is impossible to develop the art without the fissionable material which can be
made to explode. Without gunpowder or T.N.T. we would not be able to find out
anything about guns and bombs.

4.) To make enough such material for tests on bomb design (and it should be remembered that there are numerous varieties of bombs) or for experiments on industrial
applications within a reasonable period would cost nearly as much as it would to
make it on a scale which might have military significance.[64]

Cherwell's conclusion is interesting for two reasons: the candour of his words to Churchill and their touch on the economic choices involved in the GEN 75 Cabinet Committee discussions which preceded the decision to proceed, in which the economic ministers, the Chancellor of the Exchequer, Hugh Dalton, and the President of the Board of Trade, Sir Stafford Cripps, had tried to halt the programme.[65] Though Cherwell does not directly mention the Cabinet Committee discussions in October 1946 there is a distinct whiff of somebody having briefed him about them:

For all these reasons I agree not only that it was right to proceed on the lines adopted but also that the scale of effort was correct weighing the importance of the matter against our economic difficulties. If you had been in power and had heard the whole story I am sure you would have come to the same conclusions.[66]

Cherwell fleshed out 'the scale of effort' involved – the two piles for producing plutonium at Windscale in Cumberland (which had absorbed one quarter of the atomic £100m); the gaseous diffusion plant for producing uranium-25 which was half completed at Capenhurst in Cheshire; the scientific work at Fort Halstead in Kent devoted to 'the design of the bomb and the method of detonating it' ('Although we only had 2 or 3 men who had been concerned with this in America during the war, a team of scientists under the leadership of a certain Dr. Penney has succeeded in working out what we believe is a good method of detonating the bomb'); sufficient plutonium for the arming of two atomic bombs would be ready 'in a few months'.[67]

Having demolished Churchill's art-rather-than-the-article notion, Cherwell now took on the Prime Minister's assertion, 'As to your experiments surely the question is not urgent,[68] responding that the go-ahead for the test had to be given soon and it had to be in Australia. The United States would not do, partly because 'the Americans . . . will only tell us what they chose about the result' and, '[a]part from the need to make sure that the bomb will detonate satisfactorily the test is designed also to discover facts of a certain nature (which I will communicate by word of mouth), which cannot be investigated in Nevada and which are of particularly vital significance to this country.'[69] (Once the test had succeeded, Churchill himself told the House of Commons about this special aspect to it: 'The object of the test was to investigate the effects of an atomic explosion in a harbour. The weapon was accordingly placed in HMS *Plym*, a frigate of 1,450 tons, which was anchored in the Monte Bello Islands [off the north-west coast of Australia].')[70]

Cherwell pressed Churchill for a decision before they travelled to see Truman after Christmas:

I am anxious for an immediate decision because it might be difficult if the question were still open to refuse to let the Americans make the test should they press you to do so in Washington. If they did they would discover all our secrets without giving us any of theirs – as they cannot do under the McMahon Act; and as I have said in the lamentable event of the bomb failing to detonate we should look very foolish indeed.

For all these reasons I beg you to accept the advice of the Chiefs of Staff, the Foreign Office and all the other Departments concerned and definitely to decide in favour of the test being made in Australia.

Beside this last paragraph Churchill drew what looks to me like an un-finished tick.[71] Cherwell plainly could not decipher it with certainty either, for on 14 December 1951 he sent a further minute to Churchill:

You know the preparations for the atomic bomb test in Australia have been going ahead steadily. I take it you approve. If not orders must be given cancelling the test immedi-ately. Expenses from now on will mount rapidly.

If a decision is postponed we shall lose a whole year as we should miss the season in Australia. I trust therefore that unless I hear to the contrary the test may go forward as planned.

The following day Churchill wrote beneath the minute: 'Proceed as you propose. WSC.'[72] Cherwell and nuclear Whitehall had prevailed. Britain would have the 'article', not just the 'art', and the test would be off Australia in British hands alone.

Churchill announced the planned test in a Commons statement in Febru-ary 1952. Just over two years later, such was the rapidity of nuclear technological developments in both the United States and the Soviet Union, Churchill led his ministers through a series of Cabinet Committee and full Cabinet meetings to the decision that Britain's place in the world required the UK to proceed to the hugely more powerful thermonuclear weapon. It was quite a leap from atomic 'art' to hydrogen 'article', but leap he did with the shadow of nuclear destruction falling ever more darkly across his mind.

The inner anxieties and special responsibilities of those in office with atomic responsibilities were discussed almost wholly in private. The rest of the country, however, had a real enough sense of how different a Third World War would be if it came. And the run-up to Christmas 1951 coincided with continuing worries about the war in Korea. The public certainly had no hint of the Churchill–Cherwell exchanges on the bomb, but with significant numbers of British National Servicemen (soon to number among them the young Michael Caine) confronting huge numbers of Chinese and North Korean troops on that desolate, freezing peninsula, the human aspects of the Cold War were apparent enough.

Attlee was not alone in appreciating the degree to which the bombs on Hiroshima and Nagasaki imprinted themselves on people's memories. The actor Alec Guinness, then still in his naval officer's uniform, is perhaps a good guide to the first and second stages involved in absorbing the significance of 6 and 9 August 1945:

When the atomic bomb was dropped ... I was stationed at Southampton without a ship, sitting in a stuffy little office facing an empty desk ... Merula and I had rented rooms in a house near Fawley ... Neither of us, to our shame, can recall [Guinness was writing in the late 1990s] how we first heard of the bomb but M. remembers us sitting on a grassy bank overlooking Southampton Water watching a distant, joyful firework display. If we had had enough imagination to appreciate the poisonous threat which had been released on the world we might have rejoiced more soberly. When it did dawn on me what it all signified. I am sure my reaction was simply one of personal relief – 'Now, surely, they can't send me to the Far East.' After two and a half years away from England the possibility of another long stint deprived of home, wife and a small son was a nightmare.[73]

Instant relief tempered (especially when Japan surrendered on 14 August 1945) by slow-burning and cumulative anxiety about what the bomb meant and could do is, one suspects, an accurate depiction of the general impact of the atomic destruction of the two Japanese cities.

The wider, personal implications of the bomb perhaps burnt their way into the collective British psyche more slowly than might have been expected. Certain individuals, however, such as Middleton Murray, the editor of *Peace News*, were understandably sensitive to such matters. The day after Nagasaki, his paper declared that, 'The power of the atom bomb allied to the robot weapon is a possibility that comes immediately to the layman's mind.'[74] Christopher Driver, historian of British peace movements during the 'short postwar', detected a delay in a general appreciation of what Alec Guinness called the 'poisonous threat' of the bomb, 'for Hiroshima and Nagasaki ... were a long way away, and the revolutionary implications of nuclear power were, despite the initial shock, hardly understood at all. In December 1945 [the month Attlee's secret Atomic Energy Cabinet Committee, GEN 75, authorized the construction of the first plutonium pile at Windscale], when the British public was asked by the Gallup Poll what changes it expected to be bought about by the splitting of the atom, only 4 p.c. of the respondents mentioned changes in military techniques and international relations.'[75]

Writing the day after the Japanese capitulation and less than a week after the dropping of the second atomic bomb on Nagasaki, George Orwell told his American readers that:

The prompt surrender of Japan seems to have altered people's outlook on the atomic bomb. At the beginning everyone I spoke to about it, or overheard in the street, was simply horrified. Now they begin to feel that there's something to be said for a weapon that could end the war in two days. Much speculation as to 'whether the Russians have got it too'.[76]

Driver maintains that, 'thanks to the effects of American censorship in occupied Japan', not until the autumn of 1946, when Penguin published John Hersey's *Hiroshima*, 'the first full description' of the fate of that city, did the wider public come to appreciate 'the precise effects of atomic weapons on their victims . . .'[77]

There were some, however, well outside official circles, who did have a clear idea of what the atomic attacks on Japan meant before the Hersey study reached the bookstands. Amazed and privately appalled that the Catholic hierarchy in Britain had issued no spiritual guidance on what to make of the destruction of Hiroshima and Nagasaki, Ronald Knox dashed off inside a month a remarkable short book, *God and the Atom*, which *The Tablet* magazine serialized and Sheed and Ward published by the end of the year. Knox was horrified by the 'signature-tune' of atomic explosions after the 'orgy of destruction that has been going on in the past five years'. He feared either that the trauma of the atomic explosions would lead to excessive doom or that some of mankind might see it as the 'symbol' of their 'release from every internal principle of self-control'.

For Knox the sudden news in the paper opened at his quiet breakfast table in Shropshire telling him that a 'Japanese town, rather more populous than Southampton, had suddenly ceased to exist' produced a protracted intellectual effort of comprehension and, within six weeks or so, the conclusion that if Heaven was to 'preserve us all from a baptism of uranium', the world's leaders both temporal and spiritual would need an 'acceleration in the tempo' of their reactions 'to meet and match what must surely be an acceleration of tempo in the material developments of history'. To Knox's immense disappointment, *God and the Atom* 'fell quite flat', as his biographer Evelyn Waugh put it, both with aforesaid leaders and with those they purported to lead.[78]

Another perceptive observer, much younger than Knox and sprung from the dissenting tradition of religion and politics, was to sit twenty years later on Harold Wilson's inner group on the bomb, his PN or Nuclear Policy Cabinet Committee,[79] and later still became a fully convinced nuclear disarmer. He was a young officer in the Royal Air Force when the war ended and by the spring of 1946 he was an undergraduate in Oxford. His name at the time was Anthony Wedgwood Benn.

In March 1946 (his diary does not specify which day) Benn went to the Oxford University Air Squadron to hear Group Captain Leonard Cheshire VC talking about the atomic bomb. Cheshire was a member of the two-man British observer team who overflew Nagasaki shortly after the plutonium bomb had shattered it. The other watcher was Dr William Penney, who by the time Cheshire stood up to address the Oxford undergraduates was already the crucial scientific figure in the embryonic British bomb programme.[80] Nearly ten years later Penney gave Cheshire's biographer, Andrew Boyle, a graphic account of their flight in a US Air Force B-29 bomber from Tinian Atoll to Japan and back:

We were about forty miles away from Nagasaki when we saw a flash, followed by the billowing mushroom cloud. There was little we could do except circle in the air, well away from the cloud, and try to see what was happening on the ground. Cheshire's experience [as a bomber pilot] enabled him to see things that were not apparent to the rest of us. The whole of the city was hidden in dust and smoke, but very few fires were visible. Cheshire drew a sketch of what he thought was happening, and the description he gave later, with the aid of the sketch was remarkably accurate. The smoke pall seemed to be ever-increasing, and after watching for nearly an hour we left for Tinian . . . All of us were in a state of emotional shock. We realised that a new age had begun and that possibly we had all made some contribution to raising a monster that would consume us all. None of us could sleep. We argued well into the night, and in our talks were raised the same tremendous issues that have been debated ever since.[81]

Cheshire that Oxford evening in March 1946 gave Benn and his fellow students an even more vivid account, which Benn recorded using the slang he had picked up in the RAF.

The CO came in and asked us not to drop our cigarette ends on the floor, then he introduced Cheshire.

Cheshire is a young man of perhaps 26. [He was, in fact, 28]. He came up as an undergraduate in 1937 and joined the Air Force. He was described as the greatest air bomber pilot ever and he is probably the most highly decorated officer of the war . . .

Cheshire did not go on the Hiroshima raid. He described the Nagasaki one. The aircraft (two for observations, one for the bomb) rendezvoused over South Japan at 9 o'clock and went in to the target at 10. They were flying at 34,000 feet. The kite was pressurised, heat and soundproofed so they were wearing khaki slacks and shirts, with no oxygen or intercom.

They put dark glasses on, so dark that the sun was just a blur in the centre and when the bomb went off it lit up the whole scene as if a light had been turned on in a darkened room. The heat generated is 10 million degrees C, very nearly as hot as the internal heat of the sun. After three minutes they were able to take off their glasses . . . They dropped radio sets with instruments attached to record pressure waves etc.[82]

Cheshire made sure that the future shadow of the bomb reached into the Oxford University Air Squadron that night: 'Cheshire said quite plainly he did not want to discuss the ethics of the thing but he sobered everyone up by putting to us quite plainly the facts. If we have another war it will mean the end of our physical civilisation, for man might survive but buildings can't. He spoke quietly and slowly. "Realise this, that if these bombs are ever going to be used there is not much point in anything that you are doing now."'[83]

It is one of the mysteries of postwar British social history that a seriously organized anti-nuclear peace movement did not form until the late 1950s, for, as Richard Hoggart has noted, from 'the late Forties to the middle Fifties the landmarks were clear and the succession at the time apparently unending: the Berlin Blockade in 1948–9, the formation of NATO in 1949, the rising in East Berlin in 1953 and that in Hungary in 1956'.[84] Driver has traced what activity there was in the late 1940s. For example in April 1948, a month before A. V. Alexander delivered his carefully framed words in the House of Commons indicating that research was underway into the making of a British bomb, an anti-nuclear meeting was held at Caxton Hall in Westminster at which Vera Brittain, Alex Wood and Ritchie Calder spoke.[85] The Minister of Defence's announcement seems to have stimulated very little concern, partly, no doubt, because of the absence of any fuss in Parliament and the very matter-of-fact way it was reported in the press.[86]

It took the war scare of the summer of 1948 associated with the Berlin crisis and the formulation of a new civil defence programme in the autumn that followed to raise levels of concern.[87] Four months after Stalin reopened the land routes across the Soviet zone to Berlin and the Western air lift ended,

President Truman announced in Washington on 23 September 1949 that the Soviet Union had successfully tested an atomic bomb the previous month, some eighteen months sooner than British intelligence had expected[88] (not that Parliament or the public were privy to this or any other Joint Intelligence Committee estimate). The shadow of the weapon was no longer hypothetical. The public debate about civil defence and the degree to which the crowded British Isles could be protected acquired still more urgency, as did private Whitehall anxieties about a possible clandestine Soviet nuclear attack on the UK.

During a House of Lords debate on civil defence in November 1949, Lord Trenchard, the founding father of the Royal Air Force, declared that an atomic attack could kill between 10 and 20 million people (or nearly half the UK population) in a month.[89] During the summer and autumn Churchill asked for and got a series of discussions on defence matters among four of his privy counsellors and Attlee's ministers at a series of meetings in a specially convened Cabinet Committee, GEN 293.[90] Attlee later described the Berlin crisis of June 1948 and the subsequent air lift to sustain the western sectors of the city as 'the decisive thing'[91] in terms of the swinging of Western, particularly American and Congressional, opinion into a realistic appreciation of what the Cold War involved: 'It was quite a danger. But it [the air lift] was a risk that had to be taken. I don't, as a matter of fact, believe that Russia was in a position to attack at that time [neither did British intelligence[92]], although one couldn't be sure ... it could have been very nasty.'[93] Despite the reassurance provided by the Joint Intelligence Committee that the closing of the land routes was not stage one of a planned Soviet transition to global war, Mr Attlee's inner group of ministers on the Berlin crisis, sensibly enough, contemplated that conflict might come through miscalculation.

Less than a month after the western sectors of Berlin had their road, rail and canal links with their occupation zones severed, Attlee's special Cabinet group on the crisis, GEN 241, the Germany Committee (also known as the 'Berlin Committee'), discussed what the minutes, in their understated way, called 'Plans to Meet a Possible Emergency', which, decoded, meant a direct clash between Russian and Anglo-American forces, i.e. a Third World War. The Foreign Secretary, Ernest Bevin, was the driving force behind this as indeed he was simultaneously the main motivator in getting the air bridge to Berlin off the ground.[94] Bevin told the Berlin group that 'he had been turning over in his mind the question of preparations for a possible emergency and thought that it was very important that a full assessment of the position should be laid before ministers as soon as possible. Moreover, whatever the outcome of the current situation, it was important that a permanent plan for action in an emergency should be prepared and kept constantly up to date, since there might be other situations in which it would be useful.'[95]

At first glance, the shock of the Berlin blockade stimulated impressive results. By November 1948, the first Government War Book of the Cold War was finished, meeting Bevin's requirements for transition-to-war planning on paper at least.[96] A Civil Defence Bill was drafted and put through Parliament very swiftly.[97] The Cabinet Secretary, Brook, presided over an invigorated Defence Transition Committee which oversaw the preparation of the War Book and the drills for its implementation.[98] As we have seen, within days of the blockade Attlee and Brook began to sketch out plans for a War Cabinet and supporting structure for a Third World War.[99] The progressive uncovering of the Soviet spy networks in Britain and North America led to successive internal security reviews which left a positive vetting system for those in the most sensitive posts ready for the incoming Conservatives to implement.[100]

What did this new Cold War capacity amount to by the time Churchill inherited it? The real Whitehall insiders, including Attlee and his inner group of secret state ministers, certainly understood that the answer was not very much. Take civil defence. One week into the Korean War (the next great 'other situation' for which prior planning 'would be useful', as Bevin had put it to the Berlin Committee two years earlier), the Home Secretary, Chuter Ede, sent Attlee a very revealing minute about just how *un*protected the home base still was. This was a moment, it should be remembered, when there was real anxiety in Whitehall that, as the Chief of the Air Staff, Sir John Slessor, put it, 'there was a view held by certain responsible Americans that the present aggression in Korea was a feint by the Russians to attract attention from a move that would take place in Europe, possibly Yugoslavia [where Tito had broken with Stalin's Cominform two years before]'.[101]

Ede attached to his minute to the Prime Minister a briefing on 'Civil Defence' prepared by the Home Office on day nine of the Korean crisis:

You will see that, although progress had been made in rebuilding the organisation, our resources in men and equipment are not such that we could deal effectively with an attack if it were on a scale at all comparable with [the Blitz of] 1940–41. In the event of a crisis, we should not be able to do much more than we planned to do in 1948, that is, to appoint Regional Commissioners and rely on them, with the co-operation of

the Police, the Fire Service and the nucleus [of] local authority Civil Defence organisations to make the best of existing resources.[102]

Attlee, characteristically, scribbled 'noted' on Ede's memo, having (again characteristically) read it on the day it reached him.

The fuller Home Office brief added grim detail to its Secretary of State's
summary. Money (lack of) and sensitivity (probably too much) were at the
root of the problem:

Since the passing of the Civil Defence Act, 1948, good progress has been made with
paper planning both at the Whitehall level and, since the beginning of this year, at the
Local Authority level. There are, however, a good many gaps in planning (e.g. we have
not made a start with industry) and effective measures to implement planning have been
precluded by the general policy of doing nothing which would interfere with economic
recovery or alarm public opinion.

In brief, the civil defence organisation is in no position to cope effectively with attack
of the 1940–41 scale, let alone anything worse, and the deficiencies are such that they
could not be remedied at short notice.[103]

Attlee, remember, had been one of the first to appreciate in August 1945
that the atomic bomb rendered the Second World War level of civil defence
provision a 'futile waste'.[104] He was reading this brief nearly five years after
writing that and almost one year on from the testing of Stalin's atomic bomb
in the steppes.

The brief went on to list 'the major deficiencies' in provision: warning systems ('there would be many important areas where the RAF system, on which
the civil system depends, would be incomplete owing to absence of radar
cover'); shelter ('it is estimated that of the public shelter of the last war only
some 20 per cent remains and no steps have been taken, or could be taken at
short notice, to organise and equip most of what remains'); respirators ('There
are sufficient to supply about 30 million people [i.e. roughly 20m too few]');
Civil Defence Corps and Fire Service ('Personnel are quite inadequate for war
purposes ... The Fire Service is probably better off than any Service, but, at
best, it could not at short notice be expanded to more than about one third
of its 1941 strength and there are no emergency water supplies'); hospitals
('... time would be required to redistribute patients in order to make beds
available in the right areas'); evacuation ('The Ministry of Health think that
evacuation schemes could be operated at short notice, but there would be some
disorganization in the reception areas'); homelessness ('Nothing has been done

beyond paper planning and there would be serious deficiencies of equipment for rest centres, etc.'); and regional organization ('There are gaps in staff and premises, but something could be improvised at short notice').[105]

What about active defence as opposed to passive? Percy Cradock, a former diplomat and chairman of the Joint Intelligence Committee, caught the very real sense of vulnerability in Britain and western Europe during the first days of the Korean War when it looked as if

events in the Far East were merely a Soviet feint, a prelude to a further Soviet attack nearer home at a time when America was bogged down in the Far East, fighting 'the wrong war' against the Koreans and perhaps the Chinese. The diplomatic and economic foundations for Western European security, the NATO alliance and the Marshall Plan were, happily, already in place; but little had been done to provide the necessary forces. The Alliance had 12 poorly equipped divisions with little air support; the Russians enjoyed an immense military preponderance, with 27 divisions in East Germany alone, where in addition they had recently built up a 60,000-strong East German Volkspolitzei. The Berlin blockade had just ended, but it seemed an ideal time for the Russians to revive it now that Allied air strength was called to a new theatre. The successful test of the first Soviet atom bomb well ahead of Western predictions, added to the fears.[106]

On 6 July 1950, Attlee and the members of the Cabinet Defence Committee (which he used as his 'war cabinet' for Korea[107]) were told that the British Chiefs of Staff believed, given current defence policies, plans and readiness that an *eighteen-month* period of warning (or even longer) would be needed for the UK to be prepared for war, the minutes adding candidly, if superfluously, that 'it was clear from events in Korea that it was more than possible that there would be little, if any, warning. In these circumstances the peace-time forces maintained by the United Kingdom were hardly more than bluff.'[108]

What about the 'enemy within'? Under the supervision of Attlee's Cabinet Committee on Subversive Activities, GEN 183, a working group sat throughout that first Korea summer with a brief to tighten up Whitehall's very flimsy defences against penetration by Stalin's Brits. In November 1950 they came up with a scheme for positive vetting, a system of private inquiry into the background of those officials in the most sensitive Cold War related jobs, especially those involved in the making of the British atomic bomb.[109] Attlee and his ministers on GEN 183 met to agree the new arrangements in November 1950, though it fell to Churchill to announce them early in 1952.[110]

With a commendable sense of both restraint and the requirements of an open society, there was to be no widespread purge involving naming (and, thereby, shaming) suspected officials. And, quite rightly, the British secret state realized that clandestine Soviet agents, as opposed to open communists in the British Crown Service, were the problem, and that the 'detection of such persons can only be secured by the scientifically planned study of Communist activities which it is the task of the Security Authorities to carry out'[111] (a euphemism, no doubt, for the VENONA signals intelligence breakthroughs which exposed Fuchs, Maclean et al.[112]). Without still-classified files that are likely to remain so, it is very difficult to assess the overall effectiveness of the UK's post-1952 vetting arrangements. It is probable, however, that they were devised at the same time as the deepest-ever Soviet penetrations were being uncovered in both the USA and the UK and that subsequent Soviet efforts came nowhere near to recruiting agents comparable to the 'Cambridge Five'.[113]

That said, there were elements of naivety in the counter-intelligence apparatus Attlee bequeathed Churchill, not least the view that there was little need to worry about 'most regular civil servants: the difficulties would be greatest in Departments of recent growth employing staff who had not absorbed the traditions of the public service'.[114] Similarly, it was delusory to think that PVing (as it became known*) could be confined to a thousand or so posts and that it did not need to be extended to the Armed Forces.[115]

In press terms, early Cold War Whitehall was a remarkably leak-proof place, though the *Daily Express*'s star reporter, Harry Chapman Pincher, was a great gatherer of scoops and wrote candidly in retirement about the leaks he uncovered and their genesis.[116] Yet the secret state's private preoccupations were the stuff of public anxiety and the cinema, still the dominant visual medium in late-Forties and early-Fifties Britain, reflected this sometimes in a manner that had an insiderish feel. Take, for example, a pair of films by the Boulting brothers which spanned the transition from Attlee to Churchill. *Seven Days to Noon* (1950)[117] combines the shadow of the nuclear (the bomb smuggled into London) with evacuation and touches of the Fuchs-induced anxiety about who can be trusted. The cool head who saves the capital in the nick of time is Superintendent Folland of the Metropolitan Police Special Branch (played by André Morell), who does the same in *High Treason* (1951) when he thwarts a communist attempt to bring down the British government by a conspiracy to sabotage the power stations.

---

* It is now called 'developed vetting'.

High Treason has its moments but it overdoes its theme in an implausible plot embracing the senior leadership of the CPGB and its mixture of intellectual and working-class members, a KGB officer, a treacherous civil servant in the Ministry of Supply and a smooth lawyer and leftist MP, Grant Mansfield, who is to lead an alternative government dedicated to a 'people's peace' once the collapse of the national grid has brought the British economy and its democratically elected government to their knees. Written and directed by Roy Boulting when the real-life government was led by Attlee, its release was delayed until the days after the 1951 election which returned Churchill to No. 10. The excitement aroused in the press by the delay and the film's alleged sensitivity did not convert into box office and *High Treason*, unlike *Seven Days to Noon*, was successful in terms of neither esteem nor takings.[118] As Stephen Guy has noted, '*Seven Days to Noon* ... was a model film: it was both a popular and critical hit' which plainly caught the mood of 1950. 'It is less well-known than other films from that rich clutch of late-1940s productions – *Brief Encounter* (1945), *The Red Shoes* (1948), *The Third Man* (1949) and so on – partly because its subject and narrative structure became clichéd in the cycle of 1950s sci-fi disaster films that followed.'[119]

Seven Days to Noon is about a British atomic scientist who, like Fuchs, worked on the Manhattan Project in America before returning to a research job with the British bomb team. But in the script by Paul Dehn and James Bernard, the fictional Professor Willingdon, unlike the real Dr Fuchs, is not a Soviet agent. The Professor, played by Barry Jones, is a devout Anglican who disappears from the Experimental Supply Station near Wallingford (a composite of the real Harwell and Aldermaston) with the inner core of the prototype British bomb in a Gladstone bag. He sends a letter to the Prime Minister threatening to detonate it at noon a week later unless the British government stops making the bomb and renounces the use of atomic weapons.

There are some apt contemporary touches in the film. Before the PM eventually takes the public into his confidence and the search for Willingdon is on, rumours of evacuation and the reasons for it begin to circulate. In Willingdon's hearing in a pub, the standard barrack-room-lawyer type (Geoffrey Keen) opines:

There won't be no declaration of war this time. Someone presses a button and it's goodbye Sally ... Just for a change, we can press a button first. Load 50 ruddy great bombers with a couple of hundred atom bombs. We've got 'em you know. There's no doubt about that. We've been turning them out like pineapples for the last five years. Load the ruddy planes and blast their big cities to hell.

Not too much historical accuracy in that outburst.

There is rather more when Willingdon's assistant tells his daughter (to whom he is engaged) that the anxiety surrounding her father's initial disappearance isn't that unusual: 'It's just that we're so damned scared – we can't trust anybody.' Before the Special Branch and the prospective son-in-law (Hugh Cross) and the daughter (Shelia Manahan) eventually find Willingdon and his device in a church near Westminster with minutes to spare, there has been time for some popular education of what a nuclear weapon on the seat of government would do as the army, the police and the Civil Defence wardens evacuate the usual array of cockney characters of all ages and start their house-to-house search. There is much chat about, it being just like the war as old rolling stock unused since the trains evacuated London's children to the country in 1939 is brought back into service.

Seven Days to Noon remains powerful and with its combination of nostalgia for the home-front solidarity of the recent past and future nuclear/Cold War anxieties, it is easy to appreciate its impact. The Prime Minister, more Attlee-like than Churchill, summons up the recent past as the teacher of lessons in his wireless broadcast about the threat and the planned evacuation:

Were we to bow to [Willingdon's] threat, we might well be exposing this country – indeed the whole free world – to a danger far greater than any that confronts us now . . . Our recent history has taught us that to make ourselves weak provides an irresistible temptation to the tyrant.

In other words, Munich-style appeasement is both out of the question and unnecessary, provided Britain, as part of the free world, has an atomic bomb with which to deter. This is more Attlee of 1950–51 than Churchill in the same period – no nonsense here about the 'art' rather than the 'article'.

The film went on release in September 1950 at the height of the Korean anxiety and has an uncanny if unknowing relationship to the Soviet-bomb-in-a-west-London-garage scenario which Norman Brook was to place before Attlee just under a year later. Stephen Guy quotes a review of the film on 15 September 1950 in the *Daily Express*, in whose critic's opinion *Seven Days to Noon* evoked 'all the nasty fears and terrors of the ordinary citizen . . . it is the sort of threat which all of us – over bar counters, in the kitchen, across the work desk and in the intimacy of our bedrooms – have been talking about for months. Here is the threat of the atom bomb brought home in all its close horror.'[120]

How much more anxious might that early-1950s public have been had they known of Ede's briefing for Attlee on Britain's civil defence capability a mere two months before *Seven Days to Noon* first packed them into the cinemas? Attlee, like the fictional Prime Minister in the film, believed that there were limits to the amount Britain could spend on civil defence if its armed forces and their equipment were to be in the condition required. From the chair of his post-Berlin Cabinet Committee on Civil Defence, GEN 253, in October 1948 Attlee had declared that it was

essential to avoid a situation in which the Government would be driven to devote resources to civil defence on a scale which would cripple the national economy, detract from our power of defence and alienate our allies in Europe ... the Government were not prepared to devote resources to passive defence at the expense of weakening our striking force or impeding our economic recovery.[121]

The same dilemma confronted his successor.

Oddly for one so sensitized to Cold War matters, Churchill did not seriously grapple with the subject of civil defence until mid-1952, when Ede's successor at the Home Office sent him 'a note on the anticipated effect of Atom bombing ...'[122] True to form, the Prime Minister asked Cherwell to comment on it[123] and, perhaps surprisingly, given the number of ministers and departments involved in civil defence planning, he instructed his Private Office that: 'This file may be read or re-read by the Home Secretary and the Minister of Defence.'[124]

At first glance, the opening section of the Home Office brief for the Prime Minister reads like an idiot's guide to the atomic bomb – and all the more insulting given Churchill's close attention to the atomic bomb programme from 1941 to 1945 and his being the only Brit then or since to have authorized its use. 'Atom bombs,' the Home Office told him with a sublime lack of necessity, 'are differentiated from "conventional" weapons in two main ways – (a) the radiological effects and (b) the scale of damage and casualties which they are capable of causing.'[125]

It is the second section, which the Home Office's chief scientific adviser had plainly drafted,[126] that is interesting given the contents of the Strath Report into fall-out from the hydrogen bomb in which Churchill was to take such a justifiably intense interest in the last days of his premiership less than three years later:

As regards the radiological effects, the *immediate* effects are only one of the factors (the others being blast and heat-flash) which cause casualties. The possibility of *continuing* effects has been greatly exaggerated; on the basis of available experience and scientific theory there is no reason to think that so-called radioactive contamination would persist to any appreciable extent from a bomb burst at or about the height used for the two bombs dropped over Japan; it is true that some persistent radioactivity would result from a low burst but (i) this is operationally less probable and (ii) in any event the radioactive area could be detected and it would probably be possible for it to be entered after a few hours for short periods without risk.[127]

Churchill neither queried nor heckled this section.

But his fabled imagination and curiosity about detail were aroused concerning the direct effect of a bomb on the ground. The civil defenders explained that, once the weapon had fallen, 'within a radius of half to three quarters of a mile from ground zero, the devastation would be very great and even if there were survivors in shelters in this area rescue and fire-fighting operations might be impracticable. But beyond that radius the effects rapidly diminish and a point is soon reached at which the conditions are comparable with those which we experienced in World War II though the area affected would be larger.'[128]

The degree to which the last war remained the yardstick and comparator as late as 1952 (within another three years minds, measurements and imaginations had shifted to a remarkable degree, as we shall see) is very pronounced in the Home Office paper. For example, 'it would take three atom bombs to produce something like the damage caused by the Allied raids on Hamburg in July/August 1943 [one of the most devastating firestorms of the war]. It must be recognized, however, that the concentration in a short space of time of the effects of an atom bomb as compared with the spread of the "Hamburg" attacks over several days would greatly increase the difficulties of any civil defence organisation.'[129]

The Home Office at this point make their pitch for a shelter policy as they were to do again, with even greater urgency and advocacy when the shadow of the H-bomb had usurped that of the A-bomb. And the rudiments of the argument were all there at this stage – shelter was both practicable *and* part of the spectrum of deterrence as the 'result of any other policy might well be that public morale would break at an early stage in war and by breaking destroy the will to win of the Armed Forces'.[130]

Churchill was intrigued by the radius of damage around 'ground zero' and he quibbled with a part of the Home Office's use of the Second World War blitz experience. Protection, mitigation and relief, the planners told him, could be organized in a fashion 'comparable with . . . World War II'. It was the footnote to this upon which the Prime Minister seized – 'It was not the normal object of shelter policy,' the Home Office said of coping with the Luftwaffe, 'to give protection against direct hits or near misses; even the inadequate Japanese shelters stood up well at half a mile from the atomic bomb and in some cases at shorter distances.'[131]

Churchill told Cherwell there was 'nothing in the footnote . . . which I have marked in red. A single "direct hit" by an ordinary bomb might inflict destruction within a circle of 150 yards diameter. When the direct hit covers a mile and a half the "directness of the hit" or the "nearness of the miss" lose much of their meaning.' Churchill wondered, too, what the chances were of hitting targets accurately 'with modern gadgets from so high up'.[132]

Cherwell told him that the 'probable error in bombing from great heights would be about 1,000 yards'. He took his boss through the damage a 20-kiloton (the equivalent of 20,000 tons of TNT) atom bomb would create (this was the size of the Nagasaki bomb[133] on which the British bomb was based; the power of the first British weapon tested was 25 kilotons[134]):

> The Civil Defence people believe, probably rightly, that a 20,000 ton equivalent atom bomb would cause complete destruction of buildings over a circle of $1^1/_2$ miles in diameter. This circle would cover an area of $1^3/_4$ square miles or 175 times that of the circle of 200 yards diameter in which a 10 ton block-buster [conventional weapon] would cause similar destruction.
>
> The general view seems to be that the air burst atom bomb will be more effective than one bursting on the ground, against most types of target. It is said that the air burst bomb would cause most of the demolition by blast, whereas if it burst on the surface an atom bomb would waste much of its energy in evaporating the ground on which buildings had already been completely destroyed. On the other hand, there is very little radioactive contamination from an air burst atom bomb whereas one exploded on the surface would make the ground unhealthy for quite a number of days.[135]

Cherwell acknowledged the lack of 'precise information' the UK had on this subject and alluded to the Churchill government's attempts to mitigate the consequences of the McMahon Act, adding that 'I hope we shall be able to get much more from the Americans next year if all goes well. Without this information, we can only make the best estimate possible and opinions differ considerably. I, personally, am by no means sure that a concrete shelter with a roof 3 or 4 feet thick at ground level would not stand up to an air burst of a 20,000 ton equivalent atom bomb 1,000 ft above.'[136]

On 1 November 1952, exactly four months after Cherwell finished his minute for Churchill and just under a month after the first British atomic test, the Americans let off a device in a huge steel case bigger than a house in the Eniwetok Atoll in the Pacific which showed that a fusion, or hydrogen, bomb was viable, making all the Whitehall calculations of damage radius and thickness of concrete beneath the blast a matter of what Attlee might have called 'futile waste'. The American test produced a yield of 10.4 megatons – equivalent to twice the amount of *all* the explosives used in the Second World War – vaporizing the coral island of Elugelab on which the vast steel box had been placed and leaving a crater 200 feet deep and trees and brush scorched fourteen miles away.[137]

Not until the spring of 1954 did Whitehall begin to absorb fully what this meant for policy. And only when an individual copy of the Strath Report on fall-out from the H-bomb reached every Cabinet minister in the spring of 1955[138] were the wartime comparisons and extrapolations finally dispelled.

None the less, during the spring of 1953, as the country readied itself for the Coronation, the planners produced an atomic (as distinct from a hydrogen) damage ledger that was alarming enough. They assumed that 5.2 million women, children and elderly would have been evacuated by the authorities from the cities and large towns in time, with a further 4 million evacuating themselves. Even so, they estimated that 132 Russian atomic bombs 'of the Nagasaki type' dropped on the UK would leave 1,378,000 people dead and 785,000 seriously injured. Some 2,163,000 homes would be destroyed or irreparably damaged and a further 10,163,000 made temporarily uninhabitable based on Second World War experience.[139]

These figures may be put into context by comparison with the statistics for the whole Second World War period, during which 440,000 Britons died (including those killed in battle) and 750,000 UK homes were destroyed or severely damaged.[140] A new vocabulary and an enlarged arithmetic of death and destruction was now needed, and was, indeed, in place two years later.

In January 1955 Whitehall's top economist, Robert Hall, was asked to join the Strath inquiry. Intriguingly, he thought it was 'a very Top Secret affair [as indeed it was; the Strath Report was not declassified until 2002[141]] ... not I think because the material we are using is secret ... and it seems to be almost common talk in the USA – but because the facts are not absorbed here and are so unpleasant that it is very tricky to know how best to act to get them absorbed'.[142] Churchill made the same point during a House of Commons debate on the H-bomb on 5 April 1954, when he told MPs how surprised he was that a speech in the United States by Sterling Cole, Chairman of the Joint Congressional Atomic Energy Committee on what the H-Bomb did to cities, had attracted so little attention in the British press.[143] The news of Japanese fishermen contaminated by fall-out from the latest American tests in the Pacific when their boat, the *Lucky Dragon*, was eighty-five miles away from the test site on Bikini Atoll and *outside* its exclusion zone, had triggered alarm not just in the Far East but in the United States, too, in the spring of 1954.[144]

Not until the early 1960s, though, when the Campaign for Nuclear Disarmament rose to prominence[145] and Ian Fleming's James Bond made the successful transition from novel to screen, did the unpleasant facts of which Hall had written enter fully into the national consciousness. Once the British Cold War archives began to emerge over the counter of the Public Record Office in Kew, I was struck by just how close Fleming, a former member of the Admiralty's Naval Intelligence Department, had been to insider analyses and anxieties of various kinds. Indeed, he modelled 'M', his fictional version of SIS's 'C', on his wartime chief, Vice-Admiral J. H. Godfrey, Director of Naval Intelligence 1939–42.[146]

The pathfinder volume of the phenomenally globally successful Bond series[147] was *Casino Royale*,[148] which Fleming wrote at high speed in his Jamaican retreat, Goldeneye, during the early months of 1952.[149] In it, the beautiful Bond assistant, Vesper, turns out to be a Soviet agent inside the British Secret Intelligence Service. (No such woman, it should be said, ever existed, though Kim Philby was already under suspicion[150] and George Blake, the SIS station chief in Seoul, South Korea, when it was overrun in 1950, was in the process of turning himself into a Soviet agent while incarcerated in the North.[151]) But the element of *Casino Royale* which really resonates with the workings of British intelligence in the early Cold War years is the notion of a possible fifth column in France, the country identified by the Joint Intelligence Committee in the early postwar years as 'valuable to the Soviet Union as a centre for the propagation of Communism throughout the rest of Western Europe'.[152] Compare the opening paragraph of a memo to 'M' in the 1952 *Casino Royale* with the French section of the JIC's summer 1947 assessment of 'Soviet Interests, Intentions and Capabilities':

... Monsieur Le Chiffre ... one of the Opposition's chief agents in France and under-cover Paymaster of the 'Syndicat des Ouvriers d'Alsace', the Communist-controlled trade union in the heavy and transport industries of Alsace, and as we know, an important fifth column in the event of war with Redland (Fleming).[153]

Communist influence ... already amounts virtually to complete control over French industry, in particular the armaments industry. They are in a position to embarrass, by large-scale strikes, any Government in which they are not represented ... The Commu-nists are believed to have detailed operational plans for a *Coup d'Etat*. They are, however, unlikely to put these into effect on their own initiative owing to the belief that time is on their side ... (JIC).[154]

A knowledge of the power of communist influence in the French trade union movement did not require insider access to the intelligence world, but the accuracy of Fleming's *mise en scène* is striking nevertheless.

As David Cannadine has pointed out, though the Bond novels were well produced by Cape and well received in serious literary circles, 'the early books did not sell particularly well and it was only with the appearance of *From Rus-sia With Love* [in 1957[155]] that Fleming emphatically entered the best-seller lists. Thereafter, the Bond boom was not just a literary but a social phenom-enon ...'[156] (Achieving that last phenomenal status, certainly in international terms, had to wait until 1962 when *Dr No*, also published in 1957,[157] was the first of the novels to be adapted for the silver screen, transforming an Edin-burgh milkman-turned-actor born Thomas Sean Connery into cinematic gold.[158] By the 1990s it was estimated that 'half the world's population has seen a Bond film'.[159])

A real-life equivalent of Fleming's 'M', a former 'C', once told me the Bond-perpetuated myth of his service's ubiquity and omniscience was a great aid to agent recruitment in tough terrains abroad. When one of his officers made the final pass and acknowledged for whom he was really working, as often as not the target stood to attention, metaphorically speaking, so great was the honour of being invited to assist Her Majesty's Secret Service.[160]

I have heard it said by intelligence insiders that the Bond films became much sought after for private viewing by the KGB in Moscow and that, even allowing for filmic exaggeration, a degree of envy about the gadgetry and women at Bond's disposal aroused a degree of envy about the lifestyles of their Western counterparts.[161] But, naturally enough, the malign brilliance of the KGB spymasters acquired a considerable hold on Western imaginations.

The KGB's ability to recruit 'Stalin's Englishmen'[162] fascinated and alarmed the cinema-going and novel-reading public alike, certainly from the early 1950s when Fuchs, Burgess and Maclean were exposed in quick succession. And the home-grown but Moscow-tainted Communist Party of Great Britain (CPGB) came to be seen as a potential 'enemy within'. The Boultings' *High Treason*[163] played powerfully upon this in the cinemas of 1951.

In reality, albeit one concealed from the viewers of *High Treason*, British counter-intelligence took a much less alarmist view of all but a handful of the CPGB. Certainly the 1948 Government War Book anticipated that in the run-up to a Third World War the home Security Service, MI5, would send to the Home Office 'lists of persons in respect of whom detention orders might be required', and that some of these orders might be served on 'prominent trade unionists'.[164] But not until early 2005, when MI5 declassified its file on the rounding up of both British subjects and aliens 'In the Event of Emergency' for the late 1940s and early 1950s could outsiders gauge the magnitude of the operation for which the Security Service planned in the last days of peace. On receipt of a signal bearing the codeword HILLARY, the police were to round up some 3,000 people – 1,000 British subjects (of whom about 200 would be women) and 2,000 aliens (including around 500 women). The British males living in England south of a line from the Severn to the Wash would be interned initially on Epsom racecourse in Surrey; northerners would be kept in a holiday camp near Rhyl in North Wales. Southern-based aliens would be sent to Ascot racecourse in Berkshire; northern ones again to Rhyl. The women were earmarked for Holloway jail in north London and an unnamed northern prison. Once processed, all of them were to be transferred to various holiday camps on the Isle of Man. The plan was prepared jointly by the Home Office and MI5.[165]

Yet, in terms of possible UK detainees, the early postwar MI5 was quite well disposed towards the rank-and-file of the membership of the CPGB, which, in 1947–48, it reckoned consisted of 43,500 regular members, 2,000 in the Young Communist League and 'the secret members of the Party, who, contrary to estimates frequently given in the press, cannot number more than a few score at the most'.[166] MI5 split the CPGB 'into two distinct sections. By far the larger of these sections, consisting of the full-time executives and the working class members, is mainly concerned with domestic policy; wages, housing, education, taxation, unemployment, health, pensions and so on.'[167]

It is plain from, for example, reports to the Home Office from the Metropolitan Police Special Branch on the body which ran the Party's newspaper, the *Daily Worker*, in the late 1940s and early 1950s,[168] and especially the personal files MI5 kept on individual members, that the CPGB was under extremely detailed continuous surveillance by the security authorities, which had both telephone taps and bugs inside the Party's headquarters at 16 King Street in Covent Garden.[169] Their conclusion based on such close familiarity was that '[t]he most striking feature about the British Communist Party is that it is, first and foremost, a political party like other political parties. In so far as it partakes also of the character of a subversive or conspiratorial organisation, it does so to a secondary degree.'[170]

In their own version of class analysis, MI5's CP-watchers had a certain tendresse for the Marxist working man or woman, however misguided. Not so for those higher up the socioeconomic scale:

The smaller section, the intellectuals of the Party, comprising university students and graduates [then a tiny proportion of the population], civil servants and members of the professions, is on the other hand primarily concerned with international issues and this is the interest which it has in common with the amorphous body of 'communist sympathisers', who are less sympathetic to the British Communist Party than to the ideological conception of international communism. If there were any subversive activity on behalf of a foreign power carried out in peace-time, one would expect it to be carried out by individuals of the intellectual group acting on their own initiative. The working class group is unlikely to be the source of peace-time espionage.[171]

This description certainly fitted the clutch of Soviet agents who came to public attention in the last phase of the Attlee government.

In the United States, similar exposures, as we have seen, led to widespread fear, loyalty oaths for public servants and attempts by the Republicans to portray the Democratic administrations of Roosevelt and Truman as harbourers of subversives and being soft on communism.[172] Despite films such as *High Treason*, the Britain of Attlee and Churchill was almost startlingly free of such paranoia. Why and how the UK avoided McCarthyism is an intriguing question.[173] It was partly that the British political system was much more of an elite phenomenon. The Whitehall executive powerfully dominated the Westminster Parliament, and there was no chance of a House of Commons Select Committee on Un-British Activities being formed in imitation of its notorious American counterpart.[174] (Sir Waldron Smithers, at the time the organ-playing right-wing Conservative MP for Orpington, would call for one at regular intervals and would, just as regularly, be rebuffed.[175])

Edward Shils, who brought a remarkable, sociologically attuned observer's eye to both societies, found the explanation of the differing approaches in US and UK public and political life in the competing impulses of privacy, publicity and secrecy. Writing in 1956, Shils produced the only explanation of the British genius for secrecy that has come anywhere near to persuading me of its virtues. He was, of course, describing a different country, for the lessening of deference to authority is one of the great changes of the UK in the second half of the twentieth century:

Although democratic and pluralistic, British society is not populist. Great Britain is a hierarchical country. Even when it is distrusted, the Government, instead of being looked down upon, as it often is in the United States, is, as such, the object of defer-ence because the Government is still suffused with the symbol of monarchical and aristocratic society . . .

The acceptance of hierarchy in British society permits the Government to retain its secrets, with little challenge or resentment. The citizenry and all but the most aggres-sively alienated members of the elite do not regard it as within their prerogative to unmask the secrets of the Government, except under very stringent and urgent conditions . . .

The deferential attitude of the working and middle classes is matched by the uncom-municativeness of the upper middle classes and of those who govern. The secrets of the governing classes of Britain are kept within the class and even within more restricted circles. The British ruling class is unequalled in secretiveness and taciturnity. Perhaps no ruling class in the Western world, certainly no ruling class in any democratic society, is as close-mouthed as the British ruling class. No ruling class discloses as little of its confidential proceedings as does the British.[176]

Thirty years after Shil's *The Torment of Secrecy* was published, a security-related file was declassified which so reinforced the American sociologist's account that it was almost as if he had read the document before framing those paragraphs.

In 1955 the reappearance of Burgess and Maclean in Moscow, plus the frenzy about a 'Third Man' who had tipped off 'B and M' (as the popular press liked to call them) in 1951 enabling them to flee the attentions of MI5 and Special Branch (this was revealed by Vladimir Petrov, a KGB officer stationed in Australia who had defected the year before[177]), saw the finger of suspicion publicly (and accurately) being pointed at Philby by Marcus Lipton, the Labour MP for Brixton, under parliamentary privilege, in the House of Commons on 25 October 1955.[178] There was insufficient evidence to confirm suspicions of Philby's treachery (until 1962[179]) but, understandably enough, there was intense pressure on the Eden government (Churchill had retired in April 1955) to mount an inquiry.

It was Eden's successor at the Foreign Office, Harold Macmillan, who produced the Cabinet paper of 19 October 1955 on the pressure for an inquiry which was so utterly Shilsian in tone and content. Macmillan said the suggestion of a select committee inquiry should be ignored. A public investigation was highly undesirable: 'Nothing could be worse than a lot of muck raking and innuendo. It would be like one of the immense divorce cases which there used to be when I was young, going on for days and days, every detail reported in the press.'[180]

Macmillan told the Cabinet the following day that 'he was concerned that there was nothing to be said for holding an inquest into the past. This would give currency to a stream of false and misleading statements which could never be overtaken and corrected in the public mind.'[181] The Cabinet settled instead for a privy counsellors' inquiry which led to a tightening of positive vetting procedures.[182]

Given the hold that the quintet of spy-men (First Man, Guy Burgess; Second Man, Donald Maclean; Third Man, Kim Philby; Fourth Man, Anthony Blunt; and Fifth Man, John Cairncross) have come to exert on the British mentality, one that has outlasted the Cold War, it is surprising that Churchill, with his active penchant for intelligence, should have taken so little interest in numbers 1 and 2.* Churchill's Joint Principal Private Secretary, Jock Colville, recalled that Churchill was not very interested in the diplomats who had disappeared in May 1951:

In fact I had to press him to ask the Cabinet Office to provide a Note on the incident. I think he merely wrote them off as being decadent young men, corrupted by drink and homosexuality, and the whole story lowered his not very high opinion of the Foreign Office ... He certainly did not look upon it as an indication of widespread Communist infiltration – and I doubt if he had ever heard of Philby.[183]

According to Senator McCarthy's highly critical biographer, Richard Rovere, Churchill so disliked the witch-hunting of early-1950s Washington that he inserted 'an eloquent anti-McCarthy passage into Elizabeth II's Coronation speech'.[184] I have not been able to verify this, though Churchill introduced the

---

* The dubbing by the press of the missing 'Third Man' owed everything, of course, to the classic Carol Reed film of that name set in late-1940s Vienna. Its Third Man, Harry Lime, played by Orson Welles, is a drug dealer deeply involved with all the occupied sectors while sheltering in the Soviet one.

Queen's Coronation broadcast on 2 June 1953[185] and it did indeed include the following resonant passage: 'Parliamentary institutions, with their free speech and respect for the rights of minorities, and the inspiration of a broad tolerance in thought and its expression – all this we conceive to be a precious part of our way of life and outlook.'[186]

Churchill may not have been excited by Burgess and Maclean, but he took quite a lively interest in the activities of the Communist Party of Great Britain, the local manifestation of a doctrine he likened during the House of Commons debate on the North Atlantic Treaty in May 1949 to a 'theme' which was 'almost a religion'.[187] Harry Pollitt, the Communist Party's General Secretary, in particular roused his ire. Understandably, this was reciprocated. Pollitt produced a lurid denunciation of Churchill's 'Iron Curtain' speech in 1946 at Fulton, Missouri, describing it as a call for 'an anti-Soviet bloc and a bloc against the working class and all it stands for in social progress', and bizarrely saw it as a Churchillian plot against the Attlee government as well. For Pollitt, Churchill was 'seeking to use Labour for reactionary ends meant to lead to war on the U.S.S.R., to slow down Labour's domestic policy, to strengthen reaction all over Europe'.[188] Churchill, for his part, thought that the BBC gave undue prominence to communists, Pollitt and the miners' leader, Arthur Horner, in particular, arguing in 1948 that communists 'were enemies of the country' and members of 'an unconstitutional party' and, for good measure, warning Sir William Haley, Director-General of the BBC, to watch out for communist penetration of his own organization.[189]

Once back in No. 10 he became quite exercised by Pollitt's remarks to the 19th Congress of the Communist Party of the Soviet Union in Moscow in October 1952. Churchill was an avid reader of the newspapers and it was the *Daily Express*'s Moscow dispatch – 'Pollitt tells Russians his campaign plan "WE'LL GET INTO THE UNIONS"' – in its 10 October 1952 edition that caught his attention, particularly the paragraph reporting Pollitt as saying, 'The Communist Party is increasingly waging the struggle for creating the broadest possible unity within the workers' movement, utilising all forms of trade union, political and mass actions to make it impossible for the Churchill Government to remain in power.'[190] Churchill wrote by the cutting: 'Is there anything in this? What did they say?'[191]

His Foreign Affairs Private Secretary asked Guy Liddell, the Deputy Director-General of MI5 (who had recruited Anthony Blunt to that organ in 1940 and was wrongly suspected by some of having been a Soviet mole in the British Security Service[192]), to comment. The Foreign Office sent No. 10

the text of Pollitt's speech which the BBC's monitoring service had picked up (presumably from Radio Moscow). Liddell reported that Pollitt had said nothing new 'and the whole of his speech seems, apart from a eulogy of the Soviet Union, to have been no more than a summary of the British Communist Party's published policy as it appears in "The British Road to Socialism" [published in January 1951[193]] and elsewhere'.[194] Liddell took from the Reuters' tapes a fuller version of the Pollitt passage on which the *Daily Express* had based its story:

The Communist Party in England incessantly wages a struggle for the creation of the widest unity in the Labour Movement, using all forms of Trade Union and political mass action to make it impossible for the Churchill Government to stay in power; so that a crushing defeat may be dealt the Conservatives and a new Government may come to power obliged by mass pressure to conduct a new policy.[195]

This profound misunderstanding of the nature of early 1950s British politics Pollitt seems to have based on the Bevanite left's gains on the Labour Party's National Executive Committee at the fractious annual conference in Morecambe a few days earlier.[196]

Two sections of Liddell's paragraph on communist penetration of the trade unions have been deleted from the photocopy available at the Public Record Office on grounds of continuing sensitivity: 'There is nothing new in the Party trying "to get into the Unions". [deleted section] More recently the General Council of the T.U.C. has become alive to the threat presented by Communists in the Trade Union Movement, with the result that Communist infiltration has been slowed down and in some cases checked altogether. [deleted section]'[197]

As Liddell indicated but did not specify, MI5 had described for Attlee's ministers the emphasis the CPGB placed on capturing the general secretaryships of trade unions and places on their executive committees, reporting in 1948 that the Party had 'already made considerable progress toward attaining ... [its] ... aim' of securing control of individual unions and, through them, the TUC partly due to an 'active Communist fraction', directed from Party headquarters, existing in 'all the important trade unions' and partly thanks to the 'personal qualities' of individuals such as Arthur Horner of the Mineworkers Union and James Gardner of the Foundry Workers Union.[198]

After Eden replaced Churchill in No. 10, the Cabinet Secretary, Norman Brook, summarizing MI5 material in April 1956, explained to him that the CPGB was not behind the current rash of industrial unrest as 'the advocacy of strike action would more often hinder than help it in its primary objective of penetrating and eventually controlling the trade union movement . . . While its members account for less than one in 500 of the national trade union membership, the Party now controls the Executive Committees of three trade unions; and thirteen General Secretaries and at least one in eight of all full-time officials are Communists.'[199]

Churchill, unusually, did not scribble a comment on Liddell's brief in October 1952. We do know that it coincided with a burst of prime ministerial concern about clandestine Soviet offensive actions against the UK which was a recurrent theme of his last years in No. 10, embracing the bugging of British embassies and, perhaps, the most secret parts of Whitehall, and the possibility that the Russians might drop '20,000 parachutists into this country as the curtain raiser to the next war'.[200]

It was the ubiquitous 'Prof' Cherwell who alerted Churchill in October 1952 'that a small bit of apparatus has been found in an Embassy in Moscow by means of which the Russians can listen into conversations going on in a room without any wire connections. It is, of course, impossible to say whether anything like this has been smuggled into important London offices. But the risks are so enormous that it seems to me we should waste no time and spare no effort in examining the question.' Churchill agreed with Cherwell and passed it on to Field Marshal Lord Alexander, the Minister of Defence, with the injunction 'Pray take all necessary action with MI5 and "C" and please keep me informed.'[201] The flurry this caused ran well into 1954 with Sir Frederick Brundrett, the MOD's chief scientist, leading the investigation. Whitehall, it transpired, was relatively safe, as a room was vulnerable only if the transmitting and receiving equipment was stationed within fifty yards with no obstacles in between – difficult for the Russians to do in London if not in Moscow where, it was thought, the installation of fluorescent lighting might thwart them.[202]

Ironically, Churchill did a pretty good job of bugging himself in his own Cabinet Room, leading to a breach of security once described as 'the swiftest and most comprehensive Cabinet leak in the long history of unauthorised disclosure'.[203] Churchill became increasingly deaf as his last premiership deepened. He could pick up only the loud and the articulate, so microphones and loudspeakers were distributed around the Cabinet table. It was another Prime Minister, Alec Home, who told me the story:

Winston put these machines in front of everybody and there was a button that you pressed when you spoke and you released when you listened . . . Anyhow, it had been going for a very short time, not very satisfactory because none of us really were very successful with our machine, and then a . . . messenger came in to say that a [radio] taxi driver had come into No. 10 to say he's heard everything going on in his taxi in Whitehall. So that was the end of that experiment![204]

The cabbie could have made a fortune on Cabinet mornings had he alerted a political journalist or two instead of doing his patriotic duty.

The thought of Soviet paras falling from the skies all over Churchill's beloved British Isles preoccupied him in the early 1950s, using up a good deal of Whitehall time and partly stimulating the romantic, if wasteful, revival of the Home Guard on which he insisted. This theme was bothering him before the electorate put him back into Downing Street. In March 1951, as part of a general correspondence with Lord Trenchard about the state of Britain's defences, he expressed concern about the possibility of 'large-scale paratroop raids – twenty thousand or so – in our present defenceless condition, where our troops are out of the country, or to be sent away, and we have no Home Guard'.[205] To the alarm of the Treasury, as the head of its Economic Section, Robert Hall, recorded in his diary, 'Winston got a statement in the King's Speech [following the Conservatives' return] that the Home Guard was to be restored. He did not say whether it was inside, or extra to, the £4.7mn programme [the Attlee government's rearmament-boosted budget for 1951–3; it should have been billion, not million, in Hall's diary [206]].' 'In a good many ways,' Hall continued, 'he seems to be acting as if it were 1945 again and that everything we had or did then must be better than anything that has been changed.'[207]

In the spring of 1952 Churchill told the House of Commons that, if war should come, 'it will be with violent speed and suddenness' (a judgement rather out of kilter with the late 1940s and early 1950s JIC analyses – these consistently stated that the Soviet Union and its allies would be in no position to wage global war at least until the mid-1950s, though they added a regular caveat about war-through-miscalculation. It is possible Churchill had these assessments in mind.[208]) Thirty thousand men had already registered for the revived Home Guard, he told MPs, and he had rethought his original decision not to give them uniforms. He would now find the money to kit out 'at least the first 50,000'.[209]

This Commons performance was a Churchillian classic in another sense, too. When his No. 10 papers were declassified it was plain that he had chilled the MPs' bones long before asking his professional military advisers whether such a sneaky Soviet paratroop attack was either feasible or likely. It was only on 6 March 1953, a whole year after his Commons speech, that Churchill asked the Chiefs of Staff to prepare a study on whether it would 'be practicable for a potential enemy, from existing bases, to drop something of the order of 20,000 parachutes in this country'.[210]

As the country began to prepare to celebrate the Coronation, the following month the Chiefs, in suitably polite but firm language, hosed the old warrior down. The Russians could do it, they told him, but only at night, without fighter cover and at great risk to planes and paratroops:

The assembly, dispatch and delivery of 20,000 parachutists some 600 to 700 miles from their bases, with few navigational aids, is an operation of great difficulty and complexity, particularly at night. It would entail the risk of losing practically the whole of the Russian Air Transport Fleet employed [between 800 and 1,000 aircraft]; in consequence, no follow-up attack could be expected.

... The Chiefs of Staff feel that the Russians will need their transport aircraft in the early stages of war for operations on the mainland of Europe, particularly in attempts to secure the Rhine crossings and the Baltic Exits. Moreover, since the problem of airborne attack would be greatly simplified if the Russians obtained bases nearer this country, they would be more likely to defer their airborne attack against these Islands until they had advanced far enough into Western Europe to bring their fighter bases and ground navigational equipments within range of the targets.[211]

There was no likelihood of Russian paratroops descending to spoil the Coronation fun – or in the foreseeable future:

A surprise attack – that is before a declaration of war – would necessitate the postponement of the Russian preparations for war, including mobilisation. In the face of this the Chiefs of Staff believe that the Russians would not contemplate such a step – with or without atomic bombardment – unless, without prejudice to their operations in Western Europe and the Baltic, they could be certain of virtually paralysing the United Kingdom as a base for strategic air bombardment during the critical opening weeks of the war.[212]

The bomb. Its shade intruded everywhere. As Edward Shils put it, writing of America and Britain in Churchill's last years, 'Every strain of the postwar world has been accentuated by the atomic bomb.'[213] Churchill certainly saw it that way – and not just the military strains. It overshadowed his last premiership in a thoroughly civilian (and not just civil defence) sense, too. In the Coronation summer of 1953, when he was determined to overcome the effects of his stroke and have one last crack at easing the Cold War before the hydrogen bomb broke the world, he made exactly this connection in a conversation with Colville, who noted in his diary that 'Winston is firmly hoping for talks which might lead to a relaxation of the Cold War and a respite in which science could use its marvels for improving the lot of man and, as he put it, the leisured classes of his youth might give way to the leisured masses of tomorrow.'[214]

By this stage it was the shadow of the H-bomb and its 'unimaginable horrors'[215] beneath which Churchill brooded and plotted his paths to what he called 'easement'[216] with the Soviet Union (as opposed to the 'appeasement' of prewar Nazi Germany which he abhorred). It was during the 1951 general election, over a year before the United States achieved the world's first thermonuclear explosion, that Churchill had mapped his pathway to 'that lasting peace settlement which the masses of people of every race and in every land fervently desire'. This, he told a rally in Plymouth in October that year, 'is the last prize I seek to win'.[217]

The 'prizefight' with the Americans and several in his Cabinet began in earnest only after Stalin's death in March 1953, however. Once he had got through his 'art rather than article' phase (which the files suggest did not survive Cherwell's early and persistent briefing) Churchill, like Attlee in 1945, plainly thought a British bomb was the only way to deter an atomic attack on British cities. And he took a characteristically intimate and energetic interest in the preparations for the first British atomic test. This he did from the end of March 1952 when his 'APEX' committee began to meet. But first the British public and the world had to be told of the forthcoming trial. This was done in what Christopher Driver noticed was the 'first official communiqué in Queen Elizabeth's reign'.[218] The Press Notice of 18 February 1952 continued the practice of minimum openness:

In the course of this year, the United Kingdom Government intend to test an atomic weapon produced in the United Kingdom. In close co-operation with the Government of the Commonwealth of Australia, the test will take place at a site in Australia. It will be conducted in conditions which will ensure that there will be no danger whatever from radio activity to the health of people or animals in the Commonwealth [of Australia].[219]

There is an especially intriguing aspect of the test's preparations which was not divulged for nearly fifty years – the deliberate deception involved. On 9 April 1952 Alexander told Churchill that counter-measures were needed to keep would-be Russian 'spies and saboteurs from gaining intelligence about or interfering with the operation'. He listed for the PM the vulnerabilities in 'order of priority':

(i)   Risk of sabotage of the fissile material while in transit.
(ii) The prevention of intelligence gathering by enemy agents in the area, and also by scientific observations elsewhere, so far as this is possible.
(iii) Interference with the return of the scientists, their records and instruments.

'My own view,' Alexander explained, 'is that we should take all possible action to safeguard the operation, and particularly to avoid any risk of sabotage, which would be a major political triumph for the Russians.'[220] Churchill agreed. 'As proposed,' he scrawled on Alexander's minute on 17 April.[221]

But what was proposed? And who was deceived? The story is a bizarre little vignette of Britain and the bomb, the workings of the secret state and the fading mental powers of the Prime Minister even in an area – the clandestine – which had long excited his once formidable grey cells. First, the cunning plan drawn up by the Directorate of Forward Plans, the suitably vague cover name for the early-1950s Whitehall deception organization, heir to the legendary London Controlling Section which had engineered great feats of misinformation in the run up to D-Day in 1944.[222]

The idea was to fool the Russians into thinking 'that the explosion will take place later than the date we have selected' by imparting 'false information to the effect that there had been some hitch in our plans and that it was now unlikely that the arrangements for the trials could be completed until some weeks later'. Alexander explained to Churchill that the method of deception 'would be to rely upon the enemy drawing reasonably accurate conclusions from the information which we cannot hide from him and then to introduce other material designed to falsify those conclusions'.[223]

But what if friends and allies were deceived too? The Directorate of Forward Plans had thought of this. Whitehall's deception experts, Churchill was told, 'feel that they can feed in their false material through covert channels to a sufficient extent to ensure that all the pieces in the jigsaw will be in the possession only of the Russians. Any pieces of information fed in through overt channels, and thus available to the public in the western countries, would have little or no significance by themselves, and in consequence would not be likely to attract any public interest.'[224]

The Directorate of Forward Plans refined their deception still further and Alexander primed Churchill on this in early June 1952: 'The idea . . . is that we should impose on him [the enemy, i.e. Russian intelligence] the belief that there will also be an air burst at Woomera [another test site in South Australia], this second bomb being flown from Woomera to Monte Bello.'[225]

It was plainly a convincing tale because Alexander's explanatory paragraph which followed succeeded in fooling Churchill himself!

Apart from any merits which it may have of confusing the enemy's intelligence services, this second plan can be manipulated by the deception organisation to give support to the scheme for falsifying the date. Thus, it will be suggested that the reason for the late date of the trial is the lateness of the production of the second bomb. In effect our story will be that as it would be technically necessary to explode the ground bomb first and then within a week the air bomb we have had to put back the ground burst until the air burst was ready to take place.[226]

This was all too much for Churchill when he read Alexander's brief two days after it arrived in No. 10. He thought Alexander was warning him of a real, not a fictional, delay and minuted his Military Secretary, General Ian Jacob: 'What delay is involved?'[227] A no doubt embarrassed Jacob had to spell it out carefully for the old man:

I think there has been some misunderstanding. No delay in the Operation is proposed. What is proposed is to deceive the enemy about the date and make him think that it is to take place later than the actual date fixed. We want him to imagine that the trial is to take place some weeks after the real date, so that the plans of his Intelligence Service to find out the details will mature too late . . . The proposal in the [Alexander] minute is merely reinforcement of the Deception Plan.[228]

Churchill, we know from other and intimate sources, was struggling with his prime ministerial paperwork even before his stroke in July 1953. On 21 February 1952 he had suffered a small arterial spasm. Shortly afterwards his doctor, Lord Moran, and his Principal Private Secretary, Jock Colville, had a very private session about Churchill's ability to carry on. Colville said: 'I hate to be disloyal, but the PM is not doing his work. A document of five sheets has to be submitted to him as one paragraph, so that many of the points of the argument are lost.'[229]

Matters got even worse when the overt bit of the deception plan was put into place in mid-August 1952. John Drew, who ran the Directorate of Forward Plans, alerted Colville on Friday 15 August that the following Sunday's edition of the *Sunday Express* was to carry an article

inspired by us in connection with a deception operation which we are carrying out in support of Operation HURRICANE. Its intention is to assist in confusing the Russians about the precise nature of the tests (one of the objectives of the operation approved by the Prime Minister). The article takes one stage further speculation (uninspired by us as it happens) which has already appeared in the press about the nature of the weapons to be exploded. It is an inextricable mixture of the true and the doubtful, the idea being that the true facts – all of which are harmless – should give weight in the minds of the other side to the points we are trying to put across to them. I should add, of course, that the article is only part of a campaign which we are conducting mainly by covert means.[230]

But the whole operation had by this stage slipped from Churchill's mind. When he was alerted to the *Sunday Express* piece as the presses were rolling in Fleet Street, he was enraged and dictated a minute to the Cabinet Secretary, Norman Brook, which sizzles on the page to this day: 'Please find out whether the Minister of Defence or the Minister of Supply have been consulted upon this business. Why is it, if it were necessary to consult me at all, was this left until matters were so far advanced that they could not be stopped without causing much disturbance?'[231]

He went on through a little bit of constitutionalism a touch like the one he displayed when told first of how Attlee had concealed the £100m spent on the bomb from Parliament. This time he railed against an operation he himself had approved four months earlier: 'The idea of stimulating, through an inspired article, information both true and false, so mixed up as to be deceptive, to any particular newspaper, is not one hitherto entertained in time of peace.'[232]

The following day the offending article appeared on the front page of the *Sunday Express*. Under the misleading headline 'Tactical Atom Bomb Exercise Planned', the paper's features editor, John Garbutt, declared that 'Britain's first atom bomb has arrived in Australia' (it had not; the plutonium core did not get there for another month) and that in addition to the bomb proper, 'It is believed that a "tactical" atomic weapon will be tested as well' (which was untrue). The delay element, intended to supplement the material planted on Soviet Intelligence by covert means, appeared in the assertion that 'the button will be pressed, sometime towards the end of this year'. In a ringing conclusion, Garbutt wrote: 'Such is the climax to eight years' British research. In fact Britain has for four years been in a position to make an atom bomb.'[233] (That wasn't true either. As Norman Brook minuted Churchill, Penney did not receive 'his first lump of plutonium' from Windscale until the first days of April 1952.[234])

To Brook fell the delicate task on Monday 18 August of reminding the Prime Minister that: 'The Minister of Defence made two submissions to you

. . . recommending that deception techniques should be used in order to mislead the Russians about the date and the nature of this trial. You approved these submissions; and the Minister of Defence told Mr Menzies [the Australian Prime Minister], while he was in London, that these attempts to confuse the Russians would be made. The officials in the Ministry of Defence who handle deception work regarded the publication of this particular article as covered by this decision of principle . . . The Features Editor, who wrote the article, and to a lesser extent the Editor himself, were aware that we wished this information to be published for our own purposes and that it was not in all respects accurate.'[235] We do not know if Soviet intelligence was 'confused' by all this. The British Prime Minister certainly was.

What about the opposition in Parliament? Did any members of what Mrs Thatcher would later call the 'awkward squad'[236] raise difficulties for Whitehall on the first atomic test? Churchill's chief tormentor in the period before Monte Bello was Emrys Hughes, the very independent minded Labour MP for Ayrshire South. Long forgotten now – in a way that Bertrand Russell and CND are not – Hughes peppered Churchill with a series of questions about the Anglo-American relationship, the fate of bird and animal life on or near Monte Bello, and whether or not the Archbishop of Canterbury should lead a delegation of churches to witness the test. All of these were reprised for Churchill in a Ministry of Supply brief ahead of the adjournment debate Hughes had succeeded in securing on the forthcoming test in the House of Commons late at night on 27 May 1952.[237] The brief made no attempt to smear Hughes as a fellow traveller, as Brigadier Terence Clarke, the Conservative MP for Portsmouth West, ludicrously sought to do during the debate.[238] The Whitehall view was that, 'As a pacifist, he [Hughes] presumably believes that this country should have nothing to do with atomic weapons; and he regards the forthcoming test as a peg on which to hang his general argument.'[239]

On the night of the test itself, Hughes, with some verve, recalled Churchill's warnings, when Leader of the Opposition, about the vulnerability of the UK to Soviet atomic attack thanks to the US bomber bases in Britain. In the House of Commons on 28 March 1950, Churchill had speculated that fifty Russian atomic bombs on the UK would produce fifty 'fearful experiences far beyond anything we have ever endured' and Hughes quoted the Hansard entry for that day.[240] 'To think,' he said, 'as the Prime Minister did, if 50 atom bombs [dropped on the UK's industrial areas] with a possibility of 200,000 casualties with each bomb, it would perhaps result in making this country untenable . . .'[241] In fact, as we have seen, the secret Whitehall estimate drawn

up a year later, was that 132 atomic bombs 'of the Nagasaki type' dropped
on the UK's largest cities and towns would have left 1,378,000 dead and a
further 785,000 seriously injured (not quite the appalling ratio of bombs to
deaths Hughes envisaged, but ghastly enough).[242]

There is in Churchill's brief from the Ministry of Supply an intriguing aside
on the justification for there being, in Bevin's image, 'a bloody Union Jack' on
top of the bomb. Hughes, according to the brief, had told the Parliamentary
Secretary to the Ministry of Supply, Toby Low, 'that he intends to argue that
if we had had closer co-operation with the United States throughout we should
not have needed to develop our own weapons at all'. This, understandably,
was deemed an odd line to take for an MP who objected to all nuclear
weapons on moral grounds. But it's the touch of Bevin which follows that
is interesting:

Moreover, even if there had been the fullest collaboration with the US, the UK Government might still have considered it necessary, for the sake of our national prestige and
national safety, that we should acquire and practise the technique of manufacture of
atomic weapons, and produce some operational weapons for ourselves. It is true that
with full co-operation we might have reached the goal earlier . . .[243]

This was very much Bill Penney's view. A year earlier he had judged that
the 'discriminative test for a first-class power is whether it has made an atomic
bomb and we have either got to pass the test or suffer a serious loss in prestige both inside this country and internationally'.[244] Yet another indicator of
great-power status, it might seem, was in the process of being added to the
Empire/Commonwealth and the sterling area in the lexicon of British self-
worth. But the bomb could equally, perhaps more justifiably, be seen as Attlee
saw it – as the only way, *in extremis*, of preserving the UK from atomic attack,
a prime duty of the state even if it were no longer running a territorial empire
or sustaining a reserve currency.

Penney – and Britain – passed what Britain's leading bomb-maker saw as
its first-order test. Churchill took some pains over the final details. He was
briefed in mid-September on the nature and speed of the communiqué to be
released if the test succeeded, and warned by Cherwell that, 'Unless the official
statement is out within an hour of the explosion it will be forestalled by the
Australian Press which has set up a post on the mainland from which the
explosion cloud will be visible.'[245] 'Make sure it has gone off before you issue
the Communiqué,' Churchill responded. 'Otherwise we might look silly.'[246]
The PM also had two telegrams drafted: 'Thank you, Dr Penney' (if it failed)

and 'Well done, Sir William' (if it didn't).[247] Penney got his knighthood.

Just before 9.30 a.m. in Monte Bello and 1.00 a.m. in London on 3 October 1952, the bomb was detonated inside the hull of the Royal Navy frigate HMS *Plym*, at anchor in Bunsen channel between Trimouille Island (whose southern tip was named Churchill Point) and, in a nice touch of nuclear and political bipartisanship, Hermite Island (whose southern extremity was named Attlee Point).[248]

Churchill was staying with the Queen at Balmoral and was asleep when HMS *Plym* 'vanished, mostly to a vapour in the fireball', leaving 'a gluey black substance' on the shore of Trimouille.[249] While Churchill was in Scotland with Colville, a new foreign affairs private secretary joined No. 10, Anthony Montague Browne (who was to stay with Churchill for over twelve years until his death[250]). It was Montague Browne who took the call from the Admiralty. His first introduction to Downing Street life, he later recounted, 'was being telephoned in the early hours of the morning to be told by an Admiral that our first nuclear bomb experiment had been a success. He suggested that I should wake the Prime Minister at Balmoral and inform him, but even at this early stage I concluded that this would be imprudent!'[251] As Cherwell had feared, the press, watching from the mainland, were ahead of the officials. Reuters got the news to London six minutes before it reached the Admiralty.[252]

Initial calculations suggested that the explosion in *Plym*'s weapons room was equivalent to 20,000 tons of TNT, roughly the same as that of the plutonium bomb dropped on Nagasaki. The estimate was later raised to 25 kilotons.[253] Churchill, reporting on the test to the House of Commons on 23 October 1952, by which time MPs had returned from the party conferences, avoided giving any figures bar one: 'When the first flash burst through the hull of *Plym* the temperature was nearly one million degrees [fahrenheit]. It was of course far higher at the point of explosion.'[254]

It took another two years for the final report on 'Hurricane' to be completed, which, naturally, was not divulged to Parliament. Churchill had told the House of Commons on 23 October 1952 that the 'object of the test was to investigate the effects of an atomic explosion in a harbour'.[255] Though the destruction of HMS *Plym* had not produced a base surge of water, this kind of explosion was, in Brian Cathcart's words, 'far dirtier and deadlier than any other known'.[256] As the secret official report put it, 'the residual contamination due to the deposited fission products provide a major contribution to the effect of a weapon detonated in this way'.[257] The radiation produced by a harbour burst would be between two and four times as great as that from an identical bomb detonated in the air. So, as Cathcart put it, 'If London or Liverpool suffered such an attack [from a bomb in a boat], a larger number of people – perhaps a far larger number – would probably be killed by radiation than at Hiroshima or Nagasaki.'[258]

In mid-November 1952, the analysts in Whitehall's Atomic Energy Intelligence Estimates Unit circulated a brief to those inside the JIC loop reporting that: 'We believe that Russia has an appreciable stockpile of atomic bombs ... We consider that the primary target will be the UK, the balance being divided between USA, Europe, Middle East, bomber bases, elsewhere one or two "targets of opportunity", such as a fleet, together with a small reserve.'[259] Britain was the main target because Russian bombers could not at the time reach the USA. From material yielded by a highly secret intelligence venture, Operation Nomination, 'designed to obtain a measure of Russian plutonium production ... [which had] ... been in progress for some years', Whitehall believed that 'Russian production was very small indeed up to the middle of 1951', after which there had been evidence of an increase.[260]

The end result of the Monte Bello test was a weapon that could be used to deter the Russians. The first of these vast 'Blue Danube' weapons (twenty feet long and five feet across) was delivered to RAF Wittering alongside the A1 in Rutland on 7 November 1953.[261] By the time the final appraisals of 'Hurricane' were completed in 1954, Churchill – and, in the later stages of policy-making, his full Cabinet – were in the process of taking a decision to authorize the production of a British hydrogen bomb, of which more in Chapter 7.

But, just as the shadow of the bomb affected all UK citizens in 1951–2 whatever their politics and wherever they were, from the playground of St Michael's Convent kindergarten in Finchley (me) to the front-line in Korea (Michael Caine), the first British nuclear weapon was a thing of consensus, at least on the front benches of the House of Commons, as Churchill made plain in his parliamentary statement on the Monte Bello test: 'All those concerned in the production of the first British atomic bomb are to be warmly congratulated on the successful outcome of an historic episode, and I should no doubt pay my compliments to the Leader of the Opposition [Attlee] and the Party opposite for initiating it.[262]

In this respect, as in several others, the returning Churchill, in the first (and subsequent) months of his final premiership, was a natural coalitionist.

4

The Natural Coalitionist

'Went to Chartwell this evening. Alone with the P.M. who is low. Of course, the Government is in a trough, but his periods of lowness grow more frequent and his concentration less good. The bright and sparkling intervals still come, and they are still unequalled, but age is beginning to show. Tonight he spoke of coalition. The country needed it he said, and it must come. He would retire in order to make it possible; he might even make the demand for it an excuse for retiring. Four-fifths of the people of this country were agreed on four-fifths of the things to be done.'

Jock Colville's diary entry for 16 May 1952.[1]

'Now that there is a tiny Conservative Majority the persecution of the rich by the politicians will be greatly intensified so that they can display class impartiality.'

Evelyn Waugh to Nancy Mitford, 29 October 1951.[2]

'Beneath all the party malice there is a realization of the facts. But the nation is divided into 2 party machines grinding away at one another with tireless vigour.'

Winston Churchill to his wife, 21 July 1952.[3]

'We have really in a way an advantage. The Labour Party has taken [a] violent line against them [the British communists] . . . Our Labour Party is very sensible. Attlee and Morrison have a very great deal of courage . . .'

Winston Churchill to Eisenhower in the White House, 26 June 1954.[4]

'It's likely to be my last innings. So it had better be a good one!'

Winston Churchill, September 1951.[5]

During his career as an England stalwart Churchill liked nothing more than to hit the Labour front bench for six when the noise and the abuse from the House of Commons crowd rose and the Opposition bowled him a bouncer or a loose delivery. For all his genuine desire to maximize amity between the political parties he could, when the occasion demanded, be as partisan as any other senior politician. But during his last innings Churchill seemed suffused with a mellowness exhibited by no other twentieth-century Prime Minister to quite such a degree. It was the product of a long and romantic association with Parliament, a respect for the patriotism of most of his Labour opponents, a strange tendresse for the more right-wing trade union leaders (to whom he would lend his doctor when they were ill and invite to dinner at No. 10 when they were well[6]), and, above all, a sense of bafflement, awe and fear about the world in which he was, once more, the King's First Minister.

This he expressed with special eloquence when Queen Mary died in March 1953 at the age of eighty-six (a mere eight years older than himself): 'The chasm which scientific invention and social change have wrought between 1867 and 1953 is so wide that it requires not only courage but mental resilience for those whose youth lay in calmer and more slowly moving times to adjust themselves to the giant outlines and harsh structure of the Twentieth Century.'[7]

The bomb fused these themes in a way that linked the three Cs of consensus, Cold War and consumption. It also reinforced those impulses that led him in his last premiership to try to transcend the narrow boundaries of class and politics. In the slightly over-egged language of romantic benevolence at which he excelled, Churchill would occasionally make these connections in a manner quite similar to Michael Ramsey's paradox of welfare/warfare. Sometimes it was in the context of his devotion to the royal family that these rhetorical flights would soar. For example in welcoming the accession of Queen Elizabeth II on the death of her father in February 1952, Churchill told the Commons: 'She comes to the Throne at a time when a tormented mankind stands uncertainly poised between world catastrophe and a golden age.'[8]

A few months later, he told the diners at the Press Association's annual lunch: 'Around us we see the streets so full of traffic and the shops so splendidly presented, and the people, cheerful, well-dressed, content with their system of Government, proud, as they have their right to be, of their race and their name. One wonders if they realize the treacherous trap-door on which they stand.'[9]

In this instance, it was less the bomb and more the balance of payments that Churchill had in mind. But that remarkable mind often linked the two. 'We live in a time,' he told a meeting of Scottish Conservatives in Glasgow in April 1953, 'when science offers with benign prodigality to mankind the choice between a golden age of prosperity and the most hideous form of destruction.'[10]

This 'easement' in international relations, as Churchill called it, he wished not only for the general peace of the world but as the bringer of social peace and material plenty to Britain. In the summer of 1953, while recovering at Chequers from his stroke of June that year, he was, as Jock Colville's in his diary has already told us, 'firmly hoping for talks [with the new, post-Stalin leadership in Moscow] which might lead to a relaxation of the Cold War and a respite in which science could use its marvels for improving the lot of man and, as he put it, the leisured classes of his youth might give way to the leisured masses of tomorrow'.[11]

A few days earlier, he had put it even more crisply to his doctor, Lord Moran: 'You realise, Charles, I'm playing a big hand – the easement of the world, per-haps peace over the world – without of course giving up proper means of defence. If it came off, and there was disarmament, production might be dou-bled and we might be able to give to the working man what he has never had – leisure. A four-day week, and then three days' fun.'[12] Such thoughts were both the public and the private leitmotifs of Churchill's final burst of statecraft from the first to the last days of his peacetime premiership.

Initially, however, the theme of Churchill and the bomb added more than a touch of acid to the election campaign which put him back in 10 Down-ing Street, for Labour tried hard to portray him as a potentially dangerous warmonger in a nuclear age. In the deeper collective memory the lasting impression of the 1951 contest is as the 'Whose Finger on the Trigger?' general election. On polling day, 25 October, the *Daily Mirror* (the biggest mass-circulation newspaper of the age with a readership of nearly 5 million in 1950–51)[13] ran a front-page spread in the boldest type which was broken up only by a finger on the trigger of a revolver and on which was emblazoned 'BIG ISSUES OF 1951' and pictures of Attlee and Churchill. It read like this:[14]

WHOSE FINGER?

Today
YOUR
finger is
on the trigger

SEE YOU
DEFEND
PEACE WITH SECURITY
and Progress with
FAIR SHARES
VOTE FOR THE PARTY YOU CAN REALLY TRUST
The 'Daily Mirror' believes that Party is Labour

Though this front page burst across Britain only as the polls opened, Conservative party managers 'attributed much of the swing back to Labour during the campaign to the "warmonger" scare, exploited at the grass roots in Labour leaflets and speeches'.[15] Churchill was outraged by the *Mirror*'s front page as he had been two weeks before when the paper began to run its 'warmonger' theme. But the late swing back towards Labour was insufficient, and virtually Churchill's first action as peacetime Prime Minister was to sue the paper for libel. He secured costs and a full apology, and the paper offered to pay an undisclosed sum to charity.[16]

Churchill's more fruity anti-socialist tirades during the Attlee years could certainly be taken at face value and led those on the left to fear the welfare state would indeed not be safe in his hands; the right gleefully anticipated that he really would try to turn the policy clock back to the 1930s.[17] But only the crudely partisan could have failed to sense the early-1950s centrality to that extraordinary Churchillian persona of his desire to engineer an 'easement' of the Cold War.

During the 1950 election campaign, he had added the word 'summit' to the geopolitical lexicon. In an important speech in Edinburgh, Churchill, who was very conscious that he and Stalin were the surviving veterans of the wartime 'Big Three' conferences at Tehran, Yalta and Potsdam, declared,

[it] is my earnest hope that we may find our way to some more exalted and august foundation for our safety than this grim and sombre balancing power of the bomb ... I cannot help coming back to this idea of another talk with Soviet Russia upon the highest level. The idea appeals to me of a supreme effort to bridge the gulf between the two worlds, so that each can live their life, if not in friendship at least without the hatreds of the cold war ... It is not easy to see how things could be worsened by a parley at the summit, if such a thing were possible.[18]

During the 1951 election, especially once Guy Bartholomew, the editor of the *Daily Mirror* had begun hammering the finger-on-the-trigger theme,[19] he took every opportunity to refute this 'false and ungrateful charge', as he put it, telling an election meeting in Plymouth two days before polling day that preventing another world war and increasing the chances of peace was 'the last prize I seek to win'.[20]

As modern British historian Paul Addison has written, the finger-on-the-trigger line was a dubious one to push given 'the fact that a Labour Government had already sent British troops to fight in Korea, and almost blundered into a war with Persia' over the Mossadegh government's nationalization of British-owned oil interests in Iran accompanied by the expulsion of Anglo-Iranian (later known as BP) staff from the huge oil installations at Abadan.[21] Churchill was prone to using excessive language about the perils of socialism, the 'insatiable lust for power' of the Attlee government and apocalyptic prophecies in front of Conservative audiences that at least a quarter of Britain's population would 'have to disappear in one way or another' as Labour's economic policies meant the country could sustain no more than 36 million.[22] Yet attempts to portray Churchill as a reactionary on the home front were equally absurd.

In reality he accepted, albeit sometimes with reluctance, the essential core of the British New Deal, with the Conservative manifesto for the 1950 election, *The Right Road for Britain*, declaring 'the maintenance of full employment as the first aim of a Conservative Government'.[23] This was vividly apparent in Huddersfield Town Hall on 15 October 1951 when he travelled north to speak in support of the *Liberal* candidate for Colne Valley, his longstanding and beloved friend Lady Violet Bonham Carter. The glorious Lady Vi, daughter of Asquith (whose nickname with her 'Beloved Winston' was 'Bloody Duck'[24]) thought Churchill 'in wonderful looks and form' with the packed crowd inside the Town Hall (there were another 7,000 outside) 'like a loaded gun – going off at full-cock whenever the trigger was touched'.[25] And the Grand Old Man, who still sometimes pined for his Liberal roots, knew exactly where those triggers were. 'I look back with pride,' he declared, 'to the great measures of social reform – Unemployment Insurance, Labour Exchanges, Safety in the coalmines, bringing the Old Age Pensions down from seventy to sixty-five years of age, the Widows' and Orphans' Pensions – for which I have been responsible both as a Liberal and a Conservative Minister.'[26]

He then turned to his own great party political purpose as the 'last innings' approached – to change the nature of the political centre by reversing the original Lib–Lab pact that allowed the Labour Party its first real parliamentary breakthrough in the general election of 1906. Unknown to all (except perhaps

Lady Vi) that evening in Huddersfield Town Hall, he had been trying, albeit vainly, to get Conservative Party managers, especially the chairman, Lord Woolton, to think seriously about proportional representation for the urban constituencies – plus local pacts of the kind prevailing in Colne Valley where no Conservative candidate was up against Lady Vi – as a way of boosting the Liberals in the House of Commons.[27]

That autumn night in the West Riding, however, Churchill geographically and publicly showed himself to be, in Addison's vivid phrase,[28] 'a politician without a permanent address':

I find comfort in the broad harmony of thought which prevails between the modern Tory democracy and the doctrines of the famous Liberal leaders of the past. I am sure that in accord with their speeches and writings, men like Asquith, Morley and Grey, whom I knew so well in my youth, would have regarded the establishment of a Social-ist state and the enforcement of the collectivist theory as one of the worst evils that could befall Britain and her slowly-evolved, long-cherished way of life.[29]

This, Lady Vi recorded in her diary, 'was rapturously received by Libs and Conservatives alike'.[30]

The great man and the glorious lady then moved to a floodlit balcony and addressed the 7,000 massed outside in the chilly autumn air before moving off to Churchill's train, drawn up in a Huddersfield siding, where he and his entourage would shelter for the night. Though they did not know it, the age of the great public meetings linked by the grand railway progression, which Churchill adored and Mr Gladstone (whom Lady Vi had met) had pioneered nearly seven decades earlier, was about to end as what Churchill called the 'vast new organisation of television'[31] progressively changed the terms of political trade both during and between general elections.

Churchill, too, was wonderfully *pre*-1914 in never knowingly travelling without a well-stocked larder and drinks cabinet. Aboard the train, Lady Vi recorded, they 'had a voluptuous meal ... champagne and brandy flowed – innumerable attendants male + female appeared + put thro' telephone calls at W's behest. He was in marvellous form ... He said he cldn't get Electoral Reform past his people ... We didn't leave him till after midnight. He shunts off to Newcastle at 8 o'clock next morning.'[32]

'The Valley', as Lady Vi wrote to Churchill three days later, may have been 'still aglow with your presence and the echoes of your speech ... still ringing through it',[33] but Labour's Glenvil Hall (the *nice* old sheep', she called him) still beat her by 2,189 votes,[34] to Churchill's great disappointment. (He shed a few tears when Lady Vi lunched at No. 10 with the new Prime Minister and his staunchly Liberal wife, Clemmie, on 7 December and 'told them that our [Huddersfield Town Hall] meeting was one of my greatest and proudest experiences . . .'[35])

Churchill, back with an overall majority (albeit one of just seventeen), none the less tried his best to form an informal coalition with the Liberals by offering the Education Ministry to the Liberal leader, Clement Davies. Davies wanted to accept but his colleagues in the greatly reduced Parliamentary Liberal Party talked him out of it.[36] Education was where Churchill wanted to send Lady Vi had Colne Valley done its duty ('I shld have gone in unhesitatingly,' she wrote in her diary[37]). Churchill also tried and failed to get Lady Vi's younger brother Cyril ('Cys'), a newly appointed law lord, to join his Cabinet as Lord Chancellor. He sat under an Asquith in his first Cabinet and seemed determined to have one in his last, but Cyril Asquith was unwell and he had to decline.[38]

I suspect Churchill would have made a pitch for a Liberal or two in his 1951 Cabinet even if his Commons majority had been greater. The coalitionist impulse throbbed deep within him. Indeed, the absence of inter-party co-operation could be seen as one of his more consistent political threnodies because, as Paul Addison has put it,

over the long run he was a freelance who resented the restraints imposed by parties on the liberties of Cabinet ministers. He would have liked to govern the country with an inner circle of friends and non-party administrators, at the apex of some broadly-based government. Hence his preference for peacetime coalitions. If matters had been arranged as Churchill wished, there would never have been an exclusively Liberal Government in 1906, or an exclusively Conservative Government at any time after 1918 . . . in 1940, and again in 1951, he managed to create something very close to the type of government he desired.[39]

The Liberals may not have wished to have Clem Davies in the Cabinet, but they were hugely instrumental in getting Churchill back into No. 10, at some cost to themselves in terms of a 33 per cent reduction in their Commons representation (from nine seats to six). Two elections in quick succession were ruinous to a small third party with neither the business nor trade union heavyweight backers of their big rivals. In 1950 they had put 475 Liberal candidates in the field. In 1951 they could manage a mere 109.[40] It has been estimated that in constituencies without a Liberal candidate, the Party's vote split 3:2 in the Conservatives' favour and that without this Churchill would not have won.[41]

There were two other, linked, factors contributing to Churchill's victory. For all his anti-socialist rhetoric, Churchill did not give the impression either that he would put a match to the welfare state or ignite the Cold War into a hot one. The public felt safe in voting for a less bureaucratic and better fed version of the status quo. Churchill's greatest little helper here was the ration book. The researches of Ina Zweiniger-Bargielowska have skilfully linked the factors that tilted sufficient votes in the autumn of 1951 to turn a Labour majority of six into a Conservative one of seventeen:

[It was the] Conservatives' skilful exploitation of popular dissatisfaction with rationing, austerity, and controls [which] deprived Labour of its landslide majority in 1950 when the party lost support among women and middle-class voters, especially in south-eastern suburban seats, to the Conservatives. The renewed shortages following the outbreak of the Korean War, the prospect of permanent economic controls, and public discontent with the lowest-ever meat ration further strengthened the Conservative critique of Labour policies in 1951. In this context the Conservatives were able to broaden their appeal across the class divide by capturing the bulk of the former Liberal voters. The party also won a majority of the female vote.[42]

The pledge to build 300,000 new homes a year during the course of the Parliament was a comparable vote-turner. Churchill understood all this perfectly when he said privately to his Civil Service and Parliamentary Private Secretaries (Jock Colville and his son-in-law Christopher Soames) in a late-night conversation at Chequers in spring 1952 that the essence of his government's programme was 'houses and meat and not being scuppered'.[43] Colville also recorded, from the same conversation, how 'he feels strongly about class distinction: he loved Canada for its absence . . .'[44] This explains his desire to secure good relations with the solid, decent men he saw in a majority of the membership of the Trades Union Congress and atop most unions. Though much criticized by later Conservatives for appeasing the unions in an excessive desire for social and industrial peace,[45] on one level Churchill was both following his own instincts in 1951 and calculating carefully both the class and the party arithmetic of the October election. Given the vagaries of first-past-the-post, it could have gone either way – Labour won more votes (13,948,605 to 13,717,538)[46] but the Conservatives more seats (321 to 295 with six Liberals and three others).[47]

On a huge turnout of 82.5 per cent, nearly 97 per cent of those voting went virtually evenly for one or other of the two political armies (48.0 per cent to the Conservatives; 48.8 per cent to Labour[48]). This was real electoral

competition. Churchill and the Conservatives were back – but only on probation – and the parties and the electorate both knew it. Even if he had wanted
to do otherwise (and give or take a denationalization or two, some dismantling of controls and the shedding of a few plans and planners, he did not[49]),
Churchill would have been obliged to keep within the chief parameters of the
British New Deal. This was reflected both in his Cabinet appointments, Rab
Butler at the Treasury especially, and in his desire almost to place personality
above party in creating a coterie of 'overlords' to supervise them: a kind of
inner directorate of those with whom he felt most at ease.

Despite the warnings and pleas that he think again from both the techni-
cians-of-state (exemplified by the very influential Sir Norman Brook, Secretary
of the Cabinet) and an intended beneficiary of the wartime style as adapted
for peace (John Anderson, Viscount Waverley, a non-party figure who had
served Churchill as Lord President of the Council and, later, as Chancellor of
the Exchequer, in his War Cabinet), Churchill insisted on an experiment
whereby a small group of peers in the House of Lords would co-ordinate a
cluster of lesser ministers in the House of Commons, thus streamlining Churchill's peacetime Cabinet as the War Cabinet had been streamlined between 1940
and 1945. There were several difficulties with this. Anderson would have overseen the economic departments, including the Treasury and the Chancellor of
the Exchequer, but he would have nothing to do with it and told Churchill such
an arrangement would be both inefficient and unworkable in peacetime.[50]

Another defect in the system was that it offended the Conservative Party
because the overlords were not great political figures. Anderson did not belong
to any party. Lord Woolton (who was appointed to oversee Food and Agriculture – then in separate ministries) had joined the Conservatives only in
1945, having been an independent during the war and appointed to serve in
the coalition because of his business skills.[51] Lord Leathers, who became overlord of fuel, power and transport, was another businessman and not exactly
a pillar of the Conservative Party. Lord Cherwell, whose narrow, if important,
brief to oversee atomic energy matters did not match the width of Woolton's
or Leathers' remits, held views certainly to the right, but he was chosen because
of his boffinry and brains rather than his conservatism.

Neither Anderson nor Brook used the point about party in their attempts
to wean Churchill off his 'supervising ministers' idea. The crux of their argument was a mix of the constitutional and the practical – that in peacetime the
House of Commons expected individual ministers to be answerable for
specific policy areas without intermediary 'overlords' floating around in the

Upper House as well as in Cabinet between those the Commons wished to call to account and the policy decisions requiring scrutiny. Brook's plea was for co-ordination to be carried out by Cabinet committees rather than by super ministers.[52] Anderson and Brook won – but not for two years, by which time the post-stroke Churchill was asking Brook and Bridges to discover for him how the 'overlords' related to their subordinate ministers, adding that: 'A statement should also be prepared showing how wise and necessary this was [Leathers' job as Secretary of State for the Co-ordination of Transport, Fuel and Power] and how what has been achieved justifies me (a) in having created, and (b) in now abolishing the post in question.'[53]

I suspect that if Churchill had decided to send the strong-minded free-marketeer and City man Oliver Lyttelton to the Treasury rather than Rab Butler, the question of Anderson's economic overlordship may well have not arisen. In terms of personnel the choice between Lyttelton and Butler has been regarded as the single most crucial he made in influencing what 'Setting the People Free' (the actual 1951 manifesto was called *Britain Strong and Free*[54]) would actually mean, for Conservative policy-making in opposition, from which Churchill remained distant, had left the party 'facing both ways' on many of the crucial questions of political economy.[55]

Butler was the chief maker of *The Industrial Charter* of 1947,[56] seen by subsequent generations as the vehicle of Tory adaptation to the changed world which lifted them successfully out of the wreckage of 1945, propelling them along the road to thirteen years of political dominance after 1951. He was genuinely different in temperament, outlook and formation to Lyttelton, who sat with Oliver Stanley (the man who almost certainly would have been Chancellor had he lived beyond 1950) on the Party's Finance Committee. It had been Stanley and Lyttelton who took on Labour's big guns such as Cripps and Bevan during economic debates in the Commons. Lyttelton succeeded Stanley as chairman of the Finance Committee and was widely regarded as having replaced him as Chancellor designate too.[57]

Churchill himself does not seem to have read *The Industrial Charter*, even in part. Reggie Maudling, one of the bright young things brought on by Butler within the Shadow Cabinet's Secretariat after the war, recalled the moment in the autumn of 1947 when

I was working for Winston on his concluding speech to the [Party] Conference and we came to the topic of the Industrial Charter. 'Give me five lines, Maudling,' he said, 'explaining what the Industrial Charter says.' This I did. He read it with care, and then said: 'But I do not agree with a word of this.' 'Well, sir,' I said, 'that is what the conference adopted.' 'Oh well,' he said, 'leave it in,' and he duly read it out in the course of his speech . . .'[58]

If he had read it carefully, Churchill would have seen Butler's careful embroidery where he had stitched together traditional motifs of freedom with more modern themes of careful intervention. As John Ramsden has indicated, a close reading of the charter in the summer of 1951 would not have given any decisive clues as to whom the Treasury prize would go that autumn:

On industry as such, *The Industrial Charter* can be seen as demonstrating the party's theoretical commitment to the case for a mixed economy, partnership with the trades unions and state responsibility for public welfare that had been emerging by accretion under all parties for the previous twenty years, but which the Conservative Party had never considered in principle – not least because it had no full-scale policy review at all since 1924. It has thus often been interpreted in that way by historians who believe that the Tories moved towards a left-leaning 'consensus' after 1945. If some on the Tory right lamented all of this as 'pink-socialism' barely distinguishable from the fully blown red variety of Attlee and Bevan, they, like later historians, tended to miss the point that, by setting down the party's principles more clearly than before, Butler's team had not only endorsed the interventionist ideas that Macmillan had been peddling for years but had also endorsed the free enterprise ideas articulated by Oliver Lyttelton and Oliver Stanley.[59]

Yet at first glance, little of this personal or ideological fine-tuning appears to have featured in Churchill's choice for the Exchequer at the end of October 1951.

Churchill characteristically appointed his first tranche of senior ministers from his bed in 28 Hyde Park Gate bedecked, as Lyttelton recalled, 'in a quilted flowered bed-jacket' and smoking a cigar. After regaling him with how awful the economic position was – 'almost irretrievable: the country has lost its way. In the worst of the war I could always see how to do it. Today's problems are elusive and intangible . . .'[60] – he told Lyttelton that Butler, not he, would be Chancellor: 'It was touch and go, but the Chief Whip [Patrick Buchan Hepburn] thought the House of Commons stuff was a handicap to you.'[61] Lyttelton, it is true, did not care for the repetitive tedium of the House of Commons chamber and 'loathed all-night sittings perhaps more than most, because I had to earn my living, and run my company [he was chairman of Associated Electrical Industries]'.[62]

Churchill asked him to be Minister of Materials and Rearmament. Lyttelton's clear lack of enthusiasm led the Old Man to offer him the Colonial Office instead (then a senior and taxing job). In his memoirs Lyttelton admits that, had he been offered the Treasury, 'I should have taken it with zest . . . I thought I could make a contribution, perhaps even a decisive contribution, to the immediate financial and economic problems of the country.'[63] This was perhaps a cryptic reference to his wish, which he had expressed to Churchill during the sterling crisis of August 1947, 'to unpeg the pound in relation to the dollar . . . at one sweep of the pen it would be necessary to abolish most of the controls and allow price rises to take place'.[64] It is very likely that Churchill had forgotten Lyttelton's radical proposal or that he had not absorbed its implications at the time. On appointing John Boyd-Carpenter Financial Secretary to the Treasury a few days after sending Lyttelton to the colonies, Churchill, after attempting to summarize the economic position Butler and his team would be inheriting, gave a broad smile and admitted with engaging candour that, despite five years as Chancellor of the Exchequer, he had never understood it! 'But I know there is much work to be done at the Treasury and that you will be able to help Mr Butler.'[65]

When summoned to the Churchill bedroom, Butler had noticed on the Old Man's coverlet a sheet of paper with his planned senior appointments in large type.

He handed it to me gravely and silently. Chancellor of the Exchequer: R. A. Butler. 'I have thought much about this offer,' he said, 'and in the end Anthony [Eden] and I agreed that you would be best at handling the Commons. In this crisis of our Island life, when the cottage homes could so easily be engulfed in penury and want, we must not allow class or party feeling to be needlessly inflamed.'[66]

Here there is a clear hint that there might have been both a policy and a temperamental reason for Churchill's choice of Chancellor – that Lyttelton's strong style and aggressively free-market views could have aroused feeling on the Opposition benches in a manner not to the taste of the natural coalitionist romantically brooding about the needs of the humblest homes and the most meagre of hearths. Supporting this benign disquisition from the coverlet was a notably anti-capitalist measure, an excess profits levy, which 'was invented by Churchill himself' and which had been squeezed into the Conservative manifesto at the last moment.[67] Putting this 'into force', Churchill told Butler, would 'show our goodwill'.[68]

Churchill's bafflement by early-Fifties economics plainly did not incline him to appoint a Chancellor from among the relatively unbaffled such as Lyttelton, who had lived 'a lifetime of figures, after the desiccated study of applied economics, after having lived with imports and exports, the volume of bank deposits, balance of payments and monetary theory . . .'[69] 'It is no great matter that you are not an economist,' Churchill told Butler. 'I wasn't either. And in any case I am going to appoint the best economist since Jesus Christ to help you.' Butler was curious to know who this might be and was told it was Sir Arthur Salter, an Oxford economist, whose knowledge of shipping during the war had impressed Churchill sufficiently to appoint him Chancellor of the Duchy in his brief caretaker government of 1945.

So although Viscount Waverley (as John Anderson had become) had, as we have seen, declined to be placed above Butler, a rather nebulous group of ministerial advisers including Lord Woolton and Lord Swinton was assigned to him instead and Salter was put beneath him to prop him up. This Salter notably failed to do. His first impact on Whitehall was to underwhelm its professional economists, such as Robert Hall, with the humdrum and sometimes vague nature of his contributions. The 'main trouble', Hall wrote in his diary, 'was that he has to do this sort of thing at all. I do wish he could get some work and not just attempt to think'.[70] Salter only lasted just over a year in the Treasury before being moved to become Minister of Materials, the job Lyttelton had declined. The Chancellor's verdict on 'the best economist since Jesus Christ' was very Rab: 'Arthur, a nice man with a record of progressive thought but very many years my senior [Salter was seventy; Butler forty-eight], was accordingly provided with a high-ranking ministerial title [Minister of State for Economic Affairs] and for thirteen months wrote me numberless minutes in green ink, with which I did not always agree.'[71] This is Butlerian understatement, as we shall see.

Evelyn Waugh's views on the excess profits tax are not known, but it would, no doubt, have struck him as exactly the kind of 'persecution of the rich' in which Churchill would indulge because of his desire to appear impartial between the classes. What might be called this soft-edged approach both to men (Florence Horsbrugh was senior minister at Education but remained outside the Cabinet until September 1953) and to measures was noted at the time on the Labour benches by Dick Crossman, a Bevanite intellectual gossip and diarist, who wrote up the first day at Westminster after the election when most Labour MPs were 'so enormously relieved at having got back' with only nineteen seats lost in the unexpectedly tight finish:

On the Tory side I got a slight sidelight yesterday [30 October] when I ran into Bob Boothby drinking with John Junor of the *Daily Express*. Boothby has not been given a job, despite his loyalty to Churchill. He and Junor both described Lyttelton's anger at being fobbed off with the Colonies, and Boothby said, 'Rab Butler, Chancellor! Why, that's Gaitskell all over again, but from Cambridge.' With David Eccles excluded, at least from Cabinet office [he was appointed Minister of Works outside the Cabinet], and Brendan Bracken sulking [he was ill and had retired from the Commons; Churchill made him a Viscount early in 1952[72]], the real free enterprisers and deflationists seem to have been kept out and there is a good deal in the view that the general make-up of the Churchill Cabinet means that it will only be very slightly to the right of the most recent Attlee Cabinet. Just as Attlee was running what was virtually a coalition policy on a Party basis so Churchill may well do the same.[73]

Crossman's diary anticipates by over forty years the lament of some younger late-twentieth-century Conservatives that no trace elements of Mrs Thatcher's game-plan were detectable during Churchill's final innings.

Andrew Roberts, for example, in his *Eminent Churchillians* published in 1994, declared (with justification) that: 'In 1951 Churchill chose a Government which was the least recognizably Conservative in history ... Talented free-marketeer Conservatives, such as Ralph Assheton and Oliver Lyttelton, were either exiled to non-economic posts or did not receive the call-up at all.'[74] Not only did Churchill, in Roberts' eyes, err by omitting market-minded people, he sinned by commission – by appointing an emollient lawyer, Walter Monckton, to the Ministry of Labour and National Service rather than making him Attorney General. It was indeed curious to many during the years of inflation when the trade-union question dominated British domestic politics that Rab Butler could write in the early 1980s of Monckton as 'a genius appointment on the part of Churchill ... He made it possible for Winston Churchill to rule in comparative peace during his last period of office.'[75]

This was retrospective generosity. At the time Butler had sometimes been very irked by the special relationship between PM and Minister of Labour. In his affectionate portrait of Monckton in *The Art of Memory*, Butler recalled a midnight phone call from Churchill just before Christmas (a festival he was determined not be disrupted) telling Butler: 'We cannot have a railway strike, it would be so disturbing to all of us. You will never get home, nobody will be able to see their wives.' The late-night conversation ran as follows:

CHURCHILL: 'Walter and I settled the railway strike so you won't be troubled any-more.'

BUTLER: 'On what terms have you settled it?'
CHURCHILL: 'Theirs, old cock! We did not like to keep you up.'[76]

Yet Butler recognized that Monckton's 'serene non-political outlook produced all the effects Churchill hoped for from his appointment'.[77] He even acknowledged his wholesale abdication of Treasury power in this crucial area: 'I had no wages policy . . . my wages policy was governed by Walter's friendship with trade union leaders.'[78] Extraordinary. Not surprisingly, there was, as the then young Treasury economist Robert Neild noted, something 'curiously plaintive' about Butler's voice in conversations at the Treasury.[79]

To say that Churchill's last administration pursued social and industrial peace at almost any cost is tempting but too easy. Almost out of the blue, within four months of taking office, a very Lyttelton-like plan to float the pound (thereby in one bound, so its protagonists claimed, breaking free of the economic shackles that hobbled British policy-makers, the City and the industrial and commercial sectors), was sprung on a surprised Cabinet – by Rab Butler of all people. If ROBOT, as the plan was called,[80]* had been the centrepiece of the 1952 Budget, the country's economic and political history would, without question, have read very differently and the postwar consensus would have lasted but eight years, as the new exchange rate policy would have torn up the full-employment pledge which lay at its heart together with a sheaf of other undertakings of an international character.

ROBOT deserves attention in any history of Britain since 1945 for another reason. It was the economic equivalent of the Suez affair just over four years later which, for all its clandestine aspects, was visible, protracted and ultimately shaming as well as leading to the political ruin and resignation of its chief protagonist. As Edmund Dell, himself an experienced economic minister with spells of office in the 1960s and 1970s (including the substantial sterling crises of 1975–6[81]), put it:

At Suez Britain discovered how little it could do in foreign and security policy without American support. At the time of Robot, Britain discovered how constrained were its options in economic management . . . Never again would a British government contemplate the possibility of imposing its policy on its external economic environment. In 1952, for the last time, the thought was there that it might be attempted.[82]

---

* A fusion of the names of its chief begetters: Leslie ROwan, head of the Overseas Finance Section of the Treasury; George BOlton, Executive Director of the Bank of England in charge of its Overseas Division; and OTto Clarke, Rowan's number two in the Treasury.

What lay behind that 'thought'? Who had thought it up?

First, there is some catching up to do. As watersheds go, ROBOT was a very private affair. There were rumours of a possible float in early 1952 when the difficulties of the British economy were no secret. There had been two very public sterling crises in the seven years since the war ended: August 1947, when the convertibility of the pound into dollars was suspended after six weeks as the UK's gold and dollar reserves melted away; and June to September 1949, which ended with the devaluation of sterling against the dollar from a rate of $4.03 to $2.80. Butler's first Budget in November 1951 had been tough, as we have seen. He had signalled a severe overload on the British economy by rephasing Labour's huge and insupportable £4.7 billion rearmament programme over four years instead of three[83] (in the end, after later scale-backs, the Conservatives trimmed it by about 20 per cent[84]). Imports were cut back, too, using the direct controls inherited from the war economy and the Labour years.

But the gloom persisted within the Treasury and the Bank of England even as Butler delivered his Budget. Predictions were made that the country would in effect go bankrupt by the autumn of 1952 and would be powerless in the face of world economic forces unless something drastic was done both to stem the haemorrhage of the reserves and to put in place an alternative policy-regime that would stop the punishing cycle of balance of payments and currency crises punctuated by spluttering recoveries (crises which had also exhausted and demoralized the men in the Treasury and the Bank of England who had advised successive Chancellors and Cabinets on how to cope with the consequences).

Just as Suez was a desperate and risky act by a Prime Minister driven to distraction by an Egyptian leader, Colonel Nasser, and the sapping of British power in the world (and in the Middle East in particular, which Nasser was so effectively exploiting), so ROBOT was the desperate and risky response of frazzled yet clever men who had run out of both caution and alternative ideas. Yet it did not leak. As Roy Jenkins wrote over a quarter of a century later, ROBOT illustrated

the incredibly high standards of secrecy which were observed in British government in those days compared with anything which we have seen under Lord Wilson or Mr Heath or Mrs Thatcher. At the time of the Robot argument Hugh Gaitskell, only six months out of the Treasury himself, was Shadow Chancellor and I was one of his two or three closest parliamentary collaborators. I knew nothing about Robot, and I believe that he knew very little. It was like living next door to the Borgias and being surprised to discover that the diet there was not exclusively made up of health foods.[85]

There is no doubt who was the Cesare Borgia of this campaign – R. W. B. 'Otto' Clarke, one of the most mercurially brilliant minds in the postwar civil service[86] and father to Charles, a future Secretary of State for Education and Skills and Home Secretary in the Blair years. ROBOT was well named as it was meant to be a kind of automatic pilot for the British economy. Rab Butler saw a floating pound as 'an external regulator for the balance of payments corresponding to the internal regulator provided principally by Bank rate'.[87]

When ROBOT was sprung upon an unexpecting Cabinet at a 10 p.m. meeting on the night of 28 February, Harold Macmillan was both outraged that such a 'startling and quite dramatic proposal' should be put to ministers with the Budget but days away, and rightly fearful that, if adopted, ROBOT would put paid to his drive towards 300,000 new houses along with much else.[88] Brooding on it a couple of days later, he put his finger on the root of the problem:

I feel very unhappy about the way things have been managed ... For, if the plan was right, it was right in November [the time of Butler's first Budget]. Really, it was right in 1945! For the whole basis of the plan is that it is impossible to carry on a central banking business as large as the Bank of England with such slender resources. To have nearly £3000m [of sterling balances] 'at call' and to have some of the huge debt by the Bank to its customers funded, it is an impossible position.[89]

Yet ROBOT was not intended by its framers to get Britain out of the business of being banker for the world's second trading currency after the dollar, nor was it motivated by a sudden realization that the UK was no longer a world financial player and could not, should not, aspire to be one ever again. As Alan Milward has indicated, George Bolton, the key figure in the Bank, saw ROBOT as the sustainer – not the diminisher of 'national prestige ... To restore Britain to its role as the chief decision-making power in the international financial system after the United States was for him the only international policy which guaranteed the nation's survival in worthwhile form.'[90]

At first glance, floating the pound and 'letting the rate take the strain', rather than the gold and dollar reserves, while solving the balance of payments problem too (a depreciating pound would cheapen British exports in world markets), without the humiliation of a second devaluation inside thirty months, was very attractive. To its inventors ROBOT looked simple, bold and brave. It struck Churchill that way too, though, as he later admitted to Salter (much as he had to Butler and Boyd-Carpenter in October 1951), 'I don't know much about these technical financial matters myself.'[91]

But ROBOT was anything but simple. Its inherent complexities and the very substantial economic, political and diplomatic uncertainties attached to them halted the plan in its tracks. Firstly, the Bretton Woods international monetary system had come nowhere near to being fully implemented since 1945. Despite its overwhelming position as the only source of finance and manufactures in a largely war-wrecked and dollar-starved Western economy, the United States could not impose its favoured regime of free trade in both goods and currencies. And, from 1947 and the formulation of the Marshall Plan, Cold War considerations trumped the pure milk of economic doctrine and practical western European economic recovery was given priority. But the one piece of the Bretton Woods architecture which was firmly in place was the regime of fixed exchange rates for currencies (individual countries could devalue but not without prior consultation with the IMF and at least its most important member, the USA). Never again would a free-for-all of competitive devaluations be permitted, as in the years after the gold standard had collapsed in 1931, which it was thought (with some justification) had triggered beggar-my-neighbour policies, a shrinkage in world trade and a rise in both aggressive regimes and international tension.[92]

Devaluations were permitted only in conditions of 'fundamental disequi-librium' and only after negotiation with the US-dominated International Monetary Fund in Washington. A fluctuation of but 1 per cent either way was permissible. So the UK $2.80 exchange rate, after the devaluation of September 1949, could oscillate between $2.78 and $2.82; no more. ROBOT would have set it free – and it would have fallen probably to around $2.40. (That was the going informal rate in New York for sterling holders outside the sterling area who wanted to and could evade exchange controls by cashing in their pounds for dollars. This leakage of so-called 'cheap sterling' was another reason for those Dell called 'the Roboteers' to press for a radical rethink as it was costing the UK reserves up to £1m a week.)[93]

So, setting the pound free would most likely have wrecked the key disci-plines of the Bretton Woods system and, with it, the IMF. In 1950, as a way of coping with their acute dollar shortage, the sixteen nations participating in the European Recovery Programme, as the doling out of Marshall Aid was formally known, set up their own European Payments Union as the main instrument of non-dollar multilateral trade among themselves. Britain, given the relative size of its economy, was the keystone of this. If ROBOT had gone ahead, the EPU would have collapsed as well. Given the Truman administration's keenness for Europe to integrate its national economies under the stimulus of Marshall Aid, this would have been only slightly less welcome in Washington than the effective dismantling of the IMF and the world's fixed-rate currency regime.

The Roboteers were fully aware of the dislodgings of which their brainchild was capable as they were of the possibility that the unloosed pound would go into free fall, bringing down with it the very sterling area whose future it was intended to invigorate. So safeguards were added to the simple, so-called 'clean' float: the Bank of England insisted on a 'dirty' float of 15 per cent either side of $2.80 (i.e. a range of $2.40 to $3.20) and the reserves would be used to police each extremity. There were great problems with this, too, as the 30 per cent spectrum would not be announced for fear of the pound plummeting straight to the $2.40 floor and the reserves disappearing in the autumn of 1952. It was a possible collapse of these that had initially led Otto Clarke to shed his longstanding objections to floating. (The Treasury anticipated a fall in reserves from $2.3 billion on 31 December 1951 to $1.1–1.3 billion by mid-year and between $0.6 billion and $1.25 billion by the end of 1952.)[94] Clarke had become convinced that only by blocking the sterling balances and freeing the pound quickly could the UK retain any control of its economic and financial destiny[95] because if the reserves fell as expected by the autumn of 1952 'it will be impossible in any event to maintain a fixed rate'.[96]

As for blocking the £3,000m sterling balances of which Macmillan spoke in his diary, this was not straightforward either because the holders of sterling came in many guises. In total, they were rather larger than Macmillan suggested – around £3,430m in May 1952, about £872m of which was held by governments and institutions outside the formal sterling area.[97] The sterling area itself was in deficit to the tune of about £750m with the non-sterling world (of which the UK itself accounted for nearly £600m at the end of 1951[98]).

As well as a 'dirty' float of the pound on the world's money markets ROBOT included an attempt to solve the sterling balances problem once-and-for-all by splitting them into their component parts and tackling them in different ways.

- So called 'overseas' or 'external' sterling held outside the sterling area would become free of any control and could be exchanged for gold, dollars and any other currency on the open market.
- 80 per cent of the sterling balances held by the Bank of England for members of the sterling area would be frozen to prevent them being changed into gold or dollars and they would be compulsorily 'funded' by the Bank using 'long bonds at low rates of interest'.[99]
- 90 per cent of the sterling balances held by non-sterling area members who were outside the dollar area would be similarly frozen.[100]

The key, the Roboteers thought, was to severely limit the amount of sterling made freely convertible as, 'with the world greedy for dollars and awash both with current sterling and the sterling balances, a convertible pound would be sold for dollars and its exchange rate would drop like a stone',[101] breaking the $2.40 floor in a manner the depleted UK reserves would never be capable of preventing.

This immensely complicated plan was put together by the Treasury and the Bank of England in a tremendous rush with neither the Americans, the IMF, nor the Commonwealth finance ministers consulted. From Otto Clarke's original paper on 'Convertibility' of 25 January 1952 through to Rab Butler's buying of the idea in mid-February to the full Cabinet's three attempts to formalize it on 28–29 February was an extraordinarily short span for such a revolutionary proposal brimming with serious implications. It was a sign of the combination of deep frustration and anxiety on the part of some – though not all – of the guardians of British economic policy, and the looming Budget due on 4 March. Butler was persuaded to postpone his Budget speech until 11 March, to give more time for ROBOT to be discussed. When he dined at the House of Commons on 19 February with Churchill, Cameron Cobbold (the Governor of the Bank of England) and Harry Crookshank (Leader of the House of Commons), it was agreed that ROBOT, were it to proceed, had to be outlined in the Budget. The postponement was announced on 25 February and still the reason for it did not leak.[102]

ROBOT had been first outlined by Butler to a small group of ministers on 20 February, including Churchill and Lyttelton, who were in favour, and Cherwell, who was not.[103] They resumed their discussion two days later. By the 25th the political detractors and ROBOT's technical opponents among the Whitehall advisers had begun to mobilize with speed and determination. The key ministerial figure was, in fact, Cherwell, whose Prime Minister's Statistical

Section, and most notably the economist Donald MacDougall, provided Churchill with an alternative supply of economic advice to the Treasury. Salter weighed in on their side. From the Cabinet Office Economic Section Robert Hall was ferociously opposed to the Clarke–Bolton–Rowan trio. His diaries seethe through mid-February to late March 1952 and the rifts between Hall and his allies (who included Edwin Plowden, the Treasury's Chief Planning Officer) and the Roboteers in the Treasury Overseas Finance Division remained serious for quite a time. Here is Hall on 27–28 March:

The atmosphere is very unpleasant whenever OF [Overseas Finance] people are there. Leslie Rowan will hardly speak to Plowden or me and Otto Clarke and [Sir Herbert] Brittain [a Treasury second secretary] are apparently afraid to show signs of friendliness. It is a dreadful thing to have our overseas finances in the hands of an emotional man with a stomach ulcer [Rowan] . . . He is at present completely in Otto Clarke's hands. Otto himself is of course open to argument in spite of his instability. But Leslie gets angry at any sign of opposition.[104]

. . . it is almost impossible to have a rational conversation with Leslie and George Bolton. In discussion, Otto is a model of sweet reasonableness compared to them.[105]

It is unknowable whether a Cherwell–Salter team pitted against Butler and Lyttelton would have been sufficient to halt ROBOT, for it was a key minister who was abroad during the first skirmishes, the Foreign Secretary Anthony Eden, who returned to tip the political scales against the perilous dash for economic and financial freedom.

Eden had been in Lisbon for a NATO negotiation on sharing the burdens of rearmament and defence spending. Plowden, Britain's lead official in the burden-sharing exercise, was there too. A decision of this magnitude with wide international implications could not be made without the Foreign Secretary's concurrence. Two senior Whitehall figures, Brittain from the Treasury and Eric Berthoud from the Foreign Office's economic section, were despatched to Lisbon bearing briefings and letters. Two of them were for Plowden, one from the Permanent Secretary to the Treasury, Sir Edward Bridges, the second from Plowden's friend and ally, Hall. Bridges' letter, Plowden recalled many years later (after having exhumed the file from the Public Record Office)

seemed to imply that a decision to introduce 'Robot' had more or less been taken; the Foreign Secretary's acquiescence to this being virtually a formality. For his own part, he was glad. He saw 'Robot' as a 'chance of remaining in control of the situation and not just venturing in mid-ocean'.[106] Robert Hall, by contrast, indicated how disturbed and upset he was by developments. He was convinced that ministers did not really understand what the proposals might mean. If we put 'Robot' into operation in the Budget, he envisaged 'a considerable shrinking of world trade' with 'severe' political effects worldwide, 'a considerable increase in unemployment' and more domestic inflation as sterling depreciated.[107] At best, 'Robot' could be successful only at enormous cost.[108]

Eden's briefing included a letter from Churchill telling him the economy was in a 'super-crisis'.[109]

Plowden set off from his Lisbon hotel to call on Eden in the British embassy. Their accounts differ about what happened that weekend. Plowden implies that he helped Eden make up his mind; Eden that it was already made up when Plowden arrived. According to Plowden, Eden, after talking to Brittain and Berthoud,

was generally supportive of 'Robot', although also in favour of a general election to achieve a mandate for this policy [a ruinous idea, if true, as the $2.80 fixed rate would have been subject to overwhelming pressure had the world's money markets been treated to several weeks' electioneering over floating-or-not]. Eden was never strong on economic issues and I realised that he had been greatly influenced by the rhetoric [of Churchill's letter] . . . I told him the contents of Robert Hall's letter and argued that he simply must not allow a decision on 'Robot' to be made in his absence. After some persuasion he agreed, and I sat down to help draft a letter to be taken back to the Prime Minister.[110] In it Eden said that 'Robot' should be very much a last resort because of its implications for employment and Britain's foreign relations.[111]

Eden's account in his diary is rather different about the genesis if not the conclusions of his thinking:

While I was in Lisbon Berthoud came out with a senior Treasury man, sent by Winston, with an outline of Budget intentions. I did not like them at all. They seemed to me ill thought out and I was by no means convinced that they would work. In such conditions I couldn't endorse proposals that would strike a grievous blow at some of our Commonwealth friends, throw Europe into disarray and impose increased unemployment (so I judged) on our own people . . . Next day saw Plowden, who I found took much the same view. Wrote to W urging no commitment . . .[112]

Plowden believes that Eden's intervention was crucial as he 'stepped in at a critical moment to arrest the momentum which the plan had developed and gave its opponents more time to organise'.[113]

The stage was set for a mighty battle, though both Eden and Butler believed that Churchill had already decided not to risk ROBOT before the showdown in the Cabinet Room at the end of February. Eden said of Churchill in his diary that he 'was not enthusiastic himself' (this could have been a reflection of what transpired between them when they dined alone on Eden's return from Portugal).[114] Butler in his memoirs recalled that Churchill 'was perplexed by the controversy, felt in his bones that it was right to free the pound, seemed impressed by the support I had as Chancellor from Oliver Lyttelton but was persuaded not to make a dash for freedom by the marshalled arguments of Lord Cherwell and the cautious conservatism of the elder statesmen'.[115]

Harold Macmillan's diary account of the first late-night, ROBOT full Cabinet confirms this conclusion: 'At this meeting, it was clear that the P.M. had turned against the plan . . . Butler seemed very tired and uncertain of himself. I sensed that Churchill had encouraged the plan at the early stages, but had been intellectually put off by Cherwell's advice and politically alarmed by Eden's clearly hostile view . . .'[116]

In one sense, Cherwell's intervention a week earlier had been crucial to the debate on 29 February. For at the meeting of ministers on 22 February it was intended that Butler's paper proposing ROBOT should be read and digested at the gathering and left on the table, so sensitive were its contents. Cherwell insisted on taking his copy away to dissect it with his economic adviser, Mac-Dougall.[117]

As Edmund Dell has noted, Butler and the Treasury Roboteers were 'so confident that there was no alternative' that they 'had no hesitation' in making the risks of floating 'absolutely clear' so Cherwell 'was able to make a major part of his case simply by quoting Butler'.[118] It was, without question, desperate stuff. For example, the great antagonists – Otto Clarke and Robert Hall – agreed on the likely consequences for unemployment. Hall thought if ROBOT went ahead, it might rise from around 400,000 to between 700,000 and 900,000.[119] Clarke thought 'you need about 3% unemployment . . . but if you get up to 1,000,000 or more it is self-destroying, as it was in the '20's and '30's'. Nor did Clarke disguise the inevitability of 'most drastic internal action' on the 'Budget, credit policy, defence, housing – all the most vigorous policies possible to release resources for exports' if ROBOT was to cure the balance of payments.[120]

Macmillan was right to see this not just as a threat to his housing programme, but as a 'revolutionary' decision to take in wider terms.[121] He had a sneaking feeling 'that, in essence, the plan may be right' but it 'cannot be *rushed*, to coincide with our Budget . . . it is very likely that we shall come to this in April or May. But that wd be after some show (at last) of consultation and discussion; not as a panic matter . . .'[122]

Macmillan thought that ROBOT would be politically ruinous to a Conservative government with a small majority less than six months into its probation period with the electorate. But as he told his diary,

it's no good 'panicking' or we shall be in real trouble, and perhaps revolution. If the people are both unemployed and hungry under a Tory government, they will be very angry . . . I think Churchill (although he doesn't understand the niceties or so-called technique of finance etc.) understands in a dim way the salient features of the problem.[123]

It was quite plain to the anti-Roboteers that the norms of postwar politics – the British New Deal, no less – were facing a sudden death if it went ahead and, in effect, returned Britain to an interwar political economy.

Had a passer-by eavesdropped on Macmillan and Eden as they left the morning Cabinet meeting on 29 February together (this was thirty years before the gates went up in Downing Street), the following is very much the drift of what they would have overheard. Macmillan wrote in his diary that Eden

was strongly against the plan on political grounds. 'The country are not ready,' according to him, 'to cast away the whole effort of years and return to "Montagu Normanism"* without a struggle. For (apart from the writing off or funding the Bank's debt) the plan is really one to restore solvency by bankruptcy; large-scale unemployment etc. How could a huge armament programme survive the semi-revolutionary situation wh wd follow?'[124]

Later that day, after the afternoon meeting of the Cabinet, Woolton told Macmillan that Eden had threatened to resign if ROBOT went ahead: 'If this is really so, it wd explain Churchill's sudden change of front and abandonment of Butler.'[125]

Had Gaitskell overheard that snatch of conversation between Eden and Macmillan, he, too, would have agreed with their line. In fact, Gaitskell did not acquire details of the inside story of ROBOT from Berthoud and Plowden for more than two years. Gaitskell put in his diary that both

were strongly opposed to convertibility, Edwin on logical grounds, Berthoud because he mistrusted the people who were in favour of it. Berthoud's account of the matter,

---

* Norman was the financially orthodox Governor of the Bank of England 1920–44.

when we stayed with him recently in Copenhagen [Sir Eric was Ambassador to Denmark 1952–6], was perhaps natural – that he was the person who had persuaded the Foreign Secretary to reject it. Edwin's account shortly afterwards, when we happened to be dining at his flat, was a little different. He agreed that Berthoud had supported him, but made it plain that he had provided all the arguments ...

I said to Edwin, 'I wish you had not advised him that way. If they had been so foolish as to go for convertibility, we might now be back in power, or at least have a much better prospect of getting there.'

'That,' said Edwin, 'is exactly what I told the Foreign Secretary. "If you want to stay in power," I said, "do for heaven's sake reject this proposal."'[126]

What Gaitskell almost certainly never knew was that the minutes of the Cabinet discussions on ROBOT over 28–29 February 1952 (which were so sensitive that they were kept out of the standard Cabinet Conclusions Book and placed in a special Treasury file) contain a fascinating passage about Gaitskell and his colleagues on the Labour front bench as possible coalition partners if the pound did indeed collapse and the reserves melted during the coming autumn:

Under democratic government with universal suffrage such violent reversals of policy were hardly practicable. Even if the case for this change were made abundantly clear on the merits, there would be very great difficulty in persuading the public to accept it. Moreover, the adoption of this policy would create an unbridgeable gap between the Government and the Opposition; and, if it were thought possible that an even more grave economic crisis might develop later in the year, it would be unjustifiable to take at this stage a step which might exclude all possibility of forming a National Government to handle that situation.[127]

This sounds very much like Lord Salisbury, one of the 'cautious elder statesmen' to whom Butler ascribed the scuppering of ROBOT in Cabinet. Indeed, Henry Pelling found in Butler's papers at Trinity College Cambridge a letter from Salisbury to Butler comparing ROBOT with the Hoare–Laval Pact of 1935 (another sudden switch of policy – foreign this time – shortly after a general election). 'I am becoming more and more conscious', Salisbury told Butler, '... of the fact that it is likely to prove impossible to get through our present difficulties on a pure party basis; yet the plan ... would be bound to widen still further the cleavage between the parties.'[128]

The ROBOT episode raises two wider questions, both related to the 'great debates' about postwar British history. First, how does it play into the 'consensus' question? Second, was it one of the key moments when, as Lyttelton claimed to Butler in a note tossed across the table during the ROBOT Cabinets, the guardians of Britain's future preferred 'a genteel bankruptcy'[129] to the kind of bold exposure to world market forces that, after initial uncertainty and disruption, might have wrenched the British economy out of its downward spiral?

At this point, a famous composite figure, 'Mr Butskell', strides onto the page. Butskell was the creation of a marvellously gifted, mercurially brilliant free-marketer journalist, Norman Macrae, who gave the readers of *The Economist* a stream of coruscating commentary in the early postwar years and was still sparkling away when I was briefly on the paper in the early 1980s (by which time he had also added the word 'stagflation' to the lexicon of political economy). Macrae never penned a more enduringly influential articlethan his 'Mr Butskell's Dilemma' in *The Economist* of 13 November 1954:

Mr Butskell is already a well-known figure in dinner table conversations in both Westminster and Whitehall, and the time has come to introduce him to a wider audience. He is a composite of the present Chancellor and the previous one ... Whenever there is a tendency to excess Conservatism within the Conservative Party – such as a clamour for too much imperial preference, for a wild dash to convertibility, or even for a little more unemployment to teach the workers a lesson – Mr Butskell speaks up for the cause of moderation from the Government side of the House; when there is a clamour for even greater irresponsibilities from the Labour benches, Mr Butskell has hitherto spoken up from the other.[130]

Butler, who was deliciously strong on irony both on his own account as well as others', must have relished the idea that he was the restrainer of those who wished to free the pound.*

---

* Churchill's Chancellor, who loved 'building up a little scene', as one Whitehall connoisseur of his behaviour, the late Sir Philip Woodfield, put it to me in conversation in July 1997, could get cross with *The Economist*. Derek Mitchell was private secretary to Butler's permanent secretary, Sir Edward Bridges, from 1954 to 1956, and he told me a classic Rab story of a Friday evening (publication day for *The Economist*) when the Chancellor suddenly appeared in the private office, clutching the magazine and seeking out Bridges. Mitchell told him that Sir Edward unfortunately had already left for the evening but could he help? He could, said Butler: 'I work very hard indeed for this country and they are very critical of me in here. Could you ask Sir Edward to cancel my subscription?'

Sir Derek does not think it was the actual 'Butskell' piece which triggered this little scene, but another article of 1954 vintage.

Butler in his memoirs linked ROBOT with Macrae's conflation and, quite rightly, judged that if

the pound had been set free in 1952 the word 'Butskellism' might never have been invented ... Gaitskell was known to be, indeed, expressed himself as being, violently opposed to the 'disastrous turn in our policy' which the Cabinet had resisted and rejected. Despite our friendship, which became warm, we never discussed the 'doctrine' that united our names and each of us would, I think, have repudiated its underlying assumption that, though sitting on opposite sides of the House, we were really very much of a muchness ...

I shared neither his convictions, which were unquenchably Socialist, nor his temperament, which allowed emotion to run away with him rather too often, nor his training which was that of an academic economist. Both of us, it is true, spoke the language of Keynesianism. But we spoke it with different accents and with a differing emphasis.[131]

This is undoubtedly true.

Macrae knew this perfectly well, as he admitted to a young PhD student, Scott Kelly, in conversation over forty years later,[132] and Macrae's analytical polemic *Sunshades in October*, which appeared in 1963, made it plain he was well aware that Butler had economic instincts different from Gaitskell's.[133] Dr Kelly, in his *The Myth of Mr Butskell*, has shown vividly from his meticulous trawls through the files of the two Chancellors in the National Archives, that there were very substantial differences of approach, including but not confined to the convertibility question.

Butler favoured decontrol; Gaitskell thought full employment needed the maintenance of a combination of subsidies for certain essential goods and some physical controls, not least over sterling. Butler believed in using monetary policy, that is variations in Bank rate; Gaitskell in so-called 'cheap money' (consistently low interest rates).[134] They might have both been 'Keynesians' in pushing a full-employment policy, but, Keynes' intellectual legacy was a house of many rooms and the freedom versus planning arguments at the heart of the 1950 and 1951 general elections were not just synthetic differences polished up to satisfy the partisanship of Labour and Conservative activists. Had Butler won on ROBOT, unemployment would have risen sharply – at least in the short term.

Butler was, again characteristically, ambiguous about both ROBOT and consensus. In a reflective note to himself written after Suez (probably with his archive and history in mind) he talked of his core idea of 'rendering ... the traditionalist regime respectable in the eyes of the prosperous working class which it had begotten'.[135] And his dislike of the coarser shores of Conservative activism on social and penal policy, whose beachcombers 'quite clouded' his time as Home Secretary and Chairman of the Party, are well known.[136] He was no temperamental partisan; quite the reverse. But Roboteer he was until the end – or was he?

He appears to have changed his mind, then changed it back. When Salter finally left government in 1953 Churchill told him: 'You did a great public service in that affair about sterling last year – and Rab knows you are right.'[137] Edwin Plowden, whose personal relationship with Butler was quickly restored despite his having provided Eden in Lisbon with weaponry to wreck ROBOT, wrote in his memoirs that, 'In subsequent years "Rab" Butler admitted to both Robert Hall and me that he was wrong about "Robot".'[138] Yet in his own memoirs, Butler was unrepentant:

In the long-term . . . I believe that the decision not to free the pound was a fundamen-tal mistake. The absence of a floating exchange rate robbed successive Chancellors of an external regulator for the balance of payments corresponding to the internal regula-tor provided principally by Bank rate. If such a regulator had existed and a floating rate had been accepted, Conservatives would have been saved some of the uncertainties and indignities of 'stop-go' economics and socialists the traumatic experience of a second formal devaluation [in 1967 from $2.80 to $2.40].[139]

Who knows? Certainly Butler seems to have relied more on the Hall–Plow-den combination for post-ROBOT advice than on the Roboteers and wrote with great warmth of them in *The Art of the Possible*, Hall as 'our strong, silent man who came to have more and more influence. But I depended on Edwin Plowden ... to interpret and give political edge to advice generated by the less voluble and extrovert Hall ...'[140]

A narrow approach to the 'consensus' question can only see ROBOT, and other of Butler's instinctive preferences for allowing what he called 'the fresh winds of freedom and opportunity ... to blow vigorously through the econ-omy',[141] as showing the consensual notion to be a mythical beast, exposed by the passage of time and the prosaically cumulative archive at the Public Record Office. A broader look at the extraordinary economic spat inside the private government, which lasted barely more than a month (though the convertibil-ity argument rumbled on), shows just how powerful the wider constraints were even upon a vigorous Chancellor and a Prime Minister with an instinct for bold strokes and dashes for freedom. For it was the British New Deal which prevailed during those late February ROBOT Cabinets and the spectres of Beveridge's 'Idleness' and 'Want' that pushed ROBOT beyond Butler's 'art of the possible'.

We have heard Macmillan and Butler on this theme. Cherwell spelt it out for Churchill once more in late March as Leslie Rowan put round another paper pressing the case for ROBOT to be implemented the following March.[142] Fearing that the Old Man was still hankering after setting sterling free, Cherwell drove home the difference between the world Asquith's Cabinet faced and that confronting Churchill's in 1952:

It is at first an attractive idea to go back to the good old days before 1914 when the pound was strong and we never had dollar crises ... if a 6% Bank rate [very high by early Fifties standards], 1 million unemployed and a 2/- [10p] loaf is not enough, there will have to be an 8% Bank rate, 2 million unemployed and a 3/- loaf. And so on until the gap is closed. If the workers, finding their food dearer, are inclined to demand higher wages, this will have to be stopped by increasing unemployment until their bargaining power is destroyed. This is what comfortable phrases like 'letting the exchange rate take the strain' mean; nothing more and nothing less ... To rely on high prices and unemployment to reduce imports would certainly put the Conservative Party out for a generation ...[143]

Churchill forwarded this Cherwell philippic to Butler with the words: 'This is a formidable statement and arises I am sure from a purely objective view. No decision is called for at the present time but all should be borne in mind.'[144]

As we have seen, Churchill's anxieties sometimes pushed him in a consensualist direction and led him to brood about a coalition (as Salisbury had done), again telling Colville in mid-May 1952 that the 'country needed it and it must come'. Naturally, in public his preference was for 'knocking hell' out of Labour 'for the awful mess we found', as he told Moran when preparing his big Commons speech before the House rose for the 1952 summer recess.[145] There was no trace of consensus let alone coalition when he rose to his feet in the Chamber on 30 July and berated Gaitskell for being 'so smiling and carefree at the Dispatch Box' after, as Chancellor, bringing the country to 'the verge of bankruptcy, and when he has left to his successors heart-tearing problems to face and solve'. There are, he continued, 'fifty million of us here standing at a level of civilisation not surpassed in the world, and barely yet able to earn our living and pay our way and dependent for the food for two-fifths of our people on how we can do this in vast swirling world'.

Those Treasury estimates of gold and dollar reserves draining away had clearly burnt their way into the Old Man's mind and, battling on through Labour laughter which brought from him a brief, consensualist flash ('Why is there laughter? Surely it is not a Party matter?') and a great final flourish: 'Tragic indeed is the spectacle of the might, majesty, dominion and power of the once magnificent and still considerable British Empire having to worry and wonder how we can pay our monthly bills.'[146]

In fact, the figures had improved markedly between the ROBOT Cabinets and Churchill's parliamentary spat with the Opposition, and this was before Butler's import cuts had begun to bite. (The ROBOT-free Budget, when finally delivered, raised Bank rate to 4 per cent and, with new savings, brought the total of import cuts up to £600m since the previous November.[147]) When the Cabinet sat down late on the night of 28 February, the reserves had plunged by $521m over the previous eight weeks. Over the next five weeks they dropped by $114m and in the last week of March (as Cherwell chilled Churchill's bones with tales of inflation and soaring unemployment) they actually rose by $50m as the government's attempts to cut imports began to bite and the general terms of trade improved. During the last quarter of the year they rose strongly and by New Year's Eve 1952 were at $1,850m – $600m higher than the best forecast the Treasury had made.[148]

Disaster had been averted. Partial convertibility was introduced in 1955; full convertibility in 1958.[149] The pound remained within the Bretton Woods system at the fixed rate of $2.80. The Korean War ended in July 1953 (it was instability in stock purchases that had produced those volatile reserve figures in 1951–2[150]) and there was a peace dividend. Defence spending was reduced as a proportion of gross national product (down from 9.7 per cent in 1953 to 7.9 per cent in 1955).[151] The terms of world trade continued to move in Britain's and the developed world's favour. 'The same imports into the UK required 12 per cent less exports to pay for them in 1954 than three years previously ... a real windfall,' as modern British historian Peter Clarke observed.[152] The two-year period 1953–4 was relatively golden for the British economy and for Rab Butler's reputation as Chancellor – the first burst of 'having it so good', no less – a matter of great and continuing pride to Butler in his old age. ('I don't think we ever had such good expansion in the economy as in 1953 and 1954,' he told the makers of the fine television series *The Day Before Yesterday*, screened in 1971, while admitting that he had capitalized on 'a great opportunity, which you haven't got nowadays, in that everything [in 1951] was war-controlled'.[153]) But wasn't Lyttelton right in that scrap of paper he tossed to Butler across the Cabinet table at the end of March 1952? Wasn't it but a gilded patch, thanks partly to Butler's determination to 'liberate some of these controls',[154] in an otherwise shabby, if genteel, decline that braver hearts and more radical minds might have averted if a combination of cautious conservatism and British New Dealery had not trumped them?

There were some, like Otto Clarke, who thought this till their dying day. Indeed, Clarke believed not implementing ROBOT was the greatest policy error of the postwar period.[155] His friend and fellow economic policy-maker, Eric Roll, to whom Clarke confided his conviction, asked would ROBOT have 'freed us at a stroke from the incubus of the balance of payments constraints and enabled us to pursue more rational domestic policies? Would it have made it impossible to avoid a more stringent use of resources, particularly for external purposes than was in fact done?'[156]

Great prizes lurk in that pair of sentences. 'Rational domestic policies' means not having to deflate domestic demand every time a balance of payments crisis put pressure on the pound and securing the sterling balances – that 'sword of Damocles' over the postwar British economy, as William Armstrong (Butler's Principal Private Secretary as he was Gaitskell's, and a future Permanent Secretary to the Treasury) liked to describe them.[157] In other words, the stop/go cycle could have been avoided and a more generous and sustained growth path for the British economy charted. 'A more stringent use of resources, particularly for external purposes' means having to face up to Britain's reduced position as a world power, rethinking foreign and defence policies and cutting back the proportion of national wealth absorbed by military spending.

It is true that West Germany's economic miracle which began first to shimmer, then to shine and, by the end of the Fifties, to dazzle, was partly based on *not* running a world reserve currency and *not* devoting such a high proportion of its GDP to defence even after the Allies permitted it to rearm and welcomed it into NATO in 1955. Defeat had also removed from it the burden of running a territorial empire in Europe or anywhere else. France was more analogous to the UK but did not run the franc as a world currency, always put growth ahead of deflation and devalued, almost casually, when growth was threatened.

Sterling and its rate against the dollar were treated as totemic – an indication of both national virtue and strength – by successive batches of both Labour and Conservative ministers even after the age of fixed rates finally came to an end in 1972. And not until the aftermath of the great 1976 sterling crisis was

Jim Callaghan (whose 1960s chancellorship had been blighted by trying and then failing to maintain the $2.80 rate) as Prime Minister able finally to blunt the Damoclean sterling balances once and for all.

ROBOT was a genuine turning-point in postwar British history. Had Butler been allowed by the Cabinet to put it in his March 1952 Budget, the consequences of the first bang could have been big enough:

- Opposition outrage. Resistance from some Conservative MPs and, as the relatively apolitical Salter pointed out at the time, it would only take twenty rebels to deprive the government of a majority[158] (in fact, a mere nine).
- Profound shock across the finance ministries and financial institutions of the United States, the Commonwealth and western Europe as well as the IMF.
- A plunge in the pound's value to $2.40 at least, the rate at which 'cheap sterling' was trading in New York.
- Resignations from the government which, if they had included Eden, could have ended Churchill's premiership after but a short 'innings' closed by an inglorious hit-wicket dismissal.

If, somehow, the shock across the financial membranes diminished to be followed by relatively swift adjustment and if the government, like the rate, somehow took the strain, the postwar settlement – the British New Deal – almost certainly would not have, could not have, survived. Labour Party hostility would have been guaranteed. Union antipathy would have been fierce towards the cuts required and the inflation-engendered wage claims would have overwhelmed even the accommodating Walter Monckton. The vectors of relative forces which underpinned the New Deal and prevented the more ideological from making the political weather on either front bench would have been dramatically altered.

For the consensus-as-genteel-decline school, of whom Lyttelton was the flag carrier during the ROBOT Cabinets, a dramatic change in those politico-economic vectors was exactly what Britain required. For if – and just count the *ifs* involved in the Roboteers' case – freeing the pound had triggered a big, powerful and relentless reality check, cosy wage claims, food subsidies, an over-heavy welfare state, unsustainable overseas and defence commitments and an overloaded state machine would *all* have been confronted by the time the new Queen was crowned (for King George VI had died on 6 February as Otto Clarke's first floating memo was circulating within inner Whitehall).

It is unknowable whether or not confronting so many fixations and, more than that, serious and genuine international commitment would have loosened up the possibilities with British trade, industry, finance, politics, government and society to the point where a new post-postwar settlement could be pieced together to form a platform for a true and sustained UK economic miracle. But for those like Roll and Clarke who used up much of their professional lives coping with under-resourced, overstretched gold and dollar reserves, repeated balance of payments crises and the dispiriting cycle of stop–go – as well as for those political partisans who believe that until Mrs Thatcher arrived in No. 10 romantic delusions of social cohesion and the desire for a soft life had enfeebled successive premiers of both parties – ROBOT presents a huge, retrospective and counterfactual temptation. There is also, of course, the distinct possibility that Cherwell and Gaitskell might have been right and that the impact of ROBOT would have kept the Conservatives out of power for a generation.

Even without the stimulus of a ROBOT-induced agonizing reappraisal of the cost of slaying the Beveridge giants, the incoming Conservative government felt themselves to be under huge fiscal pressure with, as we have seen, no real scope for extra tax-raising measures to ease it. The continuing need for homes and the defence spending burden of the Korean War added to the pressure. Though Labour's rearmament programme was trimmed, construction of Macmillan's new homes, weatherproofed by the great human political roof that was Winston Churchill, surged ahead. Education and health, in particular, lost out to guns and houses.[159]

There were, as so often, political and personal ironies involved here. The architect of the 1944 Education Act, Rab Butler, did not lift a finger to help the hapless Minister of Education, Florence Horsbrugh, finance the implementation of his great programme. Churchill did not warm to Horsbrugh.[160] Nor did he particularly warm to the educational theme. So, as journalist and welfare historian Nick Timmins put it, 'it was Macmillan's houses that were built not Horsbrugh's schools. Virtually Butler's first act as Chancellor was to declare a moratorium on school building, and Horsbrugh spent much of her three years repeatedly fighting off a series of Treasury proposals to raise the school entry age to six, to drop the school leaving age back to fourteen, and to reintroduce school fees in all state schools or, failing that, to charge those staying on beyond school leaving age.'[161]

Churchill's dismissive and doubtful attitude towards 'the dedicated but uninspiring' Horsbrugh, as Colville described her,[162] and to secondary education for all was captured in an aside to his doctor, Lord Moran, in February

1953 after Horsbrugh had tried to economize on adult education the previous year:

[P]oor old Florence Horsbrugh has been making all the educational world her enemy. She wanted a reduction of 10 per cent in the grants for adult education. All to save £250,000 out of £2,000 million [in fact, the proposed cut was £25,000[163]]. Besides, these are the very people who ought to be helped – because they are helping themselves, far more than a stodgy boy of fourteen, sulkily doing his lessons.[164]

As a result of this hugely unequal line-up of disdainful Prime Minister and absent-parent Chancellor (Attlee's Minister of Education, George Tomlinson, went so far as to accuse Butler, father of the 1944 Education Act, of the 'murder of his own child'[165]), school building to house the postwar baby boom came to a halt, and pupil–teacher ratios in primary schools declined in 1953–4. At the other end of the process, the total of university students fell from 85,000 in 1950 to 82,000 in 1954.[166] Not until a strong-minded minister, David Eccles, succeeded Horsbrugh in October 1954 and remade the case for education as a national investment rather than a taxpayer burden, did matters improve.

Churchill, however, did have more of a feel for social security, taking great pride in his part as a builder, with Asquith and Lloyd George, of the 'New Liberal' welfare state, and he carried with him from those days his favourite formulation that 'the magic of averages' must be brought to 'the rescue of millions'.[167] In his last premiership, however, the Old Man was rather better at the verbal magic than the dry statistics – 'He had the phrases but no longer the facts.'[168] In this, there was a period of consolidation and relative stability during the Churchill twilight. Butler commissioned a review of the National Health Service, but he resisted the suggestion from Peter Thorneycroft, his fellow economic minister as President of the Board of Trade, that the inquiry should be primarily directed at cost savings and the further suggestion that it should embrace social services as a whole. Butler was determined that the Conservative government should not be seen as planning a destructive assault on the welfare state.[169] The force-field of the British New Deal was at work once more.

There were, however, retreats from the Beveridge blueprint partly because Sir William had been over-optimistic in his forecasts of how his schemes and the financing of them would work out. For example the ultimate provider of the social-security safety net, the National Assistance Board, found far more people fell into its mesh than anticipated because the benefits paid out under the national insurance schemes were insufficiently high. 'From 842,000 clients in July 1948 [when it replaced the old Poor Law regime], the National Assistance Board found itself with a million on its books by 1949 and 1,800,000 by 1954 . . .'[170]

Health costs, too, proved more of a problem than early forecasts suggested. Nye Bevan, who bemoaned the initial bill for the 'cascades' of medicine pouring down British throats now that it was free, believed none the less that once the catching-up period following decades of deprivation was over, the budgetary pressure would ease.[171] Not all his colleagues agreed and, as early as 1950, a Cabinet Committee chaired by Attlee himself was put in place to try to stem the flow;[172] and the great political crisis surrounding the 1951 Budget, which precipitated Bevan's resignation (he was, by this time, Minister of Labour) arose from Chancellor Gaitskell insisting that the principle of a National Health Service that was free at the point of delivery should be breached with the limited introduction of charging for part of the cost of dental treatment, spectacles and prescriptions.[173] Harold Wilson, President of the Board of Trade, and John Freeman, junior minister at Supply, joined Bevan in resigning in April 1951.[174]

It was the same combination of cascading medicine and the need to make financial space for rearmament that caused the incoming Conservatives to look for substantial health savings. The NHS was – and has remained – the most popular of the reforms implemented by the Attlee administration ('The people have willed it; therefore, they must have it,' as the *laissez-faire* Enoch Powell, a future Health Minister, liked to put it[175]); by the mid-1950s it was 'rapidly proving to be *the* real success of the Attlee government'.[176]

In March 1952 Harry Crookshank, Churchill's first Minister of Health, unveiled the legislation needed to implement extra charges. (Crookshank combined the job with leading the House of Commons, an unsatisfactory arrangement which Churchill soon ended by appointing Iain Macleod as Minister of Health in May 1952 after a mere two years in the Commons – he'd heard Macleod attack the titanic Bevan to great effect during the March debate.)[177] Crookshank had no feel for health policy, and did not spend much time in the Ministry,[178] but at least under him it had the seat in the Cabinet it deserved. His performance in Parliament was interesting, however, because he claimed the raising of the prescription charge and the imposition of a new one for dental treatment was merely extending a process begun by Labour, arguing that the NHS, in whose creation the Conservatives had played an important part in coalition days, would be in danger if the country's economy were not restored – a nice example of the kind of partisanship-within-consensus which gives so much of that great debate its life and piquancy. Crookshank even adapted Bevan's metaphor, claiming that Nye's ceaseless cascade of medicine had become a Niagara Falls.[179]

In those days of reticence and closed government, the protagonists in even the bigger rows about spending cuts did not leak selectively to arouse interest groups and backbenchers in a manner likely to help see off the Treasury – part of the British political routine since the mid-1970s. If they had, lurid stories could have been written about the NHS being about to bleed to death within weeks of Butler becoming Chancellor because, as Nick Timmins has itemized,

no fewer than sixteen different cuts in the service or new charges were being considered by the Treasury and by Harry Crookshank . . . These ranged from prescription and further dental charges (on top of the charges for dentures which Labour had introduced), through 'hotel' charges for hospital stays, ambulance charges, restrictions on the type of drugs available, to extending pay beds or even to abolishing NHS dental and opticians' services entirely. Each of these, save for the 1s. prescription charge and the new dental charges, foundered.[180]

A combination of New Deal pressures and administrative practicalities limited the Conservative recutting of the jewel in Labour's welfare crown.

The Treasury spent much of the 1950s seething about the prices and the procedures of the British way of health. On top of the failure to recoup still more money and to remake the structures, they faced a wage and salary spiral when the Danckwerts Committee showed that general practitioners required £40m in back pay (10 per cent of the current health budget) and a new pay structure as they had been underpaid since vesting day on 5 July 1948. Though it was the GPs' own fault (their pay 'had been fixed on the basis of their pre-war tax returns; and, given that family doctors were no more honest with the taxman than anyone else, it had been fixed rather low'[181]), the government felt obliged to pay up.[182]

This world of cascading medicine and cash could not go on. At the end of 1952 the Treasury insisted the NHS be subject to a rigorous review. A committee was established in January 1953 under the Cambridge economist Claude Guillebaud, who had been Macleod's undergraduate supervisor. It ground on for nearly three years, during which the Treasury could but fret and wait. Yet, as the technical work undertaken by Guillebaud, Brian Abel-

Smith and Richard Titmuss eventually showed, Butler's axe may have been blunted, but health spending in proportional terms fell from 3.75 per cent of GDP in 1949–50 to 3.24 per cent in 1953–4.[183]

To the Treasury's dismay, the Guillebaud Report came out firmly against extra health service charges. One reason for this was the lack of hospital building, another casualty of the housing drive. The Ministry of Health calculated that capital spending in the late 1930s was three times higher than in 1952–3, if adjustments were made for inflation.[184] In preventive health, epidemiologists Richard Doll and Bradford Hill made their great breakthrough in 1950[185] when they established the link between smoking and lung cancer, but ministers did nothing serious to curb the spread of the weed in the 1950s, partly because, as Iain Macleod admitted privately in January 1954, 'we all know that the welfare state and much else is based on [taxes raised from] tobacco smoking'.[186] Tobacco duty, as Macmillan – by this time Chancellor – reminded his colleagues in May 1956, brought the Exchequer £670m a year.[187]

Another less-public aspect of social policy in the Fifties was just how similarly the parties viewed what was then called coloured immigration from the British Commonwealth. This is best described as a consensus-in-embryo as it did not result in restrictive legislation until the early 1960s, by which time it was a matter of contention between, rather than consensus among, the parties.

In *Never Again* I traced just how close the second Attlee government came to imposing immigration controls. After a Cabinet Committee had sat under the Home Secretary, Chuter Ede, the Cabinet on 12 February 1951 accepted the Ede group's advice that such controls would have serious consequences for Britain's economic partners and its colonies, as well as for citizens of the Irish Republic. (Eire had shed its 'Free State' within the Commonwealth status and become a republic in 1949. Irish citizens enjoyed unrestricted access to the UK.) But the Colonial Office was instructed to keep a close eye on the pace of immigration with a view to possible legislation to curb it.[188] It was thought that by 1950–51 about 5,000 New Commonwealth immigrants had arrived in the UK, the bulk of them from the West Indies.[189]

Neither the work of GEN 325, Ede's committee, nor the Cabinet's contemplation of possible legislation reached the domain of Parliament, press or public. Mel Risebrow, who was one of the first historians to examine the files, noted that the 'secrecy surrounding the work and findings of GEN 325 was absolute. Certainly the press was oblivious to its existence, and no subsequent literature has been found to suggest that any knowledge of it had emerged until the records became available in 1982.'[190]

I talked to Sir Alec Atkinson, the civil servant who had taken the minutes at the GEN 325 meetings, and he recalled that it convened in an 'era of absolute security (except in the sense of Burgess and Maclean, but we did not know about them then). Nothing leaked from the Cabinet committees in those days. We would have been very surprised if it had.'[191]

The privacy of these late Ede/Attlee deliberations is very important because, as immigration historian Randall Hansen has noted, the archives of the Attlee administrations 'reveal an approach and attitude similar to those of subsequent Conservative governments . . .'[192] Yet by the time the Macmillan government brought forth legislation to restrict immigration in 1961, Labour was bitterly and eloquently opposed to curbs. Gaitskell, a Commonwealth man to his last fibre, declared that with citizens of southern Ireland beyond the reach of the Commonwealth Immigrants Bill (originally they were included), 'all pretence has gone. It is a plain anti-Commonwealth measure in theory and it is a plain anti-colour measure in practice.'[193]

To be fair to Gaitskell, one of the most powerful restraints holding back the Churchill and Eden governments (a Bill reached draft form in 1955[194]) was the political difficulty of distinguishing between white would-be immigrants from the old dominions, and non-white from the newly independent Commonwealth countries such as India, Pakistan and Ceylon and from British colonies in the West Indies and Africa. Conservative ministers simply could not contemplate barring Canadians, Australians and New Zealanders with the pull of emigrant 'kith and kin' so strong.[195]

In fact, the British Nationality Act of 1948, framed in response to changes in Canada's citizenship laws in 1946 (which threatened the seamlessness of the rights of entry to the UK of Commonwealth and Empire subjects of the Crown), was passed as 'the institutional expression of the primary relationship between the UK and the Old Dominions . . . because politicians and bureaucrats believed that migration to the UK would be dominated by British subjects from the Dominions'.[196] But the old troopship, the *Empire Windrush*, sailing up through the summer mist of the Thames estuary to Tilbury after bashing across the Atlantic from Jamaica on 22 June 1948 with 492 official migrants (several of whom had served in Britain with the RAF during the war) and eighteen stowaways,[197] began changing the whole nature of the politics of immigration before the ink on the British Nationality Act was dry.

It was the increasing though still small flow of immigration from the West

Indies (stimulated by Caribbean unemployment and, from 1952, restrictive legislation in the USA – till then the West Indian destination of choice[198]) that led Attlee, Churchill and Eden to set up Cabinet Committees, ministerial groups and interdepartmental working parties between 1950 and 1956. In Hansen's words:

As in 1950, it was the Old Commonwealth that continued in 1956 to work against ending the right of free entry . . . [successive Colonial and Commonwealth secretaries] with the support of the Cabinet, would not countenance restrictions on the Old Dominions. Migration controls were thus delayed [until 1962], and British multiculturalism furthered by an elite attachment to the Old Commonwealth in the context of selective, but not the less genuine, opposition to racially discriminatory restrictions.[199]

Yet for a time in the early 1950s it looked within Whitehall as if restrictive legislation might well happen. If it had, the Labour front bench might have been in an awkward position. Even by 1961, had the work of GEN 325 and the Attlee Cabinet's 1951 thinking been in the public domain, it would have been difficult for Gaitskell to mount such a principled opposition to the Bill the Macmillan government placed before Parliament.

Within governing circles Oliver Lyttelton, the Colonial Secretary 1951–5, was convinced that the increasing flow of the Queen's Caribbean subjects (up from 2,000 in 1953 to 11,000 in 1954 and 27,500 in 1955[200] with travel costs falling, the British economy beginning to boom and the demand for labour rising) would soon lead to curbs. In 1955, by this time out of office, he told a Kenyan businessman: 'You are quite right about the colour problem in England. If it is not tackled, which it will be, we may easily get a situation of great proportions in twenty-five years.'[201]

The most persistent voice inside Whitehall in favour of immediate immigration controls was that of Lord Salisbury. Like Lyttelton, Salisbury foresaw serious trouble ahead without such controls and, unlike Alan Lennox-Boyd (Lyttelton's successor as Colonial Secretary) or Lord Swinton (Ismay's successor as Commonwealth Secretary), discriminating between the white and black sons and daughters of Empire did not cause him difficulty. Salisbury told Lyttelton in the spring of 1954 that the chief cause 'of this sudden inflow of blacks is of course the Welfare State. So long as the antiquated rule obtains that any British subject can come into this country without any limitation at all, these people will pour in to take advantage of our social services and other amenities, and we shall have no protection at all.' Salisbury argued that without such 'protection', the problem of immigration could become 'quite unmanageable in 20 or 30 years time. We should recognize that this coloured problem is potentially of a fundamental nature for the future of our country.'[202]

It is, at first glance, surprising that the argument did not tilt the Lyttelton/Salisbury way as Churchill's feelings were strongly in their direction. Just as he was distressed by the break-up of the British Empire, he was, for all his imperial romance, deeply disturbed about its black or brown members coming to the mother country. Perhaps if his premiership had lasted a little longer, there would have been legislation. As Macmillan noted in his diary for 20 January 1955: 'More discussion about the West Indian immigrants. A Bill is being drafted – but it's not an easy problem. P.M. thinks "Keep England White" a good slogan!'[203]

The Bill was not ready until June 1955,[204] two months after Churchill had reluctantly retired. Shortly before leaving No. 10, Churchill told Ian Gilmour, the editor/proprietor of the *Spectator*, that the question of immigration from the West Indies 'is the most important subject facing this country, but I cannot get any of my ministers to take any notice'.[205] Earlier, in 1954, he had told Sir Hugh Foot, the Governor of Jamaica, over lunch at Chequers, that if coloured immigration was not curbed, Britain 'would have a magpie society: that would never do'. (Foot was appalled at the Prime Minister's attitude and choice of words.)[206] Perhaps, as his Foreign Affairs Private Secretary, Anthony Montague Browne, later told Andrew Roberts, it was, on this question as others, a matter of Churchill being 'simply too tired to deal with the immigration problem. He could only concentrate on a few big issues at a time – like the Russians – and the rest of the time he could only give a steer and not see it through.'[207]

It is important to remember, too, the novelty of the problem for Churchill in the early Fifties. For the late Forties story of imperial population movement was chiefly one of emigration from the UK to the colonies and dominions. Between 1946 and 1952, about 50,000 left the UK for Southern Rhodesia alone. But the bulk of the 720,000 who emigrated between 1946 and 1950 went to the old dominions, Australia especially, whose governments offered subsidized sea passages for families granted permission well into the 1960s. In fact, the net flow of UK migration was an outward one for the quarter century after the war.[208]

In the early 1950s immigration was one of those questions which rose in importance in a way ministers had not anticipated when the Conservatives returned to power. There was no mention of it in the Party's manifesto, the theme of which was the removal of existing state restrictions rather than the imposition of new ones.[209] The manifesto, however, was no clarion call for a general roll-back of the state despite nationalization being the key area of non-consensus between the two main parties. As Henry Pelling noted, the incoming government 'was pledged to "simplify the administrative machine", to repeal the Iron and Steel Act and to give private [road] hauliers the chance to return to business'.[210] Steel had been the most bitterly fought and, for fear of the House of Lords blocking it, the last of the Attlee nationalization measures and the only one to break into the core private sector.[211] One of the Churchill Cabinet's first acts was to prevent the nationalized Iron and Steel Corporation, which had only come into being that year, from integrating and refashioning the structures and finances of the private companies, which would have made a future break-up and sell-off more difficult.[212]

The next steps were far more difficult. Framing the legislation tested the Parliamentary draftsmen and their political customers partly because the lead minister, Duncan Sandys at Supply, wanted a Bill that would effectively make it impossible for a future Labour government to take the foundries and the mills back into public ownership. When this proved impossible[213] and it was plain to Sandys and the Cabinet by the summer of 1952 that returning the firms to the private sector would take 'some years',[214] the reality of the slimline Conservative majority and the real possibility of a Labour resumption of power – the shadow of being on political probation, as it were – fell across the Cabinet Room causing the ever independent Salisbury to urge a change of approach. The steel question provoked one of the many resignation threats from 'Old Sarum',[215] as Churchill liked to call him, particularly at moments of exasperation. Salisbury, for his part, was pretty exasperated with Churchill over what Kathy Burk has neatly called 'the first privatisation'. 'I remain opposed and rather depressed,' he wrote to Swinton after a particularly difficult Cabinet meeting in July 1952. 'I find myself more and more out of sympathy with Winston, who seems to me purely out to reverse what has been done, instead of trying to create a new and healthier atmosphere of co-operation in meeting our difficulties.'[216]

On 14 July Salisbury told the Cabinet the 'wiser course would be for the Government to seek every means of finding some base of agreement, within the steel industry and between the Parties, which would take the industry out of politics'[217] and he threatened to resign if his colleagues did not follow his advice.[218] Old Sarum's threat worked. The following day the Cabinet agreed that the 'Minister of Supply should revise the draft White Paper so as to lay greater emphasis on the proposals for the future supervision of the industry and less on the proposals for returning it to private ownership'.[219]

As a result, a hybrid solution was reached. In 1953 a new Iron and Steel Board came into existence to supervise the national capacity on behalf of the public with a particular eye, as Sandys told the Commons during the passage of the legislation, on 'prices, development and raw materials'.[220] Senior figures from the trade union movement sat on the board, one of whom, Lincoln Evans, took its vice-chairmanship.[221] It took a while for the private sector to pick up the ingots. Not until the merchant bankers Morgan Grenfell got into their stride, underwriting the sale of the English Steel Corporation's stocks in May 1955, was real momentum acquired. By 1957, '86% of the productive capacity of the iron and steel industry had been denationalised'.[222] There was only one big company that failed to get away – and stayed in public hands until the privatized companies were all renationalized back to join it when Labour, fuelled by its large 1966 majority, undid the 1953 Act (and Salisbury's compromise) with its own legislation. This was Richard Thomas and Baldwin, 'which was known to be considering a £100 million steel works and strip mill development programme; as a result, it would be impossible for some years for investors to check its earning power against actual results . . .'[223]

Deregulating the lorries was hardly the stuff of political legend either. Its faltering progress was partly due to a shortage of cash in that part of the transport sector. It was complicated, too, by plans for a £4m annual levy on road hauliers to be paid to the British Railways element of the British Transport Commission in return for the extra competition to which it would be subjected when BTC lost its lorries to the private sector.[224] Salter, with some justification, told the Cabinet Committee on Transport Policy that the calculations involved in assessing the railway's loss to the newly unleashed knights of the road would be 'intricate and progressively unreal'.[225]

The Transport Bill, which emerged after a near chaotic process in which Lord Leathers utterly failed to achieve the co-ordination for which his 'overlordship' was intended,[226] satisfied nobody. The idea of a levy was abandoned by the Cabinet on 29 October 1952,[227] but it was a privatization that still did not fly. Over 90 per cent of the British Road Services (BRS) vehicles were to be sold off: when sales began in January 1954, 32,500 vehicles were available plus their depots. In the first six months, a mere 6,000 were taken by the private sector.[228] In 1955 it was announced that BRS would be able to keep sufficient vehicles to operate its long-distance routes[229] and its lorries remained a part of the furniture of British trunk roads well into the 1960s.

When it came to extending consumer choice, it turned out to be far easier to create new private assets than to free up state-owned ones. For the great private enterprise success of the last Churchill government was an activity of which there was not a whisper in the 1951 manifesto – commercial television. Yet, just under four years after Churchill returned to No. 10 and five months after he left it, a new force burst into British life which, bit-by-bit, night-by-night, began to change it for ever. And 'burst' is the right verb because the first ever British television advert came out of a starburst at precisely 8.12 p.m. on the evening of 22 September 1955 when Associated Rediffusion began transmitting to the London area.

Viewers saw a block of ice standing in a stream with a tube of toothpaste thrust into it at an angle delivering its product on to a toothbrush at its base. 'It's tingling fresh. It's fresh as ice. It's Gibbs SR toothpaste,' declared the cultured voice of Alex Mackintosh (ironically, a BBC presenter).[230] The man who wrote the words, Brian Palmer, was watching on his newly acquired TV set at home. He had no idea his words would become such an historic piece of advertising copy – the Gibbs ad was selected from twenty-four contestants by drawing lots.[231] Palmer leapt from his chair and danced round the room crying, 'Wow! It's my ad!'[232]

Mr Palmer's ad and its successors wowed the British public more than anything else the Churchill government did and affected their consumption patterns more directly than a string of Budgets. Yet the making of the Television Act 1954, which gave Brian Palmer and his block of ice their fifteen seconds of fame, is one of the most peculiar stories of early-Fifties law making. I suspect that long after the name of Selwyn Lloyd has ceased to be associated with the Suez crisis of 1956 (when he was Foreign Secretary) or the 'Night of the Long Knives' of 1962 (by which time he was Chancellor of the Exchequer) when Macmillan figuratively butchered a third of his Cabinet, Lloyd most prominent among them, social, media and economic historians of postwar Britain will keep his memory alive as the politician who made toothpaste on TV possible so soon after 1945 (of course, the BBC's monopoly of television broadcasting would have been broken at some point).

Lloyd, by background, was not a natural standard-bearer for the televisual advance of Mammon. There was much religious non-conformity in his professional middle-class Liverpool upbringing, but there was a powerful Liberal streak too, much of which remained with him when, fresh from a war which saw him rise to the rank of brigadier and a spell with Montgomery, he won the Wirral for the Conservatives in the 1945 general election.[233] A natural staff officer, in peace as in war, Lloyd was quickly useful to the pair of key remakers of the Conservative policy and organization, Butler and Woolton. And it was their patronage which resulted in Lloyd becoming the Tory member of the Beveridge Committee on the future of broadcasting[234] announced by Herbert Morrison on 12 May 1949 for the purpose of considering 'the constitution, control and finance and other general aspects of the sound and television broadcasting services of the United Kingdom ... and to advise on the conditions under which these services and wire broadcasting should be conducted after the 31st December 1951'.[235]

Two things, in retrospect, strike one as extraordinary about Beveridge on broadcasting: first, the degree to which radio dominated the committee's agenda and how little television featured; and that Lloyd was alone in pressing the case for the BBC's monopoly to be broken. This became his passion, rather than simply his position, because of the arch defender of monopoly, Lord Reith, whose own passionate evidence to the Beveridge Committee in 1950 seared him. Reith declared that:

It was the brute force of monopoly that enabled the BBC to become what it did; and to do what it did; that made possible policy in which moral responsibility – moral in the broadest way; intellectual and ethical – ranked high. If there is to be competition it will be of cheapness not goodness. There is no reality in the moral disadvantages and dangers of monopoly as applied to Broadcasting, it is in fact a potent incentive.[236]

Ironically, in old age Lloyd confessed that one of the great disappointments of his life was how independent television turned out.[237] But, at the time, even a trip to America to experience sponsored and commercial television did not persuade him that there might be something in the cheapness versus goodness argument advanced by Reith. His dislike of monopoly trumped all. As Lloyd later told TV producer and Labour politician Phillip Whitehead, 'I got more and more worried about there being so much power in the hands of one man or a group of people, and when Lord Reith talked about the brute force of monopoly I thought it was wrong.'[238]

Lloyd's minority dissenting report attached to the main body of Beveridge when it appeared in January 1950 was well written and strong on both detail and philosophy,[239] as was his speech in July 1951 during the Commons debate on the future of broadcasting.[240] His biographer, Richard Thorpe, reckoned that: 'Arguably Selwyn never left a more important legacy than his Minority Report. Its tone of quiet yet forceful reasonableness, based on sound, practical first-hand evidence allied to the remorseless logic of a lawyer-politician made the document the standard under which the Young Turks fought.'[241] As the official historian of the BBC, Asa Briggs, expressed it, Lloyd's minority report was 'the real dynamite'[242] which, within four years, had completely exploded the central finding of the majority Beveridge Report that the BBC's monopoly should continue.[243]

Breaking the BBC monopoly found some support on the Labour benches, but the 'Young Turks' who made the running were Conservatives and the party set up a Committee on Broadcasting in February 1951 whose charter was Lloyd's minority report. Younger MPs such as Ian Orr-Ewing and John Profumo were to be especially important in running the argument when the Conservatives returned to power and Lloyd became a minister of state at the Foreign Office and bound, therefore, by collective responsibility.[244]

The change of government did not necessarily mean a stronger or fairer wind would blow in favour of the anti-monopolists. As Lord Orr-Ewing recalled nearly twenty years later:

When we first became a government in 1951 we were unable to move nearly as fast as we had hoped. We had, after all, been elected on 'Set the People Free', and that first Christmas rationing was tighter than ever ... Here was a field in television where we could go and where we could introduce some competition. We were prepared to give up sound [the BBC's monopoly was not broken there until 1973[245]] because we felt then that television was a really important medium of the future with a tremendous growth. Many of us felt that the BBC was going far too slowly in grasping the opportunities in television which existed.[246]

Worse still for the 'Young Turks', several of the Tory grandees were against them and only Lord Woolton seriously with them. Despite the Shadow Cabinet being 'divided on the issue', Woolton, when preparing to speak in the Lords debate on Beveridge, had real concerns in private about the dangers of monopoly but, in public, carefully suggested that the development of VHF (Very High Frequency) transmissions meant that, in future, more television broadcasting stations would be possible and he could see 'no reason why such stations should not be installed and supported by local interests'.[247]

The younger anti-monopolists like Orr-Ewing knew Woolton was 'a staunch ally' and easily decoded his signal during the Lords Debate.

... it was quite clear that he was in favour of breaking the BBC television monopoly. On the other side ... there was Lord Salisbury and Anthony Eden, both of whom I think had considerable reservations ... We had to fight the BBC, we had to fight the newspapers, we had to fight the bishops, and last but not least we had to fight the films ... because they thought [with very good reason, as it turned out] that if television was more successful ... then people would stay away from the cinemas ...[248]

It's intriguing that Orr-Ewing did not mention Churchill – perhaps the trickiest patch of the battleground for independent television as he disliked both the BBC *and* the medium of television.

Jack Profumo could recall with great vividness fifty years later how difficult it was to try to persuade the Old Man that TV was the coming medium (Profumo had to do this as the Conservative Party's Head of Broadcasting); of how Churchill would be both unusually silent and immensely courteous when he did speak if you were telling him things he didn't wish to hear.[249] Churchill was persuaded in 1954 to have a trial run in great secrecy in No. 10 before the camera. He was awful. He addressed it like a public meeting, referring to 'this thing they call Tee Vee'. When the film was shown to him, Churchill loathed what he saw and said he should never have agreed to appear.[250] As Jock Colville explained: 'He hated the lights, he hated the glare and he hated the heat.'[251]

Churchill also loathed the BBC. He raged about it when his beloved Violet Bonham Carter, one of its most distinguished governors in the early postwar, visited him at Chequers a few weeks after his stroke in 1953:

At moments he became suddenly and unreasonably angry – like a violent child. He blazed forth against the BBC. 'I hate the BBC. It kept me off the air for 11 years [during the 1930s]. It is run by reds –' Abuse of Reith followed – who cld certainly not be described as a 'red' ... 'The BBC behaved very badly over the chimpanzee in the Coronation* – publicizing it.' 'It was not the BBC but your friend Ld Beaverbrook who splashed it. I saw it first in the *Sunday Express*.' ... 'Well I don't care tuppence about this business of Sponsored Television but I am not going to have anyone forced to vote for it. *There must be a free vote.*' I was glad to hear this – glad also when he said, 'Do you know that ever since Anthony went sick [Eden had a disastrous operation on his biliary tract on 12 April 1953[252]] he has not expressed an opinion of any kind on politics or foreign policy. No message has been received from him of any kind, except one sentence, "No sponsored Television."'[253]

But sponsored television there was. Lloyd lobbied discreetly from within[254] and a hugely effective pressure group led by a brilliant ex-BBC man, Norman

---

* The chimp was called J. Fred Muggs; it appeared on US television during the commercial breaks in their coverage of the event – an enormity seized upon by the BBC's defenders.

Collins, from without (it was Collins who coined the phrase 'independent television').[255]

The Conservative Party conference in October 1953 passed a motion in favour of commercial television.[256] A Government White Paper outlining a regulated rather than a sponsored system was published in November.[257] Yet more high quality salvoes were fired by the good and the great (who split on the question) across the floor of the House of Lords.[258] The Television Bill was placed before Parliament in March 1954. On 30 July 1954 it became law. On 4 August 1954 the new regulatory body, the Independent Television Authority, met for the first time under the chairmanship of the high-minded patrician and cultural connoisseur Kenneth Clark.[259] Morrison pledged that Labour would dismantle the whole apparatus if they won the next election.[260] In May 1955 Labour lost it, and Britain was made safe for commercial television. It is most unlikely that Churchill watched it. A few days after retiring from the premiership he wrote to Earl De La Warr, who as Postmaster-General had piloted the television legislation through the House of Lords: 'I am no enthusiast for the TV age, in which I fear mass thought and actions will be taken charge of by machinery, both destructive and distracting.'[261] The Old Man had no liking for what he called 'this age of clatter and buzz, of gape and gloat',[262] but he had some feel for what its new technologies might bring, whether they were the television or the hydrogen bomb.

Early-Fifties Britain, however, had quite a feel for him and his government. No doubt anxieties would have arisen had the general public been aware of his inability to grapple with the breadth of problems affecting the administration as his ministers were. Had he seriously uprooted the postwar settlement, the acceptability of his last ministry would have undoubtedly been jeopardized. As it was, the Conservatives increased their electoral popularity in the early 1950s. They took Sunderland South from Labour in May 1953, the first time a sitting government had taken a seat from its opponents in a by-election since 1924,[263] and went into the 1955 general election with one more than their tally of seats in 1951.[264] Churchill might not have entirely understood early-Fifties Britain but, if the electoral arithmetic was a guide, early-Fifties Britain was noticeably at ease with him.

Churchill found increasing solace in the midst of the baffling modern age from one ancient British institution in particular, to which his devotion, if anything, reached its zenith in those twilight days in government – the monarchy. The planning of the Coronation stirred every romantic fibre in his considerable frame about royalty, pageantry, the Empire and his 'island race' behaving in his imagination as he liked them to – jolly, loyal and united from the humble cottage to the greatest stately home. And, above all, he adored the young Queen. His private secretary, Jock Colville, had no doubt 'that at a respectful distance he fell in love with the Queen'.[265] One of the greatest treats of his last premiership were his weekly audiences at the Palace. They lasted longer and longer.[266] The Queen enjoyed them too; they were 'always such fun', she said.[267]

On the night of 3 January 1953, aboard the *Queen Mary* somewhere off Newfoundland, on the way to New York and Churchill's meeting with the soon-to-be-inaugurated President Eisenhower, Jock Colville sat up with the Old Man after a good dinner in the great Cunarder's famous Veranda Grill and 'fired at him about thirty questions which he might be asked at his press conference on arrival in New York. He scintillated in his replies, e.g.

'Qn: How do you justify such great expenditure on the Coronation of your Queen, when England is in such financial straits?

'An: Everybody likes to wear a flower when he goes to see his girl.'[268]

5

Coronation, Kingdom and Empire

'I cannot forget that I was crowned Queen of the United Kingdom of Great Britain and Northern Ireland. Perhaps this Jubilee is a time to remind ourselves of the benefits which union has conferred, at home and in our international dealings, on the inhabitants of all parts of this United Kingdom.'

HM Queen Elizabeth II addressing both Houses of Parliament, 4 May 1977.[1]

'She had a love affair with the country.'

Lord Charteris, former Private Secretary to the Queen, undated.[2]

'Do such things as "national cultures" really exist?'   George Orwell, 1944.[3]

'The Prime Minister said that it remained for him to wish his colleagues all good fortune in the difficult but hopeful situation which they had to face. He trusted that they would be enabled to further the progress already made in rebuilding the domestic stability and economic strength of the United Kingdom and in weaving still more closely the threads which bound together the countries of the Commonwealth, or, as he still preferred to call it, the Empire.'

Winston Churchill's final remarks at his last Cabinet, 5 April 1955.[4]

The first days of June 1953 were deep-etched in the memories of every six-year-old in the kingdom, one of whom was me on Coronation Day. There was the Coronation mug that came to each child free. (I never thought who paid. In my case I assume it was the Education Committee of Finchley Borough Council.) There was the visit to friends who had a television to watch the spectacle. And, with perfect timing, the news reached London that very day about Everest – the highest peak in the world scaled for the first time by a British Commonwealth expedition with a rangy New Zealander, Edmund Hillary, and a plucky, stocky Nepalese Sherpa, Tenzing, pulling off the final assault. To postwar Britons there was no question about the existence or ethicality of national identity. Britishness was beyond debate. (As a white colonial Hillary was, of course, British by association.)

It rained on Coronation Day, 2 June 1953, but that didn't matter. Rain was part of Britishness too. And the newspaper splash coverage that damp morning – 'The Crowning Glory', the *Daily Mail* called it,[5] juxtaposing the Coronation and Everest's conquering, was exactly the kind of fusion that made even a six-year-old in north London come to think quite naturally that his country was different and special.*

It's intriguing how even today the most evocative 1953 stories link monarchy, mountain and Commonwealth/Empire in a way that, for my generation, evokes an era much as does sniffing coal smoke in the chilly and damp autumn air. When Jan Morris, the only journalist with the expedition,† published her memoir *A Writer's World* in 2003[6] she recalled breaking the news of Everest being climbed to *The Times* and to the world, adding a previously untold story that only the combination of Crown, Empire and class could produce. On returning to London, the victorious Everest expedition, led by a hugely efficient army officer, Colonel John Hunt, were fêted everywhere, culminating in a very grand celebratory dinner at Lancaster House, just across Green Park from Buckingham Palace. Morris recalled how she found herself

sitting next to the major-domo of the occasion, a delightful elderly courtier of old-school charm, while opposite me sat Tenzing Norkay, away from Asia for the first time in his life. The old gentleman turned to me half-way through the meal and told me that the claret we were drinking was the last of its particularly good vintage from the cellars of Lancaster House and possibly the last anywhere in the world. He hoped I was enjoying it. I was much impressed, and looked across the table to Tenzing, who most certainly was. He had probably never tasted wine before, and he was radiant with the pride and pleasure of the occasion – a supremely stylish and exotic figure. The lackeys respectfully filled and re-filled his glass, and presently my neighbour turned to me once more. 'Oh, Mr Morris,' he said in his silvery Edwardian cadence, 'how very good it is to see that Mr Tenzing knows a decent claret when he has one.'[7]

---

* Everest had a particular resonance in our household as my uncle, George Wood-Johnson, had been a member of the unsuccessful British expedition to the mountain in 1933 (see Hugh Ruttledge, *Everest 1933* (Hodder, 1934), p. 26). He moved from Lancashire to India to become a tea-planter near Darjeeling in order to 'learn Nepali, the lingua franca of the hills, and to have an opportunity for mountaineering in the Sikkim Himalaya'.

† Morris underwent a sex-change operation in 1972, before which she was James Morris.

Tenzing, as Hillary noted, acquired something of a taste for Western affluence and was saddened in later life when his pension from the Indian government was insufficient to support such a style of life.[8]

It is difficult for a more sceptical age that neither marches to even the faintest sounds of late-imperial drum and trumpet nor expects, Bagehot-like, to be affected by the spectacle of a '*family* on the throne' bringing down 'the pride of sovereignty to the level of their own lives',[9] to appreciate how easy and natural it was to get a touch carried away in 1953. As Lord Charteris, who served the Queen in her private office for twenty-five years, put it in conversation with me in 1994:

The expectations of the monarchy were very high in 1950 . . . The stature and the position of the monarchy had made a complete recovery from the near disaster of the Abdication [of King Edward VIII in 1936]. And when in 1952 the Queen came to the throne, she was dazzling. She was radiantly beautiful, or so it seemed to me anyway, and I think it seemed to everybody . . . She was married to this marvellously attractive and dazzling Prince. And it was pretty strong magic, I can tell you. One's got to remember that Winston Churchill was old enough to be her grandfather . . . and I think she had him around her little finger. I think he was absolutely crazy in love with her.[10]

It was quite plain on that spring morning more than forty years after the event as Lord Charteris and I sat in the Royal Library at Windsor that he too was still enamoured by his former boss. But this did not disqualify him as a re-creator of the mood of 1952–3. Equally important was his careful acknowledgement that the Queen was at ease with the relative consensus within the party strife that the constitution required her to be above:

You might say that the Queen prefers a sort of consensus politics rather than a polarized one, and I suspect this is true, although I can't really speak from knowledge here [I suspected that he could – but was too polite to say so]. But if you are in the Queen's position, you are the titular, the symbolic head of the country, and the less squabbling that goes on in that country, obviously the more convenient and the more comfortable you feel. Therefore, I suspect – and I think it's only natural – that politics which are very polarized are very uncomfortable to the sovereign. I think it must be so.[11]

At the time Edward Shils and Michael Young depicted the Coronation service in a deeply consensual fashion as

a series of ritual affirmations of the moral values necessary to a well-governed and good society. The key to the Coronation service is the Queen's promise to abide by the moral standards of society. The whole service reiterates their supremacy above the personality of the Sovereign. In her assurance that she will observe the canons of mercy, charity, justice and protective affection, she acknowledges and submits to their power. When she does this, she symbolically proclaims her community with her subjects who, in the ritual ... commit themselves to obedience within the society constituted by the moral rules which she has agreed to uphold.[12]

Sceptical early-twenty-first-century eyes reading that passage may suspect that this was Shils and Young writing cod anthropology for the purpose of sending up an excessively deferential society mired in what Walter Bagehot called the 'cake of custom',[13] its people the prisoners of ancient atavistic tradition and ritual. For example during a symposium organized by the Churchill Archives Centre in Cambridge on 14 January 2004 to commemorate Michael Young (who had died in 2002 and whose papers were deposited there), Piers Brendon, former archivist at Churchill and a scholar of strong republican sympathies, raised exactly this point. How could a pair of top-flight social scientists have failed to see through the whole show?

Shils, as he made plain in a famous article on 'British Intellectuals in the Mid-Twentieth Century' which appeared in *Encounter* in April 1955, highlighted the alienation from their country felt by many on the left in the 1930s, contrasting their 'repugnance for its dreary, unjust and uncultured society, with its impotent ruling class and its dull and puritanical middle classes'[14] with 'the forties and early fifties ... [when] ... [d]eeply critical voices became rare'.[15] Michael Young had himself been a member of the Communist Party of Great Britain in the 1930s,[16] but by early 1945, when he joined the Labour Party Research Department, he was firmly in the democratic-socialist camp.

In a near-perfect illustration of the shift in opinions and attitudes described by Shils (which should not be exaggerated – the Communist Party of Great Britain retained both a sizeable membership and the loyalty of many impressive intellectuals certainly up to the Soviet invasion of Hungary in 1956), Michael Young's views on the shared values of British politics and culture verged on the elegiac as Attlee's government pushed on with its social and economic reforms in the late 1940s. Though Young became increasingly uneasy with the emphasis on large state corporations as the bringers of both economic efficiency and social justice, as his *Small Man, Big World* pamphlet of 1948 made plain, that same document revealed the deeper thinking that underlay Young's view of the polity over which the young Queen was soon to preside as its head of state. The UK, he wrote, 'is already the most mature democracy in the world, in its traditions as well as in its constitution. Tolerance, the very sinew of democracy, is part of our character. We have a generally accepted code of decency. Our sense of humour is a deadly barb for autocrats. They must be used to the utmost extent so that we pioneer again, not in the world of power and wealth, but in the new frontiers of the human spirit.'[17]

Young, when turning his attention with Shils to the Coronation five years later, couched their anatomy of its rituals within a treatment of deep consensus Britain, which went beyond the politico-economic component examined in Chapters 1 and 2. 'We do not claim', they wrote, 'that men always act in conformity with their sense of values, nor do we claim that the measure of agreement in any society, even the most consensual, is anywhere near complete . . . Yet inter-twined with . . . conflicts are agreements strong enough to keep society generally peaceful and coherent.'[18]

They plainly thought that early postwar Britain possessed in abundance the moral values which bonded society – 'generosity, charity, loyalty, justice in the distribution of opportunities and rewards, reasonable respect for authority, the dignity of the individual and his right to freedom'[19] – and that the Coronation symbolized their conversion into something of a 'sacred form'.[20]

After tracing the impact of the Second World War as a generator of social solidarity, they noted that the Attlee government's 'concern for the underprivileged . . . its success in avoiding the alienation of the middle and upper classes, and by the embodiment of certain prized British virtues in its leaders', had boosted the 'moral unity of British society to a remarkably high level' and helped to complete the return of 'alienated and cantankerous' intellectuals to 'the national fold'. They added full employment and 'a growing repugnance for the Soviet Union' to the mix before concluding that the 'central fact is that Britain came into the Coronation period with a degree of moral consensus such as few large societies have ever manifested'.[21]

The Coronation ceremony, in the Shils–Young analysis, represented a symbolic expression of this huge claim – perhaps the biggest, as well as the most unverifiable, of all the assertions and counter-assertions that have gone into the making of the great consensus debate. They treated the Christmas 1953 readers of the *Sociological Review* to a step-by-step analysis of each bit of morality-affirming ritual:

The Recognition: When the Archbishop [of Canterbury] presents the Queen to the four sides of the 'theatre' [i.e. Westminster Abbey], he is asking the assembly to reaffirm their allegiance to her not so much as an individual as the incumbent of an office of authority charged with moral responsibility . . .

The Oath: The Queen is asked whether she will solemnly promise and swear to govern the people of the United Kingdom and the Dominions and other possessions and territories in accordance with their respective laws and customs.

The Queen undoubtedly took – and takes – very seriously all she undertook to do on that day.

But according to Anglican legend, solemnity might have been a bit of a problem. The cause? The Bishop of Durham, Michael Ramsey, who, like previous princes of the northern church, had the job of 'standing at the right hand of the sovereign throughout the coronation as her chief supporter. Since this was the first coronation to be televised to a nation, Ramsey was suddenly famous among the people of England; all the more so because the vast head, baldness girt by flowing white locks, mobile expressive eyebrows and waddling gait drew the attention of millions of viewers.'[22] It was reported, according to Ramsey's biographer, Owen Chadwick, that the Queen 'begged him, during a rehearsal for the coronation, to keep his eyebrows still because they made her smile and she did not wish to smile in the wrong place'.

In the event people were impressed by the immense care Durham took over his sovereign.[23] She arrived at Westminster Abbey, made sure the train was straight, turned to her six maids-of-honour and said calmly, 'All right, girls,'[24] and got on with it. There was much dignity, no Ramsey-induced giggles and only one smile, when her husband, the Duke of Edinburgh, was the first to pay homage.[25]

For Shils and Young, the Queen's swearing of the oath showed her acknowledging 'the superiority of the transcendent moral standards and their divine source, and therewith the sacred character of the moral standards of British society'. Further, the presence at the ceremony of the Catholic Duke of Norfolk, who organized the event, and the Moderator of the General Assembly of the Church of Scotland (alongside Archbishop Fisher and Bishop Ramsey) 'served the vague religiosity of the mass of the British people without raising issues of ecclesiastical jurisdiction or formal representation. As with so much else in the Coronation service, behind the archaic façade was a vital sense of permanent contemporaneity.'[26]

There was to be trouble later in the year when the Queen went to St Giles' Cathedral in Edinburgh, but it was the Moderator who presented the Bible to the Queen with the words: 'Here is Wisdom; This is the Royal Law.'[27] But the section which stuck in my six-year-old mind (and those of many others) was the spectacle of the Queen suddenly simply dressed without her regalia as the choir sang Handel's *Zadok the Priest* for

The Anointing: When the Queen . . . is presented as a frail creature who has now to be brought into contact with the divine, and thus transformed into a Queen, who will be something more than the human being who has received the previous instruction . . . He anoints her by saying 'And as Solomon was anointed King by Zadok the priest and Nathan the prophet, so be thou anointed, blessed and consecrated Queen of the Peoples' . . . she shows her submission before the Archbishop as God's agent, kneeling before him while he implores God to bless her.[28]

Presenting the Sword and the Orb: The Queen is . . . told that she will be given power to enforce the moral law of justice and to protect and encourage those whose lives are in accordance with the law . . . The sword is an instrument of destruction . . . and its terrible power, for evil, as well as good, must never be forgotten by the Queen . . . she is next invested with the bracelets of sincerity and wisdom and is dressed in the Robe Royal, which enfolds her in righteousness. With these dramatic actions, she is transformed from a young woman into a vessel of the virtues which must flow through her into society . . .

The Benediction: The communal kernel of the Coronation becomes visible again in the Benediction when the duties of the subjects are given special prominence by the Archbishop. In his blessing, he says: 'The Lord give you faithful Parliaments and quiet Realms; sure defence against all enemies; fruitful lands and a prosperous industry; wise counsellors and upright magistrates; leaders of integrity in learning and labour; a devout, learned and useful clergy; honest, peaceable, and dutiful citizens . . .'[29]

Quite a manifesto for a reign.

As I write, the Queen has seen fourteen general elections, five of which produced a change in the governing party; fourteen parliaments; a patchy economic performance (to put it kindly) by the Realm in which she resides; sets of counsellors, trade union leaders and one or two vice-chancellors who did not quite match the lofty standards of that Coronation Benediction; an Anglican clergy who, amidst shining patches of traditional tolerance, have exhibited a growing animus towards those whose theological practices or sexual identities do not meet certain austere criteria. As for the citizenry, though still admirably well behaved in comparison with much of the world, it cannot claim to exhibit the perhaps historically unusually high levels of social and individual peaceability that prevailed when Archbishop Fisher pronounced his blessing and Bishop Ramsey strove to keep his eyebrows tamed. And those 'quiet Realms'? The overwhelming majority of the Queen's overseas territories in 1953 are now neither.

One must be careful here. Coronation Day behaviour was singular even when set in the context of the morals and values of early-Fifties Britain. Subjects from the colonies and overseas realms were part of the glorious politico-military pageant of an exotic extended family rather than unwelcome job/asylum-seeking intruders into traditional working-class areas. Even the petty criminal classes became the object of police approval for being 'entirely inactive on Coronation Day'.[30] Critics and sceptics would say it was one huge self-indulgent confection both inflated and bonded by deference – a sickly and demeaning trait by which early postwar Britain was trapped and, worse, willingly so.

But the rest of the world way beyond Britain and its Empire/Commonwealth got carried away, too, during that Coronation spring and summer. *Time* magazine declared, with absurd hyperbole, that: 'The whole world is royalist now.'[31] The historian of the first Elizabeth, A. L. Rowse, thought it was 'silly ... a mere matter of nomenclature'[32] when the notion of a new Elizabethan age began to catch on for a time. Whether in the form of a comic for children (*The New Elizabethan*[33]), on the rails (British Railways trumpeted a new non-stop King's Cross to Edinburgh express service called 'The Elizabethan'[34]) or in gushily celebratory prose (Philip Gibbs' *The New Elizabethans* pictured on its cover the latest RAF Hawker Hunter juxtaposed with a sixteenth-century galleon in full sail[35]), the idea had a certain cachet for a while. Even Michael Young, when drafting *The Rise of the Meritocracy* in the mid-1950s, referred to the period as 'Elizabethan times', noting that 'well on into' the period, 'succession to jobs was much more common in the lower than in the middle classes' and that dockers wished their sons to work on the waterfront, miners their boys down the pit, as they were 'the finest callings in the world'.[36]

Young and Rowse were, like many clever people, paradoxical in their treatment of new Elizabethanry. Young, for example, had an acute sense of the degree to which the monarchy helped suffuse a wider 'ancestor-worship' which

took the form of reverence for old houses and churches, the most amazing coinage, the quaintest weights and measures. Guards, regiments, public houses, old cars, cricket, above all the hereditary monarchy and in a less obvious way the class around the monarchy, namely the aristocracy, which could trace its descent from a more splendid past. Even politicians, as Privy Counsellors, borrowed some of the royal glamour; civil servants coyly called themselves HMG [Her Majesty's Government]. The state itself had high prestige because it attracted some of the status of the aristocracy who used to govern the government. In the United States (without an aristocracy) it was for long assumed that all government was bad, whereas in Britain people were always indignant that governments were not better.[37]

In Rowse's case, the awfulness of the Sixties (as he saw it) caused him to revisit new Elizabethanry in a noticeably different frame of mind. Writing in his diary in early 1968 Rowse unleashed a tirade against the journalist, critic and polemicist Malcolm Muggeridge: 'Whatever asset Britain had, he would be sure to attack it, to discredit it, denigrate it and demean it.' Rowse roared on, declaring

I am no more sold on monarchy than he is – but it happens to have been an asset of Britain's, particularly overseas, particularly in the United States where it matters most. Anything that helps keep things together, especially at a time when things are falling apart. It was a good thing, in the bleak and gloomy post war years, to have a radiant young woman coming to the throne, against the background of elderly bald-pated generals and presidents on the international scene.[38]

Was there anything much to the new Elizabethanry apart from the undoubted star quality of the young woman around whom it shimmered and swirled? What, for example, might it have amounted to if the Coronation had been held behind closed doors with the television cameras kept out, as was the original plan? The Queen herself gently dissociated herself from it during her Christmas broadcast in December 1953, in what sounded like a gentle, but unmistakable, siphoning of inflated expectations:

Some people have expressed the hope that my reign may mark a new Elizabethan age. Frankly, I do not feel at all like my great Tudor forebear, who was blessed with neither husband or children, who ruled as a despot and was never able to leave her native shores. But there is at least one very significant resemblance between her age and mine. For her kingdom, small though it may have been and poor by comparison with her European neighbours, was yet great in spirit and well endowed with men who were ready to encompass the earth. Now, this great Commonwealth of which I am proud to be the Head, and of which that ancient kingdom forms a part, though rich in material resources, is richer still in the enterprise and courage of its peoples.[39]

Nicely done. A careful lowering, a syringing of hyperbole, followed by a swift uplift. There is a trace of Martin Charteris in here. Forty years later he told me he was always dubious about the new Elizabethanry.[40]

Of the Queen's star rating – he called it her 'tonic' quality[41] – Charteris had no doubt. And, because the Coronation was televised and beamed across the world (not least to the United States, which was already a fully fledged televisocracy), this aspect – celebrity rather than royalty – carried all before it. Unsurprisingly, therefore, several players have taken the credit for getting the BBC's cameras into Westminster Abbey.

On first succeeding her father the Queen was, as Ben Pimlott put it, 'nervous of cameras', refusing to let her first Christmas broadcast be shown on television and, as Pimlott discovered from the royal archives, asking the BBC not to allow their cameras to linger too long on her face during Trooping the Colour on Horse Guards Parade.[42] Initially she, her Prime Minister and her Cabinet were as one in not wishing the Coronation to be televised. Colville briefed Churchill in July 1952 that, 'Whereas film of the ceremony can be cut appropriately, live television would not only add considerably to the strain on the Queen (who does herself not want TV) but would mean that any mistakes, unintentional incidents or undignified behaviour by spectators would be seen by millions of people.'[43] The Cabinet agreed that the monarch should be spared the TV cameras.[44]

When the decision leaked, the *Daily Express* led the campaign for it to be reversed. The BBC lobbied as hard as it could in the same direction.[45] The inner circles thought again, but it is not clear which of their loops was crucial in bringing about the U-turn. Many years later Jock Colville, who had served as Private Secretary to Princess Elizabeth in the late 1940s, said it was the sovereign herself who, at an audience with Churchill, had told her Prime Minister that 'all her subjects should have an opportunity of seeing it', and, on returning from the Palace, Churchill told Colville, 'After all it is the Queen who is being crowned and not the Cabinet. And if that is what she wants it shall be so.'[46]

One insider account has been overlooked in the reconstructions of the about-turn on the Queen, the Coronation and television – that of Lord Swinton, veteran sage and fixer in the last Churchill Cabinet. He was convinced it was the Prime Minister, not the Queen, who made the first decisive move. In the mid-1960s Swinton, in a series of interviews with James Margach of the *Sunday Times*, published as *Sixty Years of Power*, recalled how perfunctory had been the first Cabinet discussion on the recommendations of the Coronation Committee of the Privy Council, which they reached at the end of the meeting 'when everyone was late for luncheon and a number of Ministers had to get down to the House . . . The Prime Minister said: "These need not occupy us long"; and I am afraid we all took for granted that there was nothing to bother about, and the recommendations were passed.'[47]

After the meeting Swinton sifted through the proposals and

found there was one which recommended that the ceremony should be filmed for the cinema, but not televised. I went to the Prime Minister and said I hoped he would agree that this should be reconsidered, for I thought it would be a disaster if the Coronation ceremony was not televised when millions of people had television sets in their homes. Winston, who rather disliked television and did not know very much about it, said: 'Oh you want to have hot, bright lights shining in the Queen's eyes.'

I said: 'Nothing of the sort, there would be no hot bright lights. The television equipment would be silent and requires less light than the cinema film. In fact, I am sure the Queen will not know that she is being televised at all.'

Winston then said: 'All right, we had better have a small preliminary meeting with the Archbishop [Fisher] and the Earl Marshal [the Duke of Norfolk] and the Queen's Private Secretary [Sir Alan Lascelles] and you and one or two others. Meanwhile you can go and talk to the Queen's Private Secretary and see what impression you make on him.[48]

The small meeting took place. Swinton reckoned he had turned Norfolk and Lascelles but Fisher proved tougher to move:

'Do you realize,' he said to me, 'that this is a religious ceremony?'

This got me on the raw and I said: 'Yes, I certainly do, Archbishop. It will not be the first Coronation I have attended and it is the most moving service I have ever been at, but what is the objection? I saw you conduct a religious ceremony on television and I found it impressive, and, if I may say so, helpful.'

The Archbishop then said rather unwisely: 'But these television sets are everywhere. If the service is televised it will be seen not only by people in their homes but in public houses.'

This roused Winston, who broke in with, 'My dear Archbishop, if this great and moving service is witnessed in all the public houses of the realm, I will guarantee that it is followed with at least as much decency and reverence as by the more distinguished people who will be attending Her Majesty and you in the Abbey.'

I knew then we had won . . .'[49]

And so it proved.

Macmillan attributed the change of line to *demos*: 'The people insist on the Coronation being televised and the Cabinet have had to climb down as gracefully as possible,' he wrote in his diary for 31 October 1952.[50] Churchill always wanted the Coronation to be a big hit with the public, partly to 'beat' Labour's Festival of Britain.[51] In February 1952, when the Cabinet first discussed it, Churchill wanted the Coronation to be a deferred gratification. This was ROBOT time and the spectre of economic collapse was flitting in and out of the Cabinet Room.

Macmillan's diary entry for 11 February 1952 caught this very well. After ministers had returned from hearing the parliamentary eulogies to George VI, passing his catafalque in Westminster Hall en route, the Cabinet met at five that evening: 'We discussed the date of the Coronation. There was general agreement that it shd not be this year. This year the bailiffs may be in; the Crown itself may be in pawn. "It'll have a steadying effect next year," said Churchill.'[52]

Because of the well-remembered swerve on televising the Coronation, the televisual impact of the King's funeral fifteen months before is usually forgotten. As Richard Thorpe has put it: 'One of the persistent myths about television in the 1950s was that its popularity was established by the Coronation broadcast of 2 June 1953, whereas it was the television coverage of King George VI's funeral on 15 February 1952, watched in countless shared "front rooms", that sparked off the mass purchasing of sets *in time* for 2 June 1953.'[53]

Nevertheless, at the beginning of 1953 fewer than 2 million UK homes had a television set. Substantial parts of the Queen's kingdom would have received no signal even if they had spent the £80 plus (roughly eight times the average weekly wage for an adult male) required to buy one. Once the decision to televise was made, the BBC began the process of erecting temporary transmitters to put this right. As Kingsley and Tibballs record, 'in the build-up to the great day 526,000 sets were sold as Coronation fever swept the country ... and 3,000 tickets for a large-screen showing at the Festival Hall went in under an hour'.[54]

For a mere £44,000, the BBC laid on continuous coverage from 10.00 in the morning to 11.30 that night, when Richard Dimbleby said goodnight from a silent Westminster Abbey. Dimbleby was for evermore established as the country's Greek Chorus, a national treasure – 'Gold Microphone-in-Waiting', as Malcolm Muggeridge christened him,[55] – as a result of his broadcasting marathon on 2 June 1953. His voice resonated across the televisual world and film versions followed. It was estimated that 277 million people eventually saw footage of the Coronation.[56]

For the Queen's own in her closest realm, 2 June 1953 became quite simply for media historians television's '"take-off" date'.[57] With but 2.5 million sets in her kingdom, an extraordinary 20 million of her subjects watched the Queen on television that day, 40 per cent of the population – easily outstripping the 12 million who listened to it on the wireless. Over the next year the sale of televisions surged by another 50 per cent.[58]

The Coronation played very strongly on American screens too and that, in turn, played back powerfully into the British television debate. The Coronation was, as cultural historian Richard Weight has observed, a moment for more than a whiff of British 'cultural superiority' to be directed towards the economic and military superpower across the Atlantic.[59] Even the ultra-gentlemanly Richard Dimbleby succumbed to this. Writing in the *Sunday Dispatch* five days after his marathon in Westminster Abbey, he noted how visitors from abroad 'were envious of everything they saw, and none more so than the Americans – a race of such vitality but so lacking in tradition – who know that they must wait a thousand years before they can show the world anything so significant or lovely'.[60]

Churchill was right about the Coronation – it did trump the Festival of Britain in popular perception and memory. It was bound to – everything building up to one glittering moment which, to so many, encapsulated how the Brits liked to imagine themselves and the thousand years of history that had gone into their making. In this limited sense there was a feeling of 'new Elizabethanry'. It was, I think, valid in another and related aspect. The juxtaposition of past and present, tradition and modernity was 'steadying' in the mid-1950s, as Churchill hoped it would be. Optimism was its product, incremental improvement its trajectory, whether it be in economic, welfare or social terms. This moment was fleeting. It did not survive Suez and the rather anguished introversion that crisis produced in its short-term and long-range aftermaths.

The most serene 'having-it-so-good' period was from autumn 1952 to autumn 1956, from the time when neither the economy nor the currency collapsed as the Treasury had feared, to the Anglo-French invasion of Egypt. It predates both Macmillan's Bedford speech in July 1957 when he gave the phrase its British currency (it had been the slogan of the US Democrats during the 1952 presidential election[61]) and the UK general election in October 1959 with which it will be forever associated.

The phenomenon, if such it was, is more New Deal than New Elizabethan.

Sir Philip Gibbs finished his 1953 paean to the new reign hoping for 'a renaissance of genius, and talent, and high spirit, and high hopes, in this new Elizabethan England'.[62] The special flavour of 1952–6 is, I believe, more of easement amidst the cumulative righting of old social and economic wrongs in such a way that a benign self-sustaining cycle would take hold permitting progress with stability. I am, however, just as biased a witness as Sir Philip. The early compost which nourished my mind was not so different from his, even if mine was less the history of Arthur Bryant and more the adventures of the *Eagle*'s Dan Dare. In retrospect it is easy to see why many in my generation took our country's decline so badly: our expectations were so high.

The generation before mine also contained those who saw this having-it-so-good time as something of a shining hour. Brian Palmer of Gibbs SR ad fame described it as

this feeling overall that, by and large, next year was going to be a bit better than this year and the year after that was going to be a bit better still. You had a situation where there was full employment; there were low interest rates; we were building 300,000 houses a year and very proud of it; we had a Health Service; we had an education system we were confident was going to work and you had a feeling that something was going to happen.[63]

Brian Palmer's age group and my own did not talk about 'national identity', partly because the phrase was not then in the lexicon but chiefly because we didn't have to speak about a thing we felt instinctively at ease with and were sure of. But then Brian Palmer and I were not only British but *English*.

If I had grown up in the suburbs of Glasgow or Cardiff I would, no doubt, have felt and thought rather differently – reflecting what Braudel called 'the centuries-long distillation of collective personality'[64] resulting from the merging of three and a bit different but equally ancient kingdoms. Certainly when I paid my first visits to Wales (1954) and Scotland (1957) I knew I was somewhere very different from London, Liverpool or Cumberland, which marked the extent of my previous forays from Finchley.

The Coronation, and events following it, roused emotions in Scotland of a divisive rather than a unifying kind, leaving a rather different folk-memory from that deposited in England, despite special efforts made by the organizers of the ceremony to head off potential trouble north of the border. Amazing as it is to recall, given the disappearance of Scottish Conservative MPs from the House of Commons after the 1997 general election, the Unionist Party (as it was still called there) and its allies in Scotland took a majority of both the votes cast and the seats contested in the 1955 general election. Churchill let the country be run as a fiefdom by a pair of prime upper-crusters, James Stuart (the very influential former Chief Whip) and Lord Home, the future premier and the first minister of state to be appointed to the Scottish Office (as pledged in the Conservatives' 1950 manifesto in recognition of a groundswell of nationalistic unease in early postwar Scotland).[65]

In the early hours of Christmas morning 1950, a quartet of nationalist students, pupils of John MacCormick, Professor of Law at Glasgow University, had indulged in a dash of Coronation-related larceny: the 'reivers' (or plunderers), as they styled themselves, led by Ian Hamilton (who was to become a distinguished Scottish QC), snatched the ancient Stone of Scone from beneath the Coronation Chair in Westminster Abbey and carried it back to Scotland, with whose kings it was irredeemably associated. (King Edward I had purloined it after defeating the Scots in 1296.) Eventually it was spirited to Arbroath Abbey by the students (the Abbey was the scene of the Declaration of Scottish Independence in 1320), placed before the high altar beneath a St Andrew's flag and left in the care of the Church of Scotland in April 1951. The 'reivers' were not punished and the Stone was safely back beneath the Queen on her Coronation Day[66] and, partly as a consequence of Hamilton and co., so was the Moderator of the Church of Scotland, J. Pitt-Watson. The proposal that the Moderator should be present came from a Scotsman, Alan Don, the Dean of Westminster. He had been furious at the stone-napping, but within a few days of the death of George VI in February 1952 had felt it necessary to remind the Archbishop of Canterbury that 'nationalist feeling is very strong in Scotland at the moment' and to suggest that the Moderator, for the first time, should have a role in the Coronation. Fisher, as we have seen, concurred.[67]

The Cabinet had also discussed the delicacy of the Scottish dimension to the Coronation. At the Cabinet which ministers attended after paying their respects to the deceased monarch on 11 February, Macmillan recorded in his diary that Churchill 'was in good form' and 'chaffed James Stuart very much about the Scottish pedantries regarding Elizabeth 2nd or 1st [as she was in Scotland]. There was a paper before the Cabinet about the Stone of Scone. We decided to take it [the Stone] out of the cellar in which it is now guarded, and put it back in its place ...'[68]

The importance of the Queen's numeral went far beyond mere pedantry in Scotland. Arnold Kemp, who later became editor of the *Glasgow Herald*, recalled Churchill coming to Edinburgh during the February 1950 general election and sympathizing with the Scots for having the 'serfdom of socialism' thrust upon them because of Labour's majority at Westminster[69] (although this speech is more famous as the one in which the word 'summit' was coined and mooted as a way of easing Cold War tensions – see p. 188[70]). As a result, Kemp wrote:

> In our house there was particular resentment over the decision, confirmed by Winston Churchill with a certain arrogant hypocrisy given his willingness to exploit Scottish national sentiment as a means of attacking Labour, that the new Queen . . . should be known as Queen Elizabeth II (she was the first since the Union created the United Kingdom). This caused widespread and genuine outrage. I remember my parents' fulminations very well. They went on about it for years.[71]

Some did rather more than 'go on about it'. When Scottish pillar boxes began to appear emblazoned with 'E II R', some of the Queen's Scottish subjects removed the 'II' and a few posted explosives through the slot. Sensibly, the Scottish Office later decided that a design with a crown separating the 'ER' instead would be prudent north of the border.[72]

Elizabeth's dress sense as well as her pillar boxes managed to cause offence in the Kemp household, where Arnold's parents, the writer Robert Kemp and his schoolteacher wife Meta Strachan, 'were also put out when after her Coronation the Queen came to Edinburgh to receive the Honours of Scotland (the regalia restored to public acknowledgement and view thanks to the efforts of Sir Walter Scott) wearing not her sovereign robes but a coat and carrying a handbag'.[73] The Kemps were not alone in their opinion that a handbag was an insult to the dignity of the occasion.

Scotland had its equivalent of Archbishop Geoffrey Fisher, the prelate who had famously declared in a broadcast shortly after the Coronation that 'the country and Commonwealth last Tuesday were not far from the Kingdom of Heaven'.[74] He was not the Moderator, Pitt-Watson, but Charles Warr, Dean of the Thistle and of the Chapel Royal of Scotland and minister of St Giles' Cathedral in Edinburgh where the Queen, at the suggestion of Stuart and Home, was to have the Scottish regalia – the crown, sceptre and sword – paraded before her.[75] Warr, naturally enough, was 'thrilled' by the plan but nervous lest the pillar-box wreckers should attempt sabotage in St Giles' and asked the Edinburgh police to search 'every nook and cranny', which they obligingly did. Like Fisher, Warr was carried away by the beauty, the pomp and the sanctity of it all. In his memoirs, he recalled that of all the 'moments of high emotional excitement in my life, none equalled that when I took in my hands the ancient Crown of Scotland and placed it on the Holy Table'.[76] But for many, the lasting image of 24 June 1953 in St Giles' is not this pious and poignant moment, but that handbag.

The photograph of the royal party on the Cathedral steps following the ceremony shows the crown, sceptre and sword (this last held by Lord Home in his peerage robes), the Duke of Edinburgh in uniform and white-plumed hat, the Reverend Charles Warr, heavily bemedalled, and the Queen, in smart dress and hat but with the offending item clearly visible on her right arm. Richard Thorpe, Home's official biographer, blames the faux pas on the Queen's Private Secretary, Lascelles, and the Home Office Deputy Secretary, Sir Austin Strutt, neither of whom foresaw how the Queen might appear if she wore what were then called 'day clothes' while everyone else was in full rig.[77]

Such (over)sensitivity was a sign of the times. Arnold Kemp, recounting by far the best joke of the day, put it all in perspective nearly forty years later: 'There is an old *Glasgow Herald* anecdote about the service of state in St Giles'. Its reporter was waiting in the queue for admission. The befeathered and richly garbed man in front identified himself as the Marchmont Herald and was admitted. Our man, of course, then said: "I am *The Glasgow Herald*."'[78]

The Orcadian artist Stanley Cursiter was commissioned to capture the service for posterity. Should he place her Coronation robes on the Queen at St Giles'? No. He compromised. There is no handbag in the picture which now hangs in Holyrood House to remind the Queen, on her annual summer visit to Edinburgh, of her Coronation-year miscalculation.[79]

James Stuart was one of the most influential and intriguing national politicians that Scotland produced in the twentieth century and was a descendant of one of its kings, James V.[80] He was a good friend of the Windsors, indeed some have speculated that he was the love of Queen Elizabeth the Queen Mother's life. If so, it is ironic that he was also the man who introduced her to her husband. In the summer of 1921, the future George VI was the Duke of York and Stuart his equerry. During the annual RAF ball at the Ritz in Piccadilly, 'H.R.H. came over to me and asked who was the girl with whom I had just been dancing. I told him that her name was Lady Elizabeth Bowes-Lyon and he asked me if I would introduce him, which I did. It was a more significant moment than it was possible then to realise but it is certainly true to say that from then on he never showed the slightest interest in any other young lady and they were married in 1923.'[81]

In the early 1920s Stuart was quite the most glamorous, dashing and eligible aristocrat in Scotland. He had won an MC on the Somme in 1916 at the age of nineteen. ('Having survived the battle of the Somme I felt for a long time that I could weather anything.'[82]) For Stuart and his future brother-in-law, Harold Macmillan (they were both to marry into the Cavendish family), the experience of the trenches broadened their Etonian education into a warm appreciation of the bravery and stoicism of the 'other ranks', the sergeants in particular. In Stuart's case it was his comrade in the Royal Scots, 'a company sergeant-major (an Aberdeen police sergeant), a big, strong man who had developed a remarkable degree of fatalism – so much that some of the men really believed he possessed some supernatural quality. He would sit down on an ammunition box in the trench, with his back against the parapet, and read a book during the mortar bombardments, and the men would sit down as near to him as possible and not even bother to look up to see the approaching danger.'[83]

Sarah Bradford, the biographer of George VI, has caught the flavour of the debate about James Stuart and Elizabeth Bowes-Lyon by recounting the different views of her friends: '[H]e was in love with her but she was not the least bit in love with him. If she had been she would have married him,' said one. 'Well, he was certainly in love with her and perhaps she was just a little with him. He was awfully attractive. Everybody was in love with James Stuart,' said another.[84]

Stuart died in 1971. Plainly he and the Queen Mother were great chums till the end. She used to say he was 'such fun to be with as one caught up with all the gossip from Whites!'[85]

Whatever the truth about the emotional geography of the upper reach of Scottish society after the Great War, Stuart was a figure of high regard and influence in early-1950s governing circles. Churchill rarely made a senior ministerial appointment without consulting him,[86] just as for a while Mrs Thatcher would never do without consulting Stuart's protégé, Willie Whitelaw, thirty years later.[87] Macmillan reckoned that, when Chief Whip, Stuart was 'the only man I think I have ever known who rather frightened Churchill'.[88] Though he supported ROBOT in Cabinet,[89] Stuart was, on a broader canvas, a natural consensualist in terms of both UK and Scottish politics. Indeed, he thought Churchill would be replaced pretty swiftly by a Prime Minister heading a coalition.

Lunching at home in Morayshire, in his 'tiny ... cottage, surrounded by wind and waves' with Macmillan in late August 1951, Stuart, as his brother-in-law recorded, 'thinks they [Attlee and his colleagues] have decided for an autumn election. He thinks that we shall win. Churchill in that event will form as "broad" a Govt as he can; but he will not get much in the way of left-wing recruits. He will retire in a year. James does not think we shall get through the next period without a Coalition . . . J.S. sees a lot of Churchill so this has some importance.'[90]

Stuart quite liked 'left-wing' people provided their hearts and their patriotism were in the right place. He adored Ernest Bevin,[91] and was hugely fond of old Glasgow firebrands like George Buchanan who, as he put it to a prewar Unionist Scottish Secretary, Walter Elliot, had 'lost the power of hating'.[92]

Stuart, like Elliot and Labour's Tom Johnston before him and Willie Ross after him, was one of the few twentieth-century Secretaries of State for Scotland to have real clout in the Cabinet Room. And the country over which he presided was enjoying what Christopher Harvie calls a strange 'Indian summer', economically and industrially.[93] (By the end of the 1950s its great nineteenth-century industrial staples would tip into protracted and eventually terminal decline.) And for all of what Arthur Marwick calls its 'carefully articulated class structure'[94] and quite powerfully felt religious divides, Scotland's politics in the Fifties were relatively 'tranquil'.[95] Stuart could be quite witty about this. Willie Whitelaw loved to recall the story of Stuart saying, 'I never discuss politics with my constituents. They're all Liberals really,'[96] an interesting view of this north-east protuberance of Scotland south of the Moray Firth on the part of the third son of the Earl of Moray. This partly explains why Alec Home once said of his mentor that 'his political enemies could never get the measure of him'.[97]

Did Stuart's special clout produce special benefits for Scotland during his lengthy tenure at the Scottish Office (October 1951 to January 1957)? He did not want the job but succumbed to Churchill's blandishments and secured 'Home sweet Home', as Sir Winston called him,[98] as Minister of State. As Home's biographer Richard Thorpe put it, he 'joined the Scottish Office when its shares were riding high; when he left for the Commonwealth Office on Churchill's retirement, the special links with Whitehall did not survive, and Stuart's successor, John Maclay . . . did not carry the same weight with Macmillan'.[99] Stuart and his juniors were backed by a seasoned team of Scottish Office civil servants in a department 'on the move'.[100]

It is difficult, however, to disagree with Christopher Harvie's terse, but considered, verdict: 'James Stuart, the aristocratic Secretary of State, got on well with Labour MPs, exceeded Labour's public housing programme by over a third, and at last secured substantial transport investment – with the Forth

Road Bridge and Glasgow railway electrification. But this masked a failure to tackle the fundamental economic and social problems of the country.'[101]

As part of its appeal to Scottish voters, the Conservative and Unionist Party had pledged, in recognition that Scotland is a nation (as Stuart had put it in the 1947 policy document *Scottish Control of Scottish Affairs*),[102] a review of Scottish affairs and the Balfour Royal Commission was duly created for this purpose. When it reported in 1954, it concentrated chiefly on administrative matters, arguing that, in 'the absence of convincing evidence of advantages to the contrary, the machinery of government should be designed to dispose of Scottish business in Scotland'.[103] But it did not urge that the Scottish Office be given the Whitehall Board of Trade's powers over regional and economic development.[104] In that twilight of the Scottish industrial economy which *had* once illuminated the heavier end of the world economy, 'industrialists, trade unions, government ministers and civil servants failed to foresee the imminent collapse of shipbuilding on the Clyde, on which so much else depended'.[105]

For Scotland's central industrial belt had flourished at its height as an economy with a tiny hinterland when measured in miles but into which were packed the mines of Lanarkshire and Ayrshire, the steel mills and the shipyards of the Clyde valley as well as the North British Locomotive Company in Glasgow despatching its engines across the British Empire.[106] Within six years of Balfour reporting, this highly productive interlocking had begun to unravel to a degree that the greatest pessimist could not have foreseen, let alone the aristocrats and the administrators in St Andrew's House.

It is interesting, in this context, to compare the view from the windows of the aristo-ministers in St Andrew's House, the Scottish Office on Calton Hill above Edinburgh Waverley Station, with that of the Jack household not so very far away in a Fife village up the railway line shortly after it had crossed the Firth of Forth on that great nineteenth-century triumph – the railway bridge. Ian Jack, future editor of the *Independent on Sunday*, was a boy in the 1950s. On 'still summer mornings, when a fog lay banked across the water and the foghorns moaned below [we] could still see the top of each cantilever poking up from the shrouds; three perfect metal alps which, when freshly painted, glistened in the sun'.[107]

Jack has a special feel for the great coal, steam and steel late-nineteenth/early-twentieth-century Scottish economy inherited from his engineer father and from his own experience of living in a council house in the shadow of the Forth Bridge when the steam engines still roared and struggled up the gradient to it on their way south. Like me, he can still recite the names of the locomotives for which he kept ready a young connoisseur's eye. Writing shortly after his father's funeral in the mid-1980s, Jack noted that the crematorium stood

near the site of one of the first railways in the world. The moorland to the east held mysterious water-filled hollows and old earthworks, traces of an eighteenth-century wagonway which had carried coal from Fife's first primitive collieries down to sailing barques moored at harbours in the Firth . . . The world's first industrial revolution sprang from places such as this; it had converted our ancestors from ploughmen and their wives into iron moulders, pitmen, bleachers, factory girls, steam mechanics, colonial soldiers, and Christian missionaries. Now north Britain's bold interference with the shaping of the world was over. My father had penetrated the revolution's secrets when he went to night school and learned the principles of thermo-dynamics, but as its power failed so had he. His life was bound up with its decline, they almost shared last gasps.[108]

How much of this could be sensed whether one was briefing Stuart and Home in Calton House or listening to the thoughts of the Jacks in their council home in the early 1950s? After all, as the economist Alec Cairncross noted at the time, in the early 1950s Scotland's 'dependence on the heavy industries has grown rather than diminished'.[109]

It is no wonder that the sharply remembered interwar catastrophes of slump and unemployment – the recovery triggered by the late-1930s rearmament; the mines, mills and shipyards working flat out during the war; the sustenance of full employment after it; and a gritty, smoky central Scotland reeking and roaring heavy industry deep into the 1950s – powerfully shaped the mind of Ian Jack. Even a young and fleeting visitor like me can see and smell even now the Clyde one early June morning in 1957 as we clanked across it with a swathe of the local workforce on the Erskine Ferry – and I can still feel the contrast it made with the Highlands and Islands from which we were returning in our tiny green hired Ford Prefect.

There was a strong sense as one left the mountains by Loch Lomond and, with scarcely a pause, drove straight into the great central industrial belt that, as Braudel put it of certain parts of the Mediterranean, 'Life was simply not the same in the hills as in the plains. The plains aimed for progress, the hills for survival.'[110] Certainly, for all the postwar subsidies, hill farming, crofting and fishing fitted the Braudel juxtaposition, even if the big aluminium works near Fort William did not. There was even a whiff on that first Scottish journey of mine, partly because we stayed in a remote cottage on Skye close to the sea, of the very first Scot whom history has recorded – Calgacus the Swords-man, in whose mouth Tacitus placed the words: 'There is nobody beyond us, nothing but the rocks and the surging sea.'[111]

Thirty years on, Ian Jack had his own version of having it so good as a mix-ture of old tradition and new optimism in that brief stretch between the Coronation (which he does not mention) and Suez (which he does):

The past sustained us in a physical as well as a mental sense. It came home from work every evening in its flat cap and dirty hands and drew its weekly wages from industries which even then were sleep walking their way towards extinction ... From quite an early age I sensed that my father was at odds with his surroundings, that something had gone wrong with his life – and hence our lives – and that I had been born too late to share a golden age, when the steam engine drove us forward and a watchful God still held the helm. Scotland, land of the inventive engineer! Glasgow, the workshop of the world! I hoped that the future would be like the past, for all our sakes. I day-dreamed. I drew plans for new railways powered by old breeds of steam locomotive; devised time-tables for old Clyde ferries which would burn coal and resume their journeys to long-abandoned piers in remote sea-lochs. Paddle steamers would again slide down the shipways ... The people, meanwhile, would be filled with goodness. They would aban-don Freemasonry and flee the public houses (both peculiarly Scottish evils, according to my father) and board tramcars for evenings organised by the Independent Labour Party. They would flood out of football grounds (the ruination of the working class, according to my father) and cycle off, with tents, to the Highlands.[112]

Allowing for certain family differences (ours, 400 miles to the south, was a Tory household and we were Catholics), I find that passage of Ian Jack's both elegiacally satisfying and personally reassuring.

Catholicism certainly gave me a sense of being religiously different in north London, though not, I suspect, quite in the Scottish way. For all that I was raised in a strongly Irish-flavoured Catholic parish in north London *before* Vatican II,* I think the metropolitan south had softened matters a little. Not for us – or not all of us, anyway – conviction Catholicism pitted against 'con-viction Protestantism' (to borrow Eamon Duffy's phrase[113]) of the kinds that confronted each other in Scotland with its powerful Calvinist tradition and somewhat embattled Catholic counterpoint. As Grace Davie put it (writing in 1994): 'In Scotland, things were, and still are, rather different. No *via*

---

* The Second Vatican Council was convened by Pope John XXIII in 1962 to reinterpret the Roman Catholic faith in the light of modern circumstances. It was continued by his successor, Paul VI, until completed in 1964.

media here. For most, if not all, of Scotland has been straightforwardly Protestant for several centuries, and its Protestants remain overwhelmingly Presbyterian.'[114]

Scotland in the short postwar remained a noticeably more religious society than England (as did Wales and, especially, Northern Ireland), with church memberships nearly three times greater than in its neighbour to the south.[115] This was a reflection not just of the conviction Protestantism of the established Kirk – i.e. the Church of Scotland – but also of the intensity of churchgoing in the 'survival' communities of the Highlands and Islands (with their more austere versions of Calvinist churches, as well as the Kirk) and the substantial immigration from Ireland into the western end of the Scottish industrial plain in the nineteenth and early twentieth centuries. This gave Glasgow and its environs a substantial Catholic minority who suffered a degree of discrimination in the jobs market until nationalization or the arrival of foreign multinationals beat back old prejudices.[116]

Not only has the Kirk, along with the Scottish legal and educational systems, added to the distinctiveness of Scotland (as well as the Manse supplying several Westminster political luminaries such as David Steel and Gordon Brown), it has also opened a window into the Protestant parts of continental Europe in a way unmatched by the Church of England, 'for Scottish Calvinism has a continental home in Geneva, a home denied to the state church south of the border. The Scots have, for a variety of reasons, made the most of these opportunities. Motives, however, may well be mixed in these undertakings, for it is undoubtedly true that Scotland's aspirations towards a greater European identity . . . are related to its somewhat negative feelings towards England. And it so happens that the religious factor can, and does, operate to reinforce this Europeanness.'[117]

Perhaps the power of religion in Scotland, as the Scottish radical schoolteacher R. F. Mackenzie argued, also served to 'temper' the 'claims of the controlling group' who 'mined the earth and looted the sea in the singleminded pursuit of profits'.[118] I doubt it on one level, because the great nineteenth- and early-twentieth-century Scottish entrepreneurs tended to brandish their bibles as easily as they waved their chequebooks at the latest opportunity to expand across homeland and Empire alike. And that ultimate Scottish nineteenth-century hero, David Livingstone, gave the two a virtuous fusion when he declared, 'Wherever a missionary lives, traders are sure to come, and if they had European goods to exchange, they would not have to deal in slaves.'[119]

For those on Calton Hill or in the boardrooms of the (unlike the mines) *un*nationalized shipyards along the Clyde in that Indian summer of Scotland's nineteenth-century industrial economy, as for Ian Jack's dad in his council house in Fife, it would have taken a rare mixture of realism and pessimism to absorb the magnitude of what awaited in the remainder of the twentieth century. I remember calling on Alec Home for a BBC interview in the late 1980s and seeing on his table at the Hirsel an illustrated copy of Macaulay's *History of England*. He told me it had been favourite reading since his boyhood. Part of Macaulay's 'purpose', as he declared it on the first page, was to show 'how Scotland, after ages of enmity, was at length united to England, not merely by legal bonds, but by the indissoluble ties of interest and affection'.[120] And one ingredient of Macaulay's mid-nineteenth-century mission was to remind his English readers of just how ignorant they had been of Scotland and the Scots until fairly recent times:

> It is not easy for a modern Englishman, who can pass in a day from his club in St James's Street to his shooting box among the Grampians, and who finds in his shooting box all the comforts and luxuries of his club, to believe that, in the time of his great-grandfathers, St James's Street had as little connection with the Grampians as with the Andes. Yet so it was. In the south of our island scarcely anything was known about the Celtic part of Scotland . . .
>
> We may well doubt whether, in 1689, one in twenty of the well read gentlemen who assembled at Will's coffee house knew that, within the four seas, and at a distance of less than five hundred miles from London, were many miniature courts, in each of which a petty prince, attended by guards, by armour-bearers, by musicians, by a hereditary orator, by a hereditary poet laureate, kept a rude state, dispensed a rude justice, waged wars, and concluded treaties.[121]

Alec Home was sprung from just such an ancient line that 'fitted well into the company of brigands and chieftains in a bloody era of Scotland's stormy history'.[122]

Macaulay had no doubt about the factors that had transformed Scotland and placed it on the mental maps of those both in St James's Street, London SW1, and far further. Writing as the recently elected Whig MP for Edinburgh, he declared in 1840 in the *Edinburgh Review* (in a review of Ranke's *The Ecclesiastical and Political History of the Popes of Rome*):

> It cannot be doubted that, since the sixteenth century, the Protestant nations have made decidedly greater progress than their neighbours . . . Edinburgh has owed less to climate, to soil, and to the fostering care of rulers than any capital, Protestant or Catholic. In

all these respects, Florence has been singularly happy. Yet, whoever knows what Florence and Edinburgh were in the generation preceding the Reformation, and what they are now, will acknowledge that some great cause has, during the last three centuries, operated to raise one part of the European family and to depress the other.

No prizes for guessing what Macaulay judged to be the 'great cause':

Our firm belief is that the North owes its great civilization and prosperity chiefly to the moral effect of the Protestant Reformation, and that the decay of the southern countries of Europe is to be mainly ascribed to the great Catholic revival.[123]

Alec Home never showed the slightest prejudice towards Catholics. But add to his absorption of Macaulay on the ingredients of greatness his early reading of Henty and Kipling,[124] and it is easy to appreciate just how difficult it would have been for him and his generation to live with the magnitude of Scotland's (and Britain's) relative decline, let alone to anticipate it.

For later generations, it is easier to attribute Britain's apogee as an economic and military superpower to being the world's first industrial trailblazer and the special circumstances of the nineteenth century after the collapse of French power in 1815, before the rise of the first supercompetitors in the shapes of the United States and Germany by the 1890s. Scotland benefited particularly from both the economic and the territorial expressions of that extraordinary surging and spreading of British power, possessing both the ingredients of a coal-and-steel economy and a generation or three of wider-world-viewing entrepreneurs, administrators and missionaries, makers of the 'Scottish Empire' with Macaulay as their bugler and the political economist and historian Michael Fry sounding their last post in his study of that name published early in the twenty-first century.

From creators of great shipping fleets and shipping companies and industrial pioneers and innovators to seekers of riches in a very different globalized economy was a transition hardly foreseeable in 1914 (in 1913 the Clyde yards produced more shipping, for example, than the whole of Germany), and one not that much easier to predict in 1954.[125] From the 1970s, the Scottish Development Agency worked bravely and to some effect to create the conditions where some of the world's hi-tech pacemakers, attracted by cheap but skilled labour and entry into the European market, would locate in Scotland. It provided many greatly needed jobs, but it was not the stuff of legend.

Yet if the period from Macaulay's 1850s to Stuart's and Home's 1950s was the aberrational exception for Scotland, it was not alone in the UK. Historian of modern Scotland T. M. Devine's judgement on the early postwar boom in Scotland's heavy industries as being dependent 'on the temporary conditions of replacement of demand after 1945 and the virtual absence of international competition while the ravaged economies of Europe and the Far East recovered from the devastation of war'[126] could just as easily be applied to the great extracting and manufacturing concentrations of north-west and north-east England, and South Wales too. And once the European economies had recovered, there was a shared and 'serious error' on the part of British manufacturers generally in not redirecting their export efforts to the now fast-growing continental economies.[127]

What of the politics that a combination of tradition, religion and staple industries had bequeathed Fifties Scotland? Despite Stuart's remark about Moray and Nairn brimming with Unionist-voting Liberals, the Scotland which filled the Cabinet Room with home-grown Liberal Prime Ministers (such as Campbell-Bannerman and Rosebery) or imported ones (Gladstone and Asquith; Englishmen who sat for Scottish seats) had witnessed the dramatic collapse of the Liberal Party. By the 1950s the once-great party of non-conformity and free trade was reduced to a single MP, Jo Grimond, son-in-law of Lady Violet Bonham Carter, who won Orkney and Shetland in the 1950 election against the expectations of Lady Vi, who flew out of Kirkwall feeling 'that the heritage which meant such glory in my youth has been frustration + a lost cause to them [Grimond and his wife, Laura]'.[128] The Orkney and Shetland result (given the scattered diaspora of remote islands) was not declared until the Monday following the election (27 February 1950), when the news reached London that Grimond had won by 2,950. 'I didn't believe my ears,' wrote Lady Vi in her diary. '. . . Where Jo has pulled out these thousands of votes from I don't know . . . It is an *amazing* personal performance.'[129] Indeed it was. Not until 1964 did Scotland give Parliament another Liberal (three more, to be precise, and the youthful David Steel winning Roxburgh, Selkirk and Peebles at a by-election the following year).

The big battalions of the Labour and Unionist parties had seen off nearly the last traces of the party that had dominated Scottish politics for much of the period 1868–1918. The Scottish National Party, a very recent creation, being founded in 1928,[130] fared even worse in the Fifties' elections, despite a promising flurry in the 1940s. In 1945 the SNP's leader, Dr Robert McIntyre, won their first ever seat at Westminster at the Motherwell by-election during the unusual conditions of a truce between the three wartime coalition parties. Though McIntyre lost Motherwell at the general election in July that year, and the party was not to win another seat until Winnie Ewing took nearby Hamilton in a 1967 by-election, there was a fleeting but impressive moment when an appetite for home rule, if not full independence, manifested itself in Scotland.

Its moving spirit was not McIntyre but a Glasgow law professor, John MacCormick, the SNP's former party secretary and, a little later, the man behind the lifting of the Stone of Scone. MacCormick was aware of the danger of the SNP turning inward towards an intense and narrow nationalism. Instead, as Devine put it, MacCormick resigned from the SNP during the war, and, after it, 'with a number of allies, established a body eventually named the Scottish Convention which would stand outside party politics but would seek to demonstrate to government the national desire for Home Rule by mobilizing all sections of Scottish opinion in pursuit of that primary objective'.[131] This development partly explains the siphoning of support from the SNP and its feeble performance in the general elections of the Fifties.[132]

The Convention was consensual in approach and did not put up candidates in elections. It met as a 'Scottish National Assembly' in March 1947 and produced a plan for a Scottish Parliament with powers very similar to those enjoyed by the actual Parliament which came into existence in 1999 (embracing within its reach most domestic affairs but not defence, foreign policy or macroeconomics). Two years later the movement launched a Covenant which attracted 2 million signatures (out of a total population of just under 6 million, though including 'some forgeries and the names of a few dead celebrities'.[133]) But however farsighted it might have been in the long term, the Covenant failed to convert sentiment into political capital which could be cashed in at the ballot box. The two big class- and interest-based parties saw it off with little difficulty.[134]

For a brief moment MacCormick thought he had transcended the old and new divides in Scottish political life. When displaying the Covenant to the third meeting of the National Assembly on 29 October 1949, he looked around him and, as he later recalled:

Unknown district councillors rubbed shoulders and joined in pledges with the men whose titles had sounded through all the history of Scotland. Working men from the docks of Glasgow or the pits of Fife spoke with the same voice as portly business-men in pin-striped trousers. It was such a demonstration of unity as the Scots might never have hoped to see and when, finally, the scroll upon which the Covenant was inscribed was unrolled for signature, every person in the hall joined patiently in the queue to sign it.[135]

The spirit and the mood of that moment took years to penetrate the citadel of the Union, the Scottish Office atop Calton Hill. Attlee's Secretary of State, Arthur Woodburn, regarded the whole thing as a front for Labour's enemies.[136]

The moment passed. Why? One of the most intriguing speculations has to do with two linked Braudelian notions – that in the 'slow pulse' motions of Scottish history, there existed (and still does despite the turn-of-the-century Parliament on the Mound and, later, in a purpose-designed building in Holyrood) a great cleavage which its anatomist, Neal Ascherson, called the 'St Andrew's Fault'.

For Ascherson, writing in his remarkable early-twenty-first-century study of his homeland, *Stone Voices*, defines the St Andrew's Fault as 'the traumatic chasm dividing the confident minority from the mistrustful majority, which seems to date from the wholesale uprooting of traditional society between about 1760 and 1860'[137] (the period so vividly seized upon by Macaulay). Ascherson, who carried a copy of the Scottish Covenant in the tin trunk that accompanied him to the Far East to fight the communist insurgents in Malaya as a National Serviceman in the Royal Marines,[138] believed in 2002 that the 'deep geographical fault running underneath national self-confidence' was still there[139] – that the 'wholesale uprooting of Scottish society within a few years and its forcible replanting in physically transformed landscapes, in new industrial cities or in other hemispheres altogether, has left a persistent trauma'.[140]

This, he explained, 'is to do with self-doubt (sometimes masked in unreal self-assertion), with sterile speculations about national identity and – as I guess – with suspicions of "otherness" which so often poison relationships between Scottish neighbours'.[141] This strange but understandable and persistent phenomenon has never been better put.

Its special value in the context of postwar Britain is the explanation it offers for the ambivalence which meant the Covenant spirit was not converted into votes that counted until the 1990s, when another Scottish Convention made the running on a path which really did lead to a home-rule Parliament. For, as Ascherson expressed it, the 'trauma' of the St Andrew's Fault showed and shows itself 'above all . . . in a chronic mistrust of the public dimension. The invitation to "participate", especially to offer critical comment in public, touches a nerve of anxiety.'[142] The 'dream' of those who were bitterly disappointed when Scotland failed to vote in sufficient numbers in the 1979 referendum (which incorporated a requirement that 40 per cent of those eligible to vote voted in favour) for a Scottish Parliament was that, one day,

Scottish politics would be able to 'throw bridges across that historic' St Andrew's 'gap, the chasm which separates those who are accustomed to be heard and those taught by centuries of uprooting that their lot is to survive change, not to plan it'.[143]

How comparable is the Welsh experience? Is there a 'St David's Fault' to match the St Andrew's Fault? On one level, there are several: between urban and rural (with the heavy industry, until the deindustrializations of the 1980s at any rate), concentrated on the south-east and north-east shores of the principality; between south and mid-Wales; between south and west Wales; between mid and north Wales (mountainous) against north-east Wales (industrial from Wrexham to Shotton).

The biggest is obviously that between the small country to the west of Offa's Dyke and the dominant neighbour to its east. The more eloquent chroniclers of national defiance and resentment, like Jan Morris in her exquisitely written *The Matter of Wales: Epic Views of a Small Country*, make it plain that if the Scots think they have grievances, they might ponder how it feels to be at the receiving end of the English hegemon across the Severn and the Wye:

History and geography . . . have made the Welsh one of Europe's most absolute minorities. They do not form a detached fragment of a wider whole, like the German-speakers of Poland or Czechoslovakia, or the Austrians of the Italian Tyrol, or the Swedish minority in Finland, or even the Scots-Irish in Ulster. The Welsh are on their own. Nobody else speaks their language or shares their history. There is no Greater Wales to which they can look as irredentists, whose spokesmen can back their cause at the United Nations . . . the truth is that the Welsh are engaged in a perpetual protest often without knowing it, a protest less in the intent than the instinct – a protest with which many of them vehemently disagree, in fact, against a force which does not always understand what the protest is about.[144]

Morris was writing a few years after Wales had come out strongly against its own national assembly in Cardiff as outlined in the Callaghan government's devolution proposals. On St David's Day 1979, the Welsh electorate voted 956,000 to 243,000 not to have its own elected assembly. In the Welsh-speaking north-west lay the most concentrated support for devolution, but even here it amounted to no more than 22 per cent. In Glamorgan and Gwent, at the other extremity (in both the geographical and voting senses) only 8 per cent and 7 per cent were in favour. Across the country as a whole, only 12 per cent wanted devolution.[145]

For a member of Plaid Cymru, the Welsh national party, such as Jan Morris, this was a deeply depressing moment. For could not the English – and the *British* government – ask,

> Is not the majority of the Welsh populace quite content with the way things are? Look what happened in 1979, when they held a referendum about Welsh autonomy – five to one against the idea.

Yet oppression it is, by the nature of things, just as the referendum was only such a pale inkling of self-government that almost nobody really believed in. The Welsh relationship with England, 2.75 million beside 46 million, 8,000 square miles beside 50,000, half a million speakers of the Welsh language against the hundreds of millions of English-speakers across the whole world – the colossal imbalance so affects the Welsh sense of identity that the protest has long been dispersed, like a mist, through the whole landscape of Welsh life, revealing itself in sudden flares of half-realized resentment, and in a profound sense of mingled sadness and frustration: the neurosis of a family that no longer quite knows itself, its personality having been so long rebuffed, denigrated, overawed or patronized by the heedless grandeur of the people next door.[146]

In Morris's lifetime, Wales did get its Assembly after a referendum produced the narrowest of 'yes' votes in 1998.

Had she been writing thirty years earlier, the prospect for even the thinnest sliver of greater self-determination for Wales and its political outcomes would have seemed very remote, not least because Nye Bevan – the man she rightly remembered as 'compelling' and 'majestic' with something of the 'elements' about him which made him 'a prince' of the South Walian valleys[147] – was dead set against it. In a famous intervention in a House of Commons debate in 1944, this ardent believer in centralized socialist economic planning turned all his powers of sarcastic irony against any such atavistic notions. As Kenneth O. Morgan put it, Bevan 'ridiculed the very idea that there were distinct social and economic problems peculiar to Wales and separable from those of Britain generally'. Bevan, who also had an 'ingrained suspicion of the Welsh-speaking population of the rural areas', asked how 'did Welsh sheep differ from those which grazed in Westmorland and in Scotland?'[148]

To the internal St David's Faults, the late-nineteenth and early-twentieth centuries added another – the radical socialist/Marxist advances amongst the great labour forces in the South Wales collieries, ironworks and steelworks which, even before the process of political and economic radicalization took off, had drawn in large numbers of *non*-Welsh immigrants to the valleys and the southern coastal strip during the Welsh equivalent of the great Clyde valley heavy-industrial boom. This changed all the balances within Wales including its economic and political dynamics. It had led by the 1920s to the usurpation of a Liberal hegemony by an increasingly Labour political dominance fuelled – in every sense – by the South Wales industrial belt which, for all its own distinctive culture, overwhelmed where it did not disdain the rural, Welsh-speaking way of life. Non-conformity, which might have built a religious-cum-cultural bridge between the two, was in rapid retreat after the Great War following the evangelical revival of the Edwardian period, associated with the brilliant if unstable Evan Roberts, which had suffused and enthused pit village and farming village alike.[149]

As long as the first of the two political geniuses offered up by Wales to twentieth-century British politics, David Lloyd George, was Prime Minister, an observer could be forgiven for thinking that the peculiar magic of the Welsh social, cultural/politico mix was as potent as ever. Lloyd George's special force was recognized by one of his few antagonists who could match him in both brilliance and word power, John Maynard Keynes, who had watched him in action at the Versailles peace conference. Keynes saw Lloyd George as 'the Welsh *witch*' taking on the 'non-conformist clergyman' (Woodrow Wilson) and 'an old man of the world' (Clemenceau). Keynes, a fellow Liberal it should be noted, set out to 'try and silhouette the broomstick as it sped through the twilight air of Paris': 'How can I convey to the reader, who does not know him, any just impression of this extraordinary figure of our time, this syren, this goat-footed bard, this half-human visitor to our age from the hag-ridden magic and enchanted woods of Celtic antiquity?'[150]

LG, though far more a man of the flesh than the (Christian) spirit, paid a degree of 'obeisance'[151] to Evan Roberts as non-conformist membership shot towards its peak and 'chapel life all over Wales was galvanised by spontaneous Bible readings and prayer meetings and revivalist passion' in 1904–6.[152]

The second genius delivered by Wales into twentieth-century British politics, Aneurin Bevan, was born about twenty miles, as a red kite might fly, north-west from Newport, at one of the heads-of-the-valleys towns, Tredegar, in November 1897. Michael Foot, Bevan's beloved friend, biographer and successor as MP for Ebbw Vale after his hero's death in 1960, caught the shifting cultural and political compost into which Bevan arrived in the year of Queen Victoria's Diamond Jubilee: 'The family background was that of Welsh non-conformity in its heyday, with its self-reliance, pride, resource, music and the nurture, through its own logic and past struggles, of the richest soil for the cultivation of new heresies.'[153]

Bevan had a real nose for relative power,[154] wherever it lay, from Tredegar (initially) to (eventually) the suites of those who controlled the atomic arsenals of the nuclear powers. He had a nicely self-ironic story about his near life-long pursuit of it from local council to county council to Parliament to the Cabinet Room, each time only to see its 'coat-tails' disappearing round the corner.[155] By the time he entered the House of Commons in 1929, the serious motive power of Welsh input into British political life was unarguably urban-trade-union/Labour rather than Liberal/rural, even though Plaid Genedlaethol Cymru, 'the first nationalist political party in the history of Wales', had come into being but four years earlier 'in very obscure circumstances at a meeting in a temperance hotel during the Pwllheli *eisteddfod* in August 1925'.[156] It was primarily a cultural and intellectual movement initially, with romantic and organic views of society with a somewhat right-wing hue. Its dominant figure was the writer, playwright and arch defender of the Welsh language Saunders Lewis, who, with his colleague Ambrose Bebb, 'saw the new party as embodying the organic unity of Wales and of medieval European Christendom as it had existed long ago, before the sectarian divisiveness introduced by the statist nationalism and the Protestantism of the sixteenth century had fragmented Welsh culture'.[157]

Such nationalistic, Catholic-tinged atavism was without the slightest echo in 32 Charles Street, Tredegar, where Bevan grew up. He was and remained tone-deaf to its threnodies. By the time he had followed the coat-tails of power into the Ministry of Health, however, there were some in Attlee's government, fashioned no less than Bevan had been in the bowels of South Walian Labourism, who treated Welsh cultural and political claims with noticeably more sympathy. The most notable among them was James Griffiths, another miner-turned-MP, who eventually became the first ever Secretary of State for Wales in the Welsh Office freshly created by the incoming Wilson government in 1964.

As a Minister of National Insurance, he had protested when some of the great nationalizations, of which Bevan so strongly approved, showed complete insensitivity to Welsh concerns, especially the merging of Welsh power supply to two electricity boards – one in the south and another in the north which brigaded it with Merseyside. Attlee and Morrison swiftly dismissed in 1946 any suggestions that Wales should have its own ministry à la Scotland.[158] Paradoxically, it was only when the Conservatives announced that a returning Tory government would appoint a Minister for Welsh Affairs that the Attlee government softened – if only a little – by agreeing in 1948 that an advisory council for Welsh economic and industrial affairs would be created (though Morrison and Bevan combined to kill Griffiths' idea that it should be chaired by a Cabinet minister). The council was intended to be generally toothless, and so it transpired. As Morgan put it, the 'Welsh Council for the next eighteen years proved to be largely "the dead letter" that Morrison had visualised. Labour's leaders were quite unwilling to go any further.'[159]

It was a flaccid Labour response to a 'vague' Conservative promise made by Rab Butler during a debate on Wales in the House of Commons on 26 January 1948 that the proposed minister would act as 'a watchdog' or an 'ambassador' for Welsh interests in Whitehall.[160] The incoming Churchill government in 1951 combined the job with the Home Secretaryship in the person of Sir David Maxwell Fyfe, who was immediately nicknamed 'Dai Bananas' in Wales (Fyffes were then the leading British importer of the fruit).[161] The appointment did not arouse expectations in Whitehall or in Wales. There was no equivalent nationalist push in Wales to that rightly sensed in Scotland by Churchill, Stuart and Home.

From 1951 the Griffiths' line had valuable support from some existing younger Labour Welsh MPs and a promising new one, the charming and effective Cledwyn Hughes, a Holyhead solicitor who had ousted Lady Megan Lloyd George from one of the old family seats in Anglesey – a potent symbol in itself of the near extinction which now faced the once supreme Welsh Liberal tradition. But the multiple St David's Faults thwarted them.

The paralysis of the political and cultural cleavages was hardly affected when Lady Megan's brother, Gwilym Lloyd George, the Welsh-speaking son of LG, replaced Dai Bananas at the Home Office in 1954. Lloyd George was a 'National Liberal', a label created by those of the tradition who had supported the national governments of MacDonald, Baldwin and Chamberlain. They had formally merged with the Conservatives in 1947 after sixteen years of working together[162] and Lloyd George sat for a Newcastle seat very different from the Caernarfon Boroughs where, as a boy, he had seen his father in action.

It was the flooding of a valley thirty miles south-east of the old LG stronghold that united virtually the whole of Welsh opinion against Gwilym Lloyd George's successor, Henry Brooke,* in a way that flew far above all the St David's Faults in the late 1950s and led to a brief, if limited, surge of sympathy for Plaid Cymru as the party which championed rural Welsh causes. A

---

* He combined the posts of Minister of Housing and Local Government and Minister for Welsh Affairs between 1957 and 1961.

Bill was presented in Parliament[163] which gave Liverpool a free hand both to flood Tryweryn, between Ffestiniog and Bala, 'and to drown a Welsh-speaking community of peculiar cultural significance to Welsh speakers in the process. There was no authority anywhere in Wales which could challenge the decision and Liverpool were free to do what they liked with the water, resell it if they wished.'[164] Every Welsh MP voted against it, but the protests were in vain.

Bevan was, of course, among those who voted against the Bill, though his biographers, both friendly (Michael Foot)[165] and critical (John Campbell),[166] are silent on this as they are generally on Bevan and nationalism. He and those who thought like him could argue that the nationalization of coal and iron and steel and the industrial policy which seeded the South Wales valleys with state-funded advanced factories *had* put right the 1930s, but that without Labour's push to central economic planning in an integrated *British* fashion, neither this nor his beloved National Health Service (modelled, to some extent, on his cherished Tredegar Medical Aid Society[167]) would have revived the lives and the livelihoods of the people of Wales. That this last boom of the great Victorian and Edwardian heavy industries would prove as fragile in south-east and north-east Wales as it did in central and eastern Scotland Bevan failed to foresee, just like his Scottish counterparts, whatever their ideological persuasion.

This was the Wales I first encountered in 1954 when I travelled with my mother to my Aunty Molly's pub in Newport. It struck me, as a seven-year-old (as did Scotland three years later), as a genuinely different place from industrial England. But Welsh historian Gwyn Williams was convinced that after the Second World War, 'a whole generation of the Welsh moved into a quite novel prosperity and an unprecedented integration into British society'.[168]

Economically this was undeniably true. But in social terms, it didn't seem like that to everyone at the time, whether they were a north London boy like me or the mother of the incomparable Welsh footballer John Charles, who told the manager of Leeds United, when he called at the Charles household near Swansea in 1947 to persuade young John to move to Yorkshire, that her boy couldn't travel to England as he didn't have a passport![169]

Wales in the 1950s had a considerable presence in national politics on the Labour side, though not the Conservative, thanks largely to Bevan's capacity to affect the mood on the left. And, though no statistics are available to demonstrate it, the Welsh presence in English schoolrooms reflected its capacity as an exporter of teachers. But to visit any part of it, except perhaps Deeside which was an extension of the economy of the English north-west, brought a sense of being in a different country in a way that a trip to Lancashire did not.

There are, however, degrees of separation and there is no doubt that in the early 1950s Northern Ireland, in historian Dervla Murphy's phrase, was *A Place Apart*.[170] There were several reasons for this, many, but not all, stemming from the multiple 'St Patrick's Faults' which, in turn, were in part (but only in part) rooted in religious cleavages. It was more, as the great scholarly interpreter of the baffling ingredients of nineteenth- and twentieth-century Irish experience, F. S. L. Lyons, put it, a matter of 'colliding cultures'. And 'the fact that historians are inarticulate about the different cultures which collide with each other in this island [i.e. Great Britain] is merely a symptom of a more profound ignorance which runs right through our society and is exhibited *in excelsis* on the other side of the Irish Sea'.[171]

As a British historian of, on my father's side, Liverpool Irish ancestry, I have quite naturally shuddered when, as has been commonplace in England since the Troubles re-erupted in Northern Ireland in 1968, antagonist groups, parties and paramilitaries are casually and indiscriminately labelled Catholic or Protestant. It was, and remains, in effect an abdication of thought about the multiplicity of factions and factors at work in a relatively tiny area of a small island. As Roy Foster, Lyons' pupil, put it in an essay on the man and his work:

In Ireland, Leland Lyons came to think, there were several distinct 'cultures' . . . sometimes overlapping, more often sealed into separate, self-justifying compartments. It was not simply a 'Protestant' versus a 'Catholic' tradition: varieties of identification certainly took religious labels, but as often as not the religious identification was simply a flag for a whole range of attitudes and values. And within Protestantism, for instance, there were the utterly distinct cultures of Ulster Presbyterianism and Southern Ascendancy identity. The resources of the country (psychological, geographical, political) could not accommodate the implicit friction, which broke out again and again. Nor could one really hope for a 'solvent', so to speak, which would meld or blend them into a less confrontational whole.[172]

In the early 1950s the frictions, though palpable to those who lived there, were not in a 'break-out' phase.

I can recall a very senior British civil servant, deep in retirement in the early 1990s, saying just how ignorant Whitehall was about Northern Ireland in those years. The governors-general in Hillsborough Castle did not offer or add enlightenment. What secret intelligence there was on actual or potential paramilitary activity came solely from the Special Branch of the Royal Ulster Constabulary. He had hoped, he added, that the relative tranquillity would see him out. When it didn't, he reflected, perhaps London should not have been surprised when a province with roughly the same population as the English West Midlands failed to produce from within its political class leaders of a calibre to cope with the stresses and strains unleashed.[173]

Yet Whitehall, probably without fully realizing it, was responsible for the changes in welfare services provided by Northern Irish government to bring the province into line with the rest of postwar Britain, if not its culture, that might – just might – have eased some of the frictions to a degree that made the question of the North more manageable as a whole. Friends of mine in Belfast would sometimes muse that it was a great shame the effects on consumption of the great postwar western European economic boom reached its north-western extremity so late. If only they had done so a few years before the old tensions surged once more, perhaps the population would have become more secularist, their identity more that of consumers, like the bulk of the rest of the UK.[174] James Molyneaux, when leader of the Ulster Unionists at Westminster, remarked to me in 1976 (when I was the lobby correspondent of the *Financial Times*) that he had hoped Ulster politics would move more and more to a left/right, capital/labour model more along Labour/Conservative Westminster lines than those created by partition fifty-six years earlier.[175]

Ulster's slightly belated adoption (with variations) of post-Butler and Beveridge Whitehall/Westminster education and welfare provisions could have helped such an outcome. As historian J. J. Lee has shown, the 'combination of war and welfare helped raise income per capita in the North, which had lagged at between 55–57 per cent of the United Kingdom level in 1937–8, to about 68 per cent by 1950 . . . The social legislation arising from Westminster initiatives, heavily subsidised by Britain on the parity principle, brought a marked refinement in the quality of life.'[176] Health improved markedly thanks to Stormont's 1948 statute. The 1947 Education Act put down more ladders of opportunity at secondary-school and higher-education levels. There was, too, a mini-housing boom to match Macmillan's and Stuart's – some 113,000 houses being built between 1945 and 1963, though this was nowhere near enough to expunge the province's appalling housing blackspots.

But the deeper problems of the North vitiated crucial aspects of the arrival of welfarism which, whatever their reservations about the Labour government in London, Unionist ministers felt obliged to facilitate. The educational improvements, for example, fostered the creation of a professional Catholic middle class in Northern Ireland which, by the mid-1960s, provided many of the civil rights activists who turned ever brighter spotlights on the multiple layers of discrimination in what historians Paul Arthur and Keith Jeffrey call this 'extremely parochial place' where the 'proximity both of the communities to each other and of politicians to the people they represent has enormously enhanced the primacy of specifically local issues and tragically reduced the capability of politicians of one tradition to empathize with their colleagues of the other'.[177]

It was what Roy Foster called 'the structure of the social divide and different patterns of life between the two communities [that] sustained the impression that social disadvantage adhered to religious lines'. And the figures backed this even after a decent interval had elapsed since the late-Forties welfare improvements. 'An analysis of the 1971 census showed that while both a Protestant and a Catholic middle class existed in Northern Ireland, Catholics were still disproportionately represented in unskilled jobs, and Protestants in skilled employment.'[178]

The 1947 Education Act, for example, did not confront the near complete split of schooling along denominational lines. As Arthur and Jeffrey explain, although the first years of devolved government in the 1920s saw an Act passed by Stormont declaring that the state education system should be non-sectarian,

it also stipulated (as was the case elsewhere in the United Kingdom) that Christian religious education should be included in the syllabus. To qualify for a full government subsidy, however, a school had to provide distinctively Protestant 'Bible teaching'. In effect this meant that the state primary-education system was a Protestant one. A similar state of affairs obtained after 1947 when the Northern Ireland government, following the British Butler Education Act of 1944, introduced free secondary education for all so long as they stayed within the state sector but still restricted the state assistance available for the province's specifically denominational (mostly Catholic) schools.[179]

Teacher training was similarly divided.

Health was also a sensitive topic. Even in sickness, the cleavages divided provision, overshadowing 'the fact that the health services available to Catholics in the North were superior to those in the South'.[180] This arose because the 1948 Stormont health legislation did not follow the 1946 National Health Act which applied to the rest of the UK as it declined 'to follow British practice in supporting voluntary hospitals ... and excluded the Catholic Mater Hospital from the service because it refused to accept complete government control'.[181]

The early Fifties, more than any other, was the period when, in Joseph Lee's phrase, both London and Dublin 'played Pontius Pilate on the North',[182] willing, despite the rhetoric of the new Republic of Ireland, to let the partition of thirty years before take the strain of those 'colliding cultures'. And yet, as Lyons himself expressed it, the enduring question of partition and the welfare advances of the late Forties and early Fifties *were* linked in a highly significant manner. For within a decade, he explained, 'Northern Ireland passed from the status of an exceptionally backward area to full membership of the welfare state. The picture was not without its dark shadows ... but it is necessary to insist on the extent of the improvement, since this improvement opened a wide gap between the social services in the two parts of Ireland and in doing so did more to reinforce the partition of the country than perhaps any other single factor.'[183]

To ministers in London, the division of Ireland was a solution to a rupture in the British Empire devised by a previous political generation best left undisturbed. But other vexing imperial residuals could not be ignored around the Cabinet table in the Downing Street of the 1950s. The Indian Empire may already have been dismantled into three independent nations (India, Pakistan (East and West, now Bangladesh and Pakistan) and Ceylon (now Sri Lanka), all three of which remained within the Commonwealth), but elsewhere in Africa and the Far East, with a string of military bases between them, there was a variable-geometry Empire with a host of relationships to the home country (colony, protectorate, dominion) that was still intact, with but a few colonies on the road to independence in 1953. The variety of strategies adopted towards them[184] and a host of insurgencies of various kinds from Malaya to Kenya (and, shortly, Cyprus)[185] absorbed a great deal of ministerial time and energy.

In the early 1950s Churchill could not bear the long retreat from Empire, including Britain's 'informal Empire' in the Middle East. His foreign affairs private secretary, Anthony Montague Browne, shared his boss's 'deep misgivings over our "scuttle" (his own words)' of Eden's – and the Cabinet's – policy of negotiating with Egypt a withdrawal from the huge British military base in the Suez Canal Zone (apart from a residual care-and-maintenance presence). Montague Browne recalled how

The Prime Minister was often unwontedly silent as the Middle East scene deteriorated, though from time to time the lava overlipped the volcano's edge, and he expressed himself in vehement and melancholy terms. To one tirade he added, as if in answer to the unspoken question 'Why don't you put a stop to this disgraceful capitulation, since you see its consequences so clearly?' the following deeply sad conclusion, spoken in calm and meditative terms. 'You must remember that the Office of Prime Minister is not a dictatorship, certainly not in peacetime. I am surrounded by hungry eyes. Poor Anthony' (not me – the other one [i.e. Eden]).[186]

His very last words at his very last Cabinet meeting showed just how shot-through with imperial sentiment the Old Man was when he urged his colleagues to weave 'still more closely the threads which bound together the countries of the Commonwealth or as he still preferred to call it, the Empire'.[187]

But just how imperially did others think in the early to mid-1950s before the jolt of Suez? James (now Jan) Morris, in *Farewell the Trumpets*, the final evocative volume of his trilogy on the British Empire, noticed on returning from Everest in 1953 how the wording of the Coronation ceremony had been diluted:

Victoria's great-great granddaughter was crowned Queen of England on a drizzly day in June . . . The Coronation ceremony was still recognizably imperial, and all the Commonwealth Prime Ministers were there: Nehru svelte in his silken jacket, bluff Robert Menzies from Australia, D. S. Senanayake, the Ceylonese tea-planter, even the dour Dr Malan of South Africa, who had been a frank pro-Nazi, who was an outspoken Republican . . . The imperial symbols were paraded as always, the flags and the bearskins, the battle-honours and the horse-drummers . . .

But when, amid the arcane splendour of Westminster Abbey, before the hushed peers and the silent trumpeters, the ninety-ninth Archbishop of Canterbury proclaimed Elizabeth Queen, he did so in evasive terms. Her father had been 'by the Grace of God of the United Kingdom of Great Britain and Northern Ireland and of the British Dominions beyond the Seas, King, Defender of the Faith, Emperor of India'. His daughter was 'of the United Kingdom of Great Britain and Northern Ireland and of Her other Realms and Territories, Queen, Head of the Commonwealth, Defender of the Faith'. The fanfares blared, the congregation stood, *Vivat! Vivat!* rang out across the fane: but there was no denying the bathos of this grey title, or hiding the process of retreat that had given birth to it.[188]

The wording may have changed since her father had sat where she now sat, but the lady to whom the cries of 'Vivat!' were directed was, and remained, a true believer in what she conceived to be the vitality of the best of the imperial legacy – the Commonwealth ideal. As her loyal and worldly private secretary Martin Charteris put it to me many years later: 'Has anybody ever thought of a more dignified way of getting out of Empire?'[189] The Queen had imbibed the views not only of her father but also of her tutor Sir Henry Marten on the importance of the Commonwealth and she expressed it unambiguously during her twenty-first birthday broadcast in April during the royal tour of South Africa when she famously said: 'I declare before you all that my whole life, whether it be long or short, shall be devoted to your service and the service of our great Imperial family . . .'[190]

Six years later, during Coronation week, there was still a great deal of vitality in sentiment. Indeed the official souvenir programme was dripping with it. Its first page listed no fewer than fifty-seven imperial varieties of dominion, colony or protectorate,[191] an eloquent testimony both to the rag-bag accumulation of the territorial empire and to what Anil Seal has called the 'simultaneous chess on innumerable boards', increasingly 'running into stalemates' on which the range of Empire-oriented Whitehall departments were now ever more having to play.[192]

But how deeply had the imperial experience permeated the home country in 1953 beyond every schoolchild's memory from the late 1880s to the late 1950s of maps on the wall of a world with great swathes tinted in British imperial pink? A considerable debate about the degree to which Empire and imperial enthusiasms aroused the curiosity or loyalty of the bulk of the population developed among historians in the years after the governors-general and the district commissioners had come home to Gloucestershire or Perthshire or, if still young, to berths in the Civil, the Diplomatic or, in some cases, the Queen's Secret Service.*

It was another Englishman with a special feel for Empire, India in particular, who first aroused my interest in this question. This was Cyril Radcliffe, eminent lawyer, wartime civil servant and, after 1945, an outstanding figure among the 'Good and Great' summoned by governments of all kinds to chair royal commissions and committees of inquiry.[193] As was very apparent when I called on him towards the end of his life early in 1976 when preparing a piece on good-and-greating for *The Times*,[194] Lord Radcliffe had never really

---

* It was one of this special breed, a devotee of Kipling's works who prefers not to be named, who, drawing on his long experience of palm, pine and sand, answered a question of mine about what MI6 officers did better than their CIA counterparts with the words: 'We are better at understanding those people and those places who do not want to be Americans or America.'

recovered from drawing the boundary lines in 1947 between what were to become India and Pakistan in the knowledge that wherever the final decisions lay, the lines would be crossed by thousands of refugees and streaked with much blood.[195]

On 2 October 1947, five weeks after returning to England and two months after British rule in India ended, Radcliffe broadcast his 'Thoughts on India as "The Page is Turned"'. As he would later do in beautifully crafted essays on such great imperial figures as Mountstuart Elphinstone, Governor of the Bombay Presidency in the 1820s,[196] Radcliffe evoked the people and purposes in a manner few could match. To his BBC listeners he confessed that:

I find it something of a mystery that the life and doings of the British in India should have made so slight an impress upon the imagination of their countrymen at home . . . They were doing an almost unbelievable thing – rightly or wrongly, well or ill, let us forget that question for the moment – a small section of the people of these islands for 150 years exercised in our name a direct sovereignty over larger and larger parts of this huge sub-continent . . . Yet somehow the imagination of our people, which is reflected in its art and literature, remained untouched.[197]

Radcliffe in the same broadcast caught perfectly what David Watt called the opening of Elgar's Symphony No. 1 side of Empire, the passage marked *nobilmente*,[198] though pride was tinged with a recognition that, in the end, imperialism was an imposition of one people's culture on another, however careful the imposers were not to rub up excessively against the grain of the imposed-upon culture.

'The gifts we brought', judged Radcliffe, 'were Roman: peace, order, justice and the fruits that those things bring.' Such benefits were admirable but, of themselves, insufficient:

They are the structure, but not the heart or the brain in the life of a people. It may be that somewhere on our course we mistook the means for the end and, absorbed in our practical tasks, we failed to penetrate to the heart or soul of India. It may be that the government of one people by another can never be the best government in the long run, since benevolence and fairness are no substitute for national inspiration.[199]

Gazing across the 'five continents in which British soldiers lie buried', Radcliffe concluded that: 'We have been such wanderers that the mud of every country is on our shoes . . . In all recorded history up to the present no people has ever mixed its dust with the dust of the wide world.'[200]

As the great exodus from Empire neared its end in the mid-1960s, Radcliffe returned to the lack of imperial imprint in the wax of collective British memory. He thought it absurd how so many commentators had seized upon the remarks of Harry Truman's Secretary of State, Dean Acheson, when he told his military audience at West Point on 5 December 1962 that 'Great Britain has lost an empire and has not yet found a role.'[201] To Radcliffe, as he told students at the London School of Economics during its 1965 annual oration, 'this shows a complete misunderstanding of the British mentality . . . The fact is that the British people are not grieving over their lost empire at all. When it existed the people as a whole had very little to do with it, and, except for one or two brief, Mafeking-like periods, they felt no more than a detached and tepid pride in its existence.'[202]

Even of the 'special case', India, was this true, 'but then the whole British relationship with India, astonishing in its achievement, was conducted either by incurious military professionals or by a minute section of the people, little more than a handful of families from England, Ireland and Scotland, while the remainder of the population pursued its lives with a stolid indifference to what was going on'.[203]

This is roughly the conclusion most British analysts have subsequently reached about the popular, as distinct from what two of them, Robinson and Gallagher, famously called the 'official mind' of imperialism.[204] One can, as John Mackenzie, a historian of public opinion and imperialism, has warned, overdo the lack of popular interest in what some in the nineteenth century liked to conceive of as Greater Britain (which was as absurd as calling Scotland 'North Britain'). Mackenzie nicely sends up the view that 'by the time decolonisation had been achieved, Empire was already forgotten, surviving in the national consciousness as little more than a source of nostalgic philately'.[205] Certainly the imperial and, later, Empire/Commonwealth notion *did* impinge at moments of spectacle (such as royal jubilees or coronations), trauma and anxiety (declarations of war in 1914 and 1939) and relief and celebration (November 1918 or VE Day and VJ Day in 1945). It would be wrong, however, to overplay the imperial element in the genuine mass interest in monarchy, certainly from the time Victoria made her transition from the Widow of Windsor to the Empress of India in the 1880s right through to the Queen's Coronation in 1953 and the highly successful, crowd-pulling Commonwealth tours which followed in the remaining Fifties and early Sixties.

There was, too, for those of us who had a late late-imperial childhood, as David Cannadine has put it,[206] an empire presence on the table (Camp coffee with its Indian bearer on the label) or on the living-room floor (the toy soldiers with which we played usually had 'Empire Made' embossed on their base). And, of course, every Sunday there was *Family Favourites* on the wireless, whose soothing ballads were often accompanied by the vexing percussion of insurgency in Malaya, Kenya or Cyprus; these are the moments that impinged.

This accumulation of impressions was real enough, but it did not give my generation its heroes or celebrities, none of whom would today have been invited to spend time in either the jungle or the Big Brother house. In America, as the US political and social historian Daniel Boorstin brilliantly illustrated, the 'famous for being famous' phenomenon was already well developed;[207] in the UK it was confined to one or two prototype television panellists such as Gilbert Harding and Bob Boothby. Our heroes had to earn their celebrity, as Tom Finney, Stanley Matthews and Roger Bannister, the world's first sub-four-minute miler, did.

When I first met Bannister in the 1990s for an interview at the same Iffley Road, Oxford, track on which he had set the record of 3 minutes 59.4 seconds on 6 May 1954, he turned out to be exactly as I had imagined him – charming, thoughtful, modest and quietly patriotic – the epitome of the understated hero. He was, for me and many of my generation, much more a shaper of our notion of what Britishness meant than any imperial artefact or figurehead. Sir Roger talked me through the race. He had rested for five days, he recalled, so felt full of running. His pacemakers, Chris Brasher for the first lap, then Christopher Chataway, did their stuff. Chataway 'took me round to the three-quarter mile and I overtook him on the far side of the track and just managed to beat the record by a fraction of a second, so that was all right'.[208]

The three friends set off for London to celebrate. Not until the early hours of the next morning when they 'saw the papers' did they realize 'it was going to be quite big news'.[209] The *Daily Express* I read that day set the typically jingoistic tone: 'AT LAST – THE 4-MINUTE MILE: English victory beats world'.[210]

Bannister's patriotism was of a quieter variety than that of the Beaverbrook newspapers, but still palpable forty years on:

It was a lot of fun to be an athlete in those days. We were poor. The only way to travel round the world was to represent your country so we also had a curious kind of loyalty to country and even patriotism. The war was over. Everest had been climbed. And we were part of this scene. And I was going to have to do my National Service anyway. So that again linked you to the country.[211]

Sir Roger's reflection captures exactly in a few sentences the mood of the fleeting having-it-so-good patch between the Coronation and Suez. One of the great pictures of 1954 is that of Chataway, Brasher and Bannister in Downing Street in their sports kit, being greeted by a beaming Churchill, no doubt purring with pleasure at this latest example of British pluck, pride and prowess. Not all of the sporting patriotism was so gentlemanly or so understated.

Moving from Iffley Road to Wembley Stadium, for example, you might well have heard the England fans singing at a team of uncomprehending Hungarians on 25 November 1953 that 'if it wasn't for the English, you'd be Krauts'.[212] And the cumulative impact of television was slowly changing notions of fame and celebrity in politics as well as sport. A choice illustration of this occurred on a bizarre and very Fifties-like journey taken over a year before Roger Bannister joined the sporting immortals by an unlikely trio of politicians: Robert Boothby, a maverick Conservative MP, the equally odd left-winger Tom Driberg, and Lady Violet Bonham Carter.

The three of them were to appear on the Good Friday edition of *Any Questions?* on the BBC Home Service in April 1953, which was to be broadcast from Minehead in Somerset. 'I have never spent an *odder* Good Friday,' Lady Vi recorded in her diary:

Bob Boothby called for me by arrangement about 10 to drive down to Minehead. To my amazement I saw a stowaway in the back of the car whom I recognized as Tom Driberg . . . We had a long + beautiful drive in a vast silver Jaguar of Bob's – on a most radiant day – the roads packed with Easter traffic to begin with – but clearing after we got past Basingstoke. We went the old familiar Andover–Amesbury road – Driberg bleating the whole time to be put down in a church and Bob firmly refusing. D is apparently an Anglo-Catholic – loving church councils, Liturgies, + Masses + knowing by heart all the churches in which these things are practised.

Combined with his Churchiness is a strong Bevanite loyalty + a tendresse for Communism . . . We lunched at Amesbury where lots of old tabby cats crawled out of corners in the hotel + hailed Bob like a God. They had seen him on Television. Our waiter said 'In the News [the name of the BBC's prototype political discussion programme] – + now in the George' – with infinite pride. Television fame beats all others.[213]

No change there, then.

For all the shifts in notions of national and international, from lasting greatness to fleeting celebrity, the most noticeable fixture, despite the shrivelling of Empire with Indian independence but a few years before, is that the early-Fifties notion of great-powerdom and global influence remained the expectation for successive UK governments and the bulk of the population over which they presided. Fifty years later, despite the near total disappearance of empire and thirty years spent within (though often at loggerheads with) the differing versions of the European Community, it was this enduring trait that would strike the most knowledgeable of overseas observers.

A few days before writing this page I had lunch with Mel Cappe, former Clerk of the Privy Council (Cabinet Secretary) in Ottawa and now Canadian High Commissioner in London. We talked about the overhang of empire and great-powerdom. Mel told me that he and his fellow 'old Commonwealth' high commissioners sometimes talked about this among themselves. Their conclusion? That it was far easier for the former dominions (Canada, Australia and New Zealand) to shed the old impulses: 'We have grown up, but the British elite has not woken up to that. It's still deep in their psyche. There are elements of the elite here that still have an old, world-class mentality.'[214]

Few mentalities came more 'world class' than Winston Churchill's, and his post-1945 version of it took a very distinctive shape and very special geographical configuration.

6

The Geometric Conceit

'I attended most of the meetings with Truman in the White House Annexe. Thought him a very cheerful and nice man, though performing an act of continuous hearty efficiency, romping through the agenda with a loud, gay voice. He was quite abrupt on one or two occasions with poor old Winston and had a tendency, after one of the old man's powerful and emotional declarations of faith in Anglo-American co-operation, to cut it off with a "Thank you, Mr Prime Minister. We might pass that to be worked out by our advisers." A little wounding. It was impossible not to be conscious that we are playing second fiddle.'

Evelyn Shuckburgh, Private Secretary to Anthony Eden,
diary entry for 5 January 1952.[1]

'I think Churchill was trying to develop a somewhat emotional as well as a very grand strategic plan for Europe. I remember tackling him on this at the time when I was trying to push Eden into some gesture towards Europe in 1952. I remember tackling Winston about this and saying, "But you, Prime Minister, made this speech yourself and spoke of the 'European Army in which we would play an honourable and active part.' What did you mean by that?" And he said, "Well, I really meant it for them and not for us."'

Sir Anthony Nutting, minister of state at the Foreign Office, 1951–6.[2]

'[Eden] used to put it rather simply . . . he used to put it to me this way . . . "Well, you see, in my constituency in Leamington there are many of my constituents who have relatives in Canada or Australia or New Zealand or . . . in South Africa. But I don't know any of them who talk about their relatives on the Continent of Europe" . . . That settled it for him.'

Sir Frank Roberts, former senior diplomat, recalling the early 1950s in 1993.[3]

'[Churchill] gave me a lecture on the three intersecting circles – those represented by the United States, by the Commonwealth and by Europe. And he said to me, "Young man, never let Britain escape from any of them."'

Lord Franks, Ambassador to Washington, 1948–52,
recalling a 1948 conversation in 1980.[4]

'You cannot ignore the facts for they glare upon you.'

A sentiment frequently expressed by Churchill during his last premiership.[5]

Did Churchill ignore the facts? As his foreign affairs private secretary, Sir Anthony Montague Browne (who heard him utter those words), put it long after: 'The transition from being a really great world power downwards is a very difficult one and one that can hardly be managed. It runs itself.'[6] And it still had far to run when Churchill stepped out of No. 10 to offer his resignation to his beloved Queen in April 1955.

But was Churchill's notion that Britain should use its special place at the triangulation point of Atlantic/Empire-Commonwealth/European relationships to maximize its power so out of kilter with the glaring realities of the mid-twentieth-century world? In 1991 international historian David Reynolds wrote in his *Britannia Overruled*,

Today this geometrical conceit seems far-fetched, but it grew out of international circumstances in mid-century. Britain did have a place in all three arenas. The problem was that those circumstances did not last. In a decade from 1955 Britain's relationship with America became one of dependence, the Commonwealth and Sterling Area crumbled, and Western Europe was transformed by the creation of the EEC without British participation. Underlying all three developments was the country's rapid and catastrophic economic decline.[7]

In 1951, or even 1955, only the greatest pessimist could have anticipated the scale of the economic and industrial undertow pulling against national resources, including those accumulations which, together, shape a country's influence abroad.

Apply Napoleon's test. Think of the world when the man was aged twenty rather than the seventy-seven years and 331 days Churchill was when he resumed the premiership in 1951. For Churchill's generation when young, the reach of British policy, territory and trade was both extraordinary (given the size and population of the home islands) *and* the norm. That it was the exceptional product of an unusual combination of circumstances and, there-fore, fleeting was lost on them until the debilitating and cumulative effect of a blend of the Kaiser, the interwar slump, Hitler and the superpower confron-tation of the Cold War exposed in the raw the harsh and unwelcome new realities of Britain's diminishing position in the world.

Churchill was far from alone among British twentieth-century prime min-isters in wishing to maximize his country's influence beyond its borders. He was, however, the last of them whose decisions truly shaped the course of world history (in 1940–41, when the UK really did stand alone in Europe and Churchill's leadership had profound and beneficial global consequences). In peacetime he remained convinced that the whole world benefited from Britain being a global power. He had not the slightest doubt that those places where the British imperial lion had trod were the better for it – what Anthony Montague Browne called 'the romantic side of his belief . . . the fact that where we had been, people were happier and where our writ ran there was not much murder and look what happened when we cleared out'.[8]

Churchill's and Britain's shared experience during the Second World War could be seen as a vindication of keeping a metaphorical foot in three camps, not as a conceit but as a saving and genuine reality. Keeping open the sea lanes from North America and mobilizing the shared resources of its vast imperial expanse, financially and materially lubricated by the critical Lend-Lease arrangement with the United States, had enabled Britain to remain free and, eventually, Europe to be liberated, with the inviolate United Kingdom as the indestructible dockyard-cum-army base and aircraft carrier for the greatest amphibious assault in history on D-Day in June 1944. This helps to explain why Churchill told General de Gaulle in 1944 that: 'Each time we have to choose between Europe and the open sea, we shall always choose the open sea.'[9]

There has long been a debate among historians of postwar Britain about the degree to which those glaringly hard facts about the realities of Britain's position were confronted by ministers, officials and the military after 1945. Our long and scratchy arguments about the UK and the European Union in its various stages and forms has brought the country's political class into this scholarly dance to a degree true of no other of our postwar debates, not even those that pirouette around consensus and decline. I am one of those who has some sympathy with the political and Whitehall generations in place between 1945 and 1955. Only so much adjustment of personal mental maps, as well as the wider geography of Britain's power, can be expected even from those whose minds tend towards the tougher end of the spectrum of synapses.

For me the most important question is the degree to which Britain's weakening position was seen as temporary, explicable by the national resources consumed by the war and the huge debts and obligations with which that conflict saddled the country. Ernest Bevin was classically and influentially of this school and saw the economic possibilities of continuing the Empire, in Africa especially.[10] Others, such as Oliver Franks, realized much earlier (in his case during the Marshall Plan negotiations which he chaired in Paris in the summer of 1947) that permanent diminution in Britain's position was the new reality that had to be faced.[11]

The question of British attitudes to the nascent European Community in the early 1950s turns very much on these perceptions of the temporary/permanent nature of the problems besetting a once-great power grappling with tough times. Bevin, for example, was a great patron and admirer of Franks. They breathed as one on the Marshall Plan in 1947 and NATO in 1949, but not on Britain's participation in the negotiations which led to the creation of the European Coal and Steel Community in 1952 when six nations (France, Germany, Italy, Belgium, the Netherlands and Luxembourg) pooled their needs and shared resources in the two industries which at the time formed much of the basis of advanced manufacturing capacity.

The prism of subsequent events has, for some analysts, thrown certain of the more important early-Fifties' players into stark and unflattering relief – just short of a group of myopic, hubristic grotesques. The foreign secretaries Bevin and Eden have suffered especially. The European question has envenomed and distorted the picture still further. I am hardly an apologist (see, for example, my treatment of Eden's June 1952 Cabinet paper on 'British Overseas Obligations' on pp. 38–42), but I am closer to Alan Milward than to Edmund Dell in my understanding of the swirl of calculations and emotions which led the Attlee and Churchill Cabinets to view Europe and to deal with it the way that they did in 1950–54.

Edmund Dell's was a special voice within the cacophony of historians who engaged in the rolling conversation of the 1990s about Britain's postwar history. He was the only heavyweight author who had also been a practising politician and Cabinet minister, yet he was by far the most astringent about the failings of the political class of which he had been such an intellectually distinguished member. This equally true of his contributions to the study of both economic policy-making by successive Chancellors of the Exchequer[12] and the rational conduct of Cabinet government.[13] No possible prisoner remained untaken by this Maigret among contemporary historians. And nowhere was he fiercer when clapping on the handcuffs than in his *The Schuman Plan and the British Abdication of Leadership in Europe*, which was published in the mid-1990s.[14]

Dell castigated the Whitehall insiders for failing to see that a Franco-German rapprochement through the creation of a coal and steel pool – the sinews both of war (whose possibility would thereby be diminished between the old antagonists) and of economic recovery (which would thereby be quickened and strengthened) – was in both Europe's *and* Britain's interests. That it could be achieved without jeopardizing Britain's own engines of military production if, once again, the country stood alone, or without seriously diminishing UK sovereignty, might not be understood that easily beyond Whitehall. But, surely, in Dell's argument, it is the job of career diplomats and senior civil servants to bring those capacities of foresight and intelligence for which they were recruited to bear on those problems on which most ministers and the bulk of the public remain atavistically benighted. The Whitehall insiders are Dell's guilty men (with a few notable exceptions such as Franks). If only they had persuaded ministers to join the negotiations, as the French proposed out of the blue in May 1950, the UK, wrote Dell, might have 'succeeded in sucking federalism' out of the proposed supranational high authority for the Coal and Steel Community as it had out of the Organization for European Economic Co-operation (which oversaw Marshall Aid and continued beyond it) or the initial proposals for the Council of Europe.[15]

Dell's peroration is formidable in the width of its castigations: Bevin was old and dying. There were younger, fitter men who could have replaced him. 'A major responsibility falls on Attlee for his complacent acceptance that Britain could be governed by invalids.'[16] As for the Foreign Office, it may have lacked sympathy with the European integrationists but it failed in 'its most elementary duties' because its job was 'to understand what was happening' on the Continent, 'the movements of opinion, what initiatives might therefore emerge, and how Britain might act and react'.[17]

The Conservatives go straight into Dell's dock along with Attlee and his ministers: 'The truth is that, despite the brave European vapourings of Churchill and his colleagues while in opposition, there was in practice nothing to choose between Conservative policy towards Europe and Labour policy towards Europe ... The Conservative Party's attitude in opposition was one of unprincipled opportunism. It began a tradition in which, with considerable damage to British interests, opposition parties exploit the European question against the government of the day by making speeches and proposals to which they have no intention of living, once back in office.'[18]

For Dell, this was an irreversibly pivotal moment. The second half of the twentieth-century British experience was profoundly different in consequence of our collective failure to think European:

Britain had played a positive role after the war in ensuring European security. But so far as economic integration and reconciliation with Germany were concerned, the story is very different. Dragged along by the USA, repelled by Europe, the UK could only criticize the ideas of others not elaborate ideas of its own. France could usurp Britain's leadership role in Europe only because the UK was not perceived as playing that role. The Schuman Plan was a political initiative in economic guise . . .'[19]

Britain's refusal to join the negotiations (both Attlee/Bevin's in 1950 and Churchill/Eden's in 1951) deprived the UK of the capacity to shape the European Coal and Steel Community Treaty.

It demonstrated to Western Europe what it had previously scarcely believed, that it could integrate, and achieve Franco-German reconciliation, without any assistance from the UK . . . It entrenched a Franco-German leadership in Europe into which the UK, even after twenty years membership [Dell was drafting his book in 1993–4] of the European Community, has never been able to penetrate.[20]

For Dell, the eighteen months either side of the 1951 general election was the period in which the country 'had spared itself the intellectual effort of actually reappraising Britain's position in the world',[21] with deleterious consequences for the rest of his life (Dell died in 1999).

As the Cabinet Office's historian of the UK and the European Community, Alan Milward (who, as we shall see, portrays the objections to Britain joining the Coal and Steel Community as both serious and, in many cases, valid), put it: 'Readers who expect government to have greater capacity for imaginative and drastic changes of direction than I allow for should turn to Dell's robust but scholarly text as an antidote to mine.'[22] Dell was right to emphasize the degree to which the final version of the ECSC had had much of the would-be federalism of its chief designer, Jean Monnet, siphoned from it during the process of negotiating the Treaty on which it rested. But, even so, the direction of the deep-set and widely shared British notions of the nature of the country's power, reach and international relationships went so strongly against the Monnet grain that it would have been very surprising indeed in the early

1950s if an accommodation had been reached (things might have been different a few years later – see Chapter 8).

Dell, as he wrote in its preface, had two men at his shoulder as he wrote his book:

Lord Franks was Provost of the Queen's College, Oxford when I was a history don there. During his time as Provost, 1946/8, he was also chairman of the Committee for European Economic Co-operation. He told me of his regrets that Britain seemed so unwilling to play a leading role in European integration. Robert Marjolin was one of the wisest men I have known. I was totally in sympathy with his unideological attitude to European issues. He told me that Britain could have held the leadership in Europe, in the years immediately following the Second World War, if it had had the will to do so. These two distinguished Europeans were much in my mind as I studied the British reaction to the Schuman Plan.[23]

But Marjolin's great friend and colleague, Jean Monnet, was both monomaniac *and* flexible about the step-by-step means of achieving European integration. It was his monomania about federalism which was like holding a crucifix to Dracula for most of those in the late 1940s and early 1950s Whitehall, whether ministers or officials. By 1950 Monnet was very well aware of this, which, no doubt, explains why he and Schuman gave London no advance warning of the coal and steel plan for fear that the British would seek to pluck out its federalist entrails before negotiations with Germany, Italy and the Benelux countries even began.

Marjolin was very revealing about this in his own memoirs. He captures the flexible monomania of Monnet perfectly:

At the same time Jean Monnet, dominated as he was by one idea, was aware that it was unrealistic to think of a federation in the near future. He had become persuaded of this in 1949, when he proposed to the French and the British a Franco-British union, a merging of the French and British economies . . .[24] This would have been the first step towards a European federation. But the British would hear no talk of federation nor of delegation of sovereignty; it is not even certain that they understood what the latter expression meant. Edwin Plowden, a senior Whitehall official, was later to say to Jean Monnet: 'We'd won the war, [we had worldwide responsibilities] and we weren't ready to form special links with the continent.'

Jean Monnet found that his attempt to create a federal nucleus around which Europe might be formed had failed to interest the one great power in the Old World then in a position to take on a political responsibility of that magnitude. Even in France, national sentiment was still too strong for the idea of a federation to have any chance of winning acceptance. It was necessary to come up with a scheme of smaller compass, one that would go some way towards the final goal without offending public opinion, which was as yet unreceptive.[25]

To understand the chasm between most British policy-makers in the late 1940s and early 1950s and the Monnet position, filled as it was with a mixed but dense detritus of emotion, calculation, pride, illusion and incomprehension, one needs a touch of social anthropology to set alongside the unsentimental and highly intelligent technocratic analysis Edmund Dell brought to everything he wrote.

One needs, in fact, a touch of Harold Macmillan – a serious player in the Churchill government's approaches to Europe in its various guises but already showing his simultaneous capacity for a lofty, historically infused detachment. Macmillan, along with the Home Secretary, Sir David Maxwell Fyfe, and the President of the Board of Trade, Peter Thorneycroft, was one of a very small number of Europe-minded ministers in that Cabinet who genuinely regretted the Prime Minister's continuing the Attlee–Bevin line. Churchill had a long and eloquent record of urging the western Europeans towards closer co-operation in the late 1940s, unlike the Foreign Secretary, Eden, from whom there were no rousing postwar speeches in Strasbourg or Zurich to foster false expectations. The letters home from the Empire to Leamington and towns and villages across the UK were the mood music for his ears, rather than Beethoven's Ninth-style odes to joy from European assemblies or councils. He told Shuckburgh, 'What you've got to remember is that, if you looked at the postbag of any English village and examined the letters coming in from abroad to the whole population, ninety per cent of them would come from way beyond Europe.'[26]

But for all his general Europhilia, Macmillan did not care for the way the continentals conducted the business of government – and he told them so. Speaking at Strasbourg on 15 August 1950, only a couple of months after the Attlee government had declined to take part in the negotiations on the Schuman Plan, he declared that,

The difference is temperamental and intellectual. It is based on a long divergence of two states of mind and methods of organisation. The continental tradition likes to reason *a priori* from the top downwards, from the general principle to the practical application. It is the tradition of St Thomas of [sic] Aquinas, of the schoolmen, and of the great continental scholars and thinkers. The Anglo-Saxons like to argue *a posteriori* from the bottom upwards, from practical experience. It is the tradition of Bacon and Newton.[27]

A few months later, Macmillan elaborated on this theme in private when the *Observer* journalist Nora Beloff asked him over lunch what he thought of the Schuman Plan: 'He told me that he was an old acquaintance of Jean Monnet who was a delightful person but with a foible for constructing enormous constitutional blueprints that had hardly any practical application. He advised me not to take the thing too seriously.'[28]

Macmillan, one of those whom international historian John Young labelled the 'Tory Strasbourgers' who had sat in the Assembly of the Council of Europe which met in that city from 1949,[29] told that same assembly in 1950, in the context of the proposed ECSC and the supranational High Authority which was to oversee its operations, that, 'Fearing the weakness of democracy, men have often sought safety in technocrats. There is nothing new in this. It is as old as Plato. But frankly the idea is not attractive to the British. We have not overthrown the divine right of Kings to fall down before the divine right of experts.'[30]

So much for Monnet. When one ponders the Macmillan theme, Monnet and his fellow planners represented a combination of several things old-fashioned Brits (certainly in the 1950s) found rather toe-curling. They were clever, French, left wing, Catholic and intellectual. And they were bureaucrats, too.

As Macmillan made plain at the time, the British would not let any such person lay a single finger on their heavy industries: 'One thing is certain. And we may as well face it. Our people are not going to hand any supranational authority the right to close down our pits or steelworks. We will allow no supranational authority to put large masses of our people out of work in Durham, in the Midlands, in South Wales, or in Scotland.'[31]

As for Robert Schuman, the French Foreign Minister who ran with Monnet's *grande idée* for coal and steel as the scaffolding for an eventual west-European federation, Macmillan saw him as a 'strange melancholy, quixotic figure, half politician, half priest', prone to delivering 'well phrased, philosophic, and rather impractical' speeches.[32]

Writing fifty years after Macmillan and Monnet, who, for all their quicksilver intellects, spoke past each other, the Foreign Office and European Union diplomat Robert Cooper focused on a general 'lesson' that every generation of would-be geopoliticians needs to relearn that, I think, applied to the circumstances of the European question in the late 1940s and early 1950s. In his view, 'foreigners are different. They have been brought up differently; their thoughts are structured differently by the different language they speak and the different books they have read; their habits have been influenced by different schools, different social customs, different national heroes, different churches, mosques and temples.'[33]

For all their close wartime collaboration (Monnet had worked for a time in the *British* Supply Council in early 1940s Washington[34]), even sophisticates like him and Macmillan could buttress their tendency to fall short of complete empathy by emphasizing national experiences. And, thanks to their war work, few politicians knew more about each other's countries than Monnet and Macmillan.

Michael Charlton used his microphone to great effect for BBC Radio in reconstructing the clash of British and continental approaches to the question of Europe in the 1950s and early 1960s:

Many years later, in Paris, I spoke to the man who had first tried to enlist Britain for the leadership of Europe. While often taken to task in England for what was considered a simplistic belief, that a proposition only had to be self-evidently true for it to become practical politics, he had however done more with an *idea* to unite Europe, in that crucial decade of the 1950s, than those in history who had tried to do it by force of arms. That former British civil servant, old Jean Monnet:

MONNET: 'I never understood why the British did not join this, which was so much in their interest. I came to the conclusion that it must have been because it was *the price of victory* – the illusion that you could maintain what you had, without change.'[35]

It was almost as if Monnet had received British Cabinet papers and eavesdropped on discussions in the Downing Street Cabinet Room in November 1951 shortly after the Conservatives had returned to power. On 29 November Churchill circulated a memorandum to the Cabinet shot through with 'price-of-victory'-style thinking. Referring to the Schuman Plan's bursting upon Whitehall in 1950 and the Labour government's refusal to join in the coal and steel negotiations, the Prime Minister declared that he welcomed the plan, partly as it probably rendered 'another Franco-German war physically impossible'.

I never contemplated Britain joining in this plan on the same terms as the continental partners. We should, however, have joined in all the discussions and, had we done so, not only a better plan would probably have emerged, but our own interests would have been watched at every stage. Our attitude towards further economic developments on the Schuman lines resembles that which we adopt about the European Army [the French plan for a European Defence Community]. We help, we dedicate, we play a part, but we are not merged and do not forfeit our insular or Commonwealth-wide character. I should resist any American pressure to treat Britain as on the same footing as the European states, none of whom have the advantages of the Channel and who were consequently conquered.[36]

The Churchill view, also the predominant Whitehall one in the early 1950s, was of a benign and skilful Britain bringing its statecraft to bear for the benefit of the Europeans and, incidentally, of the UK itself. It was as if Britain could be the manager of the new European team without joining the other six on the playing field. Much the same applied to European, as distinct from NATO, defence. Five days later, the Cabinet discussed the Pleven Plan (as the European Army proposal was called, after the French Defence Minister who initially made the running). Churchill followed Eden's line that the UK should continue to keep out of the negotiations, at which point, Macmillan recorded in his diary, Churchill

then turned to me and Maxwell Fyfe ... and asked if we were satisfied. I said that I thought the present position tragic, but that, in view of what Eden had said, we must accept it. But I thought that both the Schuman plan and the European army (on the Pleven–Monnet model) might break down. But was there not a danger that if it went through, the position in ten years would be still worse. There would be a European Community which would dominate Europe and would be roughly equal to Hitler's Europe of 1940. If we stay out, we risk that German domination of Europe which we have fought two wars to prevent ...[37]

Macmillan became more and more convinced that Britain's policy, by standing aside and offering its good offices plus certain military guarantees to whatever European Army emerged from the discussions, 'does not save us from the risks but deprives us of the control ...'[38]

Macmillan struck a crisis point in May 1952 and briefly considered resigning from the government over the European question. Thirty years later, in conversation with his official biographer, Alistair Horne, he reckoned resignation 'would have been a terrible mistake. We only had a sixteen majority and no enthusiasm in the country whatsoever for Europe.'[39] His despair about the Churchill Cabinet's European policy is quite apparent in his diary entry for 15 May:

A long Cabinet, and a very painful discussion about Europe and Strasbourg. The politicians in the Cabinet (of wh there are still a few) are divided, Salisbury being almost a disciple of Beaverbrook in his isolationism. The functionaries [almost certainly a swipe at Churchill's 'overlord' ministers such as Woolton, Leathers and Alexander[40]] (of which there are almost a majority) cannot make out what it is all about. The P.M. is puzzled and unhappy. It seems to me that he now turns avidly to minor problems (like railway fares) because he cannot grasp – or at any rate sees no way out of – the big ones.[41]

Churchill was indeed puzzled and low in May–June 1952. This affected, perhaps infected, his closest confidant, Jock Colville, who in the early hours of a Sunday morning at Chartwell, after listening to a long after-dinner discussion between Churchill and Cherwell which left him feeling 'wearied by the prospects of the future', penned an extraordinary entry in his diary:

It is foolish to continue living with illusions. One may bury one's head in the past, reading James Boswell or the privately printed letters of Labouchere to Lord Rosebery; or one may talk of forcing reality on the people by a slump with the accompaniment of hunger and unemployment and the consequent acceptance of a lower standard of living. But the facts are stark. At the moment we are just paying our way. A trade recession in America will break us; the competition of German metallurgical industries and the industrialisation of countries which were once the market for our industrial products will ruin our trade sooner or later and sap the remaining capital on which our high standard of living is based . . .

What can we do? Increasing productivity is only a palliative in the face of foreign competition. We cannot till sufficient soil to feed 50 million people. We cannot emigrate fast enough to meet the danger, even if we were willing to face the consequent abdication of our position as a great power and even if there were places for two-fifths of our population to go . . .

The Prime Minister is depressed and bewildered. He said to me this evening 'The zest is diminished.' I think it is more that he cannot see the light at the end of the tunnel.

Nor can I. But it is 1.30 a.m., approaching the hour when courage and life are at their lowest ebb.[42]

Earlier that weekend Cherwell had played upon Churchill's fixation with the 'English-speaking peoples', even suggesting a reverse take-over was possible by the older group of speakers within the British Empire. As Colville noted, 'Lord Cherwell sees hope in the union of the English Speaking World, economically and politically. He thinks that just as the Scots complained of

Union with England but ended by dominating Great Britain, so we in the end should dominate America.'[43]

Frustration in early 1952 could thus trigger some pretty extraordinary thinking. Even Macmillan, though, apart perhaps from the Home Secretary, Maxwell Fyfe, the most consistently pro-integration Cabinet figure, was not immune at moments of irritation with Europe. On 18 February, after a day of two Cabinet meetings, he noted, 'of course, the facts of European life remain. The French are frightened of the Germans; the Germans are frightened of themselves. (For they know that Hyde is there, always ready to replace Jekyll.)'[44] By the end of May frustration had led even him to succumb temporarily to the old imperial drumbeat when he confided to Colville in the Turf Club 'that he thought development of the Empire into an economic unit as powerful as the USA and the USSR was the only possibility'.[45]

This combination of atavism and pessimism exerted a pull on Churchill too. In that same Cabinet paper of 29 November 1951 Churchill told his colleagues:

... I never thought that Britain or the British Commonwealth should, either individually or collectively, become an integral part of a European Federation and have never given the slightest support to the idea ... Our first object is the unity and consolidation of the British Commonwealth and what is left of the former British Empire. Our second, the 'fraternal association' of the English-speaking world; and third, United Europe, to which we are a separate, closely – and specially – related ally and friend.[46]

With half of its trade flowing to and from the Empire and Commonwealth, and with its currency at the heart of a (largely) Commonwealth-based sterling area, was a late imperial flurry so absurd as a solution? Or did it merely bring nocturnal solace to those with governing authority on particularly disturbed nights in 1952?

As a permanent answer, it was certainly impossible. The General Agreement on Tariffs and Trade (the GATT) had been established in 1947 for the purpose of progressively freeing world trade by negotiated, mutual agreement. It was but a pale shadow of the planned International Trade Organization foreseen at Bretton Woods which the Americans, in particular, hoped would be the engine of worldwide reduction in customs barriers[47] (gradually dissolving Britain's imperial trading system as it went). And at the GATT's conference in Annecy in 1949, the 'tariffs registered' by the participating countries 'were generally high' and 'for all its fine rhetoric, the United States administration saw all pressuring to reduce tariffs through concerted action in GATT as presenting a domestic political problem which it preferred itself not to face, whatever it called on the others to do'.[48] But the trend of the world's advanced economies was towards freer trade and away from the protective systems thrown up in the 1930s, including that of the British Empire constructed on the basis of the 1932 Ottawa Agreement.

As Alan Milward put it, much of the domestic UK political debate about Commonwealth relations in the early 1950s was conducted in a 'sentimental half-light'.[49] Sentiment was strengthened by fear about competition from a resurgent West German economy, especially among British manufacturers who, as Milward observed,

had a wonderful opportunity really between 1945 and 1960 with Germany absent from world markets. They simply couldn't produce the goods that they could have sold. And the goods they did produce were really of such an inferior quality that they were very easily eliminated by German exports as soon as they began . . .

It's a huge defect in the structure of British manufacturing which is to blame. The Treasury was admitting in '49 that there'd been only the smallest addition to the capacity in British engineering, in spite of this huge demand for British engineering products. And it was also admitting that, with the very first German exports returning, then a lot of the additional capacity might have to be wound down again.[50]

A kind of anticipatory pessimism afflicted British industry. In 1949 several top firms joined *The Times* in a campaign to protect the UK from scarcely renascent German exports.[51]

As Milward also pointed out, the 'priority of sterling and international policy over manufacturing industry'[52] further exacerbated the position and this was reflected, too, in Whitehall's geography of power where industry 'was represented in government by the Board of Trade, a ministry whose influence was small after 1951 compared to that of the Bank [of England], and even smaller compared to that of the Treasury'.[53]

But the chance combination of political and civil service personalities atop the Board of Trade after 1951 in the persons of the President, Peter Thorneycroft, and the Permanent Secretary, Sir Frank Lee, led to at least one clearing in the forest of late-imperial sentimentality and economic half-reality. In his younger days Lee, a stocky, untidy, unorthodox figure, had been a man of empire. After Cambridge he had joined the Colonial Office and had 'served as a District Officer in Nyasaland [now Malawi], where he vigorously organised football as an alternative to tribal feuds'.[54] During the war as a Treasury official, he worked with Keynes in Washington as the great man tussled with the Americans, whose 'main goal was the elimination of imperial preference [while] the British were after reductions in the US tariff'.[55] Lee adored working with Keynes ('. . . we felt like Lucifer's followers in Milton, "Rejoicing in their matchless chief". His industry was prodigious, his resilience and continual optimism constant wonder to those of us more inclined to pessimism . . .'[56])

Lee was long remembered in Whitehall for his energy and for his realism about Britain's postwar economy and its place in the world. In the early 1950s he encouraged Thorneycroft to wean his colleagues off imperial preference, just as in the early 1960s he more than any other public servant shifted the official mind of Whitehall towards Europe. In fact, from his first day in office, Thorneycroft realized that he and his permanent secretary breathed as one on trade policy. As Lee later told his son-in-law, Richard Wilson (who rose to the very top of Whitehall himself as Cabinet Secretary during the Blair administrations), he walked down the corridor at the Board of Trade to call on Thorneycroft not at all sure they were going to get on: 'But the first thing Thorneycroft said was, "You don't believe in all this Imperial Preference nonsense do you?" From that moment they hit it off.'[57]

Thorneycroft, aided by Lee, persuaded the Cabinet and, more difficult still, the Conservative Party conference delegates, that to sustain great-powerdom they could not rest on imperial trading.[58] As economic historian Charles Feinstein put it, 'The long crusade for imperial preference was fatally crushed at the 1954 party conference. An amendment to an official motion demanding "such revision of the General Agreement on Tariffs and Trade as will restore freedom of action in respect of imperial preference" was defeated by a substantial majority. Britain was firmly committed to the fundamental principles of a worldwide multilateral trading system promoted by GATT.'[59] Though vestiges of the Ottawa system ran on until Britain's accession to the European Economic Community in 1973, after 1954 it was a question of lingering residuals rather than any attempt to buck the developing multilateral trend. Imperial preference was doomed from this point on. Lord Thorneycroft was terribly pleased when I talked of 1954 with him forty years later. Nobody remembered it, he said, what he and Frank Lee had done. But he believed it was one of the most important things he had achieved as a politician.[60]

It fell to Oliver Franks, back from Washington and now Chairman of Lloyds Bank, to preach trading reality to a wider British public when he delivered the 1954 BBC Reith Lectures on 'Britain and the Tide of World Affairs'. He told his listeners firmly that the tide had gone out for empire trade for ever:

A group of people in Britain rightly seeing the importance of maintaining and increasing trade with the Commonwealth, advocate a policy of increased imperial preference. It is pointless to argue the merits of this proposal for the simple reason that it is out of date and has no chance.

I am under the impression that we have raised the matters two or three times at Commonwealth conferences and have got nowhere. At the end of the last discussion the Rhodesias were willing, New Zealand reminiscent, Australia oracular, and all the rest opposed: Canada absolutely, on principle and on expediency, for it would involve living next door to a violently opposed United States; the Asian countries because the idea reminded them of colonialism and imperialism.[61]

For Franks, however, the sterling area in 1954 remained crucial to the country's fortunes and 'continuing greatness'. Though the Bank of England's acting 'as central banker to the Sterling Area can add to the risks we run . . . the Sterling Area is a great market for us, and it is a natural market . . .' And if Britain was 'to maintain the style of living to which we are accustomed, if we are to play the part in the world which we assume, we need great markets overseas'.[62]

Those sentiments would have struck Franks' listeners on the BBC Home Service as both natural and reassuring. They might have sounded a less comforting note had those same listeners been privy to the ROBOT story two years before or had they been able to foresee the future pressure on the pound from 1955 right through to 1977 caused by the country's relative economic underperformance and the Bank of England's role as holder of the sterling balances and maintainer of the world's second reserve currency after the US dollar.

The lecture in Franks' Reith series which was arresting in the context of 1954 was the one devoted to 'Britain and the Making of Europe'. That Franks intended it to be so is plain from his opening sentences: 'I think most of you would be surprised if I suggested that August 10, 1952, was likely to be regarded by future historians as the most important date in the post-war decade of western Europe. But that is what I think. Why? It was the day on which the Schuman Plan became a reality.'[63]

There are a number of reasons Franks' assessment rang – and still rings – true. Firstly, the integration of coal and steel is not high on the list of world questions that would have induced a racing pulse in 1954. Secondly, the real heat within the European question then and for the previous three years was the possibility of a European Army – a live issue from the moment during the crisis months of the Korean War in late 1950 that the Truman administration in Washington became convinced that without a serious West German contribution towards NATO's conventional forces, the alliance's front line in Europe would undoubtedly remain shaky. In early-Fifties Britain it was the defence question, rather than implementation of the Coal and Steel Community, which caught public and political attention.[64] And it was the EDC, rather than the ECSC, that fuelled the most memorable rhetorical flights that encapsulated Foreign Secretary Anthony Eden's general attitude towards Britain and European integration. One, in particular, has resonated down the decades, from Eden's address at Columbia University in New York on 11 January 1952 when accepting an honorary degree: 'The American and British peoples should each understand the strong points in the other's national character. If you drive a nation to adopt procedures which run counter to its instincts, you weaken and may destroy the motive force of its action.'

Eden knew only too well that Dean Acheson, his opposite number in Washington, was keen for Britain to be part of a wider western-European integration and had been from the moment the Marshall Plan negotiations got underway in the summer of 1947. This explains Eden's next passage, dealing with what allies should and should not do to each other, which served as a preamble to the physiological metaphor for which he will always be remembered:

This is something you would not wish to do – or any of us would wish to do – to an ally on whose effective co-operation we depend.

You will realise that I am speaking of the frequent suggestions that the United Kingdom should join a federation on the continent of Europe. This is something which we know, in our bones, we cannot do.[65]

The man who helped Eden draft his Columbia speech, Evelyn Shuckburgh, later explained (long after he had become a convert to Britain in Europe) that in 1952 'we *thought* in our bones that we had this wider role which we ought to keep ourselves free to play. That we were not the sort of people who could give over control of armed forces, or political decisions, to other people. That's what he meant by "We know in our bones that we cannot do it."'[66] Churchill would not have been shocked by this. In his Cabinet paper on 'United Europe' the previous November he told his colleagues that '[w]e must not lose all consciousness of our insular position', adding that the 'American mind jumps much too lightly over the many difficulties of European federation'.[67]

Eden's talk of the 'unalterable marrow' of the British character at Columbia did not play well in Washington, where Acheson, in the words of his assistant Luke Battle, thought the EDC 'the only game in town' in terms of German rearmament generally and in Paris in particular. The power of Eden's words in New York helped cause the delay in the vote on EDC ratification in the French parliament.[68]

Of this factor, Oliver Franks, still Britain's Ambassador in Washington when Eden spoke at Columbia, was very well aware. He had known since chairing the Marshall Plan negotiations in Paris in 1947 that the 'Americans believed that the key to European recovery lay in economic integration, and they put pressure on Britain'.[69]

In 1990 I had a conversation with Lord Franks about this. Ernest Bevin swore by Franks on Anglo-American, if not European, matters and, as Foreign Secretary, was responsible for prising him away from the provostship of The Queen's College Oxford to head the Marshall talks, and, later, persuading him to become British Ambassador in Washington. I began by asking Franks how he would have replied if Bevin had sought his advice about the Schuman Plan in May 1950.

FRANKS: I should have [mentioned] the idea of Monnet, put into practice by Robert Schuman, persuading Adenauer to bring France and Germany together, as Schuman described to me, 'in an embrace so close that neither could draw back far enough to hit the other'. I thought this was worth everything for the peace of Europe. And the Coal and Steel Community was the vehicle that Schuman foresaw as the way of doing this. And, of course, it produced the Six – the three Benelux countries, France, Germany and Italy. No, I think we ought to have gone in.

HENNESSY: Did anybody ask you that at the time?

FRANKS: No.

HENNESSY: It was what Acheson thought too; what you thought, wasn't it?

FRANKS: Yes. But he was in London at the time. No, nobody asked me. Why should they?[70]

At the time Franks was well aware of the dichotomy between what Eden called national character (and what we would now call national identity) and national interests. This, as a former British diplomat of a later generation, Sir David Goodall, rightly observes, has been at the root of the UK's 'ambiguous relationship' with the European community in its various forms over the past fifty years arising from 'the fact that British interests, which dictate wholehearted membership [Goodall was writing in the spring of

2004], are in conflict with its identity, which flinches from it'.[71]

Oliver Franks, in his Reith Lectures fifty years earlier, had to deal with another British trait vis-à-vis an integrating Europe which certainly did not apply when David Goodall was writing – indifference. Franks in 1954 thought that

> most of us have assumed that the Europe we knew so well continues today. I believe there is an important sense in which this assumption is mistaken. The old Europe of independent, quarrelling, sovereign nations is no longer fully alive. We have made this mistake because, on the whole, we have been uninterested in what has been happening in Europe since the war. Indeed, there is no subject of absolutely first-class importance to Britain on which the great majority of the British people have thought less and cared less.[72]

For Franks, therefore, it was a matter for regret, but not surprise, 'that the Government since the war has faithfully reflected the conviction of the electorate that Britain must not be absorbed into Europe'.[73]

By the time Franks delivered his Reith Lectures, the French Assembly had finally rejected the European Defence Community. So the proposed European Army, which Churchill had derided as 'a sludgy amalgam' (telling Roger Makins as they drafted a speech together in the Paris embassy early in 1952, '"What soldiers want to sing is their own marching songs",' before breaking into the 'Sambre et Meuse'[74]) collapsed in ruins. Out of the rubble, however, Eden (at his negotiating best) had proposed another instrument for levering-in German rearmament – via a new Western European Union building on the Western Union created by Bevin in 1948 to give substance to the Brussels Treaty (which preceded the creation of NATO).[75] To create confidence, the Churchill government pledged to keep a tactical air force and four divisions of the British Army in West Germany (unless an overseas emergency or a financial crisis triggered their negotiated withdrawal).[76]

This apparent British rescue of a failed European attempt at supranational-ism seemed to underscore the wisdom of *us* helping *them* to integrate sensibly while not getting drawn in ourselves. This was exactly the domestic political climate in the autumn of 1954 when Franks stepped inside BBC Broadcasting House to record his Reith Lectures. He tried to turn the collapse of the EDC and the utility of the WEU to advantage before the microphone, noting that Britain's 'life and security are not independent of western Europe: they cannot be decided separately from the fate of western Europe' and that the UK had 'recognised this in our relations with western

Europe, in the North Atlantic Treaty, in the original Brussels Pact and in the new Western European Union'.[77]

'We are positively involved together. Together we sink or swim,' Franks told his listeners. 'Our attitude to western Europe should be based on this hard fact.'[78] And here Franks the pragmatist swung in in a manner, I think, which demonstrates how he showed at the time why successive British governments, Whitehall and the electorate could not contemplate a fully fledged British integration with Europe until several years and many economic vicissitudes had intervened (and, even then, why a serious and sustained ambiguity continued to vitiate that relationship). Franks in 1954 told his BBC audience that London clubland (of the stolid male rather than the musical or exotic sort) provided the model. Many in that audience would have understood, in a way that many fewer do half a century later, what 'country membership' of a London club meant – a reduced subscription for out-of-town members who dip in and out of those club facilities they wish to use when visits to London permit.

Franks urged an 'empirical' approach – the best, no doubt, he could hope for in late 1954:

I think it means neither joining a political union nor rejecting it, but taking out what I shall call a country membership. We pay our subscription and take on our obligations, but not the full subscription nor all the obligations of the regular members, our continental neighbours. It seems to me that recognition of our positive involvement, and giving real effect to it in something like this way, was responsible for the great success of the negotiations for a Western European Union.[79]

A 'country membership' of Europe is exactly what the British have hankered for once more in recent years.

In 1954, Franks wanted the Churchill administration to adopt this approach to the European Coal and Steel Community:

Up to the present we have stood aloof and maintained relations with it through a mission as if it were a foreign Power. In my opinion it would be to our advantage if we made an agreement for country membership. We are in a good position, for our steel industry is efficient and highly competitive.[80]

And shortly after Franks uttered those words, an Anglo-ECSC agreement on association was signed in London in December 1954 by Jean Monnet, who ran the Community's High Authority in Luxembourg, and the UK's Minister of Supply, Duncan Sandys.

This established a Council of Association that would meet alternately in London and Luxembourg. The Council would swap information and data and consider joint action on coal and steel prices and supplies, research and development and safety.[81] It was 'country membership' of a kind. But in less than a year, a much wider European 'common market', which went way beyond the great war-material industries, was under consideration by the ECSC 'Six' which chilled Anthony Eden's by then prime ministerial bones to the marrow.

That was when the great 'geometric conceit' was really exposed, not the period 1950–54. It could be argued that the relinquishing of the Indian Empire was the moment for an agonizing reappraisal of British great-power-dom – that and the successive currency crises that buffeted the pound sterling in 1947, 1949 and 1952 showed that in terms of territory, firepower and economic strength the great game was over. If so, Britain's position at the trig point of world politics – 'the three circles of our life and power', as Franks put it[82] – could have been realistically enhanced to considerable advantage as a means of niche *influence* rather than globe-spanning *power*.[83] But for Churchill and Eden, as for Attlee and Bevin before them, this would have sounded pessimistic to the point of defeatism as well as immensely difficult to achieve with a reserve currency and a still large territorial empire to support, not to mention a Cold War to manage.

Before returning to that – the single greatest anxiety of all – it is necessary to survey those simultaneous chess games that even a raddled and over-stretched great-powerdom required British ministers and officials to play in the early 1950s, whatever might or might not have been fructifying in Monnet's mind or happening down the coal mines and in the steel mills of the ECSC Six. It is useful to recall the wording of Churchill's peroration on Britain's interests in his November 1951 Cabinet paper on 'United Europe': 'Our first object is the unity and the consolidation of the British Commonwealth and what is left of the former British Empire.'[84]

Those late imperial chess games – with but a few exceptions (limited mainly to West Africa, the Gold Coast in particular, and Malaya, provided the communist insurgency could be suppressed) – were not intended in the early 1950s to be end-games. As imperial historian Larry Butler has emphasized, even though much of Labour's colonial policy ran on in Churchill's Whitehall, 'the Conservatives did not strain to step up the pace of change, applying brakes to a process which some ministers, including Churchill himself, felt had already gone too far, too quickly. A small, but revealing, linguistic detail which illustrates this point is the [Churchill] government's preference for the phrase "full self-government" instead of "independence" in the colonial context.'[85]

It was Ernest Gellner, a disciple of Bronislaw Malinowski, whose approach to social anthropology was part of every district commissioner's training during the last two generations of Empire,[86] who noted that it was America, rather than Britain, which had 'a specially strong and rather distinctive tendency to absolutize itself. Notoriously, those who declared the USA independent [of the British Empire] found their own moral and political intuitions self-evident, humanly and universally . . .'[87] Old British Empire hands were well aware of this American tendency to denounce territorial empire while seeking vigorously to extend US influence through money and goods. So were British ministers, who never failed to be irritated by lectures from successive administrations in Washington about the evils of colonialism – though this abated a little with the death of the greatest of presidential preachers against European imperialisms, Franklin Roosevelt, and the developing Cold War, which usually, though not invariably, trumped strictures against British imperialism for reasons of solidarity against the consequences of the infinitely nastier Russian one.

This found a powerful – if secret – expression in the growing closeness of the American and British intelligence communities as the Cold War chilled. More than a faint whiff of Empire lingered on in MI6 headquarters, however, well into the 1980s, partly because some of the seasoned old 'retreads' from the Colonial Service worked there[88] and partly because, thanks to the special intelligence relationship with Washington, British intelligence still retained a global reach. It did not seem entirely far-fetched even in the early 1990s, for example, when the then Deputy Chief of SIS, Sir Gerry Warner, replied (after a lunch at what was then MI6 headquarters, Century House, in Lambeth) to the question from Sir Robert Fellowes, the Queen's Private Secretary, on what he should tell Her Majesty her Secret Intelligence Service was for, by saying, 'Please tell her it is the last penumbra of her Empire.'[89] And in the mid-1990s, another senior MI6 officer wondered aloud whether Britain's retention of its worldwide intelligence capacity was not merely 'the itch after the amputation'.[90] (This conversation took place several years before the attacks on the World Trade Center and the Pentagon at a time when the UK's intelligence and security budgets were under pressure from the Treasury.)

The more than 200 years of Britain's experience of operating a multivariate empire from territorial to informal, white settler to indigenous, hot to cold, wet to arid, palm to pine, prairie to Himalaya, was mirrored in the multiplicity of approaches to the vexing question of imperialism in the early 1950s beset, as it was, by a variety of nationalisms and pressures. It is easy to portray the 1950s as a decade of relentless imperial retreat and national-ist advance. But imperial historian John Darwin is right to emphasize that what was 'really striking about the pattern of British relations' with the phe-nomenon was 'not the uniform tendency towards the collapse of British power but the wide variation in British attitudes and policy between one region and another, and the very different kinds of accommodation which they reached, or sought, with different nationalist movements'.[91]

The Cold War added a serious and growing complication to late imperial management from Whitehall, quite apart from the fear that Russia and, later, China might play a growing and harmful role in post-independence territories in both Asia and Africa, all in the name of colonial liberation. As Michael Quinlan, a former Permanent Secretary at the Ministry of Defence, wrote of the postwar armed-service ministries, it was a matter of 'wrestling with the tensions between post-imperial rundown and the rising demands of the Cold War'.[92]

But for many policy-makers, 'post-imperial' was still not quite the phrase they would have applied even with, as it were, India gone. For example, take the human capital successive governments continued to expend on the Empire. Looking back, one might have thought Hilaire Belloc's 1939 eulogy to what he saw as a dying breed of Jeeves-style gentlemen's gentlemen might have applied, certainly after 1945, to Jeeves' imperial equivalents – the district commissioners – whose job often seemed 'to demand the qualities of both parish priest . . . and wild west sheriff'.[93] ('They rose', wrote Belloc, 'to meet a need. They played a national role triumphantly. That role is now near to extinction and they are ready to depart.'[94]) But one would be quite wrong to do so.

Fuelled by the attempts to better the colonies under the Colonial Develop-ment and Welfare Acts of 1940 and 1945[95] and through such agencies as the Colonial Development Corporation created by the Attlee government in 1948,[96] the numbers of administrators and specialists recruited by the Colo-nial Office's appointments department rose sharply. In the last five years of peace, the figures were 206 (1934), 276 (1935), 315 (1936), 286 (1937) and 409 (1938). In the five years after the war ended the numbers amounted to 2,182 (1946), 1,127 (1947), 1,230 (1948), 1,679 (1949) and 1,916 (1950).[97] Sir Ralph Furse, the great Colonial Office recruiter of the first half of the twentieth century, noted that the £1.5m he obtained to fund training over the coming ten years under the Colonial Development and Welfare Act 1945 was extracted from the Treasury with less difficulty 'than . . . had some-times been [experienced] in the past to secure a modest rise in salary for one of my staff'.[98]

Those men on the spot, the last of Furse's consignments (he retired in 1950), by and large had no notion that the great game would be almost entirely up within twenty years. For example the Governor of Kenya, Sir Philip Mitch-ell, remarked in 1948 that the notion of his colony becoming an independent African state was about as likely as the installation of a Red Indian republic in the United States.[99] Though Mitchell was no admirer of the white settlers who continued to pour into Kenya just after the war (far from it),[100] in the late 1940s, at a conference of colonial governors in Cambridge, he had come out strongly against full democracy in Kenya as it would undermine British author-ity and assist the cause of extreme and irresponsible nationalists.[101]

White settlerdom was one of the key factors in Whitehall's dealings with its variable-geometry, multispeed territorial empire in Africa. In West Africa, where it was minimal, the initial strides down the road to eventual independ-ence could be – and were – longer. In the Gold Coast, for example, as early as 1951 Kwame Nkrumah had been released from jail (into which he had been placed the year before for leading strikes and demonstrations against the colonial authorities) in order to become Chief Minister in the new assem-bly set up in the pacemaker colony. In 1957 the renamed Ghana would be the first piece of British West Africa to achieve independence. Nkrumah's Convention People's Party had won an election while he was in prison.[102]

But in the long white-settler finger thrust northwards from South Africa, through the Rhodesias and into Kenya, entirely different political and eco-nomic calculations were in play. The Attlee government, mindful of the need to curb moves to an all-out white supremacist style of government north of the Limpopo after Dr Daniel Malan's Nationalist Party won the 1948 general election in South Africa, developed the scheme for what became in 1953 the multiracial Central African Federation consisting of the two Rhodesias (North-ern and Southern) and Nyasaland. The internal power configurations of the federation, while noticeably different from South Africa and intended 'to form a physical barrier to the spread of South African influence', nevertheless involved 'favouring the region's white settler minority with disproportionate political power at the expense of the African majority'.[103] The Central African Federation lasted but ten years, absorbing a great deal of the Macmillan governments' time and, on its break-up, bequeathing a white supremacist government in Southern Rhodesia which presented the Wilson, Heath, Callaghan and Thatcher administrations with, cumulatively, probably the most vexing of all the African imperial disposals.[104]

But the most baffling and alarming of the early-Fifties colonial crises was the Mau Mau insurrection in Kenya. Because of the extreme brutality practised by the Kikuyu, both on each other and on white settlers, the level of repression the colonial authorities mustered in response and the sheer body count over the period 1952–6 (95 white deaths; over 14,000 Kikuyu – 1,000 of them by execution[105]) this was the colonial matter that dominated the front pages of the first newspapers I read – challenged, but not surpassed, from 1954 by the campaign by the Greek Cypriot nationalist organization EOKA against the presence of British troops and police in Cyprus.[106]

Why baffling? Even now, reading the most accomplished reconstructor of the Mau Mau phenomenon, John Lonsdale, it is very difficult to understand the multiplicity of factors which produced the breakdowns and the internal violence within the Kikuyu and the impact this had on white settlers, the authorities in Nairobi and the Colonial Secretary's Private Office in Great Smith Street, Westminster. (Oliver Lyttelton, as he read the reports of the 'bestial, filthy' Mau Mau bloodletting and penned memoranda or instructions in response said he felt 'the horned shadow of the Devil himself' fall across the page.[107])

Mau Mau (opinion differs as to the origin of the name) began in a small way just after the end of the war in response to the pressures on agricultural land, increased by new land-conservation techniques, on top of the immense Kikuyu resentment at the best terrain being reserved from the 1930s for the settlers in the 'White Highlands'.[108] Landless black squatters in rural areas designated for whites and young displaced Kikuyu men, poorly paid labourers in booming postwar Nairobi, used traditional manhood initiation rites as entry to 'their secret political army', Mau Mau.[109] Soon they were at war with traditionalist Kikuyu elders and those within the tribe who collaborated with the colonial authorities as much as with the colonial rulers themselves. As John Lonsdale expressed it, it was 'a story of a concentric circle and three generations':

The outer circle was the colony of Kenya in which the Colonial Office both needed and distrusted the white settlers, the inner circle was that of the Kikuyu people in which some had a vision of a tribal unity of the future that perhaps most people distrusted and where some of the most important players were in fact off-stage, not in Kikuyuland

16. A cocktail of pollutants: the Great Smog of London, December 1952.

17. The 'blizzard of obscenity' begins: young men from all backgrounds about to shed their civilian clothes and liberties for twelve weeks of National Service basic training.

18. Espresso Gaggia: coffee-bar chic, Soho, 4 November 1955.

19. Juke-box surly: coffee-bar Teds, Elephant and Castle, 13 July 1955.

20. Bill Haley and His Comets: no cinema seat was safe.

21. Bringing the Empire to its knees: The Goon Show,
29 September 1955 (*left to right*: Peter Sellers,
Harry Secombe, Spike Milligan.)

22. 'Tingling fresh': Gibbs SR toothpaste in ice-block, the first advertisement shown on Independent Television, 22 September 1955.

23. 'Do people really want more culture?' Hughie Green doubling the people's money.

24. Diamonds are Forever: Ian Fleming at play.

25. Barry Bucknell doing it himself.

26. Percy Thrower potting.

27. The Empire comes home: a Jamaican family arrives at Victoria Station, 4 January 1955.

28. But home was not always welcoming: Notting Hill riots, 31 August 1958.

29. Traditional valuer, Patrick Devlin.

30. Traditional questioner, Herbert Hart.

31. User of literacy and liberator of Lady
Chatterley, Richard Hoggart.

32. Reformer, Sir John Wolfenden:
late-Fifties politics was insufficiently pink
for gay rights.

itself but in the outer circle of the white man's country of Kenya colony, as black farm squatters on the so-called White Highlands ...[110]

The best of the district commissioners on the ground understood this.[111] But the complexities were lost, not just on schoolboy readers of the *Daily Express* back in London but on others living within Lonsdale's concentric circles in Kenya. As John Darwin put it, in 'official eyes, and even more in the minds of the settlers, Mau Mau was not the articulation of grievance and fear but a barbaric throwback, deliberately engineered by Jomo Kenyatta and other radical Kikuyu politicians and held together by the use of oaths and "unspeakable debauchery", playing on the lowest and most primeval instincts'.[112]

By 1956 the worst (in the sense of colonial policing) was over. Kenyatta had been jailed for seven years for 'managing an unlawful society' in 1953 following a trial whose procedures and fairness remain controversial to this day.[113] It had taken a huge effort in terms of a mixture of pursuit, capture, punishment, numerous executions, resettlement, the construction of 'safe' villages and land reform in the White Highlands. Almost a third of the Kikuyu's adult males – some 80,000 of them – had at one time or another been put through detention camps for screening where the authorities attempted rehabilitation.[114] In the short run, 'the effect of Mau Mau was to confirm European primacy in Kenya and to give it new conviction ... the result seemed not only the repression of a savage rural uprising ... but also a shattering setback to African nationalism in Kenya and the dream of African majority rule on the model of Ghana or Nigeria'.[115] In fact, Kenya achieved its independence under Kenyatta himself in 1963, a mere three years after Nigeria, but not before it had blown back seriously once more into British politics in 1959 atrocities perpetrated on Mau Mau detainees at the Hola Camp which discredited and discomfited the Macmillan government (of which more in Chapter 13).

In the history of British imperial withdrawal, the early 1950s can seem but a pause between the end of Indian empire in the late 1940s and the rush to dispose of the tropical empire in the early 1960s, a mere punctuation mark. This is not the way it felt at the time. Progressive Colonial Service officials such as the star of the early postwar Colonial Office and, later, the Governor of Uganda, Sir Andrew Cohen, might have pushed the cause of independence sooner rather than later ('self-government is better than good colonial government', he would tell his largely sceptical colleagues in the late 1940s[116]). But incoming Conservative ministers did not share the Cohen view. Lyttelton, for example, did not want him to come back from Uganda to become Permanent

Secretary to the Colonial Office. 'He was a man of obvious integrity,' Lyttelton wrote in his memoirs, 'and of powerful intellectual equipment. Both he and his wife were dedicated perhaps with more enthusiasm than judgement to the swiftest advancement of Africans.'[117] (Cohen eventually did become a Permanent Secretary – to the new Ministry of Overseas Development in 1964.[118])

Nobody could accuse Lyttelton (or his Prime Minister) of excessive enthusiasm for African majority rule. As Larry Butler put it, the Churchill administration 'was anxious to avoid giving the impression that it was in retreat from its colonial responsibilities, or that it no longer had the stomach to be a colonial power'.[119] When Whitehall pondered in 1954 those colonies that might reach independence by the mid-1970s, 'its list of candidates was confined to the Gold Coast and Nigeria, the Central African Federation, a Malayan federation, and a still-to-be-created West Indian federation. Up to 20 colonies were considered unsuitable for full independence, and were thought to be candidates only for internal self-government.'[120]

Malaya is a particularly interesting case as it powerfully fused both colonial and Cold War problems. On taking office as Colonial Secretary in October 1951, Lyttelton saw Malaya as his most pressing problem:

> I read and talked Malaya for two days. It was evident that we were on the way to losing control of the country, and soon. The repercussions of such a loss on South-East Asia, one of the most troubled and tender parts of the world, were incalculable. Moreover, rubber and tin were amongst the most important exports and dollar earners of the Commonwealth.[121]

Lyttelton had a great affection for Malaya and knew it well, having been chairman in the late 1930s of both the London Tin Corporation and the Anglo-Oriental Company.[122] Just over a month after the Churchill government was formed he flew to Malaya to see for himself how 'a few thousand terrorists held the country in fee'.[123]

Probably no Colonial Secretary ever knew a colony as well as Lyttelton knew Malaya. Equally probably, no officers in the Colonial Service ever knew the guerrillas in the jungle as well as some in Singapore. John Davis, a Malayan policeman before the war, became an officer in the Special Operations Executive during it and fought in the jungle against the Japanese alongside the largely Malay Chinese Malayan Communist Party, the MCP. Davis became a good friend of a young MCP commissar, Chin Peng, who led the communist guerrillas from 1948 in attacks on rubber planters, tin miners and policemen in an attempt to force the British out of Malaya. In late 1955, Davis persuaded

Chin to leave the jungle for talks with Tunku Abdul Rahman, who, two years later, led the country to independence.[124]

In the meantime the colonial authorities, aided by substantial numbers of regular soldiers and British National Servicemen, suppressed a communist insurgency and set the country on course to one of the more rapid decolonizations. In the process the system of safe strategic hamlets, the so-called 'new villages' (as adopted later in Kenya and, less successfully, by the Americans in Vietnam in the 1960s), was pioneered and designed by Sir Harold Briggs and implemented rigorously by his successor, General Sir Gerald Templer.[125] The key to British strategy was to isolate the communists from disaffected sections of the population, such as the largely Chinese landless squatters, and to compete for the 'hearts and minds' (a phrase first made familiar during the Malayan emergency) of the population alongside a vigorous counter-insurgency military strategy amid considerable efforts to reduce the strife between the different ethnic groups in the colony.

Malaya was one of the most successful of Britain's post-1945 colonial/independence operations and it was achieved against a particularly difficult backdrop. As John Darwin put it, the UK's imperial interests in South-East Asia 'were far more vulnerable to external pressures and disruption than they were in any part of sub-Saharan Africa in the 1950s. The struggle against communist insurgency in Malaya and the defusing of racial tensions between Malays and Chinese in the colony had to be pursued against a background of communist China's growing influence, of Indonesia's new found independence and of a colonial war in Indo-China.'[126] Darwin could have added the war in Korea to this list, at least up until the armistice in July 1953.

For the Churchill administration, as for Attlee's, these late imperial chess games competed for attention with – and were linked to – the wider problems of international security and the sustenance of Britain's world role in general, including its economic aspects. They added hugely to the overload on postwar Cabinets and Whitehall, imposing a multifaceted, detailed and relentless burden of case work on both ministers and senior officials. Some analysts have suggested this overarching problem was made worse by the failure to adapt the systems of British central government to the new realities.

International historian Anthony Adamthwaite has drawn the important and often overlooked contrast between pre-1939 external relationships and the multilateral world bequeathed by the wartime experience and added to still further by Cold War-related international institutions:

Before the Second World War traditional bilateral relations between states were the staple of British diplomacy. Apart from occasional visits to the League of Nations at Geneva, a Foreign Secretary stayed at home. By 1951 the Foreign Secretary, junior ministers and aides were a travelling circus. The Council of Ministers of the Council of Europe brought together European foreign ministers, and the Consultative Assembly of the Council provided an open forum for the debate by parliamentarians from both government and opposition parties. Foreign ministers of the three western occupying powers – Britain, America and France – met regularly for discussion of German and European questions and NATO Assembly meetings gathered fourteen foreign ministers, defence ministers and advisers. In addition permanent delegations were maintained at the United Nations, NATO, OEEC, the Council of Europe and the European Coal and Steel Community. The many overlapping levels of the new diplomacy, plus the fact that everything had to be translated, lengthened negotiating times, making it harder to keep overall objectives in sight.[127]

This new multilateralism seriously stretched postwar Whitehall. The plethora of ministries involved (Foreign Office, Commonwealth Relations Office, Colonial Office, Ministry of Defence plus the three service departments) led to a huge amount of time spent on interdepartmental co-ordination, often complicated still further when the economic ministries were part of the discussion.[128]

The sheer slog imposed on the busiest secretaries of state such as Eden (who was seriously ill both before and after his botched bile-duct operation* in 1953[129]) left little time for serious strategic thinking, even if ministers were so inclined (which Eden's critics say he generally was not). For Adamthwaite, 'Eden's main disability was ... intellectual. He had great flair but no genius. Unlike Bevin he was a tactician not a strategist ...'[130] This was certainly true, but in Eden's defence, it could be argued that though he was a failure at sensing and coping with the big, 'slow pulse'[131] shifts that made the conduct of British policy – economic and domestic as well as foreign and imperial – so difficult in the early 1950s, his negotiating gifts and tactical skills brought some genuine 'quick pulse' successes for British diplomacy. The Western European Union solution to the problem of German rearmament was certainly one of these.

Eden's skills as a negotiator also contributed to a number of important developments during the mid-1950s, including the creation of the WEU and

---

* Eden's bile duct was severed in the course of his surgeon's examination of both it and his gall bladder.

the success of the Geneva Conference of 1954 which led – albeit temporarily – to a cessation of serious warfare in Indo-China. Many of Eden's substantial pre-1956 achievements have been retrospectively overshadowed by the Suez affair, which, for some commentators, threw into starker relief many of Eden's less-appealing traits as well as aspects of their own country and its past which made their toes curl.

Consider the residue left by the acidulated Malcolm Muggeridge in his famous 'Boring for England' critique which linked Eden with all the postwar illusions contained within the geometric conceit of the 1950s. Eden, Muggeridge declared, was an 'eminently suitable' Foreign Secretary and Prime Minister for that era

conveying as he did so exactly in appearance and personality, the benevolent intentions and earnest purposes whereby an almost extinct ruling class seeks to protract itself a little longer. His somehow slightly seedy good looks and attire, his ingratiating smile and gestures, the utter nothingness of what he had to say – did it not all provide an outward and visible manifestation of an inward and invisible loss of authority and self-confidence? . . . As has been truly said in his days as an active politician, he was not only a bore; he bored for England.[132]

Muggeridge was certainly right about outward poise camouflaging inner anxiety, but that is not fair to Eden. Old-world courtesy and the careful use of blandness in both poise and speech had their place at the international negotiating table then as now. Indo-China, for example, marked 'the apogee of Eden's Foreign Secretaryship', as Richard Thorpe noted,[133] and he was 'to cling to the Geneva Conference as his undisputed claim to a place in history'.[134] The nature of the problem of the two Vietnams and the mixture of great powers who were the external protagonists made Geneva 1954 a near perfect opportunity for niche diplomacy by the British. To keep the American Foster Dulles, the Russian Vyacheslav Molotov and the Chinese Chou En-lai at the negotiating table, not to mention the French (the wholesale collapse of whose colonial position in Indo-China after losing the fortress of Dien Bien Phu to the communist Viet Minh in May 1954 had precipitated the crisis), was no mean feat – but Eden managed it.

Eden knew full well that if a settlement was not reached in Indo-China, the 'Communists would soon mop up' not just all of Vietnam but Laos and Cambodia too.[135] That the 1954 settlement and the partition of Vietnam into communist north and non-communist south was all undone in ten years leading to a war that cost over a million lives between 1965 and 1975 (it had already cost 600,000 between 1945 and 1954[136]) does not alter the fact that Eden was instrumental in an outcome at Geneva whose result was 'to arrest a process that showed every sign of spiralling out of control'[137] and just might have led to a second and more destructive Far Eastern confrontation between the United States and China only a year after an armistice had been reached in Korea.

Britain's role in ending the Korean War was not central,[138] though in its last months Churchill (who was also Acting Foreign Secretary while Eden was absent owing to his gall-bladder problem) had annoyed Eisenhower and Dulles by making it plain that the South Korean President, Syngman Rhee, should not be allowed to stymie negotiations indefinitely over the question of prisoner-of-war repatriation.[139] Churchill saw the death of Stalin in March 1953 as an opportunity both to ease the tensions of the Cold War and to ensure that the military stalemate in Korea that had prevailed since 1951 would not be a barrier to improving the relationship between East and West. The nuclear threat was Churchill's primary concern during 1953–5, and these two prizes, if they could be won, would lighten its shadow considerably.

It was the hydrogen bomb, too, which was the 'turn factor' in the Cabinet. This led to the deeply reluctant Churchill being persuaded that there was no point in hanging on indefinitely to the vast British base in the Suez Canal Zone, a huge installation with a garrison of 80,000 which it was becoming increasingly difficult to protect against guerrilla attacks by Egyptian nationalists.[140] Eden had been driven to distraction on the question both by Churchill ('If he has so little confidence in me, I had better to go,' he exploded to Shuckburgh in January 1953[141]) and by the so-called Suez group of Empire-minded backbench Conservative MPs led by Julian Amery and Sir Charles Waterhouse.[142] Not until mid-1954 was the matter resolved when Sir William Dickson, Chief of the Air Staff, told the Cabinet that in the thermonuclear era, the weight of an air attack on the Soviet Union in the early days of a global war would not leave the Russians in a position to thrust south through the Caucasus into the oil-rich Middle East.[143] An agreement was signed between the UK and Egypt on 19 October 1954 whereby the last British troops would quit the base in June 1956, leaving it in the hands of a care-and-maintenance team of British and Egyptian technicians.[144]

But the settlement of the base did not, as Eden hoped, ease the Egyptian leader, Colonel Gamal Abdel Nasser, into the Baghdad Pact (concluded in February 1955) between Pakistan, Iraq, Iran and Turkey designed to prevent Soviet influence from seeping into the Middle East and North Africa. Eden travelled to Cairo that month to turn his fabled charm on Nasser. Their one and only meeting failed on every level. And from that dinner in the British Embassy in Cairo began what Shuckburgh called the 'descent to Suez' and the confrontation intended by Eden to topple Nasser which in the end toppled himself.

It is easy – too easy, perhaps – in retrospect to see why Nasser was left (as he recalled many years later) feeling as if Eden 'was talking to a junior official who could not be expected to understand international politics'.[145] Sir Ralph Stevenson, the British Ambassador, had pulled out all the stops in line with Palmerston's old adage that 'dining is the soul of diplomacy',[146] but even that backfired. 'What elegance!' Nasser was reported to have said to a colleague as they left the British Embassy. 'It was made to look as if we were beggars and they were princes!'[147]

The evening reception, on 20 February, began with a gambit by the British Foreign Secretary that startled his guests. When Nasser arrived at the embassy Eden, to Nasser's astonishment, greeted him in Arabic and talked of his long experience of Egypt, which he demonstrated by exchanging proverbs in Arabic.[148] Field Marshal Lord Harding, then Chief of the Imperial General Staff, recalled the crucial moment, which came a little later:

The object of the meeting was to try and persuade Nasser that it was in his interest to become an active member of the Baghdad Pact. We got down to business after dinner and Anthony Eden started off by a few remarks about the political situation and then I was put on to explain our strategic thinking about developing the Baghdad Pact, that is to say, Turkey, Iraq, Iran and Pakistan would provide the front-line defence and we and the Americans would provide the major logistics and air support. And for that Egypt was vital, because it had a double entry through the Mediterranean and the Red Sea, it had airfields, it had an industrial capacity; it was absolutely suited in every way as the main support area. After I had finished, Anthony asked Nasser if he would like to comment and Nasser said, 'Well, I agree, I agree completely.' What flummoxed me was that Anthony then went on for the best part of an hour to try to convince Nasser of what I would have thought was the logical conclusion, that they should join the Baghdad Pact. But Nasser said the time was wrong. I think that meeting was the beginning of Eden's complete mistrust of Nasser.[149]

The number two in the Cairo Embassy, Ralph Murray, thought a deal was simply not on:

Eden tried rather insensitively to lecture Nasser on what his defence arrangements should be. It produced a rather bad effect on Nasser, who didn't like being lectured.

Eden seemed to think he could make common cause with Nasser in defence arrangements concerned with the possibility of Soviet eruptions from the north. But it was perfectly plain that Nasser wasn't interested in that kind of thing.[150]

Within two months of that evening, Eden was Prime Minister. Within fifteen Nasser had nationalized the Anglo-French company controlling the Suez Canal, which then, as Lady Eden famously put it, began to flow through their drawing room in No. 10 Downing Street.[151] And in less than two years it had swept Eden out of office. The sustenance of 'informal empire' in the Middle East and, with it, the maintenance of British prestige (that great Eden word) and of Britain as a serious player on what an American National Security Adviser, Zbigniew Brzezinski, would later call the 'Grand Chessboard' of world affairs,[152] had crowded out virtually everything else at a crucial moment in the mid-1950s – crucial for western Europe as well as the UK.

Nearly fifty years later, in conversation with Chris Patten (then a significant figure inside the European Union), the subject of Britain's place in the world came up. (I had just urged him to read Franks' 1954 Reith Lectures – especially that section on Britain's wishing for no more than a country membership of the European club). 'Ah,' he said with both feeling and resignation, 'that is psychodrama as much as it is history.'[153] So it was – and is. And, in the mid-1950s, it coincided with the penultimate phase of the 'psychodrama' of British imperialism. Perhaps the jagged mental terrain where international geopolitics grinds against national identity usually comes into that elusive category – part reality, part fantasy – much like dreaming.

The historian and strategist Sir Michael Howard is very tough on those early-Fifties illusions, recalling in his memoirs that the 'media wrote excitedly about a new Elizabethan age, more accurately than they knew, for once again we were, as we had been then, a power of the second rank, teetering on the verge of bankruptcy and punching far beyond our weight in international affairs'.[154] Yet looking back to the early Fifties, there were almost too many shifts underway for even the professional diplomats and politicians to absorb, let alone a public still suffused with the attitudes and assumptions of great-powerdom. Empire was still very real; Europe a vague and far from entrancing notion; global reach a natural expectation, for all the economic difficulties of the early postwar which, by 1954, seemed visibly to be easing. It is not hard to see why the Suez affair was such a shock two years later when the weaknesses inherent in the 'geometric conceit' of British power were starkly exposed.

Before returning to Britain, the Middle East, Europe and the *mentalité* of Sir Anthony Eden (as he had become when installed by the Queen as a Knight of the Garter on 20 October 1954[155]), we need to examine the greatest single potential mid-Fifties nightmare of them all – the hydrogen bomb – and Churchill's valiant efforts to save it from smashing the globe's Grand Chessboards (plural) possibly irreparably in a future thermonuclear war between East and West.

7

The H-Bomb and the Search for Peace

'We touched the nerve of the universe.'
Victor Weisskopf, American physicist who worked on the Manhattan Project, 2002.[1]

'Hydrogen bomb war would be total war in a sense not hitherto conceived. The entire nation would be in the front line.'   The Strath Report, March 1955.[2]

'We cannot reasonably expect to give the date or hour of an attack; it is probable that the detection of enemy aircraft on Allied radar screens will be the only warning of actual attack.'   Joint Intelligence Committee Report, January 1955.[3]

'History was suspended for 40 years.'
          Air Chief Marshal Sir John Willis, former Vulcan Bomber captain, 2004.[4]

'The day may dawn when fair play, love for one's fellow man, respect for justice and freedom, will enable tormented generations to march forth serene and triumphant from the hideous epoch in which we have to dwell. Meanwhile, never flinch, never weary, never despair.'
          Sir Winston Churchill concluding his final speech to the House of Commons as
          Prime Minister, 1 March 1955.[5]

Churchill took twenty hours to prepare his farewell speech and composed every word of it himself.[6] Formally, he was presenting the 1955 Defence White Paper to Parliament and its key announcement that his government had decided to manufacture a British hydrogen bomb. In reality, it was the most eloquent of personal swansongs, its theme the unique peril posed by thermonuclear weapons to his beloved United Kingdom and the world and the question of what would 'lie before' the children of the mid-1950s 'if God wearied of mankind'.[7]

That 'never despair' speech had an extraordinary and durable resonance. For example, its last stanza was quoted with force and passion by Sir David Omand almost exactly forty-nine years later when, as the Cabinet Office's Co-ordinator of Security and Intelligence, he spoke at the opening of the National Archives' 'Secret State' Exhibition and contrasted the era of the Strath Report with the contingency planning underway as part of the post-9/11 'protecting state', as he called it.[8] As one of those young children of 1955 to whom Churchill had referred, I said that same evening in Kew that, 'for those in my generation and older who spent the bulk of their lives in the shadow of the bomb, that the Cold War ended at all is probably the greatest shared boon of our lifetime. That it ended without global war and nuclear exchange verges on the miraculous.'

John Willis's phrase about the forty-year suspension of history reminded me of George Steiner's description of the 'armistice with history' under which those in western Europe lived 'from the time of Waterloo to that of the massacres on the western front in 1915–16'.[9] Sir John grew up in south London as the Battle of Britain raged above his head. It was this that led to his wish to become a pilot in the Royal Air Force.[10] The twentieth century is piled high with the bodies of British dead but not the second half of it – Sir John's and my half. In that specific sense history was suspended.

Reliable, timely and usable intelligence on the Soviet Union, its capabilities and, above all, the intentions of its leadership was like gold dust in the 1950s. Churchill's most famous line about Russia – that it was 'a riddle wrapped inside a mystery inside an enigma', delivered in a radio broadcast in 1939[11] – still applied emphatically twelve years later when the British intelligence product was once more delivered to him in No. 10.

The hunger and range of Western intelligence was vast and central to the conduct of the Cold War. As a distinguished British practitioner-turned-historian, Michael Herman, speaking shortly before the fall of the Berlin Wall, put it, 'The Cold War was in a special sense an intelligence conflict . . . Never before in peacetime have the collection of intelligence and its denial to the adversary been such central features of an international rivalry.'[12]

Later, when the Cold War was over, he likened Western efforts to penetrate the Soviet bloc's secrets and mysteries to 'a multinational Great Game, played out not only along the German border, but also in Berlin and around the rest of the Soviet periphery – the Baltic; North Norway and the Barents Sea, the Black Sea, the Sea of Okhotsk and elsewhere: tough men rolling for weeks on station in small ships; patient monitors on quiet islands; aircraft of many nations flying every day, packed with technical equipment; and much else'.[13] The overriding priority of this 'twenty-four hour surveillance' was to provide warning of a Soviet attack on the West.[14]

One of the most fascinating and revealing runs of documents to emerge from the National Archives, once the 'Waldegrave Initiative' had provided the key to open several Cold War-related records kept locked beyond the normal thirty years,[15] were the 'Red' and 'Amber' warning lists maintained by the Joint Intelligence Committee. They disclosed the range of Western espionage and the mixture of electronic and human intelligence that went into its making, from an agent at a railway station somewhere in eastern Europe looking for a particular cap badge that might indicate a rocket regiment was on the move following its missiles up towards the front where the forces of the Warsaw Pact and NATO stared at each other[16] to the electronic yield from constant radar and signals surveillance.

Throughout the Cold War, as the list of indicators grew, what the mid-Fifties 'Red List' called 'Indications Relating to the Nuclear Bombardment' remained right at the top of the 'Highest Priority Preparations'. The 1956 JIC paper on 'Indicators of Soviet Preparations for Early War' placed seven items in the 'nuclear bombardment' category:

1. Redeployment of Long-Range Air Force, or abnormal signal activity which points to unusual activation of the L.R.A.F.
2. Issue of Nuclear Missiles to airfields of Long-Range Air Force.
3. The deployment of Strategic Ground-to-Ground Ballistic Missiles.
4. Unusual activation of ... ground-to-air defences.
5. Redeployment and Dispersal of Soviet ground forces, particularly in East Germany.*
6. Dispersal of ships and submarines from Fleet bases.*
7. Dispersal of Government Headquarters to safe zones.[17]

This version of the 'Red List' was prepared in the weeks following the surge of anxiety when, briefly, it looked as if the Soviet Union might intervene in the Middle East as the Suez affair reached its climax.

The December 1956 report was designed 'to provide for the guidance of collectors of intelligence, a list of those measures which might be significant indicators of Soviet preparations for early war during the period *up to the end of 1959* ...'[18] The JIC's own italics here indicate that the Committee was anticipating significant strides in Soviet rocketry. As we have seen from the

* These might be concealed by holding large-scale training exercises, the JIC warned.

JIC quotation at the head of this chapter, it was assault by bomber which pre-occupied defence watchers in the mid-1950s, that the planes coming up on British and American radars would be 'the only warning of actual attack',[19] even if some of the 'Red List' indicators had already been flashing.

In the later 1950s some very British refinements were added to the lists. It has been claimed that the first British Prime Minister, Sir Robert Walpole, invented that grand national institution, the long weekend.[20] In a backhanded tribute to the understanding of our funny British ways by the KGB Residency within the Russian Embassy in late-Fifties London, the JIC warned, in a June 1958 paper on 'Timing of Attack', that in 'a premeditated war the Soviet Leaders might select a day during the period April to October to take advantage of more favourable weather conditions for Soviet air defences. This day would probably be selected to coincide with a Western national holiday, festive season or perhaps a weekend.'[21]*

In line with a consistent series of assessments from the very beginning of the Cold War,[22] the mid-Fifties Joint Intelligence Committee believed, as a May 1956 paper expressed it, 'that the Soviet leaders do not want war. We believe that their views will remain unchanged, certainly over the next few years and probably over the whole period under review [they were looking ahead 'up to 1965'], unless the political situation changes in some unexpected fashion (such as through the emergence of more aggressive Soviet leaders) and provided the West maintains its strength and cohesion and continues to act with restraint.'[23]

This May 1956 assessment, which re-examined both the likelihood of war over the coming nine to ten years and the warnings that might be gleanable by intelligence methods if indeed it was about to happen, was nevertheless eloquent (in the traditionally understated JIC fashion) about the difficulties faced by the range of intelligence collectors and systems. As the JIC told its customers among senior ministers, the most sensitive inner-groups of White-hall and the military:

If the Soviet leaders make active preparations for war we expect to learn of some of them. The extent of our knowledge will depend on whether they are made solely inside

* Or, as we discovered many years later, a Test match. During the last fraught over of the June 1963 Lord's Test against the West Indies when the outcome could have been a draw (which it was), a tie, or victory for either side, I am reliably informed that all the British early-warning screens were tuned to the BBC's transmission from Lord's. As my anonymous informant pointed out, the need for England's Colin Cowdrey to return to the field, despite having earlier retired hurt with a broken arm, meant the whole thing took much longer than four minutes to complete (the warning period to which RAF Fylingdales was geared) and 'the Russians could have had us cost-free!'

the USSR or also in the satellites ... If the Soviet leaders decide to carry out full deployment and mobilisation, we expect to be able to forecast, at least a month ahead, the date by which the USSR would achieve such a state of preparation.[24]

Whitehall's intelligence analysts thought it 'more likely' in the event of another world war 'that the Russians would wish to achieve surprise for their nuclear air attack'. To strike North America on a large scale, the Soviet Long-Range Air Force 'would have to carry out an extensive and lengthy programme of construction, stockpiling and redeployment'. In 1956 the JIC did not think the Russians would have the capability to launch 'a large scale surprise attack' on the United States mainland for another three years – 'They could, however, achieve surprise against the United Kingdom ... now.'[25]

It was this factor that lay behind the special report the JIC produced for the Strath inquiry in January 1955 (cited at the head of this chapter) which added to the urgency propelling the work of that group. The May 1956 JIC assessment made plain how it would be virtually impossible for either signals intelligence (provided by the Government Communications Headquarters in alliance with its US equivalent, the National Security Agency) or human intelligence (i.e. the British Secret Intelligence Service, a.k.a. SIS or MI6, or the US Central Intelligence Agency through their agent networks) to provide the key warnings which were the overriding priority of the entire Western intelligence apparatus:

We could be certain that a decision to attack had been made only if we succeeded in intercepting the decision. We have virtually no chance of doing this and we must, therefore, rely on interpreting the significance of military and other moves and preparations [hence the importance of the 'Red' and 'Amber' lists]; in the event of a surprise attack we may never obtain such information.[26]

So the decision in the Kremlin to go for war was almost certainly beyond reach at any time. As for picking up the timing of the initial assault, 'We cannot expect to give the time of attack much in advance. At best we might get warning of the assembly or take off of enemy aircraft at or from their bases.'[27]

The Soviet air crews would be maintaining strict radio silence; the instruction to go would come by landline and, therefore, be beyond the reach of the GCHQ and NSA aerials tuned to northern, eastern and southern Russia or in the Far East. So, presumably, human agents were the best hope here. Such clandestine operatives were very difficult to place near the airfields; equally difficult for the agents, if in place, to get the warnings back to the SIS and the CIA in time. The JIC conclusion was that 'it is probable that the detection of those aircraft on Allied radar screens would be the only warning. At present, in the case of ballistic missiles, there would be no warning.'[28] (The US Ballistic Missile Early Warning System, of which RAF Fylingdales was a part, was a development of the early 1960s.)

Few around even the JIC table in the mid-1950s would have appreciated just how parlous was the position of MI6 at that time in terms of its networks behind the Iron Curtain. Fathoming the intentions of the Soviet leadership was, in Sherlock Holmesean terms, a multi-pipe problem, and SIS had, for most of the postwar period, hardly a shred of tobacco on which to puff.

As a very senior SIS figure with long experience of Cold War operations explained to me later, 'the recruitment and running of secret agents' is the chief purpose of MI6 and its 'influence in, and importance to, the government depend upon the value and uniqueness of its intelligence product'. The Soviet bloc, he continued, 'was a hugely difficult target. It took great confidence to quietly maintain that Soviet and Eastern European officials, scientists and military officers could be not only recruited but securely run.'[29] Not until the late 1950s was such confidence gradually built up (and soon undermined by a series of unfounded allegations of security breaches in the early 1960s).[30*]

The conversion of SIS into an effective gatherer of human intelligence from the Soviet bloc – with methods that continued to shape its operational techniques in the early twenty-first century long after the end of the Cold War – was largely the work of one scarcely known figure, Harold Shergold, known universally within his service as 'Shergy'. Shergold was utterly dedicated to the idea that the SIS should sustain the secrecy of its people and its operations beyond the grave.

But if you canvass Shergold's own generation in the British Secret Service, and the two that followed, 'they all unhesitatingly agree' that 'he was by a long way the most important and influential officer of the postwar period', as one of them put it to me. He was 'in many ways the founder of the modern serv-

---

* The allegations were made by Anatoli Golitsyn, a KGB defector who persuaded top figures in the CIA, and rather fewer in MI6, that their countries and their secret services were penetrated to a scarcely imaginable degree by Soviet agents-in-place (a claim not finally exposed as a fraud until the Soviet Union disintegrated and Vasili Mitrokhin's KGB archive was smuggled out to Britain by the Secret Intelligence Service in 1992).

ice – at least the rock on which it stands', though he never became 'C', the SIS chief. From 1954 until 1971 (he spent his thirty years of retirement fund-raising for a charity which provided guide-dogs for the blind) 'he was in charge of all operations against the Soviet Union and Eastern Europe'.[31]

Shergold had been a teacher until the Second World War. A fluent German speaker, he joined up as a private and finished as a lieutenant-colonel in the Combined Service Interrogation Centre attached to the Eighth Army. In 1949 he was transferred to the Secret Intelligence Service and was posted to Germany to work against the East Germans and the Soviet occupation authorities. In 1954 he came back to London to the SIS headquarters in Broadway Buildings opposite St James's Park Underground Station to take over what were then thought to be the most important UK secret operations against the Soviet Union – the networks SIS was running in the Baltic states.

Shergold was seriously alarmed by what he found and quickly came to the conclusion that these networks were, in fact, under KGB not SIS control, so thoroughly were they penetrated by Russian intelligence. There was great resistance in Broadway Buildings when Shergold proposed that the Baltic networks be closed down. Eventually he prevailed and it was the KGB which confirmed the accuracy of Shergold's judgement when they themselves shut down the remaining SIS networks in Poland, Hungary, the Ukraine and Byelorussia. The human intelligence position was, therefore, truly disastrous when the JIC fashioned its mid-Fifties assessments about Britain's intelligence-gathering assets inside the Soviet bloc.[32]

Shergold concluded that operating agent networks behind the Iron Curtain was an inescapably insecure business but individual agents could be run safely if tight new standards and operational procedures were applied to security and tradecraft. In the late 1950s these began to pay off when SIS began the recruitment of some extremely valuable agents in the Soviet bloc which, with a flow of defectors, increased the chances of SIS discovering if any of its own people had been 'turned' and were now being run *against* British intelligence. In 1960, for example, George Blake, the SIS station chief in Seoul in 1950 who was captured by the invading North Koreans and turned in captivity, was exposed by a defector and confessed to Shergold.[33]

This turnaround in the UK's human intelligence capability was some way off when the JIC was briefing the Strath Committee on the Soviet H-bomb threat to the UK in 1955. The lion's share of British intelligence resources – in terms of people and money – went into signals and electronic attacks on the Soviet bloc's secrets in the early Cold War and, indeed, throughout its duration.[34] And not until the restructuring and reordering of intelligence priorities and provision in the United States after the SIGINT failure in Korea in 1950 did the American National Security Agency become the dominant partner in the pooling arrangements enabled by the secret UKUSA Treaty of 1948.[35] It is impossible for an outsider to judge GCHQ's effectiveness as a provider, given the understandably intense security surrounding which codes and ciphers it could break, when and for how long. There is evidence that it had considerable successes against the atomic-capable elements of the Soviet Air Force.[36] But the 1956 JIC assessment on the warning of attack suggests that GCHQ in Cheltenham would need to be particularly fortunate if there were the slightest chance of a Soviet decision to go to war being intercepted.[37]

The theme of the H-bomb resonates through Churchill's last premiership like a sombre recitative. He told his doctor, Lord Moran, in the spring of 1954, 'I am more worried by the hydrogen bomb than by all the rest of my troubles put together.'[38] Churchill had been briefed by the Home Office on the effects of an atomic attack on the UK in mid-1952[39] and took a close interest in the details (see Chapter 3). It is intriguing to see how the likely cause of an *atomic* war continued to infuse his thinking even after the Americans had detonated their huge, two-storeys-high device codenamed 'Mike' on the islet of Elugelab in Eniwetok Atoll, part of the Marshall Islands in the Pacific, on 1 November 1952 (with its vast yield of 10.4 megatons).[40]

In June 1953 he told the Commonwealth Prime Ministers gathered in London for the Coronation of his hopes for an Anglo-American-Russian summit meeting to test the new Soviet leadership's intentions and the possibility of what he called 'settlement' or 'easement' (of course he *never* used the tainted word 'appeasement' in this context) between East and West. He incorporated in his speech the merely ghastly atomic scenarios rather than the still scarcely imaginable apocalyptic thermonuclear ones. During the 3 June meeting in No. 10, Churchill told the eight Commonwealth premiers that he

did not pretend to know the extent of any changes in Soviet policy, but he felt that if all held together in the anti-Communist front and strengthened their unity no risk would be run in trying to ascertain how important these changes were and to reach some settlement with Russia ...

The Soviet Government must have their own anxieties about a future war. Though they had the power to overrun much of Western Europe they must know that their central government machinery, their communications and their war potential would be shattered by atomic attack. A future war would differ from any experience before, for both sides would suffer at the start the worst that they had both feared ... The development of atomic warfare would deter the regime, since it would face them with the certain loss of power to wage modern war within a few months of the start.[41]

The thermonuclear age put paid to any prospect of that kind of months' long, 'broken-backed' war as it became known. The sheer destructive power of one H-bomb meant that when both sides had the weapon and the means to deliver it, it would be 'beyond the imagination until it happened', as it was expressed in the British study commissioned by the Churchill administration in the last months of his premiership on the impact of H-bomb war on the UK's central government machinery, communications, war potential and its people. The Strath Committee estimated that ten 10-megaton Soviet H-bombs dropped on the UK would kill 12 million people and seriously injure a further 4 million (nearly a third of the population) even before the poisonous effects of radioactive fall-out spread across the country.[42]

The documents and the diaries of the time are eloquently revealing of Churchill's realization of this. Just a couple of months after the Commonwealth premiers had returned home, Churchill, recovering from the stroke he suffered later in Coronation month (on 23 June) of which the British people knew nothing,[43] came to appreciate the horror and force of the H-bomb with ever greater vividness and sense of doom. Shortly after returning to No. 10 from Chequers (where he went to recover from his stroke) and still far from well in mid-August 1953, he told his doctor,

'I was very depressed last night. I would have liked to see you. I nearly asked you to come over. I get anxious about myself, though,' he hastened to add, 'I don't mind what happens to me. I was conscious of my heart. How? Oh, just like it feels when you are troubled with wind. Then Oliver Lyttelton came to dinner and cheered me up ... I was depressed not only about myself, but about the terrible state of the world. That hydrogen bomb can destroy two million people. It is so awful that I have a feeling it will not happen.'[44]

Those last two sentences capture the motivating power of Churchill's determination to recover from his stroke and hang on to the premiership for as long as he could.

At the end of the previous month, while still recuperating at Chequers, he had told Moran: 'You realize, Charles, I'm playing a big hand – the easement of the world, perhaps peace over the world – without of course giving up proper means of defence.'[45] Herein lay what a more modern generation would call his twin-track approach which culminated in that last glorious, 'never despair' speech to the House of Commons in which he both announced the plan to make a British thermonuclear weapon *and* delivered his eloquent plea for a safer world in which all would realize, as he told Moran in the summer of 1953, that the H-bomb was 'so awful' it would 'not happen'.

It is interesting to speculate, however, about the slimness of the margin that enabled him to have another twenty-two months in which to have a last crack at world 'easement'. In the first days after his stroke, it looked as if he would not last the weekend and plans were discussed to make Lord Salisbury acting premier until Eden was out of the hands of the surgeons in America and back in Whitehall.[46] Had Eden been fit (he was horrified at the prospect of an interim Salisbury government[47]) would not the pressure have been overwhelming for Churchill, had he survived, to stand down in his favour in the summer of 1953?

But Eden himself was another powerful factor in Churchill's determination to hang on. He did not share Churchill's desire to push for a summit. Like the Foreign Office he headed, Eden thought it wrong-headed, premature and dangerous. It led, as we shall see, to one of the most acrimonious clashes to disturb the calm of the postwar Cabinet Room and to a hardening of Churchill's conviction that Eden was not up to the job of Prime Minister. The showdown, over several Cabinet meetings, took place in the summer of 1954 as the twin threads of Churchill's peacemaking and bomb-making reached the knotty and intertwined point of decision-making.

Churchill's stroke interrupted his campaign directed at a reluctant Eisenhower for a joint meeting with the 'new men' in the Kremlin,[48] but it did not put an end to it. In August 1953, the Russian Prime Minister Georgi Malenkov told the world the Soviet Union had successfully completed a thermonuclear test.[49] ('Joe 4', exploded on 12 August 1953, was, in fact, a 'hybrid' not a 'true' H-bomb – a boosted fission device.[50] Not until the 1.6-megaton 'Joe 19' explosion on 22 November 1955 did the Soviet Union show that it had a fully fledged hydrogen bomb[51]). On 7 November 1953, with no prime ministerial announcement, the RAF took delivery of its first weaponized Blue Danube atomic bomb.[52]

For Britain, 1954 was H-bomb year in both a very public and a very private sense. Paradoxically, it was not the first American thermonuclear test which, to adopt Victor Weisskopf, touched the nerve of the world, but the second set of tests, the 'Castle' series at Bikini Atoll in the Marshall Islands in March 1954, designed to explode the first weaponized H-bombs,[53] that were metaphorically heard round the world. By the end of the month Harold Macmillan was noting in his diary that: 'The Hydrogen Bomb panic is spreading'[54] (though not to Churchill, who was merely 'astounded'.[55] A few weeks ahead of the public 'panic', he had read in the *Manchester Guardian* the full text of a speech in Washington by Sterling Cole, Chairman of the Joint Congressional Committee on Atomic Energy, in which Cole released for the first time substantial and detailed information about the power and the magnitude of the 'Mike' explosion at Eniwetok fifteen months earlier.[56])

Public anxiety both in Britain and abroad was aroused not by the Cole revelations but by the plight of the crew of the *Lucky Dragon*, a Japanese fishing boat plying its trade eighty-five miles east of Bikini Atoll and 'outside the declared danger zone'[57] when the 'Bravo' explosion took place. That was a 15-megaton blast, nearly three times more powerful than most had expected and the largest test the USA ever made.[58] When the *Lucky Dragon* reached Japan, nearly all the crew showed signs of classic radiation sickness. Unsurprisingly, given events at Hiroshima and Nagasaki, violent anti-American protests erupted in Japan and the world's press ran the story in bold headlines.[59] Nerves had been touched, including those of Westminster and Fleet Street. As Churchill himself told the House of Commons in July 1954: 'Very little notice was taken over here at first by Mr Sterling Cole's revelations, but when some Japanese fishermen were slightly affected by the radioactivity generated by the second explosion at Bikini [one of the fishermen died two months later from hepatitis caught from a blood transfusion necessitated by his irradiation[60]], an intense sensation was caused in this country . . .'[61]

Churchill, as he later admitted in the Commons, was 'deeply concerned at the lack of information we possessed . . . in view of all the past history of this subject' – in other words, that the US administration had not given HMG 'Mike'-related information in confidence – and that he, the Prime Minister, intended 'a personal meeting with President Eisenhower at the first convenient opportunity'.[62] Martin Gilbert, Churchill's official biographer, found a long and fascinating letter from Prime Minister to President in the Eisenhower archives in Abilene, Kansas, probably written in the second week of March 1954;[63] it marks, I think, the moment Churchill's mind shifted finally and irrevocably from fission to fusion, from A-bomb to H-bomb. For, as part of his preamble, the Prime Minister told the President: 'On the day that the Soviets discovered and developed the Atomic Bomb the consequences of war became far more terrible. But that brief tremendous phase now lies in the past. An incomparably graver situation is presented by the public statements of Mr Sterling Cole at Chicago on February 17.'[64]

In the short interval between reading Cole's speech and writing his letter to Eisenhower, Churchill had been heavily briefed on the conclusions of a group of officials, scientists (of whom Sir William Penney was the key figure, as he had been since the start of the British nuclear programme) and the military on the significance of 'the latest available information concerning the development of the hydrogen bomb by both the Americans and the Russians'.[65] The meeting, given the Cabinet Committee code GEN 465,[66] was chaired by the 'omni-competent'[67] Cabinet Secretary Sir Norman Brook, who was convinced, as he told the key meeting in his office on 12 March 1954, that 'the development of this bomb had now reached a stage which required us to re-assess first, our foreign policy and general strategy and, thereafter, the "size and shape" of the Armed Forces, our civil defence policy and our atomic weapons programme'.[68]

Churchill, who had a wonderfully vivid way of converting technical advice into living and human images, told Eisenhower his expert advisers had explained to him 'that the 175 feet displacement of the ocean bed at Eniwetok Atoll may well have involved a pulverization of the earth's surface three of four times as deep'. Then, in a few sentences, he anticipated the essence of the Strath Report a year later:

This in practice would of course make all protection except for small staff groups, impossible. You can imagine what my thoughts are about London. I am told that several million people would certainly be obliterated by four of [sic] five of the latest H bombs. In a few more years these could be delivered by rocket without even hazarding the life of a pilot. New York and your other great cities have immeasurable perils too, though distance is a valuable advantage at least as long as pilots are used.

Another ugly idea has been put in my head, namely, the dropping of an H Bomb in the sea to windward of the Island or any other seaborne country, in suitable weather, by rocket or airplane, or perhaps released by submarine. The explosion would generate an enormous radio-active cloud, many square miles in extent, which would drift over the land attacked and extinguish human life over very large areas. Our smallness and density of population emphasize this danger to us.[69]

Churchill wondered why there had been 'so little comment' about Cole's 'searing' statement in Chicago. Perhaps, he mused to Eisenhower, the 'reason is that human minds recoil from the realization of such facts. The people, including the well informed, can only gape and console themselves with the reflection that death comes to all anyhow, some time. This merciful numbness cannot be enjoyed by the few men upon whom the supreme responsibility falls. They have to drive their minds forward into those hideous and deadly spheres of thought.'[70]

The arrival home of the *Lucky Dragon* and an answer to a journalist's question by Eisenhower's special adviser on atomic energy at what was meant to be a soothing press conference dramatically raised public anxiety in the West about the possibility of a thermonuclear war. The special adviser, Lewis Strauss, just back from observing the tests in the Marshall Islands, read out what Lorna Arnold described as 'a reassuring statement at the President's news conference' on 31 March 1954 saying, among other things, that the Japanese fishermen would soon recover from the effects of their 'inadvertent trespass'.[71] A journalist asked him how big and powerful a hydrogen bomb was.

STRAUSS: '... in effect it can be made as large as you wish, as large as the military requirement demands, that is to say an H-bomb can be made as – large enough to take out a city.'
JOURNALIST: 'How big a city? Any city? New York?'
STRAUSS: 'The metropolitan area, yes.'[72]

Strauss went on to explain after the press conference that, as the *New York Times* reported the next day (in one of the most famous of its Fifties front pages: 'H-BOMB CAN WIPE OUT ANY CITY, STRAUSS REPORTS AFTER TESTS'), by the 'metropolitan area' of New York 'he meant the heart of Manhattan and not the actual metropolitan area which covers 3,550 square miles'.[73]

Despite Strauss frantically backpedalling, the full horror of the H-bomb was out and the thermonuclear question burst way beyond the inner circles and those 'few men upon whom the supreme responsibility' for nuclear weapons then fell. The *New York Times* front-page map alone (showing the zones of destruction up to fifty miles beyond downtown New York of an H-bomb exploding over Manhattan)[74] made the story compelling to everyone.

There was no British equivalent of Lewis Strauss on Norman Brook's GEN 465 to blurt out at a press conference what a hydrogen bomb would do to London (though Churchill plainly knew when he wrote to Eisenhower). At the meeting in Brook's office on 12 March, however, Penney first told the meeting (accurately enough) that the 'Russians had already developed the "hybrid" bomb, and they were likely to develop the "true" hydrogen bomb before too long.' Then

Sir William Penney said that a 5 megaton 'true' hydrogen bomb would have the following effects. A bomb dropped on London and bursting on impact would produce a crater $3/4$-mile across and 150-ft. deep, and a fire-ball of $2^1/4$ miles diameter. The blast from it would crush the Admiralty Citadel [built during the Second World War on the north-west corner of Horse Guards Parade to house a signals intelligence centre – and still there] at a distance of 1 mile. Suburban houses would be wrecked at a distance of 3 miles from the explosion, and they would lose their roofs and be badly blasted at a distance of 7 miles. All habitations would catch fire over a circle of 2 miles from the burst.[75]

Penney was basing his estimates on the 'Mike' explosion at Eniwetok in November 1952 (he thought it had been a 14-megaton blast rather than the 10.4 megatons final calculations indicated,[76] closer in other words to the 15 megatons of 'Bravo' at Bikini that very month of which he had no details to impart to GEN 465 beyond stating that the 'Americans had now embarked on a series of six more test explosions of bombs ranging from 100 kilotons to 10 megatons'[77]).

The minutes of GEN 465 illustrate plainly how effective the McMahon Act of 1946 had been in cutting off US–UK nuclear weapons information pooling. They also provide a vivid contrast with the collaboration restored in 1958, including the sharing of warhead designs and the joint-targeting of the US Air Force's B-52 bombers and the Royal Air Force's V-bombers and, later, the Polaris and Trident submarine forces of the US Navy and the Royal Navy.

Penney, for example, told GEN 465 on 12 March 1954 that the 'details' of the Eniwetok test, on which his presentation was based, 'had recently been revealed in a public statement by Mr Sterling Cole, the Chairman of the Joint Congressional Atomic Energy Committee'.[78] It is hardly surprising, given the toughness of the Soviet Union as an intelligence target, that GEN 465's knowledge of the Russian effort (partly derived from US/UK sharing of information on debris from Soviet tests which was permitted by the so-called *modus vivendi* of 1948 allowing co-operation on 'detection of a distant nuclear explosion'[79]) was a mixture of the certain and the tentative:

Whatever progress the Russians might make from now on in developing the hydrogen bomb, we should be justified in advising Ministers now that the Russians had already developed the material for an attack on this country, the intensity of which far exceeded our previous assumptions and the plans which we had based on them.[80]

As we have seen, this is the point Churchill made forcibly to Eisenhower a few days later. But the knowledge within this innermost of British nuclear circles about *American* capabilities was remarkably thin:

Sir William Penney had said that by the end of this year the United States Strategic Air Force would rely on hydrogen bombs. But it was not clear whether the Americans now excluded the possibility of strategic bombing with conventional high explosive bombs. Up till now it had been thought that they were basing their plans for dropping atomic bombs on the 'queen bee' method whereby a bomber carrying an atomic bomb would be accompanied by a large number of bombers carrying conventional bombs ... It was agreed that it would be valuable if the Chief of the Air Staff could discover what change, if any, had taken place in American theory on the dropping of atomic bombs.[81]

GEN 465 did know, however, that '[t]hough the Russians were rapidly reducing the Western lead in atomic development, it was not certain that they were making the same progress in developing the means of delivering an atomic attack'. Nevertheless they 'could bomb the United Kingdom, but not the United States (even by means of one-way missions), with T.U.34 aircraft, which were the equivalent of the obsolete B.29 [the US propeller-driven aircraft which had dropped the atomic bombs on Japan]'.[82]

GEN 465 was one of Norman Brook's most important pitch-priming Cabinet Committees. He had, he told its members, already prepared the way by suggesting

to the Prime Minister that it was necessary to re-assess, in the light of the new information about the hydrogen bomb, the following points:

(i)   The likelihood of war.
(ii) The form which war was most likely to take if it came.
(iii) The changes which would need to be made in the pattern of our defence arrangements, active and passive, in order to adjust them to meet the most likely contingency.
(iv) The extent to which we should ensure against the possibility that war might take some other form than that which now seemed most likely ...

He agreed that to these four issues should be added a fifth, namely, 'consideration of the bearing of this re-assessment on our atomic weapons programme'.[83]

No doubt if Churchill had been present he would have added a sixth – the need to push for a summit to head off the entire thermonuclear horror. As he put it in his letter to Eisenhower a few days later:

Of course I recur to my earlier proposal of a personal meeting between Three [i.e. the USA, USSR and the UK]. Men have to settle with men, no matter how vast, and in part beyond their comprehension, the business in hand may be. I can even imagine that a few simple words, spoken in the awe which may at once oppress and inspire the speakers, might lift this nuclear monster from our world.[84]

And it was this mixture of sentiments – oppression and inspiration – which infused the thermonuclear spring and summer of 1954 that gave flavour to Churchill's last great political cause. It also precipitated the gravest Cabinet crisis of his final premiership as high diplomacy in pursuit of summitry mingled with grinding out the decision to manufacture a British H-bomb.

The greatest single leap in the technology of weapons of mass destruction (apart, naturally, from the making of the first atomic bombs) – the jump from fission to fusion – came at a time when the UK's atomic production was fully stretched to meet a programme for the manufacture of 10-kiloton Blue Danubes, getting them up to a yield of 30 kilotons 'by means of improvement in design' and designing a smaller version that the new Gloster Javelin aircraft could carry, as Penney told his colleagues on GEN 465.[85] And, just a few days before Brook's session on the interlocking questions of great nuclear magnitude now facing the Churchill government, the Old Man was presiding over a meeting of ministers to see how one embarrassing British atomic secret could be kept from Parliament, the British public, the Russians and the Americans alike: that, as the Minister of Supply Duncan Sandys put it, 'the rate of build-up of our stockpile of atomic weapons is exceedingly slow and that for several years to come Britain's atomic power is not a factor to be reckoned with ... Apart from gratuitously assisting foreign intelligence services,' Sandys continued, 'it is surely most undesirable, from the standpoint of our influence for peace, that information of this kind should be disclosed.'[86]

The problem had arisen because a new Atomic Energy Department (a step towards a proposed Atomic Energy Authority) was about to be created, and Parliament, unless the system of financial reporting was changed, would be able to work out that in the fiscal year 1954–5, the Ministry of Supply would be paying the new Department some £14m for atomic weapons work. 'It is true,' Sandys told his colleagues, '... that the payments from the Ministry of Supply cover expenditure on research as well as expenditure on weapon production. But, so far as the deterrent effect of our atomic stockpile is concerned, this only makes matters worse.' He suggested that the nuclear element should be mushed in with conventional bombs under such vague headings as 'Ammunition and Explosives' and 'Extra-Mural Research'.[87] Remember how Churchill had been exercised by Attlee's concealing of the original £100m bomb-making programme from Parliament but had reluctantly agreed that MPs should continue to be kept in the dark? The Cabinet Committee which met on Sandys' proposal agreed 'in principle that the Estimates of the Department of Atomic Energy should be so presented as to conceal the total receipts of atomic weapons and uranium sales'.[88]

Sandys' paper for GEN 458 reflected a deeper and more enduring factor even than the degree to which much of the detailed story was kept from Parliament at the time – the psychology of an ever shakier great-powerdom. Sir Michael Quinlan, the former Permanent Secretary at the Ministry of Defence and very much its high priest of deterrence theory,[89] captured the essence and importance of this aspect of early postwar nuclear policy-making during a conversation about the bomb at the National Archives as part of its 2004 'Secret State' Exhibition.

Citing the diplomat Robert Cooper on the importance generally (and not just in the UK context) of sensing those times and those questions on which policy 'grew out of national identity, not out of interest',[90] Sir Michael turned to the standing-alone period of British nuclear history after US–UK collaboration had been severed by the McMahon Act 'in a way that was, to put it at its most polite, unfriendly – you could argue treacherous . . .'[91] For Attlee's GEN 163 ministerial group, Quinlan continued, to authorize the manufacture of a British atomic bomb in the absence of US co-operation was 'psychologically quite inevitable – it was an "of-course" decision'.[92]

Sir Michael's general characterization of the early postwar *mentalité* fits, I think, all the 1954 ministerial and official nuclear groups too, not least Sandys' determination that Parliament and the world should not know on how meagre and slowly growing a stockpile of bombs British influence rested:

For all our economic problems, we saw ourselves as one of the three great victors of the war. We still had global responsibilities. We still had quite a lot of an Empire even if we knew that the sun was setting on it. And given all that, it would have been enormously counter-identity, counter-cultural for us to do anything other than to decide to get into the [nuclear] business . . . This must be the sort of thing that Britain, as it perceived itself in those days, did.[93]

This was equally true of Churchill's consistent pushing of the need for 'a parley at the summit', as he put it when coining the term in his Edinburgh speech during the 1950 general election,[94] when he was acutely aware that Truman, Stalin and he (once he resumed the premiership) had unfinished business as leaders of the three victorious powers who had met at Potsdam in July 1945.

Much of the subsequent history of the secret ministerial and official discussion on Britain and its bombs involved, in essence, finding 'a set of rationales to clothe that gut decision', as Quinlan put it.[95] The nuclear spring and summer in 1954 Whitehall was classically a part of that pattern. I have written in detail elsewhere about the work of the interlocking committees through which the thermonuclear question flowed during those months.[96] The clothing rationales, to borrow Michael Quinlan's metaphor, were present throughout, for essentially there were two.

The first was the great-power impulse. Once the 'atomic knights' (Penney, Sir John Cockcroft from Harwell, the nuclear research laboratory, and Sir Christopher Hinton, who oversaw the series of plants which produced the necessary ingredients for the bombs) had convinced him the costs of Britain going thermonuclear were manageable – though Aldermaston, the weapons research station, still had no precise idea of how to design an H-bomb warhead[97] – Churchill was in no doubt that the programme should go ahead. Sir Edwin Plowden, head of the Department of Atomic Energy, presented the Prime Minister with the collective scientific advice in his room at the House of Commons one afternoon after lunch. As Plowden told me many years later,

When I'd explained what the effort necessary would be, he paused for a time, and nodded his head, and said in that well-known voice of his, 'We must do it. It's the price we pay to sit at the top table.' And having said that, he got up and tied a little black ribbon round his eyes, and lay down on his bed in his room, and went to sleep.[98]

The 'top table' impulse was linked to the second motivator or rationale – the need when sitting at that table atop, as it were, a British nuclear weapon with, Bevin style, 'a bloody Union Jack on top of it', to press the case for peaceful restraint on a potentially aggressive United States as well as a truculent Soviet Union.

Churchill could be very direct with the Americans on this front and had been so even before the detail of the American tests emerged in 1954. He was well aware that, as so often in the history of weaponry, the armourers had outrun the ethicists, and that, in the new world of the H-bomb, this meant 'living in a time when at any moment London, men, women and children might be destroyed overnight', as he put it to the entourage that accompanied him to the Bermuda meeting with Eisenhower in December 1953.[99] That same evening before the conference opened, he mused on the possibility 'that we are living in our generation through the great demoralisation which the scientists have caused but before the countervailing correctives have become operative'.[100]

The late 1953 Bermuda discussions were an important prelude to the year of the hydrogen bomb. Once underway, the anxiety levels inside what Churchill called 'this old carcass of mine'[101] rose even higher. On 5 December 1953 Churchill had informed Eisenhower that the first British atomic bomb had 'recently been delivered to the RAF' and Cherwell had explained that the UK was 'not intending to do any work on hydrogen bombs' as Aldermaston could get sufficient destructive power from 'boosted fission weapons'. Eisenhower came up with a sentence which, once it had sunk in, seriously alarmed the British party, saying it was his belief that atomic weapons 'were now coming to be regarded as a proper part of conventional armament and that he thought this a sound concept'.[102]

The British team was even more alarmed over dinner that night when Churchill and Eden dined with Eisenhower and his Secretary of State, Dulles (the French Prime Minister, Joseph Laniel, was excluded because his country did not then have a nuclear weapons capability). As Churchill described it to Colville afterwards, the 'grim conversations' included Eisenhower saying the United States was prepared to drop an atomic bomb on North Korea if the truce, agreed the previous July, broke down. Churchill 'strongly resisted' this suggestion.[103] This, as Colville noted the following day in his own diary, had left the British delegation 'in rather a state' as the previous night's discussion 'far outstrips in importance anything else at the conference'.[104]

Later that morning, Eisenhower waxed alarmingly to Colville once more on the profound difference of approach to nuclear matters in Washington and Whitehall:

Eisenhower was in his sitting-room, cross-legged in an armchair, going through his speech. He was friendly, but I noticed that he never smiled: a change from the Ike of war days or even, indeed, of last January in New York. He said several things that were noteworthy. The first was that whereas Winston looked on the atomic weapon as something entirely new and terrible, he looked upon it as just the latest improvement in military weapons. He implied that there was in fact no distinction between 'conventional weapons' and atomic weapons: all weapons in due course became conventional weapons. This of course represents a fundamental difference of opinion between public opinion in the USA and in England.[105]

And this difference was sharpened by Eisenhower's failure to link the bomb to the need for a summit, which left Churchill near despair as the Bermuda conference closed and it preoccupied him for the next eight months.

The Old Man was tired in Bermuda and this made everything worse. He became furious when told Eden did not wish to stay the extra day Churchill had suddenly decided upon and he shouted at Christopher Soames, his son-in-law and Parliamentary Private Secretary, who had come to tell him Eden wanted to get back to London to keep lunch and dinner appointments: 'To hell with his engagements. He's not running this show.'[106] 'When we were alone,' his doctor noted, 'his mood changed.' Moran later wrote down his patient's broodings and all their pent-up resentment of his own and his country's waning powers:

'. . . I cannot make it out. I am bewildered. It seems that everything is left to Dulles. It appears that the President is no more than a ventriloquist's doll . . . This fellow preaches like a Methodist Minister, and his bloody text is always the same: That nothing but evil can come out of a meeting with Malenkov.'

There was a long pause.

'Dulles is a terrible handicap.' His voice rose. 'Ten years ago I could have dealt with him. Even as it is I have not been defeated by this bastard. I have been humiliated by my own decay. Ah, no, Charles, you have done all that could be done to slow things down.'

When I turned round he was in tears. That was the last I heard of Moscow while we were at Bermuda.[107]

The glorious thing about Churchill, the bomb and the pursuit of peace is that he simply would not accept defeat at the hand of any 'bastards', whether they be the Americans, the Foreign Office or certain of his Cabinet colleagues.

As Whitehall's nuclear committees began to pave the way towards the decision to build a British H-bomb three to four months after Prime Minister and President flew away from Bermuda, Churchill became even more aware of the danger of the Americans returning to active warfare somewhere in east Asia. For in April 1954 the Eisenhower administration proposed a joint Anglo-American military intervention in Indo-China to prevent the French collapse from leading to a communist takeover by the Viet Minh. The President sent to London the hawkish Admiral Arthur Radford, Chairman of the US Joint Chiefs of Staff, to try to persuade Churchill of the need to put GIs and Tommies into the jungles of Vietnam and to use air power against China, in Radford's eyes 'the source of the trouble'.[108] Radford, 'whom we did not think very intelligent, and who is obviously raring for a scrap', as Evelyn Shuckburgh noted in his diary,[109] got extremely short shrift from Churchill, who lectured Radford over dinner at Chequers on 26 April 1954 on his favourite interlocking themes.

'The British people,' he told the American admiral, 'would not be easily influenced by what happened in the distant jungles of SE Asia; but they did know that there was a powerful American base in East Anglia and that war with China, who would invoke the Sino-Russian Pact, might mean an assault by hydrogen bombs on these islands'. Churchill, as the No. 10 record of the conversation makes plain, endeavoured 'to impress on Admiral Radford the danger of war on the fringes, where the Russians were strong and could mobilise the enthusiasm of nationalist and oppressed peoples. His policy was quite different: it was conversations at the centre. Such conversations should not lead either to appeasement or, he hoped, to an ultimatum; but they would be calculated to bring home to the Russians the full implications of Western strength and to impress upon them the folly of war.'[110]

April 1954 was a strange month for Churchill and matters nuclear. It began badly when, in a Commons debate on the hydrogen bomb on the 5th, he got himself into a nasty and unnecessary fight with Attlee over the severance of Anglo-American atomic collaboration after the war. It came as the culmination of what Dick Crossman called in his diary next day, 'the fortnight of the H-bomb, the fortnight, incidentally, when the whole political situation here was completely transformed, with Labour suddenly holding the initiative'.[111] Another Labour MP, the youthful Tony Benn, caught the moment and honed it down to its irreducible minimum: 'Commons debate on H bomb. Attlee made a superb speech, Churchill's mean party attack misfired, Boothby walked out. Tory backbench embarrassment.'[112]

Crossman, who always patronized Attlee (who privately couldn't stand him, seeing Crossman as the worst kind of volatile intellectual – 'Dick is irresponsible and unstable,' Attlee told his official biographer, Kenneth Harris[113]), recorded that

Attlee began quite well but, as we had all heard the dress rehearsal, the edge of our pleasure at the little man's carefully prepared rhetoric had been blunted. [The Parliamentary Labour Party had agreed the previous week that the party line would be to stress the need for talks between the Americans, the Russians and the British about the peril of the H-bomb and to let drop any push for a British renunciation of nuclear weapons.] Then came Churchill's extraordinary performance. He started quietly enough but in a few minutes he was attacking Attlee on the ground that British inability to obtain information from the Americans was due to Attlee's abandonment of the secret Quebec Agreement [of 1943 requiring the US and the UK to consult and agree before either used an atomic weapon]. Gradually the scene worked up to a fever, with all of us shouting, 'Guttersnipe! Swine! Resign!' with Churchill standing there swaying slightly and trying to plough through his script. There came a terrible moment when Bob Boothby got up from his seat below the gangway, turned his back to Churchill and strode out beyond the Bar [of the House of Commons], stood there glowering and then disappeared.[114]

Crossman, perhaps, on occasion, a better man than many on both sides of the House imagined, wrote down how amid 'the turmoil I suddenly detached myself from myself and thought how nauseating we were, howling for the old bull's blood. I think we really would have lynched him if we could.'[115]

Churchill's mistake was to allow his anger at the taunts of left-wing backbenchers about his lack of influence in Washington to stimulate an attack on Attlee and the Labour front bench: 'I do not say that there were not many reasons and facts operative at the end of the war which were different from those during its course. But considering that the abandonment of our claim to be consulted and informed as an equal was the act of the Socialist Administration I feel they have no ground for reproaching their successors with the consequences.'[116] Churchill's ministerial colleagues and his officials were dismayed. Some by what their boss said and others by how he faltered in the face of Labour's onslaught.

His foreign affairs private secretary, Anthony Montague Browne, recalled later that this was 'the first time' he 'realised unmistakably how much his powers had waned. In days gone by he would have put aside his notes and devastated the opposition ...'[117] Shuckburgh, in the House as back-up for Eden, wrote in his diary that night 'that the PM has made a real bloomer and exposed his aged feebleness to the House'.[118] Shuckburgh was well aware that Lord Cherwell and Sir Norman Brook had tried to persuade Churchill *not* to expose the secret Quebec Agreement of 1943.[119] But Churchill, needled by media attacks on him during that heated H-bomb fortnight (particularly one on television three days earlier by the Labour MP Michael Foot, who had declared, 'I am attacking the British Prime Minister, the British Foreign Secretary, and the British Government because of their failure to demand from the Americans full information about this [hydrogen] bomb'[120]), persisted and read out for the Commons (with Eisenhower's permission) the text of the Quebec Agreement.[121]

Macmillan's diary coverage of that extraordinary afternoon in the House of Commons is perhaps the most interesting of all the contemporary reports, not least because it flowed from a sympathetic pen:

There *was* 'one hell of a row' yesterday afternoon [5 April 1954] . . . It was really a very strange performance. Attlee made a speech wh commanded general approval and respect – with a 'non party' approach and full of worthy sentiments . . . It was a strange contrast to the flood of partisan questions last week, and violent attacks on the PM by Michael Foot on the TV and by Crossman in the *Sunday Pictorial*.[122]

The House (and the press) expected that the PM wd make a similar sort of speech – perhaps a little more realistic and better phrased, but on the same note. This he did for the first part of his speech. Then he started on the story of the Churchill–Roosevelt agreement of 1943, and its 'abandonment' by the Socialist Govt. In other words, we had a veto on the use of the atomic or any other nuclear bomb by the USA now the veto has gone.

This sudden change of tone infuriated the Opposition, and shocked the Government back-benchers. A long and angry scene followed. Attlee made some effective interventions, and Churchill muddled his case in answering.[123]

Attlee seems to have been genuinely disappointed by this. He told his brother Tom: 'I had given him the opportunity to make a great speech on a high level – to give a lead to the world so to speak. Instead of responding he plunged into the gutter, to everybody's disgust. It would have been an eye-opener to him if he could have seen the faces of his own party. It was a great pity as I had been strictly non-party.'[124]

It would have been even more of an eye-opener for Churchill if Macmillan's diary had fallen into his hands, in which the following day's entry continued:

He was thrown off balance by the violence of the reaction. After about 20 minutes of storm . . . he was able to finish the speech, the latter part of which was in the tone wh had been expected, but coming after the attack, was ineffective and not appreciated, even where good points were made. Bob Boothby, with a characteristic gesture of disloyalty [Boothby was still involved in a long-running affair with Macmillan's wife Lady Dorothy[125]], walked out – apparently to show his disapproval of Churchill.[126]

In fact, as Boothby told Beaverbrook, his walkout was partly due to the pain of a dental operation earlier that day. 'By half-past four the anaesthetic had worn off, all I had got from the PM was an attack on Michael Foot, and the House was a bear-garden. I hated the speech, the Labour Party and my bleeding gum in about equal proportions. So I decided to go home to aspirin, and to bed, and went.'[127]

Macmillan's overall verdict was deeply damning of his old chief: 'It was the greatest failure – on the surface at least – since Churchill's speech [in 1936] on the abdication of King Edward VIII.'[128] Of this occasion Roy Jenkins, himself no mean connoisseur of great parliamentary moments, wrote that Churchill 'had come in with all his heavy guns primed. It was not so much what he said – indeed he was bludgeoned into silence before he could say very much – as that it was a classic example of running completely against the feeling of the House.'[129]

From a distance of fifty years, Macmillan's judgement on Churchill's performance in the spring of 1954 is hard to fault. The peril of the hydrogen bomb *was* the greatest of Churchill's concerns. Attlee *had* constructed a platform from which the Prime Minister could have delivered a public *tour de force*, as he sometimes did in private,[130] whose echoes would have been heard in the White House and the Kremlin alike. He blew it, and for all his bluster to his doctor afterwards ('It will be all right in the morning papers'[131] – it wasn't[132]), Churchill must have known it. Indeed, the next morning he admitted as much to Moran:

'Things didn't go as well as I expected. When one gets old one lives too much in the past. I ought to have told the House that I was very happy the Opposition had come round to my view that the Heads of the three states ought to meet, instead of ...'

He was silent for a while, lost in thought.[133]

Churchill soon bounced back in pursuit of his two favourite causes: keeping Britain a serious player in the highest counsels of the world and the creation of sufficient British nuclear weapons capital to fund this. In the middle of April a special Cabinet committee, GEN 464, met under his chairmanship to approve moves to acquire the raw materials needed for the H-bomb ahead of the decision to make it (the Americans were engaged in stockpiling and buying up large quantities of thorium[134]). On 13 April 1954 the Prime Minister told the small group of colleagues on GEN 464 'that he would like to invite the Cabinet at an early date to decide in principle that hydrogen bombs should be made in the United Kingdom'. Eden, Butler, Alexander (Minister of Defence), Swinton (Commonwealth Secretary) and Salisbury (Lord President) agreed.[135]

On 22 April Churchill wrote to Eisenhower inviting himself to Washington for talks.[136] Eisenhower was not keen, cabling back in a manner which suggested that Prime Minister and President had come no closer on the issue of the hour since those awkward meals and conversations in Bermuda four months earlier. 'The United States and Britain seem to reach drastically different answers to problems involving the same set of basic facts,' read his telegram to Churchill dated 26 April.[137] Nevertheless, there Churchill was, two months later on 25 June, after sleeping for nine hours on *Canopus*, the BOAC* Stratocruiser he used for such journeys,[138] preparing to land at Washington, accompanied by a highly sceptical Eden.

Moran was pessimistic:

No one, save Winston, seems to think that much will come out of this visit to Washington. Christopher [Soames] says the Americans are hopping mad with us ... Winston, for his part, has never been a Doubting Thomas. He seems to have taken a new lease of life since we left London. At ten o'clock this morning by English time he called the steward and ordered him to take away the whisky and to bring champagne. Then he proceeded to make a meal of caviar and toast, though he had had a hearty breakfast only an hour before.

Four hours later the *Canopus* made a bumpy landing. We all waited for Winston. Presently he appeared shuffling down the space between the seats of the aircraft. Christopher reminded him that he was wearing his spectacles, whereupon he stuffed them in his pocket without putting them in a case. Then Christopher said something in his ear, and he took the unlighted cigar from his mouth and handed it to the detective, while Anthony watched, with a grim smile, all these preliminaries to taking a curtain.[139]

On the tarmac Vice-President Richard Nixon and the greatly disliked 'Methodist Preacher' Secretary of State, John Foster Dulles, waited to greet the Prime Minister and his Foreign Secretary.[140]

Between inviting himself to talks with Eisenhower and driving with Nixon to the White House, Churchill had made a good deal of progress on the British hydrogen bomb within his most secret Cabinet Committees. But, as his

* British Overseas Airways Corporation.

official biographer Martin Gilbert noted, at the last full Cabinet meeting he chaired on 22 June before boarding the *Canopus* there was no mention 'of the decision [in the Defence Policy Committee] to build a British hydrogen bomb'.[141] This was to result in immense problems for Churchill in the Cabinet Room once he and Eden returned.

Acting along the lines prescribed by his Cabinet Secretary, Churchill created a special Cabinet Committee on Defence Policy, DPC, to assess the magnitude of the multiple changes in prospect thanks to the H-bomb and, mindful of the brittleness of the British economy, he sought to use the thermonuclear leap as a way of evading some of the more costly aspects of conventional defence. The Chiefs of Staff* prepared a paper, 'United Kingdom Defence Policy', dated 1 June 1954 for the ministers on the DPC.[142] (Later, shorn of certain sensitive detail on the number of H-bombs envisaged, a copy would be made available to every member of the Cabinet.[143])

Attached to the Chiefs' memo for the DPC was a highly eloquent annex prepared by the Working Party on the Operational Use of Atomic Weapons chaired by Sir Frederick Brundrett, the Ministry of Defence's chief scientist. It was revealing in several ways. For a start it put figures on the anxiety that had rippled through GEN 464 about the meagreness of the UK's existing atomic capacity. By the end of 1954, the working party estimated, Britain's stock of Blue Danube bombs would be just twenty.[144] And at 10 kilotons the weapons would not be powerful enough to destroy the UK's priority targets in the Soviet Union 'such as airfields or ports, with a single bomb'.[145]

The military planners and the scientists on the working party were particularly concerned that the RAF should be capable of swiftly immobilizing the bases of the Soviet Long Range Air Force. For that purpose even the improved Blue Danubes that were planned would not be enough:

The time factor for the destruction of Russian airfields will be so critical that we must be certain of putting them out of action in the first attack, and be prepared to overhit these targets. The possession of a bomb in the 5 and 10 megaton range offers this possibility and would go a long way towards overcoming the need for improved terminal accuracy ... A hydrogen bomb to give a yield of 5–10 megatons would weigh from 9,000 to 12,000 lbs and could be carried by the V-Class bombers [the Valiants, Vulcans and Victors then in the process of testing and construction].[146]

* Field Marshal Sir John Harding, Chief of the Imperial General Staff; Admiral of the Fleet Sir Rhoderick McGrigor, First Sea Lord and Chief of the Naval Staff; Marshal of the Royal Air Force Sir William Dickson, Chief of the Air Staff.

This paragraph of the technical annex was a clear signpost to Churchill and his inner nuclear group of ministers.

From the early studies undertaken by the JIC in 1949 of the use of atomic weapons against the Soviet Union if war broke out in the mid-1950s (1957 was the hypothetical date they used), it was plain that huge numbers of bombs would be needed to hit the Soviets' communication centres, economic concentrations and military installations sufficiently hard to impede a Red Army advance into north-west Europe. Moreover, as a last throw it was planned to bomb French Channel ports and those in the Low Countries if the Red Army looked set to invade Britain.[147]

Science-fiction nightmare had become conceivable reality. Under the laconic heading 'Safety', Brundrett's working party drafted a paragraph that can only have fuelled still further the desire of their avid reader in No. 10 to secure his cherished 'parley at the summit':

We wish to draw attention to the fact that there is a limit to the cumulative quantity of certain products of explosions of atomic and hydrogen bombs which can be tolerated (in the medical sense) without endangering the health of the animal, including human, populations of the world. Similarly, there is a limit, depending on many factors, including upper wind structure, to the total number of megatons which can be exploded in an area (such as the British Isles) without causing deadly contamination hundreds or even thousands of miles away. It is extremely difficult to assess what the safe levels are. A total of 40,000 megatons of explosive power is the lowest figure that has been quoted by reliable sources for world contamination. A total of 1,000 megatons exploded in a limited area might well cause intense contamination thousands of miles away, over areas of hundreds of square miles.[148]

Such paragraphs, as his doctor noted, 'got Winston down'. When he was at Potsdam Churchill told Moran

about the explosion of the first atomic bomb. He saw the scene as an artist, but I remember that he had not yet grasped what it meant to the world . . . The hydrogen bomb is another matter . . . I came across him brooding so that he does not seem to know I am there.

'You are unhappy about the hydrogen bomb?'

'Terrible, terrible,' he replied, half to himself. 'Nothing so menacing to our civilization since the Mongols.'[149]

That exchange took place in Churchill's last days as premier. But the cumulative feed he received of scientific, military and intelligence material all but consumed him with 'foreboding' from the spring of 1954.[150]

In the main text of the 1 June memorandum from his Chiefs of Staff Churchill found confirmation for his own view that the H-bomb enabled Britain to keep its place at the 'top table' and made keeping that seat ever more important to the peace of the world, not least because the 'danger', as the Chiefs put it, that 'the United States might succumb to the temptation of precipitating a "forestalling" war cannot be disregarded. In view of the vulnerability of the United Kingdom we must use all our influence to prevent this.'[151]

The Chiefs led their ministerial readers on the DPC through a series of briefings on the power of the H-bomb, the UK's extensive vulnerability to thermonuclear assault, the likelihood of the Russians launching one and the danger of the US dealing the Soviets 'a quick knock-out blow' with its H-bombs before the USSR acquired the capacity to destroy New York and Washington. The report finished with some 'deductions' for Churchill and his Cabinet Committee to ponder.

Reading that paper fifty years later, it could be said that the Cabinet's military advisers were moving their political overseers towards another 'inevitable' decision comparable to the one taken by Attlee and his inner group of ministers in 1946–7, provided the costs of going thermonuclear were manageable. They began and ended by saying that it was indispensable to the preservation of peace that the UK should remain a leading power. This is how the Chiefs' argument flowed in possibly the single most important paper they drafted in the 1950s:

... we must maintain and strengthen our position as a world power so that Her Majesty's Government can exercise a powerful influence in the counsels of the world ...

The world situation has been completely altered by recent progress in the development of nuclear weapons. The Americans have exploded a weapon approximately 1,500 times more powerful than the 'nominal' atomic bomb ... There is no theoretical limit to the destructive power which can be achieved with the latest techniques ...

A provisional estimate of the effect of 10 bombs dropped one each on 10 selected cities in the United Kingdom indicates that if they are of 100 times 'nominal' power, the death roll would be 5 millions, and, if 1,000 times 'nominal' power, 12 millions ...

Another factor of immense significance is that these weapons can now be made with much smaller quantities of fissile material than was originally thought. Thus the availability of fissile material is no longer a critical factor. The cost of producing these weapons should not be beyond our financial capabilities.[152]

The 'Deductions'?

(a) Short of sacrificing our vital interests or principles, we must do everything possible to prevent global war which would inevitably entail the exposure of the United Kingdom to a devastating nuclear bombardment.

(b) The ability to wage war with the most up-to-date nuclear weapons will be the measure of military power in the future.

(c) Our scientific skill and technological capacity to produce the hydrogen weapon puts within our grasp the ability to be on terms with the United States and Russia.[153]

Today the last point reads as little short of hubris, but at the time, and in the circumstances of 1954, that trio of deductions represented a powerful and rational argument to support the gut instinct that it was essential for the UK to be a leading actor on the world's thermonuclear stage. The H-bomb decision, as it worked its way through Churchill's Cabinet Committee and his full Cabinet, represented a technical fix that somehow would compensate for the wasting of more conventional ingredients of great-powerdom, whether it be economic clout, territorial control or conventional military superiority.

Writing in 1956, a year after the British decision to manufacture an H-bomb had been announced in the House of Commons, Raymond Aron, the incomparable French historical sociologist and politico-military observer, likened the UK's private 1954 thermonuclear 'rationale' to a modern 'certificate of grandeur' comparable to the colonies, divisions and battleships a country needed to 'possess' to 'enter the exclusive club of the world's masters' in late-Victorian and Edwardian times.[154] The British H-bomb decision, Aron wrote,

represents, for the Atlantic Alliance taken as a whole, an unnecessary expense ... But, in taking this step, the British Government qualifies for entry into the great-power club which is no longer reserved for states that merely boast of millions of soldiers or dozens of heavy units, but for those who know how to manufacture the Bomb. Is this simply a question of pride and prestige, or a recovery, perhaps more apparent than real, of diplomatic sovereignty, in the traditional sense of the term, which expresses itself by the capacity to choose between peace and war?[155]

Like Monnet and Churchill's 'United Europe' Cabinet paper of November 1951, it was almost as if Aron had had a glimpse of the Chiefs' memorandum on 'United Kingdom Defence Policy' in June 1954.

Even before the Chiefs' paper was quite ready for circulation to its members, Churchill had shown just how open was the psychological door at which the Cabinet's military advisers would be pushing when he summed up the DPC meeting of 19 May 1954. From the minutes, it is apparent that the PM identified the problem as deciding

what practical steps could be taken to effect the saving [in overall defence spending] of £200 million a year, with the least risk of weakening our influence in the world, or endangering our security. Influence depended on possession of force. If the United States were tempted to undertake a forestalling war, we could not hope to remain neutral. Even if we could, such a war would in any event determine our fate. We must avoid any action which would weaken our power to influence United States policy. We must avoid anything which might be represented as a sweeping act of disarmament. If, however, we were able to show that in a few years' time we should be possessed of great offensive power, and that we should be ready to take our part in a world struggle, he thought it would not be impossible to reconcile reductions in defence expenditure with the maintenance of our influence in world councils.[156]

This very Churchillian peroration, the force of which even the dry Cabinet Committee minutes captured, was Bevin-like in its determination to keep a 'bloody Union Jack' on top of the bomb whatever the pressures on public expenditure.

It is no surprise, therefore, to find the DPC at its next meeting in No. 10 on 16 June 1954, after considering the long paper on UK defence policy from the Chiefs and the shorter technical report from Brundrett's group, deciding to do just that. The minutes in the confidential annex incorporating the nuclear element of that discussion record that the meeting '[a]uthorised the Lord President [Salisbury] and the Minister of Supply [Sandys] to initiate a programme for the production of hydrogen bombs . . .'[157]

This was the decision Churchill had in his pocket when he travelled to meet Eisenhower and the Canadian Prime Minister, Louis St Laurent. (The 16 June meeting had decided that the Canadians should be asked, in strict confidence, if they could supply sufficient tritium to enable the UK's H-bomb programme to start 'somewhat earlier'.[158]) A man on a mission, the PM set off without informing the full Cabinet of the huge step authorized by his Defence Policy Committee, a failure that was to have serious repercussions.

When they arrived in Washington on a sweltering Friday 25 June 1954, most of Churchill's party mingled perspiration with pessimism about the prospects of the talks. Not the Old Man himself, however. He might have sweated with the rest of them ('The White House', as Colville noted, 'is not attractive

... all the lights burn all the time which is extremely disagreeable at high noon – particularly as the sunshine is bright and the temperature in the 90s'[159]), but he went for broke straightaway with Eisenhower, and, before he went to bed that night, it looked as if he had succeeded against all expectations. As Colville recorded in his diary,

I spent most of the day at the White House where, on arrival, W. at once got down to talking to the President. The first and vast surprise was when the latter at once agreed to talks with the Russians – a possibility of which W. had hoped to persuade the Americans after long talks on Indo-China, Europe, atoms: on all these the first impressions were surprisingly and immediately satisfactory while the world in general believes that there is at this moment greater Anglo-American friction than ever before in history and that these talks are fraught with every possible complication and difficulty.[160]

Churchill, naturally, was elated. He had, he thought, been vindicated. 'It's my show entirely; I have been working for this for a long time,' he told Moran as he dressed for dinner that night in the White House, adding that he might be in Russia the following month.[161]

That night, I think, Churchill reached the apogee of his last premiership. He really thought, as he told Moran, his breakthrough with Eisenhower might 'lead to results which will be received by the world with a gasp of relief and amazement'.[162] So fluent and wide ranging were Churchill's outpourings that his doctor spent a restless night 'piecing together what Winston had told me'.[163] So great was the Prime Minister's excitement that he didn't go to bed till two in the morning, twenty-four hours after he had woken up on the Stratocruiser as it approached the Canadian coast – amazing for a 79-year-old.[164]

As so often when he had cranked himself up for a great exertion in his last premiership – especially after his stroke – Churchill's thoughts would range back to the war and forward to the perils now confronting the world. 'They were terrific times,' he told Moran that evening, 'and yet I am more anxious now than I was then. My thoughts are almost entirely thermo-nuclear. I spend a lot of time thinking over deterrents.'[165] It was the Old Man's belief, Moran continued,

and this he holds with a fierce, almost religious intensity – that he, and he alone, can save the world from a frightful war which will be the end of everything in the civilized globe that man had known and valued. And, he keeps saying, time is short.

No doubt there are other instincts at work . . . He knows that to bring about a lasting peace with Russia is now the only plausible reason for hanging on to the leadership of the Party. If there was no change of heart in the Kremlin, if a policy of peaceful co-existence was only a myth, it would be difficult to justify his holding onto power in his eightieth year, when he has not completely recovered from his stroke.[166]

Moran was certain that the 'warmonger' taunts directed at him during the early-Fifties elections still hurt Churchill: 'They had to admit that he had been a great war Minister. He would show them that he was as great a peace-maker. He would like, he once owned to me, to end his days with that final, resounding triumph, which would round off his story in war and in peace.'[167] He told Moran 'that he would like once more, before he went, to speak for England as he had done in the trough of the war, if that would avert another war', and then lapsed into silence. Moran looked round to find Churchill weeping.[168] Almost from that moment Churchill's last great cause began to unravel, though it would take another month before he realized it.

Part of Churchill's singularity was his ability almost to screen out what he did not want to hear in conversation even from the most powerful individual in the world, for the discussions that morning in the White House, as the record in the Presidential Library makes plain,[169] provided rather less than 'vindication' as Eisenhower began to surround Churchill's Russian initiative with a curtain of restraining caveats:

The President then brought up the topic of 'reconnaissance' in force which the Prime Minister had referred to in conversation the previous night (i.e. a meeting of the leaders of Soviet Russia, Great Britain and the United States?).

The President would not agree to a meeting anywhere under the present Soviet rule, but did not object to Churchill's suggestion of either Stockholm or London.

The President tried to urge the Prime Minister to (1) make the first move through diplomatic channels, and (2) include France. As to the first, the Prime Minister feels he can approach the matter obliquely, either through Malik [the Russian Ambassador in London] or directly to Malenkov, by saying something to the effect, 'How would you feel if you were asked to go to a Big Three meeting?' etc. The President tried to stress that opportunity should not be given to Malenkov to 'hit the free world in the face'.[170]

Note the frequent use of the word 'tried'.

The observant Colville noted how Dulles stiffened Eisenhower's resistance to Churchill's big idea. His diary for Sunday 27 June recorded that the 'Russian project has shrunk again as Dulles has been getting at the President'.[171] That lunchtime Dulles 'got at' Churchill, too, in a private talk which, on the Secretary of State's side, was entirely free of Eisenhower-style conversational 'trieds'. Dulles wrote his own record of his exchanges for the President:

I pointed out to Mr Churchill that it was extremely dangerous to have such a meeting unless it would have positive results. An illusion of success would be bad, and also an obvious failure would be bad and might create the impression that the only alternative was war ... I pointed out that if Mr Churchill should make an exploratory mission alone, it would not be looked upon well in this country, and also we might have to make it clear that Mr Churchill was in no sense speaking or acting for the United States. Sir Winston said he fully understood this.[172]

I wonder if he did; or if he did, perhaps Churchill thought his powers of persuasion would induce Eisenhower to overrule his Secretary of State. What is certain is that Dulles did not succeed in dampening Churchill's spirits that Sunday lunchtime in Washington. 'The PM,' Colville noted, 'went to bed ... elated and cheerful.'[173]

There were those in the Prime Minister's party who privately believed Churchill was deluding himself on the grand scale, not least about his friendship with and influence upon Eisenhower. The top Foreign Office diplomat in the group, Sir Harold Caccia, Deputy Under-Secretary at the Foreign Office, certainly thought so. When Churchill and Eden were back in London and in the middle of the fearful row in Cabinet about the summit and the bomb, Macmillan (taking great and characteristic pains to find out what had gone on in Washington and on board the Cunarder carrying Churchill and Eden home),

learned subsequently from Harold Caccia who was in Washington, that some such conversation [about a great-power meeting in London] did take place, but that Eisenhower treated it all rather lightly, if not jocularly. He hates all these telegrams and visits from Churchill, and is acutely embarrassed by them. However, since it seems Eisenhower passionately wants to be asked by the Queen to a state visit to London, there is the simple explanation of his rather light references to the matter.[174]

For all the allure of the Queen in 1954, I doubt if it was as simple as that. Caccia on Ike's irritation with Winston, however, is fully credible.

Churchill's high spirits had a thermonuclear element, too. At the Saturday morning meeting in the White House, Churchill had told Eisenhower that the British were going to manufacture a hydrogen bomb. He asked for an easement of the McMahon Act (of which Eisenhower would later tell Macmillan he was 'personally ashamed'[175]). Churchill wanted US information on the 'weight, dimensions and ballistic characteristics' of American H-bombs to help with the design of the RAF's V-bombers.[176] And on 30 August 1954 Congress did pass a new Atomic Energy Act which permitted the sharing of information on the external characteristics of nuclear weapons but not their design. It turned out to be of only limited use to the British bomb makers.[177] Real collaboration had to await the 1958 Agreement for Co-operation on the Uses of Atomic Energy for Mutual Defence Purposes[178] which Macmillan, as Prime Minister, concluded with Eisenhower.[179]

Telling the US President about the UK H-bomb before the British Cabinet was told might, to adapt Lady Bracknell, have been unfortunate if necessary. But informing the Canadian Prime Minister, too, could have looked provocative to Churchill's ministers without a seat on the Cabinet's Defence Policy Committee, not least when the Prime Minister slipped it out just before the Cabinet broke for lunch on 7 July 1954, admitting both that the DPC had taken its key decision on 16 June and that his 'recent discussions in Washington and Ottawa had been conducted on the basis that we should produce hydrogen bombs'.[180]

To be fair to Churchill, he had kept the DPC decision from the Canadian Cabinet when he and Eden addressed them on Wednesday 30 June 1954. The Canadian Cabinet minutes, however, show that he gave them a broad hint: 'Before concluding, Sir Winston went on to emphasize that he felt the best and perhaps the only defence against the terrible nuclear weapons that had now been developed was the deterrent effect of the power to retaliate in kind, which must be preserved and multiplied.'[181]

Two of the Canadian ministers present that morning *did* know the full story, however. The crucial meeting had taken place the night before over dinner in Churchill's suite in the grand Château Laurier Hotel overlooking the Canadian Parliament building and the Ottawa River. Churchill and Cherwell briefed Louis St Laurent and his Defence Minister, Clarence Howe, on the H-bomb decision and the need for Canada to help with its ingredients. 'St Laurent dumb and a little glum – possibly even a bit shocked,' noted Colville,[182] as well he might be since Churchill opened by telling the Canadians that the decision to go ahead was not known to the Cabinet as a whole and it was, therefore, a matter of great secrecy.

Lorna Arnold, the official historian of the British H-bomb, records that Churchill told St Laurent and Howe that ministers had reached the decision because firstly ... it was necessary in order to belong 'to the club' and, secondly ... [because] ... possessing effective deterrents was the only sure way of preventing war. Moreover, if we had it, the Americans would respect our intervention in world affairs far more than if we did not. Then he came to the point. Britain needed tritium for the bomb and he understood that the Canadians could produce it in their reactor at Chalk River, Ontario. If so, this would save a year. Would they provide tritium as part of a Commonwealth defence effort, or on a commercial basis? Payment could perhaps be made with 'finished articles'.[183]

This last was an odd offer as Canada was the first and, for forty years, the only country which could have made a bomb (given its wartime participation in the Manhattan Project) but decided not to. St Laurent swiftly put him right, saying Canada did not want H-bombs, but saying also that they could talk about supplying tritium. (In the end, no supplies were forthcoming.)[184]

Two nights later, to the relief of his doctor, Churchill was on board the *Queen Elizabeth* in New York harbour preparing to leave for home.[185] From that Thursday night to the following Tuesday evening, there took place the most extraordinary sea voyage in the recent history of British high politics. For what soon began as a 'domestic' between the Prime Minister and his Foreign Secretary (Churchill and Eden embarked on what would today be described as a series of hissy fits) over the following weeks developed into something approaching a Cabinet meltdown. Churchill's edginess on the voyage stemmed from anxiety about whether Eisenhower would approve of the alacrity with which he contacted the Russians from the ship; from Eden's furious but failed attempt to talk him out of doing so until the Cabinet had been consulted; from Churchill's decision to retire three months later to make way for Eden (about whose fitness for the premiership he harboured growing doubts); from the short time he had left in which to pull off his heart's desire of a summit; and, perhaps most of all, from his own appreciation of the greatest and most painful fact glaring upon him – that Britain, even a Britain led by himself, could no longer move the world on great global matters.

The first day at sea on the *Queen Elizabeth* did not help tempers. Ice floes in the North Atlantic forced the great liner to take the southerly Gulf Stream route, and the weather was initially 'more oppressive' than it had been in Washington. Eden had only agreed to join Churchill on the voyage in order to obtain a 'firm date for Winston to hand over to him', as Colville noted in his diary.[186] Eden consulted Colville on the right moment to make his pitch:

I thought, and said, how strange it was that two men who knew each other so well should be hampered by shyness on this score. This morning the opportunity came and W. tentatively fixed September 21st for the hand-over and early August for the Moscow visit. Returning to his cabin he then dictated to me a long telegram to Molotov* proposing talks with the Soviet leaders in which the US would not, indeed, participate but could, W. thought, be counted on to do their best with their own public opinion.[187]

Eden's morale may have risen a tad because of the 'tentative' September date (though, by this stage, there must have been an element of 'I'll believe it when it happens'), but the stress came piling back after 'a gay luncheon in the PM's dining room',[188] when the eternal go-between, Colville ('never an admirer of Eden'[189]), turned up in the Foreign Secretary's cabin with the draft of Churchill's telegram to Molotov:

Eden told me he disliked the whole thing anyway: he had been adding up the pros and cons and was sure the latter (danger of serious Anglo-American rift, effect on Adenauer† and Western Europe, damage to the solid and uncompromising front we have built up against Russia, practical certainty that the high hopes of the public would be shattered by nothing coming out of the meeting) far outweighed the pros. However, what he really disliked was Winston's intention of despatching the telegram without showing it to the Cabinet. Why couldn't he wait till we were home and let A.E. deliver the message to Molotov when we saw him at Geneva [at the forthcoming talks on Indo-China]? Would I tell W. that if he insisted, he must do as he wished but that it would be against his, Eden's, strong advice.[190]

Back shuttled Colville to convey the message. Churchill 'said it was all nonsense: this was merely an unofficial enquiry to Molotov. If it were accepted, that was the time to consult the Cabinet, before an official approach was made.'[191]

To his credit, Colville warned his boss 'as strongly as I could, that this was putting the Cabinet "on the spot", because if the Russians answered affirmatively, as was probable, it would in practice be too late for the Cabinet to express a contrary opinion'. The Old Man would not budge and set the scene for a great showdown over several very rough meetings in Downing Street:

W. said he would make it a matter of confidence with the Cabinet: they would have to choose between him and his intentions. If they opposed the visit, it would give him a

---

* Vyacheslav Molotov, Soviet Foreign Minister.   † Konrad Adenauer, West German Chancellor.

good occasion to go. I said this would split the country and the Conservative Party from top to bottom. Moreover, if he went on this account, the new administration would start with a strong anti-Russian reputation.[192]

Colville, not only a trusted private secretary, almost an adopted son to the Prime Minister, could not shift the Old Man. Eden was summoned to the cabin

and eventually agreed to a compromise which put him 'on the spot'. The PM agreed to send the telegram to the Cabinet provided he could say that Eden agreed with it in principle (which of course he does not). Eden weakly gave in. I am afraid that the PM has been ruthless and unscrupulous in all this, because he must know that at this moment, for both internal and international reasons, Eden cannot resign – though he told me, while all this was going on and I was acting as intermediary, that he had thought of it.[193]

On 4 July Eden and Churchill had a silly spat over a telegram relaying the assertions of a right-wing senator that the two of them had gone to Washington intent on getting China into the United Nations. The problem with Eden, Churchill told his doctor, was that he could not distinguish between big and small things.[194] Yet on their last night on board, 'Anthony and Winston talked as father to son, as if [Churchill] were only concerned for [Eden's] future happiness.'[195] Possessing the knowledge of what was to come at Suez, every later reader of Moran's published diary must have been struck by what followed when, speaking 'very earnestly', Churchill 'implored' Eden 'not to quarrel with America . . .'

Describing himself as a link to the days of Queen Victoria, Churchill treated Eden and his entire Washington team seated round the dinner table to a disquisition on the waning of British power since its Victorian apogee: 'Up to July 1944 England had a considerable say in things; after that I was conscious that it was America who made the big decisions. She will make the big decisions now . . . Without . . . [American] . . . help, England would be isolated; she might become, with France, a satellite of Russia.'[196] The Old Man's voice broke and he wept once more.[197]

Late the following afternoon, 6 July, the *Queen Elizabeth* docked at Southampton. One can almost sense the seething frustration in the picture of a sulky and anxious Eden standing behind Churchill at the Prime Minister's quayside press conference that Tuesday evening. Within hours the hard facts – the realities that glared, to apply Churchill's own metaphor – were upon the Prime

Minister. The first difficulty took the form of mishap through miscomprehension. Churchill's draft of the telegram to Molotov had reached R. A. Butler, the acting chairman of the Cabinet, on the previous Saturday. As it was marked 'personal and very secret' Butler thought it was 'personal' to him. Eden thought it would be copied to the whole Cabinet.[198] This emerged late the same evening when a tense meeting took place in No. 10 between Churchill, Eden, Butler, Salisbury and Macmillan.[199] Macmillan recorded in his diary that the gathering 'was ostensibly to help draft a telegram to the President. I think it was really to try and lessen the shock to the Cabinet by breaking it first to the leading members.'[200] Once that meeting broke up after midnight, Eden took Salisbury and Macmillan to the Foreign Office and spared them no detail about recent life on the *Queen Elizabeth*.

So began the four days that, for Macmillan, amounted to 'the most extraordinary which I can remember since the Govt was formed – or indeed at any time which I can recall'.[201] Historians have had a good idea about the *Sturm und Drang* in the Cabinet Room in July 1954 since the Cabinet Office files were declassified in 1985, for they are interleaved with confidential annexes – near-verbatim minutes taken by Norman Brook as is the Cabinet Secretary's custom when ministerial resignations are threatened. But not until Harold Macmillan's diaries became available could we gauge fully the ferocity of the exchanges and the extraordinary animosity towards Churchill felt by several of his Cabinet ('All of us, who really have loved as well as admired him, are being slowly driven into something like hatred ...'[202]), leaving Churchill frequently 'speechless' and, at the worst moments, looking 'as if he were going to have another stroke'.[203]

The Cabinet met at 11.30 a.m. in No. 10 on Wednesday 7 July. 'There was', Macmillan recorded, 'a good deal of business before we came to the "bomb-shell" [when,] at about twenty minutes to 1, the PM began to unfold his tale. He was obviously nervous ... As he proceeded, the general look of blank surprise was strange to see. Harry Crookshank [Lord Privy Seal] sits (on the PM's side) opposite me. His look of disgust was a picture!'[204] Crookshank was Macmillan's best friend from Eton.[205] After his failure at the Ministry of Health his irritable partisanship perhaps found a happier outlet in the leadership of the House of Commons. He was among the tetchiest of early-Fifties politicians – but he had much to be tetchy about. As Peregrine Worsthorne put it, it was 'well known in high Tory circles ... [that he] ... had had his balls blown off in the trenches' during the Great War.[206] Understandably, therefore, he had taken very ill Churchill's offer in February 1942 of an hereditary peerage. Of what use could it be to a castrato incapable of producing an heir? Crookshank mused bitterly in his diary.[207] But, as Simon Ball puts it, there is 'no independent evidence to say whether the peerage offer was a cruel joke or the result of poor staff work. Churchill did have other things on his mind – most pressingly the fall of Singapore and the collapse of the British Empire in the Far East.'[208] Even the most benign political temperament would not have easily assuaged such a painful memory. Crookshank's certainly did not. The seventh of July 1954 may have involved a tweaking of it.

The Foreign Secretary, as both the Macmillan diaries and the fuller Cabinet minutes make plain, voiced anxieties about the Molotov telegram, though with 'great chivalry, Eden did not actually say he had opposed the whole idea'.[209] Salisbury, Macmillan continued, spoke tensely and in

carefully prepared phrases, said he thought the Cabinet should reserve the discussion until the President's reply [to the previous night's telegram from Churchill] was known. This was agreed ... Then followed a most extraordinary scene.

It was now about 1.20 pm Ld Cherwell had been asked to tell the Cabinet what had happened in Washington in connection with the exchange of information on thermo-nuclear matters ... This he did. [The US would provide the UK 'with full information of the effects of their hydrogen bombs. They were also ready to give us details of the dimensions and characteristics of their bombs, so that RAF aircraft could be adapted to carry the United States type of bomb ... The Canadian Government had undertaken to explore the possibility of providing us with supplies of tritium ...'[210]]

It all appeared very satisfactory. Then PM [dropped] his second bomb. He told us that the decision had been taken to make the hydrogen bomb in England, and the pre-liminaries were in hand. Harry Crookshank at once made a most vigorous protest at such a momentous decision being communicated to the Cabinet in so cavalier a way, and started to walk out of the room. We all did the same and the Cabinet broke up – if not in disorder – in a somewhat ragged fashion.[211]

The bizarre end to the meeting, of course, could not be divined from the Cabinet minutes. The great charlady of 1950s Cabinet government, Norman Brook, had tidied everything up and rounded them off like this:

The Lord Privy Seal said that the Cabinet had had no notice that this question was to be raised and he hoped they would not be asked to take a final decision on it until they had had more time to consider it.

The Cabinet – Agreed to resume their discussion of this question at a later meeting.[212]

That evening Colville and Macmillan had a conversation which reflected the drama of the day. Colville asked what Macmillan had judged to be the effect of the Molotov telegram upon the Cabinet.

I said, 'Terrible.' He said, 'The PM has definitely decided to resign in the middle of September and has so informed Eden.' I said, 'But the Government, and probably the Party will have broken up before that. He must go at once, on grounds of health, to avoid a disaster.' He said, 'You are very severe.' I said, 'As you know, I am devoted to Winston and admire him more than any man. But he is not fit. He cannot function. If there were a strong monarch of great experience, he would be told so by the Palace.' He said, 'What will happen in Cabinet tomorrow?' I said, 'I beg of you to urge him not to try to ride this one off so easily. He must take it seriously and realise how deeply he has hurt us.'[213]

In fact, the following day's Cabinet turned out to be something of a lull between dramatic eruptions. It was mostly memorable for a discussion on the morality of nuclear weapons, for Crookshank making it plain it was the method by which the decision had been reached, rather than the decision itself, that had bothered him, and for a disquisition, almost certainly from Churchill, about the need to face 'the fact . . . that, unless we possessed thermo-nuclear weapons, we should lose our influence and standing in world affairs' before it was agreed that the Cabinet would return to the subject by the end of the month.[214]

The Friday Cabinet ('the most dramatic . . . which I have attended,' wrote Macmillan[215]) took place at lunchtime in the Prime Minister's Room at the House of Commons. This time it was Salisbury who made the emotional weather. Again, it is instructive to place the official minute alongside Macmillan's diary. First, the version on which history would have relied but for the diarist at the Cabinet table:

THE LORD PRESIDENT said that he wished to make it clear that he was opposed in principle to the idea of holding a high-level meeting with the Russians without the participation of the United States . . . The projected meeting, if it took place, would be an important act of foreign policy; and, if he remained in the Government, it would fall to him, as Leader of the House [of Lords] and spokesman for the Foreign Office in that House, to defend it publicly. This he would be unable to do. Therefore, as at present advised, he feared that he would have to resign from the Government if it were in the event decided that the Prime Minister should go forward with this project for a bilateral meeting with M. Malenkov.[216]

And from Macmillan:

... Salisbury opened the discussion. The pros and cons of the telegram to Moscow he would not discuss. But he was concerned with the method. Of course, he accepted the right of the PM to communicate with heads of state or of Govts. But this involved, as the PM would be the first to admit, a corresponding obligation upon other members of the Cabinet either to accept the collective responsibility or resign. In this case, the PM had chosen an unfortunate moment. Two days at sea, he had left the President uninformed. Two days from home, he had kept his colleagues in the dark. He (Salisbury) had the special task, as Leader of the House, of expounding and defending Govt policy. To do so properly, he must believe in it . . . If therefore it was pursued, he must leave the Govt.

Churchill was very much moved. At one moment his face went dead white – at the next it was puce. I really thought he was going to have another stroke. As Salisbury spoke, there was a tense, dramatic silence. When he finished nobody spoke. After a few moments, PM said – with great dignity and much emotion – 'I should deeply regret a severance. But I hope our private friendship wd survive.'[217]

That evening, after calling on Eden at the Foreign Office ('Churchill has begun to get him down again. He knows, in his heart, that he ought to have resigned on the boat . . .'[218]) Macmillan motored to Hatfield to dine with the Salisburys at Hatfield House in an attempt to persuade Bobbety (with whom he had also arrived at Eton in 1906, along with, not just Crookshank, but Oliver Lyttelton, too – and all four had served in the same battalion of the Grenadier Guards in the Great War[219]) not to resign. This Macmillan managed so to do, albeit temporarily.[220]

Macmillan was, bit by bit, converting himself into the Churchill Cabinet's psychiatric social worker. The following week, as one extended meeting followed another, Macmillan went to call upon Lady Churchill just before lunch on Friday 16 July:

She was charming, and pleased to know accurately what she had only heard partly by rumour and partly by what Winston had told her. She has for a long time thought that Winston ought to resign. Indeed, the strain of it all has made her ill. She feels that he ought to go; but he is like a child in many ways. If he wants something, he must have it. This Russian visit has been a sort of obsession for a long time. She would speak to Winston at luncheon . . .[221]

This she did and induced a 'domestic' which Colville witnessed:

She began by putting her foot into it saying that the Cabinet were angry with W. for mishandling the situation, instead of saying that they were trying to stop Salisbury going. He snapped back at her – which he seldom does – and afterwards complained to me that she always puts the worst complexion on everything insofar as it affected him. However, he did begin to see that Salisbury's resignation would be serious on this issue, whereas two days ago when I mentioned the possibility to him he said that he didn't 'give a damn'.[222]

It had been, as Macmillan noted with some understatement, 'a very strange week. It would be stranger still if the public knew what was going on. Curiously, the press has got very little so far . . .'[223] (What was then 'curious' would today be 'amazing'.)

Macmillan had almost exhausted his reserves of hyperbole in describing the July Cabinets – but worse was to come. It was now Eden's turn for an emotional dam burst. Back from the Geneva conference on Indo-China, which, as we have seen, ended with Eden sporting at least a small halo, the Friday Cabinet in Churchill's Commons room on 23 July, all two and a half hours of it, led to, in Macmillan's words, a 'most painful morning, even shattering'.[224] To Whitehall insiders (the public still knew nothing of what was happening) it must have appeared that the Cabinet really was on the verge of a collective nervous breakdown. The Molotov telegram (and the proposed new one to the Soviet Foreign Minister) fused with the H-bomb question into a debate about the constitutional proprieties of collective Cabinet responsibility, the heated nature of which (no surprise here) is much more apparent from Macmillan's note than the Cabinet Secretary's Confidential Annex:

PM: I will now ask the Cabinet for approval for the following telegram to M. Molotov – copies are before you.

The telegram was then read out, and we followed it, like schoolboys, from the text which we were given for the lesson. It was taken away afterwards, as too dangerous . . .

There was no interval for silence, as often occurs. Salisbury took up the argument at once. He spoke from notes, carefully prepared, with restraint, but white and tense. He reverted to the domestic question, as he called it – the constitutional propriety in the PM's sending the first telegram from the ship. He maintained vigorously, but courteously, his view of this matter.[225]

Churchill countered: 'On the constitutional question, I absolutely deny the validity of Lord Salisbury's argument. I have always, in all my years as PM, claimed the right to correspond with Heads of State, friendly or unfriendly. I could not relinquish this right.' At this point, he lit Eden's blue touch paper by saying, 'Of course, I have always acted after full consultation with the Foreign Secretary, and with his agreement.'[226]

According to Brook's record, at this point, 'THE FOREIGN SECRE-TARY said that it had been his view that the Cabinet should be consulted before the message was sent, and he had made this clear to the Prime minister at the time.'[227]

As W. C. Sellar and R. J. Yeatman put it in their spoof examination paper in *1066 and All That*, 'contract, expand and explode'[228] that Cabinet minute and compare it with Macmillan's diary:

Eden: You really cannot say this. You know that I did everything possible to dissuade you for one whole day at least on the voyage. I told you that if you sent the telegram 'it would be against the advice of the Foreign Secretary'. I told you that it ought to be referred to the Cabinet. What else could I do? Resign on board the ship, I suppose?

This outburst was rather a shock to C who turned very white and then very red.[229]

Churchill promptly dug another pit for himself by rounding on Salisbury, claiming that he had 'acted in just the same [way], when he connived, or really promoted, a similar concealment from the Cabinet about the H-bomb. He authorised going into production, four months before the Cabinet was informed . . .' Now Salisbury could take no more and he interrupted the Prime Minister:

I cannot accept that. There was no question of entering production. The materials are not in our possession [and, as we have seen, Aldermaston did not know how to make a hydrogen bomb]. It was not 4 months but 4 days, and it was agreed to tell the Cabinet after your return from Canada . . .[230]

As so often when in desperation, several politicians (including Macmillan) at this point said the time had come to look forward not back. The Cabinet would resume the discussion on Monday.[231]

In the event, it was the Russians who hosed down Churchill and his seething ministers. As he told them when they resumed on the morning of Monday 26 July, since they last met, 'the Soviet Government had publicly proposed an early conference of all European Governments to consider the establishment of a system of collective security in Europe . . . he was satisfied that he could not proceed with his proposal for a bi-lateral meeting with the Russians while this suggestion of a much larger meeting of Foreign Ministers was being publicly canvassed.'[232]

At the same meeting, the Cabinet finally took the decision to manufacture hydrogen bombs.[233] There would be a Union Jack on a British thermonuclear device. And so, some seven years later, during the second Macmillan premiership, 'Yellow Sun' H-bombs were fitted to the V-bombers in Lincolnshire and East Anglia.[234] A generation of RAF pilots, navigators and bomb aimers, when gathered together for historical purposes, can still graphically recall their endless exercises with the disembodied voice coming over the loudspeakers and the earphones from Bomber Command's bunker under the Chilterns near High Wycombe: 'This is the Bomber Command Controller. Exercise EDOM. Readiness 05.' And, in five minutes, they would be aloft.[235]

Unlike the making of a British H-bomb, Churchill's meeting with the Russians to start the process of ensuring that the world did not suffer thermonuclear war never took place. When Jock Colville's diaries were published, we discovered that the old boy had deliberately kept the Cabinet in the dark about his Molotov telegram. After his burst of anger towards his wife that Friday lunchtime on 16 July, Colville recorded that Churchill

admitted to me that if he had waited to consult the Cabinet after the *Queen Elizabeth* returned, they would almost certainly have raised objections and caused delays. The stakes in this matter were so high and, as he sees it, the possible benefits so crucial to our survival, that he was prepared to adopt any methods to get a meeting with the Russians arranged.[236]

The whole episode was absurd and marvellous, egotistical and altruistic in equal measure – part of the explanation of why Roy Jenkins and many others have treated Churchill as the most exceptional human being they have encountered, albeit (as Jenkins put it) a specialness relieved by 'strong elements of comicality'.[237]

But after the tantrums and his glorious failure to pull off a summit in the summer of 1954, Churchill's last administration thereafter lacked a theme – like the famous pudding he sent back during his opposition years at a Savoy lunch for just this reason.[238] He soldiered on to April 1955 – well beyond his proposed mid-September departure date – still hoping for a sudden glimpse of that elusive summit, his doubts about Eden's fitness for the highest office accruing all the time.

A few weeks before his final Cabinet he lunched with one of its number, Lord Swinton, who recalled the scene for James Margach:

He said to me: 'I wonder if I have done right, not morally, but politically.' I replied, 'Well, your home affairs have been eighteenth century, and in Imperial affairs you've been in the nineteenth century. But in the things that matter, foreign affairs, defence and the war, you've been a hundred per cent right.'[239]

This is quite a revealing statement in itself from the Commonwealth Secretary, a shrewd and clever man, showing that in mid-Fifties Britain domestic and economic questions, in Swinton's mind at least, were relegated to the second division of what 'matters'. But Churchill was not musing about any of this:

Winston said: 'Oh no, you damn fool, I don't mean that. I'm talking about my successor. Do you not think that Rab would be better?' I said: 'Well, frankly, Winston, anybody would be better than Anthony. I think Anthony would be the worst Prime Minister since Lord North. But you can't think like that now – it's too late. You announced him as your successor more than ten years ago.'
   Winston replied: 'I think it was a great mistake.'[240]

During the very first days of the Eden premiership, Colville committed to his diary an account of Churchill's last night in No. 10, 4 April 1955. The Queen and the Duke of Edinburgh had come to dinner in the evening with the Edens and the senior members of the Cabinet.

When they had all gone, I went up with Winston to his bedroom. He sat on his bed, still wearing his Garter, Order of Merit and knee-breeches. For several minutes he did not speak and I, imagining that he was sadly contemplating that this was his last night at Downing Street, was silent. Then suddenly he stared at me and said with vehemence: 'I don't believe Anthony can do it.'

'His prophecies', Colville appended, 'have often tended to be borne out by events.'[241]

'So', wrote Harold Macmillan in his diary on 6 April, 'the old PM is out, and the new one in. It is a pretty tough assignment to follow the greatest Englishman of history, but I feel sure Eden will make a good job of it . . .'[242] It is by no means certain that Macmillan did actually so feel. Twenty years later he gave a slightly different version to a young schoolmaster, Richard Thorpe, who was to become Eden's second official biographer.[243]

8

Out of the Stalls

'The trouble with Anthony Eden was that he was trained to win the Derby in 1938; unfortunately he was not let out of the starting stalls until 1955.'

Harold Macmillan, 1975.[1]

'Yep. It's the heavy roller, you know. Doesn't let the grass grow under it . . . He [Eden] has never had any experience of running a team.'

Clement Attlee to Hugh Gaitskell on the lingering shadow of Churchill, January 1956.[2]

'He was a creature of politics, hardly even thinking of, let alone following, any other significant occupation. But he disliked many aspects of political life: men's clubs, the purlieus of the House of Commons, and the Conservative Party. He liked private life punctuated by bursts of public adulation . . . He won an election, but beyond that he did not have much touch or luck, even before Nasser erupted.' Roy Jenkins, 1986.[3]

'Televise tonight In the News *with [Walter] Elliot, Boothby and Crossman . . . Most amusing part of the evening is at Boothby's house afterwards, where all gossip freely. Boothby is sure Churchill is going on Tuesday (the 5th), but it's awful for him that London newspapers will still be out of action owing to strike! Eden, they say, is accepted but without enthusiasm. Eden, Butler and Macmillan are "not a triumvirate but a trinity". No friendship at the top here. But no present challenge from outside the three. Physically, Eden, though he was three times cut up, has made a wonderful recovery . . . Butler is very tired . . . and felt the loss of his wife very much. And Macmillan shuffles along like an old man. He [Macmillan] had a gall bladder operation not long ago. Boothby thinks the others will be watching Eden and that he may well be pole-axed in eighteen months' time.'* Hugh Dalton, diary entry for 1 April 1955.[4]

For a brief while it looked as if Anthony *could* do it. He made a quick dash for an election, not needed before the autumn of 1956, which took place on 26 May 1955. The Conservatives attracted the highest proportion of the votes cast of any party in the postwar period to date (49.7 per cent to Labour's 46.4 per cent). Not since Palmerston's time had a party in power increased its majority (in this case from seventeen to fifty-four).[5] Churchill was a touch hurt when kept in the background of the spring election campaign.[6] He was even more irritated when it was announced that Eisenhower and Eden would meet the Russians at a summit in Geneva the following July. 'How much more attractive a top-level meeting seems when one has reached the top!' he grumbled to Macmillan, who had replaced Eden as Foreign Secretary.[7]

The gilded moment for Eden as premier was less a shining hour and more a shining minute in the longer sweep of political history. As James Margach put it,

Scarcely had he succeeded Churchill and with astonishing flair won the 1955 general election than decay set in. Of all Prime Ministers' honeymoons his was the briefest. It is a complete misreading of history to regard him as a one-issue man, for long before Nasser even thought of nationalising the Suez Canal in July 1956 Eden was fighting desperately for survival ... In January 1956, six months after his convincing election victory, an 'Eden Must Go' campaign was sweeping through the Tory Party.[8]

A shrewd journalist like Margach would not have failed to notice (as did Dick Crossman – there as a *Daily Mirror* columnist) at the press conference to launch the Conservative manifesto that 'Eden was at ease in foreign affairs but Butler took over from him on any detail of home affairs'.[9] This was a quite deliberate and not evidently benign action on Butler's part. He had planned to do it even while Churchill was still in office, as is apparent from the memoirs of John Boyd-Carpenter, Minister of Transport at the time. Recalling the narrowness of Eden's formation as the premiership beckoned, Boyd-Carpenter wrote of him that

he had no understanding of economics or finance. And even less knowledge of or interest in the social services. He seemed to feel these were hardly subjects with which gentlemen should concern themselves. He was absorbed in the great issues of foreign and imperial affairs played out on the world stage on which he knew personally all the chief actors. So marked was his detachment in such wide areas of the business of Government that it provided occasion for one of R. A. Butler's highly entertaining indiscretions.

He had been good enough to come to speak for me in Kingston – my constituency. As, under the strictly austere Churchillian rules then operating he could not use his ministerial car for the purpose, my wife drove him back to his house in Smith Square. The date was early in 1955, with Eden's succession imminent, though not yet actual. Rab commented in his discursive way about the next Prime Minister's limitations. But he reassured my wife – who had of course sought no such reassurance – that these would not matter; at least in home affairs, he (Rab) would 'manage him from behind'.[10]

In fact, Eden's lack of confidence on domestic and economic matters was there for all to see – a very considerable weakness and, in the general elections that followed, very damaging indeed for any Prime Minister or Leader of the Opposition who showed such a gap in his understanding (as Alec Douglas-Home was to find during the 1964 election when his minimal grasp of economic policy attracted derision). The general election of May 1955 was probably the last in which a premier could get away with it. Some of his ministers, like Boyd-Carpenter, were content to console themselves privately by 'saying it's a pity he knows nothing about economics or social security or finance, but at least we shall be all right with foreign affairs'.[11]

By the time of the 1959 general election, television had begun to play a serious part in campaigns and both parties (Labour first; then the Conservatives in swift imitation) began the practice of a daily press conference at party headquarters.[12] Thereafter no Prime Minister or Leader of the Opposition could escape with the kind of division of labour Eden and Butler displayed when launching *United for Peace and Progress*[13] in May 1955. For, as Richard Thorpe noted, the '1955 Election was the last of its kind, in that the party leaders and senior figures from the Cabinet and Shadow Cabinets [sic] travelled the country, largely without security, mixing freely with ordinary voters. Unlike 1959, it was not so dominated by television. Big evening meetings were open to the public on a first-come, first-served basis and were not the carefully screened, all-ticket events of later years.'[14]

Eden did not even want a detective to accompany him but was eventually persuaded to have one.[15] He referred affably to the Labour leadership as 'our Socialist friends',[16] and, in a nice backhanded tribute to Attlee, who was fighting his final general election as party leader, he spurned a grand Humber car offered by the manufacturer for something more modest, telling his entourage, 'Attlee is driven everywhere by his wife, Violet, in a Standard Eight. It doesn't look too good to be in a boss's car.'[17] Ironically, the Attlees had long since replaced the Standard Eight they used in the 1945 election – with a Humber.[18]

This anecdote could serve as the template for a much wider political issue central to the 'short postwar', one to which both Harold Macmillan and Rab Butler were especially sensitive at the time. On the Sunday following the previous general election in 1951, Macmillan had reflected on the wider factors behind Labour's doing better than expected, leaving 'the nation ... evenly divided – almost exactly even' between the two main parties with the 'Liberal party ... practically disappeared':

The truth is that the Socialists have fought the election (very astutely) not on Socialism but on Fear. Fear of unemployment; fear of reduced wages; fear of reduced social benefits; fear of war. These four fears have been brilliantly, if unscrupulously, exploited. If, before the next election, none of these fears have proved reasonable, we may be able to force the Opposition to fight on Socialism. Then we can win.[19]

Whether or not Macmillan's 'four fears' were a conscious or unconscious echo of Beveridge's 'five giants' we cannot know. What is true is that the Macmillan quartet did prove to be unreasonable. The Churchill government did not put a match to Beveridge, full employment was sustained and the Grand Old Man proved to be a stubborn peacemaker. Had he and his Cabinet implemented ROBOT (see pp. 199–210) there might well have been something in three of the 'four fears' – an intriguing 'what if?'.

For Butler, Eden's victory at the polls in 1955 had finally exorcized the demon of the 1945 defeat and the fear that Britain's political sun was shining brightly upon Labour's way. The increased majority, Butler declared in a private note to the Conservative Research Department, 'destroyed the myth that 1945 represented the beginning of some irreversible revolution'.[20] As Conservative Party historian John Ramsden has observed, in the 1955 and 1959 general elections, 'Labour's vote ... fell away from its 1951 zenith ... , for Labour voters – or at least enough of them – had finally had their "memories" of the 1930s moderated by happier, and more recent experience of Conservative government.'[21]

Given this confidence-restoring change in the nation's political ecology, would the Conservative government shift to the right and come out of the shadow of Mr Attlee and the 'postwar settlement' to which historians would later attach the Labour leader's name? Certainly, party activists had their own strong views on curbing, for example, both trade union power and what was then called 'coloured immigration'. It is one of the rolling paradoxes of the consensus debate that the late 1940s and 1950s, which so many members of its political class (on both sides) retrospectively saw as a consensual apogee,* was also the period marked 'by the highest ever level of membership of the parties, historically high levels of turnout at elections, and a strong degree of partisanship shown by the electorate when asked by opinion pollsters whether they felt that they "belonged" to any particular party or whether they felt it mattered to them who won elections'.[22]

So Eden had two shadows over him in the spring of 1955 – Attlee's and Churchill's. And perhaps a third, a very personal one, the complex shadow of his poor health, his brittle temperament and proneness to anxiety and fussiness. All three shadows clouded the question of whether Anthony could do it as he finally came 'out of the stalls'.

In one sense, he was similar to the figure whose shadow preoccupied him more greatly than any other, for Eden and Churchill were people requiring heavy maintenance, in both physical and psychological senses. Churchill as premier required a constant flow of attention, drink, conversation (or, at least, listeners) and pills. Eden needed pills and the kind of reassurance which is self-defeating that expressed itself in constant and fussy phone calls about matters great, middling and trifling that interfered with the work of his increasingly irritated ministers.[23] Within days of becoming premier he wrote to all his departmental ministers, asking, 'Have you any problems to which we shall have to give our early attention? If so I should be glad to have a short note

---

* On 31 January 1997 Simon Forshaw, a student at St John's College, Southsea, and a pupil of Bernard Black, the most entrepreneurial teacher of politics I have known, wrote to Jim Callaghan, Roy Jenkins, Ted Heath and Margaret Thatcher asking them when, in their view, the 'post-war consensus' ended. Their replies were revealing in two ways. All four were with Healey and Hailsham in believing such a thing had existed but, Jenkins and Heath apart, there was no agreement on when the political milieu in which all four had been raised actually came to an end. Lord Callaghan told Forshaw he was 'sure that you recognise that the date you seek is purely a matter of judgement. One possible date for the ending of the post-war consensus would be the mid-seventies, but I realise that it would be possible to select a number of other dates.' Lord Jenkins, like Jim Callaghan, believed that 'The question is not subject to any precise factual answer. But probably most people would put it down to Mrs Thatcher and therefore pinpoint the decade as the (late) seventies.' Lady Thatcher disagreed. Her Private Office relayed her view in a single, characteristically caveat-free sentence: 'The Post War consensus ended in 1970.' For his part, Ted was with Roy and thought it was Margaret. Jay Dossetter in his Private Office said, 'Sir Edward has asked me to point out that setting a precise date for such an event as the end of the post-war consensus is an almost impossible thing to do. Consensus between the Conservative and Labour parties has existed to various degrees on different issues. There is a case to argue that Parties [sic] policies began to diverge on defence in the 1950s, education in the 1960s and on housing in the 1970s. However, perhaps the most significant departure from consensual politics came with the advent of neo-liberal economic ideas with the Thatcher government of the 1980s.' The Heath reply showed the greatest sensitivity to the ingredients of the historical debate and his concluding line (via the Private Secretary) went to the heart of it: 'The political date you are searching for will depend largely on your own definition of the post-war consensus.'

from you upon them since I am trying to review the position generally.'[24] In a calmer, more self-confident Prime Minister, such an initiative would have been seen as evidence of strategic grip. Not so in Eden. Iain Macleod, the Minister of Health, sent a courteously canny reply: 'The Health Service has rarely been so placid and it is my policy to keep it so. It had its fill of politics in the early years. All the same difficulties can arise out of a clear sky . . .'[25]

The same most certainly could not be said of domestic, social and economic policy generally. Eden's anxiety, stemming from ignorance, led to his taking a close interest in such matters, perhaps because for the first time in his ministerial life he needed to be fully briefed on them. His lack of experience, however, produced a period of questioning rather than decision-taking. To his credit, there was one deep-seated problem linking the whole front for which he had a genuine feel – and, here, something did get done. Given the darker colours in which most aspects of his premiership are painted and remembered (Eden's first official biographer, Robert Rhodes James, applied the words on Curzon by Churchill – 'The morning had been golden; the noontide was bronze; and the evening lead'[26]), it is fair and fitting to stress this area of insight and imagination at the outset for fear of its being overshadowed later. It had to do with deeper sources of British power than a succession of polished performances in the negotiating halls of Geneva – the technical prowess of the UK's labour force.

For Anthony Eden, the winner of a First in Persian at Oxford (a fact lost on Churchill, incidentally, until the let's-make-up dinner on the last night of that fractious voyage home on the *Queen Elizabeth* in July 1954[27]), had a real passion for technical education. And if his premiership had lasted even up to a general election in 1959 or early 1960, this just might have been his enduring legacy to his country. On the first day back from their New Year break over the turn of 1955 and 1956, Eden had placed on the desk of every Cabinet minister a paper on technological education he had requested from Churchill's favourite boffin, Lord Cherwell. 'During the recess', the Prime Minister explained, 'I have been thinking over the problems of scientific and technological manpower and education which are so vital to the future of this country.'[28] Two aspects of Cherwell's paper now look particularly striking. The first is the degree to which in the mid- to late 1950s Soviet technical prowess exerted a mesmeric hold on those in a state of anxiety about the West. ('Russia with only about four times our population has some 300,000 scientists and technologists in institutions of university status and a further 1,600,000 in institutions at least equal to our best technical colleges. Per head of the population we have only a fraction of these numbers in training.'[29])

The second is the degree to which Britain was doomed to a dramatic relative economic decline, even within Europe, if serious remedial measures were not taken. In his final paragraph Cherwell dramatically fused all the anxieties:

We have seen how quickly Germany with her army of technologists has recovered from the catastrophic damage inflicted by the war. Russia with her enormous man-power and vast mineral resources may well in 30 or 40 years' time overtake and even dominate the West if she is allowed to build up a similar preponderance. Unless Britain takes speedy action she seems doomed to sink in wealth and influence to the level of Portugal within a generation.[30]

It is interesting how politicians, when wishing to shock for effect, used the fate of other European countries with experience of empire and decline for this purpose. Nearly seven months later, for example, in the early days of the Suez crisis Harold Macmillan (by this time Eden's hawkish Chancellor of the Exchequer), told Robert Murphy (President Eisenhower's emissary and an old wartime chum of Macmillan's from Algiers days) over dinner in No. 11 Downing Street with Field Marshal Lord Alexander on 30 July that unless the government made a stand against Nasser in the Middle East, its position in the world would be reduced to that of the Netherlands.[31] 'We certainly did our best to frighten him . . .' Macmillan later wrote of the evening.[32]

Just before Christmas 1955, Eden's Minister of Education, David Eccles, had circulated a Cabinet paper on 'Technical Education',[33] out of which was to come a White Paper in 1956.[34] This was the Siamese twin of Cherwell's paper, although Cherwell had included data on the universities whereas Eccles's paper did not. (As he reminded his colleagues, 'The Universities are outside my province'[35] – the University Grants Committee worked directly to the Treasury.[36]) Eccles is one of the most intriguing postwar education ministers and, unusually, held the post twice, in 1954–7 and 1959–62. He occupies no great place in the pantheon of postwar British political figures but he has a claim, in Noel Annan's words, to be 'arguably the best minister of education since the war . . . Opinionated, self-assured, a Wykehamist with the manner (so Etonians said) of a Harrovian, he was a manager.'[37] Annan believed that, in Eccles's opinion, the Butler reforms (secondary school for all within a triangle of grammar, technical and secondary modern schools) had run out of steam in the drab Horsburgh years at the ministry and that he was also determined to fill the greatest gap in post-Butler provision: 'In Germany industry trained boys after they left school. In Britain few educationalists gave them a second thought. But David Eccles did.'[38]

Eccles felt education as a whole needed a boost to dispel the lassitude and depression of the early Fifties almost amounting to shock tactics.[39] His Yuletide paper was very much part of this and it did have a German feel to it:

The technical colleges are a complementary means of training technologists, catering for those students who prefer to mix earning and learning, and whose ambitions are not fully stirred until they [have] had some experience of making a living. I suspect that this mix of practice and theory is particularly suited to our people, and that many boys, and also their parents and employers, prefer this start in life to a university.[40]

Notice the degree to which technical education was viewed as a boy's world. Eccles certainly saw it that way:

This year out of some 250,000 boys who left maintained schools 70,000 went on to further education. The programme I propose will raise this figure to 120,000 out of the 300,000 who are expected to leave in 1965. (Not many girls become technicians; separate figures for those are, therefore, not given in this memorandum.)[41]

Another paragraph leaps out for what it does not say. Subtitled by Eccles 'Technical Education and Liberal Studies', it warns that the

clamour for scientific and technical education is so great that we shall have continually to watch the courses given in technical colleges to see that they are broad enough. In particular, the ability to speak and write clear English seems to be declining, and I should think it wrong if the technical colleges did not make an effort to improve the knowledge and use of our language.[42]

The whole initiative was predicated on the notion of an enhanced skills base as a booster of British manufacturers in export markets – but not a whisper of the need for foreign-language training.

This, too, was the motive power behind Cherwell's words which appeared in Cabinet ministers' red boxes a few weeks later: 'Britain will only be able to survive in the modern world if we can continue to sell at competitive prices manufactured goods equal in quality to those ordered by other countries.'[43] Cherwell had his eyes on the further education provided not just by technical colleges, but by those institutions at the very apex of British higher education, too, at the top of the university structure:

Our technical colleges are, it seems, good – some indeed very good; nevertheless they should be encouraged and perhaps further expanded. [Cherwell was no longer a member of the Cabinet and would not, therefore, have seen Eccles' paper of 19 December unless Eden had authorized it.] But technical colleges only teach the non-commissioned officers of industry.

What the country is really short of is what might be described as the officer class, the really highly trained technologists such as exist in large numbers of other countries where the applied scientists are trained in technological universities like Massachusetts Institute of Technology, Zurich, Charlottenburg and so on. To produce anything like the number we need, technological universities of equal standard and status should be built up here.[44]

Within days Eden used part of a speech in Bradford on economic themes to counteract a growing campaign of criticism against him in a right-wing press disappointed by his lack of decisiveness, delivering what Macmillan described as a 'calm and dignified reply to his critics . . .';[45] another section was devoted to the Eccles/Cherwell theme. 'The prizes,' he said, 'will not go to the countries with the largest population. Those with the best systems of education will win.' Eden declared his determination to make good Britain's shortage of scientists, engineers and technicians.[46]

To his great credit, Eden, like Eccles, saw education spending not as a burden on the taxpayer but as an indispensable investment for the country. And he would return to this theme in the dark days of late December 1956, amid the Suez-shattered ruins of his premiership which had then but a few days to run, in five pages of 'thoughts' on 'the lessons of Suez' which but a tiny handful of people in Whitehall saw. (He restricted its circulation to three ministers: Selwyn Lloyd, Foreign Secretary; Lord Salisbury, Lord President; and Anthony Head, Minister of Defence. Significantly it did not go to Harold Macmillan at the Treasury.)

We have to try to assess the lessons of Suez. The first is that if we are to play an independent part in the world, even on a more modest scale than we have done heretofore, we must ensure our financial and economic independence. Since we have no raw materials but coal, this means that we must excel in technical knowledge.[47]

Eden drew two 'lessons' from this: too many scientists were working for military purposes and there should be a rebalancing in favour of civil programmes; 'the cost of the welfare state' should be cut back and its 'alarming increase' should be curbed apart from 'education ... a necessary part of our effort to maintain a leading position in new industrial developments' as '[o]ther aspects of this spending are less directly related to our struggle for existence'.[48]

Part of Eden's legacy, therefore, must include the ten colleges of advanced technology which came into being in 1957* 'to be backed up by twenty-five regional technical colleges'. The CATs, as they were known, grew rapidly in student numbers and became fully fledged universities with degree-awarding powers in the mid-1960s on the recommendation of the Robbins Report on higher education in 1963.[49]

Eden's passion for technical education tends not to figure in the scales of this most toughly judged of postwar premierships (and not just on its Suez-related aspects). He has come in for a good degree of retrospective criticism from some critics as an exemplar of the kind of benevolent Toryism which powerfully contributed to a cumulative mess that only the more abrasive conservatism of Margaret Thatcher seriously started to address twenty years later. Historian Andrew Roberts, for example, in his *Eminent Churchillians* published in 1994, was highly critical of Eden for keeping the ever-emollient Walter Monckton at the Ministry of Labour instead of pursuing a policy of resisting strikes, curbing trade union power through pre-strike ballots and generally facing up to the fact that in 'Germany, Konrad Adenauer and Ludwig Erhard [his Finance Minister and architect of West Germany's social market philosophy[50]] were achieving incredible advances in productivity and efficiency ... [while] ... Britain desperately needed someone to crack employer and employee heads together, and that man was not Walter Monckton.'[51]

Roberts is equally critical of Eden for not stemming the flow of Commonwealth immigrants along lines proposed by Lord Salisbury, who argued for a 'guest-worker' system establishing 'the possibility of admitting Colonial immigrants for temporary employment for a period not exceeding five years ... [as] ... [t]his might meet the need for labour with less prejudice to long-term social considerations.'[52] For Roberts, the light of history shines harshly on the Conservative administrations of the mid-Fifties on the matters of trade union power and immigration control:

---

* Aston, Battersea, Bradford, Bristol, Brunel, Cardiff, Chelsea, Loughborough, Northampton and Salford.

The emollience [Monckton] showed, while probably necessary at the very beginning to prove that the Conservatives could work with the unions, ended by sending entirely the wrong messages to organized labour. By the 1960s and 1970s trade union militancy threatened the British economy and even brought down a Conservative Government.[53]

And the lack of immigration legislation until the early Sixties meant, for Roberts, that: 'By that time ... the pass had been sold. For good or ill but certainly forever, Britain had become what Churchill had feared, "a magpie society".'[54]

Andrew Roberts' critique concentrated on two turning-point aspects of the mid-1950s of particular interest to those on the same section of the political spectrum as himself, but union power and immigration were only part of a wider picture of Britain-on-a-cusp. The years 1955–6 are a period in which a whole range of assumptions about society, economy, finance, trade and the instruments of British power and influence in the wider world were thrown into sharper and more critical relief. This was true – and would have remained so – even if the Suez crisis had not occurred over the summer and autumn of 1956. Indeed, it could be argued that Suez was so much an affair of primary colours that it has dazzled historians and taken their eyes off the range of problems that confronted a country which, superficially, was already having it so good in material terms to a degree experienced by no previous generation (except those small groups for whom a profoundly unequal society had provided a very high degree of personal comfort and security).

Of all the senior figures in political authority, Harold Macmillan was probably the most acutely aware of the paradox of rising affluence on top of an economy whose foundations were shaky, whose currency was fragile and whose overseas commitments too great. It emerged (as we shall see) in a series of papers he wrote for his ministerial colleagues and Whitehall officials – the first of these drafted in the summer of 1955 was evocatively titled 'Dizzy with Success'[55] – which turned on the theme of 'overload'. His great obsession was that Britain's foreign and defence policy, and its government and society more generally, were placing immense pressure upon an economy which, at some point, would break under the strain, jeopardizing the improvements which were being enjoyed on a wider scale than ever. Linked to this was the European question. Macmillan was fixated upon the possibility of an economically buoyant West Germany dominating an ever more successful European economy of the six ECSC nations to the detriment of an economically faltering

Britain doomed to lose power and influence unless it could, through some grand interlocked design, break through all of its intermeshed constraints at home and abroad, not least by shaping the emerging Europe along lines that would serve British interests.

This theme, in different forms, dominated Macmillan's tenure as Foreign Secretary (1955), Chancellor of the Exchequer (1955–7) and Prime Minister (1957–63). It makes him the single most fascinating political figure of the period and it also made the political weather during his years at the top. Even without the trauma of Suez, 1955–6 would have seen some crucial turning points, on Europe especially. The decision, scarcely noticed outside the private world of the Whitehall Cabinet Committee Room and the negotiating suites in Brussels, taken by the Eden government (with scarcely a dissenting voice amongst ministers or officials[56]), in November 1955 to have no further part in the discussions that might lead to a Common Market, was far more significant both intrinsically and in its long-term consequences for Britain than the view of the Attlee and Churchill administrations in 1950–51 that Coal and Steel Community membership was not for them.

Why? As the official historian of this most vexing of British relationships, Alan Milward, has put it, 'partly because it led to a complete separation from what was to become the most powerful and distinctive of western Europe's post-war international organisations, and partly because that separation weakened, economically and politically, Britain's links with the USA'.[57] And, as Milward laconically noted nearly fifty years later, the choice 'presented to the United Kingdom by the Six's progress towards the Treaty of Rome thus opened a divide in British politics and public opinion over the country's relationships to European institutions which persists' today.[58]

The fascination of Eden's years in No. 10 and Macmillan's time first in the Foreign Office and then No. 11 Downing Street is the degree to which they represent the hinge of the Fifties – the moment when the inadequacies of past solutions were perceived, deeper problems identified, anxieties raised and decisive action (the disastrous Suez invasion apart) forsworn. As with so many key moments in the short postwar, there was only so much adjustment the government and the country could contemplate, let alone manage. And the question remains, would a better primed and more decisive premier than Anthony Eden have been capable of tougher analysis, greater foresight and more determined action (technical education excepted) in 1955–6? This miniature 'age of postponement', as it might be called, is the context in which the array of policy concerns and possibilities of those years must be examined.

And the pair of policy questions on which Andrew Roberts focused in *Eminent Churchillians* are revealing illustrations of this.

The immigration question was bound up with one of the factors Macmillan itemized in 'Dizzy with Success' – 'over-full employment'.[59] The early-Fifties boom was very labour intensive and sucked in a large number of workers from Ireland, an immigration flow far greater than from the Old and New Commonwealths combined. A Whitehall working party reported to the Churchill government in 1953 that some 60,000 a year were arriving from the Irish Republic (which had left the Commonwealth three years earlier), compared to the 3,000 'coloured immigrants' from the Queen's own territories.

But the 1953 working party and a ministerial group which reported to the Eden Cabinet in 1955 were 'united in wishing [Irish immigration] to continue because of the labour shortage and its contribution to economic growth, and because of the fit young men and women being added to the population'.[60] The 1955 committee considered complaints about the overcrowding of Irish immigrants in certain urban areas, but the families whose sons and daughters attended Our Lady of Lourdes Primary School in North London with me were deemed acceptable because of their northern European provenance and their pasty skin colour:

> . . . it cannot be held that the same difficulties arise in the case of the Irish as in the case of coloured people. For instance an Irishman looking for lodgings is, generally speaking, not likely to have any more difficulty than an Englishman, whereas the coloured man is often turned away. In fact, the outstanding difference is that the Irish are not – whether they like it or not – a different race from ordinary inhabitants of Great Britain, and indeed one of the difficulties in any attempt to estimate the economic and social consequences of the influx from the Republic would be to define who are the Irish.[61]

There was a difference between the pressures felt in the Whitehall of Coronation year and those of 1955. As yet another report to Eden's Cabinet from a committee of ministers chaired by Lord Kilmuir, the Lord Chancellor (as the former Sir David Maxwell Fyfe had become), noted in June 1956, coloured immigration had risen from 3,000 in 1953 to 10,000 in 1954 and to 35,000 in 1955.[62] The number of MPs, across all three parties, raising the subject in the Commons had also increased. Eden, however, was happy to play the Irish card in the House of Commons in November 1955 when he informed a Conservative MP, Cyril Osborne (who had been campaigning for immigration control since 1952) that the government was not about to introduce such controls, pointing out that the largest source of immigrants was the Irish Republic.[63]

The surge in new arrivals from the New Commonwealth in 1954 had prompted the new Home Secretary, Gwilym Lloyd George, to press upon his colleagues the view that this altered the immigration question. In December 1954 he and Alan Lennox-Boyd, who had replaced Lyttelton as Colonial Secretary the previous July, were commissioned by the Cabinet to prepare a draft Bill to impose controls.[64] The draft legislation was ready for the Cabinet in the autumn of 1955. As Randall Hansen has observed, at first glance it looked 'tame', but, in fact, had it been put to Parliament and passed, it would have given ministers 'considerable' discretionary powers, using orders in council, to restrict the entry of Commonwealth immigrants, to impose conditions on those admitted and to deport those who broke them.[65]

The politics of postponement, however, pervaded the Cabinet Room on 3 November 1955. Lennox-Boyd was determined that any legislation should not be directed specifically at colonial immigration as this would seriously harm Commonwealth relations.[66] He made it plain, too, that he simply could not agree to such legislation, implying thereby that it was a resignation matter. The Cabinet did not wish to contemplate this. The question, yet again, remained frozen and the public unaware of what ministers had been considering.[67]

Norman Brook applied his oil can, advising Eden that he should appoint another committee of ministers to look at the technical problems and allow time for the need for controls to be more widely appreciated. Eden agreed this was 'the best we can do'.[68] When Kilmuir's committee reported back to the Cabinet in June 1956 it confronted a 'dilemma' which the Commonwealth Relations Office had described a year earlier as lying 'at the heart of this question, viz that there must either be more or less open legislative or administrative discrimination as to which people should be allowed to enter freely, or else the controls will be liable to keep out a great many citizens of other Commonwealth countries whom no-one wishes to keep out'.[69] Alec Home, the Commonwealth Secretary, believed legislation could be framed to avoid this, arguing in a memorandum to the Cabinet in September 1955 that it 'would probably be quite easy to discriminate in favour of white members of the "old" Commonwealth countries'.[70]

Kilmuir's committee recognized that the principle of free entry to the mother country for all the subjects of King George VI 'grew up tacitly at a time when the coloured races of the Commonwealth were at a more primitive stage of development than now', a time when the means did not exist in the colonies to stimulate a 'coloured invasion of Britain'.[71] When the Cabinet discussed Kilmuir's report on 11 July 1956,[72] the old desire not to jeopardize white immigration from the Old Commonwealth had sufficient remaining force to trump the impulse to curb it from the New. Immigration controls did not occur in mid-Fifties Britain, because of divisions within the Cabinet and ministerial unwillingness to restrict immigration from the white dominions.[73] Against these combinations, the determination of Lord Salisbury, the consistent dissenter in all discussions at every level on immigration matters, that there should be curbs had no chance of prevailing. Given the other views around the Cabinet table, it is unfair to argue, as historian Richard Lamb has done, that it was Eden's weakness and love of 'his own rhetoric about a new multi-racial Commonwealth' plus a dislike of 'controversial legislation which might spoil his image as a moderate in home politics' which led to the decision not to proceed with legislation in 1956.[74]

Lamb was the first author to make extended use of the archives for 1955 and 1956 when they reached the Public Record Office. In his 1987 study *The Failure of the Eden Government* he not only claimed that the 'nation might have been spared many tears' if an immigration Bill had been placed before Parliament in 1956,[75] but went on to argue in a similar vein that a 'great opportunity for trade union reform was missed in 1955, because at that time the union leaders were moderate and might well have agreed or made little opposition to a sensible package deal'.[76] It is true that, as political and labour historian Robert Taylor expressed it, 'the Eden government believed that on balance the trade unions were more of an asset than an obstacle to dealing with the country's economic troubles',[77] and that, as Lamb noted, the official trade union leaders in 1955 were men of moderation. This became apparent when a formidable figure who was not, Frank Cousins, was elected leader of the huge Transport and General Workers Union in 1956. Cousins' appointment upset the TUC 'old guard' as much as it worried ministers because, in Geoffrey Goodman's words, it marked 'the end of the economic truce that had existed between the Conservative Government and the TUC leadership' which Churchill 'had forged' and Eden had 'inherited'.[78]

Yet Eden was sufficiently alarmed by a rash of *unofficial* trade union militancy, which the old 'right-wing' junta that had dominated the TUC since the war[79] (Arthur Deakin of the T & G; Will Lawther of the miners, Tom Williamson of the General and Municipal Workers) could not handle, that he quickly set up a Ministerial Committee on Industrial Relations to explore the possibility of curbing 'wildcat' strikes.[80] A year into his premiership, MI5 and Norman Brook briefed him that, although individual communists might be active in the current unofficial strikes, the unrest was not in any way stimulated by the Communist Party of Great Britain as 'the advocacy of strike action would more often hinder than help in its primary objective of penetrating and eventually controlling the trade union movement . . .'[81]

In the end, a policy of exhortation prevailed over not just industrial relations legislation but pretty well everything else – even Eden's long-held desire for a companies profit-sharing scheme to encourage the growth of a mutual interest of capital and labour in sustained national prosperity.[82] As his second official biographer Richard Thorpe observed,

Eden's Government failed, as did later administrations, to grasp the particular nettle of fundamental Trade Union reform, backed if necessary by legislation, that was to be such a central part of the Thatcherite agenda in the 1980s . . . he believed that legal sanctions would have alienated the Trade Union leaders, who were mainly moderates.[83]

So, apart from acceptance by trade union leaders of a 'voluntary' three-week 'cooling-off' period between a decision to strike and an actual strike,[84] nothing came of Eden's attempts to reconcile the two sides of industry.

Robert Rhodes James, Eden's first official biographer, was very critical of his subject's submission. Walter Monckton's view from the Ministry of Labour was that secret pre-strike ballots would not be an aid to improved industrial relations. This was an idea pressed strongly on Eden by the motor magnate Lord Nuffield.[85] 'Eden', wrote Rhodes James, 'was definitely interested, and a more confident and experienced Prime Minister might well have overridden Monckton's characteristic irresolution and caution about doing anything that might possibly evoke trade union hostility . . .'[86] The shadow of wartime was still visible in 1955–6. The unions, in Taylor's phrase, had emerged from Bevin's days at the Ministry of Labour in the 1940s 'as a recognized and accepted Estate of the Realm'.[87] And they still were. It did not seem to Eden, Monckton or the Cabinet that the co-operative model of industrial relations was broken beyond repair. For all the industrial problems they faced, a switch to confrontation with the unions would, in mid-Fifties terms, have been both precipitate and difficult to justify.

But, for that brooding and inveterate memo writer and shameless interferer in other ministers' business, Harold Macmillan, full employment and the banishing of the shadow of the 1930s had changed the balance of power between the industrial and economic estates of the realm. As he put it to Eden and Butler in the summer of 1955 in 'Dizzy with Success' (in the paraphrase of it contained in his memoirs), 'We had travelled a long way from the terrible old days of massive unemployment, although in the years between the wars I had never dared hope to see such a transformation. But we could not disguise from ourselves the new problems which this situation of overload had produced, both mentally and morally.'[88]

And five months *before* the responsibilities of the chancellorship fell on his shoulders, Macmillan was preparing to think very radically indeed about possible solutions to such material and moral 'overload' lest it produce 'either a collapse of the reserves or a million on the dole'.[89]

In his memoirs, Macmillan says that he drafted 'Dizzy with Success' at Eden's request.[90] Its theme was plainly critical of current policy. Both Eden and his Chancellor, Rab Butler, must have anticipated that long before they sat down to lunch with Macmillan at his 'flat' (presumably his word for the Foreign Secretary's personal living quarters in the very grand No. 1 Carlton Terrace overlooking St James's Park) on 26 August 1955. Of this occasion, Macmillan recorded in his diary that: 'Both the PM and Chancellor of Ex liked my paper on the economic situation and the remedies to be applied. I thought PM in good heart, but Butler seemed very tired and rather more "distrait" than usual.'[91]

In fact, Butler had had a terrible year. His wife, Sydney, had died from a particularly cruel cancer in December 1954 and, as Butler himself put it, 'the domestic shock was not at once fully apparent but gained increasing force during the year'.[92] His expansionary pre-election Budget, with its sixpence off the income tax, had placed extra pressure on an economy which, as Sidney Pollard put it, 'was growing fast, and since there had been no capacity increase to provide the supply for that growth, there were obvious bottlenecks at home and a sharply rising import bill'.[93] The humiliation of the deflationary measures Butler was forced to take in October when 'compelled to reverse his pre-election Budget concessions virtually entirely, apart from the 6d cut in income tax',[94] lay ahead as Macmillan drafted 'Dizzy with Success'. But already on 25 July Butler had come to the House of Commons with interim measures increasing hire-purchase charges, encouraging the banks to cut advances and reining back both the investment plans of the nationalized industries and with them coal and steel prices.[95]

At Macmillan's lunch table on that late-August day sat a battered Chancellor who, in the judgement of a historically minded Conservative successor at

373

the Treasury, Nigel Lawson, had miscalculated hugely in the spring as 'the election prospects were good, and in any event tax cuts announced in the Budget would not have had time to reach the pockets of the people before polling day. So there was not only no economic case for a give-away Budget: there was no political case either.'[96] (Intriguingly, Lawson thinks Butler's authority *within* Whitehall, with his Cabinet colleagues especially, never recovered from his failure to prevail over ROBOT and that this formed a stark, if private, contrast with his public image as Chancellor.)[97]

Also there at lunch was 'a Prime Minister innocent of the least economic sophistication', in Edmund Dell's blunt assessment,[98] an opinion probably shared by both Butler and Macmillan as they ate and drank that day. In his memoirs, Macmillan expressed his belief that his lack of economic knowledge was a very real source of anxiety to Eden.[99] Time did not soften the views of Butler and Macmillan in old age on their former boss:

Anthony's father was a mad baronet and his mother a very beautiful woman. That's Anthony – half mad baronet, half beautiful woman [Butler].[100]

He was always very excitable, very feminine-type, very easily upset, easily annoyed . . . [Macmillan][101]

Eden did not warm to them, either. In October 1963, when Butler was in the throes of failing to secure the leadership of the Conservative Party yet again, Eden told Lord Beaverbrook, 'I wish Butler were a man I could respect. LG [David Lloyd George] once called him "the artful dodger", but if this is important in politics, it is also not enough.'[102]

Eden thought Macmillan was devious, too – the difference probably being that he was a touch frightened of Macmillan and he wasn't of Butler. Both of Eden's official biographers dwell on the mutual dislike of the two key figures in the Eden government, Robert Rhodes James talking of a 'longstanding personal antipathy'[103] while Richard Thorpe traces it right back to schooldays:

For Macmillan, the King's Scholar at Eton, Eden was always a junior Town House Oppidan. For Eden, Macmillan was self-advertising and immodest. The constant harking back to Passchendaele and the Durham Miners made Eden cringe. It was not the way a gentleman behaved . . . Eden considered Macmillan a vulgarian and at heart untrustworthy . . .[104]

All three thought they would make a better job of being Prime Minister than the other two.

So why had Eden invited the Foreign Secretary he disliked and feared to produce a paper on a subject which intruded directly into the personal terrain of the two figures – the First and Second Lords of the Treasury[105] – who, if a government is to work properly, have to represent its most central human relationship? Divide and rule? Unnecessary. There was no real chance of a Butler–Macmillan axis leading to a putsch against the incumbent in No. 10; they would never have been able to agree upon whose head should be placed the crown. The reason, I suspect, has to do with a combination of Eden's anxiety about his economic illiteracy and his preferred way of operating in the only department of state he knew well – the Foreign Office. For, as Victor Rothwell observed in his political biography of Eden,

The Foreign Office had been ideal for his preferred work style: seldom being alone, but rather being at the centre of attention, presiding at endless meetings and conferences or discussing policy more informally with advisers ... Another problem stemmed from his difficulty in switching from one subject to another, as a Prime Minister has to do several times a day. He had become used to concentrating all his energies for long periods on one issue. In that respect the Suez crisis was to transform him back into almost a caricature of his earlier self.[106]

Eden, too, as his diary entry for 24 August 1955 (just two days before the 'Dizzy with Success' lunch) indicated, was disappointed in Butler's performance as Chancellor: 'In the midst of this economic turmoil it is fair to recall that I did sound a note of warning last December. He was firm in his denial of any faltering in our economy + even rather contemptuous of the suggestion.'[107]

In this aspect of his premiership Eden resembled Clem Attlee, whom he still faced across the despatch box (Gaitskell did not become leader of the Labour Party until December 1955). Harold Wilson said of Attlee that he was 'tone deaf as far as all economic questions were concerned'.[108] And Douglas Jay, who had served Attlee as his economic assistant in No. 10, thought that 'Clem treated economics very much like medicine – a subject ... on which it is wise to find a second opinion.'[109] Whatever the cross-currents which carried the Eden–Butler–Macmillan trio to that lunch table in the summer of 1955, Macmillan's paper had assumed a significance that could not have been foreseen, and one enhanced when he became Prime Minister and First Lord of the Treasury seventeen months later.

What was the wider Macmillan analysis? In his memoirs he describes his 'Dizzy with Success' proposals as 'within the limits of orthodoxy'[110] before, less than two pages on, appearing to contradict himself by arguing that 'it was clearly right to use conventional weapons before embarking on so uncharted a course' and commending Butler for his deflationary measures in the autumn 1955 Budget.[111] Indeed, a good deal of his 'Dizzy with Success' was orthodox – a credit squeeze through a higher Bank rate; reduction of government subsidies 'including high housing subsidies and the bread and milk subsidies' – slowing down capital investment; ending National Service; abandoning obsolete or unnecessary weapons; reducing direct taxation; boosting savings; and helping 'the managerial and entrepreneur class'.[112]*

If these 'more orthodox measures' did not work, then it would be time to think again (hence the apparent contradiction). It would be ROBOT once more (which is ironic – as Butler could hardly have failed to notice – because Macmillan himself was not a Roboteer in the political circumstances of early 1952). On exchange rates, Macmillan quoted 'Dizzy with Success' directly in his memoirs:

Do *not* devalue to a *fixed* rate. Go on to a *floating rate*. The rate may fall violently at first. But, if so, a lot of people will get their fingers burned. In any case, in present conditions, it may be safer to take the strain this way than any other way. In the second half of the twentieth century sound government in our country is more likely to be endangered by either a collapse of the reserves or a million on the dole than by occasional fluctuations in the value of sterling in relation to the dollar. Of course, it reduces the use of sterling as a long-term store of value. But no currency in the world, except the dollar, can really be that today.[113]

Less than a month later Eden offered the Treasury to a surprised Macmillan, who confessed himself 'staggered' in his diary for 23 September 1955:

'When?' 'At once.' 'What about Rab?' 'He can be Ld Privy Seal and Leader of the House.' 'Have you spoken to him?' 'Yes, last night. He seemed to rather like the idea.' We then discussed the effect on Rab's position and the prestige of the Govt. Wd it not seem a confession of failure? Wd not the whole Govt suffer accordingly? What about the autumn Budget? PM seemed in a great hurry to settle it, but I said I must think about it . . .[114]

Macmillan left for Foreign Office work in America. On his return, on 8

---

* Eden did absorb some of this thinking about the desirability of easing the tax burden as well as the sustainability of high public spending. In December 1955 he commissioned a secret review of long-term social service provision. And, for a time, it seemed likely that NHS funding might switch from general taxation to compulsory contributions. But the idea was dropped in 1957 for short-term political reasons: National Insurance contributions could not be raised without triggering unwelcome demands for higher pensions.

October, Eden asked him for his decision. Eden wanted Macmillan out of the Foreign Office as much as Macmillan wanted to stay. 'It was quite clear,' Macmillan told his official biographer, Alistair Horne, many years later, 'that Eden wanted to get rid of me; he kept on sending me little notes, sometimes twenty a day, ringing up all the time. He really should have been both PM and Foreign Secretary . . .'[115] (It was this side of Eden-as-premier which was long remembered right across Whitehall, 'his awkwardness in dealing with ordinary business – testy and impatient'.)[116]

It says something for the relative power of Macmillan and Eden in early October 1955 that Macmillan, when Eden spoke to him 'again about the Treasury, and asked me if I had yet been able to decide', could flatly reply that he hadn't. Eden thought it could wait until early December.[117] With a stronger premier, Macmillan would most certainly have overplayed his hand during the intervening weeks by his prima donna-like attitude, which had the side effect of rubbing Butler's nose in his demotion.

This is detailed in perhaps the most bizarre correspondence I have ever read in the National Archives between a senior Cabinet minister and a premier. In Paris for a NATO summit, Macmillan reached for his pen in the British Embassy on 24 October after dictating a letter to his wife, and scrawled on a covering note to Eden: 'DO NOT be alarmed. Dorothy typed it for me.' He did not, he told Eden, want to leave the Foreign Secretaryship, which was 'the fulfilment of a long ambition'. There was no point in moving 'to be an orthodox Chancellor of the Exchequer. I must be, if not a revolutionary, something of a reformer. However, to reform the Treasury is like trying to reform the Kremlin or the Vatican. These institutions are apt to have the last laugh . . . As Chancellor I must be undisputed head of the Home Front under you. If Rab becomes Leader of the House and Lord Privy Seal that will be fine. But I could not agree that he should be Deputy Prime Minister.' If Butler was so designated, Macmillan told Eden, 'my task would be impossible'.[118]

What Macmillan certainly did not know is that Eden really wanted someone else at the Treasury as much as he wanted Macmillan out of the Foreign Office. That man was Oliver Lyttelton, who had left government over a year earlier. Eight days before Macmillan despatched that truly insubordinate letter from Paris, Eden had recorded in his diary, after lunching with Lyttelton, 'I wish he were with us + free to go to the Treasury now.'[119]

Two days after the Macmillan letter left the Paris Embassy the hapless Butler rose to his feet in the Commons to present what instantly became known as the 'Pots and Pans' Budget, which, as Richard Thorpe records, was to prove a turning point for the Eden Government, quite apart from its deleterious effect on Butler's own career. Butler announced savings of £112 million in public expenditure, including a one-fifth increase in purchase tax, and the inclusion of previously exempt goods such as kitchenware – from which the Budget got its dismissive name – together with increases in telephone charges and a reduction in the housing subsidy, effectively wiping out the concessions from April.[120]

Butler was in a very low state and his senior officials, who held him in affectionate regard, knew it. As Robert Hall noted in his diary, 'The Chancellor has been very unhappy and rather demoralized; it began with his dislike of having to have a Budget at all after the April one and it was added to by the cool reception of the Budget by his own party and by the violent speech Gaitskell made against it the next day ... On the following day, Friday, he came into the office looking like a defeated man ...'[121]

Butler never recovered his poise as Chancellor. As Hall observed after the Macmillan appointment had been announced, Butler had

lost his nerve at the Treasury lately and is almost unable to take a strong line or to give firm instructions. He was very rattled after the reception of the Budget and depressed by the course of the debate. He felt on the whole that the April Budget was a mistake, although he himself was responsible for it and it was put clearly to him that it was a risk unless credit restrictions were made to work. I do not think he got really good advice from the Treasury all through the year but if he had been firmer the advice would have been better.[122]

Under the new incumbent of Whitehall's Vatican-cum-Kremlin, infirmity of purpose would not be a problem.

Just how unorthodox were Macmillan's economic instincts? The economist who had most influenced his thinking was a great one – John Maynard Keynes. Keynes had been a contemporary of Macmillan's elder brother Dan at Eton and the Macmillan family published him (Harold Macmillan had been closely involved, for example, in the publication in 1940 of Keynes's *How to Pay for the War*).[123] Macmillan, on occasion, could flaunt his devotion to the great man, whom he knew quite well, in a manner deliberately designed to irritate those to the left of him politically. For example at the European Assembly in Strasbourg during its debates on the Schuman Plan in the summer of 1950 he 'made a very short (and a little teasing speech) congratulating [Hugh] Dalton [on his speech]; reminding him of the great progress made in monetary policy since the days which he and I remembered when the classical theory imposed itself on all parties; dominated even such minds as Churchill and Snowden . . . I added a tribute to the memory of Maynard Keynes. He did not like that at all . . .'[124]

It was Keynes himself, in one of the most famous passages in his classic 1936 work, *The General Theory of Employment, Interest and Money*, who warned of the danger of those in power falling into excessive intellectual thrall to some particularly persuasive thinker in their past:

[The] ideas of economists and political philosophers, both when they are right and when they are wrong, are more powerful than is commonly understood. Indeed the world is ruled by little else. Practical men, who believe themselves to be quite exempt from any intellectual influences, are usually the slaves of some defunct economist. Madmen in authority, who hear voices in the air, are distilling their frenzy from some academic scribbler of a few years back.[125]

Keynes then proceeded to give his version of Napoleon's dictum that one needs to recall the way the world was when a man was twenty:

I am sure that the power of vested interests is vastly exaggerated compared with the gradual encroachment of ideas. Not, indeed, immediately, but after a certain interval; for in the field of economic and political philosophy there are not many who are influenced by new theories after they are twenty-five or thirty years of age, so that the ideas which civil servants and politicians and even agitators apply to current events are not likely to be the newest. But, soon or late, it is ideas, not vested interests, which are dangerous for good or evil.[126]

Macmillan was slightly beyond Keynes's zone of maximum receptivity when the *General Theory* was published, being forty-two in 1936, but the advancing years seem to have had little detrimental effect on either Macmillan's or Keynes's supple mind.

Macmillan made his farewells at the Foreign Office on 22 December and walked over to the Treasury to be greeted by its Permanent Secretary, Edward Bridges, 'whom I had known from school days and whom I greatly admired'.[127] (The degree to which public life was one Old Etonian after another was still very marked during the Fifties' Conservative administrations.) Characteristically, Macmillan in his memoirs paid Bridges something of a double-edged compliment: 'He was a typical product of all that was best in the tradition of the Civil Service, both in character and in intellectual gifts. A humanist and a scholar, he concealed under an almost boyish humour great strength and resolution. If he had no pretensions to being an authority in economics in the modern sense, he was a supremely sensible and wise man.'[128] Note Macmillan's use of the word 'modern'. Modern economics for him meant Keynesianism (above all, the demand-management approach to avoiding serious unemployment), as it did for his adviser Robert Hall (though both men came to be more worried in the mid-1950s about over- than underemployment). Their mentor's posthumous triumph over classical *laissez-faire* economics was by no means complete among those, in Keynes's words, whose economic thinking was 'not likely to be the newest'.

Macmillan's self-belief, therefore, in his own relative economic literacy and modernity meant that, given the overlordship of the 'Home Front' he had laid down with Eden as a condition of taking the job, it looked as if Whitehall was about to experience a command chancellorship of the kind it had experienced during Neville Chamberlain's spells at the Treasury in the interwar period and under Stafford Cripps after the war (and as it would once more during Gordon Brown's stewardship as the centuries turned). It did not turn out that way, partly – but only partly – because the Suez affair pulled him, just over a year later, from what he probably thought would be the crowning political office of his career. Eden, after all, was a younger man and, for all his health problems and brittleness of temperament, it would have been difficult in December 1955 to have foreseen circumstances in which he might soon depart.

Few Chancellors have begun their tenure so briskly. Over the Christmas holiday Macmillan drafted an array of questions for the Curia figures at the top of his Whitehall Vatican which he entitled 'First Thoughts from a Treasury Window', of which, sadly, no copy survives (we have to rely on his memoirs for a précis).[129] He relished the company of the Curia. On 22 December he wrote in his diary: 'The Private Secy (Petch) is absolutely charming – and, thank God, not too clever! Everyone else is brilliant. It's like going back to Balliol . . .'[130] On 30 December, as these 'first thoughts' were falling into place (Macmillan wrote them in the immensely grand setting of Petworth House in Sussex, home of his great friend John Wyndham, over New Year's Eve and New Year's Day[131]), he recorded: 'A good morning at the Treasury. I am just beginning to get a glimpse of some of the problems, and how they fall into place. The position is *much worse* than I had expected. Butler has let things drift, and the reserves are steadily falling. If and when they are all expended, we have total collapse, under Harold Macmillan!'[132]

That preoccupation with the country's gold and dollar reserves ran through 1956 like a red thread of possible insolvency for Britain and for sterling as the world's second reserve currency even before the rising tensions associated with Suez put them under yet greater threat of depletion.

The problem of what Edmund Dell called 'this era of mercurial reserves'[133] is that at no point were the Treasury and the Bank of England operating with sufficient gold and dollars to have any kind of margin of safety; quite the reverse: 'For most of the 1950s, the reserves varied between 2 and 3 billion dollars and never exceeded 4 billion dollars. On the other hand liquid liabilities, the sterling balances, never fell below 4 billion dollars.'[134] Hence 'the Sword of Damocles' constantly hanging over the postwar Treasury until the Callaghan–Healey partnership finally had the remaining balances placed inside a safety net funded by the IMF and leading central banks in 1977.[135]

In the mid-Fifties, as in the mid-Seventies, Britain's faltering relative performance as a producer of goods and services and as a trader was the root cause of the pressure. As Dell wrote of the 1950s, the 'reserves were also inadequate measured against the level of imports. Reserves averaging about 2.5 billion dollars were not much more than enough to pay for three months' imports in the first half of the decade and even less in the second half. The only hope of building the reserves and thereby providing more adequate defence for sterling, was for the UK to achieve a much larger surplus in its balance of payments.'[136]

One of Macmillan's first thoughts from his Treasury perch was the drafting of a 'short paper', a 'very pessimistic' paper, as he explained to Louis Petch, designed for the Cabinet's Economic Policy Committee 'to make their flesh creep and to use on the Cabinet at an early meeting'. He knew that a combination of strong words and alarming figures would be needed as it 'takes a lot to make Ministers' flesh creep – they are all hardened'.[137]

Four days later the paper was ready for the Cabinet and, amid other gloom, Macmillan took his colleagues to the gold-and-dollar-paved brink and invited them to peer into the abyss as the balance of payments position, crucial to the adequacy of the reserves, was worsening: 'Preliminary indications of the December trade returns suggest that the visible deficit will be at best about £75 millions and that it may easily reach £100 millions. These figures compare with about £50 millions for September and October, and about £70 millions for November. These figures support the view that our position is getting worse.'[138]

Macmillan then moved on to the reserves, the neurosis-inducing economic indicator in that era of fixed exchange rates, and established a benchmark which was to be of immense significance as the Suez crisis reached its peak eleven months later to the day: 'The gold and dollar reserves at the end of December stood at $2,120 millions. They are therefore approaching the critical level, which is between $2,000 and $1,500 millions, at which experience shows that speculation against sterling can be expected. When this happens the reserves themselves are in danger of falling so low that confidence in our ability to maintain the value of sterling will be lost.'[139]

Eden rather plaintively minuted his Cabinet Secretary in May 1956 (after agreeing to a Macmillan suggestion that the Cabinet's Economic Policy Committee be reconstituted and more involved in early policy formation) that 'I should like to be kept in touch with the main economic questions. How could this most easily be done?'[140] The answer was partly by keeping him in constant touch with the fluctuating gold and dollar reserves. Macmillan sent him a regular (usually weekly) minute on the treasure left in the Bank of England.

This cannot have helped the state of Eden's nerves. For example on the very day Macmillan told Petch he intended to make ministers' flesh creep he had sent Eden the latest figure of $1,956m, which was within the bracket of heightened anxiety as outlined in the Cabinet paper Eden would have read four days later. Here are some of the UK dollar and gold reserve figures to mid-July 1956, i.e. *pre*-Suez:

27 December 1955: $2,120m[141]
2 January 1956: $1,956m[142]
29 May 1956: $2,369m[143]
2 July 1956: $2,385m[144]
16 July 1956: $2,373m[145]

In the era of fixed exchange rates, there were tight and narrow limits within which the pound could take the strain ($2.80 was the official rate and it could rise to $2.82 or fall to $2.78[146]). Macmillan's reports to Eden in the last quarter of 1956 showed a great deal of bumping and grinding just above that lower limit even after heavy interventions by the Bank of England.

While watching the pound, Macmillan developed and impressed upon his ministerial colleagues several firm ideas he thought central to the avoidance of its throwing fits in the future. Some of them had a melodramatic side (especially given his relationship with Eden). His 'First Thoughts from a Treasury Window' undoubtedly shaped his first, 'flesh-creeping' paper for the Cabinet and the subsequent Cassandra-like productions which followed. All we have to go on is Macmillan's own account in his memoirs. 'I felt strongly', he wrote, 'that if we accepted the need for action to restrict inflation we must work quickly and effectively. This was clear from the increasing pressure on the reserves. Unless we were to adopt an entirely revolutionary policy by a new devaluation or by instituting a floating rate, it was necessary to restore confidence at home and abroad as rapidly as possible. Once this was done we could pass to methods of stimulating production and savings.'[147]

The flesh-creeper Cabinet memo which emerged very quickly from those first thoughts concentrated on overload and over-employment as the cardinal culprits:

We are trying to do more than our resources allow. The effect of this excessive demand shows itself in expanding imports and using up home goods that we ought to be export-ing. This endangers the balance of payments and consequently the reserves . . .

At home, the preliminary figures of unemployment for December show that unem-ployment in mid-December was about 216,000. This is 10,000 below the figure for December, 1954 and is by far the lowest December figure since the end of the war.[148]

Such an argument very much went with the grain of Treasury thinking, including the most thoroughly Keynesian officials like Robert Hall who appre-ciated that wage restraint was very difficult to achieve under conditions of truly full employment. 'Ever since about 1948', Hall recorded in his diary in the spring of 1956, 'I have thought that full employment could not be recon-ciled with price stability unless there was some sort of self-restraint by labour, in the sense that they could get a number of possible wage increases, leading to varying price increases, without any difference in anything else. In the long run of course there would be balance of payments effects and if wages rose too fast a series of devaluations,'[149] he concluded (rather presciently – this was more or less exactly what happened over the next twenty years).

Hall warmed to Macmillan as Chancellor.[150] Macmillan liked him even though he privately described him as 'our tame economist' who 'is very inar-ticulate – even on paper he is not very clear. But I find him sensible.'[151] Hall was particularly pleased when Macmillan quickly agreed to publish a White Paper on wages, prices and full employment as a kind of public flesh-creeper. 'We have drafted a number of White Papers on this subject,' Hall later wrote, 'but for one reason or another Ministers (Labour or Tory) would not agree to publish them. However the last round of wage increases was so alarming that they actually did publish the current draft as a White Paper, *The Economic Implications of Full Employment*, before the Budget.'[152]

The White Paper's good sense was rather smothered by its tone, which combined blandness and preachiness: 'The Government', it declared, 'is pledged to foster conditions in which the nation can, if it so wills, realize its full potentialities for growth ... But the Government must no less seek to ensure that the pressure of domestic demand does not reach a level which threatens price stability and endangers the balance of payments ... To maintain full employment without inflation necessarily involves continual adjustments.'[153] How about that for a rallying-cry?

Macmillan called in the press and tried to sell the White Paper to them. He found them resistant, 'rather hostile', in fact. 'They regard the White Paper as too much of the old policy of exhortation ...'[154] If only the press had had an inkling of the full story of the battle royal between the Chancellor of the Exchequer and the Prime Minister that took place in the run-up to the 1956 Budget, that press conference might have been vastly more interesting.

Historians can pick up its opening skirmishes in the scribbles Eden wrote on the second of Macmillan's Cabinet papers on 'The Economic Situation' in January 1956. In it, Macmillan invited the Cabinet to bite the bullet:

So long as inflation continues our reserves will be further run down and internal wages and prices will continue to be forced up. We must now decide on the measures we must take to remedy this state of affairs ...

What is needed is to take a substantial block from the load now pressing on our resources. I believe that the measures we have already taken [presumably Butler's autumn Budget] have begun to reduce the overload and will become progressively more effective once it is believed that we are serious. This will give us a tide in our favour instead of against us, as it is now.

But we cannot afford to wait. Nor need we fear that we shall overdo it.[155]

Against the last two sentences Eden placed a '?'.

Of more than passing interest in this paper is Macmillan's willingness to hammer those spending areas for which he had quite recently been ministerially responsible in one way or another. For example he proposed that the 'next step in housing must be the abolition of the general needs subsidy ...' The Minister of Defence who had circulated the Strath Report to his colleagues and presided over the Cabinet Committee on its implications now proposed to hack £17m out of the £55m planned for Home Defence in 1956–7 by *not* buying food, medical supplies and oil for the post-attack stockpile and by stopping the building of protected headquarters and control rooms. As for the RAF, in the coming age of missiles, there was no point in Fighter Command – there should be progressive reductions on spending, starting with research and development work on new fighters. Eden circled Macmillan's suggestion that the Cabinet's Defence Committee should discuss this. The British Army of the Rhine should also lose one of its divisions to help ease the balance of payments.[156]

It was on these last two proposals that Macmillan anticipated trouble from Eden. The day before the paper was to be circulated to the rest of the Cabinet, the phone duly rang with Eden on the line: 'He had been reading my paper. He seemed very concerned, not to say excited. "I can never agree to *two* of your proposals. It's absolutely unthinkable." "Which do you mean?" I replied. "I suppose about the Army in Germany and the ending of Fighter Command." "No, no! About bread and milk!"'[157]

In fact, on his copy of the Cabinet paper Eden had scored a line through much of the paragraph headed 'Bread subsidy' in which Macmillan had written: 'I propose that the bread subsidy should be abolished. It costs £41m a year. It involves a subsidy and price control – methods which have been almost entirely abandoned by this Government as instruments of our economic policy.' On milk, Macmillan had proposed a subsidy reduction of a halfpenny per pint to save £20m a year.[158]

'A long conversation followed – chiefly talk by him,' Macmillan noted. 'It is quite clear that (a) he does not understand the serious character of the crisis (b) will shrink from unpopular measures . . . Also, to be fair, he cannot follow how taking off a subsidy will help . . .'[159] Macmillan clearly believed his Prime Minister was both weak and economically illiterate ('his mind concentrated on wages and labour relations'[160]).

Following a good deal of Cabinet argument about the subsidies, the Chancellor summoned the Cabinet Secretary to tell him on 11 February he would resign if he did not get his way.[161] Such was the relationship between Eden and Macmillan, who had been front-bench colleagues for nearly sixteen years by this stage, that they dealt with each other through a proxy. Perhaps this was one of the effects of Macmillan's laying down those cheeky and elaborate conditions before agreeing to go to the Treasury in the first place. I have some sympathy with Eden here: Macmillan was very difficult to deal with, being both haughty and touchy to a degree, and Eden could not have lost a pair of Chancellors in the space of two months without considerable political and personal damage.

Three days after Brook conveyed Macmillan's resignation threat to Eden, Iain Macleod (the Minister of Labour) and Walter Monckton (now Minister of Defence) turned up at the Treasury:

I shewed [sic] them a formula which I wd accept. This was 1d off bread subsidy (out of 2¹/₂d) at once; rest later. Milk in July, as I proposed originally. After a few verbal changes they went off to see PM. (This seems an odd way of doing business – with these emissaries between the two High Contracting Parties – but it is really rather a good way. It saves everybody's face and is less embarrassing.) I was summoned to No. 10 at 12.45. PM accepted the formula, and all was settled. This has been a strange, tense and very tiring crisis – all the more because it has been, as it were, 'suppressed'.[162]

Was this Macmillan the ambitious power-playing politician exploiting a weak Prime Minister with scant grasp of economic affairs or Macmillan the would-be reforming Chancellor? He did not fool himself about being the latter, not so far, at any rate. Brooding upon this very private crisis, given the failure of press and Parliament to hear of it, he told himself (through his diary) that: 'after all this effort and excitement, I have managed – by threat of resig- nation – to get 4/5 of my plan. But will it be enough? Will it do the trick? Or shall we drift into bankruptcy and devaluation in the summer? It's a tremen- dous gamble, and really worries me. Everyone else (including the PM) seems quite unconscious of the danger . . .'[163]

His one and only Budget as Chancellor followed in April. Raising income tax by 6d (thereby undoing Butler's election cut of a year earlier) was consid- ered but ruled out. Instead, ministers would have to find £100m savings in public spending.[164]

The 1956 Budget is remembered largely for Macmillan's introduction of Premium Bonds for savers and his joke about the difficulty of micro-managing the British economy from Whitehall: 'We are always, as it were, looking up a train in last year's Bradshaw.'[165] Macmillan basked briefly in the 'best press I have ever had . . . Now we must work.'[166] 'Work' meant coping with still more anxiety about the pound, its exchange rate and the gold and dollar reserves. Following the 1956 Budget, Macmillan was particularly vexed by a complica- tion caused by Butler's decision in February 1955 to make sterling freely convertible into dollars for non-resident holders of pounds at a rate lower than but close to the official parity with the dollar of $2.80 (plus or minus the 1 per cent margin permissible).[167] He began conversations with the Bank of England about moving to across-the-board convertibility (this, in fact, did not happen until December 1958[168]).

The problem for Macmillan in the spring of 1956 was 'the rapid movement of the rates of official and transferable sterling together'.[169] Freeing the pound in any manner (floating, convertibility) was all too difficult given the perpetual fear in the Bank of England and the Treasury that sterling holders would rush to convert their pounds into dollars the moment they were free to. But Macmillan continued to hanker for radical measures, particularly when it became apparent, as he told Eden in his 'Half-Time' paper ('halfway between the Budget and the Summer Recess' – or the Suez crisis, as it turned out), that finding the £100m savings was proving difficult, as was restraining wages at a time when 'the great investment boom which was stimulated by our policies in 1953 and 1954 cannot easily be checked'. (Manufacturing investment increased by 50 per cent between 1952 and 1956, stimulated in part by the 'investment allowance' tax-credits Butler introduced.)[170] But what is especially eye-catching for the historian about 'Half-Time' is Macmillan's gift for cocooning his immediate concerns within a sense of the ancient flows of history with which his classical education had endowed him. This led the Chancellor, for example, in his section on military expenditure, to tell Eden that 'it would be absurd to decay like the Roman Empire in the 4th century, because we insisted on spending money which we have not earned on defence measures which are probably ineffective'.[171]

Historians have to be especially careful with Macmillan for several reasons, not least because of his appetite for writing our first draft for us. He placed a polished miniature of declining-and-falling in the middle of 'Half-Time':

If the financial economy of this country collapses, by which I mean another devaluation becomes necessary, followed by the break-up of the sterling area and the removal of the many cushions which have sustained the British people at a standard of living which is higher than they really earn, historians will attribute this collapse to three reasons.

First, the refusal of democracy to face the realities and the implications of 'full employment'. There is little we can do about this. Second, the excessive investment boom of 1953 and 1954 – not checked in time by monetary restraint – and the return to a free economy without, perhaps, sufficient controls having been retained in the background. Third, to the weight of defence expenditure and commitments overseas far beyond the power of this country to sustain.[172]

Over-full employment we have pondered. What about those controls for which Macmillan pined? He had in mind building controls, especially 'on non-productive building (which includes office-blocks), and by returning to the sponsoring of industrial building'.[173]

But it was defence above all that he had in his sights in June 1956:

Some £700 million a year has been added to defence expenditure since the Korean War.* Moreover, much of this falls on the most valuable part of the modern economy, that is the metal-using and engineering industries. As textiles fall away it is these industries on which we must rely more and more ... we must take a number of calculated risks in defence. After all there is such a thing as over-insurance ...[174]

What did he mean by this?

... we should deliberately take some chances, both in the field of research and development and in production (e.g. in fighter programme and ship construction) ... Even if these decisions do not give us much immediate relief in terms of money (for instance because of compensation payments), they will give very great relief in terms of reality. For if men are stopped from working on armaments, they can readily be used on productive work and make things which could be sold abroad.

It may well be better in our present economic plight to leave a ship or an aeroplane uncompleted, thus showing industry that we are in earnest and encouraging the transfer of men and materials to something else.[175]

Five months later, Britain was at war in the Middle East after months of scrabbling together a naval task force in Malta, covering the Cyprus bases with aircraft and calling up the reserves. One aspect of Macmillan's wish list had come to pass – the taking of chances on defence – but not in the way he had imagined.

Five days before the Suez crisis erupted with Colonel Nasser's nationalization of the Canal Company, Macmillan penned one of the most evocative of his broody diary entries, a combination of gloom and analysis at which, as we have seen, he excelled:

The Government's position is very bad at present. Nothing has gone well. In the M East, we are still teased by Nasser and Co; the Colonial Empire is breaking up, and many people view with anxiety the attempt to introduce Party Democracy in such places as Nigeria and the Gold Coast. Cyprus is a running sore [the terrorism campaign begun in 1955 by the Greek Cypriot EOKA organization seeking independence from the UK and union with Greece]. The situation regarding Russia is better, but the defence burden goes on. At home taxation is very high [about 1s 10d or 9p in the pound for a married couple with two children sustained by average male earnings]; the inflation has *not* been mastered [it reached 4.5 per cent in 1956]; no one knows whether the new Chancellor will be a great success or a crashing failure (least of all does the Chancellor know!)

* Though by 1956 the Conservative governments had reduced defence spending to 7.8 per cent of gross national product from its Korea-related high of 9.8 per cent in 1952.

Meanwhile, we see Germany – free of debt, and making little contribution to defence – seizing the trade of the world from under our noses.[176]

The 'German question' took a particular and hugely important form in Macmillan's mind. The phrase is usually used in a geopolitical context, as in Timothy Garton Ash's depiction of Germany as the European pivot of the great East–West confrontation 'and especially divided Berlin, [which] was a thermometer of the worldwide struggle between the two blocs . . .'[177]

For Macmillan it went wider and deeper. He never forgave the Germans for the Great War and, deep into his old age, as Chancellor of Oxford University, he would recall for the undergraduates of the 1980s those of his own generation who were 'sent down by the Kaiser'.[178] He could not bring himself to return to Oxford after the war to complete his degree. 'It was not just that I was still a cripple,' he recalled nearly sixty years later.* 'There were plenty of cripples. But I could not face it. To me it was a city of ghosts. Of our eight scholars and exhibitioners who came up in 1912 [to Balliol], Humphrey Sumner and I alone were alive. It was too much.'[179] He had, too, a daily reminder of his injuries on the Somme as he carried 'a piece of best Krupps steel in his left thigh until the day he died'.[180]

Macmillan simply could not stand the Germans. Ted Heath recalled in his memoirs that, when Prime Minister, Macmillan 'astonished' the Duke of Edinburgh at a private lunch by 'proclaiming with a staccato emphasis' that 'Huns are always the same. When they are down they crawl under your feet, and when they are up they use their feet to stamp on your face.'[181] And as Chancellor the spectre of an economically buoyant West Germany confronted him at every turn. For 1955–6 was as much a benchmark economically and geopolitically in that country's fortunes as it was in Britain's – and the shift was very definitely not in Britain's favour. This position was worsened in terms of relative trade and productivity performance as the early West German 'economic miracle' (its traditional manufacturing prowess restored, its currency strong and without a world reserve role and no overseas or imperial commitments) gave an immense boost to the economies of the other five members of the European Coal and Steel Community.

Pursuing his thoughts through his Treasury window in Whitehall, Macmillan would have been more aware than any other Cabinet minister, except perhaps

---

* The most severe of several war wounds was caused by a bullet which struck him in his left thigh at the Somme on 16 September 1916, ending Macmillan's war. Surgeons were unable to remove several fragments embedded in his pelvis, and they caused him pain for the rest of his life.

Peter Thorneycroft at the Board of Trade, that, over the period 1945–55, 'the national incomes of the Six had grown on average almost twice as fast as that of the United Kingdom'.[182] Macmillan, no doubt, would have added his rider about Germany carrying no equivalent of the sterling balances or having to pay for armed forces around the globe. But, as Alan Milward judged:

It seemed increasingly reasonable to link this disparity in part to the rate of expansion of the Six's foreign trade, also on average almost twice as rapid as that of the United Kingdom. This correlation only appeared in the popular press in the context of Germany's more successful post-war performance. The fact that European trade expansion depended so much on trade with Germany was no consolation because Germany was seen as Britain's most dangerous rival. The year 1955 was one in which German manufacturers made sudden inroads into the share of Britain's manufactures in European markets, especially in the Netherlands and Scandinavia. The territory of the Federal Republic accounted for 70 per cent of the pre-war Reich. On that basis 1955 was the year in which the Federal Republic recaptured and then surpassed its pre-war share of European markets, mainly at Britain's expense.[183]

Here lies the key difference in economic context between the Coal and Steel Community proposals presented to Attlee, Bevin and Cripps by Robert Schuman, the French Foreign Minister, in the late spring of 1950 and those pressed on Eden, Macmillan and Butler for a European Economic Community, or Common Market, by Johan Beyen and Paul-Henri Spaak, respectively the foreign ministers of the Netherlands and Belgium, in the summer and autumn of 1955.

To say, as Butler did nearly thirty years later, that 'Anthony Eden was bored with this. Frankly he was even more bored than I was . . . Well, we just thought it was not going to work. That's where we were wrong, you see,'[184] tells only part of the story of 1955–6 and the British reaction to the Messina talks, opened in June 1955 by the Coal and Steel Community. The purpose of Messina was to pursue the idea of a wider Common Market, and this drove the Brussels negotiations that followed. Yet you cannot be entirely bored if you are frightened, and fear of its possible success was very much the Whitehall emotion about this latest attempt at European integration.

In his last days at the Foreign Office Macmillan was convinced nothing would come of Messina and after. For example he flew to Paris for a meeting of the Western European Union (the body created to ease a rearmed Germany into NATO). The WEU was itself a crucial element in the Whitehall 'it-won't-work lullaby',[185] as it had been built to a British design atop the ruins of the integrationist European Defence Community. Macmillan recorded in his diary of 14 December 1955 that:

Beyen (Netherlands) and Spaak (Belgium) opened rather a sharp attack on UK policy regarding the 'Messina' or '6 Power' plans for a common market etc. I replied. I said that always before (e.g. with EDC and Steel) we had been accused for concealing our policy till it was too late. Now they complained that we had revealed it prematurely.[186]

Eight days earlier, the British Ambassador to the Organisation for European Economic Co-operation (the body created to oversee economic co-operation during the Marshall Plan and after), Sir Hugh Ellis Rees, had announced at an OEEC meeting also in Paris that Britain could not join a Common Market as the motive behind Spaak's report (which fleshed out the Messina proposals for a European economic community) was political, not economic: that it would break up the OEEC and split western Europe into two; that it was discriminatory against GATT rules.[187]

Macmillan was confident that rough and difficult day at the Quai d'Orsay that he knew what was really going on – or *not* going on:

Of course, there's a good deal behind this. Neither the Germans nor the French spoke up at all. The French will never go into the 'common market' – the German industrialists and economists equally dislike it, altho' Adenauer is attracted to the idea of closer European unity on political grounds. This of course is very important, and I made it clear that we wd welcome and assist the plan, altho' we cd not join, so long as a proper relation cd be established between the inner and outer circles – the 6 and the 15 – Messina and the OEEC.[188]

Here were the early glimmerings of the ideas for a looser approach to European economic integration which would later emerge as 'Plan G', the British government's attempt to both envelop and make palatable (to UK interests, that is) a Common Market of the Six.

But as he prepared to shift his gaze from a Foreign Office window to a Treasury one, Macmillan did not think it would come to that. Sir Edward Bridges, about to welcome him to Great George Street, was a firm anti-Common Market man just as he had been anti-Coal and Steel Community, and he harboured doubts about his new Chancellor on this score. He had told the old one, Rab Butler, on 20 September 1955 that 'I remain firmly convinced that Britain's interest certainly does not lie in this direction.' The government should not fall for 'the kind of mysticism which appeals to

European Catholic federalists and occasionally – I fear – to our Foreign Secretary'.[189]*

Yet six weeks after his knockabout in Paris with Spaak and Beyen, Macmillan was sharing his anxieties with the same Bridges that something might come of the Spaak findings on the next steps towards economic integration. On 1 February 1956, he minuted his Permanent Secretary asking, 'What then are we to do? Are we to just sit back and hope for the best? If we do that it may be very dangerous for us; for perhaps Messina will come off after all and that will mean Western Europe dominated in fact by Germany and used as an instrument for the revival of power through economic means. It is really giving them on a plate what we fought two wars to prevent.'[190]

To eyes and minds not wholly attuned to the Whitehall of the mid-1950s it might appear baffling that, if the anxiety about a European Common Market working without Britain inside was so acute, so few voices were raised among officials (not a single Cabinet minister was pro[191]) in favour of UK participation from within. Especially as the Board of Trade official who had sat in at the Messina/Brussels talks until November 1955, the economist Russell Bretherton, was convinced, as he had informed the Treasury the previous August in a telegram from Brussels, that: 'We have, in fact, the power to guide the conclusions of this conference in almost any direction we like; but beyond a certain point, we cannot exercise that power without ourselves becoming, in some measure, responsible for the results.'[192]

Until the moment he was summoned home for good, Bretherton tried to convince London something of importance was very likely to emerge from the talks – and he had excellent contacts with the French (especially with Bernard Clappier, the deputy to the Paris representative at the Brussels negotiations).

On 29 October 1955, less than a week before his last attendance at the Spaak Committee as UK observer, Bretherton reported to his home department, the Board of Trade, that 'I do not myself think that the movement for European economic integration is losing ground and will collapse: rather the reverse.' His reading of the Brussels meetings was that the Six were 'more and more inclined to go for drastic "across-the-board" solutions like the Common Market, and to be impatient with the sort of piecemeal work which has so far been accomplished in OEEC, GATT etc.'.[193]

---

* Shades here of Ernie Bevin, who thought, as did his junior minister, Kenneth Younger, that Robert Schuman, a devout Roman Catholic, was excessively influenced by priests; Bevin did not care for priests.

To begin to understand the 1955–6 UK resistances to European economic integration requires, naturally, an understanding of how the Common Market finally enshrined in the 1957 Treaty of Rome worked and the differences between it, a customs union and a free trade area. Few people naturally throb with excitement when confronted with the intricacies of trade policy, but they are essential to an understanding of Whitehall and wider attitudes.

A customs union is an arrangement whereby a group of countries erect tariff barriers against goods imported from outside the union, while tariffs and quotas within the union are reduced to promote free trade among members. The German Zollverein was the pioneer customs union (the word's literal translation) in the mid-nineteenth century. In a pre-echo of the early 1950s, 'Palmerston and his successors neglected to countervail the lead assumed by the [Prussian] Hohenzollern dynasty in formation of the Zollverein.'[194] Joseph Chamberlain's great, but failed, early-twentieth-century crusade to move Great Britain and its Empire away from global free trade was based on the same idea, a 'form of transoceanic Zollverein – a massive imperial free trade area, protected from the rest of the world by high tariff walls, within which the colonies would provide both the raw materials and the markets for the goods produced by revived British industry'.[195]

The European Common Market (or European Economic Community, to give it its formal title), incorporated by treaty in 1957 and operational from 1 January 1958, was a customs union *plus*. And the plus was a huge one, designed to be of ever growing importance. For as international historian James Ellison put it, its ambition rested in its aim 'to achieve free movement of persons, services and capital, to adopt common policies on agriculture and transport, as well as creating a European Social Fund and a European Investment Bank. It would achieve these objectives within the supranational framework of a European Community administered by an Assembly, a Council, a Commission and a Court of Justice.'[196]

All this was planned to be a dynamic process leading, in the core phrase of the Treaty of Rome,* signed by the Six on 25 March 1957, 'to lay the foundation of an ever closer union among the peoples of Europe', by which was meant political as well as economic union – much, much more than a relatively static customs union arrangement. But, as journalist and author Hugo Young noted of that essential passage in the treaty, 'few of the British, even

---

* Or 'Treaties', to be precise, because a separate if simultaneous one created the European Atomic Energy Commission, EURATOM.

among the political leadership, properly absorbed this. They never really penetrated the words, and, if they did happen to be vouchsafed a moment of enlightenment, it was to see them as a challenge, rather than a credo that had much to do with the island race.'[197]

In 1956 the problem for the Foreign Office, the Whitehall economic ministries and No. 10 was to fashion an alternative to the Common Market, once it was plain to London that it was indeed going to be created – a surrogate that would absorb it into a wider design crafted by the British for Europe but to very definite UK specifications. And here we come to the difference between a free trade area, or FTA (Britain's preferred solution), and both a customs union and a common market. The British idea was this:

An FTA would be established in manufactures which would aim to eliminate tariffs and quotas internally. Externally, however, member states would retain autonomy in setting tariffs against third countries. Agriculture would, of course, be excluded [sustaining a 'cheap food' policy for imports from the British Empire/Commonwealth was a powerful factor in UK calculations] and the FTA would work within the OEEC via an intergovernmental Managing Board, avoiding the creation of a new institution. In simple terms, what the British envisaged was a concurrent reduction of tariffs and quotas between the FTA and the Common Market in manufactures; the FTA would include none of the more wide-ranging commitments of the Rome Treaties . . .[198]

It contained no trace of the Monnet–Schuman or Beyen–Spaak Catholic continental mysticism – ever closer union and all that – which so horrified Sir Edward Bridges about Europe's would-be integrating federalists.

Before plunging into the range of quibbles, caveats and fundamental resistances which greeted the Common Market idea in Whitehall during 1955 and 1956, another question must be placed around it – the Bretherton one, in fact. Why did the British government never contemplate becoming a full and participating member of the Spaak Committee, shaping it from within *and* purging it of both the problem elements (as the British saw them) and the mysticism? As Miriam Camps, the earliest historian of Britain and Europe from the mid-Fifties to the failure of the first UK application for membership of the EEC, noted: 'Had the British at any time been willing to accept a customs union it seems clear enough that they would have had little difficulty, at this period [the mid-1950s], in negotiating the kind of sweeping exceptions for agriculture and the Commonwealth that, later, it became impossible for them to do.'[199] The French, another imperial power after all, managed to do precisely what Camps believed was possible 'for their agriculture and overseas territories within the Treaty of Rome'.[200]*

It is important, in any history of Britain and Europe, to divine the mixture of certainties, fears and prejudices sculling around Whitehall during the crucial month of November 1955 when Bretherton attended his last meeting of the Spaak Committee on the 7th[201] and the Cabinet's Economic Policy Committee decided on the 11th that it was 'against the interests of the United Kingdom to join a European Common Market'.[202] Butler as Chancellor chaired the crucial meeting. Its key briefing paper rested on the work of the interdepartmental Working Party on a European Common Market, chaired by the influential Treasury under-secretary Burke Trend, which reported to the official Cabinet Committee on Mutual Aid, MAC.[203] (On 27 October MAC had concluded that 'on the whole the establishment of a European Common Market would be bad for the United Kingdom and if possible should be frustrated. But if it came into being with us outside it we should pay an increasing price commercially. But even this would not necessarily outweigh the political objections to joining.')[204]

There were two absentees from that pivotal meeting of the Economic Policy Committee: Harold Macmillan, who was in Paris on Foreign Office business, and Eden himself, who usually left its chairing to his Chancellors.† For historians, Eden's absence from the EPC meeting is a small boon as Butler's private secretary sent a copy of its Common Market briefing paper to No. 10 for him to read and comment upon.[205] The paper, entitled 'European Integration', is of great intrinsic interest because it incorporates the story up to that point which Whitehall was telling itself, including the 'motives which have prompted this new Brussels initiative, [which] are complex'.

'European Integration' began with some basic contemporary history, perhaps because the officials drafting it sensed or knew that ministers on the

---

* Many years later, by which time the EEC had mutated via the European Community to the European Union, one of Nigel Lawson's best jokes had to do with his decision to live in France for a good part of the year as 'it gives me a chance to get away from the EU!' (as he confirmed to me in conversation, 26 January 2005).

† The day after, Macmillan had a chat about the Middle East with Alan Hare, the SIS Station Chief in Paris, and noted in his diary that 'Alan Hare (who has excellent contacts here) believes that the Israelis are now seriously considering an attack on Egypt, to destroy the Egyptian army and bring down Nasser. Everyone seems to think this wd be a great disaster – because of the other Arabs. But there wd certainly be compensations ...' *Exactly* the temptation for which Eden and Macmillan fell the following autumn.

EPC, not least its chairman, Rab Butler, as he later admitted, found the whole business a distraction and a bore. And certainly several of them would have known how unsatisfactorily Butler's recent meeting had gone with Beyen when the Dutch Foreign Minister had come to London, for the second time since the Messina talks and just before Bretherton's last attendance at the Spaak Committee, in an attempt to persuade the Eden government to join the proposed Common Market. A quarter of a century later Butler recalled what he described as 'The Beyen business' for Michael Charlton at the BBC:

BUTLER: . . . I was rather surprised that the Dutch Foreign Minister should take such a big part. I got very bored with him, and so did everybody else; and so in the early part we, I'm afraid, rather cold-shouldered him. Then on the second occasion when he came over, which was more businesslike and there were all these talks, I think it possible that I listened. And the word 'listened' is very important, because what I mean by that is that I was not combative, or against him, or rude; and I think that I may have given him the impression that he had made an impression. But after he had gone – I consulted with my colleagues – I had not betrayed my country in any way by wrong words, but I think that I had been sensibly sympathetic to him, and had overcome (on the advice of some of my advisers) my personal repugnance to him.

CHARLTON: Repugnance? Why repugnance?

BUTLER: Well, he was a very pushing man. And he was always telling you what to do. I was sort of looking rather to the bigger nations, you see, and he rather took the lead, you know.[206]

Butler was right about the initial lead for what became the Messina talks. It came very much from the three small Benelux countries, the Netherlands especially.[207]

The 'European Integration' paper prepared by officials for Butler and his EPC colleagues began its historical section with the meeting in Sicily five months earlier:

At the Messina Conference in June, the Six countries . . . resolved that further progress must be made 'towards the setting up of a united Europe, by the development of common institutions, gradual merging of their economies, the creation of a Common Market, and the gradual harmonization of social policies'.

The means by which this Resolution might be implemented have been under study in the last few months at a preparatory conference in Brussels. At this conference the

UK has been represented by a spokesman, who, while he has taken an active part in the discussions, has done so on an expressly non-committal basis.

The Spaak Report was imminent; its objectives would go to the ministers of the Six for agreement and deposition in a draft treaty giving them 'concrete expression'. A line from the British government was now needed.[208]

What did the best minds in Whitehall make of the motives 'which have prompted this new Brussels initiative . . .'?

To some extent, it derives from the enthusiasm for integration which has been endemic in Western Europe since the end of the war, and has found expression, in varying degree, in OEEC, in the Coal and Steel Community, and in the Council of Europe (and in this respect the Brussels movement undoubtedly owes something to the acute disappointment which the sponsors of a united Europe experienced on the collapse of the EDC). To some extent it derives from genuine dissatisfaction with the leisurely and apparently ineffective method by which business is conducted in OEEC itself. And to some extent it derives from a desire on the part of certain Foreign Ministries to weld Western Germany firmly into Western Europe while Dr Adenauer is still alive.[209]

There is a striking gap in this list of motivations which is hinted at, but no more, in the bracketed section of the official paper on the disappointments experienced over the failure of the EDC. For, in Alan Milward's words,

Flowing beneath the tumultuous history of the EDC was a powerful current of economic expansion strongly sustained by the growth of trade between the Six. It transformed the concept of tariff unions from one of threats to national economic stability into the opposite idea that they were instruments for continuing economic growth. In that transition the dynamic expansion of the Federal Republic's foreign trade after 1950, faster even than that of its economy, was the major influence. Whereas the EDC was born out of fear of Germany, the EEC was born out of the increasing need for the Federal Republic as market and supplier in sustaining the industrialisation and economic growth of its neighbours.[210]

Here lay the crucial difference between Europe's two leading, if fading, imperial powers: 'When British ministers like Macmillan or Thorneycroft saw the expansion of Germany's exports as a threat, small western European countries, and an increasing number of French politicians, saw it as a benefit. Their eyes were fixed on the reciprocal gains to be made in the rapidly expanding German market.'[211] The 'official mind' in Whitehall during that autumn of 1955, however, knew that the dilemma they faced was tougher and more 'complicated' than before. The briefers wrote, 'We have faced the prospect of economic "integration" (in varying degree) with Europe several times since the war; and each time, after much heart-searching, we have drawn back.'[212]

America, once more, was a 'complication'. President Eisenhower was an especial enthusiast for the Common Market idea and no fan of the British alternative of a free trade area. Like Truman before him and Kennedy after him, he was keen on greater collective economic self-reliance on the Europeans' part and attracted by the idea of having one big community with whom to negotiate on trade matters rather than a scattering of individual nations.[213] Peter Thorneycroft, the President of the Board of Trade, was particularly vehement about the dangers of this. His brief for Eden to read as he and Selwyn Lloyd sailed across the Atlantic to meet Eisenhower and Dulles in January 1956 declared, 'I am convinced that the Americans are in a fool's paradise about Messina, and I strongly recommend that you and the Foreign Secretary should seek to bring home to President Eisenhower the gravity of the dangerous situation which is rapidly developing against the interests of both our countries and all our joint work since the war to build up a "one-world" trading system . . . The Americans think in terms of customs unions, and the idea of a customs union in Europe has a strong appeal for them. But this is all an illusion.'[214]

Not long before he died, Lord Thorneycroft told me that with hindsight he regretted that a minister rather than a civil servant from his department, Bretherton, had not represented the UK in the Spaak Committee. But, he explained, 'the opinion in the Cabinet was too strongly averse to Europe to commit a Cabinet minister to those negotiations at that time. I wish I *had* gone. If we had managed to get an accommodation – or start to get an accommodation with them – the history of Europe would have been very different.'

Was it, I asked, the single greatest lost opportunity of the postwar period? Lord Thorneycroft thought for a while (this was in 1993) and said: 'It has had the biggest effect of any lost opportunity . . .'[215] At the time, however, Thorneycroft was, as he put in his memo to Eden, a convinced 'one world' free trader.

There is no commentary from Eden himself on the full text of the November 1955 EPC brief on 'European Integration', but we know he did read the summary prepared by his private secretary, Neil Cairncross, as he wrote 'AE. Nov 18' at the base of it. Alongside the section of Cairncross's brief encapsulating the principle that 'Her Majesty's Government should lean towards supporting OEEC and try to keep out of the more far-reaching schemes that the Continental countries favour' he wrote, 'I agree.'[216]

If Eden had read the full paper, he would have picked up the extra degree of anxiety induced in Whitehall by those continentals in 1955 which surpassed the fretting inspired by the ECSC and EDC plans earlier in the 1950s, for all the understatement in which it was couched:

It is tolerably clear ... that membership of a Common Market – in the sense of a customs union, in which there would be no tariffs on trade between members, and a common tariff against the outside world – would present us with very considerable problems, both economic and political. Speculative though our predictions on this subject are (and must necessarily be), they suggest two things: –

(a) That we should not, on balance, benefit from joining a European Common Market, and that it would be to our advantage that the project should collapse.

(b) That, if it did not collapse, we should be faced with a very difficult decision in choosing whether to join it, at the cost of all the disadvantages implicit in any drastic readjustment of our economy (involving perhaps some degree of surrender of Sovereignty), or to hold aloof from it, at the cost of losing our competitive commercial position in Europe and possibly facilitating the establishment of a German political hegemony.[217]

So the answer was 'to take advantage of the various political stresses and strains within the Brussels group and to encourage the project to die of its own accord'.[218]

The briefing papers and discussions of 1955 on Britain and Europe strike an early-twenty-first-century reader as very familiar. The debate was, unlike today, very much an internal Whitehall matter which rarely broke surface in public. When it did, it failed to excite Parliament and the press, which thought it boring (which it was) and marginal (which it most certainly was not). Perhaps its greatest significance lay in its marking the moment when both ministerial and official circles came to realize just how little sway Britain as a global power could exert on that part of the world to which it was closest in geographical terms.

There were only a few dissenting voices against this mixture of anxiety, disdain, hubris and wishful thinking in the Whitehall of autumn 1955. Very few. The Economic Section of the Treasury concluded that, in *economic* terms, it was in the UK's interest to become a member of a European Common

Market.[219] And Sir Frank Lee, Permanent Secretary to the Board of Trade, was the sole voice arguing on the same grounds at the Economic Steering Committee of senior officials, which worked to Butler's EPC, at its meeting on 1 November 1955.[220] (Lee, as we shall see in Chapter 13, would be one of the most crucial figures in the tilt towards Europe in the summer of 1960.)

What if the 'political stresses and strains' within the Spaak Committee did not wreck the idea of a Common Market? The 'European Integration' paper for EPC had thought of that:

The most hopeful [outcome] appears to lie in our taking the line that, if the Six intend to try to create a Common Market (which, as they must realise, we should not join) their activities will impinge on the wider interests of the OEEC at many points, and that, in order to avoid the embarrassing division of Europe into two rival camps, a closer liaison between Paris [the OEEC headquarters] and Brussels should be devised. We should then take advantage of the ensuing period of discussion – which might, with luck, be quite lengthy, and might also, with skilful management, bring to light several fresh obstacles in the way of the Six – to develop a new counter-initiative of our own with OEEC.[221]

Out of this would emerge Plan G, the free trade area ploy. But even this was not without a degree of difficulty because influential official voices within the Treasury argued against the need for any British counter-initiative at all. The most powerful of these was Sir Leslie Rowan, head of its overseas finance division. Rowan was a tough operator who had been Downing Street Principal Private Secretary to both Winston Churchill and Clement Attlee. He was Whitehall's primary keeper of the 'collective approach', the financial expression of Churchill's geometric conceit based on the desirability of sterling as a secure global currency buttressed by growing multilateral trade within a 'one-world' rather than regional system.[222] Rowan's in-house Treasury adversary was equally formidable: the mercurial Otto Clarke,[223] now head of the Home and Overseas Planning Staff into which the old Central Economic Planning Staff had mutated.

By the end of 1955 Clarke believed Rowan's views were unrealistic and that the growing importance of Britain's influence (or lack of it) in Europe required recognition in the form of a fresh study on the trade question.[224] In early February 1956 Clarke declared himself 'in favour of a little bit of a tilt towards Europe'.[225] The incoming Chancellor, Macmillan, had already asked Bridges for a new plan to be prepared, 'however sketchy'.[226] Macmillan resisted Rowan's fightback and supported Clarke (who was to do the work), making it plain that 'I want this study to be made. But I don't want the study to be limited by any other doctrinaire assumptions. Let it be objective.'[227]

By late April Clarke and his team had produced six 'Elements of Initiative': [228]

A. More cooperation within the OEEC.
B. Merger of the Council of Europe and the OEEC.
C. Tariff reductions on a list of European commodities.
D. Free trade area in steel.
E. A general free trade area for western Europe.
F. A new Commonwealth/Europe preferential scheme.[229]

Rowan still thought the Messina Six, about to meet for a summit in Venice, would fall apart, minuting: '. . . it is quite likely that the Six will not progress very much further in fact at Venice, and it may be thought that the risk is negligible of our receiving any embarrassing invitation to join. Unless the French run very contrary to form it is not very likely that there would be any very clear cut decisions to which we could possibly be asked to subscribe or show any sympathy.'[230]

As the Six met in Venice at the end of May, a meeting of ministers and officials in Macmillan's room agreed that element E should form the basis of the British counter-initiative, with a crucial rider that there be 'an exclusion list of goods, including the whole of the agricultural sector', and 'being in essence a different [initiative] from Element E, it was given a new letter and a more purposive title. It became "Plan G", the basis of all subsequent commercial negotiation with the European Communities until the formal Cabinet decision in 1961 to seek entry into the EEC.'[231] Macmillan's timetable for fleshing out Plan G anticipated a final Cabinet decision in September, by which time a very different set of troublesome foreigners was dominating the agenda in Whitehall.

Paradoxically, as anxieties about *western* Europe increased in London in 1955 and early 1956, those about eastern Europe and the Soviet bloc generally eased. As Eden toured the country during the 1955 general election campaign, Macmillan, as Foreign Secretary, was in Vienna preparing to sign the Austrian State Treaty, which would remove all the occupying powers from that country, leaving it neutral and self-governing. Nikita Khrushchev, who was beginning to emerge in Moscow as the dominant figure in the post-Stalin leadership, was keen on domestic reform, which required the cutting of military expenditure, and he overrode his Foreign Minister, Molotov, to make the final changes needed before the Treaty could be signed.[232] The shadow of the

H-bomb was also having its effect on both sides, as Macmillan noticed during
the dining and the diplomacy in Vienna:

At dinner, nothing of very great importance was said, but M [Molotov] was going out
of his way to be pleasant – kept talking about the need for mutual understanding and
the 'reduction of tension'. The American ambassador at Moscow – Bohlen – says (a)
his own position is not as strong as it was (b) the Russians are very much more frightened by the American strategic air force and the hydrogen bomb (c) are anxious about
the economic strain upon their economy by the double demands of armaments and
providing heavy industry for China.[233]

The Vienna meeting and the Austrian Treaty enabled the first post-1945
summit, which met at Geneva in July 1955 and witnessed Khrushchev's emergence as a world figure, to open in a promising international climate.[234] The
irony of the 1955 summit occurring under an Eden premiership rather than
a Churchill one was not lost on the retired PM: 'Anthony,' he told his doctor
in May, 'has changed his tune about top-level talks; he is pressing for them
now, though it was he and Bobbity [sic: Salisbury] who were so much against
them when I wanted them.'[235]

Eden, in fact, shone at Geneva in July 1955. He was back in his element.
Over dinner with the Russians in his villa, Macmillan recorded, 'Eden conducted the whole affair brilliantly. He exerted all his charm ...'[236] The
Russians, however, did not accept his idea for a demilitarized zone in Germany,[237] nor did they accede to Eisenhower's suggestion that an 'open skies'
policy should allow for each superpower to overfly and gather photo reconnaissance on each other's weaponry as a confidence-building measure. Nikolai
Bulganin, the Soviet premier (Khrushchev's nominal equal), said the proposal
had 'real merit' when Eisenhower unveiled it on 21 July 1955. As journalist
and author André Fontaine noted, 'A few moments later everything had
changed. As the delegates were going to the bar during recess, Khrushchev
approached Eisenhower and told him he didn't agree with Bulganin.'[238] Eisenhower recalled in his memoirs that 'I clearly saw then, for the first time, the
identity of the real boss of the Soviet delegation.'[239]

Macmillan thought as Geneva started that the Russians 'will play for a
draw'.[240] In fact, both sides did – and that, in essence, was what the 'Spirit of
Geneva', as it was dubbed, amounted to. The Russians left Macmillan believing they didn't want a war: 'So long as nuclear weapons exist, they know it to
be impossible.'[241] Both superpowers had come to this conclusion. Eisenhower
told the Russians that nuclear weapons technology now meant that any mas-

sive use of them, because of prevailing wind patterns, could 'destroy the Northern Hemisphere'. Khrushchev agreed: 'We get your dust, you get our dust, the winds blow, and nobody's safe.'[242] In this sense, a kind of reality prevailed at the first East–West summit since Potsdam a decade earlier.

One tangible result of Geneva was that Bulganin and Khrushchev expressed a desire to visit Britain. This was agreed. When 'B and K', as the British press came to dub them, arrived on their cruiser the *Ordjonikidze* in Portsmouth harbour on 18 April 1956, so began one of the most bizarre heads-of-government visits ever to British soil, not least because, despite Eden's instructions to the Admiralty to leave the vessel alone, SIS sent an ageing frogman, Commander Lionel 'Buster' Crabb, to take a look at its hull. He did not return. His headless body was washed ashore the following summer. The Russians complained of espionage. Eden was enraged and shook up SIS, transferring the Director-General of MI5, Dick White, to Broadway Buildings to become the new 'C'.[243] *

The visit had its lighter moments. Eden was particularly keen that the two Russian leaders should see as much of Britain as possible. Khrushchev completely failed to appreciate that Holyrood House in Edinburgh, which they visited, was the Queen's official residence in Scotland. He thought it the equivalent of a 'Siberian outpost where the peasants (in actual fact senior members of the General Assembly of the Church of Scotland) were being well cared for in their dotage'.[244]

Worse was to happen when the Foreign Secretary, Selwyn Lloyd, entertained B and K to lunch at 1 Carlton Gardens on 25 April. The FO's usual interpreter had fallen ill. A last-minute replacement was found whom nobody present knew. He arrived the worse for drink, of which there was already more than a sign over the pre-lunch cocktails when Lloyd introduced the Russian leaders

---

* From the swift, top-secret inquest into the Crabb affair, which Eden instructed Sir Edward Bridges to undertake in May 1956 and which was partially declassified almost exactly fifty years later, it is possible to reconstruct the essentials of what went wrong.

On 6 April 1956 the Admiralty asked the Prime Minister's permission to mount Operation Claret against the Soviet cruiser once it had docked. On 12 April Eden forbade it. The Foreign Office was informed but did not pass the decision to the SIS. Crabb, assisted by an SIS officer, carried out a practice dive on the evening of 18 April, close by the vessel. His operational dive took place in Portsmouth harbour early on the morning of 19 April. His instructions were to examine 'the rudder and screws of the Russian cruiser'. He never returned from what should have been a one-hour mission.

Eden was not informed until 4 May. His continuing rage is apparent from his copy of the report by Bridges, which reached him on 18 May and is littered with such scribbles as 'against orders AE' and 'Ridiculous!'.

to his Parliamentary Private Secretary, the raffish Lord Lambton, describing him as a 'shooting' Lord (as in hunting, shooting and fishing). Khrushchev was greatly moved and shook hands with him solemnly, thinking that Lambton was under sentence of death.[245]

Matters got truly out of hand when Khrushchev rose to reply to Lloyd's speech in a manner unappreciated until Richard Thorpe published his biography of Eden forty-seven years later. The interpreter, Thorpe wrote,

made the most of his moment in the sun. His first translation began, 'He says he is pleased to be here, but if we are pleased to have him is another matter.' Silence fell and Selwyn Lloyd's expression froze. Khrushchev, unaware of anything untoward, pressed on with his speech. To the Russian leader's comment about Britain and Russia having much in common, the interpreter added his own gloss, 'Don't you believe it, *we* haven't got eight million prisoners in Siberia!'

More followed in like vein, before the interpreter was quietly ushered from the room, while Lloyd tried to repair the damage through the Russians' own interpreter. There was no need. When Khrushchev cottoned on to what had happened, he burst into roars of laughter, clearly enjoying the episode more than Lloyd's speech. Strict instructions were given to those officials present that Eden should never hear of what had happened.[246]

There was, however, one moment of great significance in Lloyd's speech and it was made without levity of any kind. For he had 'made it perfectly plain to the Russians that Britain was prepared to defend Middle East oil supplies by force if necessary, the line Eden had emphasised in his talks earlier that morning'.[247] The following day Eden made this plain to his Cabinet, too, Macmillan recording in his diary that Eden had given an account of the whole discussion: 'The Russians understood more what we felt about the M East, and our determination to fight for the oil, if we had to. PM of course had obviously enjoyed these talks very much. He excels in all this. Ld Salisbury sat very glum.'[248]

What even the gloomy and habitually pessimistic Bobbety Salisbury cannot have imagined was that, within the space of six months, Britain would be on the brink of a war (partly for oil) in the Middle East and that, far from exhibiting the 'Spirit of Geneva', Bulganin would be threatening to launch Soviet rockets on London and Paris if the Anglo-French task force invaded Egypt.

9

To the Canal and Back

'All my life I've been a man of peace, working for peace, striving for peace, negotiating for peace. I've been a League of Nations man and a United Nations man and I'm still the same man with the same convictions, the same devotion to peace. I couldn't be other if I wished.'

Sir Anthony Eden, prime ministerial broadcast, 3 November 1956.[1]

'Anthony called a Cabinet. In the middle he adjourned them and kept Bobbety, who had risen from his sick bed for the occasion, Harold and Rab behind and told them if they wouldn't go on he would have to resign. Rab said if he did resign no-one else could form a government.'

Lady Eden's diary, 4 November 1956.[2]

'If we attacked Egypt solely on the ground that nationalization of the Canal is illegal and incompatible with the Suez Canal Convention, or in order to impose an international authority for the operation of the Canal, we should, in my opinion, be committing a clear illegality and a breach of the United Nations charter. It would in fact be a simple act of aggression, even if not an entirely unprovoked one . . . Very few people in this country realise the immense change that has taken place in the climate of world opinion on the question of the use of force, especially that particular use of it that takes the form of what might be called "gun-boat diplomacy". Justifications that would have been accepted without question fifty or even twenty-five years ago would now be completely rejected.'

Sir Gerald Fitzmaurice, legal adviser to the Foreign Office, 6 September 1956.[3]

'A history more worthy of the name than the diffident speculations to which we are reduced by the paucity of our material would give space to the vicissitudes of the human organism. It is very naïve to claim to understand men without knowing what sort of health they enjoyed. But in this field the state of the evidence, and still more the inadequacy of our methods of research, are inhibitive.'

Marc Bloch, 1940.[4]

'I have no doubt at all that history will prove that we acted rightly. It becomes increasingly evident to me if only from Moscow's anger that we have uncovered preparations which would have exploded in due course at the time selected by the Russians, through Nasser as their instrument. Indeed, the big issue that seems to me to emerge is that if we had not acted, before very long Nasser would have been the ruler of the whole Arab world on Moscow's behalf.'

Sir Anthony Eden to the Prime Minister of France, Guy Mollet, 12 November 1956.[5]

History has let Eden down. There are a few partial defenders half a century later but not many. For example, while regretting 'that Eden did not cancel the Suez invasion plans in mid-October when Anglo-French negotiations with Egypt at the UN were making some progress',[6] the historian Victor Rothwell thinks excessive attention has been 'paid to his role during Suez' in the context of his whole political life, centring on 'the secret collusion with France and Israel, and Eden's regrettable lying to Parliament about it on one occasion, a debate on 20 December [1956]. That last may be passed over without too much censure. It was a solitary lapse by an unwell man ...'[7]

The health point is important and we shall return to it. Most politico-military specialists, however, regard Eden's conduct of the Suez crisis as an object lesson in how not to do it. In the aftermath of the Iraq War of 2003, for example, Sir Michael Quinlan, former Permanent Secretary at the Ministry of Defence and the most distinguished in-house defence intellectual in postwar Whitehall,[8] writing of 'Britain's Wars since 1945', reckoned that for

those guided by the just-war tradition the first serious challenge in British history after 1945 was that posed by the Suez episode. (Few would have seen difficulty about participation in the international intervention against North Korea's 1950 attack on South Korea; and internal-security operations like those in Malaya were not wars in the normal sense.)

The Suez adventure was questionable against more than one of the classical criteria, including just and proportionate cause. But though at its launching there was much controversy about its wisdom and propriety, this was not framed in just-war terms ... In addition, because the adventure was conceived in such a closed, even clandestine way, its credentials were not fully tested beforehand; its duration was brief; and it had few subsequent defenders to sustain debate.[9]

For Quinlan's generation in Whitehall, 'not doing an Anthony', was a governing norm.[10]

For some insider commentators, Suez ranks among the worst 'intellectual errors in foreign affairs' that have led to armed conflict in the world since 1945. For the British and European Union diplomat Robert Cooper,

Suez was a mistake, at least for Britain: it was fought on the basis that Nasser was a new Hitler and a threat to order, but neither the threat nor the order really existed. Algeria was a mistake: France was fighting for a concept of state [Algeria remaining a part of metropolitan France] that was no longer sustainable. Vietnam was a mistake: the United States thought it was fighting the Cold War when in reality it was continuing a French colonial campaign. These conceptual errors had heavy costs. Clarity of thought is a contribution to peace.[11]

Eden, to his dying day, believed he was thinking with exactly that clarity and foresight, and in the cause of a wider peace, in the summer and autumn of 1956. His thinking embraced the discipline and the terrain to which he had devoted his professional and intellectual life.

Was his judgement clouded by ill health? This is often a question as central as it is vexing in historical terms but, in the case of Anthony Eden and Suez, an attempt to answer it must be made. At each end of the crisis, those who saw him in action or knew him especially well had the impression, in Keynes's marvellous phrase about 'madmen in authority', that the Prime Minister was indeed 'distilling a frenzy' about Nasser.[12] For example Sir Dermot Boyle, the Chief of the Air Staff, returned to the Air Ministry from Eden's meeting with the Chiefs the day following Nasser's nationalization of the Suez Canal Company on 26 July 1956, called his team together and, as one of them, Frank Cooper, recalled, opened his address to them with: 'The Prime Minister has gone bananas. He wants us to invade Egypt.'[13] At the other end of that extraordinary sequence of summer and autumn events, Eden's former Foreign Office Private Secretary, Evelyn Shuckburgh, turned on the television at home on the evening of Tuesday 30 October 1956

and heard that the Prime Minister had announced that afternoon an Anglo-French ultimatum, with a twelve-hour time limit, to Egypt and Israel to 'withdraw' ten miles from the Canal so that we might move in. Staggered by this. It seems to have *every* fault. It is clearly not genuinely impartial, since the Israelis are nowhere near the Canal; it puts us on the side of the Israelis; the Americans were not consulted; the UN is flouted; we are about to be at war without the nation or Parliament having been given a hint of it. We [he and Mrs Shuckburgh] think AE has gone off his head.[14]

Had he? Historians cannot, I think, be psychiatrists. But Eden was certainly unwell throughout the Suez crisis and it was ill health that was the final trigger of his departure from the premiership in early January 1957.

A member of the medical staff from the clinic in Boston, where he was treated in the summer of 1953, has published a paper dealing with Eden's health.[15] But the latest and fullest account is in Richard Thorpe's official biography, not least because, as he put it, 'The story that senior medical figures have told the author has never been told before.'[16]

Putting Eden's problem right should have been a routine matter in April 1953. In fact, it turned into a nightmare for all concerned. Eden was referred by his usual doctor to two very senior medical figures, Sir Horace Evans, probably the leading general physician of his generation, and Basil Hume, a senior general surgeon at St Bartholomew's Hospital. On 4 April 1953 they thought there might be gallstones in Eden's bile duct. An immediate operation was needed. It was arranged to take place at the London Clinic on the 12th. At this point, Churchill,

fired by the adrenalin of the crisis, took up ACTION THIS DAY [the red stickers he attached to urgent memoranda during the Second World War] stations after hearing of the original diagnosis by Evans and Hume. Consultations followed with Lord Moran, who assured Churchill that Eden would be safe in British hands, and indeed that any thought of sending him abroad at this stage (for example to the world famous specialist Dr Richard Cattell in Boston) would be regarded as a slight on the reputation of Britain's medical profession. To make the assurance doubly sure, Churchill let it be known to Hume, who was to undertake what in essence was a routine operation, that it was vitally important that nothing should be allowed to go wrong. No surgeon likes to be inhibited by others, and under this unexpected and unwelcome pressure, Hume was experiencing considerable concern about the forthcoming ordeal.[17]

Churchill, who habitually alternated between treating Eden with irritated disdain and fussing fondly over him almost as if he were a son, pursued the latter course *fortissimo* as Mr Hume prepared:

Horace Evans was drawn into Churchill's web and became, as it were, Downing Street's representative in the hospital, reiterating the Prime Minister's concerns to an anxious Hume, who was now being asked for regular updates. Even as Eden went under the anaesthetic in the operating theatre, a message came to underline the eminence of the patient. By this time Hume was in such a state of agitation that, even though Eden was now unconscious, the operation had to be put on hold for nearly an hour to allow the surgeon to compose his nerves.

When the operation eventually began, those present could not remember so much loss of blood in a patient. It was turning into a nightmare. A difference of opinion then ensued about whether the gall bladder was actually the cause of the trouble. The consequence had an air of inevitability. Further probing, in the tensest of atmospheres, led to the bile duct being severed. The problem was not now gallstones, but saving Eden's life. Hume was unable to continue, and Guy Blackburn, his main assistant, took over.[18]

Eden pulled through, but a second operation was needed. It took place on 29 April with Blackburn in the lead, and 'proved even more tense than the first ... Eden was within a whisker of death at several stages of the lengthy and traumatic process. Afterwards he was not guaranteed to be free of cholangitis [inflammation of the bile duct] – all part of a piece with the inflammation, obstructions, fever and jaundice from which he was now suffering intermittently.'[19]

The unfortunate Eden needed still more repair. For this he travelled to Boston and Dr Cattell, 'the world's greatest expert in patching up gall bladders'.[20] Before he set to work, Cattell told the British Ambassador to the United States, Sir Roger Makins, that there was a 50/50 chance Eden would die under his knife; a 20 per cent possibility of regaining a measure of his earlier fitness; and only a 10 per cent chance of a full recovery.[21]

Eden never made a full recovery. As he told his colleagues during his final Cabinet on 9 January 1957:

It is now nearly four years since I had a series of bad abdominal operations which left me with a largely artificial inside. It was not thought I would lead an active life again. However, with the aid of drugs and stimulants, I have been able to do so.

During these last five months, since Nasser seized the Canal in July, I have been obliged to increase the stimulants necessary to counteract the drugs. This has finally had an adverse effect on my rather precarious inside.[22]

And a tough fifteen months, without a holiday, over his premiership pre-July 1956 had left him very tired and desperately 'counting the days' until he could take 'three weeks' rest in August' in a villa on Malta which the local Governor had found for the Edens.[23]

Nasser took away Eden's August the moment he took the Suez Canal on the evening of 26 July 1956, triggering the seizure of the company and the proclamation of military law in the Canal Zone with a codeword – 'de Lesseps', the name of the Frenchman who built it – during a speech to a packed open-air meeting in Alexandria.[24]* From the moment the news of Nasser's action reached Eden in the dining room at No. 10 that same evening, where he was entertaining King Faisal II of Iraq and his Prime Minister, Nuri as-Said, until 23 November when, a sick and exhausted man, he flew with his wife to Jamaica to rest, the pressure upon him and his 'rather precarious inside' was intense and unrelenting. The combined stresses of those four months, I think, surpass anything any other postwar British premier has had to endure.

The strain was apparent enough to insiders who saw Eden in action on a daily or weekly basis in Whitehall during that Suez summer and autumn. And, at one point, on 5 October 1956, at a moment of supreme irritation with Foster Dulles[25] as the United Nations Security Council debated the crisis in New York,[26] Eden was taken ill while visiting his wife in University College Hospital in London and it looked for a moment as if he might not be able to carry on. As Robert Rhodes James put it:

To political strains, which were acute, with constant meetings and discussions, delayed meals and physical pressures, there were also personal worries. Clarissa Eden was unwell, and it was while he was visiting her at the beginning of October at University College Hospital on a Friday afternoon that Eden suddenly felt freezing cold, and began to shake uncontrollably with a violent fever. The doctors were summoned, and he was put to bed in a room close to his wife's. His temperature rose to 106 degrees until the fever responded to treatment. He was allowed to leave on the Monday, 'feeling much refreshed by my rest', as he later wrote.[27]

Rhodes James judged this to be 'deceptive ... these violent fevers, which were the direct result of the 1953 operation, were short-lasting but, although they left him feeling surprisingly well after treatment, even exhilarated, they were profoundly weakening, and then caused bouts of lassitude, against which Eden fought irritably. Perhaps wrongly, the doctors considered that he was well enough to carry on with his work, but a sinister bell had been sounded.'[28] Dr Hugh L'Etang, who was the leading British scholar of what he called the 'pathology of leadership', reckoned Eden was suffering from 'the toxic effects of bile-duct infection, and the chemical effects of stimulant and possibly other medication: Benzedrine was almost certainly a factor here'.[29]

* The Suez Canal was, prior to Nasser's nationalization, an international waterway owned and run by the Anglo-French Suez Canal Company through which, in the mid-Fifties, 80 per cent of western Europe's oil flowed. Free passage for the vessels of all nations was guaranteed by the 1888 Convention of Constantinople. The Canal Zone was the huge area covered by the former British base largely evacuated by agreement with the Egyptians a month earlier and now reduced to a care-and-maintenance status by the UK.

The problems of the Middle East, especially those influenced by Nasser, had the capacity like no other of Eden's worries to produce an immediate toxic effect long before the word 'de Lesseps' fell from the Colonel's lips. A turning point, after which Eden's fixation with Nasser hardened into something approaching mania, was the moment on 1 March 1956 when the young King Hussein of Jordan sacked the experienced British General Sir John Glubb ('Glubb Pasha') from the command of the Arab Legion, the Jordanian army which was largely financed and equipped by the British government. Glubb had exerted a fatherly guiding influence far beyond his formal military role. For his part, the King consistently displayed a genuine sympathy for the UK and British influence in the Middle East even at times of surging anti-British sentiment on the part of his Arab neighbours. Eden, as Percy Cradock put it, 'was only too ready to see King Hussein's dismissal of Glubb Pasha ... as evidence, not of Jordanian nationalist feeling, or simply Hussein's resentment at being under the tutelage of a much older man, but as proof of Nasser's plotting and hostility'.[30]

Thirty years later Anthony Nutting, Lloyd's Minister of State at the Foreign Office, recalled Eden's rage on the evening of Glubb's dismissal:

The telephone rang and a voice down the other end said: 'It's me.' I didn't quite realize who 'me' was for a moment. However, he gave the show away very quickly by starting to scream at me. 'What is all this poppycock you've sent me about isolating Nasser and neutralizing Nasser? Why can't you get it into your head I want the man destroyed?' I said, 'OK. You get rid of Nasser, what are you going to put in his place?' 'I don't want anybody,' he said. I said, 'Well, there'll be anarchy and chaos in Egypt.' 'I don't care if there's anarchy and chaos in Egypt. I just want to get rid of Nasser.' But the real consequences of getting rid of Nasser were never really thought out and never really investigated by the Cabinet or by anybody else.[31]

This last is a crucial point to which we shall return.

From the time of the Glubb sacking, nobody senior on a Middle East-related desk in Whitehall was immune to a phone call from Eden during which the Prime Minister's jumpiness would pour from the receiver. His Foreign Office Private Secretary, Evelyn Shuckburgh, was especially well placed to witness this as, after leaving Eden's service, he became the FO's Under-Secretary for Middle Eastern affairs. His diary entry for 3 March, the Saturday following Glubb's dismissal, is especially illuminating:

Chaos in the FO – every time I tried to talk to Kirkpatrick [the Permanent Secretary] or Nutting their telephone rang and the PM came on the line, dictating messages, asking questions, complaining about life in general . . .

At 11.45 I set off in Greeners [his car] for Chequers to lunch with the PM and Lady Eden and to meet Mr Jack McCloy, formerly US High Commissioner in Germany, now head of the Chase Bank. The Aldrichs also there [the US Ambassador to London and his wife] . . . McCloy gave a factual account of his talks with Nasser and King Saud [of Saudi Arabia], which AE interrupted with (I thought) rather light and ill-tempered comment, as if M was supporting the views expressed. He is now violently anti-Nasser, whom he compares to Mussolini, and he spoke darkly (to the Americans) of having a good mind to reverse the evacuation of Suez . . .

After the Americans had gone, AE took me aside and said I was seriously to consider reoccupation of Suez as a move to counteract the blow to our prestige which Glubb's dismissal means . . . AE summed up the whole business by saying, 'We are in a mess,' which is an understatement. He added, 'We are at our best in a mess,' and a sort of 1940 look came into his eye.[32]

Back in the Foreign Office on the Sunday morning for a meeting with Nutting and Glubb, Shuckburgh found the General 'made a most noble impression – no harsh words against the King of Jordan, and a real understanding of the boy's desire to get rid of him, Glubb, who was always preventing him from doing foolish things. He said "It would not be right to come down on Jordan like a ton of bricks. Take what they say at its face value; they want to remain friends."'

During this intriguing conversation Shuckburgh had been called to the telephone once and Nutting twice by Eden 'ringing from Chequers to ask why we were wasting our time gossiping with Glubb' instead of answering the telegrams coming in from the British Ambassador in Amman.[33] If this was Eden's *modus operandi* before Nasser's coup against the Suez Canal Company, it takes quite a leap of the imagination to conceive of how his state of mind and working patterns could have got worse when the crisis broke in full force.

During that Saturday lunch at Chequers with McCloy and Aldrich, Eden had made a rather Churchillian remark, saying, 'I never move a step without our American friends.'[34] It may have been part of the normal, semi-ingratiating chit-chat that is one of the staples of dining for one's country (to borrow Palmerston's definition of what he called 'the Soul of Diplomacy'[35]). For, as Foreign Secretary 1951–5, he had been distinctly ambivalent about those self-same friends in the privacy of his own thoughts. James Ellison and Kevin

Ruane, in a fascinating comparative study of Eden's and Macmillan's trans-atlantic relationships, 'Managing the Americans', illuminate what they call Eden's 'latent anti-Americanism' with a 1954 document from the Avon Papers* in which he bemoaned, in a private note to Lord Salisbury, that: 'They like to give orders, and if they are not at once obeyed they become huffy', observing that this was 'their conception of an alliance – of Dulles' anyway'.[36] They drew from Eden's 1952 Cabinet paper on 'British Overseas Obligations' the theme of 'power by proxy',[37] of attempting to persuade the Americans to take over more and more of Britain's global functions, albeit as unobtrusively as possible, to 'inconspicuously'[38] shore-up Britain's overstretched reach and influence to avoid an unstoppable slide in Britain's international prestige.[39]

Such a strategy was crevassed with pitfalls. It anticipated a level of public and private forbearance on the part of the Americans which is unusual in international affairs, even between the closest of allies. And it was guaranteed to produce huffiness all round if the realities of dependence and real relative power spilled over into personal dealings – as they were bound to in the case of someone as sensitive to slight as Eden when dealing with somebody as powerful and socially dyslexic as Dulles, with his penchant for preaching in primary colours rather than the subtle hues of diplomacy which, pre-Suez, had filled Eden's palette. But, to be fair to Eden and his aside to McCloy and Aldrich over the Chequers lunch table, he really did try for a joint Anglo-American approach to the great intractables of the politics of the Middle East. During 1952–3 he strove to persuade the Americans to join forces in making a Middle East defence organization, or MEDO, in which the USA would be the lead partner.

This was undermined from each end. 'Egypt, the pied-piper of Arab nation-alism, proved implacably opposed to participation in an organisation bearing a British imprimatur, and where Cairo led the bulk of Arab opinion tended to follow.'[40] On the other side, the Americans were reluctant for two reasons. They were wary of appearing to buttress the old imperial power of the region, thereby endangering the US relationship with Arabs struggling to be more independent, but the Cold War was the chief driver of American policy, and the Eisenhower administration was concentrating 'on the Northern Tier or "roof" of the Middle East' by encouraging mutual military aid between Iran, Iraq, Syria, Pakistan and Turkey as a barrier to southward expansion by the Soviet bloc.[41]

* Eden became the Earl of Avon when he entered the House of Lords.

Eden tried hard again in 1955 when Britain, Turkey and Iraq signed the Baghdad Pact for the pursuit of mutual defence (implicitly against any Soviet designs upon the Near and Middle East) in April. But in July, Eisenhower made it plain the USA would not join, preferring bilateral relationships with the northern tier countries concerned. Macmillan, as Foreign Secretary, was very blunt with Dulles about this when they met over dinner in the American Embassy in London in July 1955 to discuss Plan Alpha, a very secret US–UK attempt to resolve the Israel/Palestine problem by discovering the minimum requirements of all the protagonists and constructing a settlement around them.[42] 'I put strongly to Dulles,' Macmillan wrote, 'the difficulties which we felt ... I said that if the whole Middle East went up in flames as a result, we wd have to carry the baby. We had been left with the Turco-Iraqui [sic] pact, wh the Americans started, and then ran out of.'[43]

In fact, beneath the differences over British 'colonialism' in the Middle East and the Baghdad Pact, there was a good deal of Anglo-American co-operation, involving varying levels of secrecy, not least because Khrushchev was developing a very different policy from Stalin's on Middle Eastern nationalism, the most visible and alarming sign of which was the Czech arms deal with Egypt which was announced on 27 September 1955.[44] President Tito of Yugoslavia, now reconciled to the post-Stalin leadership in Moscow, urged Khrushchev to make a pitch at Nasser, who, said Tito, 'was a young man without much political experience', but if given the benefit of the doubt, 'we might later be able to exert a beneficial influence on him ...'[45]

The Americans picked up this new Soviet policy towards the Third World and its nationalisms around the time of the Geneva summit in the summer of 1955 and Eisenhower told his staff that 'we should make a concerted effort to "woo" Nasser'.[46] Egypt and Syria were the main worries for those concerned to keep Soviet bloc arms and influence out of the Middle East. A covert Plan Omega was developed for interventions in Egypt and Syria. The idea was to bring down the Syrian government (Operation Straggle). For Egypt, the plan was to undermine and weaken Nasser.[47] The overt, accommodating face of Anglo-American policy, however, shone on the Aswan Dam, 'Nasser's pet project',[48] which, in fact, at the time, was 'the largest civil engineering project in the world' involving the creation of a huge reservoir near the border with Sudan to regulate the flow of the Nile, irrigate its valley and generate electricity to power the Egyptian economy.[49] Such developmental aid in December 1955 was the West's counterploy to the 200 aircraft, 100 tanks and six submarines that Moscow was supplying to Cairo via Prague.[50]

The Joint Intelligence Committee produced an assessment in April 1956 of what, in the cricketing parlance to which they were then addicted (in the eyes of the CIA's Liaison Officer who attended their meetings[51]), they would no doubt have called the delicately balanced state of play in Cairo. Though Egypt was 'already in a position of increasing dependence on Russia', the JIC analysts did not see Nasser as having

consciously resigned himself to becoming an instrument of Soviet policy. He probably still believes he can steer a middle course not beholden to either side. He has tried to resist some of the Russian conditions for arms supplies, and seems to want the West to finance the Aswan High Dam if he can get firm assurances and satisfactory terms. The question is how long this balancing act can last? It is not yet clear that Nasser has reached a point at which he cannot call a halt to his involvement with Russia. But the Russians are ready to feed the Egyptian appetite until dependence upon them is irreversible, and we must conclude that Nasser will probably soon reach the point of no return.[52]

Already the JIC was out of kilter with the views of its single most important customer, the Prime Minister.

Sir Percy Cradock, who, in effect, did retrospectively for intelligence and Suez what Robin Butler forty-eight years later was to do for intelligence and Iraq,* reckoned that by the time the Committee had approved that early April assessment,

Eden's thinking had passed through several more stages. At first he was disposed to advocate Western finance for the Aswan Dam despite the September arms deal and he encouraged the United States to make a formal offer together with the United Kingdom, of support for the first phase of the project on 16 December 1955. But King Hussein's dismissal of Glubb Pasha in March 1956 provoked a violent change of mood. From then on Nasser was seen by Eden as beyond the pale.[53]

Evelyn Shuckburgh's diaries confirm Cradock's judgement. On 8 March he wrote starkly: 'Today both we and the Americans really gave up hope of Nasser and began to look around for means of destroying him,' adding, a touch incongruously, that 'Kirkpatrick thinks that the PM's description of him as a second Mussolini shows that feminine flair for which he is so famous.'[54]

Sir Ivone Kirkpatrick, Permanent Secretary at the Foreign Office, was just about the only senior official who would be wholeheartedly behind Eden

---

* Though Cradock, unlike Butler, did not have access to all intelligence material but only those JIC files that had been declassified.

throughout the Suez affair. For him Britain's continued place as an advanced nation depended upon both the maintenance of its strategic flow of oil (remember, 80 per cent of western Europe's supplies were passing through the Suez Canal in early 1956[55]) and upon the country's willingness to take on those who sought to disrupt it. This was exactly the line Eden and Lloyd had taken with Bulganin and Khrushchev during their April 1956 visit to the UK. As the crisis came to the boil towards the end of September that year, Shuckburgh (who, by this stage, to his immense relief had moved from his Middle Eastern desk at the Foreign Office to become an instructor at the Imperial Defence College) called on Kirkpatrick. 'Never', he wrote that evening, 'have I heard such black pessimism. Set off by some mild criticism I made of the PM's handling of the Suez crisis, he said the PM was the only man in England who wanted the nation to survive; that all the rest of us have lost the will to live; that in two years' time Nasser will have deprived us of our oil, the sterling area fallen apart, no European defence possible, unemployment and unrest in the UK and our standard of living reduced to that of the Yugoslavs or Egyptians.'[56] At the time Kirkpatrick had thought it very important when he heard Eden tell the 'primitive and brutish' Bulganin and Khrushchev that Britain, if necessary, would fight to preserve its Middle Eastern oil supplies.[57]

Britain's £5.5m contribution to the Aswan Dam project was being channelled via the World Bank. The American money came through its foreign funding mechanism and required the approval of the US Congress.[58] This was always likely to be a problem and Nasser made it 'immeasurably' worse on 16 May 1956 when Egypt recognized the People's Republic of China.[59]

In June reports reached London and Washington that Dmitri Shepilov, the Soviet Foreign Minister, was in Egypt with a counter-offer on the dam – an interest-free loan of $400m repayable over sixty years, together with a bid to buy all of the country's cotton crop. As Cradock wrote, 'Western financing for Aswan was effectively dead by the early summer.'[60] On the morning of 19 July Dulles told the British Ambassador in Washington, Roger Makins, that the American funding for the dam would be withdrawn. At four the same afternoon, the Egyptian Ambassador, Ahmed Hussein, was called to the State Department. Dulles, ever unpolished, told him no project was as unpopular in America as US funding for Aswan; perhaps the Egyptians should be thinking about less grand projects. The Ambassador could not quite believe what he had heard. Did Mr Dulles mean there would be no American money at all for the dam? That's right, said Dulles.[61] Seven days later Nasser nationalized the Canal Company, telling his fellow Egyptians that its revenues would be used to finance the Aswan Dam.[62]

Only one British official, Michael Johnston, foresaw this contingency and he was a Treasury man, not a JIC analyst or intelligence officer. He was the Treasury's Aswan expert and on 6 June, after Kirkpatrick had been warned by the Minister in the US Embassy in London that there was no possibility of Congress approving the funding, Johnston minuted his opposite number in the Foreign Office warning him that 'Nasser will undoubtedly be appalled by the apparent breach of faith by the two Governments and will seek to revenge himself. There is not much he can do against the United States but a lot he can do against us. Obvious examples are renewed pressure on the Suez Canal Company or stirring up trouble in the Gulf.'[63]

In Washington, only the French Ambassador, Maurice Couve de Murville, matched Johnston's insight. He told State Department officers that Dulles' action was a mistake and would cause Egypt to retaliate. 'What can they do?' came the reply. 'They will do something about Suez. That's the only way they can touch the Western countries,' said Couve.[64]

The prescience of Johnston and Couve did not reach Eden's ears. At 10.15 p.m. on the night of 26 July, when Guy Millard, Eden's Foreign Affairs Private Secretary, interrupted the Prime Minister's dinner for the visiting Iraqis to tell Eden Nasser had nationalized the Suez Canal Company, the shock was real enough. Eden told the diners, who included the Labour leader Hugh Gaitskell, what had happened. When the guests left, and still in white tie, an inner group of ministers repaired to the Cabinet Room and waited for the Chiefs of Staff to arrive. The French Ambassador to London, Jean Chauvel, and the US Chargé d'Affaires, Andrew Foster, were also summoned. They talked till 4.00 a.m. Eden said Nasser could not be allowed to prevail.[65] 'Of all the Suez meetings, this hastily convened one in the Cabinet Room was to prove one of the most fateful,' as Richard Thorpe justifiably expressed it.[66]

Many years later Lord Sherfield, as Roger Makins had become, told me how horrified he was in October 1956 on returning to London from the Washington Embassy to replace Bridges as Permanent Secretary to the Treasury, to find the tight group in the know about Suez were 'running in blinkers'.[67] These 'blinkers' were put on in the first hours and days of the crisis. Sadly, no Macmillan diaries survive for Suez beyond 4 October 1956 as he destroyed the entries dealing with the bulk of October and all of November–December.[68] But his entry for 30 July 1956 encapsulates the essence of the affair as seen from the British end. Eden's Egypt Committee was already in existence as, in effect, an 'inner Cabinet' for the crisis[69] (though Macmillan had yet to commit its name to memory) and the seasoned US diplomat who had worked alongside Macmillan in North Africa during the Second World War, Robert Murphy, President Eisenhower's special envoy, was already in town:

Bob Murphy arrived yesterday. The Suez Committee met and heard the For Secy's account of the first talk. It is clear that the Americans are going to 'restrain' us all if they can. I lunched at No. 10 – Bob Murphy, Mr Foster (American Chargé) M Pineau (French Foreign Minister), For Secy, Harold Caccia [senior FO diplomat]. We had a good talk, and the PM did his part very well. The French are absolutely solid with us, and together we did our best to frighten Murphy all we could ... We gave him the impression that our military expedition to Egypt was about to sail. (It will take at least 6 weeks to prepare, in fact.)[70]

In fact, it took twice as long as that.

Within seven hours of Eden's pre-dawn white-tie meeting breaking up his Cabinet were discussing the nationalization and swiftly confronting the 'fundamental question' of 'whether they were prepared in the last resort to pursue their objective by the threat or even the use of force, and whether they were ready, in default of assistance from the United States and France, to take military action alone'. The Cabinet gave Eden what he wanted, agreeing 'that our essential interest in the area must, if necessary, be safeguarded by military action and that the necessary preparations to this end must be made'.[71]

The pursuit of that 'essential interest' involved, over the next three months, a tangled trail of open diplomacy (through conferences in London, negotiations and debate at the United Nations in New York and bilateral disagreements and misunderstandings with the Americans), secret war planning (with the French and the Israelis), changing military preparations (two different plans) and, finally, a joint Anglo-French assault on Egypt, using the pretence of separating Egyptian forces from Israeli invaders in the teeth of unsurprising opposition from the Soviet Union *and* surprisingly active dissent from the 'special relation' across the Atlantic. Amid the shifting scene, one consistent element shone through: Eden's unswerving determination that Nasser should be forced to disgorge the Suez Canal, and should preferably topple as he did so. It is rare to be able to claim, historically, that but for one person, the course of history would almost certainly have been different. In the case of Suez, one can.

Eden pursued these overriding aims in the teeth of attempts to divert or warn him off by President Eisenhower, his two law officers, one Chief of Staff,

Whitehall's leading Arab experts, the Joint Intelligence Committee and the Treasury (Chancellor Macmillan excepted, until the last hours). It caused uproar in the House of Commons, split government and country to a degree not seen since the Munich crisis eighteen years earlier and would not be experienced again until the invasion of Iraq forty-six years later. It stimulated a series of strategic reassessments of remarkable width and significance in the years that followed and its repercussions were felt even in 2002 and beyond when Tony Blair, a Labour Prime Minister this time egged on rather than discouraged by a US President, agreed that the country and the world needed a line to be drawn in another stretch of sand.

One of the most intriguing resonances of Suez in the Whitehall of the early twenty-first century rang through the British intelligence community when John Scarlett, Chairman of the JIC 2001–4, and Sir Richard Dearlove, Chief of the Secret Intelligence Service 1999–2004, picked up from a study of the workings and influence of the Joint Intelligence Committee by Sir Percy Cradock the degree to which, during the build-up to the invasion of Egypt in 1956 (in Cradock's words), intelligence had been neglected 'because the estimates and forecasts of the JIC were disregarded by the policy-makers. While the Prime Minister was ready to call on individual officials or parts of the intelligence community to do his bidding, he and his colleagues were clearly not prepared to listen to the collective wisdom of its senior body.'[72]

Scarlett and Dearlove were aware that the JIC had had a 'good Suez' (the austere Sir Percy prefers to describe it as 'a creditable job', given that the JIC's was 'by no means a flawless performance' in 1956[73]) and that the Committee's assessments and forecasts had not been heeded by the man with a mission in No. 10. Dearlove and Scarlett believed, too, that in the recent past the combined UK intelligence product had not enjoyed the place it deserved in the inner decision-making circles of Whitehall. They were determined that, wherever those circles were located, they and their material would be inside the circumference.[74] They were to be so[75] – and too closely so in the judgement of the Butler Committee, whose members believed that the traditional and much-prized British division between intelligence *analysis* and policy *formation* and *advocacy* on the basis of it had been insufficiently observed on the road to Baghdad.[76]

Critics of the road Eden took to Port Said and the banks of the Suez Canal in 1956 view the degree to which what Cradock called the 'collective wisdom'[77] of the JIC was ignored as a matter of particular regret because the JIC did its job of speaking truth (as its members saw it) unto power within a matter of days of the Cabinet of 27 July. The JIC might not have foreseen the link between the cancellation of Western funding for Aswan and the nationalization of the Canal Company, but within eight days of the 'de Lesseps' moment it had to some extent redeemed itself with a measured and prescient study of its implications and how matters might unfold.

The JIC paper of 3 August 1956 on 'Egyptian Nationalization of the Suez Canal Company' is, I think, among the most significant it produced in the postwar period, even allowing for Eden's disregard of its most striking warning: 'Should Western military action be insufficient to ensure early and decisive victory, the international consequences both in the Arab states and elsewhere might give rise to extreme embarrassment and cannot be forecast.'[78]

The document, circulated on 10 August, the day after the Chiefs of Staff had approved it, took the measure of Nasser without demonizing him. As reticent British males of that generation, no doubt the members of the JIC could not help recoiling at the sight of 'a considerable element of emotion in Nasser's actions. As a demagogue he is liable to be carried away by the violence of the passions he himself has whipped up.' But the JIC knew a skilled operator when they saw one: 'As a dictator, his actions over the past three years show subtlety and calculation and have so far all resulted in gain to Egypt. We should be prepared for any action that may enhance his prestige and maintain him in power.'[79]

How did the JIC assess Nasser's seizure of the Canal? His 'declared motive', they noted, was to use its dues to finance the Aswan enterprise:

We doubt however whether this is the real reason for his action. There have been a number of indications that he himself has recently had doubts whether the High Dam is the best way of solving his power and irrigation problems, and he must have realised that the net annual profit likely to be derived from the Canal is only a fraction of the Dam's cost.

The building of the Dam had, however, come to be seen in the popular mind as the cure for all Egypt's ills and Nasser's own position and prestige were staked upon its accomplishment. When the Western offer of financial aid was withdrawn, therefore, he urgently needed to distract public attention and at the same time find a new method to arouse their enthusiasm and to repair any damage his stock might have suffered in other Arab countries. As a means to this end his nationalisation of the Canal has been a triumph; it has also served the subsidiary purpose of retaliation against the West for the withdrawal of the High Dam offer.[80]

Two months on, the JIC had caught up with Michael Johnston and Couve de Murville. But what next? It was not the JIC's function to tell ministers what to do, but saying what might work and what might not was part of the Committee's tradition: 'We do not believe that threats of armed intervention or preliminary build up of forces would bring about the downfall of the Nasser regime or cause it to cancel the nationalization of the Canal.'[81]

Armed intervention to regain control of the Canal 'would lead to a state of war with Egypt', but the JIC did not think other Arab states would offer more than sympathy to Nasser. It must be remembered that throughout its course the Suez affair was also a grade-one Cold War crisis. Eden was convinced the Soviet Union had designs on Egypt with not just the Middle East in mind, but Africa too. His Commonwealth Secretary, Alec Home, also believed this. Writing to buck Eden up at the end of a difficult month, Home told him on 24 August: 'I am convinced that we are finished if the Middle East goes and Russia and India and China rule from Africa to the Pacific.'[82]

The Suez affair, as Eden, his ministers and Whitehall knew, involved a series of overlapping crises which intertwined and worsened in the three months between Nasser's seizure of the Canal in July and the opening Anglo-French assault at the end of October when RAF bombers crippled the Egyptian air force on its airfields. First, there was the problem of restoring the international status of the Canal, without which Nasser would be in a position to jeopardize Western oil supplies. Military preparations were started in London and Paris while a tortuous diplomatic process began in parallel in the hope of a peaceful outcome which the Eisenhower administration made plain its wish to see. For British ministers, American, Commonwealth and world opinion generally had to be considered at every stage.

As diplomacy faltered the military option loomed ever larger and the French tempted Eden into a secret deal with Israel whereby Israeli forces would invade Egypt, allowing British and French troops to intervene in the guise of peacekeepers. But would sterling be able to take the strain if Britain, with French and Israeli connivance, invaded in the teeth of US and world opinion? Above all other worries was that the Suez affair would develop into a Cold War crisis of substantial magnitude, as Eden, Home and several other of his ministers were convinced a stand had to be made against communist expansion through the Middle East and into Africa as well as facing down Arab nationalism. The very real fear was that Suez would escalate from a regional crisis to an East–West confrontation that could trigger global war. But would it?

British Intelligence thought not. For example, the JIC in its 3 August appraisal expressed

doubt whether the Soviet Union would take any action. She has no treaty of alliance with Egypt and as far as we know, no secret agreement. The support of Egypt in peacetime as a thorn in the side of the West accords with the policy of competitive co-existence, but we do not believe she would embark on global war on behalf of Egypt. The Soviet Government might send technicians and further arms to Egypt but we doubt whether, in the event of hostilities, these would greatly affect the issue.[83]

Towards the end of the crisis, as the Anglo-French task force approached Port Said, Bulganin did threaten rockets on London and Paris (the first indication that the so-called 'Spirit of Geneva', or, as Macmillan rather crudely put it, 'There ain't gonna be no war',[84] did not preclude Khrushchev succumbing to the temptation 'to try to use his nuclear capabilities to *alter* the status quo'[85]).

The JIC papers were retained for several years after most of the other Suez-related files were declassified. They do not appear in the No. 10 archive as, by tradition, the PM's copies of JIC briefings are returned to the Cabinet Office with only the pristine master copies reaching the National Archives. So, unlike Eden's economic briefs from Macmillan for example, we do not have access to Eden's copies of JIC material and any comments he might have written on them. But the Cold War element in the Suez crisis must, I suspect, have fostered the belief that, in the end, Eisenhower and Dulles would not interpose the USA between an Anglo-French force and Egypt, however great Washington's distaste for the colonial/imperial impulses at work in London and Paris (the French were enraged by Nasser's vociferous support for the uprising in Algeria). After all, creating a barrier to Soviet expansionism in a line from the Bosphorus to the Himalayas really interested the President and his Secretary of State. And didn't Foster Dulles blow hot and cold about the desirability of a new regime in Cairo?

Eden appeared determined not to take at face value Eisenhower's frequent and consistent urgings that force should be ruled out as a means of solving the Canal crisis. As Cradock says, this 'lively correspondence' with the President should have left Eden with 'no illusions'.[86] Eisenhower, not always the most accomplished of penmen, was utterly plain in his letters to Eden. On 3 September, for example, he told him:

As to the use of force or the threat of force at this juncture, I continue to feel as I expressed myself in the letter Foster [Dulles] carried to you some weeks ago. Even now military preparations and civilian evacuation exposed to public view seem to be solidifying support for Nasser which has been shaky in many important quarters. I regard it as indispensable that if we are to proceed solidly together to the solution of this problem, public opinion in our several countries must be overwhelming in its support. I must tell you frankly that American public opinion flatly rejects the thought of using force, particularly when it does not seem that every possible peaceful means of protecting our vital interests has been exhausted without result.[87]

So much for Eden's claim to McCloy and Aldrich at Chequers exactly six months earlier that 'I never move a step without our American friends'.[88]

Eisenhower's 3 September letter contained an ominous little coda: 'Moreover, I gravely doubt we could here secure Congressional authority even for the lesser support measures for which you might have to look to us.'[89] Could this be a hint about the *non*-availability of help should the reserves flow out and the pound scrape along its lower limit with the dollar? Finance just might trump firepower in a malign twist to sterling–dollar diplomacy.

The UK Treasury was only too acutely aware of the linkage between the volatility of the Middle East and the fragility of the pound. On 8 August Sir Edward Bridges prepared for his boss, Harold Macmillan, a financial appraisal as prescient as the JIC's politico-military assessment which reached the Chancellor two days later. Bridges warned that if the London Conference of Maritime Nations, summoned to discuss how best to maintain Suez as an international waterway, broke down after failing to find a solution to the Canal problem, various sections of the Treasury's 'Sterling War Book' would 'need working out in detail': 'The trouble here is that the action to be taken is almost totally different according to the situation which we are faced with – a limited war, or a not so limited war – a war in which we go it alone, or a war in which we have the Americans with us from the outset.' Bridges went on to warn Macmillan that measures to protect sterling might be needed in the autumn even if Britain was not pursuing armed intervention in Egypt.[90]

Just before the nationalization, the UK's gold and dollar reserves stood at $2,373m.[91] One month into the crisis, thanks to international anxiety about the vulnerability of the UK economy if war came and oil supplies were disrupted, they had fallen by $68m to $2,305m.[92] On 7 September Bridges, just a few weeks from retirement and, absurdly, cut out from the circulation list of Egypt Committee minutes on Eden's instructions,[93] minuted Macmillan once more with the Treasury's collective view:

Very broadly it seems to us that unless we can secure at least United States support and a fairly unified Commonwealth, then it is not possible to predict either the exact timing or the magnitude of the strains which are likely to come upon our currency. At the worst, however, the strains might be so great that, whatever precautionary measures were taken, we should be unable to maintain the value of the currency . . .

On the other hand, if we do get overt United States support, and support from elsewhere, including the Commonwealth, our general feeling is that our action would be regarded by world opinion as something likely to strengthen sterling.[94]

Macmillan highlighted Bridges' concluding passage in the Chancellor's traditional red ink. His permanent secretary told him: 'What this points to . . . is the vital necessity from the point of view of our currency and our economy of ensuring that we do not go it alone, and that we have the maximum United States support.'[95]

Macmillan read this paper on 10 September, writing beneath Bridges' peroration, 'Yes. This is just the trouble. US are being very difficult.'[96] His diary entry for that day shows he had fully absorbed Bridges' anxieties:

The financial and economic outlook is very bad. The great problem remains – what will make the Americans willing to give us the maximum economic and financial aid? Will it be by conforming to their wishes or by 'going it alone'? It's a nice point . . . How I wish the Presidential election were safely over! [This was to take place on 6 November.][97]

Just over two weeks later he was in the Oval Office of his old wartime chum, President Eisenhower, and in a position to probe just this.

Extraordinarily, the issue of the hour scarcely featured in Macmillan's private diary. After basking in the fact that 'it was just like talking to him in the old days at St George's Hotel in Algiers, at Allied Force HQs', Macmillan merely noted of Eisenhower that 'On Suez he was sure that we must get Nasser down. The only thing was how to do it. I made it quite clear that we could not play it long, without aid on a very large scale – that is, if playing it long involved buying dollar oil.'[98]

As Roger Makins, another old Algiers hand, told Macmillan's biographer many years later, 'Yes, the Americans were willing to see Nasser put down, *but* what they would not contemplate were military operations – especially ahead of the [Presidential] election.'[99]*

Looking back, it is amazing that Suez did not completely dominate the Oval Office session, particularly as it was surrounded by a ring of confidentiality and 'special arrangements ... to elude the press' ('Roger Makins and I went in an ordinary car (not the Rolls) and we were taken to a little used and private entrance ...'[100]). Macmillan had not mentioned the possibility of devaluation to Eisenhower, though plainly Treasury briefings were on his mind. The department's chief rate-watcher and keeper of the 'Sterling War Book', Leslie Rowan, had sent a telegram to Macmillan on 21 September, opening in that slightly strange Socratic fashion favoured by some of the Treasury figures of those days:

Rowan asks: 'Will confidence return and sterling be strong even if Nasser falls?'

Rowan replies to himself: 'The answer is, unfortunately, almost certainly no.'

Rowan urged on Macmillan the importance of stressing two things to the Americans 'on economic as well as political grounds':

First the need to maintain the maximum flexibility in their thinking and acting on future aid programmes.

Second, the need – once the Suez problem is solved – to move on very quickly to *joint* action to deal with the Middle East generally and the Arab/Israel dispute in particular.[101]

Rowan did not spare Macmillan the implications of a failure to achieve US support: 'Unless something like this is done, both soon and successfully, sterling will be in the greatest danger and our other resources – IMF [International Monetary Fund drawing rights], dollar securities etc. – will not do much to put off the day.'

Macmillan wrote beneath this starkest of warnings: 'This is gloomy, but very likely correct.'[102]

---

* When Makins' note of the 25 September conversation in the White House was finally declassified in July 2006 it contained an especially intriguing paragraph, given the American use of economic pressure against the UK a few weeks later: 'Mr Macmillan referred to the economic strain on the United Kingdom which the loss of confidence caused by the Suez crisis had brought in its train. The President seemed aware of the nature of this problem, though not of its extent. He quite understood that we could not face the prospect of purchasing dollar oil or even of bringing oil round the Cape for any length of time.'

So it proved as the gold and dollar reserve figures sent across from the Treasury to No. 10 showed in cold print:

16 July 1956: $2,373m
27 August 1956: $2,305m
9 October 1956: $2,308m
29 October 1956: $2,251m
5 November 1956: $2,206m
20 November 1956: $2,066m
26 November 1956: $2,012m
11 December 1956: $1,897m
22 December 1956: $2,373m[103]

As the Task Force sailed from Malta to Port Said on 20 October and quickly found itself harassed by the US Sixth Fleet permanently based in the Mediterranean, which shone its searchlights upon the Anglo-French vessels and interfered with their radar,* the currency slide began.[104] The exchange rate moved from around $2.78½ on 29 October[105] 'to just over $2.78¼, virtually the lower limit' by 5 November, as Macmillan minuted Eden, adding, '[h]eavy support was necessary . . . There was speculation against sterling in Continental markets also.' The reserves had fallen by '$38m over the first three days of November'.[106] As the list above shows, they continued to fall until the Cabinet had agreed to pull British troops out of Suez altogether and the US authorities unblocked Britain's IMF drawing rights ($311m arriving in mid-December from that source[107]) and ceased to stand aside watching the money markets hammer the pound. This is to jump way ahead for the purposes of illustrating that of all the Treasury's gloomiest warnings in August/September (with the exception of a devaluation) had come to pass by 11 December with the reserves at $1,897m and the pound still scraping the bottom of the exchange-rate barrel.[108]

In international affairs, there was no indicator for the limit of legality, let alone probity or morality, as there was for the currency, apart from resolutions of the United Nations Security Council which came darkly critical and fast as the Suez crisis peaked. But the legal question lurked from the outset.[109] From the very first Cabinet meeting after the nationalization, ministers knew the legal case for using force was built on quicksand:

* This, Alec Home told me when the files were declassified, 'really turned the scale . . . for all the world to see . . . announcing in effect that America was totally against us'. See p. 450.

426

The Cabinet agreed that we should be on weak ground in basing our resistance on the narrow argument that Colonel Nasser had acted illegally. The Suez Canal Company was registered as an Egyptian company under Egyptian law; and Colonel Nasser had indicated that he intended to compensate the shareholders at ruling market prices. From a narrow legal point of view, his action amounted to no more than a decision to buy out the shareholders. Our case must be presented on wider international grounds.[110]

However, Lord Kilmuir (the former Home Secretary, Sir David Maxwell Fyfe), now Lord Chancellor, argued throughout the crisis that there *was* a legal basis for retaking the Canal by force, if all else failed, under Article 51, the self-defence clause, of the United Nations Charter. As he put in his memoirs:

From the first I thought it was wrong in international law to end unilaterally and by threat of force the international control of an international waterway. The Suez Canal Company had been treated as an international entity and was the basis of the international control. I further took the view that to destroy this basis and end international control by force was forcible aggression against territory marked with an international character, which, if the other procedures of the charter produced no result, could be decided by force under Article 51 of the Charter of the United Nations.[111]

Kilmuir's view would have sounded a joyous note in the Prime Minister's ears. But it was supported by only one serious authority on international law, Professor Arthur Goodhart of Oxford University.[112]

More importantly, it was *not* supported by the government's two law officers or by the top international lawyers in the Foreign Office. Sir Gerald Fitzmaurice, its Chief Legal Adviser, expressed his doubts internally within Whitehall from beginning to end.[113] For example, as early as 1 August he had written to the Attorney General, Sir Reginald Manningham-Buller, that the

fundamental legal difficulty in the Suez Canal case is that although the Egyptian Government are committing a number of illegalities, none of them amount, at any rate at present, to a direct breach of the Suez Canal Convention [the Convention of Constantinople, 1888, which stipulated that the Suez Canal 'shall always be free and open, in time of wars as in time of peace, to every vessel of commerce and of war, without distinction of flag'[114]], and therefore they do not help us on the central issue on which we are seeking to base ourselves.[115]

However, Fitzmaurice laboured under a severe handicap whenever he tried to fulfil the Crown servant's primary duty of speaking truth unto power at the very highest level during the Suez crisis: Eden would not listen to him.

At a crucial moment when the prospect of a secret deal with Israel as well as France was in the early stages of discussion in mid-October, Anthony Nutting suggested to the Prime Minister that Fitzmaurice be brought into the tiny circle of those in the know. 'Fitz is the last person I want consulted,' replied Eden. 'The lawyers are always against our doing anything. For God's sake, keep him out of it. This is a political affair.'[116] Indeed, Eden put the secret collusive arrangement with France and Israel on an even more lofty plane once the deal was in the bag, describing it to his Chief Whip, Ted Heath, whom he indoctrinated into its details, as 'the highest form of statesmanship'.[117] Neither Fitzmaurice, Manningham-Buller nor the equally dissenting Solicitor General, Sir Harry Hylton-Foster, was so indoctrinated.

Eden probably did not fully appreciate the doubts of his two law officers, or the degree to which they disagreed with Kilmuir, until the peak of the crisis. Unlike the Lord Chancellor (who is not a law officer), the Attorney General and Solicitor General are not regular attenders at Cabinet meetings. What triggered Manningham-Buller's direct approach to Eden was the telegram sent by the Foreign Office to the British Ambassador in Jordan and all other diplomatic missions across the Middle East the day after Israeli forces moved towards the Canal and as the British and French governments, in accordance with a secret deal, called on both Israel and Egypt to withdraw their forces ten miles either side of the Canal on pain of British and French intervention. The telegram that worried Manningham-Buller read as follows:

The policy of Her Majesty's Government is to take the most decisive steps open to them to bring hostilities to an early end. They are advised on the highest legal authority that they are entitled under the Charter [of the United Nations] to take every measure open to them within and without the United Nations to stop the fighting and to protect their nationals and interests which are threatened by these hostilities.[118]

This was the pure milk of the Kilmuir/Goodhart line.

Manningham-Buller would have none of it. After consulting Hylton-Foster he wrote, on behalf of both of them, to the Foreign Secretary (with copies to the Prime Minister) on 1 November (as the RAF continued bombing Egyptian airfields). Referring to the Amman telegram, he said:

It may be that the advice given is distracted by the need to impact it into a telegram but I feel under a duty to make it plain that I do not agree with the advice Her Majesty's Government have been given if the telegram records that advice accurately.

It is just not true to say that we are entitled under the Charter to take any measures open to us 'to stop the fighting'. Nor would it be true to say that under international law apart from the Charter we are entitled to do so. Further, it is not true to say that under international law we are entitled to take any measures open to us 'to protect our interests which are threatened by hostilities'.[119]

In a passage amazing today (when the Attorney General is a constant adviser on the legality and proportionality of the use of force on British interventions great and small), Manningham-Buller told the Prime Minister, the Foreign Secretary and the Lord Chancellor that he felt

compelled to write this letter because as the Law Officers are constitutionally the legal advisers of the Government ... it will be generally assumed that we have been approached for advice as to the legality of what has been done. In fact we were not consulted on this matter nor were we upon questions relating to the Suez Canal before Israel's attack. I feel it is essential that I should make my views clear. I had no opportunity of doing so before the ultimatum was delivered.[120]

The previous day Fitzmaurice had minuted the ever hawkish Kirkpatrick, on behalf of himself and his number two in the Foreign Office's Legal Department, Francis Vallat, saying:

Mr Vallat and I have discussed the present Anglo-French action in regard to Egypt from the legal point of view, as to which we were neither of us consulted.

The decision seems to have been a political one, but whatever justification it may possess on that basis, we feel bound to place it formally on record that we can see no legal justification for it, on the facts so far as they are known to us, and as they stand at present.[121]

Fitzmaurice and Vallat, like Manningham-Buller and Hylton-Foster a day later, disassociated themselves from the legal opinion on which the Amman telegram rested and which, Fitzmaurice said, seemed not to have come from the law officers, 'who constitutionally have the ultimate, and sole ultimate responsibility as legal advisers to the Crown and hence to the government of the day'.[122]

Nasser and the Egyptian government had, in Fitzmaurice's eyes, carefully avoided taking any actions subsequent to the nationalization that could provide a legal justification for the use of force by Britain and France. As early as 10 August he had minuted one of the Foreign Office's leading Middle Eastern hands, Harold Beeley, its Under-Secretary for Middle East Affairs, that the UK was already on an extremely bad wicket legally as regards using force in connexion with the Suez Canal. Indeed, whatever illegalities the Egyptians may have committed in nationalising the Suez Canal Company, these do not in any way, as things stand at present, justify forcible action on our part, and such a justification could only arise, if at all, from some further and much more drastic step on the part of the Egyptian Government amounting to a closure of the Canal, or at any rate a definite refusal or impeding of passage through it.[123]

Beeley was another of those officials Eden wished excluded from both the full-knowledge and advice circles. As Sir Anthony Nutting told me many years later, the Prime Minister 'knew that the more Foreign Office voices I consulted, the more horror would be exclaimed against going ahead with this conspiracy'.[124] As that 'conspiracy' was being put to Eden at Chequers on 14 October by a pair of French emissaries – Major-General Maurice Challe, Deputy Chief of the French General Staff, and Albert Gazier, the Minister for Social Affairs – Beeley was with the Foreign Secretary, Selwyn Lloyd, at the UN in New York, where Lloyd was in discussion with his Egyptian opposite number, Mahmoud Fawzi, and inching towards a negotiated settlement of the Canal crisis. Eden summoned them back to Whitehall before a deal could be reached.[125]

Beeley 'thought it was foolish not to allow any of the people who were dealing with the Middle East, who had been following events in the Middle East in the [Foreign] Office, to become involved in the preparations for a policy of this kind'.[126] Lunching with Shuckburgh on 1 November with the war underway, Beeley told Shuckburgh 'that the FO, with one exception (Kirkpatrick) are equally depressed and astonished'.[127] The following day a round-robin, drafted by Paul Gore-Booth (a future Head of the Diplomatic Service) and supported by Beeley amongst other senior diplomats, was presented to Kirkpatrick conveying 'the sense of dismay caused throughout our ranks' by the government's action: 'People are doing their duty but with a heavy heart and a feeling that, whatever our motives, we have terribly damaged our reputation.'[128]

Quite apart from the morality or legality of the Anglo-French attack on Egypt, Beeley (who was Ambassador to Cairo 1961–4 and 1967–9) remained convinced for the rest of his life that 'it was crazy. For one thing, one question that didn't seem to have been asked was what we were going to do in Egypt after we'd occupied the Canal. As far as I'm aware [Sir Harold was speaking shortly after the bulk of the Suez-related British documents were declassified

33. Clem's last throw: Attlee and busmen in Walthamstow on polling day,
25 April 1955.

34. On the road to victory: Anthony and Clarissa Eden in Leeds, 14 April 1955.

35. Hands across the Middle East: Eden and Nasser meet at the British Embassy in Cairo, 20 February 1955.

36. 'All my life I've been a man of peace': Eden broadcasts on the Suez crisis.

37. 'The one overriding lesson of the SUEZ operations is that world opinion
is now an absolute principle of war ...': General Sir Charles Keightley,
Commander-in-Chief, Anglo-French Forces aboard HMS *Tyne* off Port Said,
November 1956.

38. A canal too far: halted at El Cap, British paratroops adopt a camel and call it 'Nasser', naturally.

39. Scotland the wary: soldiers of the Royal Scots patrol the streets of Port Said, November 1956.

40. The Edens leave for Jamaica and Ian Fleming's retreat, Goldeneye, 23 November 1956: 'Returned to find everyone looking at us with thoughtful eyes,' wrote Lady Eden.

41. Harold Macmillan assumes the premiership, 10 January 1957, after contriving the impression that Suez 'had been a kind of victory, and that nothing much had happened'.

42. Britain goes thermonuclear: mushroom cloud generated by 'Grapple X', the first genuine UK-made H-bomb, off Christmas Island, 8 November 1957.

43. The great white ghosts of deterrence: Vulcan bombers in Lincolnshire.

44. Those who wanted them disarmed: CND arrives at Aldermaston after the first Easter March from Trafalgar Square, 7 April 1958.

45. The 'Soviet Threat' comes to London under wraps: Nikolai Bulganin and Nikita
Krushchev at the Cenotaph, Whitehall, 21 April 1956.

in 1987], to this day there is no evidence that the sequence of events after the immediate attack on the Canal had been properly thought out.'[129]*

This deeply worried Eden's principal military advisers, too. The Chiefs of Staff were split on Suez. Even before the crisis erupted, they had shown themselves to be a particularly fractious set as chiefs went. In an intriguing diary entry after he had been to brief them 'about Israel' and 'the impossibility of going to war with the Arabs if they aggress' in early March 1956 (as the Glubb crisis swirled around), Evelyn Shuckburgh wrote:

Mountbatten [First Sea Lord] and the new CAS [Sir Dermot Boyle, Chief of the Air Staff] pressed me to produce a statement showing 'our policy in the ME [Middle East]' which they both professed to think must be stateable. Templer [Chief of the Imperial General Staff] and Dixon [sic: Marshal of the Royal Air Force Sir William Dickson, Chairman of the Chiefs of Staff Committee] were more realistic . . .

The Chiefs are not a very effective body at present. Dixon has an ulcer and talks too much, Mountbatten is full of undigested bright ideas and is really a simpleton though very nice. They all argue with one another.[130]

The Secretary of the Chiefs of Staff Committee, Sir David Lee, put it very delicately to me over thirty years later when we discussed the minutes he had taken during the toing and froing of the planning for Operation Musketeer (to attack via Alexandria); and later, Musketeer Revise (to go for the Canal directly):

Lord Mountbatten was the strongest opponent of the operation, but I think the other Chiefs of Staff, if not quite so vociferous about it, were very anxious that it was an operation which might lead us into very considerable difficulties, and, for example, get us bogged down again in Egypt, a country which we'd only left six months beforehand. We had a number of what I can only describe as conflicting treaties. So really we were the meat in the sandwich . . .[131]

The meat-in-the-sandwich problem presented itself starkly in mid-October (as Eden was pondering the French temptation of the secret three-way deal with Israel to attack Egypt) when Israeli raids into Jordan raised a genuine fear

---

* Though, to his credit, Macmillan had tried to get Eden to think about it at the end of August. In a personal minute on the 24th he suggested summoning 'a conference within a very few weeks' to consider post-conflict proposals of 'a creative character'. Britain must not appear colonialist, he said, delving, uncharacteristically, into history for his comparison: 'We must not be like Louis 18th returning [to France] in 1815 to a dull restoration, but rather like Napoleon breaking through the Alps towards the unification of Italy.'

that Britain might find herself allied to Egypt in a war *against* Israel. The Royal Air Force was warned that it might have to execute Operation Cordage[132] at short notice and destroy the Israeli air force on the ground.[133]

Alec Home, wrestling with all these problems as a member of Eden's Egypt Committee, recalled the nightmarishly complicated skein of alarming possibilities when I took the newly declassified Suez documents to him at the Hirsel, his home in the Scottish Borders, in January 1987: 'We had a treaty with Jordan which legally bound us to support Jordan if Jordan was attacked. Israel was getting very restive and the chances were that she would attack Jordan, the weakest of the Arab countries, and if she had done that we would have found ourselves fighting with Jordan against Israel, and a lot of Arab countries would come in on the side of Jordan, including Egypt. One couldn't conceivably imagine a worse scenario.'[134] The Chiefs loathed such complications and pointed out to ministers 'that they could not operate Cordage at the same time as Musketeer (Revise). But Cordage remained operational and until very late in the day some Musketeer commanders remained under the impression that they were under its direction.'[135]

Of the Chiefs, Templer was the hawk, Mountbatten the dove, as Dermot Boyle recalled for me when he re-read the old Chiefs of Staff Committee minutes for 1956 in early 1987:

He was always really doubtful. Now it's understandable, I think, that Mountbatten was in a slightly different category. He could regard himself as an elder statesman, and he'd been Viceroy of India and all that. But on the other hand Gerald Templer had done that wonderful job in Malaya, and therefore I took a lot of encouragement from his attitude, which was 'Dermot, this is a military business, don't let your mind be wasted on swanning around what might or might not be the political implications.'[136]

But it was not as simple as that; the political could not be separated from the military – and all the Chiefs of Staff knew this in the late summer and autumn of 1956.

As late as 24 October, the Chiefs' own Joint Planning Staff presented them with a paper on the 'Military Implications of Mounting Operation Musketeer'. In it, the planners established 'HM Government's Political Aims' as '(a) The securing of international administration and control of the Suez Canal, (b) The establishment of the authority of a co-operative Egyptian government throughout the country including the Canal Zone . . .'[137] In a silent but merciless comment on the failure of Eden and his Egypt Committee to think Suez through, the planners went to the heart of the 'what then?' problem as 'Musketeer plans do not extend beyond the occupation of the Canal Area. No consideration has yet been given to the military commitments which might arise after this phase.'[138]

The planners' job, as was made evident from a subsequent military inquest into Suez, was made even harder by the lack of political intelligence coming out of Egypt, making 'the assessment of Egyptian intentions very much more difficult during this operation'.[139] In the absence of any guidance from Eden and his ministers, the chiefs' planners attempted to fill this extraordinary gap, describing under four headings the huge task that would face a post-attack British Army of Occupation in Egypt whose job would be:

(a) To maintain the security of the Canal area against considerable guerrilla activity and labour unrest.

(b) To occupy Cairo in order to depose a hostile Government and to render possible the immediate installation of an acceptable successor, with possible commitment of maintaining it in power indefinitely.

(c) To assist in the rehabilitation of Egypt.

(d) To assist the Egyptian Government in the administration of the country.[140]

Yet another group of Crown servants, in uniform this time, found their analyses ignored by those to whom they were politically subordinate. Combine the JIC's warnings with the Treasury's, the legal doubts, those of Whitehall's Arab experts and the guardians of the 'special relationship' with the USA such as Makins, and the only conclusion possible is that by late October 1956 nothing could deflect Eden from his determination to topple Nasser. Whitehall had never experienced anything quite so bizarre.

It was to become even more so. On 24 October, the very day the joint planners presented the Chiefs with that hugely worrying assessment of the tasks awaiting the British Armed Forces in Egypt once Musketeer was over, what international historian Avi Shlaim called 'the most famous war plot in modern history'[141] was concluded in an old French Resistance 'safe house' in the Paris suburbs as representatives of the British, French and Israeli governments put their initials to what became known as the Sèvres Protocol. Eden had succumbed to the temptation of an apparent master stroke that would secretly and efficiently cut through every political, military and diplomatic thicket that had grown around him since the night of 26 July.

In the last of his undestroyed diary entries for Suez, Macmillan (who, recall from Chapter 8, had been intrigued by the possibility of an Israeli strike against

Egypt since the SIS Station Chief in Paris had briefed him the previous November) wrote on 4 October:

The Suez situation is beginning to slip out of our hands. Nothing can now be done till the UN exercise is over. By then the difficulty of 'resort to force' will be greater. I try not to think that we have 'missed the bus' – if we have, it is really due to the long time it has taken to get military arrangements into shape. But we must, by one means or another, win this struggle. Nasser may well try to preach Holy War in the Middle East and (even to their own loss) the mob and the demagogues may create a ruinous position for us. *Without oil and without the profits from oil*, neither UK nor western Europe can survive.[142]

Ten days later M. Gazier and Major-General Challe carried a message from their Prime Minister, Guy Mollet, to Eden at Chequers offering, in Macmillan's word, 'another' means of resolving the crisis.

The French emissaries asked what Britain would do if Israel attacked Egypt. After some discussion about treaty obligations to keep Middle Eastern borders as they were, Eden admitted he could not bring himself to fight to keep Nasser in power. General Challe then presented an outline plan which, as summarized by Keith Kyle, described Israel's ability to occupy swiftly all the Sinai right up to the Suez Canal. Britain and France would then demand that both sides withdraw from its banks to prevent damage. Anglo-French forces should then enter as policemen 'to separate the combatants',[143] while occupying the full length of the Canal from Port Said to Suez.

Eden was non-committal. He said he would think about it and travel to Paris to talk to Mollet. But, in effect, the Prime Minister had fallen for it. Guy Millard, his foreign affairs private secretary, who was present at the fateful Chequers lunch on 14 October, told me over thirty years later:

Eden was intrigued. I think he was clutching at a straw in a sense; he was looking for a pretext. The problem was that the operation, which had been planned for a long time, had either to go ahead or be scrapped altogether. The reservists had been called up, the shipping had been mobilized and so on. You couldn't disperse all that without abandoning the whole idea of the use of force. Therefore ... this plan, originally worked out by the French with the Israelis, came at a convenient moment and he saw it as a handy pretext.[144]

It does not seem to have occurred to the sick, anxious man veering towards the desperate that such a thinly disguised deception would easily be unmasked, however determined the denials.

Those who were soon to be in the know and who were *not* sick and verging on the desperate should have confronted Eden with reality. The Foreign Secretary, Selwyn Lloyd, as he told his fellow conspirators in Sèvres on 22 October, thought he was a week away from a negotiated settlement at the UN when Eden summoned him home from New York as the Gazier/Challe plan tempted him more and more.[145] His private secretary, Donald Logan, who travelled back from the UN with Lloyd and later accompanied him to Sèvres, was in no doubt of his boss's attitude to Eden's 'highest form of statesmanship':

I don't think he ever liked it from the start. It was not in his nature to be the sort of person in charge of this kind of operation. He had been Minister of Defence, it's true, and indeed in his youth he enjoyed playing with toy soldiers, he was a great reworker of military campaigns; but he was not the kind of person you would ever describe as belligerent.[146]

But Lloyd was incapable of standing up to his Prime Minister, especially when Eden had a bee in his bonnet. Harold Beeley, who came back from the UN talks with him but, unlike Logan, was not privy to the collusion discussions, told me, 'Selwyn Lloyd was a modest man and was not very confident in his own judgement ... Eden, of course, had a great reputation as an expert in foreign policy and I think Selwyn felt that he ought not to challenge Eden's judgement.'[147]

Lloyd was very much his master's instrument at the first Sèvres meeting on 22 October. He could not attend the second one on the 24th so Eden sent Patrick Dean, Deputy Secretary for Defence and Intelligence in the Foreign Office and Chairman of the Joint Intelligence Committee. It is his initials that represent the UK on the notorious document of that date.* What does it say? This was to be the order of events:

1. The Israeli forces launch in the evening of 29 October 1956 a large-scale attack on the Egyptian forces with the aim of reaching the Canal Zone the following day.
2. On being apprised of these events, the British and French Governments during the day of 30 October respectively and simultaneously make two appeals to the Egyptian Government and the Israeli Government on the following lines:

A. *To the Egyptian Government*
   (a) halt all acts of war
   (b) withdraw all its troops ten miles from the Canal

---

* Eden ordered the British copy to be burnt but posterity was not fooled; a photostat of the Israeli copy now resides in the British National Archive under reference NA, PRO 22/88, 'The Sèvres Protocol'.

(c) accept temporary occupation of key positions on the Canal by the Anglo-
French forces to guarantee freedom of passage to the vessels of all nations
until a final settlement.

B. *To the Israeli Government*

(a) halt all acts of war

(b) withdraw all its troops ten miles to the east of the Canal.

In addition, the Israeli Government will be notified that the French and British
Government[s] have demanded of the Egyptian Government to accept temporary
occupation of key positions along the Canal by Anglo-French forces.

It is agreed that if one of the Governments refused, or did not give its consent, within twelve hours the Anglo-French forces would intervene with the
means necessary to ensure that their demands are met.

C. The representatives of the three governments agree that the Israeli Government
will not be required to meet the conditions in the appeal addressed to it, in the
event the Egyptian Government does not accept those in the appeal addressed
to it for their part.

3. In the event that the Egyptian Government should fail to agree within the stipulated
time to the conditions of the appeal addressed to it, the Anglo-French forces will
launch military operations against the Egyptian forces in the early hours of the morning of 31 October.

[...]

6. The arrangements of the present protocol must remain strictly secret.

7. They will enter into force after the agreement of the three governments.[148]

How many people in Whitehall were privy to this at the time? When Eden
divulged its contents to Ted Heath on 25 October he told him that only he,
Lloyd, Macmillan and Butler 'were to know about it'.[149] Percy Cradock's tally
of ministers also included Salisbury, Anthony Head (who had succeeded the
doubting Walter Monckton as Minister of Defence) and Nutting,[150] who
resigned over it, though he refrained from blowing the full story until his
memoir, *No End of a Lesson*, appeared in 1967.[151]*

The political scars of Suez went – and remained – very deep. So, I suspect,
did *mens rea* (guilty knowledge) of quite a high degree on the part of those

---

* At which time the Cabinet Secretary, Sir Burke Trend, tried to persuade him not to, as did the by
then retired Harold Macmillan ('Dear boy . . . you are revered as a man of honour and you should
remember the damage this will do to the Party . . . ').

other Cabinet ministers who, it seemed, had not heard a whisper about the Sèvres collusion. For only when the confidential annex for the Cabinet meeting of 23 October was available for researchers in January 1987 could the British public (or that part of it still curious about Suez) know just how much the Cabinet as a whole knew of the hidden deal behind the final assault on Egypt. This was the key passage:

THE PRIME MINISTER recalled that, when the Cabinet had last discussed the Suez situation on 18th October, there had been reason to believe that the issue might be brought rapidly to a head as a result of military action by Israel against Egypt. From secret conversations which had been held in Paris with representatives of the Israeli Government, it now appeared that the Israelis would not alone launch a full-scale attack against Egypt.

The United Kingdom and French Governments were thus confronted with the choice between an early military operation or a relatively prolonged negotiation. If the second course were followed, neither we nor the French could hope to maintain our military preparations in their present state of readiness – on our side some of the reservists would have to be released, some of the requisitioned merchant ships would have to be released for commercial trading and others would have to be re-loaded – and our position of negotiating from strength would to some extent be impaired.[152]

The moment my BBC radio producer, Mark Laity, found that confidential annex during the press preview of the Suez papers at the Public Record Office, it struck the both of us as the 'smoking minute'.[153] For you did not need a background at GCHQ to decode the significance of Eden's words about 'secret conversations' in Paris 'with representatives of the Israeli Government'.

Robert Rhodes James, Eden's first official biographer, told his second, Richard Thorpe, 'that this was the single most important fact he had discovered in his researches into Eden's career'.[154] Of equal importance, in my view, is the Cabinet's collective failure in No. 10 between 11.00 a.m. and noon on that morning of Tuesday 23 October 1956 to press Eden on those 'secret conversations' and the pros and cons of an imminent military operation or a longer negotiation. Norman Brook's minute shows that they did not. This ranks as one of the single greatest failures of Cabinet government in the postwar years, not equalled until 2002–3 when the Blair Cabinet discussed the proposal to invade Iraq on the basis of what the Butler inquiry plainly saw as insufficient information and inadequate critical curiosity.[155]

At their meeting on 23 October Eden warned his Cabinet ministers that they would have to take 'grave decisions ... in the course of the next few days'.[156] Two days later, after informing his colleagues that the Israelis were 'after all, advancing their military preparations with a view to making an attack on Egypt', he warned them of the 'risk that we should be accused of collusion with Israel'.[157] What, in fact, Eden did over subsequent full Cabinet meetings was to secure ministers' approval for all the key elements in the Sèvres Protocol without disclosing that each decision was part of a single, agreed, three-way war plan.[158]

The intense secrecy surrounding the Sèvres Protocol compounded all the existing problems of who knew what and widened the yawning gap where planning for post-attack Egypt should have been. As Sir Frank Cooper, head of the Air Ministry's Air Secretariat at the time and very close to Sir Dermot Boyle, Chief of the Air Staff, told the RAF Historical Society over thirty years later, 'There were several Air Ministries at work depending on levels of knowledge.'[159] Later still he told a group of my MA students that 'the shame of Suez was in the way it was handled by people like Eden and Selwyn Lloyd and the French, who did it in such a hole-in-the-corner way'.[160]

Even some of the key commanders of the operation did not know that the Israelis were to attack Egypt at all, let alone first. Air Chief Marshal Sir Denis Barnett, the air commander, described how he accidentally discovered the plot when the Commander-in-Chief of the Anglo-French force, Sir Charles Keightley, briefly left his office:

As he went out the door opened, a gust of air came in and it unsettled a piece of paper that was on his desk in front of him and planted it absolutely straight between my feet, so that as I picked it up I couldn't help – although it was not my business, it might have been private – I couldn't help seeing what it said. In his own handwriting were a couple of notes that I couldn't help noticing. One was 'Israeli D-Day is such and such, our D-Day is such and such'. I couldn't believe that it could be so. I didn't think we would behave like that. I was appalled that political entanglement of that sort could lie at the root of this operation that we were trying to do.[161]

The French were much less discreet and it was galling for some senior British officers to learn of the collusion from their opposite numbers in Paris.

General Sir Kenneth Darling was Chief of Staff to the Army task-force commander, Sir Hugh Stockwell. Two days after the Sèvres Protocol had been initialled, they stopped off en route to Malta from London at Villacoubley airfield near Paris on a routine visit to enable Stockwell to consult his French number two in the combined operation, General Beaufre. As Sir Kenneth recalled,

The scene was really almost like a James Bond sort of set up. There were two or three rather dilapidated wartime huts, I think there were one or two odd gendarmes standing about, sucking their teeth, and General Stockwell was then taken by the arm by General Beaufre into one of these huts. Meanwhile I and the other officers of General Stock-well's staff sort of hung about kicking our heels.

Eventually he came out of the hut and took me to one side and told me what he had learnt from General Beaufre, which was, in a nutshell, that it was likely that the Israelis were going to attack Egypt and that we would undoubtedly get involved. And it was, therefore, quite obvious that we'd been living in a kind of fool's paradise up to this particular moment.[162]

Most in Whitehall still were.

It is, as Sir Percy Cradock noted, 'even uncertain how much the Chiefs of Staff knew', though there was 'a considerable degree of knowledge implicit in their comments at the chiefs of staff meeting on 1 November, though it is doubtful, even here, whether they had been introduced into the full mysteries of Sèvres'.[163] The minute to which Sir Percy referred recorded that: 'It was agreed that General Keightley would find it necessary to ensure that there was no tactical conflict with the Israelis. Any contact with the Israelis should be conducted by covert means. Pending further instructions, Israel would not be treated as an ally . . . It was essential that co-ordination of operations with the Israelis or the appearance of it should be avoided.'[164]

What *is* known is that one of the Chiefs, Lord Mountbatten, could take no more. On 2 November he wrote to Eden, declaring his 'great unhappiness about the prospect of launching military operations against Egypt' and offering his resignation. He was ordered to stay at his post by the First Lord of the Admiralty, Lord Hailsham.[165]

It is very likely that Mountbatten conveyed his doubts about Suez to the Queen,[166] who was similarly sceptical. One of her private secretaries, Lord Charteris, told me in 1994 that 'Suez was a matter which gave the Queen a great deal of concern . . . I think that the basic dishonesty of the whole thing was a trouble. She was also alarmed, once the war was underway, of its effect on both Commonwealth and American opinion.'[167] But, in their private audi-ences, Eden recalled, 'the Queen never protested strongly or otherwise to me about Suez'.[168] No minutes are kept of these occasions; indeed, no one else is present. And the Queen neither gives interviews nor gossips. It is perfectly possible, indeed highly likely, that she would not have voiced her doubts to her Prime Minister unless he had specifically requested her opinion. She has the right to be informed and her document flow included sensitive intelligence material during the Suez operation,[169] but it is highly unlikely that the Sèvres Protocol was among it.

Eden's 'risk that we should be accused of collusion with Israel' was more like a racing certainty. Shuckburgh had been until very recently an insider, but, as he noted in his diary on 1 November, there was a very public indication of a prior secret arrangement:

It looks more and more as if there has been collusion with the Israelis, for we have not said anything about the need for them to return behind their frontiers. I wrote Kirkpatrick a note yesterday afternoon suggesting that we ought to do this, if only to put ourselves alright with the other Arabs, and to give some verisimilitude to our story that we have gone in to 'separate the contestants and safeguard the Canal'. But it begins to look as if we have moved over to a policy of using Israel. Mountbatten (First Sea Lord) came to lecture this morning, and could not conceal from us the fact that he, too, profoundly disapproves of the policy. He said he had spoken against it up to the limit of what is possible, and was surprised that he was still in his job. This added greatly to our gloom . . .[170]

Needless to say, if Shuckburgh could work out the secrets of the collusion sitting in the Imperial Defence College in Belgravia, so could President Eisenhower sitting enraged in the White House. On 30 October Eden sent Eisenhower what he described as a 'hurried message to let you know how we regard the Israel–Egypt conflict . . . As you know [section deleted because, no doubt, it referred to intelligence sources, which is why the message's declassification was delayed until June 2006], the Russians regarded the [UN] Security Council proceedings as a victory for themselves and Egypt. Nevertheless we continued through the Secretary-General of the United Nations to seek a basis for the continuation of the negotiations. Now this has happened.' How Eisenhower must have been infuriated by Eden feigning surprise.

Eden went on: 'When we received news of the Israel mobilisation we instructed our Ambassador in Tel Aviv to urge restraint . . . Egypt has to a large extent brought this attack on herself by insisting that a state of war persists, by defying the Security Council and by declaring her intention to marshal the Arab States for the destruction of Israel.'[171]

Eisenhower's constant warnings against the use of force had been pointedly ignored. As the RAF began bombing Egyptian airfields and communications facilities and Britain and France used their vetoes to stymie a US resolution in the UN Security Council calling for a cease-fire and an Israeli withdrawal, he fired off one of the most extraordinary telegrams ever sent by a US President to a UK Prime Minister. Cold anger suffused every paragraph:

Dear Anthony

I address you in this note not only as Head of Her Majesty's Government but as my long-time friend who has, with me, believed in and worked for real Anglo-American understanding.

... Without bothering here to discuss the military movements themselves and their possible grave consequences, I should like to ask for help in clearing up my understanding as to exactly what is happening between us and our European allies – especially between us, the French and yourselves.[172]

Without alluding directly to it, Eisenhower at this point begins to make use of the US intelligence product:

We have learned that the French had provided Israel with a considerable amount of equipment, including airplanes, in excess of the amounts of which we were officially informed. This action was, as you know, in violation of the agreements now existing between our three countries [including the 1950 Tripartite Pact]. We know also that this process has continued in other items of equipment.

Quite naturally we began watching with increased interest the affairs in the Eastern Mediterranean. Late last week we became convinced that the Israeli mobilization was proceeding to a point where something more than mere defence was contemplated, and found the situation serious enough to send a precautionary note to Ben Gurion [the Prime Minister of Israel who had attended the Sèvres talks in person]. On Sunday we repeated this note of caution and made a public statement of our actions; informing both you and the French of our concern. On that day we discovered that the volume of communication traffic between Paris and Tel Aviv jumped enormously; alerting us to the probability that France and Israel were concerting detailed plans of some kind.[173]

Eisenhower then turned to what the outwardly implacable but deeply unhappy British Ambassador to the United Nations, Sir Pierson Dixon (who nearly resigned over Suez[174]) had said under instruction from Whitehall:

Last evening our Ambassador to the United Nations [Henry Cabot Lodge] met with your Ambassador, Pierson Dixon, to request him to join us in presenting the case to the United Nations this morning. We were astonished to find that he was completely unsympathetic, stating frankly that his Government would not agree to any action whatsoever to be taken against Israel. He further argued that the Tripartite Statement of May 1950 was ancient history and without current validity.[175]

Eisenhower's anger was fuelled by his fear that the Anglo-French-Israeli action would set alight not just a Middle East conflagration but perhaps even an East–West confrontation:

All of this development, with its possible consequences, including the possible involvement of you and the French in a general Arab war, seems to me to leave your Government and ours in a very sad state of confusion, so far as any possibility of unified understanding and action are concerned. It is true that Egypt has not yet formally asked this Government for aid but the fact is that if the United Nations finds Israel to be an aggressor, Egypt could very well ask the Soviets for help – and then the Middle East fat would really be in the fire. It is this latter possibility that has led us to insist that the West must ask for a United Nations examination and possible intervention, for we may shortly find ourselves not only at odds concerning what we should do, but confronted with a *de facto* situation that would make all our present troubles look puny indeed.[176]

A key element of Eden's strategy had failed utterly. Instead of the Cold War factor overriding US doubts about the attack on Nasser as the Soviets' chosen instrument of penetration through the Middle East and into Africa, the fear of hot war had led Eisenhower to insist that nothing be done by the British, the French and the Israelis that might increase the chances of it. So far from falling into line at the last moment, Eisenhower was to interpose the political might of the USA and, if possible, the UN between invaders and invaded in the eastern Mediterranean. He had not been fooled for one second by the Anglo-French cover story of separating the combatants.

What of Eden's early-warning system for alerting him to Soviet moves that could lead to an East–West war? The Joint Intelligence Committee was poorly placed in late October 1956 because it was not officially privy to all the government's plans and intentions. Its chairman, Pat Dean, for example, knew of the collusion as he had been Eden's emissary to the second Sèvres meeting and, as Percy Cradock points out, initialling the protocol 'must have left him with a clear enough view of the toils in which his leaders had enmeshed themselves, a degree of information he would have rigorously to exclude from any subsequent JIC discussions. It must have been a very awkward position, typical of the fragmented government of the time.'[177]

Like Shuckburgh, several among the JIC membership would have pieced together the collusion story for themselves and the heads of SIS and GCHQ (both regular members of the committee) must have known a good deal about the secret communications channels in use between the three conspirators. But the JIC assessments *do* contain some surprising sections. For example, in the paper of 4 October, which was prepared nearly three weeks before the collusion but well into the period of repeated warnings from Washington, and was addressed to 'Possible Soviet Assistance to Egypt's Military Effort in Certain Circumstances', the JIC drafters had originally written as an 'assumption' that, in the first stage of Musketeer, 'the United States will give her moral support to the operation'. This was altered by hand to 'the United States will adopt a strictly neutral attitude towards the operation'.[178] The paper was for 'Limited Circulation UK Eyes Only'.[179]

The JIC's conclusion, in essence, was that an Anglo-French invasion of Egypt would not trigger a Third World War, although the Soviet bloc

will seek to help Egypt as much as possible in order to demonstrate to the uncommitted countries of the world its dependability as an ally, to embarrass the British and the French, to support Egypt's morale, and to prolong hostilities. The Soviet bloc will probably be willing to accept considerable risks in doing this, but will stop short of anything which is likely to lead to a clash with United States forces . . .

Replacement operational aircraft might be flown in with Soviet or Satellite volunteer crews, despite the Soviet bloc leaders' expectation that Egyptian airfields would be under attack . . .

The JIC believed, too, that Russian intelligence on Anglo-French operations would be 'given to Egyptian intelligence'.[180]

The invasion of Suez was a boon for Khrushchev and Bulganin. It enabled them to engage in the ruthless suppression of the Hungarian rising in Budapest as the Anglo-French task force neared Port Said.* The Red Army attacked the twin cities on 4 November. Three days later 20,000 Hungarians and 3,000 Soviet troops were dead and the revolution was effectively over.[181]

On 5 November Dixon at the UN, linking the two events, drafted an impassioned diplomatic telegram and despatched it to Eden and Lloyd. He reminded his Prime Minister and Foreign Secretary that two days previously

---

* As a forthcoming book by Professor Jonathan Haslam will show, the Anglo-French invasion had the unanticipated effect of precipitating the overthrow of the anti-communist régime in Hungary by the Red Army. It reversed a decision taken by the Soviet leadership on 30 October to pull out completely and rearrange relations with its unhappy ally on a more equitable basis. (*Chill Shadow: A History of the Cold War*, forthcoming, 2007).

I felt constrained to warn you that if there was any bombing of open cities with result-ing loss of civilian life it would make our purposes completely cynical and entirely undermine our position here. Again . . . I urged that unless we could announce that Anglo-French forces were suspending all further military activities until we know that the United Nations were prepared to deal with the situation effectively, there would be no chance of being able to move towards our objectives without alienating the whole world.

I must again repeat this warning with renewed emphasis . . . we are inevitably being placed in the same low category as the Russians in their bombing of Budapest. I do not see how we can carry much conviction in our protests against the Russian bombing of Budapest . . . if we are ourselves bombing Cairo.[182]

British ministers were so utterly preoccupied by events in the eastern Med-iterranean that they could scarcely absorb what was happening along the banks of the Danube as the Soviet Union crushed the Magyar revolt while the Anglo-French fleet was steaming towards the banks of the Suez Canal. Unlike the assault on Egypt, the Russian attack was swift, brutal and effective (and a harsh warning to other satellites not to contemplate either withdrawal from the Soviet bloc or aspirations to military/political neutrality of the kind the new government of Imre Nagy had sought for Hungary).

The juxtaposition of British aggression and Soviet suppression was, as Dixon indicated, unbearable for British diplomats in New York, where both dramas aroused the United Nations as never before in its eleven-year history. Dixon's UN delegation contained a young diplomat who would go on many years later to become Foreign Secretary, Douglas Hurd. Until 3 November, the day Anthony Nutting resigned as Minister of State at the Foreign Office, Hurd recalled that he had

nursed in my mind a private hope that somehow, somewhere, deep in Whitehall, there was a master plan which would make everything right. In the last resort, I had thought, our influence at the UN was expendable. In the last resort it did not matter if we were embarrassed, distressed and kept in the dark – provided that we were low cards being sacrificed until the moment came to play Britain's aces and trumps . . .

Nutting, whom I knew slightly, was a young, attractive, modern Conservative minister with none of the bluster which discouraged me in Selwyn Lloyd. Moreover, Nutting was close to the Prime Minister, indeed his protégé. If there was a master plan he would have known it. Nutting had left, so there was no master plan, no aces, no trumps; just deception. Would deception now be followed by defeat?[183]

If the answer was 'yes', would it be at the behest of a Soviet threat or an American action?

On 5 November Eden received his letter from Marshal Bulganin in Moscow telling him: 'There is no justification for the fact that the armed forces of Britain and France, two Great Powers that are members of the Security Council, have attacked a country which only recently acquired national independence and which does not possess adequate means for self-defence. In what situation would Britain find herself if she were attacked by stronger states, possessing all types of modern destructive weapons? . . . Were rocket weapons used against Britain and France you would, most probably, call this a barbarous action.' He added a menacing rider: 'We are fully determined to crush the aggressors by the use of force and to restore peace in the [Middle] East.'[184]

Khrushchev, who instructed Bulganin to send that note late on 4 November,[185] was convinced it was this threat, not Eisenhower's condemnation of the Suez invasion, which halted it. In one of his memoirs he said, 'The governments of England and France knew perfectly well that Eisenhower's speech [in fact, it was a television address to the American people] condemning their aggression was just a gesture for the sake of public appearances. But when we delivered our own stern warning to the three aggressors, they knew we weren't playing games with public opinion. They took us very seriously.'[186] Whatever else, it was the last thing that Eden needed on 5 November.

No premier has had to endure greater strain than Eden did over that seven-day period in the autumn of 1956. As his wife Clarissa said shortly afterwards, she felt as 'if the Suez Canal was flowing throughout the drawing room' in 10 Downing Street.[187] On 6 November Bulganin's threat gained credibility when a FLASH signal* arrived from General Keightley: 'Information has been received that Russia may intervene in the Middle East with force.'[188] This, it turned out later, rested on an 'unconfirmed report' produced by the JIC (Middle East) based in Cyprus that eighty MiG aircraft 'were to arrive at Damascus and Aleppo' in Syria.[189] Journalist and author Tom Bower later discovered from his conversations with the then 'C', Dick White, that there was real concern in Whitehall that day about Soviet capabilities in the Middle East – all this and the US Sixth Fleet bothering the Anglo-French expedition, and the House of Commons and the United Nations in uproar. Chester Cooper, the CIA's liaison officer in London, brought some relief when he passed White the key

---

* One with overriding priority and urgency.

US intelligence estimate of 6 November that the Soviet Union would 'almost certainly not attack metropolitan UK or France – primarily because such an attack would make general war practically certain' and that the Russian leadership would not 'employ Soviet forces on a large scale in the Eastern Mediterranean', both because their capabilities were inadequate and 'because the risk of general war arising from such action would be very great'.[190]

A touch of intelligence balm might have arrived from America that day courtesy of the CIA. But it was Eisenhower, not Khrushchev, who used his superpower muscle to halt the Anglo-French forces which had reached El Cap, twenty-three miles down the Canal from Port Said, at the time of the ceasefire. And it was the economic weapon that loosed the final salvo – pressure on the pound with oil sanctions in the background. Never has the 'special relationship' reached such a low. Looking back, Alec Home's point about Eden's not going to see Eisenhower personally early on in the crisis (or at any stage during it) is very relevant. As Richard Thorpe put it, 'Home thought Eden should have gone to Washington at an early stage to see Eisenhower face-to-face, as this would have given him an insight into American feeling. By November it was too late.'[191]

On Sunday 4 November, Eden decided to lock his Cabinet into continuing with the war with a specific vote. Richard Thorpe was given access to Lady Eden's diary, which gives a far more vivid account of the outcome than the Cabinet minutes:

. . . each was asked in turn what they felt about going on. Selwyn, Alec Home, Harold, Alan [Lennox-Boyd], Antony Head, Peter [Thorneycroft], Eccles, Duncan [Sandys], James Stuart, Gwilym [Lloyd George], and Hailsham were for going on. Kilmuir, Heathcoat Amory [Minister of Agriculture], Macleod, Bobbety [Salisbury], Patrick Buchan-Hepburn were for doing whatever Anthony wanted and Lord Selkirk [Chancellor of the Duchy of Lancaster] was unintelligible.[192]

On the morning of Tuesday 6 November, a few hours after the Anglo-French seaborne forces had landed at Port Said, Eden called a 9.45 Cabinet meeting in his room at the House of Commons. The majority of the Cabinet now swung away from Eden. Of the big figures, only Lloyd, Head and Stuart supported his desire to carry on.[193] Butler and Salisbury led the others in what the minutes record as a

general agreement in the Cabinet that, in order to regain the initiative and to re-establish relations with those members of the United Nations who were fundamentally in sympathy with our aims, we should agree, subject to the concurrence of the French Government, to stop further military operations provided that the Secretary-General of the United Nations could confirm that the Governments of Egypt and Israel had now accepted an unconditional cease-fire . . .[194]

The key figure in the turnaround of mood and purpose was Harold Macmillan. Finance had indeed trumped firepower.

As the hawkish Antony Head told Macmillan's official biographer, 'Harold was very strong in his warning of what the US would do . . . he put the fear of God into the Cabinet on finances, as Chancellor.'[195] This time a Macmillan presentation really did make flesh crawl. He had telephoned Washington and the Federal Reserve in New York before the Cabinet met on that extraordinary Tuesday morning and 'was told that only a cease-fire by midnight would secure US support for an International Monetary Fund loan to prop up the pound. Secretary of the Treasury [George] Humphrey, whom he had found so "amiable" in Washington in September, was leading the pack against Britain.'[196] That, the possibility of oil sanctions against Britain and France that the US were thought to be considering[197] and, above all, the open hostility of the Eisenhower administration to Eden's actions put stress close to breaking point on the pound and upon its political guardian in the Treasury.

The Cabinet minutes for 6 November are, even by their usual standards, understated as a means of conveying the anxieties swirling round the Prime Minister's Room at the House of Commons that morning, though Bulganin's rockets, the threat of oil sanctions and the need to 'shape our policy in such a way as to enlist the maximum sympathy and support from the United States Government' were mentioned by Lloyd, who went on to stress that

we must also maintain our position against the Soviet Union. A menacing letter had just been received from President Bulganin calling on the United Kingdom to stop the war in Egypt, and stating that the Soviet Government were submitting to the United Nations a proposal to employ, together with other members of the United Nations, naval and air forces in order to bring the war in Egypt to an end and to curb aggression. We must not appear to be yielding in the face of Soviet threats . . .[198]

Norman Brook recorded that 'the following points were made' during the Cabinet's discussion:

It would still be practicable to proceed with the Anglo-French occupation of the Canal area, regardless of opposition from any quarter. But, if we adopted this course, we must reckon with the possibility of a Soviet invasion of Syria or some other area in the

Middle East, and possibly a direct Soviet attack on the Anglo-French forces in the Canal area. It was also probable that the other Arab states in the Middle East would come actively to the aid of Egypt and that the United Nations would be alienated to the point of imposing collective measures including oil sanctions, against the French and ourselves.[199]

There is no whisper of the pound, or the state of the gold and dollar reserves in those minutes.

After that Cabinet, however, Macmillan briefed Iverach McDonald, the renowned Foreign Editor of *The Times*, who recalled in his memoirs meeting Macmillan in a room at the House of Commons:

Eden was to have seen me, but he was caught in an endless talk with Mollet on the telephone ... 'We must have courage,' he said to me. 'The Government must show courage.' For a wild moment I thought he was about to say that they were going to defy the world and pile more troops into Egypt. No – they must show courage, he said, by staying united: no resignations or anything of that kind.[200]

As McDonald observed ironically, 'Macmillan was to become known as the unflappable,'[201] yet he succumbed to the near apocalyptic in the possibilities he sketched out on 6 November:

They had decided to call it off when they saw that they were not going to have quick success. 'It was risky from the beginning – perhaps it was too risky,' and now they had to face facts. Salisbury had said in the Cabinet, Macmillan told me, 'We have played every card in our hand, and we have none left.' I gathered that this intervention has-tened the decision. Macmillan said that Salisbury, for all his funny ways, had a fund of statesmanship in him. They all realized that there had to be a ceasefire. They did not take the Russian threats seriously but there was a risk of the war eventually spreading. America would come in, but it would mean the third world war. 'America would win it, but *we* should all be killed.'[202]

What next? inquired McDonald.

'Yes, how do we get out of it?' ... The most hopeful line ... was to hand the thing over to the United Nations force.* Eden had won approval for his endorsement of a UN police force in the area. And, after all, we had forced the United Nations to act. With-out our move, the Israel–Egyptian war would have spread through the Arab lands.[203]

---

* In the early hours of Sunday 4 November the United Nations General Assembly had overwhelm-ingly passed a resolution authorizing a UN peacekeeping force to occupy the Suez Canal.

The cover story for the collusion plainly had to be sustained even in the most private briefings to a journalist, especially one close to the inner circles as McDonald was. Macmillan continued, saying that it was now

for the United Nations to see if it could bring about a settlement . . . He then went on to talk about the heavy run on the pound and the other financial and economic consequences. He had to rush back into the Commons but he showed that he himself feared that the consequences would be much heavier if we delayed calling a halt.[204]

And that financial pressure remained, as is evident from the figures on page 426 for the reserves and from the continued grinding of the pound against its lower limit with the dollar, until the Cabinet (with Eden convalescing in Jamaica) finally agreed at the end of November to withdraw every last British soldier from Egypt[205] after Macmillan had told his colleagues on 27 November that: 'It was urgently necessary that we should re-establish satisfactory political relations with the United States. We should have to announce, early in the following week, the extent of the drain on our gold and dollars during November; and it was desirable that we should have secured by then the support of the United States Government for the action which we should need to take to support sterling.'[206]

The mood of the Treasury was wonderfully well caught two days later by Robert Hall. The government's Chief Economic Adviser had been in India for a month as Britain went through its greatest crisis of the short postwar. As he told his diary,

In a way the most encouraging thing is to find that *all* senior officials as far as I can see are violently opposed to the Government's action and feel that it was disastrous. I gather that Ministers have avoided officials as much as they could and only talked on detailed matters.

The economic situation is very dangerous because of the rapid rundown of the reserves. The US disapproves of our policy strongly and it has been difficult for us to borrow from the [International Monetary] Fund . . . because until we have left Egypt they are more against us than for us. Apart from the reserves, the oil position is poor and has been made a bit worse than we expected because there is no official US encouragement, though we can buy from private companies. However, it seems to me that there is a real danger we will be driven off the present exchange parity, purely for speculative purposes, and I doubt if sterling as we know it now could stand the shock of another move so soon after 1949 [when it was devalued from \$4.03 to \$2.80].[207]

Hall's contemporary testimony is important in terms of the reality of the economic and financial pressure brought to bear by the US White House, Treasury and the New York Federal Reserve Bank, as there have been suggestions since that such pressure was not irresistible and that Macmillan's move in the Cabinet on 6 November had as much to do with personal ambition as with the shakiness of sterling and the meagreness of the reserves. Antony Head was eloquent on this when interviewed by Alistair Horne: 'I could never believe it was just the US threat to withdraw money from us. It wasn't naked ambition, though if you had a nasty mind, you might have thought so. I didn't ... It's the big mystery ... I simply could not believe that the US could wreck us, or would want to wreck us, in two days ...'[208]

Eisenhower's exchanges with Eden make it very believable – those and putting the US Sixth Fleet among the Anglo-French task force, the factor that Alec Home could never forget. When the Suez papers were declassified, I asked him why all those warnings – including the Treasury's on the fragility of the pound – had been ignored until that morning in Eden's room at the Commons:

A warning is a different thing from it happening, isn't it? You often get warnings of this sort and then the results are different. I think what really turned the scale and made the Chancellor of the Exchequer that day so terribly anxious was the American action in putting the Sixth Fleet alongside us in the Mediterranean, for all the world to see, and therefore announcing in effect that America was totally against us. The effect on sterling as a result of that was catastrophic. It was the actual effect on sterling, rather than the warnings, I think. Perhaps we ought to have taken the warnings more seriously.[209]

Macmillan, Home told me, was 'very fussed and upset' by sterling's plight:

But what he had to deal with was the actual situation as to whether the fall in the pound sterling justified us in curtailing our action. And, on the whole, he persuaded the Cabinet that we had to do that. It might have taken two days to get to the other end of the Canal, it might have taken longer, and that was a consideration in the Cabinet's mind at that time. And time was the essence of the matter, as it had been from the start.[210]

Head might have been sceptical about Macmillan's assessment of the financial weapon being wielded by the US authorities, but Alec Home plainly was not.

Head's disbelief as Minister of Defence about the halting of the attack was shared by the armed forces in the field. The Chiefs of Staff despatched a FLASH signal to General Keightley:

1. Subject to separate executive signal containing code word 'STOP' repeat 'STOP' you are to cease fire at 1700 hours GMT repeat 1700 hours GMT to-day 6th November and not to reopen fire unless attacked.

2. No forward movement from your positions reached on land are to be made after the cease fire.

3. You are at liberty to land at Port Said such further fighting or administrative units or supplies as are necessary for the maintenance of your position ashore.

4. Unless attacked your air operations are to be confined to the air transport support of the forces ashore and such air reconnaissance as may be tactically necessary.[211]

The bulk of British forces heard of the news on the BBC World Service, including senior figures such as Sir Kenneth Darling: 'It was the BBC news bulletin . . . when suddenly we heard the tannoy echoing around the ship the news that there would be a cease-fire . . . We were just astounded. It came straight out of the clear blue sky. The whole thing was brought to a halt and it had hardly started.'[212]

At the very prong of the sharp end of the assault was a young National Serviceman, a second lieutenant in the Parachute Regiment called Christopher Hogg. Many years later, by this time Sir Christopher and Chairman of Reuters, he told me during the tranquillity of an interval at the Glyndebourne opera house how he had spent the night of 6 November 1956. He and his platoon were guarding a sewage farm close to the Suez Canal. Covered in filth and being eaten alive by mosquitoes he brooded both on the ghastliness of it all and the likelihood that the morning would see the start of the next world war.[213]

Unsurprisingly, many professional military men felt sullied by Suez, especially the veterans of the Second World War, the memory of which was still fresh. I shall long remember Sir Dermot Boyle, the Chief of the Air Staff in 1956, falling very quiet at the end of our BBC Radio 3 interview in 1987, after Mark Laity and I had shown him a selection of the freshly declassified documents. Asked to sum up his recollections, Sir Dermot said: 'When you compare it with the Second World War, one was proud of everything that happened in the Second World War, and one wasn't proud of everything that happened at Suez. I think that's about the summing up of the situation.'[214]

Evelyn Shuckburgh caught the mood in his diary entry for 5 December 1956, two days after Selwyn Lloyd had told the Commons that British troops were to leave Egypt without delay[215] (triggering a restoration of oil supplies and a $561.47m drawing from the IMF with a further standby of $738.5m available as the US lifted what were, in effect, economic sanctions against Britain[216]):

Now that our withdrawal 'without delay' from Suez has been announced by Selwyn Lloyd, everyone at the IDC [Imperial Defence College] has become suddenly very gloomy and all the Services feel that they have been betrayed, and that we will never be able to show any independence as a nation again. A long letter from Admiral 'Lofty' [Sir Arthur] Power, who has been on the operation, and who describes it as 'conceived in deceit and arrested in pusillanimity'. Petrol is up by one and sixpence.[217]

The deceit continued amid the wreckage of Eden's policy.

Back from Jamaica, during what was to be his last appearance in the House of Commons on 20 December 1956 replying to a question from Denis Healey ('I have never been so angry for so long as I was during the Suez affair,' Healey would write later[218]) about what Healey regarded as the 'conspiracy with Israel',[219] Eden added the final ruinous stain to his reputation when he replied: 'There were no plans got together [with Israel] to attack Egypt . . .'[220]

In winding up the debate on the same day, Eden was emphatic: 'I want to say this on the question of foreknowledge, and to say it quite bluntly to the House, that there was not foreknowledge that Israel would attack Egypt – there was not.'[221] As Richard Thorpe put it, this was 'a nadir for Eden, and a desperate end to the series of speeches he had made in the Chamber since his first . . . on 9 February 1924'.[222] Ted Heath, his Chief Whip, could hardly bear it: 'As I sat and watched him deny any "foreknowledge" of Israeli's invasion of Egypt, I felt like burying my head in my hands at the sight of this man I so much admired maintaining this fiction.'[223]

A few feet away, listening to Eden in the officials' box in the Commons Chamber, was Lloyd's Private Secretary, Donald Logan, the only man from the British side to the collusion who had attended both Sèvres meetings. I asked him about the impact upon him of Eden's unequivocal denials that there had been collusion:

LOGAN: I felt that at that moment his attempt to justify his intervention to separate the forces simply exploded.

HENNESSY: Did you feel at all that you should have done what Clive Ponting in another generation [post-Falklands in connection with the sinking of the *General Belgrano*] did?

LOGAN: In those days civil servants were not expected to betray their ministers and I certainly did not feel this, no.

HENNESSY: You don't regard lying in the House of Commons as a cardinal sin on the part of an elected politician?

LOGAN: Whatever I may think, it is, I think, for ministers to decide their own conduct in the House of Commons and the public to judge ministers on their performance.[224]

Two days earlier, Eden had told his backbenchers during a meeting of the 1922 Committee that: 'As long as I live, I shall never apologise for what we did.'[225] Nor did he. In less than a month, Eden was gone from political and public life for ever.

Real power had effectively drained from him as he left for Ian Fleming's house Goldeneye in Jamaica on 23 November. Even in the days before his sad departure from Heathrow and his three-week convalescence in the Caribbean,[226] Macmillan was in and out of the American Embassy in Grosvenor Square, in session with the ambassador, Aldrich, discussing the rescue of the pound and the flow of oil to the UK *and* hinting that he, Macmillan, might fly to see Eisenhower as Eden's 'deputy' (which he was not).[227] Butler went with him to Grosvenor Square on 21 November, but most of the visits to Aldrich involved Macmillan operating solo, leaving Aldrich with the impression 'that some sort of movement is on foot in the Cabinet to replace Eden'.[228]

At a memorable meeting of the 1922 Committee on 22 November, Macmillan made a thinly disguised pitch for the succession before the assembled Conservative backbenchers. Once Prime Minister, Macmillan admitted in the privacy of his diary that he realized Eden 'could never return and remain PM for long'.[229] He told Alistair Horne that, looking back, Suez was 'a very bad episode in my life. I feel unhappy about the whole thing.'[230] But, against the odds, the political gods had presented him with the chance to succeed a younger man.

He pulled out all the stops before the '22', completely eclipsing the dry, technocratic Rab Butler in mood, word and manner.[231] He used his famous metaphor of the British as Greeks to the Romans, leading with ideas rather than power.[232] It was the Chief Whip, Ted Heath, who set up the occasion. He later recalled that with Eden ill and off to Jamaica, there was

almost immediately . . . speculation about a successor and widespread lobbying on behalf of the two obvious candidates, Rab Butler and Harold Macmillan. I did all I could to maintain a balance between the two of them. At the last meeting of the 1922 Committee before the House rose for Christmas someone had to give the party a general survey of the political position following Suez. It turned out to be the official start of the campaign for the leadership, although the forces at work behind it were not as malign as some have since supposed.

Technically, Rab Butler had been left in control of the government, so it was natural that he should address the Committee. Nonetheless, I believed that if he alone appeared it would cause ill-feeling, so I arranged for Harold to speak after him. Butler made a balanced and worthy speech which was, sadly, uninspiring. Macmillan, on the other hand, turned in a magnificent performance. His speech was laced, as it usually was in private, with sparkling apposite historical and philosophical allusions and was lightened with the witty, ironical humour of which he was a master.[233]

Poor Butler was almost literally swept aside. As one of Heath's junior whips recalled: 'Rab was not on his best form, whereas Harold was at his most ebullient and managed to win the day, not only on the merit of what he said (as it seemed to the Committee) but also physically in that his expansive gestures nearly caused poor Rab to fall backwards from the adjacent seat.'[234] As Anthony Sampson, an early and shrewd biographer of Macmillan, put it, he 'had managed to give the impression that the war had been a kind of victory, and that nothing much had happened'.[235]

Butler was not merely outshone by Macmillan in the fevered post-Suez atmosphere of Westminster politics, he was both feeble and foolish, alienating Cabinet ministers and Conservative backbenchers alike. As Antony Head told Alistair Horne: 'The whole time he was saying "on the one hand, on the other". It did him a lot of harm. If Rab had only been more forceful throughout the period, he could have been Prime Minister . . . but there was an ambivalence in him all the way – and it did him absolutely no good in the Cabinet . . . Also I have a sneaking feeling that he himself never really wanted the responsibility deep down.'[236]

Nigel Nicolson, among the handful of Conservative MPs who dissented on Suez (and who, for his pains, was deselected by his Bournemouth activists),[237] reckoned Butler 'played a double game, which lost him a lot of backing. He would speak up for the Government in the House, and then go into the Smoking Room and say to everyone how terrible it was. He thought that would get him support; in fact it did the reverse . . .'[238]

Butler could not – or pretended he couldn't – understand any of this. In his memoirs he wrote, 'wherever I moved in the weeks that followed, I felt party knives sticking into my innocent back'.[239] And he told Macmillan's official biographer, 'I couldn't understand, when I had done a most wonderful job – picking up the pieces after Suez – that they then chose Harold.'[240] Harold understood all right. Macmillan knew the mettle – or lack of it – of the man he had to beat for the succession. Butler, he told Horne, 'had the ambition but not the will ... a sort of vague ambition – like saying it would be nice to be Archbishop of Canterbury ...'[241]

It is not easy in the British system of government to eject a Prime Minister, however battered and discredited, who does not wish to go. And it was not obvious to everybody in the inner circle that Eden would do so. On 5 December Sir Norman Brook went to lecture at the Imperial Defence College and, as Shuckburgh noted, 'showed us afterwards (in private) that he too thought the Suez expedition a folly. He thinks however that the PM will return and assume charge again as if nothing had happened, because the Tory Party would split without him, into Macmillan v Butler groups, with the Suez diehards as a third.'[242] When the Edens flew home from Jamaica, Lady Eden wrote in her diary for 14 December: 'Returned to find everyone looking at us with thoughtful eyes.'[243]

The health factor finally decided the question uppermost in every mind. How was Eden at this stage? According to Richard Thorpe, many 'inaccurate statements were made, then and later, about his medicines and the "uppers" and "downers" he supposedly swallowed ... Eden's two doctors, Horace Evans and Ralph Southwood, provided Sparine sleeping tablets for Jamaica, but Eden made no use of them ... In the last fortnight of Eden's Premiership, by which time the policy initiatives had in effect passed to Macmillan and Butler, he occasionally took small quantities of Benzedrine, but never before he went to Jamaica.'[244]

Just after Christmas 1956, on 27 December, a sextet of Cabinet ministers travelled to Chequers for lunch with the Edens (Butler, Kilmuir, Lennox-Boyd, Salisbury, Lloyd George and Head). The Prime Minister asked the Lord Chancellor to stay behind. Kilmuir later wrote:

We went into the little 'white' sitting-room where Clarissa had arranged the Christmas cards – which owing to Suez had come in unusually large numbers – really charmingly. Then Anthony asked my view as an old friend on the question of whether he should stay on.

Of course, the principal factor was his health. He put it to me that it was not illness but an inability to get back his ordinary vigour. This was accompanied by bad nights and the fact that if he took anything to make him sleep then it did not suit his stomach. There was no suggestion on this day that the old trouble of 1953 had returned. Anthony was, however, afraid – and quite naturally – that he would be a

Prime Minister at half-cock and therefore unable to give a lead over the grave questions which faced us.

I advised him strongly to carry on ... but I came away with the feeling that he was consumed with grave apprehensions about his personal position.[245]

Back in London, on 5 January Eden saw his doctors and took their advice that he should resign. On 8 January the Edens stayed overnight with the Queen at Sandringham and the head of state was told that she would need to find a new head of government.

On 9 January Eden wrote to Bobbety Salisbury telling him, 'I am too sad for words. Your friendship and your help will always be the outstanding memory of my political life.'[246] Later that morning he told his colleagues at his final Cabinet that the adverse effect of his drugs and stimulants on his 'rather precarious inside' meant he must leave the premiership.[247] That evening he called on the Queen at Buckingham Palace to resign. The Queen told him she shared his 'regret' at having to leave and, as Eden recorded, 'understood how painful the decision must have been'.[248] That morning, Eden had written to Churchill to warn him of his resignation: 'The benefit of Jamaica is not significant. More troubling is that over Christmas + the New Year I have had a return of internal pain, which, apart from its fatiguing effect, worries the doctors in relation to my past operation. In short they say firmly ... that I am endangering my life and shortening it by going on ... they give me little hope that I can continue as I am doing without collapse until Easter, + virtually no hope, if I attempt to go on, until the end of summer.'[249]

It was a dispiriting end to the most tragic premiership of the postwar period. His 'man of peace' television broadcast of 3 November 1956, with which this chapter opened, remains unfailingly moving. He meant every word. Anthony Eden's conduct of the Suez affair calls to mind Rudyard Kipling on Joe Chamberlain, as a would-be statesman 'who stepped aside from the sheep-tracks of little politicians, who put from him ease, comfort and friendship and lost even health itself ...'[250]

It is equally possible to see in him the apotheosis of the hypothetical Englishman who so worried Peter Laslett in 1950 as, in Laslett's words, the peace of the world depended 'on the Englishman being able to reconcile himself to a continuous diminution in the consequence of his country. This can only be done if he can learn to separate his personal prestige from the prestige of his nation state.'[251] Eden, though not the last figure in authority to suffer from this symbiosis, could not. In failing to do so, took his country in the summer and autumn of 1956, in Percy Cradock's words, to 'a low point in the history of responsible government'.[252] And Professor Sir Michael Howard spoke for many of the younger generation in the mid-Fifties who had fought in the Second World War when he wrote in his memoirs that Eden's conduct 'caused me real anguish, as it did so many others.

It was not so much that the affair marked the end of Britain as a Great Power: it marked our end as a *good* power, one that could normally be expected to act honourably. It was for me what Munich had been for a slightly older generation and Iraq would be for a younger; but whereas Munich and Iraq were understandable if deplorable acts of *realpolitik*, the sheer irrationality of the Suez adventure still [in 2006] fills me with melancholy amazement. [253]

Once the cause of that 'amazement', Eden, was gone, he stimulated perhaps the most remarkable series of reappraisals that the United Kingdom had experienced since VE Day.

10

Lightning Flash

'It [Suez] was like a flash of lightning on a dark night. What it did was to light up an unfamiliar landscape. It was a landscape in which the two superpowers and principally the United States had told us to stop and we'd had to stop. And this was different. This was not being a world power. This was being told by a world power what the limits were and I thought that everything was different from then on . . . a great many people in Britain perceived at that point of time that what they might have thought before was no longer valid.'   Lord Franks recalling 1956 in 1990.[1]

'Suez was the most terrible trauma, and whether we drew the right lessons from it, I don't know. But I do think that everyone realised after the event, that things would never be the same again; that the weakness of our economic position – the flight from sterling . . . – was underlined by it; the fact that we couldn't count on the special relationship with the United States in the terms we used to think about it . . . that had gone. And the whole position of our relations with traditional former allies, with the Commonwealth, I think there was a feeling that it wouldn't be the same and we've got to rethink our role.'

Lord Hunt of Tanworth, Private Secretary to Sir Norman Brook, 1956–8;
Secretary of the Cabinet, 1973–9, recalling Suez in 1994.[2]

'World War II vindicated our way of doing things. There was great and genuine pride in contrast to France's defeat and Germany's sin. It was only when people sensed the decline after Suez that there came a sense of shame.'

Sir Christopher Mallaby reflecting on Britain in the
late 1950s and early 1960s in December 2002.[3]

Those few days at the end of October and the beginning of November 1956 really do merit the over-used description of a 'turning-point'. For almost everything that could have been in flux *was* in flux – the US–UK 'special

458

relationship'; Anglo-French relations, with enormous and enduring consequences for the Franco-German axis within the European Community that to this day presents British ministers and officials with a persistent difficulty;[4] East–West Cold War relations; Commonwealth/Empire, its internal cohesion and the exposure of Britain's weakness as a wielder of imperial force to a host of nationalist movements in a swathe of UK colonies and dependencies. Not least, Suez held up a very fractured mirror to those Brits who (with much good reason since 1940) liked to regard their country as an exemplar in terms of proper international behaviour.

Christopher Mallaby's notion (which reflected this perception) that the Second World War 'vindicated our way of doing things' fitted exactly Jean Monnet's explanation of Britain's aversion to any serious integration with Europe in the early postwar years. 'She felt no need to exorcise history,' was how he put it in his memoirs.[5] The British, unlike the French, he wrote, 'had not known the trauma of wartime occupation; they had not been conquered; their system seemed intact'.[6]

Suez did not see Britain occupied or conquered. But it was a defeat and it scarred the psyche of those younger politicians who came to prominence and power in subsequent decades, including those who occupied No. 10. For Jim Callaghan, Suez was 'a terrible setback for British arms and influence'.[7] At the time, Margaret Thatcher 'fiercely supported the Suez campaign'.[8] Later, as she

came to know more about it, I drew four lessons from this sad episode. First, we should not get into a military operation unless we were determined and able to finish it. Second, we should never again find ourselves on the opposite side to the United States in a major international crisis affecting British interests. Third, we should ensure that our actions were in accord with international law. And finally, he who hesitates is lost.[9]

Lady Thatcher could well have based her more considered thoughts about Suez partly upon one of the earliest and most striking of private and personal inquests – Winston Churchill's. In late October Eden had asked the Old Man's Private Secretary, Anthony Montague Browne, to sound out Churchill by asking whether he would accept 'a seat in the Cabinet without portfolio'. Churchill was understandably amazed. Nothing came of it.[10] It is thanks to Churchill's private secretaries that we know his verdict on Suez. To Montague Browne he said, 'I would never have done it without squaring the Americans, and once I'd started I would never have dared stop.'[11] Jock Colville lunched with his former chief on 29 November 1956, who 'told me in reply to a direct question that he thought the whole operation the most ill-conceived and ill-executed imaginable ... I had begun by asking him if he would have acted as Eden had if he had still been Prime Minister. He replied, "I would never have dared ..." He also said that if Eden resigned he thought Harold Macmillan would be a better successor than R. A. Butler.'[12] Which was exactly the advice he gave to the Queen before she sent for Harold Macmillan a few weeks later.[13]

Eden's private and personal '"thoughts" on the general position after Suez', as his Principal Private Secretary, Freddie Bishop, called them,[14] appear to have been written over his last sad Christmas at Chequers. He shared them only with Bobbety Salisbury and Antony Head, the Minister of Defence.[15] They did not reach the Public Record Office with the first batch of Suez papers in 1987. When they did arrive in the early 1990s, they formed a fascinating postscript to the whole episode – Eden's own very secret mini-inquest, in fact. 'We have', Eden told his tiny readership, 'to try to assess the lessons of Suez.'

His analysis was close to Macmillan's on the dangers of excessive military spending weakening the vitality of the civil economy in a self-defeating fashion. This, allied to his belief in the centrality of technical education examined in Chapter 8, comprised the 'first' post-Suez lesson to be learned, for, 'if we are to play an independent part in the world, even on a more modest scale than we have done heretofore, we must ensure our financial and economic independence. Since we have no raw materials but coal, this means that we must excel in technical knowledge. This in turn affects our military plans.'[16]

Too many British scientists were absorbed by defence work, Eden believed – 'I think I have seen a figure of two-thirds' – which to him was unacceptable. 'On the other hand, some progress with the military aspects of the development of the hydrogen bomb can no doubt be useful for civil purposes also. It seems therefore that we have need to keep the balance between civil and military development, leaning rather more towards the former in our nuclear programme.'[17]

This was the period of high optimism about both Britain's own civil nuclear designs (Rab Butler missed some crucial Suez meetings as he was with the Queen in Cumberland opening the first civil reactor at Calder Hall[18]) and the prospect of cheap and plentiful electricity flowing from them (the first nuclear-generated electricity entered the UK national grid on 17 October 1956[19]). As part of a 'more modest' version of a British world role, Eden anticipated briefly several of the reappraisals to come under both the Macmillan and Wilson governments. What, for example, was the point of having an armoured division in Tripoli and Libya? If the purpose is to prevent this part of North Africa falling under Egyptian dominion, could that not be ensured more cheaply? ... And would not a smaller garrison be sufficient if one is needed at all? If we apply the same considerations to the Indian Ocean, can we not now dispense with the Ceylon Naval base altogether, using the Maldives instead for the air? Can we not increase the integration of the Services so far as concerns our requirements at Singapore? Do we need so many troops in Malaya?[20]

Eden knew it had been judged too risky to use the British troops based in Libya against Nasser for fear of inflaming wider Arab opinion.[21] He was also well aware, as the Chief of the Air Staff, Sir Dermot Boyle, later expressed it, that future military planning was concentrating on how to fight a 'NATO war' against Russia, 'and it meant that if we had the things we wanted for NATO we would inevitably not have the things we wanted for these little operations around the world'.[22]

The Suez operation was not so 'little'. But had Britain (and France too) had a different mixture of troops and kit and the means to project them flexibly and swiftly and if, in Richard Powell's words, it had been possible 'to compress the operation into two or three days, the world would have been faced with a *fait accompli* and would have settled down to accept it'.[23] Here for Eden lay another lesson of Suez: 'surely ... we need a smaller force that is more mobile and more modern in its equipment. This probably means that we have in proportion to our total army too much armour and too much infantry and too small a paratroop force.'

The British Army of the Rhine should be cut by half and, with it, the cost of maintaining it, Eden concluded.[24] The final passage in Eden's thoughts on politico-military matters was retained as too sensitive to reveal for over a decade after the incomplete version was declassified. It dealt with nuclear weapons and their targeting (this last explaining the extended sensitivity). Eden believed

it is of the first importance to maintain deterrent power, which means ability to deliver a destructive weapon, atomic or hydrogen, on the target. In this connection I have observed that it appears to be assumed that if, for instance, China were to attack Hong Kong, the Americans would have to deliver the atomic counter-blow. I do not see why this is necessarily so. We too have the capacity [the V-bombers operating from Singapore].[25]

The Prime Minister's brooding during his final days in office then turned to economic and domestic matters, especially the need to trim the costs of the welfare state while boosting technical education and training crucial to 'our struggle for existence': 'We shall not have adjusted to our problems until the younger generation here can feel that they live in a community which is leading in industrial development and can reasonably expect a fair reward for their brains and application', as the 'present burden of taxation leaves them with little incentive except patriotism'.[26]

Eden's final paragraph, his equivalent of Franks' 'lightning flash', is especially notable for its tone on Europe, so different from that of the pre-Suez Eden:

> The conclusion of all this is surely that we must review our world position and our domestic capacity more searchingly in the light of the Suez experience, which has not so much changed our fortunes as revealed realities. While the consequences of this examination may be to determine us to work more closely with Europe, carrying with us, we hope, our closest friends in the Commonwealth in such development, here too we must be under no illusion. Europe will not welcome us simply because at the moment it may appear to suit us to look to them. The timing and the conviction of our approach may be decisive in their influence on those with whom we plan to work.[27]

General Charles de Gaulle was eighteen months away from assuming the French premiership when Eden wrote those words.[28] But they proved markedly prescient in terms of the sixteen *years* that lay ahead until finally, in January 1973, the UK became a member of the European Economic Community.

Interestingly, de Gaulle had 'applauded the Suez expedition ... criticizing only the inadequacy of the forces used ... [and] ... the unpreparedness of the British'.[29] Though it was post-Suez anxieties about the imperial decline of France, very comparable to those experienced in Britain, that helped feed the political crisis which eventually brought the General to power[30] – in good time, amongst other things, to wreck the British free trade area alternative to the EEC. In fact, one of the swiftest impacts of the Suez crisis in Whitehall was to line up the British Cabinet behind Plan G.

The very day Suez reached its point of maximum crisis, Chancellor Konrad Adenauer was in Paris clearing away the last obstacles with Prime Minister Guy Mollet on the road to what became the Treaty of Rome the following spring. The very same day, Macmillan and Thorneycroft circulated a Cabinet paper recommending acceptance of Plan G as the great alternative to the Six's grand design.[31] The Cabinet had two cracks at it before finally deciding to accept and unveil Plan G. At the first, on 13 November, Lord Salisbury, who before Suez had been worried about imperial and Commonwealth implications, gave it his blessing.

Alan Milward, as an official historian, has seen Norman Brook's unpublished notes of that meeting which attribute views to ministers. 'The Marquis of Salisbury', he writes, 'had been convinced by Suez that the imperial link, which he had thought Plan G would weaken, did not now look so strong. More colonies would become independent and Britain was still excluded from US markets. It must therefore "turn a little towards Europe".'[32]

Given the turmoil of Suez, however, the UK Cabinet can perhaps be forgiven for not absorbing the significance of the 6 November meeting between Adenauer and Mollet. Their discussion had been rather rudely interrupted by Eden's telephone call telling a reluctant Mollet that the intervention had to stop. When it was over, Adenauer said to Mollet, 'France and England will never be powers comparable to the United States and the Soviet Union. Nor Germany either. There remains only one way of playing a decisive role in the world; that is to unite to make Europe. England is not ripe for it but the affair of Suez will help to prepare her spirits for it. We have no time to waste: Europe will be your revenge.'[33]

Not only was Britain 'not ripe for it', ministers were simply unaware of the rapid engineering of the Franco-German axis which would become the basis of the Common Market for fifty years. For example on 13 November Macmillan told the Cabinet that there 'was now some indication that, among the six Powers, both France and Germany might limit their aims to the establishment of a free trade area'.[34] The Cabinet agreed to proceed with Plan G on 20 November.[35] After consultations with an agreeable Opposition front bench (represented by Shadow Chancellor Harold Wilson[36]), Plan G was launched in the House of Commons on 26 November 1956 upon a wave of bipartisan support[37] in a sea of self-delusion.

The attention of the wider public, never much gripped by European economic matters in the mid-Fifties, was understandably elsewhere thanks to Suez and its shock waves. Perhaps the only official reappraisal which caught their imagination was the 1957 Defence White Paper (not least because most of the others, Plan G apart, were secret internal Whitehall affairs). As Alistair Horne noted, it 'was the most drastic of any White Paper on Defence since the end of the war',[38] and when it was published on 4 April, 'the country gasped'[39] because it announced the end of a practice that potentially affected every home in the land housing a young adult male. National Service was to end in 1962 with the number of enlisted personnel being reduced from

690,000 to 375,000 over the five years until the three armed services consisted of nothing but regular soldiers, sailors and airmen.[40] There would be 'no further call-up under the National Service Acts after the end of 1960'.[41]

Apart from the ending of conscription, the 1957 White Paper is significant for two other things – its reliance on nuclear deterrence as a way of both confronting the Soviet threat and saving money (Churchill's line in 1954), a policy of 'big bangs and small forces'[42]; and for Duncan Sandys, the Minister of Defence who gave the review its name. Sandys is one of but two office holders (the other is Denis Healey) who are widely remembered for their time in the MoD since it was given its own minister in 1946 as a separate entity from the premiership (as under Churchill during 1940–45).

Alec Home once told me that, had he won the 1964 general election, he would have asked either Sandys or Enoch Powell to take on the reform of the civil service. ('They were the two most ruthless politicians I knew,' he told me with a laugh.)[43] Macmillan plainly saw Sandys in the same light. He didn't care for Sandys' aggressive '*cassant* manner'[44] (a favourite word in Macmillan's French vocabulary), but he wanted a tireless, relentless brute at Defence to push through those changes and economies he had pressed for as Chancellor – someone who could take on the Chiefs of Staff and the vested interests of the armed forces.

He had pressed Antony Head, Sandys' predecessor, hard on this as Chancellor even as the last shots of Suez echoed round Whitehall. On 24 November 1956 he told Head in a personal minute that 'we face the most difficult economic situation in our history', and that the state of the reserves and the shortage of oil meant that large savings were necessary. He needed to 're-examine the bases on which our present defence policy rests . . . in our present position we cannot afford to carry too many insurance policies. We cannot hope to emerge from a global war except in ruins.'[45] Head was appalled at what he regarded as an over-reliance upon the nuclear deterrent to which this approach pointed and the peremptory manner in which arbitrary cuts would be foisted on the forces he was there to protect.

'I had to resign,' Head told Macmillan's biographer. 'Perhaps it was just a neat way of getting rid of me, knowing that I couldn't accept the cuts . . . I thought the forces would be pleased that I stood up for them, but they weren't; they got Sandys instead, which they couldn't bear!'[46] Head was Macmillan's greatest ministerial problem as he moved into No. 10 in January 1957 (once he had made his peace with Butler: 'I saw him at once, and offered him whatever office he might wish' – Butler took the Home Office after Macmillan 'steered' him away from the Foreign Office because Selwyn Lloyd had to stay there, 'one head on a charger being enough'[47]).

Macmillan's reflective diary entry for 3 February 1957 is evocative of his wonderfully sinuous approach to the tricky matter of reshuffles (which did not fail him until he sacked a third of his Cabinet in the 'Night of the Long Knives' in July 1962[48]):

The Cabinet was completed by the Sunday evening [13 January 1957], when the Queen came up from Sandringham. My chief problem was the Ministry of Defence. I felt that with Antony Head it wd not succeed. He was too much of a 'service' man. There was a lot of resistance to my plan of having Duncan Sandys – chiefly from Norman Brook who thought the rows would be too great. But the Chief Whip [Heath] felt it was politically an advantage. I also wanted a 'direction' to increase the powers of the defence minister. Brook (who is a tower of strength) drafted them, and I got the 3 service ministers to accept them before appointment. By moving Hailsham from the Admiralty to Education a possible danger was avoided. Also I think he will be a first-class Minister of Education. Anyway, he is one of the cleverest, if not always the wisest, men in the country today.[49]

The Cabinet Secretary was right. The rows were great and were remembered within the Ministry of Defence for decades, as were Sandys' working methods, some of which – such as his penchant for late-night meetings – reminded people of the practices of his father-in-law, Winston Churchill.[50] The White Paper went through thirteen 'final' drafts[51] – and there was blood on every page.

Eden had begun the long-term defence review which culminated in Sandys' report and he had also contemplated the ending of National Service.[52] And in the work overseen by Selwyn Lloyd during his brief time as Minister of Defence in 1955, greater reliance on nuclear weapons was a theme which played strongly.[53] But it was a combination of the impact of Suez, the weakness of the pound, Macmillan's presence in No. 10 and Sandys being unleashed upon the Chiefs which made the 1957 White Paper such a powerful document.

The economic argument conditioned its pages in a very Macmillanesque way, which is not surprising because the Prime Minister himself 'dictated a new version of the White Paper' at Chequers on Sunday 17 March 1957 and Sandys came to dinner that evening to read the new text ('Fortunately he accepted this,'[54] Macmillan wrote in his diary; Sandys was an 'able and obstinate' man[55]). Defence in recent years had spent 10 per cent of GNP, employed

7 per cent of the working population, used 12.5 per cent of the metal-bashing industries' capacity and exercised the minds of 'an undue proportion of qualified scientists and engineers'. Garrisons and bases strung across the world were putting great pressure on the balance of payments.[56] Just a few days into his premiership, Macmillan told Salisbury on 18 January that the Governor of the Bank of England, Cameron Cobbold, had come to see him and 'stressed very strongly that unless some reduction can be made in the total burden [of the defence budget], it will be very difficult to hold the pound in the Autumn. If we lose the pound, we lose everything. We have put our last reserves into the Government line. We cannot borrow any more dollars . . .'[57]

But it was Macmillan's conversion of this into atomic terms – 'We must rely on the power of the nuclear deterrent or we must throw up the sponge'[58] – that had, the abolition of conscription apart, the most lasting effect in terms of the thinking, the argument and the decisions that shaped the Defence White Paper. For not only was home defence 'slashed to the bone – on the pessimistic, or realistic, assumption that there could be no effective protection for the civil population against the dreadful new power of the H-Bomb', as Alistair Horne put it,[59] but also the stark phraseology of the Sandys White Paper on Britain's nuclear vulnerability shortly afterwards united a scattering of disparate peace groups into the path-breaking Campaign for Nuclear Disarmament, CND.

Both the historian of the early CND, Christopher Driver,[60] and the MI5 analyst who prepared a brief on CND for Macmillan in 1963[61] emphasized the importance of the 1957 Defence White Paper in eventually getting the Easter marchers on the road to Aldermaston and the government's Atomic Weapons Research Establishment a year later.

One of the key sections was this:

It must be frankly recognised that there is at present no means of providing adequate protection for the people of this country against the consequences of an attack with nuclear weapons. Though in the event of war, the fighter aircraft of the RAF would unquestionably take a heavy toll of enemy bombers, a proportion would inevitably get through. Even if it were only a dozen, they could with megaton [i.e. hydrogen] bombs inflict widespread devastation.[62]

Peace lay in only one direction – 'the only existing safeguard against major aggression is the power to threaten retaliation with nuclear weapons'.[63] It was with this proposition that CND would come to take fundamental issue. A further fillip to the dissenters came in the White Paper's judgement that, while Britain cannot by comparison [with the United States] make more than a modest contribution, there is a wide measure of agreement that she must possess an appreciable element of nuclear deterrent power of her own. British atomic bombs are already in steady production and the RAF holds a substantial number of them. A British megaton weapon has now been developed. This will shortly be tested and thereafter a stock will be manufactured.[64]

That Macmillan, who had an unusually well-developed sense of how his policies might strike his political opponents as well as the politically uncommitted, anticipated the appearance of something like the CND is indicated by his diary reflections a day after the Sandys review was presented to Parliament:

The Defence White Paper, on which we have worked so hard, has at last been published. It has had, on the whole, a very good press. Since it makes clear that *all* our defence – and the economies in defence expenditure – are founded on nuclear warfare, it throws the Socialists into still greater confusion. Gaitskell's position becomes more and more humiliating. Meanwhile, however, the political side of their campaign has dangers for us all. [The day before, Gaitskell had called for the British H-bomb tests to be postponed,[65] a suggestion Macmillan thought 'idiotic'[66].] The sentimental appeal is very strong. The worthy people of all types and ages are particularly easy prey and of course they will be cynically exploited.[67]

It wasn't quite true that '*all*' the UK's future defence was founded on the 'nuclear', as Macmillan liked to call it.[68] Plans were laid in the White Paper to rely less on garrisons around the world and more on a 'central reserve' of forces in the UK to enable 'despatch [of] reinforcements at short notice'.[69] The lessons of Suez were sinking in here, too.

But in 1957–8, as part of an internal Whitehall debate about the planned site of the V-bomber force, Macmillan did set down his real reasons, economy apart, for maintaining an 'independent nuclear capability for the UK'. There were four:

(a) To retain our special relation [sic] with the United States and, through it, our influence in world affairs, and, especially, our right to have a voice in the final issue of peace and war.

(b) To make a definite, though limited, contribution to the total nuclear strength of the West – while recognising that the United States must continue to play the major part in maintaining the balance of nuclear power.

(c) To enable us, by threatening to use our independent nuclear power, to secure

United States co-operation in a situation in which their interests were less immediately threatened than our own.

(d) To make sure that, in a nuclear war, sufficient attention is given to certain Soviet
targets which are of greater importance to us than to the United States.[70]

Detailed rationales of this kind were not for inclusion in public documents.
For example the need to use residual British power to *restrain* ever-growing
US power, here and in many other secret UK documents[71] was, understandably, never expressed boldly in public. Yet what J. K. Galbraith called the
'responsibly critical' role of Britain inside the 'special relationship'[72] is a consistent theme for much of the 'short' and 'long' postwars.

'Worthy people of all types', however, could read White Papers and absorb
the essential thinking behind them, as happened with the deterrent paragraphs
of Sandys' review, published as *Defence: Outline of Future Policy*. That such
paragraphs stimulated public protest in post-Suez Britain mattered. So, too,
did the private inquests and studies which, taken together, were to shape
political, official, military and intelligence minds for at least a couple of Whitehall generations afterwards, up to the ending of the Cold War and beyond.

One of the most interesting, which caught the eye of Douglas Hurd when
it was declassified,[73] flowed from the pen of the man charged by the British
and French governments to retake the canal and install a new regime in Cairo
– General Sir Charles Keightley, the Allied Commander-in-Chief of the Suez
operation. His 'Despatch on Operations in the Eastern Mediterranean
November–December, 1956' did not reach the Chiefs of Staff Committee
until October 1957 and its opening sentence was far from catchy ('The experience of the Suez operations stressed certain factors in relation to carrying
out such limited operations in future'[74]). But it was an exemplary piece of work
ranging from practical matters of military command and control, the value of
equipment (helicopters, used on the battlefield by the British for the first time,
were deemed particularly useful) and the shortage of landing craft to matters
of high policy, international diplomacy and politico-military relationships at
the very top.

Although classified 'secret', Keightley's despatch was very careful in the
elliptical way in which it dealt with the complications created by what is usually referred to as the Anglo-French-Israeli 'collusion' (a word which nowhere
appears in Keightley's pages) and the degree to which it *was* known about by
senior French commanders and *not* known about, at least officially, by most
of their British counterparts. These hints and criticisms emerged in Keightley's

sections headed 'Allied Command' and 'Political Direction'. In the former, Keightley told the Chiefs of Staff,

If in any future operations of a similar nature we are to take action with Allies, one vital factor must be rectified. In these operations the British Commanders and the French deputies at Commander-in-Chief and Task Force levels were nearly always able to agree on straight military problems. But it often transpired that the British and French Governments were giving divergent directions to their Commanders, albeit sometimes unofficially. This might have had great repercussions.[75]

Keightley became less veiled when he turned to political direction. The sudden decision in the Cabinet Room to halt the invasion on day one had left an ugly scar:

It is appreciated that in any such operations political factors must always be of paramount importance at the outset and be of constant concern throughout.

However it is urged that a sound and comprehensive political appreciation must be made beforehand, so that ideally the military operations once launched required the minimum of political intervention until they are successful ... the whole of these operations could have been successfully completed in 12 days at a maximum ...

In fact certain changes of orders required for political reasons but clearly unsound militarily inevitably cause a grave lack of confidence in Commanders at each level all the way down to the soldier, sailor or airman who is eventually given a militarily inexplicable order usually at very short notice. This makes him lose confidence in his immediate Commander and is most serious. This aspect is often forgotten when such directions are given at a high level.[76]

There is no evidence in the National Archives that Keightley's despatch was seen – or was intended to be seen – by Mr Macmillan. But his recommendations and observations from here on certainly applied to the very top of the decision-making hierarchy. Keightley plainly believed that if political factors had wrecked a military operation, it was his duty to point it out:

It is of the utmost importance that the 'supreme commander' should be given a political adviser of the highest calibre and completely in the mind and confidence of the Cabinet. I had a very high grade political adviser indeed but he had not the personal contact with the Cabinet which would have avoided many difficulties in the political/ military field. We should, in future, have direct access to the Cabinet and separate communications to allow for this.[77]

Keightley, however, told his bosses that it was their duty to sort out clashes between political and military matters – 'the "supreme commander" should be given all orders and directions through the Chiefs of Staff and it is on their level that all political issues and problems should be resolved'.[78] But, as we saw in the last chapter, the Chiefs could not get ministers to give them 'what next?' directions in October 1956.

It was in taking up his pen to draft the 'World Opinion' section of his despatch that Keightley really removed his general's kid gloves, strengthening his blows with a reminder that he and his planners had warned those in authority of its centrality before the RAF took to the air and the task force sailed from Malta. Keightley declared that:

The one overriding lesson of the SUEZ operations is that world opinion is now an absolute principle of war and must be treated as such. However successful the pure military operations may be they will fail in their object unless national, Commonwealth and Western world opinion is sufficiently on our side.

Throughout the planning period this factor was categorically stated in appreciations to Her Majesty's Government and the intervention of the United Nations and the ultimate result of the whole operations [sic] confirmed its truth.

Turning to the impact of domestic politics, Keightley said 'Her Majesty's Opposition "rocked the landing craft" in the early stages and our preparations were affected by a fear even that the dockyard workers might not reload vehicle ships once unloaded.'[79]

But the Labour Party in the House of Commons and the anti-Suez protestors in Trafalgar Square, Keightley implied, mattered not a jot compared to the man in the White House 3,000 miles away. And in a passage graphically underscoring Alec Home's point about the US Sixth Fleet in the Mediterranean, he wrote,

it was the action of the UNITED STATES which really defeated us in attaining our object. Her action in the United Nations is well known, but her move of the 6th Fleet, which is not so generally known, was a move which endangered the whole of our relations with that country. It is not difficult to appreciate the effect of the shooting down of a United States aircraft or the sinking of a United States submarine, but both these might easily have happened if EGYPT had obtained certain practical support from outside [i.e. the Soviet Union, whose planes and submarines, had they come to Nasser's aid, would have been very hard to distinguish from American ones] which she tried to get or our Commanders had not shown patience and care of the highest order.[80]

American support for the Suez operation, the General judged, 'would have assured a complete success of all our political objects with the minimum military effort'. This, he acknowledged, was 'a political matter but the effects on military operations are vital'.[81]

Keightley was in no doubt about the great lesson to be drawn from the whole Suez affair: 'This situation with the UNITED STATES must at all costs be prevented from arising again.'[82]

Macmillan had already drawn the same conclusion. And the first foreign policy initiative of his premiership was to seek a face-to-face reconciliation with Eisenhower to repair the damage. The meeting took place in Bermuda at the end of March 1957. In private, Macmillan was a very nervous man; the stylish poise he maintained in public was his best and most sustained acting performance, as he admitted in retirement. (Speaking of his parliamentary performances he said, 'I earned a certain reputation for unflappability . . . If only they knew how one's inside was flapping all the time.'[83]) The relief pours out from the pages of his diary when he recounts the twenty-minute drive he and Eisenhower took from the airport to the Mid-Ocean Club where the meetings were to take place:

In the car . . . Pres had talked very freely to me – just exactly as in the old days. There were no reproaches – on either side; but (what was more important) no note of any change in our friendship or the confidence he had in me. Indeed he seemed delighted to have somebody to talk to! In America, he is half King, half prime minister. This means that he is rather a lonely figure with few confidants.[84]

Macmillan was determined that the world should see that the US and UK were doing business again. For example, out of the Bermuda conference came the decision to station sixty Thor US intermediate ballistic nuclear missiles on British soil (which could be launched only by joint Anglo-American agreement under a 'dual key' system[85]). This put eastern England from the East Riding, through Lincolnshire and into East Anglia, even more into the nuclear front-line and, when the Thors began to arrive in September 1958, they became the early object of CND marches.[86]

The imperatives of the Cold War and Washington's anxieties about Soviet advances in rocketry trumped any late-imperial spat in the Middle East. They also paved the way, with Bermuda as its first stage,[87] for conversations which led to a restoration of serious Anglo-American nuclear weapons collaboration the following year,[88] the crucial breakthrough (which led to the amendment of the McMahon Act) taking place when Eisenhower and Macmillan met for a second time in Washington in October 1957.[89]

Behind the scenes, alongside Macmillan's deft and determined post-Suez repair work with the Eisenhower administration, came a spate of reassessments very much along the lines of Keightley's reflections. The first of them Macmillan commissioned within weeks of becoming Prime Minister, far ahead of Keightley. The General in his despatch to the Chiefs would not ignore the Empire/Commonwealth factor. 'A solid front by the majority of the Commonwealth,' he wrote, 'if achieved would have neutralised much of the opposition of other nations.'[90] But it was not achieved. And, as we have seen, Lord Salisbury noted the implications of this when the Cabinet discussed Plan G in mid-November 1956.

Salisbury, soon to resign ostensibly on a colonial matter (the release of Archbishop Makarios from exile in the Seychelles and his return to Cyprus[91]), chaired the Cabinet's Colonial Policy Committee as Lord President of the Council. And it was to him that Macmillan addressed his request for the compiling of the first ever cost–benefit analysis of the British Empire at the end of January 1957.[92] He followed it up in November 1957 with an instruction to Norman Brook that he lead a team of senior Whitehall figures 'to make a fresh assessment of the role which we can hope to play in world affairs today and of the manner in which our limited resources can best be used in support of that role'.[93] Brook called this report *The Position of the United Kingdom in World Affairs*.

The imperial review, *Future Constitutional Development in the Colonies*, was completed two months before the global one began. It is surprising that Macmillan's request for 'something like a profit and loss account for each of our Colonial possessions'[94] should, as late as 1957 (with the Gold Coast moving towards independence as Ghana), be the first exercise of this kind (1857, after the Indian Mutiny, might, rationally, have been moment for it[95]). The Colonial Secretary, Alan Lennox-Boyd, naturally agreed his department should undertake it and, underscoring the novelty of the exercise, told Salisbury that, 'If it is to be worth doing ... it must be done thoroughly; and it will take a good deal of time and involve consultations with a number of Departments.'[96] Whitehall, in fact, managed to do it in just seven months, though the final report acknowledged the cost–benefit element had been taxing ('It is difficult to present economic and financial considerations territory by territory, or even region by region').[97]

It is very difficult to judge the impact of such reports on the thinking of the man who commissioned them, especially as he had already conducted his own post-Suez review of Empire/Commonwealth and Britain's place in the world *before* reading either document, as became apparent in a fascinating section of the fourth volume of his memoirs, *Riding the Storm*, when it appeared in 1971. It took the form of 'the very full notes' he had prepared for his opening statement at the first session of the Bermuda conference on the morning of 21 March 1957. The notes, as one would expect, involve a very Macmillanesque sweep blending history, grand themes and current political matters in an immensely well-rehearsed stream of consciousness:

1. Grateful to President –
receive as host [Bermuda was British Sovereign territory]; greet as old comrade; welcome as head of the greatest and most powerful nation in the world.

2. Critical time in history –
In short time, tremendous problems of Suez Canal and Middle East, on which life of Europe depends. Also critical in secular struggle against Communism; and future of United Nations. League of Nations failed because it placed peace before justice and so lost both.

3. Some general reflections –
Balance of power changed; so quickly difficult to grasp. When I was a child – Queen Victoria's Concert of Powers – i.e. *European* powers. Austrian, Hungarian and Turkish Empires have gone. Large part of Europe and Asia balkanised. Europe destroyed itself in two internecine struggles. The immense powers of US and USSR dominate whole world.[98]

And here, Macmillan changed key; one can almost hear the slow, deliberate voice turning mournful and see the sombre look developing around the drooping moustache:

Many countries in Europe are tempted to give up struggle.
Neutralism (disguised sometimes as Third Force Concept).
I must frankly admit recent events have revived this in Britain. But I believe you cannot be neutral in a war between two principles, one of which – Communism – is evil.
With change in balance of power, change in position of Western and Christian civilisation.
For about 2,500 years Whites have had it their way.
Now revolution: Asia/Africa.
Bound to be immense stresses and great power vacuums over great areas.
Who is to fill these voids? Russia, China or free alliance.
The number of uncommitted countries must increase, as they emerge from Colonial or

other dependence to independence. We in Britain cannot stop; but we might now and then control this process.

In ten to fifteen years, India, Pakistan, Ceylon, Burma.

Now Ghana, in August Malaya; next Singapore.

Same process going on in French territories: Tunisia, Morocco, soon Algeria. Indonesia.

Within ten to fifteen years of mutually destructive European war, these immense territories have become in effect neutral.

In Middle East countries more or less under guidance have become more restless and obsessed by Moslem and nationalist propaganda.

In this confusion, Europe is divided between those who wish to watch from the sidelines – for a change – and those who are ready to play a full part.[99]

Which way would Britain jump? Eisenhower, whose presidency was punctuated by historical soliloquies from British Prime Ministers (command performances almost in the cases of Churchill and Macmillan), can hardly have been surprised by what came next: 'I believe Britain – I know my Government – will be for staying in the game and pulling our weight.'[100]

Macmillan knew full well that such Kipling-like notions of the great game were no longer playable on the old terms. It had to be, in Ruane's and Ellison's phrase, a matter of pursuing power by proxy.

That is why I welcome full restoration of confidence and co-operation between our two countries.

Partly sentiment, though sentiment may work both ways – there are people who still seem to be harking back to that Tea in Boston Harbour.

Partly interest – powerful as you are I don't believe you can do it alone.

You need us: for ourselves; for Commonwealth; and as leaders of Europe.

But chiefly because without a common front and true partnership I doubt whether the principles we believe in can win.[101]

To a remarkable degree, the two reviews of 1957–8 correspond with Macmillan's Bermudan oration – not simply because Norman Brook was there and heard his boss in full flow after having 'prepared pretty carefully'[102] for the occasion.

For there was nothing teleological between the 'lightning flash' illumination of Suez and the subsequent shedding of territory within the next ten years and the ending of sterling's role as a world reserve currency over the following decade. Suez, in John Hunt's words, undoubtedly was 'the most terrible trauma for both ministers and officials',[103] but it didn't lead to a sudden wish in Whitehall to reduce the UK to a medium-sized power with minimal overseas responsibilities. Macmillan's thinking aloud in front of Eisenhower and Dulles in the middle of the Atlantic, like the officials analysing away on the twin reviews in their Whitehall committee rooms, could only go so far in facing up to those hard realities exposed by the events of November 1956, the first time round at least.

Plainly, however, by 1957 territorial empire was no longer seen as a sustainer of British great-powerdom. Its costs and benefits were only a part of the review Macmillan commissioned in 1957, as was apparent from his minute to Salisbury of 28 January. Top of the list of information he required from the Cabinet's Colonial Policy Committee was 'which territories are likely to become ripe for independence over the next few years – or, even if they are not ready for it, will demand it so insistently that their claims cannot be denied – and at what date that stage is likely to be reached in each case'.[104]

As Macmillan was to make plain to Eisenhower in Bermuda a few weeks later, there was, as his staccato notes attested, no British intention 'to give up the struggle'. There was the intention to 'now and then control this process' of colonial independence, and the cost–benefit aspect of his instructions to Salisbury's analysts reflected this:

I should . . . like to see something like a profit and loss account for each of our Colonial possessions, so that we may be better able to gauge whether, from the financial and economic point of view, we are likely to gain or to lose by its departure. This would need, of course, to be weighed against the political and strategic considerations involved in each case. And it might perhaps be better to attempt an estimate of the balance of advantage, taking all these considerations into account, of losing or keeping each particular territory.[105]

As at every stage of the prolonged series of adjustments on Britain's road from top-flight great-powerdom, remaining influence and reach were to be maximized amid the retreat. 'There are presumably places', Macmillan concluded, 'where it is of vital interest to us that we should maintain our influence, and others where there is no United Kingdom interest in resisting constitutional change even if it seems likely to lead eventually to secession from the Commonwealth.'[106]

Macmillan's instructions to Salisbury mirrored the genuine uncertainty he felt about British territories beyond the seas when he took over from Eden.

In his memoirs he recalled how he had 'reflected that in the coming year both Ghana and Malaya were due to become independent. This process was bound to continue. Could it be resisted? Or should it be guided as far as possible into fruitful channels? Was I destined to be the remodeller or the liquidator of Empire?'[107] Would Britain under his premiership attempt to add a few more years to the '2,500' in which 'Whites have had it their way', as he put it before Eisenhower in Bermuda a few weeks later? If the process was unstoppable, exactly how might the UK 'control' it?

By posing the imperial question this way Macmillan was subtly but significantly moving away from the Churchill/Eden position on the remaining territorial Empire. And, as imperial historian Tony Hopkins has noted, the Colonial Secretary, Alan Lennox-Boyd, realized this the moment he read Macmillan's memo to Salisbury. The Prime Minister's request for ministers to 'know more clearly which territories are likely to become ripe for independence over the next few years ...'[108] was the signal. As Hopkins explained, when restored to office in 1951,

the Conservative Government continued a broadly bi-partisan policy on colonial affairs: the aim was to promote the degree of economic and political development needed to support, in the fullness of time, internal self-government in the colonies ... Independence was an entirely different matter. Indeed, Churchill and Eden wanted to ban the use of the word in any discussion of the future of the colonial empire. As far as possible, Lennox-Boyd kept the faith.[109]

Lennox-Boyd and his officials quickly produced a 'skeleton plan' of how the imperial audit should be conducted, which, as he put it to Salisbury, 'implies one or two glosses on the Prime Minister's minute ...' The Colonial Office caught the whiff of true independence in Macmillan's instructions and treated it as if it were a verbal slip on the Prime Minister's part rather than the rat, one suspects, that they truly smelt it to be.

'The Prime Minister', Lennox-Boyd noted in his memo to Salisbury of 15 February 1957, 'drew a distinction between those colonies which would qualify for "full membership of the Commonwealth" and those "which may attain 'independence' [the quotation marks around 'independence' are Lennox-Boyd's, not Macmillan's] but cannot aspire to full Commonwealth membership".'[110] It looked as if 'independence' really was a dirty word for him and his officials.

But the Colonial Secretary, courtesy being the norm of even the most heated Whitehall exchanges in those days, explained himself. Somewhat cheekily, given how famously literate his Prime Minister was, he tried to suggest to Salisbury that Macmillan had not quite meant what he had written.

I have assumed that, in using the word 'independence' in this context, the Prime Minister had in mind the status which we usually describe as internal self-government. It is generally recognised that, whereas some territories, by themselves or in federal arrangement with others, should eventually attain independence as full Members of the Commonwealth [i.e. on the model of Ghana and the Malay Federation], there will remain other territories which, in the foreseeable future at any rate, appear unlikely, for various reasons, to be able to achieve anything other than a considerable degree of internal self-government, with the United Kingdom remaining responsible for at least their defence and external relations.[111]

It was a brave try by the mid-Fifties guardians of Empire but it did not prevail over the six months it took to complete the imperial review. Nor, however, did the Treasury-driven alternative.

The Treasury view involved sustaining Britain's economic and financial interests in the territories under review without the cost and pain of policing and, if necessary, suppressing peoples – or, at least, nationalist leaders – yearning to be free.[112] This was very much in tune with Macmillan's Bermudan line to Eisenhower about the possibility of controlling the process and his own thinking, as he settled into No. 10, about guiding the independence impulses in British Africa and South-East Asia 'as far as possible into fruitful channels'. If a smooth, agreed transition to independence were possible, the former colonies could well trade at much the same level with the old mother country and treat their sterling balances as their national reserves, albeit reserves kept in London.

Britain spent £51m a year in 1956–7 on colonial development and welfare, only about a sixth of the development spending of the UK colonies as a whole (the remaining five-sixths coming out of their own resources or through external loans). 'The Colonies', Brook reported, 'are large holders of sterling assets.' At the end of 1956 they accounted for £1,311m of the sterling balances, and the 'Colonies as a whole have contributed to the strength of the Sterling area in recent years'.[113]

Brook stressed the 'considerable' continuing clout of its colonies in terms of UK trade:

UK COLONIAL TRADE, 1956

UK exports to UK colonies . . . £422m (13% of UK total)
[of this £334m were in manufactures; 13% of the UK total]

UK imports from UK colonies . . . £376m (10% of UK total)
[of this £190m were in basic materials; 17% of the UK total]

UK trade = 25% of total colonial trade.

It was the commentary of the final Brook report in which these *financial* and *trading* data were embedded which held out the possibility of a relatively quick and smooth transfer of *political* power being the best option if the UK's economic interests gained precedence over the desire, in the words of the final report, to 'retain some measure of jurisdiction or protection where this is patently required in the best interests of peoples whose system of govern-ment, of law, or administration, and of political habit, derive from United Kingdom custom and advice'.[114]

The last paragraph of Brook's report leaves the impression that it was a cautious, gradualist production which gave no hint of what was to come within a few years as colony after colony moved to independence (rather than a measured accrual of internal self-government) in the 1960s. For, Brook warned ministers, any

premature withdrawal of authority by the United Kingdom would seem bound to add to the areas of stress and discontent in the world. There are territories over which juris-diction might be surrendered without prejudice to the essentials of st[r]ategy or foreign relations, and at some modest savings to the Exchequer. But would we stand to gain by thus rewarding loyalty to the Crown which is an enduring characteristic of so many Colonial peoples? The United Kingdom has been too long connected with its Colonial possessions to sever ties abruptly without creating a bewilderment which would be discreditable and dangerous.[115]

Under the 'political' section of the review, Brook had penned a sentence as eloquent as it was alarming to buttress that final conclusion: 'The United King-dom stands to gain no credit for launching a number of immature, unstable and impoverished units whose performances as "independent" [note those quotation marks once more] countries would be an embarrassment and whose chaotic existence would be a temptation to our enemies.'[116]

But when Macmillan's review of Empire was declassified, an alternative way of looking at the after-us-the-chaos argument was contained within it. And it was the input from the real-terms cost–benefit analysts in the economic ministries, the Treasury especially, which opened out the intellectual argument for the kind of swift imperial disposal whose prospect so horrified Lennox-Boyd and his Colonial Office briefers.

In the final draft, the Treasury, as moderated through Brook's sub-editing, introduced what the Colonial Office would have seen as heretical thinking: 'In general, if there were a premature grant of independence which resulted in a serious deterioration in political and economic conditions, this might easily cause a serious loss to the Sterling Area's dollar reserves. On the other hand, postponement and only pique resulting from it would be more likely to lead to abandonment of Sterling Area connections.'[117]

The same applied to trade: 'Any premature transfer of power which resulted in serious political troubles and a lasting deterioration in a territory's economic circumstances would of course seriously affect United Kingdom trading and financial interest in that territory. On the other hand, assuming an orderly transfer of power and no appreciable falling-off in a territory's economic activity, the grant of independence need not adversely affect the United Kingdom's trading position in the territory concerned.'[118]

The economic conclusion in the 1957 balance sheet of Empire was paradoxically worded:

To sum up, the economic considerations tend to be evenly matched and the economic interests of the United Kingdom are unlikely in themselves to be decisive in determining whether or not a territory should become independent. Although damage could certainly be done by the premature grant of independence, the economic dangers to the United Kingdom of deferring the grant of independence for her own selfish interests after the country is politically and economically ripe for independence would be *far greater* [emphasis added] than any dangers resulting from an act of independence negotiated in an atmosphere of goodwill such has been the case with Ghana and the Federation of Malaya.[119]

This cost-accountant view of Empire might have been unsentimental and tone deaf to any residual white-man's-burdenry/civilizing-missionary impulses in others parts of Whitehall. But it was not wholly realistic and tinged with a degree of optimism – not least because it did not take account of the special difficulties of moving to independence of those colonies with a substantial number of white settlers such as Kenya and Southern Rhodesia.

The overall impression left by Brook's report, however, is of the slower road to shedding the tropical Empire. It would be quite wrong to see the immediate aftermath of Suez as the starting gun for a race to the door marked 'exit', as the merest glance at the 'independence' and 'internal self-government' forecasts in *Future Constitutional Development in the Colonies* shows (I have put the actual dates of independence in square brackets beside the predictions of the Brook document):

INDEPENDENCE

Federation of Malaya, in August 1957 [1957]
Nigeria, perhaps in 1960 or 1961 . . . [1960]
West Indies Federation, perhaps in 1963
    Jamaica [1962]
    Trinidad and Tobago [1962]
    Barbados [1966]
Singapore, if it joins the Federation of Malaya [it did, but seceded from Malaysia in 1965].

The 'independence' chart included the Central African Federation but recognized that Northern Rhodesia and Nyasaland were separate cases from Southern Rhodesia: the first two were the responsibility of the Colonial Office; Southern Rhodesia, which already had a high degree of independence, came under the Commonwealth Relations Office. The Federation broke up in 1963. The independence dates of its constituent parts were Nyasaland (as Malawi), 1964; Northern Rhodesia (as Zambia), 1964; Southern Rhodesia (as Zimbabwe), 1980. Uganda hovered between the 'independence' and the 'internal self-government' lists – '. . . there will almost certainly be African pressure for rapid advance, which may take the form of demands for a considerable measure of self-government in 1961 and independence in, say, 1967. Uganda cannot be expected by then to have acquired the skill in government, or to have developed the racial harmony, which would justify the United Kingdom Government in relinquishing their authority.'[120] Uganda became independent in 1962.

The second list proved even more out of kilter with reality as it did not foresee for these territories anything more than 'significant developments in internal self-government during the next ten years . . .'[121] Once more the dates of actual independence are in square brackets:

INTERNAL SELF-GOVERNMENT

Singapore [1965]
Cyprus [1960]

Gibraltar [still a UK dependent territory]

Kenya [1963]

Tanganyika (as Tanzania) [1961]

Zanzibar [1963]

Sierra Leone [1961]

The Gambia [1965]

Aden Colony (as Yemen) [1967]

Somaliland Protectorate (to Somalia) [1960]

Mauritius [1968]

British Guiana (as Guyana) [1966]

British Honduras (as Belize) [1981]

This list, though it proved one of the more vivid examples of wishful think-ing in postwar Whitehall, must (those economic and financial sections apart) have been a genuine consolation to Lennox-Boyd in his remaining two years as Colonial Secretary. In fact, in early 1958, he told Rab Butler, 'I keep the product [the final report] always by me and constantly refer to it.'[122]

The Brook paper was a template of competing possibilities and rival pess-imisms about the risks to long-term British interests if colonial independence came too late or too soon. Macmillan still faced a choice. He could act like a decent old district commissioner by moving slowly and hoping that a policy of benevolent preparation and discreet grooming of potential ministers in future independent capitals would not be hijacked by nationalist violence and insurrection. Or he could behave like a hard-nosed asset stripper and pursue a tranche of quick independence deals in the hope of salvaging much-needed British trading and financial interests under the consoling camouflage of a remodelled Commonwealth. For eighteen months he did very little. Not until he had won the 1959 election did he signal his intentions when he replaced Lennox-Boyd at the Colonial Office with the radically minded Iain Macleod and the scramble out of Africa really began.

There was, however, another element of the 1957 audit – the military/strategic value of various pieces of colonial territory – which fitted directly into the next of the post-Suez line of reassessments, *The Position of the United Kingdom in World Affairs*, which Macmillan commissioned from a group of senior officials in November 1957 shortly after receiving his balance-sheet of Empire. This was even more sensitive than its colonial precursor, being labelled 'top secret' as opposed to merely 'secret'.

In its way, the 1958 review, which reached Macmillan in June, was a statement of defiance. Suez might have been a terrible shock and setback, the British economy might remain shaky, the pound sterling precarious, the future of the Empire/Commonwealth profoundly uncertain, the relationship with an integrating Europe difficult, but the UK's global role, give or take a few modifications, was non-negotiable. This was expressed *en clair* in the report's introduction:

We can no longer operate from the position of overwhelming strength – military, political and economic – which we enjoyed in the heyday of our Imperial power. But, although we no longer have superiority in material strength, we can still exercise a substantial influence in world affairs – partly in our own right and because of our position in Europe, and partly as a leader of the independent Commonwealth. We must now bring that influence to bear, in support of the superior material strength of the United States, in the world struggle between the forces of freedom and those of tyranny.

We could not hope to exercise that influence – or to put to their best use the advantages of our special position, either as a link between Europe, the Commonwealth and the United States, or as the guardian and trustee of dependent peoples – if we took refuge in the neutrality and comparative isolation of the purely commercial Powers such as Sweden or Switzerland. Nor could we do so if we failed to maintain our position as a world trading nation and the centre of an international trading currency.[123]

Britain, however, needed to be faster on its feet and needed 'greater freedom of manoeuvre in our overseas policy . . . In the nineteenth century we had the power to impose our will. By contrast, we now have to work largely through alliances and coalitions. We must therefore be more ready to improvise, to adapt our tactics to changing situations and be quick to take advantage of fleeting opportunities to strengthen or improve our position almost anywhere in the world.'

The appetite for global reach was plainly undiminished. But Brook and his fellow permanent secretaries warned ministers that it would be impossible to 'maintain our influence if we appear to be clinging obstinately to the shadow of our old Imperial power after its substance had gone'.[124] For Brook's generation, the Commonwealth conception developed in the 1930s as a way of embracing the UK and independent dominions such as Canada, Australia, New Zealand and South Africa was most definitely not seen as a ruse to maintain the appearance of Empire after its substance had gone. It was treated as a multilateral organization of intrinsic benefit to all concerned. The report's sections on Empire and Commonwealth reflected both this sentiment and the imperial audit:

The Commonwealth. – The Commonwealth system provides an important link both between the interests of Afro-Asian countries and the West, and between the United Kingdom and the colonies. Its cohesion is necessary to ensure our position as a world power and its disruption would have a major effect on the status of sterling . . .

The Colonies. – We have an economic interest in the continual stability and development of the Colonies; a political interest in their continuing evolution within the Commonwealth, and a strategic interest in the maintenance of necessary bases and staging rights. Africa is of special importance.[125]

The cost–benefit analysis of Empire had stressed the colonies' 'essential contribution to the facilities required to maintain and control United Kingdom world-wide sea, air and wireless communications'. (It listed Gibraltar, Malta, Cyprus, Aden, Singapore, Nigeria and East Africa as the 'most important Colonial territories for military reasons'.)[126]

The geometric conceit is still plainly detectable in *The Position of the United Kingdom in World Affairs*, with Britain cast as the 'link' between Europe, the Commonwealth and the United States. But, even at this stage, Europe was the least important of the three in achieving the 'basic aims of our oversea [sic] policy', which Brook and his colleagues itemized as:

(a) We must, in concert, with our friends and allies –
    (i) prevent global war and defeat the efforts of Russia and China to dominate the world;
    (ii) maintain the stability of the free world, especially Western Europe.

(b) We must ourselves –
    (i) preserve and strengthen the cohesion of the Commonwealth;
    (ii) further our trading interests throughout the world;
    (iii) maintain the sterling area and the strength of sterling.

These political and economic aims are inter-dependent. To achieve them maximum Anglo-American co-operation is indispensable. But the Commonwealth association is equally vital to the position of influence which we seek to maintain. Commonwealth cohesion and Anglo-American solidarity are therefore major aims in themselves.[127]

Not a whisper there of Europe, the proposed free trade area or of the European Economic Community which had come into being six months earlier.

Europe, if not its EEC component, found its place in the document, however, within its section on 'Our Principal Existing Political Commitments':

We aim to strengthen our ties with Europe, and are seeking to negotiate a European Free Trade Area. We support the North Atlantic Alliance as the bulwark against Soviet encroachment in Europe. NATO involves the United States in Europe and upholds the confidence of European nations which might otherwise go neutral or lapse into Communism.[128]

The future policy preoccupation of Brook and his fellow global positioners was how to find room for manoeuvre and greater flexibility to enable this nimbler pursuit of British global reach. As ever, the British economy's persistent inability to feed the appetite for continued great-powerdom was the problem:

An adequate current balance of payments surplus is the key to meeting our economic objectives . . . The £250 millions earned in 1957 was . . . plainly insufficient in the conditions of last year . . . Broadly, we believe that in the years just ahead we require an average annual current surplus of £350–400 millions if we are to put sterling on a sound basis – and even more in good years. A high level of exports will be vital.

As ever, the gold and dollar reserves were 'demonstrably too low in relation to our liabilities . . .'[129]

How about slimming down the physical manifestations of great-powerdom – or even shedding a burden or two? Brook and his colleagues thought about that. It was plainly very difficult for them. They looked at six possibilities:

(a) *Withdrawal from Germany.* – Total withdrawal of British forces, or their reduction to a level of a purely token force, would in present circumstances threaten the basis of the Atlantic Alliance and damage our political and economic association with Europe . . .

(b) *Abandonment of the Nuclear Deterrent.* – This would free resources (e.g. scientific man-power) which could be used, among other things, to increase our exports. On the other hand, it is by no means to be assumed that a defence policy which relied solely on conventional forces would cost less than our present defence effort. The maintenance of our nuclear capability is moreover a key element in our relations with the United States and may become so in relation to Europe . . . The deterrent itself at present accounts for less than 10 per cent (£145 millions) of our defence expenditure . . .

(c) *Defence Research and Development.* – Total expenditure on this is £240 millions. It is now being reviewed. Substantial savings are not likely. We should however get better value for money in the nuclear field by the pooling of information with the Americans if the McMahon Act is suitably amended [as it was later that year].

(d) *Colonial.* – Some small savings may accrue as territories become independent. In certain territories, such as Cyprus and Hong Kong, we have military commitments which are a considerable drain on our resources; the same applies to Singapore, though this commitment is not primarily a Colonial one ...

(e) *Commonwealth.* – Australia and New Zealand are at present making a very small contribution to defence and information work in South-East Asia and the Far East. An increase would be welcome, but there would be considerable local political difficulties in these two countries if a much increased contribution were sought at the present time ...

(f) *Foreign.* – It may be possible to redeploy some of resources used oversea [sic] (e.g. in broadcasts to Western Europe) to meet more urgent requirements elsewhere, but the scope for this is limited.[130]

It was all too difficult. How heavily the past weighed upon them, and how the accretion of commitments entangled the permanent secretaries in the Whitehall committee rooms in the early months of 1958.

So what did Brook and his colleagues recommend? Their conclusion began, like their introduction, with a heartfelt passage on what ministers must not do:

It is sometimes suggested that we should do better to rely on our trading position, withdraw from the nuclear club and from our oversea commitments and reduce our status to that of a European Power with a standing similar to that of the Netherlands or Sweden. But comparison with other Powers differently situated from ourselves is dangerous. Our trading position is inextricably bound up with, and sustained by, our roles in Europe and in the Commonwealth and as the centre of the sterling area; none of which can be abandoned or modified in isolation. The question is however one of degree. We are already running down our oversea commitments as fast as circumstances allow us to do so with safety. But to do this wholesale would undermine the position of sterling and could break up the sterling area. We could not recommend such a policy as a fair risk.[131]

Nor, following the 1957 defence review, could they recommend any more 'major reductions' in military spending.

That left 'civil expenditure at home'. And here they effectively opt out (they wanted more for overseas efforts including 'information and cultural activities' as well as development and technical training). Cutting home spending, too, was an awfully vexing matter: 'We recognize that earlier efforts to reduce expenditure on the social services and education have achieved little, and there are great difficulties in reducing other forms of domestic expenditure ... Nor have we touched on the question of taxation.' But here the old great-power bias swung in: 'We suggest that it in these wider fields [i.e. domestic and civil spending] that an answer to the problem of our world position is to be found rather than in abruptly seeking to reduce our oversea and defence expenditure below their present level.'[132]

The country's economic competitors, largely free (with the exception of France) of territorial imperial burdens or (the USA apart) the duty of running a world reserve currency, were girding up as never before, with postwar reconstruction and recovery virtually complete in western Europe and Japan. Yet the best brains in Whitehall urged the Prime Minister to cut back on education and welfare before having another hack at the expenses accruing from great-power status.

Other anxieties were to intrude within eighteen months as these questions thrust themselves more and more into Whitehall's calculations. It was at this stage what Christopher Mallaby called 'a sense of shame' about British decline really began to affect the official mind and mood. The twin reviews of Empire and Britain's place in the world in 1957–8 were in effect the important and indispensable first stage of the post-Suez adjustment. Not until 1959–60 were the longer-term consequences of the 1956 wrenchings confronted fully. This was partly because of the swift and real economic success of the European Economic Community which came into being on 1 January 1958 and the collapse of Britain's alternative idea to the Common Market – the free trade area – the following autumn. French diplomacy, guided once more by General Charles de Gaulle, who had returned to power the previous June on the back of a colonial crisis in Algeria, finally sank the UK's cherished Plan G in November 1958. [133] On 6 November Maurice Couve de Murville, de Gaulle's Foreign Minister, told Reggie Maudling, the British Cabinet's Plan G champion, that the French economy could not sustain competition from both a European Common Market of the Six *and* from the wider free trade area that Britain was proposing.[134] Macmillan wrote desperately to de Gaulle the next day, begging him to see the question as a wide political issue rather than a narrow technical/commercial matter. 'I am convinced', Macmillan wrote, 'that we are already in a crisis which has the seeds of disaster for Europe in the long-term.'[135]

De Gaulle would have none of it. On 14 November 1958, his Minister of

Information, Jacques Soustelle, told the press in Paris that 'it was not possible to form a free trade area as had been wished by the British, that is to say by having free trade between the six countries of the Common Market and the eleven other countries of the OEEC [the Organization for European Economic Co-operation], without a common external tariff and without harmonization in the economic and social sphere'.[136]

This was a blow that helped inject a dose of reality into the fantasy realm of the top officials who had reported to Macmillan on Britain's place in the world a mere four months earlier. And when such adjustments do begin to occur, there is often a rush to find substitutes for the waning ingredients of power and influence.

In these terms, an important and related element was missing in *The Position of the United Kingdom in World Affairs* – the use of intelligence as a surrogate for fading military and economic power. For reasons difficult to fathom (all Brook's fellow reviewers had the highest security clearances), mid- to late-Fifties thinking about this took place in parallel rather than as a part of a wider exercise. It was Norman Brook's successor, Burke Trend, who explained nine years later to Harold Wilson that 'After the Second World War, it became apparent that we should henceforth have to make our way in the world by influence rather than by power [though the 1958 reviewers would not have put it as starkly as this] and that political intelligence would henceforth be at least as important as military intelligence, if not more so.'[137] The shift, in fact, had begun during the Eden premiership when the Chiefs of Staff (to whom the Joint Intelligence Committee still reported) urged on the Prime Minister, the Foreign Secretary and the Defence Secretary the need to reconfigure the UK's intelligence effort for a new phase in the Cold War.

This initiative arose after the 1955 Geneva Conference, 'when it became plain that the Russians were about to indulge in competitive co-existence...'[138] Out of this in early 1956 emerged the Political Intelligence Group consisting of representatives of the secret world, Whitehall's intelligence analysts and their customers, charged with trying to anticipate future Soviet efforts on the subversive side of co-existence and to plan counter-measures. By 1958 this group was influential in the setting of priorities.[139]

It was in the immediate post-Suez climate, however, that the big change in the central organization of intelligence took place when the JIC's patrons ceased to be the Chiefs of Staff and became the Prime Minister and the ministers in his inner intelligence circle. Greater emphasis, too, was placed on political and economic intelligence gathering. The JIC moved from being a sub-committee of the Chiefs of Staff Committee within the Ministry of Defence to a Cabinet Committee inside the Cabinet Office (where it has remained ever since).[140] The Chiefs and the JIC recommended this in April 1957 and Macmillan implemented it the following October. As Percy Cradock put it, the idea was to have the JIC's intelligence 'requirements set in part by the Cabinet or individual ministers rather than just by the Minister of Defence and the Chiefs'.[141]

It took a while before ministers became used to their new role as JIC task-setters and customers. Norman Brook had to ask Macmillan to encourage ministerial suggestions.[142] Given the degree to which most ministers were then sheltered from the details of intelligence provision, it is most unlikely that they fully appreciated the size of the 'power by proxy' element in this most secret of fields. For without the very special Anglo-American intelligence alliance established by the UK–USA Treaty of 1948, the UK would, even by 1957, have ceased to enjoy global intelligence reach.[143]

The 1957 reorganization also affected the intelligence feed to the Prime Minister. From 1946 Mr Attlee and his successors received a weekly intelligence summary, 'particularly on political subjects', derived from 'CX sources' (i.e. agent and other reports reaching MI6).* In the summer of 1957 Patrick Dean, still Chairman of the JIC, suggested to Macmillan's Principal Private Secretary, Freddie Bishop, that with the extension of the JIC's 'responsibilities for the collation and presentation of intelligence on political and economic matters' and the committee's 'removal . . . from the exclusively military sphere' it might be an idea if the new, JIC-provided weekly 'Red Book' of intelligence summaries replace the 'CX Weekly Summary' as '(a) it [the CX summary] includes reports from MI6 sources only which have not been fully collated with other information and (b) it offends against security'.[144] (The 'Red Book' was (and remains) a few pages, tersely written, of fully assessed intelligence with no indication as to its sourcing. The 'CX' material is purely from MI6 and unmixed with the product of other agencies or departments.)

To this No. 10 agreed, but Macmillan and his successors continued to receive 'particular CX reports of importance as soon as they are available'.[145] After discussion with 'C', Sir Dick White, No. 10 arranged for MI6 to send 'a selection of reports on important current subjects' to the Prime Minister's Private Office and Macmillan's private secretaries would draw MI6's attention

---

* Secret Service legend has it that 'CX'-marked material indicated that it emanated from 'C' exclusively.

'to specific subjects ... in which the Prime Minister is particularly interested, at any given time'.[146]

Among the greatest of intelligence gaps in a Prime Minister's red box is that relating to the social and cultural shifts of his or her own country. Other people's countries are very often British intelligence targets, and not just for military or security or economic reasons. Diplomacy, political reporting and the clandestine reach of the UK's secret services are, together, supposed to provide their customers with a proper, rounded appreciation of target societies. Quite rightly, the UK is not seen in the same terms.

It was, therefore, very easy for an overworked Edwardian gentleman in his sixties to be unaware of what was happening in the country he sought to lead. When, in 1963, the Profumo affair threatened to overwhelm him with details of a world of celebrity and sex that he did not understand, Macmillan remarked: 'I do not live among young people much myself.'[147] By that time he had been Prime Minister for over six years and he was still baffled by the changes that had gathered apace which, together, were to produce what for intellectual convenience and brand-recognition purposes has come to be known as the 'Swinging Sixties'. And this greatest of twentieth-century social dam bursts was produced by a confluence of swirling rivulets that were already becoming apparent at home when Macmillan was soliloquizing before Eisenhower in Bermuda about the 'revolutions' in Africa and Asia whose growing force he *did* perceive.

11

Dam Bursts

'I must admit ... that as the son of a Forest of Dean coalminer I am in danger of being unnecessarily sensitive about some of the subtler and more tenacious implications of class ... there are many more people like me, who, with a strange mixture of academic ambition and unwillingness, have been drawn up through the educational hierarchy by a series of examinations and fortunate accidents ... These people are a powerful force – or will be a powerful force – for the first time in British history; but they must first escape the attractions of a new kind of conformity, the security of neat suburbia.'
Dennis Potter, 1959.[1]

'In the years of struggle for economic recovery ... and of dominance by the imperatives of the Cold War, very many of these [wartime] hopes had been frustrated, but they began to emerge again at the end of the fifties. Also significant ... in creating certain of the movements so prominent in sixties society was the breaking out of the frustrations which had been dammed up since the early postwar years. Generally, the conservative and unchanging nature of institutions added to these frustrations.'
Arthur Marwick, 1998.[2]

'... in an inherently mobile and unstable society the maintenance of these social dams, separating unequal levels, is intolerably difficult. The powerful currents of mobility are ever undermining them.'
Ernest Gellner, 1983.[3]

'And so Smiley, without school, parents, regiment or trade, without wealth or property, travelled without labels in the guard's van of the social express.'
John Le Carré, 1961.[4]

Looking back, it is easy to argue that in late-Fifties Britain, the 'long 1930s' was coming to an end in economic, social and welfare terms a decade *after* it had finished thanks to a combination of Beveridge and full employment.

Even for those especially sensitive to the malign effects of old social dams such as Perry Anderson, it was hard at the time to divine the true significance of what was happening. He opened his famous 'Origins of the Present Crisis' essay on post-Suez Britain in the *New Left Review* with the observation that 'society is in the throes of a profound yet cryptic crisis, undramatic in appearance, but pervasive in its reverberations . . . But what kind of crisis is it?'[5]

Revisiting the scene nearly thirty years later, he wrote of 'the economic decline and social deadlock whose symptoms were just then coming into public focus'.[6] So they were – with a running chorus of Penguin Specials of the 'What's wrong with Britain?' variety as a kind of obbligato.[7] Nearly fifty years on, it is much clearer to those who lived through the period that the last five years of the decade really were a time when Bagehot's 'cake of custom'[8] was crumbling in a country which liked to regard itself as the most stable in the advanced world. As Eric Hobsbawm put it in 2002: 'The Fifties are the crucial decade. For the first time you could feel things changing. Suez and the coming of rock-and-roll divide twentieth-century British history.'[9]

It's important to remember that the latter came before the former as Gillian Shephard, a future Conservative Secretary of State for Education, made plain when recalling what was for her the pivotal moment within the grand sweep of Professor Hobsbawm's division. For Mrs Shephard, the daughter of a cattle-dealer in north Norfolk, the moment postwar British society changed was 'rock-and-roll. Bill Haley. *Rock Around the Clock*. I went to see it in Cromer . . . when I was 15 with a girlfriend from grammar school. Suddenly, she began to scream. I couldn't believe it. I was so embarrassed. She'd read about people screaming at the film and cinema seats being torn up. For the first time, Cromer began to behave like London.'[10]

Bill Haley and His Comets had featured in MGM's 1955 film *Blackboard Jungle*, as had the song which gave its name to the title of the 1956 film that so affected Mrs Shephard.[11] Haley was thirty in 1955,[12] getting on in years by comparison with the 20-year-old Elvis Presley,[13] by whom he was soon eclipsed in terms of both innovation (a blend of black rhythm-and-blues and white country-and-western music) and innuendo (no entertainer had ever previously used his pelvis to greater effect) from the moment 'Heartbreak Hotel' and 'Hound Dog' reached these shores in 1956.[14]

But for those who worried about the combined potency of popular music and the social (mis)behaviour of British youth, the film *Rock Around the Clock* will always be the post-1945 benchmark. As the social commentator and pop critic Ray Gosling put it, 'It seemed our whole generation stood in the cinema aisles bawling back at the screen the choruses of those songs: "Razzle dazzle," shouted Bill Haley . . . "Razzle dazzle," we all hollered back . . . As if possessed by the devil, the fit Teds did handstands in the aisles.'[15] Forty years later I found myself in a lunchtime discussion with senior officers of MI5 which, among other things, touched on the difficulty of keeping abreast of changes in society. 'Take the Fifties,' I said. 'I reckon it was the start of ITV in September 1955.' 'No,' said a physically imposing officer who seemed every inch the traditional model of the old male MI5 man, 'it was a bit after that. It was the Saturday I cycled seventeen miles from my public school [Ampleforth, in North Yorkshire] to Thirsk and seventeen miles back to buy a 78 of Elvis's "Hound Dog".'

At the time when the Presley films hit the British screens (*Love Me Tender* in 1956; *Loving You* and *Jailhouse Rock* in 1957; *King Creole* in 1958), there were some 5 million single Britons in the 15–24 age range with nearly £1.5 billion a year to spend between them.[16] Youth was not only a potential problem for the nation's guardians of morality and taste: it had become a serious engine of economic growth and product innovation in its own right. This socioeconomic phenomenon is a central element in the shift towards what posterity likes to label 'the Sixties' – the 'cultural revolution', as Arthur Marwick expressed it, which was 'no transient time of ecstasy and excess, fit only for nostalgia or contempt', but a real shift which 'established the enduring cultural values and social behaviour' in Britain, as well as much of the advanced world, 'for the rest of the century'.[17]

Most of this social churning took place far away from the world of Whitehall with its 'arid paper and shiny politicians'.[18] Occasionally aspects of it reached the Cabinet table. The Wolfenden Report (which recommended decriminalizing homosexual acts provided they were between consenting adults and in private[19]) sold 15,000 copies within three months of its publication on 4 September 1957 and was a very difficult document for the Fifties generation of politicians on all sides.[20] Capital punishment was another thorny issue,[21] and the 'problem' of youth generally which featured in the Albemarle Report on *The Youth Service in England and Wales* of 1960.[22] And there is no question about Cabinet anxieties over community relations and immigration during and after the disturbances in Nottingham and Notting Hill in the summer of 1958.[23]

Government policies – past and current – did contribute powerfully to several of the late-Fifties social and cultural changes. Good and plentiful public housing, for example, was treated as especially important and a necessary condition of wider social improvement. Yet it was starting to undergo a shift which, fifty years later, lacks a single defender. In reaching for the sky the tower block was, as the architect and historian Patrick Nuttgens put it, reflecting 'a desire to make a mark on the landscape, to display technical proficiency and to announce the arrival of a new age'. The early postwar generation of architects had been powerfully influenced by pioneering high-rise or long-landing blocks in 1930s north London such as Wells Coates' Lawn Road flats in Belsize Park and Berthold Lubetkin's Highpoint 1 and 2 in Highgate.[24] Such flats were designed for the selective rich, not the mass needy – more high society than high rise.

But it was only twenty years later that British cities entered their age of elevation, thanks to a combination of new mass-produced prefabricated building materials, an architectural profession which began using them to make reality Le Corbusier's mid-1940s notion of 'cities in the sky' and a little-noticed change in the pattern of central government subsidy for new public housing. For just as Michael Young and Peter Willmott were completing their work on family and kinship in Bethnal Green – which showed that 'very few people wish to leave the East End. They are attached to Mum and Dad, to the markets, to the pubs and settlements, to Club Row and the London Hospital'[25] – Eden's Minister of Housing, Duncan Sandys, in November 1955 put through the measure which would change the nature of their neighbourhoods dramatically.

Until then, all publicly provided flats had received the same level of grant. But because 'construction, in practice, costs more as you go higher', Sandys told the House of Commons, 'the result has been that flats in low blocks have been more heavily subsidised in relation to costs than flats in high blocks. Apart from being inadequate, this has unintentionally influenced local authorities to concentrate on building blocks of three, four and five storeys, which I believe, many honourable members will agree are most monotonous.'[26] Over the four years 1956–60, high-rise blocks increased from 3 per cent of new public housing provision to 15 per cent (it had reached 26 per cent by 1966).[27]

High-rise buildings never won the affection of those fated to live in them. As early as the late Fifties the continuing researches of Young and Willmott and their team found that in Bethnal Green, where 'the high-rise was just starting', as Young explained to me, it 'was about as unpopular as anything could be'.[28] For most young British architects, however, it offered an irresistible combination of professional thrill and practical problem-solving.

Patrick Nuttgens, for example, was converted to the ideas of Walter Gropius and Le Corbusier by Robert Matthew, the London County Council architect, who had a powerful influence as both a practitioner and, later, Professor of Architecture at Edinburgh University.[29] Looking back, Nuttgens singled out both 'idealistic' impulses ('High-rise housing was already associated for many designers with progress and the expression of a new technological age'[30]) and the 'pragmatic' solving of 'definable problems' ('the shortage of land, especially where planning policies were limiting the growth of the city outwards; and the overwhelming demand for accommodation'[31]).

Nuttgens admitted that the rush to reach for the sky owed nothing to 'demand from the prospective tenants . . . Nor . . . the outcome of sociological study.'[32] Peter Townsend, a member of the Young/Willmott team in Bethnal Green, said he and his fellow researchers quickly learned from young families perched sixteen storeys up the disadvantages of tower-block life, which simply could not replicate the old street life. ('How can kids play safely a hundred feet below watching parental eyes?')[33]

For Michael Young, old Bethnal Green had been 'the almost ideal environment for bringing up children . . . children could move, before the age of the car, from aunt to uncle, grandmother and grandad and have a choice of the relatives they felt most at home with from a wide array' in neighbouring streets. Why didn't the Bethnal Green councillors, who came from those very streets and shared the attitudes of their constituents, resist the bulldozing and break-up of those communities? Michael Young believed the Bethnal Green case was a microcosm of inner-city experience across the country: 'They were hoodwinked and out-talked by the clever architects and planners. They gave way . . . and they gave way all over the country . . . to what was thought to be the modern fashion – the architectural and planning ideologies.'[34]

Of course, the slum housing being replaced often lacked in physical amenity what, at best, it possessed in terms of human warmth. And amenity mattered, certainly when the shift from cold discomfort to indoor lavatories and heating which reached every room in the building could amount to a leap from 1859 to 1959, as it often did in the late Fifties. The 1951 census for the first time introduced an amenity index for all British households which, when read alongside the 1961 figures, shows the Fifties as a decade of considerable improvement (see table overleaf).

Between 1951 and 1960, the proportion of owner-occupiers in England and Wales rose from 31 per cent of households to 44 per cent, the number of houses and flats rented from local authorities or New Town corporations from 17 to 25 per cent, while private renting fell from 52 to 31 per cent.[35]

	1951		1961	
	Share	Lack	Share	Lack
Fixed bath	8%	37%	4.6%	22%
WC	13%	8%	5.8%	6.9%

Roy Porter caught this almost elegiacally in the preface to his *London: A Social History*. His Fifties London childhood lay south of the Thames, in New Cross Gate, which was 'not exactly the Bethnal Green beloved of Young and Willmott, but it was a stable if shabby working class community completely undiscovered by sociologists'.[36]

Writing in the mid-1990s, Porter saw this south-east London world as almost part of a past which

now seems another country: bomb-sites and prefabs abounded, pig-bins stood like pill-boxes on street corners, the Co-op man came round with a horse and cart delivering the milk, everybody knew everybody . . . locals grumbled about how run-down and old-fashioned the area was, hemmed in by railway sidings, canal and docks that had long provided secure employments but which imparted a grimy, dingy feel.[37]

In 1959 the Porters forsook their 'three-up, three-down council house' which he and his parents shared with Roy's grandparents and uncle (with its outside lavatory and tin bath 'filled from kettles and a wheezing Ascot gas water-heater' once a week) for a house in Norwood, 'five miles out into the suburbs. It cost £3,000. Its walls were pebble-dash; it had a bathroom, an inside toilet, French windows and plumbed in hot water. It was heaven. The Porters were a classic upward-social-mobility statistic in the era that had never had it so good.'[38]

None the less, Roy Porter continued to recall a happy pre-Norwood child-hood – 'though living was cramped and people had to be careful with money, the feeling was that, with the war over, with full employment and the NHS, life was secure; within limits, you could get on, be neighbourly, be respectable, grow tomatoes, save for a washing-machine and afford a week's holiday at Jaywick Sands with candyfloss and cockles'.[39] Porter wondered, forty years on, how 'different are things in SE14 now'. The picture was mixed. Many of the houses were privately owned 'and the monotony of Deptford Borough Council's bottle-green and cream paint has yielded to rainbow hues, Regency doors and louvre windows, and kerbsides crammed with cars'.[40]

The picture, however, was dappled by loss and social decay:

Docks are closed, the canal is filled in, the railway a ghost of its former self. The local sweet factory and dress makers have closed down. New Cross Road, which once wore an air of faded early Victorian elegance, is now a ceaseless roar of lorries hurtling down to the Channel ports. The big houses by the Marquis of Granby pub, once admired, are slums, squats or boarded-up, like many of the shops. Dossers and drunks litter the gardens, and some students of mine were mugged there last year. South London has gained a mean name for drug-dealing, racial violence, gangland crime and contract killing.[41]

A similar picture could be painted for a host of Fifties to Nineties British urban landscapes.

The make-up of the urban population had undergone vast changes, too. Commonwealth immigration, especially from the West Indies, had been a recurrent preoccupation for ministers and civil servants from the last years of the Attlee governments. What was new in the late 1950s, and genuinely a shock, was the first serious racial violence experienced within the United Kingdom in Nottingham and Notting Hill, west London, in August–September 1958. It occurred shortly after the Macmillan government had yet again turned to the possibility of legal curbs on immigration in line with a Cabinet decision the previous year to review the position. (By this time Salisbury was no longer in the Cabinet Room to argue the hard, restrictionist line. He had resigned at the end of March 1957. The occasion was the government's decision to release the Cypriot nationalist leader Archbishop Makarios from exile in the Seychelles. The cause was a wider discontent about Macmillan's policy centrism, including on immigration.)[42]

Lord Hailsham, who, as Lord President of the Council, chaired the Cabinet Committee on Colonial Immigrants, presented its report to the Cabinet on 1 July. The document, 'Commonwealth Immigrants',[43] was shot through with anxieties about both the pace of immigration (the figures before them for 1957 indicated 23,016 new arrivals from the West Indies, 6,620 from India and 5,189 from Pakistan[44]) and the social problems already arising from it in certain urban areas. Early returns from Home Office immigration officers at seaports and airports indicated a quickening rate in the first few months of 1958, leading the Cabinet Committee to conclude that if immigration 'were to continue at the level reached at the beginning of this year, there would seem little alternative to proceeding as a matter of urgency with legislation to restrict it'.

Employment, health and, above all, housing were the 'social and economic problems arising from coloured immigrants' which most worried Hailsham and his colleagues:

The immigrants from India and Pakistan particularly are often unskilled and illiterate and unable to speak English; many of them live in dirty and overcrowded conditions; and the health of some of them gives cause for concern. They find employment less easily than do the West Indians . . .

Social difficulties so far involving the coloured population generally (but most acutely the West Indians because they are the most numerous), have emerged in some areas – for example in parts of north-west London, and in Brixton and Birmingham, where large numbers of coloured have congregated. Property has been bought up by coloured landlords, who have then made the position of white tenants intolerable, and entire streets have gone over to a coloured population.[45]

Nevertheless, neither Hailsham's committee nor the Home Secretary, Rab Butler, thought the time had yet come to legislate. As the Cabinet paper put it, 'public opinion generally does not appear yet to be seriously concerned by the problem; legislation to curb coloured immigration from the Commonwealth would clearly be contentious and, if the rate of immigration could be held back by administrative measures and also by appropriate publicity in the countries concerned, we do not think that early legislation would be justified'.[46]

The Cabinet discussed the matter on 1 July and adopted the Hailsham/ Butler line following 'general agreement' during the discussion but the minutes picked up ministers' anxiety that 'unrestricted coloured immigration might have serious social consequences in the longer term; and although it would be desirable, if possible, to avoid legislation on this subject in the last full session of the present Parliament [i.e. 1958–9; the latest an election could be held was mid-1960], the situation should be closely watched'.[47] Less than two months later, the serious disturbances in Nottingham and Notting Hill pushed the immigration question high up the political agenda and, as Ted Heath (still Chief Whip) later noted, the late summer of 1958 was a turning point, revealing how the 'racial prejudice . . . immigrants encountered' and ongoing 'inter-racial friction eventually prompted Rab Butler to bring in the Commonwealth Immigration Act in 1962 to limit the numbers of non-white immigrants entering the country . . .'[48]

It was not just ministers who were shocked by the sudden violence; so was the country as a whole and those beyond the seas who had a certain image of the United Kingdom. As Harry Hopkins wrote not long after, suddenly the 'arclights of world publicity were switched on to the festering slums of Not-ting Dale. For days the attention of the world's press, radio, television, was focused on this mess which the "Mother Country" appeared to have been concealing under her neat official carpet.'[49]

The trouble flared first in Nottingham on 23 August following a weekend brawl outside a pub after which white youths set out on what they called 'nig-ger hunts' through the city streets.[50] The following weekend, serious violence broke out in Notting Hill, west London – once an area of Edwardian elegance, now very run down and plagued by racketeer landlords.[51] Competition for housing was a cause of social inflammation, especially when immigrants from the Caribbean settled in the area during the early and mid-Fifties.

When making the television series *What Has Become of Us?* in the mid-1990s I talked to Rene Webb, a West Indian serviceman in the RAF during the war who had returned to the UK to live in Notting Hill. He told me the tension had been building: 'We could feel the pressure was there . . . It didn't seem that they [the authorities and the police] cared. You were constantly being threatened on the streets . . .'[52]

At first the West Indian community received the worst of it, with white gangs roaming Notting Dale rampaging down Portobello Road and Colville Road chanting, 'Kill the niggers!', attacking any black person they saw and smashing property.[53] Rene Webb described the turning point: 'The riot devel-oped. We were getting the worst of it until a few of us decided to fight back . . .' They waited for the next assault. 'We prepared for that. And when they came, we attacked before they did and they ran away.'[54]

The police were severely stretched in trying to interpose themselves between rival groups especially during the biggest showdown on the nights of Sunday 31 August and Monday 1 September. Tony Benn lived close by in Holland Park and his diary entries are vivid accounts of the two worst days and nights of violence:

Monday 1 September 1958: For the second night running last night the race riots went on in Notting Hill. A very ugly situation is developing. I drove through the streets this evening and it was extremely sinister to see everyone standing out in front of their doors in the hot sultry air just waiting for something to happen. The crowds of young people gathering on street corners indicated the outbreak of some new attack.

Tuesday 2 September 1958: The trouble continued on an even bigger scale last night. I toured the area before breakfast and saw the debris and the corrugated iron behind the windows of the prefabs where the coloured families live. The use of petrol bombs and iron bars and razors is appalling. There is a large area where it is not safe for people to be out.[55]

The trouble simmered on. Then, as Peter Ackroyd put it, 'by a curious chance the great heat of these August [and early September] days was swept away by a thunderstorm, the rain falling among the debris of broken bottles and wooden clubs'.[56] A weary and dispirited Harold Macmillan ('I am suddenly feeling very old and tired') simply added 'the so-called "Racial Riots"'[57] to his long list of burdens and anxieties and the host of issues overloading the Cabinet's agenda as his diary entry for 8 September records:

Early to London. Cabinet 11–1.15, 2.30–6. An immense agenda – Cyprus; W Indians and others in UK and the riots; Iceland and the fish war; the Far Eastern Crisis [China and the threat to Formosa (now Taiwan)]; H.P. [hire purchase] deposits and the new banking policy; Scottish teachers' pay.[58]

Even the great downpour over the night of 5 September which doused Notting Hill ('PC Rain' as I once heard an old Met sergeant call it when, as a young reporter in the mid-1970s, I covered a West End demonstration) depressed the Prime Minister:

Last night there was a tropical storm all over the S of England – the most spectacular in our history, says the Press. The harvest in East Anglia and the South will now be finally ruined, I fear. What is almost worse is that the potato crop is going to go mouldy. We are certainly not having much luck in my period of office. When I think of all the troubles since 1956, I feel we have had almost more than our share – and now the weather![59]

Macmillan devoted far more space in his diary to that tropical storm than he did to the summer riots of 1958. Interestingly, his official biographer, Alistair Horne, noted that over the nearly seven years of his premiership, Macmillan, as 'is clear from his diaries ... devoted ten times as much attention to the problems of the Central African Federation as he did to the problem of Commonwealth immigration'.[60]

When the Cabinet's attention turned to the significance of the riots on the morning of 8 September, it is intriguing to trace the similarity between the content (if not the phraseology) of Butler's presentation and the ITV report filmed (by one black and one white reporter) amid the broken glass and the run-down houses of Notting Hill. One white youth tells the West Indian journalist that, in his view, of the Caribbean population, 'the majority they are bad ... I think we've got the worst in Notting Hill. They've got girls on the game and all that.' Another white man, probably in his early thirties, says, 'I happen to know plenty of white people who can't get a home ... They [the West Indians] all club together and they simply buy a place up, just like that.'[61]

Butler told the Cabinet 'that the police were confident that they could control the racial disturbances' which had arisen in Nottingham and Notting Hill: 'It would be necessary, however, to give further consideration to the circumstances which provoked these outbreaks of violence between white and coloured people. They appeared to originate largely in competition for housing and casual employment; and they were aggravated in some cases by disputes about women. It would be desirable to seek to establish some form of control over the emigration of coloured people from their countries of origin ...'[62]

During the Cabinet's discussion, the need for 'law and order [to] be maintained irrespective of the racial characteristics of individuals' was stressed and it was also suggested (by which minister is unknown) it would 'be important to avoid, if possible, any major pronouncement of policy about the principle of Commonwealth immigration. We should continue to deal with this problem empirically and should base our action on the practical consideration of the availability of housing and the capacity of the labour market.'[63] Macmillan certainly agreed with this line. In mid-September, the Prime Minister of Jamaica, Michael Manley, was in London and discussed the riots with Butler and the Colonial Secretary, Alan Lennox-Boyd. They 'seem to have got on well', Macmillan noted in his diary. 'We can, I hope, reduce the rate of immigration *without* legislation. At least, we must give this a trial.'[64] They were sticking to the line agreed on 1 July – for the moment at least.

It is not excessively teleological, however, to draw a line from early September 1958 to the passing of the Commonwealth Immigrants Bill into law four years later, as Ted Heath indicated. Butler, the Home Secretary of the day, explained in his memoirs that he

had been gravely troubled by the Notting Hill riots in 1958, and I cannot praise too highly the determined action of the Judiciary in the person of Mr Justice Salmon who pronounced the most stringent sentences on the racist trouble-makers. But whilst disturbances on this scale did not recur, I was by 1961 [he was still Home Secretary] persuaded that the rise of racial tension could be avoided only if it were anticipated. This in essence was the argument for the Commonwealth Immigrants Bill which controlled entry by a system of labour permits that in practice approximately halved the rate of net immigration.[65]*

Most observers were shocked, I suspect, not so much by the friction as by its explosion into violence. As Peter Ackroyd noted, 'during their trial some of the white rioters were told: "By your conduct you have put the clock back 300 years." But this would only take them back to 1658; they had in fact behaved like their medieval predecessors who "swarmed" upon supposed enemies or aliens with often fatal results.'[66]

For Michael Young, the anatomizer of urban life six miles to the east of Notting Hill in Bethnal Green, 'it was a surprise to me at the time – the violence and virulence of it – and certainly very saddening to me because the high-minded principles I'd had were obviously going to be buffeted in many ways from that time on. And here was a new strand in politics that hadn't been prepared for by Beveridge. Not one of the "Five Giants" is "racial prejudice".' Young concluded that the 'riots had shattered the illusion that the Queen's subjects, whatever their origins, could live together in harmony'.[67]

Things were never the same again. The comfortable shared notion within a nation which prided itself on its tolerance and civility that race riots were a blemish on other societies such as South Africa or the southern USA was gone for ever. The tone of British domestic politics shifted and, after a short lag, the politics and the statute law concerning immigration did too.

The late Fifties was also a moment of intermingling for notions of identity, faith, morals, crime and punishment. It was easy enough for Butler to raise the possibility of changing the law on prostitution on the back of the Cabinet's discussion of Notting Hill, and, a year later, he piloted to its royal assent a Street Offences Act which raised the penalties for soliciting, 'moved to take such action by the condition of the streets around Mayfair and Piccadilly which were literally crowded out with girls touting for clients'.[68]

The 1959 Act implemented a recommendation of the Wolfenden Report of 1957 which, though almost entirely remembered for recommending the legalization of homosexuality, also dealt with prostitution. In fact it was anxiety about the number of prostitutes on the streets of a London filled with visitors attracted by the Coronation that had initially led Maxwell Fyfe as Home Secretary in 1954 to commission Sir John Wolfenden, the vice-chancellor of Reading University and an ex-public school headmaster, to

*Nearly 40 years later I asked Enoch Powell (whose intervention in the immigration debate in 1968 famously caused Ted Heath to expel him from the Shadow Cabinet) how he had reacted to the Notting Hill riots. 'I think I was unsurprised,' he replied, 'but I wouldn't put it higher than that.'

undertake his inquiry. The question of homosexuality was included 'almost as a make-weight', in the words of a top Home Office civil servant.[69]

The morality of same-sex relationships, however, was simply too difficult even for the guileful Rab to tackle along Wolfenden lines, so deeply did emotions and instincts run not just within the late-Fifties Conservative Party but through society generally. Another decade had to pass before legislation could be carried here. Butler's instinct had been to legislate along the lines indicated by Wolfenden, but he could not persuade his Home Office ministerial colleague, David Renton,[70] let alone the country. He admitted as much in the Commons on 24 November 1958, explaining, 'I do not think we have yet with us a general sense of opinion which would regard it as right to alter the criminal law in the sense suggested by the Committee.' Much the same message was conveyed to Wolfenden himself.[71]

Macmillan had a deep and old-fashioned Christian faith which he was keen to talk about (early on in his premiership he wrote of Archbishop Geoffrey Fisher, 'I try to talk to him about religion. But he seems to be quite uninterested and reverts all the time to politics'[72]), but could not understand, let alone wish to discuss, what he later described to the Queen as the 'strange underworld'[73] of a society where the old values and hierarchies appeared to be receding all around him.

It would be crude and crass to depict late-Fifties Britain as a tussle between stiff and baffled old men and freewheeling angry young ones. Nevertheless, some of the first were running the government while some of the second were cutting a swathe through literate and vocal sections of the governed. And they talked past each other. Macmillan delighted in placing in his diary his thoughts on the books he had read. But the 'angries' seem to have passed him by. The ultimate insider, one suspects, may never even have heard of Colin Wilson's *The Outsider*,[74] the cult book of 1956 which swept the market and its author temporarily to heights which he seems to have found as baffling as many of his readers found his philosophical and religious digressions.[75]

The Outsider was not – is not – an easy read. Eavesdropping on a young and sensitive soul grappling with the meaning of life could not be anything else, especially if life up to that point has treated him to a series of menial jobs and a touch of rough sleeping eased by the daytime warmth of the British Library Reading Room. The book, with its mixture of religious and philosophical reflections, leaves me baffled. It may have left its author similarly perplexed if his final paragraph (which is representative of the whole) is anything to go by:

There are still many difficulties that can be touched on here. The problem for the 'civilization' is the adoption of a religious attitude that can be assimilated as *objectively* as the headlines of last Sunday's newspapers. But the problem for the individual always will be the opposite of this, the conscious striving *not* to limit the amount of experience seen and touched; the intolerable struggle to expose the sensitive areas of being to what may possibly hurt them; the attempt to see as a whole, although the instinct of self-preservation fights against the pain of the internal widening, and all the impulses of spiritual laziness build into waves of sleep with every new effort. The individual begins that long effort as an Outsider; he may finish it as a saint.[76]

Quite why, when this appeared under the Gollancz imprint in May 1956, Cyril Connolly was moved to write in the *Sunday Times* that Wilson was 'a young man of twenty-four who has produced one of the most remarkable books I have read for a long time'[77] is difficult to fathom. But he did and the work, in more recent publishing argot, acquired legs, suggesting that beneath the impulse to savour the fashionable book of the hour lay a confused fluidity of beliefs into which Wilson tapped.

It is possible to see Wilson as the early incarnation of the clever, post-Butler Act strivers beating their fists in baffled frustration as their 'internal widening' left them on the margins of still incurious, hierarchical society. Noel Annan noted that *The Outsider* was greeted by 'an ominous silence in the academic world; and none of the sixty-two books Wilson published in the next thirty-odd years was ever reviewed in this way'.[78] How then to explain its success? Perhaps, suggested Annan, this was the moment when the retreat of religious explanations gave Wilson his moment as mystical/philosophical reflection found a niche within the mind of the young and the curious.[79]

Wilson's sudden fame had much to do with the random coincidence, as he reflects in his memoirs, of the fact that 'suddenly *The Outsider* and [John Osborne's] *Look Back in Anger* had appeared in the same week. That was all the press needed to start talking about it.'[80] J. B. Priestley wrote about them in the *New Statesman*. *The Times* coined the phrase 'angry young men' and a phenomenon was launched. Wilson loathed Osborne's play when he went to see it at the Royal Court: 'It seemed to me an outpouring of self-pity and bad temper.'[81] The *Daily Express* ran a series on 'Angry Young Men'. Wilson needed the money and wrote for it. 'I had no idea how much I would come to hate this label,' he wrote nearly fifty years later.

The Osborne play was – and remains – much easier to absorb than the Wilson book. The play is set in a flat in the Midlands. Jimmy Porter, its anti-hero, is a flesh-and-blood hater of encrusted old Britain. Wilson was more anguished than anything else ('I wasn't in the least angry – except about my years of struggle; and now that I was recognised, even this hardly applied').[82] Raging, rather than self-widening, was the forte of Jimmy Porter. In the play's most famous passage, he condemns the lingering imperial past of the father of his upper-class wife and the heroic past of his working-class father who perished during the Spanish Civil War:

I suppose people of our generation aren't able to die for good causes any longer. We had all that done for us, in the Thirties and the Forties, when we were still kids . . . There aren't any good, brave causes left. If the big bang does come, and we all get killed off, it won't be in aid of the old fashioned grand design. It'll just be for the Brave New-nothing-very-much-thank-you. About as pointless and inglorious as stepping in front of a bus.[83]

It is Porter's wife, Alison, who captures the ambivalence of mid-Fifties Britain on the turn when she tells her father, 'You're hurt because everything is changed. Jimmy is hurt because everything is the same. And neither of you can face it. Something's gone wrong somewhere, hasn't it?'[84]

What Cyril Connolly did for Colin Wilson in the *Sunday Times*, Kenneth Tynan did for John Osborne in the arts pages of the *Observer*. He saw him as the exemplar of a clever yet bitter and alienated generation in whom many younger people, post-Suez, might see themselves reflected: 'The Porters of our time deplore the tyranny of "good taste" and they refuse to accept "emotional" as a term of abuse; they are classless and they are also leaderless. Mr Osborne is their first spokesman in the London theatre.'[85]

But, for me, the contemporary, though not especially angry, young man with the most impact was Kingsley Amis, whose own anti-hero, *Lucky Jim* Dixon, appeared two years before the Wilson/Osborne summer. Quite apart from an unsurpassable summary of the vilest of hangovers – 'His mouth had been used as a latrine by some small creature of the night, and then as its mausoleum'[86] – it uses wit as its weapon to carve up the absurdities of social and intellectual status in the setting of a provincial university in early postwar Britain. Dixon, who had a completely unheroic war as an RAF Corporal somewhere in the West of Scotland, is the lowest form of lecturing life in a History Department headed by the preposterous and pompous Professor Welch.*

---

* The story is tangled, relentlessly funny and it has a happy ending (which is why I adored both the film of 1957, with Ian Carmichael playing Jim, and the book when I read it later).

The book has much to say about the rise of the grammar schoolboy, up on his brains,[87] bashing gauchely on, pulling a series of grotesque faces and taking a profoundly different view of medieval history to that of the boss on whose whim his tenure hangs:

As he approached the Common Room he thought briefly about the Middle Ages. Those who professed themselves unable to believe in the reality of human progress ought to cheer themselves up . . . by a short study of the Middle Ages. The hydrogen bomb, the South African Government, Chiang Kai-shek, Senator McCarthy himself, would then seem a light price to pay for no longer being in the Middle Ages. Had people ever been as nasty, as self-indulgent, as dull, as miserable, as cocksure, as bad at art, as dismally ludicrous or as wrong as they'd been in the Middle Age[s] . . . ?[88]

In addition to the best-ever hangover paragraph in the history of fiction, Amis also managed to paint the best-ever drunken lecture-giver scene, in which Dixon, to the horror of Welch, demolishes the notion of 'Merrie England'.[89] Amis's genius was to extract and expose the absurd from all pretensions. And he, above all, did that for the 'angries', with whom he was blithely and erroneously bundled. Reviewing Wilson's *The Outsider*, Amis wrote: 'One of the prime indications of the sickness of mankind in the mid-twentieth century is that so much excited attention is paid to books about the sickness of mankind in the mid-twentieth century.'[90]

Jimmy Porter's Alison had put her finger on it. Since that glorious moment in 1940–41 when, in Len Deighton's words, 'evil was in the ascendant, goodness diffident, and the British – impetuous, foolish and brave beyond measure – the world's only hope',[91] both the guardians and the would-be destroyers of tradition had become edgier and more anxious almost with every passing year. By the end of the Fifties, against a backdrop of rising crime and falling church attendance, a multi-layered debate on faith and morals, society and public policy, crime and punishment took place in a messily fragmentary way in Parliament and pulpit, Cabinet Room and courtroom. However, one shining exception to this largely unavoidable incoherence was to be found at the most cerebral end of the legal profession.

The exchange was part of a delayed response to the section of the 1957 Wolfenden Report dealing with the criminality of homosexual acts in private between consenting adult males. It took place between a pair of finely calibrated legal minds and was judged by the biographer of one of them as 'probably *the* debate of the decade'.[92] The minds in question were those of Patrick Devlin and Herbert Hart and at issue was the power of the state to outlaw private practices it deemed immoral even if they harmed no one else.

It is a debate that has continued with scarcely a pause[93] from the moment Devlin approached the British Academy's lectern on 18 March 1959 to deliver its annual Maccabaean Lecture in Jurisprudence on 'Morals and the Criminal Law',[94] to Tony Blair's declaration on 19 July 2004, while launching the Home Office's five-year strategy document with Home Secretary David Blunkett, that it 'marks the end of the 1960s liberal, social consensus on law and order'.[95]*

The nerve Devlin and Hart exposed with such forensic skill as their exchanges ran on into the early Sixties has remained sensitive ever since and twitched into life every time social legislation affecting faith, morals or personal behaviour has come before Parliament. Patrick Devlin, a judge from his early forties, had made his name in handling commercial cases but became more widely known when he presided in 1957 over the trial for murder of Dr John Bodkin Adams and, in his direction of the jury (who acquitted Adams), declared that 'no doctor, nor any other man, no more in the case of the dying than of the healthy, had the right deliberately to cut the thread of life'.[96] So, as R. F. V. Heuson put it when Devlin died in the early 1990s, 'the injection of lethal drugs is still murder. It is different if invasive medical treatment is withdrawn from a patient who is in a permanent vegetable [sic] state.'[97] Devlin brought a Catholicism-honed 'rigorous-conscience'[98] to the law both as a judge, a Law Lord (which he became shortly after his British Academy lecture) and as an inquisitor in 1959 into the suppression of disturbances by the colonial authorities in Nyasaland.

(His subsequent report infuriated Macmillan ('I have ... discovered that he is (a) *Irish* – no doubt with that Fenian blood that makes Irishmen anti-Gov on principle, (b) *A lapsed R.C.* (c) *A hunchback ...*' he wrote with absurd intemperance in his diary [99]) by claiming that 'Nyasaland is – no doubt temporarily – a police state, where it is not safe for anyone to express approval of the policies of the Congress Party'[100] (as we shall see in Chapter 13).)

Herbert Hart, a philosopher by training (with a distinguished wartime career in MI5 behind him), became in the twenty years after 1945 'quite simply, the pre-eminent English-speaking legal philosopher of the twentieth

---

* One of the flaws in the Prime Minister's speech was its assumption that a consensus had been reached at any point in the forty-five years between the Devlin–Hart debate and the launching of the Blair–Blunkett plan for a more ordered and orderly society. As with all 'consensus' debates, victory for one or other set of protagonists is neither complete, nor, insofar as it tilts one way or the other, static.

century'.[101] Hart had lapsed from his Jewish faith to the point of being actively secular in his attitudes[102] (though the 'tension between an underlying sense of Jewish identity and an intellectual commitment to its moral irrelevance' was ever-present in him[103]). He was part of that extraordinary generation of Oxford philosophers, which included Stuart Hampshire, Peter Strawson and Isaiah Berlin, when theirs was the dominant discipline in that university.[104] Devlin and Hart were as one in wishing jurisprudence, the philosophy of law, to be rescued from the fussy and narrow by-ways into which the study of it in Britain had retreated since the early-nineteenth-century utilitarians had successfully projected it into the chief socioeconomic debates of that reforming era.[105] As Noel Annan put it, 'Our Age' (his and Hart's generation) in general scarcely recognized the concept of 'rights' because their peers in the legal profession

were so uninterested in general ideas. No one who read law ever doubted the subtlety of English lawyers. But the common law, the entrancing task of citing case against case and countering an obiter by a chief justice against a judgement by a law lord, had not given much of a welcome to jurisprudence . . . Hart had the impertinence to bring moral concepts into play with legal concepts, and his encounter with the Roman Catholic law lord, Patrick Devlin, revived jurisprudence – until that time moribund in England.[106]

That revival endures to this day.

In his opening words to the British Academy that evening in March 1959, Patrick Devlin sought to give jurisprudence its place in the legislative firmament that had been so long resistant to it and paid tribute to Wolfenden's Committee on Homosexual Offences and Prostitution for having attempted to do just that, as their report 'does what law reformers so rarely do; it sets out clearly and carefully what in relation to its subject it considers the function of the law to be'. The greater part of the laws touching upon sexual offences, Devlin continued,

is the creation of statute and it is difficult to ascertain any logical relationship between it and the moral ideas which most of us uphold. Adultery, fornication, and prostitution are not, as the [Wolfenden] Report points out, criminal offences: homosexuality between males is a criminal offence, but between females it is not. Incest was not an offence until it was declared so by statute fifty years ago. Does the legislature select these offences haphazardly or are there some principles which can be used to determine what part of the moral law should be embodied in the criminal?[107]

Devlin thought there were, and in the single most quoted passage of his lecture argued that private morals could not simply be lifted out of the public sphere as the 'suppression of vice is as much the law's business as the suppression of subversive activities; it is no more possible to define a sphere of private morality than it is to define one of private subversive activity . . . There are no theoretical limits to the power of the state to legislate against treason and sedition, and likewise I think there can be no theoretical limits to legislation against immorality.'[108]

How was immoral behaviour to be delineated? 'Immorality,' Devlin said, '. . . for the purpose of the law, is what every right-minded person is presumed to consider to be immoral.'[109] Certainly the 'limits of tolerance shift', and it 'may be that over-all tolerance is always increasing. The pressure of the human mind, always seeking greater freedom of thought, is outwards against the bands of society forcing their gradual relaxation.'[110] But, in Devlin's view,

No society has yet solved the problem of how to teach morality without religion. So the law must base itself on Christian morals and to the limit of its ability enforce them, not simply because they are the morals of most of us, not simply because they are the morals which are taught by the established Church – on these points the law recognizes the right to dissent – but for the compelling reason that without the help of Christian teaching the law will fail.[111]

For Devlin, there 'is a disintegration when no common morality is observed and history shows that the loosening of moral bonds is often the first stage of disintegration, so that society is justified in taking the same steps to preserve its moral code as it does to preserve its government and other essential institutions'[112] – hence his analogy with treason and subversive activities.

It was this connection which brought Herbert Hart to the microphone four months later. In a radio talk, 'Immorality and Treason',[113] he argued that state power should be used only where a harm test applied to a private activity; to involve the criminal law because a general sense of conventional morality was affronted was not the mark of a civilized community. To liken 'immoral' behaviour in private to treason was plain wrong. It had to be judged action by action rather than subjected to blanket condemnation.

Hart and Devlin pursued their debate in lectures and books well into the 1960s. Hart, whose own sexuality was unclear,[114] was especially eloquent in his subsequent lectures at Stanford (published as *Law, Liberty and Morality* in 1963) about the 'interference with individual liberty' by legal means 'on those whose desires are frustrated by the fear of punishment'.[115] Laws enforcing sexual morality may create misery of a quite special degree. For both the difficulties involved in the repression of sexual impulses and the consequences of repression are quite different from those involved in the abstention from 'ordinary' crime. Unlike sexual impulses, the impulse to steal or wound or even kill is not, except in a minority of mentally abnormal cases, a recurrent and insistent part of daily life. Resistance to the temptation to commit these crimes is not often, as the suppression of sexual impulses generally is, something which affects the development or balance of the individual's emotional life, happiness and personality.[116]

Hart spoke, too, to the ever present danger of invoking 'the people' and their views on crime and punishment against the reform-minded minority: 'It seems fatally easy to believe that loyalty to democratic principles entails acceptance of what may be termed moral populism: the view that the majority have a moral right to dictate how all shall live.'[117]

Quite apart from producing a classic mini-literature between them, the Devlin–Hart debate created an intellectual, legal and ethical background against which, in the British context, what Arthur Marwick has called a 'measured judgement' could be applied by 'a liberal, progressive presence within the institutions of authority'[118] when confronted by the pressures exerted subsequently by cracks in the dam visible as the Fifties and Sixties turned.

For Marwick, this had nothing at all to do with the notion of 'repressive tolerance'[119] sketched later by Herbert Marcuse: 'Many of the exciting developments in the sixties, and much of its unique character, are due to the existence of a genuine liberal tolerance and willingness to accommodate to the new subcultures, permitting them to permeate and transform society.'[120] There is much in Marwick's analysis. But it does not fit the middle-aged to elderly men in Macmillan's Cabinet charged with handling those legal and moral conundrums which Patrick Devlin adumbrated in a society that left them increasingly baffled.

Macmillan himself just wished these 'conscience questions' (as they became known) would go away, whether it was the matter of capital punishment (on which he was a retentionist[121]) or the criminality of male homosexuality. When the Commons, on an unwhipped vote, 'voted heavily against homosexuality', as Macmillan put it on 29 June 1960, he wrote with relief that: 'This should end the Parliamentary controversy for a time.'[122] Characteristically, he would resort to teasing his more liberal-minded Home Secretary, Rab Butler, about it: '... I understand,' he would say to Butler, 'what it is you want to do. You want to popularise abortion, legalise homosexuality and start a betting shop in every street. All I can say is if you can't win the Liberal nonconformist vote on these cries you never will!'[123]

Macmillan's detachment, verging on insouciance, really irritated Butler, as their exchanges on what became the Suicide Act 1961 showed. For liberals such as Herbert Hart, this statute was of special significance, for 'though it may directly affect the lives of few people, it is something of a landmark in our legal history. It is the first Act of Parliament [Hart was writing two years later] for at least a century to remove altogether the penalties of the criminal law from a practice both clearly condemned by conventional Christian morality and punishable by law.'[124]

The deeper significance of the measure was entirely lost on Macmillan, who inquired of Butler,

Must we really proceed with the Suicides [sic] Bill? I think we are opening ourselves to chaff if, after ten years of Tory Government, all we can do is to produce a Bill allowing people to commit suicide. I don't see the point of it. It is just to please a few cranky peers. I don't mind these noblemen if they commit suicide (which they seldom do) being buried with a stake through their bodies, but beyond that I do not see why we should go.[125]

Rab would have none of this. The Suicide Bill, he told Macmillan,

is far from being supported by only a handful of obsolescent peers. There has been a good deal of demand in the Commons for a change in the law, and the Bill is supported by magistrates, doctors and the Churches . . .

The main object of the Bill is not to allow people to commit suicide with impunity – still less to save them from a stake at the crossroads, which was abolished in 1882. It is to relieve people who unsuccessfully attempt suicide from being liable to criminal proceedings . . . The present position is inhumane and unnecessary and I think should be a relief for the Courts and Prisons to bring it to an end.[126]

Butler was, by nature and intellect, in the Hart camp. He thought the prospect of amending 'the social laws' left Macmillan 'bored'.

But for all the levity of his memorandum to Butler on the criminality of suicide, Macmillan did care about the moral condition of society. It was his administration which put through the Mental Health Act 1959, which began the process of freeing large numbers of people from what Enoch Powell, as Minister of Health, would later call those 'isolated, majestic, imperious [asylums], brooded over by the gigantic water-tower and chimney combined, rising unmistakable and daunting out of the countryside'.[127] In fact, by temperament and religious conviction, he was in the camp championed by his least-favourite judge, Patrick Devlin. In this area of his multifaceted mind he is remembered for a typical piece of drollery in an interview with that most thoughtful of political journalists, Henry Fairlie,* who famously drew from him in 1963 the line that: 'If people want a sense of purpose, they should get it from their archbishops. They should not hope to receive it from their politicians.'[128]

As Fairlie reported five years later (when his book was published), 'Macmillan, in fact, went further. People, he said, would not discover a sense of purpose until they had rediscovered a sense of sin.'[129] Macmillan brooded during a party planning meeting ahead of the 1959 election that 'we all really know that in the last 40 years the morals of this country have declined' (this was in the context of easing the laws regulating gambling and drinking).[130] And there is no doubt that in his mind he linked this not only with the decline of religion but also with the very affluence with which his own name would for ever be bound by the hoops of history and political memory. This emerged in a diary entry during the early summer of 1960 on his return home from a visit to Norway: 'The unattractive side of the Norwegian "affluent society" is its increasingly Pagan character. Christianity (they have a Lutheran Church) is openly despised, and a sort of vague, materialistic agnostic creed flourishes (as over a large part of British life).'[131]

As a very old man, he told an American television interviewer: 'If you don't believe in God, all you have to believe in is decency ... decency is very good. Better decent than indecent. But I don't think it's enough.'[132] Quite plainly, Macmillan was and remained ambivalent about the spiritual if not the material consequences of the 'having it so good' with which his name will for ever be associated.

The Butler policy prevailed to some degree in the late 1950s. There was an element of loosening of what Rab liked to call the 'Victorian corsetry' restraining the nation's life.[133] And much of the battle over how many social stays to remove from the webbing took place, interestingly enough, inside a Conservative Party group rather than in a Whitehall network. It was called simply the Steering Committee. It operated from the end of December 1957 to the 1959 general election and its life was as secret as if it had been a Cabinet Committee, the only difference being that officials from the Conservative

---

* Who wrote a fine book about the late Fifties and early Sixties, *The Life of Politics*, shortly before emigrating to America in an attempt to escape the consequences of a profligate lifestyle. Fairlie was quite a connoisseur of Harold Macmillan; and the Prime Minister thought Fairlie 'a queer man, but quite a good journalist'.

Research Department rather than civil servants took the minutes. Macmillan himself chaired it and its thinking was crucial to the Party's 1959 election manifesto.[134]

It was during a Steering Committee meeting in June 1959 that Macmillan acknowledged that the Butler view was (up to a point) prevailing when he recognized that 'a great number of the laws and restrictions [were] framed in a more primitive society [and] so were based on a mistrust of what people would do. But like children growing up we can all now be trusted to do more of what is right . . .'[135] This must have jarred with what he truly believed in the innermost tabernacles of his Anglican heart.

A swift result of Rab Butler's social loosening was the Obscene Publications Act of 1959. This owed much to the pioneering work of two literary-politico figures, the Conservative Norman St John-Stevas (though not yet in Parliament, he had initially produced a draft Bill for the Society of Authors in 1955[136]) and the Labour MP Roy Jenkins, whose Private Member's Bill (which became the basis of the 1959 Act) on the subject had concentrated minds in the Home Office.[137] A special Commons Select Committee, stimulated by Butler, had also recommended an easing of the laws and a defence of 'literary merit' for formerly banned works.[138]

It was the new Act which, after a landmark case heard in the Old Bailey in 1960 in which Richard Hoggart's evidence supporting publication played a crucial part, enabled Penguin Books to publish D. H. Lawrence's *Lady Chatterley's Lover* in November of that year. This, in Marwick's judgement, was 'the most celebrated and illuminating show trial of this critical time of change'.[139] ('Is it a book that you would have lying around in your own house? Is it a book that you would even wish your wife or your servants to read?' the prosecuting counsel, Mervyn Griffith-Jones, inquired of the jury – a pair of questions from which his reputation never recovered.[140])* The nature of the book and the extensive publicity it stimulated made the trial one of the most notorious and significant in legal history.

Other forms of indulgence from which Victorian inhibitions were to be partly lifted – drinking and gambling – had to wait until after the 1959 election, though the Steering Committee slipped both into the manifesto.[141] The Betting and Gaming Act 1960 put paid to much illegal back-room bookmaking, directing it instead to newly legal betting shops which have been a prominent feature

---

* *Lady Chatterley* certainly 'lay around' on my school bus in Gloucestershire that winter (introduced by the genuinely literary son of a village policeman), and obviously in many other places too: the book sold 2 million copies within a year.

of every British high street ever since. On the Steering Committee, the shrewdly cerebral Michael Fraser, who headed the Conservative Research Department (and, with Macmillan and Butler, was one of the Committee's most important members), saw the gambling reform as adding 'some colour to an otherwise colourless legislative programme' which would appeal to working-class voters as it extended to them gambling privileges which had been previously confined to the rich.[142] The Licensing Act 1961 extended opening hours in public houses, the government's argument (then as now) being that this would discourage what would now be called binge drinking,[143] and for the first time pubs throughout Wales could open their doors on Sundays.

Butler, as the title of his memoirs showed (*The Art of the Possible* – a phrase lifted from Bismarck, whose definition of politics it was[144]), had an acute sense of just how far the traditional element within the Conservative Party could be eased towards modernity. On capital punishment (for most reformers the penal/ social issue overriding all others), though not yet an abolitionist himself, Butler knew he had no chance of persuading the Cabinet, let alone the party conference, to cut the rope once and for all. Every year as Home Secretary he had the difficult task of heading off rank-and-file calls for the restoration of corporal punishment. However much Butler disliked these occasions (they 'quite clouded my time as Chairman of the party', he wrote with some understatement[145]), they were as nothing to the anguish he went through when, as Home Secretary, he had to decide which executions went ahead and which did not:

Each decision meant shutting myself up for two days or more, with only the [Home] Office, the Judiciary, and occasionally my old friend David Kilmuir [former Home Secretary; by now Lord Chancellor] ... to counsel me ... By the end of my time at the Home Office I began to see that the system could not go on, and present day Secretaries of State are well relieved of the terrible power to decide between life and death.[146]

Capital punishment, like the illegality of gay sex, would remain until swept away by the higher tide of mid-Sixties social liberalism, yet the death knell for both was sounded in 1957, with the Wolfenden Report in one case and the passing of the Homicide Act in the other. Butler realized this from his first days as Home Secretary. The law, he later wrote,

was in progress of being modified ... and I thus inherited the rather curious Homicide Act of 1957 which restricted the death penalty to certain specified types of murder. These were not necessarily the types recognised as the most wicked, but rather those on which the deterrent effect of capital punishment was believed to be the most likely to operate and those striking especially at the maintenance of law and order.

Initially it was the possibility of hanging those who murdered a police officer or a prison warder which persuaded Butler 'that the modified law should be retained'.[147]

But the ambiguous state[148] of the law on capital punishment turned Butler into an abolitionist and ensured that, with only the House of Lords blocking the way in 1956, the will of the House of Commons (which had voted for abolition in February 1956[149]) would eventually prevail, particularly if a Labour government were elected. The Homicide Act was the unsatisfactory compromise drafted by the Eden government (Eden was a retentionist[150]) on the back of the split of opinion in the two Houses of Parliament. It was initially intended to be in force only for a trial period of five years.[151] Macmillan in 1956 had supported the idea of selective capital punishment 'based [not] on moral culpability but on practical grounds. Therefore poisoning (tho' in a sense the most culpable) will not attract the capital penalty. But shooting policemen will . . .'[152] But after the Commons vote, he recognized that future Conservative intakes might swell the abolitionist vote still further, noting in his diary in February 1956 that '30–40 of our chaps (mostly young) voted for abolition . . .'[153] (In fact, forty-eight of them did with three Cabinet ministers – Macleod, Lloyd and Heathcoat Amory – abstaining; without those Conservatives the Commons would have voted for retention as the vote was 293 to 262 for abolition.)[154]

These tweakings of the corset and tugging at the rope took place against a rise in recorded crime generally which took some of the gilt off improving living standards. As criminal historian Terence Morris noted, reformers had argued, with a high degree of plausibility, that nineteenth-century levels of poverty were

almost certainly a cause of crime . . . Even during the 1930s 'genuine need' had been recognized as a cause of subsistence crime. But, as the standard of living rose during the second half of the 1950s, so the spectre of poverty largely disappeared into the mists of history and the recollections of those who had suffered in the depression years of the 1930s. It was a paradox that, as the combination of increased national prosperity and the enveloping security of a welfare state seemed to push poverty and deprivation into an increasingly remote past, crime, and especially the crime of the young, seemed inexorably to increase.[155]

No wonder Macmillan's Steering Committee found it so difficult to understand the society for whose growing affluence they tried so tirelessly to take the credit. And, as if with every rise in their level of bafflement, they sang more loudly what was to become their electoral refrain that 'Life's better with the Conservatives'.[156] In fact, as political and social historian Mark Jarvis concluded, 'the Tories found themselves presiding over an unruly modernity, which could not be tamed and could only partially be influenced by policy'.[157]

To what degree do the statistics substantiate Macmillan's – or Patrick Devlin's – pessimistic anxieties? The overall crime figures certainly show the 1955–60 quinquennium as a period of serious deterioration after a decade of *falling* crime (see table – upper panel).[158] When those overall figures are broken down (lower panel), the most significant increase (of almost 100 per cent) was in crimes of violence against the person.[159]

INDICTABLE OFFENCES KNOWN TO THE POLICE IN ENGLAND AND WALES

YEAR	TOTAL	VARIATION OVER AVERAGE OF PRECEDING FIVE YEARS	RATE PER MILLION POPULATION	VARIATION OVER AVERAGE OF PRECEDING FIVE YEARS
1955	438,085	−5.1%	11,234.7	−4.8%
1960	743,713	+69.8%	18,474.1	+64.4%

SELECTED INDICTABLE OFFENCES KNOWN TO THE POLICE IN ENGLAND AND WALES

YEAR	OFFENCES AGAINST THE PERSON	VARIATION OVER PRECEDING FIVE YEARS	OFFENCES AGAINST PROPERTY	VARIATION OVER PRECEDING FIVE YEARS	SEXUAL OFFENCES	VARIATION OVER PRECEDING FIVE YEARS
1955	7,884	+26.2%	399,924	−6.4%	17,078	+29.5%
1960	15,759	+99.9%	688,381	+72.1%	19,937	+16.7%

The rise in property crime can be linked with the spread of affluence. The greater availability of cars and televisions after 1955 meant there was so much more to steal and changes in the layout of shops (the disappearance of the counter as a barrier in more open-plan shops and the spread of self-service supermarkets) made life much easier for shoplifters.[160]

If Macmillan had wished to seek in the statistics a 'Pagan' correlation (to borrow the word he used after his 1960 trip to Norway), he might well have thought he had found one. Religious statistics are notoriously and variably unreliable.[161] But, like crime, there was a marked shift in church membership in the Fifties – and, most noticeably for the Anglican Church, it was one inverse to the rise in crime (see table).[162]

CHURCH MEMBERSHIP (LARGER DENOMINATIONS)

YEAR	ANGLICAN	PRESBYTERIAN	BAPTIST	METHODIST	ROMAN CATHOLIC
1950	3,441,000	1,860,000	337,000	772,000	2,223,000
1960	3,341,000	1,868,000	318,000	766,000	2,626,000

There is always a grave danger where God and Mammon meet of writing and thinking in absolutes. The life and thought of the Churches was no more static in the Fifties than society generally. It was, after all, the Church of England Moral Welfare Council report on *The Problem of Homosexuality* two years before the Wolfenden Committee was commissioned by the Home Secretary to examine the subject which urged an inquiry into the law affecting homosexual practices and the separation of sin from statute.[163] It would be misleading to think that, *ex officio* as it were, leading Church figures were in the Devlin rather than the Hart camp.

Archbishop Geoffrey Fisher, whom Macmillan regarded as 'a silly, weak, vain and muddle-headed man' (this on his attitude to capital punishment in 1956;[164] he was to get even more cross about his attitude to Suez[165]), was generally – and rightly – regarded as a less liberal figure than his successor at Canterbury, Michael Ramsey.[166] But Fisher was nevertheless open minded rather than censorious about the perplexing paradoxes of affluence, secularism, crime and sin. His poor relationship with Macmillan might well have precluded the Archbishop from being privy to the Prime Minister's own doubts about the moral price of affluence, as both men would have conceived it.

Fisher, like Macmillan, suspected that the country's 'spiritual capital' was running down in late-Fifties Britain. In an *Observer* interview in 1959, Kenneth Harris asked him if the world was a more sinful place than it had been fifty years earlier. Fisher replied that the world was now more complicated. There were 'many more things to do with the chance of misusing them and harming yourself or other people thereby. Bad things are no longer hushed up. They are talked about and publicised, and so, I think, do more harm than when they were hushed up.'

This particular social dam burst, Fisher thought, had left the world 'in many ways less healthy than it was 100 years ago', but 'I do not think that men are more sinful-hearted than they were. They are, however, I should say, more dangerously placed.' Here, in Fisher's analysis, affluence had tilted the balance in the wrong direction: 'The temptations to self-indulgence (which accounts for a great deal of the world's sin and misery) are multiplied in extent and made more alluring, and many of the time-honoured defences against bad thinking and bad doing are weakened. Also the incentives to good thinking and good doing are less powerful than they were. There is, or may be, a loss of spiritual capital.'[167]

Fifties Britain tends to be viewed through early-twenty-first-century eyes as stuffy and staid, but for Macmillan's and Fisher's generation, their standard of a tranquil, self-ordering society was that of pre-1914 England. Or, in Macmillan's case, Scotland. The Prime Minister was more than a little prone to the cult of the Highlander, and his attachment to the grouse moor was a boon for satirists. It was, no doubt, a part of the 'Edwardian mask',[168] as his friend Lord Swinton called it, behind which the Prime Minister liked to conceal himself. But it also reflected his need to ease the stresses of high office by regular immersion in a more serene world. He liked, for example, to shoot with Swinton on the Yorkshire moors. And the contrast between the North Riding and London stimulated some elegiac letters like this one thanking Lady Swinton for her hospitality:

I think one of the reasons why one loves a holiday on the moors is that, in a confused and changing world, the picture in one's mind is not spoilt.

If you go to Venice or Florence or Assisi, you might as well be at Victoria station – masses of tourists, chiefly Germans in shorts. If you go to Yorkshire or Scotland, the hills, the keepers, the farmers, the farmers' sons, the drivers are the same; and (except for the coming of the Land Rover etc.) there is a sense of continuity. There is also the country and the neighbourliness that goes with people who live in remote and beautiful country.[169]

Macmillan's diaries are laced with pages, particularly his August entries, which ring to the sound of aristocratic banter amid the unmistakable whiff of damp tweed as foreign alarms and domestic anxieties are briefly put aside. In fact, some of these entries are beyond parody:

20 August 1958: . . . The American messages [to Eisenhower about the full restoration of nuclear weapons collaboration] were ready by 12.30. I had already postponed my departure for Yorkshire. But I was able to approve the texts and catch the 1.20 from Kings X to Leeds.

. . . It is fun to be at Bolton Abbey again. Andrew and Debo [the Duke, Lady Dorothy Macmillan's nephew, and Duchess of Devonshire] are as nice as ever – the boy, Peregrine, is charming. He is now at Eton. The daughter, Emma, will be a great beauty. The baby girl looks, at present, a Cavendish, but with Mitford hair . . .

21 August 1958: Stayed in bed till luncheon – writing and working. Telegrams are beginning to arrive, describing the FS [Foreign Secretary, Lloyd] and Dulles conversations about the [nuclear] Tests . . . Read 'War and Peace'. We went out (Debo, Mr Hey and I) in the afternoon and had 2 little drives. We got 12 grouse. I shot 6, including 2 very high birds.[170]

Such passages can, apart from the invitation to satire, be faintly seductive in a kind of Evelyn Waugh-like *Brideshead Revisited* fashion – all part of the elegy that, for Macmillan (and for Archbishop Fisher, too), ran like a tarnished thread through British late-Fifties society entwined with the golden filigree of increasing and more widespread affluence.

It was this kind of thinking which led Fred Hirsch, one of the most gifted economic journalists and thinkers of the postwar period, later to posit his theory about the frustrations generated by 'social limits to growth'. The 'paradox of affluence', he called it[171] (though he was writing in and about the 1970s, the developments he analysed had their origins in the years 1952–64, when consumer expenditure grew in real terms by 45 per cent[172]). Hirsch argued that 'positional goods' have a finite supply which the spread and growth of wealth and educational opportunity cannot increase – prestigious and interesting jobs; country homes commanding a fine view in a peaceful setting. For example, until the twentieth century (to return to Macmillan and Lady Swinton or his afternoon on the moors with 'Debo and Mr Hey'), 'only rich aristocrats had an income sufficient to have satiated other effective demands to an extent that left something over for the purchase of land for "consumption" purposes – land to walk in, shoot in, play in, keep others out of'.[173]

Once larger numbers acquired sufficient surplus wealth to kindle an appetite for positional goods, it produced both actual and social congestion, causing frustration to both existing possessors of such goods and future aspirants to them alike. Sir Kenneth Clark, whose personal wealth and artistic connoisseurship made him one of the most fascinating figures of mid-twentieth-century Britain,[174] was eloquent on this theme in the section of his memoirs dealing with the making of his 1969 BBC Television *Civilisation* series which made him a household name among the positionally rich and deprived alike:

Filming 'Civilisation' gave me the opportunity to revisit places, like Moissac and Vezelay, that I loved and might never have seen again. The chief of these was Urbino ... Evidently my enthusiasm for that enchanting place made itself felt, for in the last few years hundreds of people have made the long journey to Urbino, and only its inaccessibility has prevented it from becoming a tourist centre. 'Each man kills the thing he loves.'[175]

There were some cultivated, aesthetically inclined souls who, though they loved to holiday in the remoter parts of Italy, simply loathed that kind of talk. Often their beef against affluence was couched in J. K. Galbraith's analysis of the contrast in the United States (whose economy and society were admittedly very different from those of the UK) between 'private affluence' and 'public squalor' in his 1958 best-seller *The Affluent Society*.[176] Their argument was that affluence had spread insufficiently to those areas where a positional problem did not exist.

The greatest British exemplar of this was the leading intellectual of the British centre left, Anthony Crosland, who declared himself 'wholeheartedly a Galbraith man'.[177] In 1956, Crosland had published his own classic work, *The Future of Socialism* (which was in effect the UK equivalent of Galbraith's US analysis which was soon to follow). In it he positively looked forward to the moment when 'the Industrial Revolution finally matures into the modern mass-production economy, as it has in the United States and is about to do in Britain', as it would 'no longer be possible for the rich to sustain the magnitude of their lead in the consumption of goods'.[178] Crosland, in the most eloquent section of his book, which he labelled 'Liberty and Gaiety in Private Life; the Need for a Reaction against the Fabian Tradition', wanted Britain to be

a more colourful and civilised country to live in. We need not only higher exports and old-age pensions, but more open-air cafés, brighter and gayer streets at night, later closing-hours for public houses, more local repertory theatres, better and more hospitable hoteliers and restaurateurs, brighter and cleaner eating-houses, more riverside cafés, more pleasure gardens on the Battersea model [with the Festival Hall, this was the surviving physical bequest of the 1951 Festival of Britain], more murals and pictures in public places, better designs for furniture and pottery and women's clothes, statues in the centre of new housing-estates, better-designed street lamps and telephone kiosks ...[179]

The state, plainly, was to have a role in providing this better, brighter Britain, but not a state with a Fabian mentality that wanted people 'to sacrifice private pleasure to public duty . . .'[180]

Crosland anticipated Hart when he turned to 'socially-imposed restrictions on the individual's private life and liberty. There come to mind at once the divorce laws, licensing laws, prehistoric (and frequently unfair) abortion laws, obsolete penalties for sexual abnormality, the illiterate censorship of books and plays, and remaining restrictions on the equal rights of women.'[181] He reacted with something like contempt to those who in any way suggested it was harmful for his constituents in Grimsby (his parliamentary seat from 1959 until his death in 1977) increasingly to enjoy any of the pleasures previously confined to the rich. Economic growth and the affluence it brought were to be embraced as an instrument of equality, not disdained as corrupters of morals and wreckers of physical amenity. 'The rich', Crosland later wrote, 'would proceed in a leisurely fashion across Europe to the Mediterranean beauty spots where they would park their Rolls-Royces and take to a boat or a horse-drawn vehicle. As for my constituents, who have only a fortnight's holiday, let them eat cake and go back to Blackpool.'[182]

The twin catalysts of Britain's transformation into a mass-consumption society were sustained full employment and a growth rate of around $2^1/_2$ to 3 per cent a year in the 1950s, fuelled internationally by the general boom in the advanced economies of the West over the decade as a whole and domestically by the ending of hire-purchase restrictions in 1958, which led to a surge of demand for cars, fridges, furniture and televisions bought 'on the never-never'.[183] One of the best-remembered political cartoons of the age (apart from Vicky's 'Supermac') is Trog's* depiction of Macmillan in the *Daily Mail* sitting back in his armchair, absorbing his 100-seat majority in the general election of 8 October 1959, surrounded by a fridge containing an abundance of food, a car, a washing-machine and a television, as the autumn leaves fall outside the window. Addressing the collection of consumer durables which carried him to victory, he declares: 'Well, gentlemen, I think we all fought a good fight . . .'[184]

The dry figures for personal consumption running through the Fifties do tell a story, with Trog's items increasingly prominent as the meeting of basic needs left an increasing amount for greater creature comfort and domestic

---

* Real name Wally Fawkes; clarinettist and saxophonist; member of the Humphrey Lyttelton Band, 1948–56 (John Chilton, *Who's Who of British Jazz* (Cassell, 1997), p. 115).

convenience. The statistics (see table)[185] illuminate a cumulative improvement in material comfort and opportunity which, when allied to sustained full employment, made the 1950s a decade of easement without previous parallel in British economic and social history.

SELECTED ITEMS AS PERCENTAGES OF TOTAL CONSUMERS'
EXPENDITURE IN THE UNITED KINGDOM (AT CURRENT PRICES)

YEAR	FOOD	DRINK	TOBACCO	HOUSING	FUEL/LIGHT	CLOTHING	DURABLES	TRAVEL/ COMMUNICATION	RUNNING CARS
1950	25.1	7.8	8.1	8.9	3.8	11.2	5.2	4.5	1.2
1955	27.6	6.3	6.7	8.6	4.0	9.9	7.1	4.2	1.9
1960	25.0	5.6	6.7	9.8	4.4	9.7	8.4	4.2	2.7

Such tangible improvements in the quality of life made politics tough for the opposition in the House of Commons. In fact, late-Fifties competition between the two main political parties was, at root, about which of them could more effectively sustain this cataract of consumables. Labour was very production-oriented under that most high-minded of economists, Hugh Gaitskell, who, in running against Macmillan, attempted to outbid him by claiming that, if Labour had been in power, economic planning would have boosted both production and the tax revenue available for 'great improvements in the welfare services . . . without increasing the present rates of taxation', as Labour's manifesto for the 1959 election put it.[186] Gaitskell, in Labour's poster campaign for that contest, was depicted as a smiling technocrat declaring, 'We want a Britain where production expands year by year and the growing wealth is fairly shared throughout the nation' (he claimed that Butler's 1954 target of doubling the standard of living in twenty years *could* be achieved if Labour was in power and engineered expansion as steadily as it had done between 1945 and 1951).[187]

Gaitskell, a professional economist by training,[188] was a strange mixture as top politicians go. He could aspire to heights of moral fervour (at the time of Suez for example[189]) and, as his protégé and acolyte, Roy Jenkins, put it: 'He was a man for raising the sights of politics . . . He could raise banners which men were proud to follow.'[190] But, as Jenkins continued, his blend of techno-cracy and emotion could weaken him when, 'in a paradoxical way [Gaitskell became] too emotionally committed to an over-rational position which, once he had thought it rigorously through, he believed must be the final answer'.[191] He was, as we shall see in the next chapter, no match for the 'deft material-ism'[192] with which Macmillan dazzled the electorate.

Gaitskell's Labour Party did not entirely neglect the moral element in polit-ical action. The worthily stodgy concluding paragraph of its 1959 manifesto, 'Our Socialist Ethic', did attempt to link 'the ethical principles of Socialism', that had 'inspired the pioneers of Socialism, and still inspires the Labour Party' to both its domestic social and economic policies and tackling 'this vast prob-lem of the hungry two thirds of the world'.[193] And shortly before he succeeded Gaitskell as Labour leader, Harold Wilson told the Labour conference that: 'This party is a moral crusade or it is nothing.'[194] But, for all the personal close-ness of both Crosland and Jenkins to Gaitskell, the Party's 1959 manifesto contained not a whisper of the social and cultural reforms of which Crosland had written in *The Future of Socialism* and about which Jenkins had solilo-quized in the final, 'Is Britain Civilised?' chapter of his pre-election Penguin Special, *The Labour Case*.[195]

If any political grouping deserved the label of moral crusader to be stitched on its banner it was a movement which represented a particularly visible dam burst in the late 1950s – the Campaign for Nuclear Disarmament. Though led largely by the middle-aged and, in one famous case, the very old (Bertrand Russell had been active in the Union for Democratic Control during the Great War and imprisoned for his pacifist beliefs[196]), it was to an impressive extent a movement of the young and its appeal, and its instruments of protest, stimulated a good deal of trouble for both mainstream political parties. It caused Macmillan anxiety, and not only because his wife was prone to aim the prime-ministerial car at CND demonstrators if they attempted to halt it while she was at the wheel. In December 1957, just a few weeks before CND emerged from a cluster of peace and anti-nuclear groups, as if sniffing the wind, he noted in his diary that the 'H of C (and the Daily Mirror led critics) have suddenly got excited about the H Bomb being in the hands of American bombers based in this country. All the pro-Russians and the pacifists and all the sentimentalists (inspired by the clever politicians) have tried to work this up into a sort of "finger on the trigger" campaign [a reference to the *Daily Mirror* in October 1951].'[197] Macmillan concluded that the 'only thing [to do] is to remain quite calm and see it through'.[198] Unlike his wife, the Prime Minister generally managed to do so. In a June 1957 letter to Dr Charles Hill, Chancellor of the Duchy of Lancaster and minister responsible for government information, Macmillan had wondered 'whether all this propaganda about the bomb has really gone deeper than we are apt to think . . .'[199] It had.

In between Macmillan's letter to Hill and his diary musings on the need to keep calm in the face of anti-nuclear sentiment, the *New Statesman* published what remains the single most influential article ever to appear in its pages.[200] It was crafted by the pen of one of the most fluently evocative literary figures of twentieth-century Britain, the novelist and playwright J. B. Priestley. Entitled 'Britain and the Nuclear Bomb', it appeared on 1 November 1957 when the British left was still reeling from the shock of Aneurin Bevan, Labour's Shadow Foreign Secretary, begging the party conference not to send him 'naked into the conference chamber' by committing a future Labour government to getting rid of the bomb.[201]

Bevan, a left-wing firebrand and natural orator with a gift for responding spontaneously to an audience's mood, did exactly that in the Brighton Conference Hall on 3 October 1957. His reputation with the left never recovered during the few years of life which remained to him (he died of cancer in July 1960 at the age of sixty-two). To shouts of 'Do it [abandon the British H-bomb] now!' from the floor, Bevan, 'his scorn . . . off the leash' (as his friend and biographer Michael Foot, who was horrified by his hero's words, put it), cried out:

'Do it now,' you say. 'Do it now.' This is the answer I give from the platform. Do it now at a Labour Party Conference? You cannot do it now. It is not in your hands to do it. All you can do is pass a resolution. What you are saying is that a British Foreign Secretary gets up in the United Nations without consultation – mark this; this is a responsible attitude! – without telling any members of the Commonwealth, without concerting with them, that the British Labour Movement decides unilaterally that this country contracts out of all its commitments and obligations entered into with other countries and members of the Commonwealth – without consultation at all. And you call that statesmanship. I call it an emotional spasm.[202]

It was those last three words that cut deep. As Michael Foot said, 'if many had not been nearer to tears, the whole place might have broken into uproar'.[203] The denunciation of emotion in politics was especially shocking coming from Bevan's lips. Rab Butler thought Bevan was 'the best speaker I ever heard in the House of Commons' because 'he spoke out of pure emotion . . .'[204]

Bevan's passion may have helped the unilateralist motion at the Brighton conference to go down to defeat by 5,836,000 votes to 781,000.[205] But Priestley's lifting of his pen proved, in its way, mightier than the verbal sword Bevan had thrust at Labour's disarmers. As wordsmiths the two men were well matched. Priestley caught the post-Brighton mood and gave the old left, the new left and, above all, the young left the possibility of mounting the kind of moral crusade beyond the reach of Macmillan and Fisher, Gaitskell or even Bevan.

His article opened by heaping scorn on Bevan, much as Bevan had heaped scorn on Labour's unilateralists. Bevan's speech, Priestley wrote,

seemed to many of us to slam a door in our faces. It was not dishonest but it was very much a party conference speech, and its use of terms like 'unilateral' and 'polarization' lent it a suggestion of the 'Foreign Office spokesman'. Delegates asked not to confuse 'an emotional spasm' with 'statesmanship' might have retorted that the statesmanship of the last ten years has produced little else but emotional spasms. And though it is true, as Mr Bevan argued, that independent action by this country, to ban nuclear bombs, would involve our foreign minister in many difficulties, most of us would rather have a bewildered and overworked Foreign Office than a country about to be turned into a radioactive cemetery.[206]

Priestley recognized how tiny the British nuclear weapons capability was in comparison to the arsenals of the two superpowers. But though Britain's 'bargaining power is slight . . . the force of our example might be great'. He turned his readers' attention back to that glorious moment in 1940–41 when: 'Alone, we defied Hitler; and alone we can defy this nuclear madness into which the spirit of Hitler seems to have passed, to poison the world. There may be other chain-reactions besides those leading to destruction; and we might start one.'

Priestley ended with a peroration inviting the British people to rise above the tide of affluence and materialism that threatened to engulf their old decencies (how common a theme this was in the late Fifties):

The British of these times, so frequently hiding their decent, kind faces behind masks of sullen apathy or sour, cheap cynicism, often seem to be waiting for something better than party squabbles and appeals to their narrowest self-interest, something great and noble in its intention that would make them feel good again. And this might well be a declaration to the world that after a certain date one power able to engage in nuclear warfare will reject the evil thing for ever.[207]

Priestley's article did trigger a chain reaction of a kind. The *New Statesman* was deluged with letters.[208] Within three months the Campaign for Nuclear Disarmament was up and running.

Christopher Driver, the mid-Sixties historian of what might be called first-wave CND (to distinguish it from its 1980s revival), believed that, after Priestley's article, 'the birth of CND was only a matter of midwifery and committee work'.[209] But Priestley's article was also the front end of a missile of protest which had been under construction through much of 1957. Its architects ranged from Macmillan's Minister of Defence, Duncan Sandys, through the American originator of 'containment' policy, George Kennan, to the Soviet leader Nikita Khrushchev himself.

Both Driver and the secret history of CND prepared for Macmillan by the Security Service, MI5, in 1963 placed emphasis on the impact of the section of the Sandys Defence White Paper of April 1957 in which, the government admitted, 'It must be frankly recognised that there is at present no means of providing adequate protection for the people of this country against the consequences of an attack with nuclear weapons'[210] (see p. 466). George Kennan, who was to spend the academic year 1957–8 as the Eastman Professor of American History at Oxford, was 'flattered' when the BBC asked him to deliver the 1957 Reith Lectures following in the glittering line of Bertrand Russell, Arnold Toynbee, Oliver Franks and Robert Oppenheimer (to cite the names he singled out[211]). Naturally, as a man who had spent his life grappling with 'the great problems of what is called the cold war',[212] East–West would be his theme, though he 'did not anticipate any great pressure of publicity'.[213]

Kennan was a man of immense foresight; but not in this instance. He is not entirely to blame. How could he have known early in 1957, when the BBC invitation arrived, that between the Bevan speech at Brighton and his taking to the microphone in Broadcasting House, Mr Khrushchev would, on 4 October, have 'startled the world by launching the first earth satellite – the so-called "Sputnik"',[214] sending a frisson of alarm about Russian superiority in missile technology in its arms race with the USA. For Kennan, that 'the dangerousness and expensiveness of this competition should be raised to a newer and higher order just at the time when prospects for negotiation in this field were being worsened by the introduction of nuclear weapons into the armed forces of the Continental NATO powers was a development that brought alarm and dismay to many people besides myself'.[215]

He said this – and much more – in his Reith Lectures that autumn using language which went far beyond his diplomatic training. To what kind of life,

Kennan asked his listeners, did nuclear-weapons competition condemn us? 'Are we to flee like haunted creatures from one defensive device to another, each more costly and humiliating than the one before, cowering underground one day, breaking up our cities the next, attempting to surround ourselves with elaborate electronic shields on the third, concerned only to prolong the length of our lives while sacrificing all the values for which it might be worth while to live at all?'[216]

Unlike Priestley and the other soon-to-be-founders of CND, Kennan 'accepted our retention of such weapons as a deterrent, but as that only. I opposed the basing of our defence posture upon them . . .'[217] For such views, Kennan was denounced by Dean Acheson, President Truman's Secretary of State when Kennan headed the State Department's Planning Staff, who accused him of having 'never grasped the realities of power relationships'.[218]

The world's press picked up Kennan's words and so did the British peace movement. In fact, Kennan's views were closer to those of Labour's leading defence thinker, Denis Healey, than to those of the nuclear disarmers, and Healey attended a late-November party for Kennan at the Adelphi flat in central London of Kingsley Martin, the editor of the *New Statesman*.[219] Neither the guest of honour nor Healey wanted to join the others (who included Priestley, Michael Foot, Bertrand Russell, the physicist Patrick Blackett and John Collins, Canon of St Paul's Cathedral) in mounting a national campaign for the abolition of nuclear weapons. 'Kennan, Blackett and I', Healey wrote in his memoirs, 'were not sufficiently impressed to attend a second meeting at Canon Collins' house, at which it was decided to support a Campaign for Nuclear Disarmament. We found the arguments of the others unrealistic, and distrusted some of their motives.'[220]

That second meeting, at No. 2 Amen Court in the shadow of Canon Collins' place of work and worship, on the evening of 15 January 1958 marks the real birth of CND. Out of it came the CND executive committee chaired by Collins with an ace campaigner, Peggy Duff, a veteran of the Campaign for the Abolition of Capital Punishment,[221] as its organizing secretary and a plan for an inaugural meeting at the Methodist Central Hall, Westminster, the following month.[222]

The historian A. J. P. Taylor, who described his fifty or so fellow attendees at Amen Court as 'an odd collection, appointed by nobody and convinced that we could change the fate of the world by our own unaided efforts',[223] was the star of the packed 17 February meeting in Westminster's Methodist Central Hall, close to Parliament Square. Taylor rose to the occasion as if he were a scion of the great dissenting tradition of foreign-policy 'Trouble-makers'[224] he had so lovingly chronicled in the Ford Lectures at Oxford in 1956.[225] Later, as he toured the great cities on behalf of CND talking to overflowing halls, he called it a 'wonderful experience', not least because John Bright 'had been there before me' when campaigning against the Corn Laws.[226]

Yet it was not to Bright but to the Women's Social and Political Union that Taylor turned as his exemplars that winter night in Westminster in February 1958. Taylor, who spoke last after Russell, Priestley, Foot and Collins, 'remembering his parents' stories of suffragettes breaking up political meetings with cries of "Votes for Women", recommended heckling Cabinet ministers with cries of "Murderer"'.[227] After the meeting over 1,000 people walked the short distance to Downing Street and stood outside No. 10, shouting, 'Ban the Bomb' and 'Murderer' at Mr Macmillan until the police dispersed them.[228] There is no mention of this in Macmillan's diary. He was just back from a long Commonwealth tour, preparing a speech on foreign policy and worrying about Nasser's designs on Sudan.[229] Macmillan did not care for Taylor or his left-wing views.[230] The previous year, influenced by eminent historian Lewis Namier, the Prime Minister had ensured the Regius Chair of Modern History at Oxford went to Hugh Trevor-Roper and not to Taylor.[231]

But first-wave CND made much more trouble for Gaitskell and the Labour Party than for Macmillan and the Conservatives. Within a couple of years Canon Collins was leading 5,000 demonstrators shouting 'Gaitskell must go!' outside the Royal Hotel in Scarborough where Gaitskell was staying during the 1960 Labour Party conference[232] (at which he was to deliver the speech of his political life, promising to 'fight and fight and fight again to save the party we love' from the 'pacifists, unilateralists and fellow travellers' who preached disarmament and neutralism in the Cold War [233]). Though it took some time for disputes within the Labour Party about the bomb to become truly poisonous, in Dora Gaitskell's words 'hostility rang through the air' that Sunday afternoon on the Scarborough seafront.[234]

CND has another claim to historical attention, as, in the words of Gaitskell's biographer, Philip Williams, it 'aroused the largest spontaneous popular movement in post-war Britain'.[235] (Williams was writing in the late 1970s; but, in terms of post-1945 political pressure grouping, I think that judgement still stands.) It is difficult nearly half a century later to recapture the éclat of very early CND. Only a decade after that supercharged night at Central Hall Bertrand Russell recognized this when he wrote, 'It seems now to many people as if the CND has been part of the national scene from the beginning of time, and it has lost its lustre and energy through familiarity.'[236] What was it that made the prototype movement seem so lustrous and energetic even as early as 4 April 1958 (the coldest Good Friday for forty-one years) as 4,000 people set off from Trafalgar Square to march to the Atomic Weapons Research Establishment at Aldermaston in Berkshire?[237]

There had been marches and protests before, not least those organized by the National Committee for the Abolition of Nuclear Weapons Tests. A year earlier, for example, the catchily acronymed NCANWT had orchestrated a demonstration reminiscent of the suffragettes with '2,000 women with black sashes and flags walking on a pouring wet Sunday from Hyde Park to Trafalgar Square'. Organized by Peggy Duff, it was this march which gave the peace activist Laurence Brown the idea of marching to Aldermaston.[238] With Pat Arrowsmith, field organizer of the NCANWT's Direct Action Committee and the march's planner, taken on as an assistant secretary by CND,[239] preparations were made by the Aldermaston March Committee from its headquarters in Blackstock Road near the old Arsenal football stadium.[240] They produced a leaflet urging 'all who are opposed on any ground to nuclear weapons, whether possessed by the British, American or Russian Governments' to walk 'for a weekend, a day, or an hour'. The organizing committee expected 300 to turn up. In the event, 'numbers never fell below 540, and between 5,000 and 10,000 people marched the last mile to Falcon Field, Aldermaston, in absolute silence'.[241]

Crucial to its sudden presence in national consciousness was the decision by newsrooms to send reporters to march with the demonstrators and not just to cover the start and the finish. And the press coverage was 'by and large respectful, conscious that nothing quite like this had been seen in Britain before'.[242] Some of the best reporting was by the right-wing press; not least, I suspect, because a fine and individualistic journalist, Alan Brien, covered the march for both the *Daily Mail* and *The Spectator*. Here he is in the former:

The marchers were mainly middle-class and professional people. They were the sort of people who would normally spend Easter listening to a Beethoven concert on the Home Service, pouring dry sherry from a decanter for the neighbours, painting Picasso designs on hardboiled eggs, attempting the literary competitions in the weekly papers, or going to church with their children. Instead they were walking through the streets in their old clothes. They were behaving entirely against the normal tradition of their class, their neighbourhood, and their upbringing . . .[243]

In his *Spectator* piece, Brien alluded to a factor which has always been stressed by the males of my generation and a bit older – in that era when 'going all the way' was as rare as it was thrilling, the Aldermaston marches of the late 1950s and early 1960s, with their overnight stops involving church halls, sleeping bags and no segregation, were a magnificent opportunity for morality and immorality to mingle rather gloriously.

Brien depicted the scene overall as 'a tremendous stimulation of ideas and arguments and witticisms and friendships and love affairs. Perhaps it would be more tactful to keep this revelation a secret – but the Aldermaston March is the rare phenomenon of a physical and social pleasure which yet has an intellectual and moral justification.'[244]*

In its way, early CND caused as much trouble to the Communist Party of Great Britain as it did to the Labour Party or to the Conservative government (as Macmillan was told in his MI5 briefing[245]). The *New Statesman* appreciated the significance of non-CP involvement at once, reporting that 'official circles are confused and alarmed about the Campaign for Nuclear Disarmament because it is a movement of a new pattern. It is unprecedented because it has no political group behind it; no showman's drum beats it up; it has no leaders serving personal ambitions; it is not inspired or indeed supported by the Communist Party, which is embarrassed by the obvious retort that the Soviet Union should also abandon nuclear weapons.'[246]

Fledgling CND might not have had a leading showman – but it had something even better than a drum, perhaps the single most memorable piece of postwar iconography, which has endured as a global symbol instantly recognizable and easily understood. Its logo, which was ready to be paraded before the press, newsreel and television cameras on Good Friday 1958.

Since the spring of 1958, countless denim jackets and rucksacks have carried that symbol round the globe. Christopher Driver described it as 'probably the most powerful, memorable and adaptable image ever designed for a secular cause'.[247] It was drawn by Gerald Holton, a professional artist who did

---

* A particularly eloquent re-creator of the marching mood amongst my friends used to hitch-hike down from Yorkshire as a grammar-school sixth former for the event, returning exhausted up the A1 once the Trafalgar Square rally was over on the Easter Monday (from Easter 1959, the march reversed direction, starting at Aldermaston). He later joined the Air Ministry and became for a time one of the Ministry of Defence's experts on nuclear retaliation. Both he and his positive vetting officer took a sensible view of his late-teenage Easters. One might think that only in Britain would such a mature approach be possible. As I noted in *The Secret State* (p. 107), a future Chief of the Secret Intelligence Service, David Spedding, went on the second Aldermaston march and wrote it up in his school magazine.

'decorative work in schools for the Ministry of Education. He brought the design – unsolicited – to the chairman of his local group in Twickenham in February 1958, and alternative versions were shown at the inaugural meeting of the London CND.'[248] In 1994, when making *What Has Become of Us?* with Rob and Gill Shepherd, I called on Pat Arrowsmith in her north London flat, full of CND banners and memorabilia, who wore the CND logo hanging on a chain from her neck. Holton, she said, had originally come up with a cross as it was to be an Easter march. 'No, no; it's not a religious march and we're not all of us religious,' he was told. So the final version consisted of a circle (symbolizing an unborn child), around an interior sign which both represented a dying man and incorporated the semaphore positions for N(uclear) and D(isarmament).[249]

Holton waterproofed his signs and placed them on top of sticks, giving the distinctive 'lollipop' effect apparent in most pictures of the early marches. After the first one, Eric Austen emblazoned the design on to ceramic lapel badges.[250] It was branding at its most brilliant. No political party could match it and CND instantly set the pace for all other pressure groups as the suffragettes had done fifty years earlier with their purple and green sashes and their marches. Both the suffragettes and the disarmers understood the need for spectacle as well as protest.

All this was very hard for the old left to take. At the time of the second march, the Communist Party of Great Britain continued to treat CND as an irritating and bourgeois distraction and as a regrettable rival to its own front organizations, the British Peace Committee and the Youth Peace Committee.[251] At its 26th Congress over Easter 1959, the party line was spelled out with a heavy-handedness that contrasted sharply with CND's light-footedness: 'Experience has shown that unilateralism only divides the movement, and diverts attention from the real issue, namely, international agreement to ban nuclear weapons. This is the only way to banish the menace of nuclear war and also the issue of which the greatest number agree.'[252]

The dourest of the CPGB's intellectuals, Rajani Palme Dutt, dismissed the CND approach as 'hopelessly inadequate and irrelevant'.[253] But for those intellectuals and others who had left the CPGB after the Soviet invasion of Hungary in 1956 (official party figures showed a membership decline of 6,000 – about a fifth – between February 1956 and February 1957), CND helped provide 'the cause and comradeship' they had lost when old loyalties were strained beyond endurance by the spectacle of Russian tanks in the streets of Budapest.[254] The best known of them was the social historian Edward (E. P.)

Thompson, who, with the economic historian John Saville, created a small but influential journal, the *New Reasoner*, as a vehicle for new thinking on the Marxist left in July 1956, before Hungary but after Khrushchev's denunciation of Stalin at the 20th Party Congress in Moscow earlier that year.[255]

Thompson, who was to become a talismanic figure in second-wave CND during the 1980s, was well aware, as he put it later, that the British Communist Party of the 1950s was 'in the impossible position of trying to follow a formula evolved for a foreign people'.[256] CND was a very British phenomenon – a very modern pressure group but one with the unmistakable pedigree of a very old dissenting tradition that predated organized political parties. Thompson understood this very well:

The young people who marched from Aldermaston do not mean to give their enthusiasm cheaply away to any routine machine. They expect the politicians to do their best to trick and betray them. At meetings they listen attentively, watching for insincerities, more ready with ironic applause than with cheers of acclaim. They prefer the amateur organisation and the amateurish platforms of the CND to the method and manner of the Left-wing professional . . .[257]

Thompson caught here the outlook that would be so swiftly appreciative of the 'satire boom' once it took off in the early 1960s with *Beyond the Fringe*[258] and *Private Eye*.[259]

CND had another overriding advantage – its cause was both grave and simple to understand. But, as Thompson stressed, it was 'a difficult generation for the Old Left to understand. It is, to begin with, the first in the history of mankind to experience adolescence within a culture where the possibility of human annihilation has become an after-dinner platitude.'[260]

It was Dennis Potter, the playwright (though before he became so), who produced the most striking work that spoke for that young group of left-wingers while still an undergraduate at Oxford. Finished in the weeks after the 1959 general election and published in 1960, it represented Potter's self-described 'scattered highly impressionable and youthful description of a few of the social and political problems of present-day Britain'.[261] On the question of CND he was ahead of most in appreciating that many of Britain's disarmers were at one with Harold Macmillan and his government's belief that Britain was an influential world exemplar – that what happened in the Cabinet Room in Downing Street or on the A4 between Aldermaston and London *did* matter to the inner groups in the White House and the Kremlin, the Pentagon or the Soviet Defence Ministry. Potter did not share this view. He was sceptical of the value of 'moral arguments' when 'linked to a conception of the status of this country, seen in its ability to provide world leadership, that is alien to most of us'.[262] In this sense, Potter saw a 'dichotomy [between] "morality" and "politics"'.[263]

This was a view espoused a few years later by the right-wing critic Anthony Hartley in his 1963 work *A State of England*: 'That the Aldermaston marches should have evoked enthusiasm from a large number of young people as well as from the old war-horses of the left is not surprising. CND, after all, is the only thing of its kind: a campaign over a live moral issue whose importance can hardly be overestimated and which can be viewed in terms of absolute good and evil.'[264] But, Hartley added, '[n]o better example can be offered of the gulf between undirected idealism and political possibility which has been opened by the decline of Great Britain's world power.'[265]

It was one of those 'war-horses' of the old left, A. J. P. Taylor, who later made this point with even greater force. In his memoirs, Taylor had no regrets about doing his John Bright impressions across the provincial halls in the late Fifties: 'The bomb was wicked. It was idiotic. It was dangerous ... But we made one great mistake which ultimately doomed CND to futility. We thought that Great Britain was still a great power whose example would affect the rest of the world. Ironically we're the last Imperialists. If Great Britain renounced nuclear weapons without waiting for international agreement we should light such a candle as would never be put out. Alas this was not true.'[266]

As the UK has not yet renounced its nuclear weapons capability, it remains impossible to know the wider effect such a move might have. It was this theme of fading power – whether military, diplomatic, financial, industrial or territorial (in the sense of colonial possessions) – that infused so much late-Fifties/early-Sixties literature, whether the author was on the left, middle or right of the political spectrum.

Potter does not occupy much of a place in the 'state-of-the-nation' literature of 1958–64,[267] but his *Glittering Coffin* is worth lingering over – and not just because of the fame that later came his way. As a working-class grammar schoolboy at New College Oxford in the late 1950s, Potter was cross, but not angry, with his country. He was positively Orwellian (in Orwell's *The Lion and the Unicorn* mode) in his love for it in contemplating what he called 'the politics of decline' – 'The atmosphere is one of polite decay and immense self-deception. But it *is* our country, the nation in transition, caught between a magnificent past and a sentimental lethargy.'[268]

Potter's threnody – which he shared with other critics – was of a glorious people stifled by overmighty and backward-looking institutions. For Potter in 1959, the British people 'have it in them to change all this – the people who queue so placidly, who have such a sense of the important, as opposed to the minor, acts of civilized living, like tolerance, compassion and prickly resentment of the grosser forms of interference with individual dignities. No one can be presumptuous enough to escape altogether the long, surging beat of his native culture, and I certainly do not wish to do so.'[269]

Potter believed that a combination of old decencies, the rise of scholarship boys and girls like himself and a rejuvenated Labour Party with 'a consistent socialist ideology'[270] could put so much right. He had no time for the 'angries' because they turned 'their resentments and suspicions into reasons for social apathy rather than the means by which they can escape it'.[271]

Potter was as uneasy, in his own way, about affluence as any of the encrusted adornments of what he would have regarded as the *ancien régime*, such as Fisher or Macmillan. He was positively Tawney-like in his denunciation of 'acquisitive community'[272] and poured scorn on what one of the commercial television companies called 'Mr and Mrs Consumer 1959'.[273]

To what extent did the politico-literary class fuel non-bomb related concerns as mass consumption filtered through Britain's social capillaries for the first time? It can be argued, for example, that that great reader of Keynes's works, Macmillan himself, contributed to this. His immortal 'having it so good' speech was clothed in warning and wrapped in worry about the fragility of the new prosperity. He delivered it before a large weekend audience at Bedford football ground on 20 July 1957 as his 'chief purpose was to warn the people of the dangers of inflation, however prosperous things might appear at the moment'.[274] It was at Bedford, he noted wryly in his memoirs, 'that I first used without exciting any particular comment, a phrase which afterwards became notorious'.[275]

Macmillan, as a very accomplished manipulator of political language, should have known that it is declamatory sentences couched in vivid language which rise up, walk and are remembered – never the caveats. The Bedford speech was a classic. Its first two sentences took flight; later ones never got off the ground:

Let's be frank about it; most of our people have never had it so good. Go around the country, go to individual towns, go to the farms, and you will see a state of prosperity such as we have never had in my lifetime – nor indeed ever in the history of this country. What is beginning to worry some of us is, 'Is it too good to be true?' or perhaps I should say, 'Is it too good to last?' For amidst all this prosperity, there is one problem that has troubled us – in one way or another – ever since the war. It's the problem of rising prices. Our constant concern today is – can prices be steadied while at the same time we maintain full employment in an expanding economy? Can we control inflation? This is the problem of our time.[276]

That is the passage for which both contemporary politicians and subsequent folk-memory recall the Bedford speech, not its darker, yet more prescient, corollary:

The great mass of the country has for the time being, at any rate, been able to contract out of the effects of rising prices. But they will not be able to contract out for ever, if inflation prices us out of world markets. For if that happens, we will be back in the old nightmare of unemployment. The older ones among you will know what this meant. I hope the younger ones will never have to learn it.[277]

It was a Conservative creation – commercial television – which added powerfully to the difficulties of Macmillan's conveying a message of warning and restraint. His was the first political generation that had to live with the aspirational impact of visual advertising. The cinemas and even the mass-consumption magazines had never reached the immediacy or the bite of commercial television. It is impossible to measure the degree to which the growth of consumer durables was quickened by the existence of ITV from September 1955. The same problem applies to the social changes in late-Fifties Britain.

The literary critic Cyril Connolly surveyed the factors of social dam-bursting and wrote, 'Television is, I suppose, the greatest single factor for change in people's lives and probably has done much to undermine English puritanism.'[278] It is hard to imagine Connolly's sense of the aesthetic made him an early fan of *Coronation Street*, which so far has run for forty-six years. Folk-memory, including my own, places *Coronation Street*'s creation in the very earliest years of British commercial television. It wasn't. It didn't bring its special pastiche of northern working-class culture to life until 1960 (four years after Granada began transmitting) – and it very nearly did not happen at all. Its creator, Tony Warren, 'an unhappy twenty-three-year-old actor and writer who was being paid £30 a week by Granada Television to adapt scripts',[279] let his mind wander from W. E. Johns' *Biggles*, on which he was working, to write something 'from the heart, acted by genuine Northerners'.[280]

He wrote episode one overnight, giving birth, as it were, to immortals such as Elsie Tanner, Ena Sharples, Ken Barlow and Albert Tatlock, calling it 'Florizel Street'.[281] Sir Dennis Foreman, who as head of Granada Television used the treasure accumulated by *Coronation Street* and Granada's other mass-audience programmes to finance such costly gems at the high-culture end of the spectrum as *Brideshead Revisited*[282] and *Jewel in the Crown*,[283] recalled for me the 'pure luck' involved in getting backstreet life in Salford an apparently permanent place in the nation's affections and collective consciousness:

I vividly remember the board meeting at which it was discussed ... The sales director was dead against it. It would debase Granada's name in television putting out stuff like this and it's not going to attract viewers ... The non-execs were against ... There was just a majority of one ... *Coronation Street* was given, I think, three or four slots to see what happened – and it was magic.[284]

The 'magic' persists.

The dry arithmetic of Britons' listening and viewing habits is eloquent about the nation's changing appetites as both television sets and the spreading commercial channel reached ever greater sections of the population between the 1954 Television Act and the coming of *Coronation Street*. Asa Briggs, the official historian of the BBC's first half-century, compiled a fascinating set of graphs, shown on p. 537. By the summer of 1958, 80 per cent of the UK was within range of both a BBC and an ITV transmitter,[285] and in 1957–8 the number of combined radio and television licences overtook the radio-only variety. By 1960 there were 10 million television sets in use and about half the population were watching at peak time on any given evening.[286]

The rationing (in terms of broadcasting licences) and regulation (in terms of content) by government of TV and radio meant that the sex and language battlefront lay elsewhere – in the theatres and the cinemas. Plays still had to be submitted for censorship by the Lord Chamberlain, who, though a Crown servant appointed on the recommendation of the Prime Minister, 'was unaccountable to government or Parliament, and was under no obligation to give reasons for refusal to grant a licence to a play, and there was no form of appeal against his decisions'.[287] His (the Lord Chamberlain was always male) major campaigns were against the portrayal of homosexuality and the more carnally related swear words.[288]

The British Board of Film Censors attempted to play Lord Chamberlain for the big screen. Though a trade body, it was supported by the Home Office and applied the 'U', 'A' and 'X' certificates which my generation and the next still associate with the spectrum ranging from the harmless to the near-taboo at the cinema.[289] John Trevelyan, the chief censor, was a cautious liberal who was none the less 'extremely resistant to any linkage of sex and nudity in a British film'.[290] He led an easement of censorship which, by 1960, when the Board considered *Saturday Night and Sunday Morning* (the toned-down film version of Alan Sillitoe's novel of East Midlands working-class life – though Sillitoe disliked the 'working-class' label – which, even so, for those days retained a strong element of sexuality[291]) allowed it to pass uncut. Local authorities retained the power of veto in their area but only one, in Warwickshire, used it.[292]

The battleground between playwright and film-maker and the Lord Chamberlain's Office and the British Board of Film Censors was a very significant one. But the line on Briggs' graph depicting the growth of advertising expenditure – a powerful transmitter of 'having it so good' – suggests that, with the jingle of coin in the pocket, this was the more powerful social transformer, certainly in the short term before changes in the social and sexual mores caught up with increased wealth and leisure time. The bedrooms of Britain may only slightly have resembled the Britain of the new, gritty novels (oddly classified 'kitchen-sink') but the real kitchens and parlours were increasingly becoming filled with 'having-it-so-good' goods.

Cultural critics such as Richard Hoggart were horrified at the aspect of independent television typified by *Double Your Money*. Hughie Green's immensely popular quiz show, which ran from September 1955, with its dreadful Hammond-organ signature tune and its '£1,000 Treasure Trail', was in many ways the tone-setter for early ITV and it made good – perhaps inevitable – commercial sense for the early investors and entrepreneurs behind the new companies. 'There was,' Hoggart told me forty years on, 'a lot in commercial television from the start which was just going for the audience as fast as it could because that means more advertising revenue. This was an appalling thing to have done to the best new [broadcasting] instrument we had.'[293]

Hughie Green, an ebullient ex-Royal Canadian Air Force officer, struck me as understandably touchy about accusations that his cherished programme was a debaucher of popular culture when I interviewed him in 1994 for *What Has Become of Us?*. And he was quite unrepentant when *Double Your Money* was taken off the air in 1968: 'For thirteen years we have been consistently in the Top Ten. My only crime, apparently, is I have been popular for a long time. They say they want more culture and that "Double Your Money" is too trivial. But do people really want more culture? I very much doubt it.'[294]

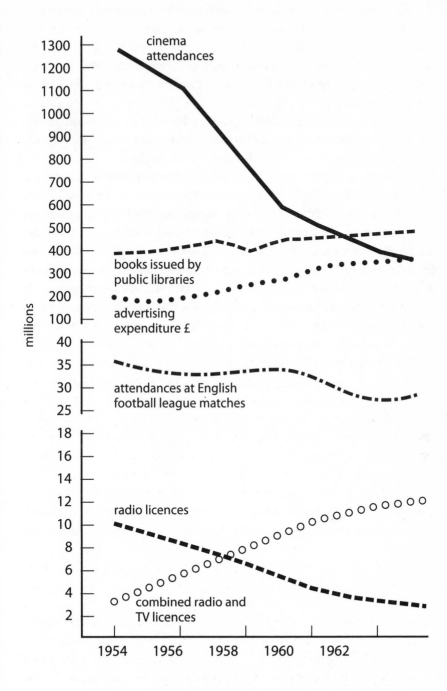

The Impact of Television: Comparative Annual UK Statistics 1954–1962

Dennis Foreman, whose philosophy was that Granada should be a provider of culture, high, middle and low, took the line that the viewer was sovereign: 'The frivolity of independent television when it first went on the air was anathema to people like Richard Hoggart – but they are nannies . . . My view has always been that people can look after their own welfare and that a bit of fun does not go amiss.'[295]

Keynes believed the British had 'been trained too long to strive and not to enjoy'.[296] Given the rise of commercial television and rich pattern of sport and leisure that large numbers began to enjoy in growing and greater measure from the late nineteenth century, this bald statement requires qualification. But in terms of domestic and personal consumption, it was increasingly ceasing to be true in late-Fifties Britain. The British debate on consumption has tended to concentrate on the skilled working-class families who by 1960 would have had a television, a washing machine, perhaps a 'baby' Austin or a Ford Prefect parked outside and, thanks to the spread of the Berni Inns and their imitators, tasted steak of the non-stewing variety for the first time.

This was certainly Macmillan's habit. He had no time, as he told Jimmy Margach of the *Sunday Times*, for 'superior' people who denounced the spread of hire purchase, seeing it as a feckless 'never-never' spree on the part of lower-income groups:

I'm *not* ashamed of 'having it so good'. The temptations of comfort and affluence are not an argument in favour of poverty. Our purpose should be to keep it good and make it better. The people who object most violently to the new affluence being shared by the mass of working class people are those who are doing exceptionally well out of the new capitalism through fat expense accounts, expensive meals and other perks on the company's account.[297]

He expressed the same sentiment to Henry Fairlie in an interview as the twilight of his premiership approached:

I usually drive down to Sussex on Saturday mornings [to Birch Grove] and I find my car in a line of family cars, filled with fathers, mothers, children, uncles, aunts, all making their way to the sea-side. Ten years ago, most of them would not have had cars, would have spent their weekends in their back-streets, and would have seen the sea-side, if at all, only once a year. Now . . . I look forward to the time, not far away, when those cars will be a little larger, a little more comfortable, and all of them will be carrying on their roofs, boats which they may enjoy at the sea-side.[298]

What Uncle Harold had failed to pick up, through his fog of benevolent paternalism, was the quiet spreading of what the *Financial Times* called in June 1959 the 'Foreign Travel off the Peg' phenomenon.[299] The newer travel agents were already pioneering the package tours to the Spanish Costa Brava which would hit older agencies like Thomas Cook[300] – and those south-coast resorts to whose traffic flows the Prime Minister paid such close attention – very hard from the mid-Sixties. By 1961, 3.5 million Brits went abroad for their holidays, double the figure for 1950.[301]

The advertising industry was maturing apace across the entire socio-economic spectrum, including those classier, comfortable sections of it about whose attitudes Macmillan himself could be so superior. One of the pacemaker agencies was Kingsley, Manton and Palmer (KMP). Brian Palmer (he of the SR toothpaste television ad – see p. 227) told me how struck he and his colleagues were just ahead of ITV's first transmissions when David Ogilvie returned briefly to Britain from the USA, where he had become a big figure in advertising, to tell those he (and the US industry) had left behind: 'The consumer is not a moron, she's your wife.'[302] Palmer and his colleagues were so impressed they made a special trip to the USA to talk more to Ogilvie.[303] Brian Palmer sees the change of approach by British advertisers and the coming of television advertising as a significant moment. Speaking in 1994, he said of KMP, 'we thought – and I still believe, incidentally – that TV and advertising and that whole marketing thing, whereby you put what people wanted first and then tried to ... get manufacturers to provide it, was a very powerful engine for change'.[304] And so it has remained from that day to this.

In making his case that a cultural revolution *did* take place cumulatively in Britain as in other advanced Western countries roughly speaking between 1958 and 1974 (the period of both sustained economic growth and social changes among the young, brought to a halt by the inflation, stagnation and recession associated with the oil price explosion of the mid-1970s), Arthur Marwick lays great stress on the pace of entrepreneurial innovation and on increasing purchasing power and widening personal horizons for the young.[305] One example on the fashion front was the 'boutique moment' in 1955 when two former art students, Mary Quant and Alexander Plunkett-Green set up Bazaar on the King's Road in Chelsea.[306] In that last grey patch of the 'long 1930s' it was a sensation, though, in a peculiar way, some of Quant's first creations reflected that fading world. As she told Joan Bakewell for *My Generation*, 'I liked to use lots of men's suitings, city suitings, which I loved, and flowers and Prince of Wales checks, and then I liked to use this with very feminine details which I always felt ... exaggerated femininity in a very provocative way . . .' Her designs, she explained, 'were what I wanted and I knew that my sort of friends wanted and people in Chelsea wanted. I thought it was entirely for Chelsea, and we were in fact a part of a group who were known as the Chelsea-set. Chelsea was a perfect place. It was a mixture of bohemia and modern.'[307] Perhaps a widening bohemianism is the way to see those early stirrings.

It is very hard to distil the mix of propellants of this kind of social mobility. Certainly the volatile mixture of fashion, sport, television and celebrity ten years after Bazaar opened when personified by Manchester United's George Best was much easier to discern than, say, when the young Bobby Charlton appeared on *Double Your Money* (he won £1,000 answering questions on pop music[308]). But the celebrity endowed by television nevertheless changed Charlton's world for ever, just as Jimmy Hill transformed the bank balances of the country's leading professionals by fighting for abolition of the maximum wage. Though the memory of those early televised matches is – literally – blurred, those programmes did add, for the masses, a new dimension to *the* mass sport in Britain.

Until the late 1950s, unless you lived within reach of one of the great industrial cities or one of a cluster of Lancashire towns such as Preston, Blackburn, Burnley or Bolton you might never witness a top-division match. 'Football', as Richard Holt put it, was 'transformed for most of those who follow it from a Saturday afternoon activity in all weathers to a Saturday night home entertainment.'[309] The players themselves became more professional as athletes too. Ted Fenton, as manager of West Ham in the late 1950s, pioneered both the use of weight-training during the week and steak as Saturday's pre-match 'dinner' in place of the traditional stodge.[310]

The notion of celebrity-cum-fashion needs a special kind of cartographer to map its shifts (it is worth a book of its own within the British context alone). Clive Priestley, who was a grammar-school lad like me but a decade and a bit ahead of me at university, traces the changes through what he and his fellow undergraduates at Nottingham experienced between 1953 and 1956. Films shown in cinemas would be largely war-related with 'God Save the Queen' played at the end of the last performance. They would listen collectively to *The Goon Show* on the wireless – 'The junior common room on the Lower Corridor of the Trent Building would always be full of a smoky crowd of chaps (almost invariably in flannels and tweed jackets) and girls (almost invariably in skirt and jumper) listening to the heroic Bentine, Milligan, Secombe and Sellers and afterwards reproducing their voices, names and catch-phrases . . .'[311]

The coming of ITV did reflect a different social reality. For example *The Army Game* (first broadcast in 1957, winning 'the ratings war for ITV'[312]) 'presented a picture of wet officers and anarchistic NCOs and other Ranks ... Bootsie and Snudge were centre stage, Alfie Bass and Bernard ... Bresslaw an unforgettable incarnation of the Common Man'.[313] With Duncan Sandys that same year announcing the end of National Service from 1960, comedies relying on shared military experiences might top the bill for a while but the realities of the Cold War and its high-tech imperatives foretold their end too. Tough, amoral ex-soldiers like Len Deighton's Harry Palmer (a role for which Michael Caine was perfectly cast in *Funeral in Berlin*[314]) were the new breed of clandestine operator in the early 1960s – fascinating, sexy to some but not very lovable.

It would be wrong to overdo the theme of hedonism creeping in beneath the shadow of the bomb – the glittering coffin approach to late-Fifties Britain. Yet it was RAF Bomber Command which provided a particularly pleasing example of just such a combination. In 1958 the first Vulcan squadrons were mustered in Lincolnshire. John Willis was among the youngest of the pilot officers on one of the airfields and many of the boring routines of nightly security fell to him. He would be driven round to inspect the great white delta-winged ghosts one by one, each guarded by a corporal armed with a revolver and protected by an Alsatian.

One night, as the jeep approached, Flight Lieutenant Willis noticed on one of his planes the rather odd spectacle of the Alsatian tied to a nose-wheel and no sign of the corporal. He stopped his driver some way away and approached cautiously. From inside there came the unmistakable sounds of passion between the corporal and his girl, making use of the padded area in the bomb-bay from which the aimer (should the worst happen) could watch the dreadful weapon drop on a Russian city. Without a care in the world for the bomb, Mr Khrushchev, Mr Macmillan or Flight Lieutenant Willis, hot nature – for a moment at least – trumped Cold War. The corporal was not put on a charge.[315] The worst did not happen, the bomb did not drop and the well-balanced Willis rose to be Vice-Chief of the Defence Staff, though the bomb remained a near-constant preoccupation for the man in No. 10 Downing Street, who could have authorized its deployment at any time during his very nuclear-minded premiership.

12

Supermac

'Not to detect a man's style is to have missed three-quarters of his actions and utterances.'
Michael Oakeshott, 1967.[1]

'. . . there was an element of the dining club or the country house party about his [Macmillan's] conduct of Cabinets and Cabinet committees. There would be quotations from Homer, there would be vague historical analogies; the trade union leaders would be described as medieval barons in the period of the Wars of the Roses. And some of them would be relevant and some of them would be mildly misleading. But they would all be amusing and detached and very carefully thought out . . . one had to watch what he was doing as well as what he was saying.'
Lord Hailsham, 1986.[2]

'Vicky [Victor Weisz, the cartoonist] . . . who created Supermac from a conflation of Harold Macmillan and the popular cartoon figure Superman, in order to ridicule Macmillan's attempt to give an impression of ubiquity, omniscience and supernatural powers, had the galling fate of seeing his subject adopt even more consciously and flamboyantly the ludicrous postures attributed to him, with immense popular and electoral success.'
Bernard Levin, 1970.[3]

'Finally it was agreed that I should go down to Macmillan's Sussex home, Birch Grove, so that subject and biographer could "look at each other". As we walked round and round the garden, lovingly laid out by his redoubtable American mother, Nellie Macmillan and improved by Dorothy, his wife, I began to realise that he was just about as diffident as I was. I recall making some flip remark about my knowing all too little about British party politics, and not even being sure that I was a very good Tory. He replied "Nor was I, dear boy!" The ice was broken . . .'
Alistair Horne, 1988.[4]

Of all the postwar Prime Ministers Harold Macmillan was, as Anthony Sampson described him, a most marvellous 'study in ambiguity'.[5] He thrilled in the swashbuckling side of Toryism. Even before going up to Oxford in 1912, he 'became entranced by Disraeli's romantic career'.[6] Yet he loathed the stodgy, small 'c' conservatism of the Conservative Party. In 1954 he 'reminded Winston . . . that it took Hitler to make him PM and me an under-secretary. The Tory Party would do neither.'[7]

Macmillan was in many ways more of a Whig than a Tory, and he all but gave his political instinct away in his loving essay on 'The Whig Tradition' nearly a decade after leaving Downing Street: 'It was not perhaps until 1917, with the failure of the last great Whig's [Lord Lansdowne's] final appeal for peace [in the Great War], that the Whig influence as such came to an end. It was a strange but not inglorious story. It had lasted in one form or another for two hundred and thirty years. It began with a protest against extremism – political or religious. It ended with a dignified but fruitless appeal for moderation.'[8]

The Whig tradition was alive and well in No. 10 forty years later once Harold Macmillan had crossed its threshold. He may 'from Disraeli . . . [have] . . . learnt that *laissez-faire* and Free Trade were not dogmas, but at the best expedients. Things could be done, and must be done, above all in the social field.'[9] But it was his sceptical detachment from policy doctrine and party orthodoxy, his restlessness with tradition for its own sake and his own dislike of extremes that made him much more of a Whig than a Tory, as he intimated to his biographer Alistair Horne when strolling round the garden at Birch Grove.

The philosopher Michael Oakeshott saw the great divide within British (and European) politics as a spectrum between two poles – faith and scepticism – pulling in perpetual if fluctuating tension.[10] In religious matters, Macmillan was a man of genuine faith (of the High Anglican variety); in political affairs he was definitely at the sceptical end. He fitted well Oakeshott's belief that 'the affirmations which the politics of scepticism make about the activity of governing will be found . . . to be based not, like faith, upon a doctrine about human nature, but upon a reading of human conduct. The sceptic in politics observes that men live in a proximity with one another and . . . are apt to come into conflict with each other. And this conflict, when it reaches certain dimensions, not only makes life barbaric and intolerable, but may even terminate it abruptly.'[11]

This fits, I think (especially that last sentence), Macmillan's approach to coping with the Cold War abroad and, in a less dramatic way, to his pursuit of social peace at home. It also accords with his assertion (though this might have been as much practical artifice as personal conviction) that on matters of morals the British people should look to their archbishops rather than their politicians, as we saw in the last chapter.

Macmillan's style, too, was a mixture of the genuine and the contrived. It was, observed Anthony Sampson, as if, 'like Disraeli, he seemed to see himself as part of a fashionable play'.[12] Whatever the ingredients which shaped it, Macmillan's personal style powerfully reinforced the aura of tradition, guile and detachment that surrounded him during his late-Fifties political apogee. It was Sampson, anatomist of Britain supreme and one of Macmillan's earliest biographers, who rightly stressed to the Mile End Group just a few weeks before he died that it was 'terribly important' for contemporary historians (especially the younger ones who, that evening in 2004, comprised the bulk of his audience) to record 'how somebody looked and talked at the time. That is what brings things to life for later readers.'[13]

Anthony Sampson did this to perfection in the first of his anatomies, published to immense critical and popular acclaim in 1962,[14] which caught Macmillan's Britain in flight, as it were:

From time to time, in one of six of the more conservative London clubs (Pratt's, Buck's, the Carlton, the Beefsteak, the Turf or the Athenaeum), a tall, grey-haired man with a drooping moustache can be observed walking slowly – almost shuffling – up the stairs alone. He walks in, orders perhaps a dry martini, and then may turn to talk to one of the members. He talks well, in a casual, relaxed way, with a sardonic wit ... Everything about him seems to droop – his moustache, his eyes, his mouth, his floppy cardigan. Even his black bow-tie, which he wears in the evening, is tucked beneath his collar, in the Edwardian fashion ...

His repertoire of languid gestures includes the pulling in of his mouth, tongue in cheek, as he prepares a quip; the pulling down of the corner of his eyes, while he pauses for a point; the fastidious wobbling of his hand, as he searches for a nuance; the opening of his mouth – squarely, like a trap, as he feigns amazement. He might be any aged clubman, imagining himself to be important. But in fact he is, of course, the Prime Minister: and it is in clubland – in this old-fashioned, faintly histrionic setting – that he seems at home.[15]

Not for nothing did Enoch Powell call him the 'old actor-manager',[16] an impression Macmillan's fruity cadences ('poe-litical' never 'poll-litical', for example) served only to reinforce.

In Powell's case, this observation was not intended to be complimentary. The two men did not care for each other. When Powell was inside Macmillan's

Cabinet as Minister of Health, Macmillan asked the Cabinet Secretary to move him to a seat out of direct prime ministerial vision as he couldn't stand Powell's 'steely and accusing eye looking at him across the table any more'.[17] For Powell too, Macmillan was, without question, a Whig. Reviewing a new biography of Macmillan[18] in *The Spectator* in 1980, he noted: 'If, as is reputed, the reviewer and Harold Macmillan did not "hit it off", that would be only to be expected. Of all political categories the Grand Whig and the High Tory are the least compatible.'[19]

Macmillan as last Whig Prime Minister drove Enoch Powell to expressions of dismay and disgust: 'Like the elephant, it is more easily recognised than described: but among its essentials are cynicism, agnosticism, bread and circuses (provided they are held at a decent distance from the ducal estate), European combinations, a readiness to try any wheeze (provided it helps to keep them in power), and a contempt for principle in politics (though some of Mr Locke's ideas may come in handy)'.[20] For Macmillan, Powell was simply 'a fanatic',[21] a description conferred in the privacy of his diary at the height of what he believed was 'a crisis . . . carefully planned by the Chancellor of the Exchequer [Peter Thorneycroft] and the Treasury ministers [Nigel Birch and Powell]'[22] over the level of public spending in early January 1958.

Macmillan, though plainly wrong at the time to suspect Thorneycroft, Birch and Powell of preparing 'a deep plot' to eventually overthrow his premiership[23] (although his Chief Whip, Ted Heath, believed to the end of his days 'that the whole episode was ultimately a challenge to Macmillan's leadership'[24]), was right, as was Powell,[25] to see the late 1957/early 1958 showdown over public expenditure as a critical moment. In prevailing over his Treasury team, Macmillan consolidated his authority over his Cabinet as a whole and paved the way for his 'Supermac' phase and the avowedly reflationary economic policy which gave it lift-off.

Together, the events surrounding the Treasury resignations of 1958, the questions of political economy at stake and Macmillan's management of the episode and its aftermath are among the most significant moments of the early postwar years, not least because, although there was remarkably little resultant political disruption at the time,[26] the ripples could still be felt during subsequent Conservative premierships. Heath, for example, remained a Macmillan man through and through and Mrs Thatcher a Thorneycroft admirer – 'the husbanding of public money did not strike me as an ignoble cause over which to resign. The first steps away from the path of financial rectitude always make its final abandonment that much easier.'[27]*

Both Thorneycroft and Macmillan tended, in their benign old age, to soften the edges of the 1957–8 tussle over economic philosophy. Thorneycroft told me in 1993: 'Dear Harold, he was a great spender. He'd been brought up [politically] in areas of great unemployment and he thought that writing cheques was the best way of dealing with it. This wasn't my view or the view of the junior ministers [Enoch Powell and Nigel Birch].'[28]

Macmillan, in an impromptu speech at *The Economist* in late 1978 to mark the publication of another volume of Walter Bagehot's collected works, took a jovial swipe at the magazine for its economic liberalism: 'I used to remember it as a rather dull looking professional paper that always rebuked me. Every article began, "Mr Macmillan has now, in the last effort of this year, destroyed the British economy for ever!" But it didn't seem to matter very much.'[29]

The 1958 resignations did matter on the level of policy. And I disagree with Macmillan on personalities too. In his memoirs he took the Svengali line, with Powell and Birch as the manipulators: 'Both these men, although nominally subordinate to the Chancellor of the Exchequer, were, in my view, largely responsible for leading him, by their powerful advice and influence, to this final step.'[30] Not only does this sit ill with Macmillan's other view that the resignations were part of a deeper plot to eventually overthrow his leadership, but it underestimates Thorneycroft as well (perhaps partly because Macmillan did not care for his combative style).

January 1958 saw the economic liberals routed.[31] Paradoxically, the Bedford speech had shown that the Prime Minister was as anxious as his Chancellor about the risk of inflation.[32] But, as so often in high politics, it was a symbolic moment – the kind of top-level showdown to which the Macmillan government was unlikely to return. Thereafter the political barriers to public

---

* As late as 2005 the significance of the resignation of Macmillan's entire Treasury team produced a stimulating mini-debate between Nigel Lawson and Rodney Lowe during a Mile End Group seminar. Professor Lowe thought it 'the second fork in the road' of early postwar economic policy (the first being ROBOT). Lord Lawson said the 'Thorneycroft resignation may have been a fork in the road to a lesser extent.' Lawson, though an economic liberal through and through, was not a wholehearted subscriber to the heroic interpretation of Thorneycroft as a full-blooded prototype for Thatcherism, given his experience of him as Conservative Party Chairman in the late 1970s and early 1980s, writing in his memoirs that Thorneycroft 'was wrongly believed to be an economic "dry"'. For Lawson he 'owed this reputation to his courageous resignation as Chancellor at the beginning of 1958 after a clash with Harold Macmillan on public expenditure. The episode gave a false impression, however, of his degree of commitment to our [that is Mrs Thatcher, Sir Geoffrey Howe and Lawson himself] sound money approach.'

spending, both as a means of reflation (which was a feature of the run-up to the 1959 general election) and as an instrument of modernization (which was Macmillan's economic theme from 1960), were distinctly lowered.

Enoch Powell, a lifelong devotee of *laissez-faire* and critic of interventionist economic policy on the part of the state, saw it as a truly profound moment in postwar British politics and government and expressed it in the language of primary colours in 1963, having refused to serve in Alec Douglas-Home's Cabinet. In his more impassioned speeches, Powell's West-Midland accented tones would rise higher and higher, like a siren warning of the Last Judgement. His writing could be similarly apocalyptic:

From 1958 to 1963 one man placed upon the Conservative Party and Government, and thus upon the political history of our time, his own stamp and express image, which will not for long be obliterated . . .

The year 1958 was even statistically a turning-point in so many trends in the course of events of the last fifteen years. At that point the state's share in the national income, which has been declining since 1951, began to rise again and has been rising ever since . . .

It is not a coincidence that it was just in the first days of 1958 that Harold Macmillan, who had been Prime Minister for little under a year, defeated his Chancellor of the Exchequer, Peter Thorneycroft, and settled for inflation.[33]

It is useful to examine the skid marks along the road taken through Westminster and Whitehall during late 1957 and 1958, especially as the drivers concerned argue about what they were swerving to avoid. The traffic was confined to what Macmillan, some sixteen months after the Thorneycroft/ Powell/Birch resignations, described in a letter to the Queen as 'the acceptable zone between deflation and inflation', which, the Prime Minister told her, was 'in present day conditions . . . very narrow'.[34] In fact Macmillan and Thorneycroft were following very similar routes, for in the final Cabinet showdown on the evening of Sunday 5 January 1958 the gap between the Chancellor and the spending ministers was a mere £48m. Thorneycroft had persuaded them to find £105m of the £153m savings on which he was insisting in order to keep the 1958–9 total in line with what has been spent in 1957–8.[35] The Cabinet tussle of late 1957 and the first days of 1958 was a political crisis rather than an economic one. Neither the pound nor the balance of payments was in immediate peril as the year turned. The debate was about the lessons of running a mixed economy since 1951 for the conduct of future policy if the UK was to break out of the tax and spending policies which, in Thorneycroft's view, left it perpetually vulnerable to crises.

Macmillan's summing up late that Sunday night was carefully framed to decrease the chances of the third resignation by a Chancellor in some eighty years, and, therefore, his chief emphasis was upon the narrowness of the divide. The Cabinet, he said,

must seek to share with the Chancellor of the Exchequer the heavy burden of managing an economy which, though potentially prosperous, was precariously balanced ... But disinflation, if enforced to the point at which it created a stagnant economy or provoked a new outbreak of industrial unrest would defeat its own ends ...

The Cabinet could and should pledge themselves to achieve as nearly as possible the Chancellor's objective of ensuring by all possible means that Government expenditure in 1958–59 should not substantially exceed its level in 1957–58. But it was doubtful whether the Government could hope to achieve a precise arithmetical equilibrium without injury to their other purposes.[36]

To rub in the lack of precision (and the implication that Thorneycroft was unreasonably seeking an arithmetical perfection not attainable in the real world of government), Macmillan stressed the cuts already agreed meant 'the residue of the increase would represent a rise of no more than 1 per cent in the outlay of the Exchequer. An increase of this order, largely attributable to factors over which the Government had no control, could not be fairly represented as indicating any weakening in the Government's resolve to resist inflation and to support sterling by all possible means.'[37]

But there was much more to the tussle between Prime Minister and Chancellor than an elusive and statistically insignificant 1 per cent on the public expenditure total. There were two related forces pulling them apart – one to do with differing economic philosophies and the other to do with the sustenance of the British New Deal. Thorneycroft's resignation speech in the House of Commons on 23 January 1958 gave a public clue to the former. Since the end of the war, he said,

we have slithered from one crisis to another. Sometimes it has been a balance of payments crisis and sometimes it has been an exchange crisis ... It is a picture of a nation in full retreat from its responsibilities ... It is the road to ruin ... I do not believe that the problem is technical at all. I do not believe it lies in an answer to the question whether we should use Bank Rate or physical controls. To tell the truth, neither of them works very well ... The simple truth is that we have been spending more money than we should.[38]

The rise in Bank rate from 5 to 7 per cent in September 1957, its highest level since 1921,[39] had convinced Thorneycroft that the cycle of exchange crises and balance of payments problems had to be broken once and for all. He did not accept the bulk of the Treasury opinion that this particular spate of pressure on the pound was but a reflection of the devaluation of the French franc in August 1957 (its immediate cause) and rumours that the West German mark was to be revalued upwards (which turned out not to be true).

Thorneycroft, like his two junior ministers, came to the conclusion that the problem was systemic rather than episodic: that the British economy was overloaded by both welfare and defence spending. In fact, in 1958 the proportion of gross domestic product absorbed by taxes and social security contributions was 29.7 per cent, down from 35.2 per cent in 1948. Defence was absorbing 6.7 per cent as opposed to 9.8 per cent in 1952 at the height of the Korean War.[40] Thorneycroft also feared that trade union power in the wages market was now exerting a permanently inflationary force. His 'never again' impulse took the form of urging cuts in the government's own spending (which were within its power) and a curbing of the quantity of money in circulation (which was more difficult as his power to coerce the banks was limited). Apart from Sir Leslie Rowan, head of its Overseas Finance Branch, the senior figures in the Treasury thought the Chancellor's economic philosophy crude, old-fashioned and plain wrong.[41]

Thorneycroft lost confidence in his officials and turned to Professor Lionel Robbins of the London School of Economics for advice. Robbins was a monetarist, an apostle of the quantity theory of money. Macmillan turned to Professor Sir Roy Harrod at Christ Church, Oxford, a Keynesian anti-deflationist.[42] (It was a neat example of Keynes's dictum in his *General Theory* that practical men 'distil their frenzy' from an 'academic scribbler' of their choice.[43]) Harrod was the 'scribbler' whose advice eventually prevailed. This, rather than the elusive '1 per cent', was the difference between Prime Minister and Chancellor – that and a differing approach to the British New Deal.

The New Deal cleavage was made public in Thorneycroft's resignation speech when he said,

For twelve years we have been attempting to do more than our resources could manage, and in the process we have been gravely weakening ourselves. We have . . . been trying to do two things at the same time. First, we have sought to be a nuclear power . . . At the same time we have sought to maintain a Welfare State at as high a level – sometimes at an even higher level – than that of the United States of America. We have been trying to do these things against the background of having to repay debt abroad during the next eight years of a total equal to the whole of our existing reserves . . .[44]

Thirty-one years later, when the minutes of Macmillan's Cabinet Committee on the Civil Estimates, 1958–9, GEN 625, were declassified, we could see the details of the struggle for some of the talismans of the British New Deal in a period when the Conservatives still sought to stress their credentials – jointly with Attlee's governments – as creators of the welfare state.

The argument that raged in No. 10 on the afternoon of 23 December 1957 is especially instructive. The minutes do not record who was the antagonist (though it is very likely to have been the Minister of Labour, Iain Macleod[45]), when Thorneycroft was tackled head-on over child benefit (then called family allowance):

The abolition of the family allowance for the second child only two years after this allowance had been increased by the present Government would be liable to be criticised as an instance of vacillation and weakness of policy. It would be regarded as particularly inappropriate in the light of the recent increase in retirement pension. It would also be regarded as undermining the structure of the social services which the Conservative Party [more accurately, the Churchill-led coalition government] had themselves originated in 1944–45 as being inconsistent with public pledges by Government spokesmen that those services would be maintained. Finally, it would be liable to provoke a fresh round of wage claims.

Thorneycroft was assailed, too, for wishing to impose hospital boarding charges for NHS patients and for suggesting the abolition of free eye tests.[46]

Such symbolic welfare cuts were among the main ingredients of the £48m separating Chancellor and Prime Minister when the break came and Thorneycroft, Powell and Birch resigned on 6 January 1958. On both economic philosophy and the British New Deal Macmillan prevailed. Never again did he have to face a serious threat from his Chancellors. Heathcoat Amory and Selwyn Lloyd were neither strong nor economically literate players. At least until Reginald Maudling replaced Lloyd in July 1962, the motive power of British economic policy came from No. 10 rather than No. 11 Downing Street. Just as ROBOT had fallen for New Deal reasons, so did the Thorneycroft version of economic liberalism plus sound money.

Unlike ROBOT six years earlier, the alternative policy never had a chance. The weight of both Cabinet opinion and the Whitehall machine was firmly against it. Twenty-two years on, with Mrs Thatcher in No. 10, Thorneycroft reckoned he had got the politics of 1957–8 wrong. He told Alistair Horne that his difference with Macmillan '... was really more fundamental than a matter of £50 million (he loved to spend – that was the element of the aristocratic Whig in him – always an element of the rake, rather than the more brutal view of the downhill descent of the country, which was my view ...).' But, 'whether we were right to resign I think was questionable ... my ideas were very out of fashion in those days, before Milton Friedman* ... we probably made our stand too early ...'[47]

How the ever affable Peter Thorneycroft, had he lived long enough to see it declassified, would have enjoyed reading the Old Whig's letter to his Sovereign just a couple of years after the resignations about the perpetual dilemma of public spending:

As always one never seems to have enough money. When one was at a private school one felt that ultimately this indigence might rectify itself with reaching manhood or middle age. On the contrary, most individuals have found that as they get older the claims upon them become more and more embarrassing. And so it is with our country.

Government expenditure, that is, the demands either of the Services, or of the new scientific methods of warfare, or of the social services, education, health and all the rest, or rebuilding Britain and repairing the neglect of many years, all these things together seem to cost more and more. The public want them all but they do not like the idea of paying for them. That is the internal problem, the perpetual public dilemma of politicians, in which indeed they merely find reflected the everlasting private dilemma of private individuals.[48]

Had he read this little soliloquy at the end of July 1960, Thorneycroft could have been forgiven for saying that was exactly the thrust of his resignation speech.

But when he rose on 23 January 1958 to make it in the House of Commons, Macmillan – transformed from Old Whig aristocrat to new Commonwealth statesman – was well into his tour of Asia, the Far East, Australia and New Zealand. His departure from Heathrow on the morning of 7 January 1958 in his specially fitted-out Britannia plane (a 'little cabin' with beds for him and Lady Dorothy[49]) gave Macmillan a platform for his best-remembered (and well-rehearsed) example of *sang froid*. The press and

---

* The US monetarist economist and free marketeer whose influence was considerable during the Thatcher years.

television cameras were gathered, avid for his reaction to the resignation of his Treasury ministers the previous day. 'Almost the whole Cabinet [were there] to see me off. This was intended, obviously, as a mark of respect and loyalty.'[50] Macmillan, as he recalled in his memoirs,

made a short and carefully prepared statement about the Commonwealth trip. In doing so I referred to 'some recent difficulties' in our affairs at home which had 'caused me a little anxiety'. However, 'I thought the best thing to do was to settle up these little local difficulties and then to turn to the wider vision of the Commonwealth.' I was conscious of seeming to minimise the crisis. Nevertheless, I was sustained by the conviction that we had nearly turned the corner.[51]

The No. 10 files for early 1958, when declassified in 1989, told a rather different story. A shiver of continuing anxiety ran through the signals to and from the Prime Minister's party as they made their way through the Middle East to Pakistan in early January. For example, a message encoded using a one-time pad was waiting for Macmillan during his brief stop-over at Bahrain on 7 January. Drafted by his Principal Private Secretary, Freddie Bishop, it read:

The Lord Privy Seal [Butler], Chancellor of the Duchy [Hill] and Chief Whip [Heath] have all been actively keeping watch on the situation today. Chief Whip has completed a round-up of political reactions and reports that the situation among Government Members of Parliament is stable and favourable. As far as we can find out, general opinion in the city is generally favourable. There is a feeling here and there that there must be something else behind Thorneycroft's resignation . . .

Sterling naturally remained unsettled during the day . . .

You will have seen from telegram No. 27 from Washington that the President and Mr Dulles are helping to counter any wrong impression.

Editor of Times, at his request, saw Lord Privy Seal this morning to endeavour to understand what was happening. Lord Privy Seal pointed out that he ought to have understood the facts before writing his critical leader. Haley departed looking worried, even 'cowed', we thought.[52]

On 8 January Bobbie Allan (about to be promoted Financial Secretary to the Admiralty in the Thorneycroft-induced reshuffle), Macmillan's Parliamentary Private Secretary, sleuthed through the City on behalf of his boss and Rab Butler, who was in charge of the government in Macmillan's absence. 'Informed opinion', he told Butler, initially 'began to swing in favour of Thorneycroft. The main argument was that private industry had been dealt with pretty roughly and it was quite right that the Government should deal equally roughly with its own expenditure.' But City opinion, according to Allan, later started to, 'swing the other way, which took notice of the wider political implications. The best summing up was something which a leading international broker said. This was: "I would like to see the Government cutting every penny of expenditure; but if it is a matter of political judgement I would prefer to trust Macmillan rather than Thorneycroft."'[53]

Despite the generally reassuring tenor of the messages from Whitehall, Macmillan did consider returning to London for the economic debate in the House of Commons on 23 January in which the old and the new Chancellors were due to speak. He was worried, too, about what Thorneycroft would say when he spoke to his Monmouth constituents in Newport on the 14th.

On 12 January the Prime Minister cabled his Chief Whip, Edward Heath, from Karachi:

Nearly a week has passed since Thorneycroft's resignation. I am afraid it must have been a very difficult week for you and I feel rather out of the fray. I cannot express sufficiently my gratitude to you for the way in which you managed affairs in those difficult days ... I am hoping that by the time the debate comes the party will have recovered from what must have been a very serious nervous shock. However I do not propose to return for the debate unless you order me.[54]

The following day Hailsham, who was also Conservative Party Chairman, sent a telegram to Macmillan containing an account of his conversation with Thorneycroft the previous Friday, when 'he struck me as in a resentful and sullen mood but he promised that he would not attempt any revolt from the party – I anticipate some quite choppy water ahead but we must take it as it comes'.[55] On 16 January Hailsham followed up with another message to Macmillan (who was by this time in Ceylon), telling him Thorneycroft had kept his word:

Peter's speech at Monmouth [in fact, it was in Newport[56]] was good, moderate and highly publicised in The Times. Perhaps in the long run this moderation is the more dangerous but for the present I feel we can write off the danger of a revolt. Nigel [Birch] flapped as usual noisily and somewhat irresponsibly in his constituency last night, but I fancy this will be the last instalment for the time being ...[57]

As so often with Harold Macmillan, public insouciance masked private anxiety.

Nevertheless, he returned to London on St Valentine's Day, 'having been away nearly 6 weeks'[58] (an absence scarcely conceivable in the early twenty-first century). He had another 'little local difficulty' to deal with at Heathrow, where Rab Butler and Alec Home were waiting to meet him:

The Rochdale by-election [which Labour won on 12 February, taking the seat from the Tories[59]] . . . where our vote fell from 20000 or more to 7000 and we were behind the Liberal [Ludovic Kennedy] (who polled 17000) has been a tremendous shock. I was, of course, asked a question by the BBC and ITV interviewers. I said that the govt cd continue to carry on its work and that a single incident in a campaign did not settle the issue.

I drove back to London with Rab; he stayed an hour with me at No. 10; then the Chief Whip; then the For Secy [Lloyd]. All the same problems – all important, and all insoluble.[60]

In fact, Macmillan returned from his Commonwealth tour a changed man. Anthony Sampson, who accompanied him for the *Observer*, chronicled the metamorphosis that took place before his eyes as Macmillan, 'as he never hesitated to point out', became the first British Prime Minister to visit India, Pakistan, Ceylon, Australia and New Zealand.[61] 'When he left,' wrote Sampson, 'just as all three Treasury ministers had resigned, it seemed doubtful whether he would have a Government behind him at all; the journey seemed in danger of becoming ridiculous.'[62]

Writing his despatches home in January 1958, or even his short biography of Macmillan in the mid-1960s, Sampson could not have known of the carefully guarded signals traffic to and from Whitehall about post-Thorneycroft developments, but that most shrewd of journalists did see an anxious, ageing figure getting off the Britannia plane in India,

looking old, stiff and uncompromisingly English. He stepped down from the plane at Delhi airport, straight from the English mid-winter into the tropical sun, wearing a dark blue suit, the usual Old Etonian tie, and an expression of nervous confusion: he looked shy as the customary garland was hung around his neck, and anxiously aloof from the hubbub around him. He walked with his slow, stiff shuffle as if half in a daze; and he spoke in each country with the same rehearsed phrases: 'my wife and I are indeed delighted' . . . 'this is the first time that a British prime minister' . . . 'this is a unique occasion . . .', with the same lack of expression. He was often nervous – clutching at the bottom of his coat, or tapping with his fingers. In the active, hospitable atmosphere of India, he seemed an apparition from the imperial past.[63]

The crowds, however, appeared to love this old parody and he responded.

' "You've only got to raise your hands and say 'my friends!' " he said one evening, "and you get an immediate response." '[64]

Harold the romantic historian and Macmillan the realist/modernizer put in a revealing appearance in Pakistan:

he was driven up to the North West Frontier, had lunch at the officers' mess still draped with imperial trophies, and chatted up the old soldiers about their campaigns under the British. In Karachi he made a private speech to bewildered British residents on a favourite theme – of how the Victorian age was only a brief interruption of Britain's more humble and practical role in the world, as a vigorous trading nation.[65]

In the evenings he would sit down with Norman Brook and Neil Cairncross from the No. 10 Private Office and work on the business sent from Whitehall. There was in 1958 an element of novelty in this 'new kind of airborne government'[66] which had replaced Churchill's grand transatlantic progress aboard a Cunarder.

Sampson's caption beneath a photo of an overcoated Macmillan, laughing, head aloft, arms outstretched walking up Downing Street through a packed and cheering crowd (kept back by a single policeman – those were the days), had the airborne statesman 'return[ing] to London with an extraordinary new expansiveness'.[67] It was as if the combination of surveying the Treasury resignations and the pleasure he always took in playing the global statesman had persuaded Macmillan he was finally through the anxieties he felt early in 1957 about the durability of his premiership.

Macmillan did his best, both publicly and privately, to inject a dash of the post-tour confidence into economic affairs. Early in March, as Sampson put it, 'Macmillan loftily congratulated himself', by claiming, 'The day I left for my Commonwealth tour I had a feeling that the strict puritanical application of deflation was in danger of being developed into a sort of creed. When I got back six weeks later I found quite a different atmosphere; people were beginning to talk about quite different problems. The real truth is that both a brake and an accelerator are essential for a motor car ...'[68]

Professor Roy Harrod had been applying his persuasive Keynesian magic. In his 12 March diary entry Macmillan wrote:

Roy Harrod to luncheon (alone). He is very keen that we should start to take 'anti-deflationist' measures. According to him, the slump is now the enemy, not the boom. I rather share his view altho' perhaps it wd be better to say that we are subject to rather divergent influences – those arising from the American 'recession' wh is also beginning to influence Germany and other European countries on one side, and our own inflation (by no means yet out of our system) on the other.[69]

Within a few hours of lunching with Harrod, Macmillan was on his feet before 1,800 people at Friends House in Euston gathered under the banner of the Conservative Political Centre to hear perhaps the best expression of his personal approach to political economy that he would deliver during his premiership. The occasion was to mark the twentieth anniversary of the publication of his *The Middle Way* and the old man found it 'a very delightful experience'.[70] Not only did he look back with aplomb, he set out his pathway to the general election nineteen months later.

That night at Friends House there were several Macmillans on display, as there always were when he was on top form. The first was Harold the bibliophile, reaching for Dickens to heap scorn on his political opponents: 'They resemble that character in *Dombey and Son* who was described as a kind of human barrel-organ, "with a little list of tunes at which he was continually working over and over again, without any variation". This temperamental affinity to a barrel-organ afflicts, I think it is fair to say, the political Left far more than the political Right. The assumption that it is the opinions of the political Left that are kept progressive and up to date is really one of the quaintest of popular fallacies.'[71]

For Macmillan, progress lay firmly in 'The Middle Ground of Politics'; the 'finest' and 'the most enduring, tradition in British political thinking made it so'. This was not a matter of 'temperament' or 'trimming' on his part but because (and here, once more, he was taking a swipe at Thorneycroft, Powell and Birch) 'economic and social problems are matters of judgement and practical approach . . .'[72] A 'national party' like the British Conservatives 'must by its very character and tradition avoid sectional or extremist politics. It must, therefore, by definition occupy the middle ground.'[73] The job of the Conservative, said this grand old Whig in disguise, was 'combating the pretensions of those who believed – or at least said they believed – that their particular brand of doctrinaire politics at any particular time could solve every problem'.[74]

Such imbalance, he went on, was classically illustrated by the current anxiety about full employment within price stability, 'Inflation and Deflation' – 'not merely *a* problem, it is for us *the* problem', as it had been for the entire postwar period.[75]

But those of us who lived through the inter-war years know that there is another problem, just as difficult to solve and certainly no less painful in human terms. It is not only inflation which can threaten the steady expansion of production and the full employment of our resources. Deflation, involving the failure of effective demand, can do just the same thing . . .

The younger ones, of course, have no recollection of it. The middle-aged remember it vaguely. But the old ones have not forgotten. I was a Member of Parliament in those days on Tees-side. As long as I live I can never forget the impoverishment and demoralisation which all this brought with it. I am determined, as far as it lies within human power, never to allow this shadow to fall again upon our country.

Macmillan then, in a single sentence, captured the significance – as well as the inevitability – of his parting of the ways with Thorneycroft (and, with unknowing clairvoyance, why he would never sympathize with the outlook of the young woman who four months later would be adopted as prospective Conservative candidate for Finchley, the 32-year-old Margaret Thatcher[76]):

Even the social injustices suffered by a minority in the post-war period – and they are very real – are more tolerable than this major injustice.[77]

For, in the end, Macmillan was a 'never againer' – a man of the centre left, the essentially social democratic middle ground staked out by the combined experiences of Thirties slump and Forties war.

No wonder Attlee had once (in 1951) mused privately to Sir David Llewellyn, Conservative MP for Cardiff North 1950–59, that, but for the coming of war in 1939, 'Macmillan would have been Labour's Prime Minister – and not me . . . His experiences of the depression, the hunger, the poverty, fathers on the dole, kids not getting food, changed Macmillan completely. That's why he was moving strongly towards joining us.' In a real outbreak of clairvoyance Attlee went on to forecast that a 'great future still awaits him'.[78]

Jimmy Margach, to whom Llewellyn had related this extraordinary conversation, told Macmillan about it in the late 1970s in the Carlton Club before publishing it in his *The Abuse of Power*:

After I had read over the exchanges he sat back, pondered for a few moments and remarked: 'That's very interesting, you know, very interesting indeed. It's a revealing flash-back to much that was happening in those terrible years.' Yes, but was it an accurate reconstruction of what was happening, or on the point of happening? 'Oh well, you know what it is for a man of eighty-two . . . one's memory is not so good when

so much was going on in the world then.' He then set off on one of those classic elliptical chats which tell more than they say . . .'[79]

Macmillan's ellipse embraced Attlee's honesty and Llewellyn's skills as a
journalist. For Margach, 'the message was clear. How could two such eminent men talking about him as the centre of a conversation in a train
travelling from Cardiff to Paddington all those years ago have got things so
wrong. He did not say so in as many words, but the moral was crystal clear
. . . Report the conversation in your book? Of course, who was he to question
the testimony of Clem Attlee and the accuracy of David Llewellyn? As ever,
the delivery was perfect.'[80] As, no doubt, was the timing and panache with
which he delivered his 'The Middle Way – 20 Years After' that evening in
Friends House.

His pitch at Friends House for the progressive centre of British politics was
all the more remarkable in the light of the thumping majority he won at the
1959 general election, as it was that very same progressive centre which had
been outraged by Suez sixteen months earlier. It was extraordinary how the
affair had been consigned to the past (unlike the Iraq War of 2003, which
plagued the Labour government, with scarcely a moment's respite, right up
to the 2005 general election and beyond). One of the differences between
1956–8 and 2003–5, of course, was that Eden resigned two months after
the invasion of Egypt and Blair stayed in office. What was comparable, however, was the degree to which the two premiers remained unrepentant about
putting Britain's armed forces into combat (as did Macmillan).

In mid-March 1958, a few days after wallowing in the middle way before
the CPC, Macmillan talked to his fallen predecessor over a Saturday lunch
after driving

down to see Anthony Eden at a house wh he has borrowed near Newbury. I lunched
with him and Clarissa alone. He seemed rather better than when I had seen him last
. . . but very thin still. He told me that he still gets these periodic attacks – but they are
less frequent and the high temperature does not now accompany them . . .

Poor Anthony has, however, no interests. He talked only about politics, and chiefly
about Suez – which is, naturally, an obsession. Yet I feel sure that, however tactically
wrong we were, strategically we were right. If the Americans had helped us, the history
of the Middle East wd have been changed. Now, I fear, Nasser (like Mussolini) will
achieve his Arab Empire and it may take war to dislodge him. Yet (in these nuclear days)
limited war is difficult and dangerous.[81]

'The nuclear', as Macmillan called it, was never far from his thoughts as Prime Minister.

Even at the peak of his political powers – from his return from his Commonwealth tour in February 1958 to the spring and early summer of 1960 – he was always aware that, however prosperous Britain might be as he paved his reflationary way to his electoral triumph, it could all end in a moment (his own version of the 'glittering coffin' argument, perhaps). His anxiety amid prosperity arose not only from worries of the kind expressed in his Bedford speech about its being too good to last. For example during the protracted Berlin crisis of 1958 to 1961 he feared, at a particularly fraught moment, a possible 'drift to disaster ... a terrible diplomatic defeat or (out of sheer incompetence) a nuclear war'.[82] Khrushchev's successive ultimatums to the West after November 1958 to negotiate away their zones of occupation in Berlin led Macmillan to press upon both his US allies and the Soviet leader the need for a summit to ease East–West tension and to find a solution to the Berlin problem. It became and remained one of the great preoccupations of his premiership.

On the domestic and economic front, the Macmillan of the *Middle Way* became fully apparent in the spring of 1958 with a near constant stream of Keynesian expansionist exhortations from Harrod to reinforce his instincts. Macmillan was now the dominant economic policy force in the Cabinet with the Treasury resignations behind him, and a far from strong new Chancellor of the Exchequer, Heathcoat Amory, set about reflating the British economy. Amory, intriguingly, had forsaken his family's traditional West Country Liberalism for Conservatism 'under the influence of Macmillan's *The Middle Way* ... and had sat with Butler and Macmillan devising the *Industrial Charter* in 1947'.[83] As Chancellor he was overshadowed by the combination of Macmillan and Butler, though he need not have been quite such a *piano* performer at the Treasury.

As Edmund Dell pointed out, 'A strong Chancellor who succeeds a comrade fallen in battle against Cabinet colleagues is in a particularly powerful position politically. The Prime Minister cannot afford to see him go.'[84] But, like Macmillan, Dell was fully aware that Amory 'had neither the character nor the experience nor the intellect to put himself in opposition'. The same applied to that other interwar Liberal at the Foreign Office, Selwyn Lloyd. 'Macmillan now had both a Foreign Secretary ... and a Chancellor ... neither of whom had regarded themselves as serious contenders for the high positions they now held and both of whom were prepared to defer to their maker.'[85]

Macmillan's diaries are an unwitting corroborator of the Dell thesis:

14 March 1958: I had Chancellor of the Exr and Ld Privy Seal (Butler) to talk and supper. We argued for some hours about the state of the economy and what should now be done. The Treasury think that the 'boom' or the 'inflation' is still on. Butler and I have our doubts.

31 July 1958: 10.30 to 1. Cabinet. A lot of work, but very successfully completed ... Agreement on the immediate injection of 30–50 millions of Govt expenditure on Housing, Hospitals, Roads etc – with special regard to the areas where some unemployment is developing. Nothing will be said about this – for it will be thought too little by some, too much by others ... At the same time, there will be certain relaxations as to the amount of deposit on Hire Purchase transactions ... (In addition, the Chancellor of the Exr has told me that he hopes to be in a position to recommend $1/2$% *off* Bank Rate quite soon.*)

The Chancellor of the Exr is really handling the economy with great skill. Cautious where necessary, but not afraid of bolder action. He is worth 20 Thorneycrofts.

22 October 1958: I had a good talk today with the Chancellor of the Exr on the 64000 dollar question – is it a boom, is it a slump? Is it slack water? If the last, will the tide go in or out? The people now have a pathological fear even of a little unemployment. Yet 1% means *over* employment and a financial crisis. 3% means almost a political crisis ...

It is a great pleasure to talk with Heathcoat Amory, after having dealt with Thorneycroft. The former is *very* intelligent, flexible and courteous. The latter was fundamentally stupid, rigid and 'cassant'. We agreed on the things we *might* do to 'reflate' the economy a little, but we did *not* reach a final agreement about what to do.[86]

Amory liked Macmillan as an interlocutor, but one suspects that much of the time he kept relatively quiet about his doubts when Macmillan pushed his version of the late-Fifties 'middle way' and he did not much care for Roy Harrod's impact on No. 10.

Macmillan, Lord Amory recalled for Alistair Horne, was

always very friendly to me. [He never] bullied me, as I think he did bully Selwyn ... He was terrified of one thing, a slump ... he did ring me up occasionally. 'Don't you think there might be a slump in a month?' – that was the influence of Roy Harrod. He

---

* It had already been reduced to 5 per cent on 19 June and was indeed further reduced to $4^1/2$ per cent on 14 August 1958.

was always pleased by anything that was expansionary, almost a wild inflationist at that time ... It was his instinct to be rebellious against the restrictive actions of the Treasury: 'What is wrong with inflation, Derry?' I'd reply, 'You're thinking of your constituency in the 1930s!' – 'Yes, I am thinking of the under-use of resources – let's over-use them!' ...[87]

Macmillan for his part thought Amory was truly other-worldly, describing for Horne his 'sweet and Christian nature ... very good ... not conscious of his great gifts. Very simple, humble man ... and a charming man; very great, generous character. A little eccentric ... he would have been a monk, I think, in the Middle Ages ...'[88]

Perhaps the saintly side of Amory had forgiven the cajoling side of Macmillan by the time the former Chancellor talked to Alistair Horne in the 1980s, for but five days after their pleasurable and courteous conversation on 22 October 1958 Macmillan received a Treasury paper signed by Heathcoat Amory on 'Public Investment and Reflation' which (though I have not seen any of Mrs Thatcher's annotations on ministerial submissions of which she disapproved) received extraordinarily abusive treatment from the outraged inflationist in No. 10. Amory, in fact, had signed it off the day after the two of them had pondered the 64,000-dollar question (a phrase then in vogue thanks to a contemporary American television game-show).

The Amory/Treasury paper began by tackling head-on the Stockton-in-the-1930s fixation which still dominated the Prime Ministerial mind:

Ever since the 1944 Employment Policy White Paper, it has been agreed that public investment should be used against the trade cycle. But this thinking was related to the traditional trade cycle – the 7–8 years boom-slump-boom swing, with unemployment rising in the cycles before World War I to 8–10%, and to over 20% in the 1930s ...

In such a situation, public investment could readily be stimulated for two or three years ahead ...

But this is not the present situation. Now, expansive long-term forces are at work. The question is whether the upturn will come within the next six months, or whether it will be delayed until next autumn ...

We now seek *short-term* stimulation of the economy. Public sector investment is on a rapidly rising trend. It would be superogatory to stimulate it for the next two or three years – the danger is that it will overload the economy anyway.[89]

'Next autumn', of course, was the likely date of the next general election (though Macmillan could have delayed going to the polls until the spring of 1960).

I have a suspicion that Macmillan read Heathcoat Amory's paper late at night with a bit of whisky inside him. His diary makes no mention of it, but if he did read it in the small hours of 27–28 October it would fit because he had gone on to a party, following the traditional eve of Queen's Speech dinner with his ministers.[90] The Prime Ministerial heckling really began when Amory's paper pressed the 'need for control':

> (i) without it, the Government and public authorities would undoubtedly become committed to long-term programmes far in excess of our long-term resources. Our long-term economic assessment in 1957, repeated in 1958, shows this beyond any reasonable doubt. At the present time, capital expenditure is regarded as the panacea for all sorts of problems – railway wages, education, dependence on Middle East oil (although nuclear power substitutes for coal, not oil) etc. etc. I would not deprecate this, for in the last 50 years we have
>
> Rot!   not been nearly investment-minded enough. But at a time of great shortage of savings, the aggregate of Ministers' desires will always outrun the constable. We then need a system of presenting the whole picture so that Ministers can take rational choices on which is the more and which is the less important.

> (ii) there are no sound economic criteria governing investment in the public sector – the capital, in the last resort, comes from the Exchequer, and the terms on which it is made available (to nationalised industries and local authorities, and indeed the Post Office) bear no
>
> these are two   relationship to the <u>prospective return on</u> the capital, nor to <u>the eco-</u>
> quite different   <u>nomic merits nor social necessity of the project</u> [Macmillan's
> considerations   underlining].

The abuse escalates as Amory declares:

Have you ever   I am bound to say that these periodic attempts to cut or increase
been in   short-term capital expenditure are likely to frustrate the whole objec-
a.) war   tive of exercising effective control over the long-term programmes
b.) business   and keeping them in line with our long-term resources to carry them
c.) active   out.
   politics?

Hurrah!

. . . if we are forced to keep on chopping and changing, our control will undoubtedly collapse altogether. It has no sanctions to back it up . . .[91]

On Amory's cover note, dated 27 October 1958, Macmillan scrawled:

Chancellor of t Ex

This is a very bad paper.

Indeed, a disgraceful paper. It might have been written by Mr Neville Chamberlain's ghost.

HM.[92]

Robert Hall, still the Chief Economic Adviser in the Treasury, cutting short a visit to Poland, returned to London on the night of 28 October 1958, to find ministers in a 'flap':[93]

The trouble is that there are now two sharply conflicting schools of thought in the Tory Party. At one end is the PM who is naturally expansionist and who is egged on by Roy Harrod on theoretical grounds and Lord Mills [Minister of Power and former businessman] out of ignorance. The PM is supported by some of his Ministerial colleagues when they think of the next election and see that unemployment may be about the only good cry that the Labour Party could have . . .

At the other end are the Nigel Birch school . . . who think inflation is the cause of all our troubles and that the country needs a bit of unemployment and that nothing will lose the Tory Party votes among its own supporters so much as appearing to get soft as soon as any results of a tough policy appear.

The Chancellor is very much afraid that he might appear to be the man who claimed that he was going to continue the Thorneycroft policy but ran away from it [though in agreeing to succeed him, Amory implicitly signalled he did not accept the Thorneycroft line of public expenditure levels for 1958–9].[94]

Which, with the real Chancellor in No. 10, rather than No. 11 Downing Street, is exactly what Amory did.

Macmillan prevailed. Another increase in public investment of between £125m and £150m was forthcoming,[95] and on 20 November the Bank rate was reduced by another half per cent to 4 per cent. The last trace of Thorneycroft had gone from the Treasury. The 1959 Budget the following April sought to drown his memory in a sea of consumerism. As Edmund Dell put it:

Now caution was thrown to the winds. The overall Budget deficit projected, £730 million, was larger than any since the war. The Budget made very considerable tax reductions. They were calculated to increase consumers' spendable incomes by £300 million in a full year. Income tax was reduced from 8s 6d [in the pound] by no less than ninepence. Purchase tax was reduced by about one-sixth. There was a cut in the duty on beer. A start was made in the more rapid repayment of postwar credits which added a further £70m to spendable income. Investment allowances, introduced in 1954, abandoned in 1956, were reinstated.[96]

The combined result of Macmillan's policy in the midst of an expansionary period for the world generally was a rise of 10 per cent in industrial production between October 1958 and October 1959, a fall of 100,000 in unemployment, a growth rate of about 4.5 per cent in 1959–60 and a deterioration in the balance of payments from a surplus of £350m in 1958 (the best performance since 1945) to a deficit of £237m in 1960.[97]

Poor Heathcoat Amory nearly fainted towards the end of his Budget speech on 7 April 1959, not because he was worried about the sustainability of this rampant expansionism (which, quite rightly, he was), but 'because he had had no lunch'.[98] It left Macmillan buoyant, rather than feeble, with a golden ballot box (rather than a glittering coffin) in mind. 'Budget', he told his diary on 9 April, 'has been *very* well received in the country and by the press. The only attack has been "Why nothing for the Old Age Pensioners?" Actually, we have done this class in the community exceptionally well ... But Gaitskell and co will exploit the old people quite shamelessly. The 64000-dollar question remains – when? I am feeling more and more *against* a "snap" election.'[99]

'Gaitskell and co' did find it hard to cope with Macmillan at his zenith. With a pronounced Whig-cum-social democrat in No. 10 and so dominant inside his own Cabinet, life was very difficult for the democratic socialists across the floor of the House of Commons. Naturally, party political rhetoric concealed this, as it was in the interests of all the competitors for power so to do (as it always is). And the differences between the Prime Minister and the Leader of the Opposition in both position and style were very much to the former's advantage as the general election approached.

Not for nothing did Gaitskell's empathetic official biographer, Philip Williams, describe the period as 'Macmillan Ascendant'.[100] As Williams put it: 'The Prime Minister was not only a splendid performer on the screen, but also enjoyed the appurtenances of power and the sympathy of the press, which praised Macmillan (and later Wilson) for the skill in party management for which Gaitskell was condemned; and gave the Prime Minister six times as many news stories as his adversary.'[101]

Paradoxically this was Gaitskell's best period as manager of his party – the relatively benign lull between the great fights with the Bevanites and the acid arguments about both nationalization and unilateral nuclear disarmament which followed Labour's electoral defeat. The truce between Gaitskell and his Shadow Foreign Secretary, Nye Bevan, led to the harmonious interlude. Neither man found it easy. They never really warmed to each other or understood the roots of the other's convictions.[102] Gaitskell's combination of deep seriousness, devotion to reason and pertinacity in pursuit of a course once his formidable mind was made up led to irritation and adoration in equal measure – a cleavage not confined to the usual left–right line-ups within the Labour Party.

His admirer and fellow Leeds MP, Denis Healey (a man whose intellectual horsepower was at least the equal of Gaitskell's), did not altogether care, however, for every aspect of the Labour leader's style: 'I was worried by a streak of intolerance in Gaitskell's nature; he tended to believe that no one could disagree with him unless they were knaves or fools . . . he would insist on arguing to a conclusion rather than to a decision. Thus he would keep meetings of the Shadow Cabinet going, long after he had obtained consent to his proposals, because he wanted to be certain that everyone understood precisely why he was right.'[103]

Healey acknowledged that, 'I was never a member of his inner circle, like Tony Crosland and Roy Jenkins.'[104] I remember as a young political journalist talking to Healey in No. 11 Downing Street in the spring of 1976 when he sought to succeed Wilson as Prime Minister. Roy Jenkins ran too and Healey was characteristically dismissive of politicians who sought disciples. All he needed was his wife, Edna.

Contrast the Healey view with that of a disciple. With Gaitskell's death in January 1963, wrote Roy Jenkins a decade later, 'a light went out of British politics which has never since returned . . . he inspired a generation . . . Gaitskell . . . people felt, would be the great head of a government. His death was not therefore merely poignant. It was the snatching away of a nation's opportunity, as well as his own.'[105] As for the ever-unsentimental Denis Healey, he 'always doubted whether the fierce Puritanism of his [Gaitskell's] intellectual convictions would have enabled him to run a Labour Government for long, without imposing intolerable strains on so anarchic a Labour movement'.[106]

Gaitskell's fierce straightness did, however, have an appeal across the party spectrum.* Nearly half a century on it strikes me how fortunate the British electorate was in 1959 to have as its choices for premier two political acts as classy, in their own ways, as Harold Macmillan and Hugh Gaitskell. Yet their regard for each other was not high; the most individual aspects of their characters brought out a mutual dislike. Gaitskell told Roy Jenkins he thought Macmillan 'cheated at politics'[107] – he 'distrusted his flamboyance and thought he sailed too close to the political wind. His own reckless honesty, accompanied by a compulsive desire to set out every argument and every move in terms which were logically convincing – but sometimes emotionally provocative – made him disdainful of Macmillan's fondness for doing everything behind a smoke-screen.'[108]

For his part Macmillan was quite brilliant at lampooning Gaitskell's earnestness. He told Henry Fairlie in his *Daily Mail* interview as election year began: 'The trouble about Mr Gaitskell is that he is going through all the motions of being a Government when he isn't a Government. It is bad enough having to behave like a Government when one is a Government. The whole point of being in opposition is that one can have fun and lend colour to what one says or does. To be colourful: that is the opportunity opposition gives to you.'[109] The clear implication was that Gaitskell was dull, boring and lacking in self-irony.

Macmillan always set great store by a Prime Minister's need to command the House of Commons. And here, too, he generally enjoyed an ascendancy over Gaitskell but one which concealed a genuine and perpetual inner anxiety. The key to dominating the House, he said in a BBC Television interview in 1971, was 'never to give in, never to show how nervous and awful the whole business is . . . I think I did seem to have what was called unflappability – if only they knew how one's inside was flapping all the time, they wouldn't have said that . . .'[110] Out of the private flapping came public flair. Macmillan had taken decades to mature his style and one mentor in particular had helped him.

After one of his early speeches in Parliament in 1924, Lloyd George 'came up to me and said, "Macmillan, that was an interesting speech of yours." I was naturally flattered. He continued: "If you don't mind my saying so, you have no idea how to make a speech."'[111] A somewhat crestfallen Macmillan

---

* It has emerged that at least one leader of the Conservative Party greatly admired him. Michael Howard, as a young Cambridge undergraduate, was considerably affected by Gaitskell's death (Philip Webster, 'New Biography Says Tory Leader Considered Joining Labour Party', *The Times*, 30 March 2005).

asked the greatest orator of the age for help. Lloyd George took him up to his room and coached him:

First of all you are a new member. You always speak in a thin house, probably in the dining-hour ... Never say more than one thing. Yours was an essay, a good essay, but with a large number of separate points. Just say one thing; when you are a Minister two things, and when you are Prime Minister winding up a debate perhaps three ... Of course you wrap it up in different ways. You say it over and over again with different emphasis and different illustrations. You say it forcefully, regretfully, even perhaps threateningly; but it is a single clear point ... there must be continual variation; slow solemn phrases, quick, witty amusing passages ... Finally, don't forget the value of the pause.[112]

This last is very much how I remember the Macmillan style from my youth.

Gaitskell made some of the most passionate and best-remembered speeches of the postwar years – combating unilateral nuclear disarmament in 1960 ('There are some of us ... who will fight and fight and fight again to save the party we love'[113]) and opposing British entry into the European Common Market in 1962 ('It means the end of a thousand years of history'[114]). But they were delivered from the party conference platform rather than across the floor of the House of Commons.

Gaitskell, unlike Macmillan, had not had a parliamentary speech-trainer of the calibre of Lloyd George and camouflage and verbal artifice did not come naturally to him. As a result, in Macmillan's view, he

might have been a lecturer in Economics. He made the mistake, which Lloyd George warned me about, of making too many points ... he would ask ten, or fourteen, questions – one of which was unanswerable, without telling him a direct lie ... I soon learned that you only answered the easy ones ... If he had asked one question which he knew I couldn't give the answer to truthfully, it would have been much more effective ... Poor man. I did it over and over again to him; he never spotted it.[115]

Unlike Macmillan, Gaitskell never saw politics as an elaborate game.

He had other disadvantages, too. One part of the Labour movement might be relatively quiescent but rarely, in the early postwar years, was all of it so at any particular time. Bevan might no longer be the left-wing thorn in the party's side of earlier years, but Frank Cousins of the Transport and General Workers Union increasingly was – and the old operator in No. 10 was sharp-eyed in his appreciation of the dividend that dysfunction within the Labour movement could engineer for the Conservatives. (During a bad patch for the

Conservatives in the autumn of 1957 he had told his diary that: 'At the moment the whole thing is swinging *away* from us – but has it swung to Labour? . . . If I can keep the battle [i.e. the general election] off for 2 years, it is quite likely they will quarrel again.'[116]) Bevan's endorsement of multilateralism at the 1957 Labour Party conference meant that the bomb could no longer work for Macmillan behind Labour's lines; but the London buses could.

Cousins, as leader of the country's largest trade union, represented the toughest industrial opposition any postwar premier had had to face so far. He was determined to take on the Macmillan government over public sector pay policy. As his biographer Geoffrey Goodman wrote: 'Until the miners' strikes of 1972 and 1974 [the 1958 strike of London busmen] remained the outstanding example of a Government decision to take on a union in the public sector in an attempt to force through a general policy of wage restraint.'[117] Macmillan chose his ground carefully. He settled with the railwaymen in order to isolate the busmen.[118] As he explained many years later, the London public wouldn't worry if they were without a bus for a few weeks. 'It's an inconvenience but not a disaster' for the government.[119] He thought, too, the public had more sympathy for the railwaymen's cause than the busmen's.[120]

Cousins and Gaitskell did not get on, and Cousins put Gaitskell in an impossible position.[121] A London bus strike might not inconvenience the electorate as much as a national rail strike, but it would – and did (I remember it) – enrage a large number of voters. Labour leaders in opposition can very easily fall between the twin stools of preaching economic responsibility and sustaining general support for the Labour movement. Gaitskell fully understood that the bus strike 'would be most unpopular and he knew it was bound to fail when the [TUC] General Council disapproved of it. Yet he was critical of the government's general policy and also rightly suspected that Cousins and the Cabinet had not tried to avert the strike.'[122] The government prevailed, leaving Gaitskell aware that 'we lost a lot by supporting the strike and got no kudos within the TUC because they hate Cousins'.[123]

Macmillan took great comfort from the busmen's failure (though he admired their doggedness[124]) and saw it as a moment of wider political significance. Returning from a week in Washington on 14 June he found the staunchly CND Frank Cousins in deep trouble with his busmen. On 20 June the strike ended. The day before, the Bank of England had brought Bank rate down to 5 per cent.

Both Macmillan's confidence and his reflationary instincts were stoked:

This second fall within a month and in a period of considerable industrial disorder, made me feel more and more certain that the time had come for a cautious reversal of policy . . .

Certainly from the political aspect the bus strike seemed to be a turning-point. Up to then, although I felt in no doubt that the Government had succeeded in maintaining itself and even imposing a moral ascendancy in the House of Commons, there had been no similar advance in the country.[125]

Until the early summer of 1958, he added in his memoirs, 'I felt little doubt that in spite of our bold attempt to ride the storm after the events of 1956 we were still slipping backwards.'[126]

Despite Macmillan's assessment of those weeks, it would be both wrong and crude to divide Macmillan's first premiership into a post-Suez storm (January 1957 to June 1958) and a smooth glide to electoral victory (June 1958 to October 1959) propelled by his twin theme of prosperity at home and peace abroad. (There was the growing possibility of a four-power summit in early 1960 which Macmillan was seeking and he 'was quite shameless'[127] in exploiting Eisenhower's visit to Britain at the end of August 1959, the two of them driving through the City of London in a white open-topped Rolls-Royce Macmillan had borrowed for the occasion from silver-screen heart-throb Douglas Fairbanks Jr).[128] Few incumbents may have had a better electoral hand than he did at the end of the golden summer of 1959, but the first days of the campaign saw Gaitskell and the Labour Party appearing to dislodge Macmillan and the Conservatives from that political middle ground the old Edwardian tried so assiduously to straddle.

Macmillan sought a dissolution of Parliament from the Queen on 8 September and polling day was set for 8 October – sufficiently late in the year for the benign effects of the spring Budget to work through the economy and sufficiently early in the autumn to increase the chances of a campaign conducted in good weather (which was indeed golden). The election saw two relatively novel political weather-makers at work – 'relatively' because both involved a heightened use of existing instruments: the opinion poll and television.[129] And it was Labour's superior use of television over the first two weeks of the campaign which was credited with halving the Tory lead in the polls from about 6 per cent to about 3.[130] Gaitskell, advised by some genuine TV experts from his own ranks (Tony Benn, Woodrow Wyatt and Christopher Mayhew, who themselves shared in the party's election broadcasts[131]), began to profit, too, from his greater exposure to the wider public, upon whom, though Labour leader for over four years, he had yet to impinge fully.[132]

Macmillan was a touch rattled. He noted in his diary on 22 September:

All our people were depressed yesterday by the Daily Mail 'Gallup Poll' wh shewed our lead had reduced from 7% to 3½%. But today the rival Daily Express poll shows our 7% lead maintained. Ld Poole [Deputy Chairman of the Conservative Party], who came yesterday afternoon, was calm – but thought we shd have to stiffen up the attack pretty soon. I thought I could use the whistle-stop speeches for this [Macmillan mostly used an open-topped Ford, rather than a train, for these[133]].

The Socialists had a very successful TV last night – much better than ours. Gaitskell is becoming very expert. All their campaign so far is concentrated on dirt (against the Tories and businessmen) with bribes to the old. They are trying to make it a Pension Election. While we must defence [sic] this flank, we must not let ourselves be diverted from the main theme – peace and prosperity.[134]

Three days later Macmillan disgraced himself by seeming to challenge Gaitskell's valour. If this was part of a deliberate 'stiffening up' of the Conservative campaign it was deeply unworthy.

Macmillan, as his diaries showed over several years, was prone to deprecate 'gownsmen' and laud 'swordsmen'.[135] Though immensely bookish, he placed himself firmly in a category which fused both.[136] But towards the end of September 1959, though he had, until then, conducted his campaign in a lofty fashion, he suddenly attacked Gaitskell for not having fought in the war, a move for which the Conservative-supporting *Daily Telegraph* criticized him.[137]

This particular animus towards Gaitskell was long and deeply felt. After standing beside him at the Cenotaph in Whitehall on Remembrance Sunday in 1960, Macmillan noted in his diary: 'Poor Mr Gaitskell always seems a little conscious on these occasions that he has no medals. However, he supported the War, from Dr Dalton's side, in the Ministry of Economic Warfare.'[138] In fact, Gaitskell regretted not having served in the armed forces, but, as an economist, he was placed in a reserved occupation and earmarked for the planned Ministry of Economic Warfare before the Second World War began.[139]

Macmillan's best-remembered assault on Gaitskell during the 1959 campaign was both fair game and effective politics. It was a classic tax-and-spend ambush; but Gaitskell set himself up for it. His devotee, Roy Jenkins, reckoned 'the hidden mood of the country was against him. There was a strong latent satisfaction with the new affluence of the past few years. People did not parade this satisfaction much, but it was there, and was well exploited by the deft materialism of Mr Macmillan's campaign. In the circumstances no radical leader could have won. Gaitskell did at least as well as anyone else could have done.'[140]

Perhaps. But what Jenkins recognized as Gaitskell's 'one significant mistake, for which he was bitterly critical of himself',[141] was deemed both at the time and subsequently by most observers as the turning point of the campaign. Gaitskell had argued consistently from the outset of the campaign that Labour's promises – including the boost to old-age pensions – could be paid for by a combination of economic growth and a tightening up of capital gains tax and business expense allowances.[142] Towards the end of September, Gaitskell's aides sensed (erroneously, as it turned out[143]) that the Conservatives were about to claim that, if elected, Labour would increase income tax by half a crown (2s 6d or 12$\frac{1}{2}$p) in the pound.[144] In a speech at Newcastle on 28 September Gaitskell said: 'There will be no increase in the standard or other rates of income tax so long as normal peacetime conditions continue.'[145]

The error was compounded at Labour's morning press conference on 1 October (a Labour innovation in 1959 which the Conservatives felt obliged to imitate[146]) when journalists were given a handout saying a Labour government would remove purchase tax from certain essential items.[147] Macmillan, who had already rubbished Gaitskell's income tax pledge in Glasgow on 29 September (which he described as 'a very queer one for a professional economist and an ex-Chancellor of the Exchequer'[148]), read reports of the purchase tax claims while on the road in south London en route to his Sussex home, Birch Grove. He turned to his speech writer, George Christ, and said, 'We've got him!'[149] 'I remember exactly where it was,' he recalled to Alistair Horne. 'And we got out of the car, and called a meeting on Wandsworth Common ... There were a few people following, and we had a sort of press conference, and I said, "If this is an auction, I am not in it!" And that finished it ...'[150] In Macmillan's view, 'those were probably the words that won the election'.[151] The opinion polls suggested this was a crucial moment.[152]

To compound Labour's woes, Macmillan found a sure touch in his last election broadcast on 6 October. It looks terribly mannered today, but it was deemed very effective at the time with the credit shared between the Edwardian actor and his producer, Norman Collins (described by Macmillan as 'a consummate expert'[153]), who prepared the Prime Minister as a one-off favour, with the Conservative Central Office press people pushed to the sidelines. Collins told Macmillan to rehearse carefully and to fly solo:

On the morning of 6 October I went along with John Wyndham [personal and unpaid Downing Street assistant] to his [Collins'] studio. We roughed out a draft and I made two rehearsals before lunch. The plan was to keep on my feet; use as accessories only a globe, a map of Britain and some letters on a table to pick up and read at random. I hoped by this plan to bring a certain life and ease into the performance. But at lunchtime I was depressed. It was an ambitious idea, but could I make it successful? If it did not come off it would be a crashing failure and the stakes were high.

After lunch we did two or three more rehearsals ... At 6 o'clock Norman Collins said to me, 'I think that will do ...' 'But,' I protested, 'I have got to go and deliver it at 8 o'clock on the BBC.' 'Oh no,' he said, 'I have got the film – we will send it along.' Without telling me he had taken film records of each performance and I was thereby saved the strain of doing it 'live' with all the risks involved.[154]

It was masterly. Macmillan managed to be both intimate and grand, speaking of the country as 'trustees, not owners' of a great national tradition ('a nation is a partnership between the living and the dead and those yet to be born').[155]

One viewer in Tredegar surprisingly thought it a great performance. Nye Bevan dismissed the criticisms of his friend Geoffrey Goodman (who was following him for the *Daily Herald*) and defended Macmillan, 'not so much the man, who[m] he despised, but the politician, the party leader; the manner of his presentation may be "hammy", he agreed, but he makes his point for his own party and his own class. That impressed Bevan.'[156]

Privately he had been as critical of Gaitskell's performance (on tax pledges especially) as he had been reluctantly approving of the Macmillan style.[157] That same evening in Tredegar, Bevan told Goodman that Macmillan had considered joining Labour in the 1930s and had talked privately to him about it. Bevan believed that Macmillan had never forgiven him for urging caution.[158]

The 1959 general election was an extraordinary triumph for Macmillan. Out of the wreckage of Suez and the Eden premiership, he had not only presided over a political recovery, he increased the Conservative majority (if not the party's share of the vote – partly because the Liberals doubled theirs). On a turnout of 78.7 per cent (2 per cent higher than in 1955), the Conservatives' overall majority on 8 October 1959 was nearly doubled from 54 to 100. The Conservatives took 49.4 per cent of the votes cast (Eden had managed 49.7 per cent in 1955); Labour 43.8 per cent and the Liberals 5.9 per cent (quite a boost for their new leader, Jo Grimond).[159] Macmillan the centrist took comfort from this, noting in his diary on 11 October that: 'What I think happened is that the Liberals (for the first time) took more from the Social-ists, in many places, than from us. This may prove important. The great thing is to keep the Tory party on *modern* and *progressive* lines.'[160]

As so often with Macmillan, at the moment of his greatest public triumph there were undertones of real anxiety about his party's, his government's and his country's true position. Unknown to anyone outside a handful of White-hall insiders that election summer and autumn of 1959, he had commissioned a highly secret assessment of the performance of the UK's economy, its place in Europe and the world and as a serious player in the Cold War over the coming decade. On 7 June he had summoned a group of top civil servants, diplomats and the Chiefs of Staff to an all-day meeting at Chequers to start the process of mapping the road to 1970.[161]

This secret *Future Policy Study* rather than a general election won on a complacent, if understandable, ticket of 'Peace and Prosperity' (with the economy as the main reason for the Conservatives' success[162]) in which 'Britain's relationship with the European Common Market was neglected',[163] was by far the more revealing indicator of the country's condition – its rela-tive wealth, power and influence. And the consummate actor, twirling his globe in Norman Collins' studio that October afternoon, knew this full well. Aided by Labour's confusion over fiscal policy and a tide of consumer goods, he might have deceived the electorate; but he had not altogether convinced himself.

13

Wealth, Power and Influence

'Even though the material strength of the United Kingdom would decline relatively, we should still have other assets which would enable us to play a significant part in world affairs. The best periods of our history had by no means been those, such as the nineteenth century, when we had a preponderance of wealth or power, and for the future we must be ready to consider how we could continue to exercise influence in the world other than through material means alone.'

Harold Macmillan in 1960, contemplating Britain's place in the world by 1970.[1]

'I'm not ashamed of "having it so good". The temptations of comfort and affluence are not an argument in favour of poverty. Our purpose should be to keep it good and make it better. The people who object most violently to the new affluence being shared by the mass of working people are those who are doing exceptionally well out of the new capitalism through fat expense accounts, expensive meals and other perks on the company's account . . . The expansionist is the optimist because he believes in the future. The deflationist is the pessimist because he fears the future.'

Harold Macmillan to James Margach, early 1960s.[2]

'I think the miscalculation that I and a lot of other people made was that we never foresaw the collapse of British manufacturing industry. I've read one or two things saying that if he studied the statistics more carefully we would have come to a different conclusion . . . I'm not sure that anybody foresaw it.'

Lord Sherfield, Ambassador to Washington, 1952–6; Permanent Secretary to the Treasury, 1956–9, reflecting in 1990.[3]

'We live in a political age. All round us we see foreign competition making itself unpleasant.'   P. G. Wodehouse, *The Clicking of Cuthbert*, 1922.[4]

'Psychologically, it ... meant as it were turning the last page in the most successful imperial history ever known.'

> Fernand Braudel on the UK's first application for membership
> of the European Economic Community.[5]

Politicians can be at their most revealing at moments when setback arouses a level of irritation that propels them close to the rim of rage. Macmillan was especially so when dealing not with a Thorneycroft within his own ranks or a Gaitskell on the hustings but with his opposite numbers abroad when their actions or behaviour reflected what he sensed all too directly was an ebbing of Britain's power. In the summer of 1958, the Macmillan government's alternative to a tariff-protected Common Market – a free trade area (Plan G) in Europe – looked doomed, as indeed it was, by the first six months of the EEC's life and the intransigence of Charles de Gaulle. In a minute of 24 June, which he intended to be read only by his Chancellor, Amory, and his Foreign Secretary, Lloyd, Macmillan let fly against the wretched Europeans, de Gaulle and Adenauer especially. He began in somewhat grand, yet self-pitying mode:

I think sometimes our difficulties with our friends abroad result from our natural good manners and reticence. We are apt not to press our points too strongly in the early stages of a negotiation, and then when a crisis arises and we have to take a definite position we are accused of perfidy. I feel we ought to make it quite clear to our European friends that if Little Europe is formed without the parallel development of a Free Trade Area we shall have to reconsider the whole of our political and economic attitude towards Europe.[6]

At this point Macmillan lit the blue touch-paper:

I doubt if we could remain in NATO. We should certainly put on highly protective tariffs and quotas to counteract what Little Europe was doing to us. In other words, we should not allow ourselves to be destroyed little by little. We would take our troops out of Europe. We would withdraw from NATO. We would adopt a policy of isolationism. We would surround ourselves with rockets and we would say to the Germans, the French and all the rest of them: 'Look after yourselves with your own forces. Look after yourselves when the Russians overrun your countries.'[7]

This was flappability of a high order. Macmillan knew that Britain could no longer see itself as the power broker in western Europe.

There was, however, always available for British policy-makers the consolation of the UK now being a thermonuclear-tipped power. Or was there? Just over a year after Macmillan's very private outburst against de Gaulle and Adenauer, it was Eisenhower's turn.

Macmillan feared the day when the two superpowers would seize summitry for themselves alone. In July 1959 – just days before a visit to the UK by the US President[8] – Macmillan sensed this danger acutely, as he confided to his diary:

My own position here will be greatly weakened. Everyone will assume that the 2 Great Powers – Russia and the USA – are going to fix up a deal over our heads and behind our backs. My whole policy – pursued for many years and especially during my Premiership – a close alliance and co-operation with America will be undermined. People will ask 'Why should the UK try to stay in the big game?'

... 'Why should she be a nuclear power? You told us that this would give you power and authority in the world. But you and me [sic] have been made fools of. This shows that Gaitskell and Crossman and Co are right. UK had better give up the struggle and accept, as gracefully as possible, the position of a second-rate power.'[9]

Graceful acceptance of decline from the top table to outer ring was something neither Macmillan the gownsman nor Macmillan the swordsman[10] could bear to contemplate. (Macmillan the penman appeared to have gone temporarily AWOL.) It was to find ways of averting this fate that he had, in great secrecy, summoned his senior officials, diplomats and military (but not a single ministerial colleague) to Chequers that June Sunday in 1959. When he finally let his full Cabinet into the secret at the end of February 1960 he told them,

In June of last year I held an informal meeting at Chequers to discuss the possibility of making a long-range study of our oversea [sic] policy during the next decade. My idea was that we should try to forecast what the state of the world would be in 1970 and what role the United Kingdom would be able to play in it. I thought that, if they had this picture before them, Ministers would be better able to formulate policies for the intervening years which would allow us to play a significant part in world affairs.[11]

The *Future Policy Study*, or FPS, outstrips in its detail and reach any comparable review of the UK's place and prospects in the world I have ever encountered. It makes a fascinating control against which to judge what actually happened in the 1960s, as I shall be doing in the successor volume to this one.

Predictably it was Sir Norman Brook, the arch fixer at the Whitehall epicentre, who first alerted the small clandestine group which was to spend the day at Chequers on 7 June 1959. Sir Patrick Dean, Chairman of the Joint Intelligence Committee, who was to oversee the entire production, received a letter, on a 'top secret and personal' basis, from the Cabinet Secretary at the end of May outlining the purpose of the gathering and explaining that, 'This study would be undertaken by officials – the Prime Minister does not wish to be troubled with it at this stage – and it is contemplated that its results should be available, in the form of a report or reports, for consideration by Ministers at the end of the year, preferably in the late autumn.'[12] Though they were to dine with the PM, it would not, said Brook, 'be necessary to bring a dinner jacket'.[13] (Brook was a stickler for 'correct' attire, frowning on tweeds in the office, for example.[14])

Macmillan summed up the 7 June session in his diary:

All day conference at Chequers on '*Future British Policy*'. The idea was to draw up a paper – for the use of the next Government. The first part would try to assess '*The Setting*' – what is likely to happen in the world during the next 10 years. The second part would deal with '*UK's resources*' – the gross national product; the calls for expenditure on Pensions, Education, Defence etc. wh are more or less inescapable. The third part would be about '*The Objectives*' – what Foreign, Commonwealth and Colonial and Economic policies we ought to follow. Today's meeting was to agree the skeleton – the general outline of the work – and to cast the parts. It is hoped to do the job in 3 or 4 months. We had Sir Norman Brook, Sir R. Makins (Treasury), Sir F. Hoyer-Millar and Sir Pat Dean (FO), Sir R. Powell (Defence), Sir W. Dickson (Chief of Defence Staff) and the 3 Chiefs of Staff – or their deputies. The meetings began at 11.30 and continued till about 7. I gave them all luncheon and dinner.[15]

Given Dean's central casting as chairman of the group assigned to do the work, his minister, Lloyd, had to be told what was up. This Macmillan did in a minute three days later.[16] It fell to Dean to put the frighteners on everyone else, warning them on 23 June that: 'It is important that the fact that this exercise is in progress should not become widely known. It would be upsetting for Departments in Whitehall generally if they got the impression that a radical review of policy was in train without their knowledge, and it could of course be positively damaging if such an impression got about in public and reached the ears e.g. of the US Government.'[17] Need-to-know was the key. When in doubt, Dean should be consulted.[18]

Unsurprisingly, therefore, the 'questions' paper discussed at Chequers (to which Macmillan referred in his diary) was appended to the formal minute of the meeting,[19] classified top secret and distributed to a very narrow circle. Had it leaked (which it did not – though Don Cook of the *New York Herald Tribune*, a seasoned journalist with excellent London contacts, got hold of the outline story by 'osmosis rather than a "leak"' in July 1960[20]) it would have been quite a scoop. Its degree of candour about the UK's position in that pre-election period would have made a stark contrast to the government's smug theme of 'Peace and Prosperity', especially its sections on 'The Objectives' and 'The Means'.[21]

Strategically important questions were posed, such as 'What is the future of Anglo-American interdependence? What differing degrees of emphasis may we have to set on maintaining our relations with the USA, with Europe, and with the Commonwealth?'[22] Some questions reprised the 1957 in-house debate on how best to sustain influence in the UK's colonies and former domains. The nuclear question had a central place:

What would be the effects of discontinuance of nuclear tests, and the achievement of nuclear sufficiency? If (a) the Soviet Union and (b) the Western Powers acquire so great a nuclear capacity that each side is afraid to attack the other, by what means do we maintain this balance of tensions?

Even pulling out of the whole business was contemplated:

In those circumstances should we still need to make an *independent* contribution to the Western deterrent? If so, what form should it take, e.g. should it be on the lines of BLUE STREAK [British-made, liquid-fuelled, ground-launched missile then under development], BLUE STEEL [stand-off missile to be launched from the V-bombers] or POLARIS [the most advanced submarine-launched system under development in the USA]? Alternatively, should we need a greater degree of interdependence in this field – with the USA, or with the Commonwealth or with Europe? Will there be a specifically European contribution to the deterrent, and what will be our relation to it?

The shadow of Suez was present, too: 'What commitments, short of global war, should we plan to meet, either on our own or in association with allies, and what Forces do we need for these purposes?'[23]

But the spectre that really haunted the Prime Minister, the officials and the military men at Chequers that June Sunday was the country's ability to pay for continuing to cut a dash in the world. It was 'The Means' section which, had it leaked before or during the 1959 election campaign, would have caused the greatest fuss:

13. How much of our economic resources can we reasonably expect to be able to afford to devote, over this period [1960–70], to: –

    (i)   defence?
    (ii) assistance to the under-developed countries?
    (iii) 'prestige' civil projects (for example, atomic energy, a supersonic airliner [what became Concorde], space research, Cunarders [what became the *QEII*])?

    Can we reasonably be expected to be able to: –

    (i)   maintain the present allocation of money for these purposes?
    (ii) maintain the present proportion of gross national product?
    (iii) increase the proportion of gross national product?

14. Within these totals, can we expect to be able to maintain or increase the level of overseas military and political expenditure?

15. What changes within (i) the United Kingdom economy, (ii) the sterling area, or (iii) the world economy would invalidate the answers to questions 13 and 14?[24]

The early papers prepared by the Treasury, with the help of the Foreign and Commonwealth Relations Offices and the Joint Intelligence Bureau, in answer to the mind-stretching possibilities suggested that 'having it so good' would not exactly be the leitmotif of the replies to the Chequers questions. For example a submission to Dean's Working Group dated 20 July 1959 noted that, for demographic reasons, the UK would 'slip back' as an economic force compared to the USA and Western Europe: 'Whether the declining relative position of the UK could be redressed by a breakthrough in productivity cannot be predicted – and there is no ground for expecting such a development.' Here the currency, as so often, put in a depressing appearance: 'UK influence and capacity for independent action has been greatly weakened in the last decade by the repeated sterling crises: if the UK could maintain a strong external financial position that would much improve its relative position within the West.'[25]

The Treasury draftsmen were too discreet either to mention the word 'Suez' in connection with this paragraph or to venture an opinion on the likelihood of the UK achieving that holy grail of a 'strong external financial position' at any point between 1960 and 1970. Money and the capacity of the UK economy cast a dark shadow over the entire *Future Policy Study* exercise and so did the nuclear question in the form of the capability, utility and cost of the British deterrent. A surprisingly large proportion of the very first discussion at Chequers was taken up by it – and the one area of minuted disagreement in the final report was about the power and the purposes of the UK's nuclear force.

When the 'questions' paper was discussed at Macmillan's 'sizing and shaping' Chequers session, the bomb dominated, starting with the 'Theory of the Western Deterrent'. Macmillan and his politico-military advisers were well aware of the differences between 1951 (when the Conservatives had returned to power and Churchill discovered how far advanced was Mr Attlee's atomic weapons programme) and 1959. As the minutes put it:

The policy of the deterrent was first evolved when the West had a clear nuclear superiority, which was regarded as a means of deterring Russia from starting a major war. In the state of nuclear parity, which we had virtually reached already, both sides were equally deterred from doing anything which might start nuclear war. Was this balance to our advantage, and if so, could it be maintained? Would it, nevertheless, permit or even encourage a whole range of minor hostile actions and encroachments?

With uncanny prescience, the meeting anticipated the Cuban crisis of autumn 1962 when the Soviet Union, miscalculating likely American reactions, began to construct missile sites on the island which, had they remained, would have brought the bulk of the United States' cities and military bases within range of Russian nuclear weapons:

The political effect of nuclear parity might be to cause the Russians to believe that the American area of vital interest would be increasingly reduced. But we should expect to see more active Communist economic and political penetration, playing on the fears and divisions of the West under cover of nuclear parity. The state of nuclear parity would thus seem to give a real advantage to the side which was ready to take risks in areas of marginal interest to the other side ... Nuclear parity might make it harder for the West effectively to counter Soviet probes and minor encroachments outside Europe.[26]

The Chequers group also anticipated a problem that was to vex the Whitehall nuclear weapons community from the mid- to late 1960s – the possibility of 'an effective anti-ballistic missile' system being developed. (The UK, as we have seen, was still developing its own ballistic missile, Blue Streak, in 1959; in the late 1960s the first of the Royal Navy's ballistic-missile carrying Polaris submarines were starting their patrols.)

The central question hovering over Chequers that Sunday was whether Britain should continue the huge effort required to sustain itself as a nuclear power. The argument was couched in the language of cost–benefit analysis rather than that of altruism and moral economy favoured by the Campaign for Nuclear Disarmament. This part of the Chequers discussion opened with a statement as bold as it was unprovable: 'In terms of foreign policy the British contribution to the Western deterrent had paid a handsome dividend up to now, but we should have to consider whether it would continue to do so.'[27]

What was this 'handsome dividend'? A place at the top table? There was every chance of a summit, with Britain present, in the coming year. The restoration in 1958 of nuclear weapons collaboration with the USA? The minutes give no clue.

But could Britain sustain its relative position as a nuclear player? It might be 'that by 1970 Soviet and American nuclear power would be so great as to dwarf our own nuclear capability; the credibility of our own deterrent would then be significantly reduced. On the other hand, having paid the entrance fee to the nuclear club, we could not easily withdraw, more particularly when others, e.g. the French, were likely to join it.'[28] (France tested its first atomic bomb in 1960 and its thermonuclear weapon in 1968.)[29]

That 'entrance fee' to restored collaboration with the Americans had caused Macmillan great worry and exertion – and had involved a degree of subterfuge. Macmillan regarded ending the application of the McMahon Act to the USA's primary Second World War nuclear partner, after twelve years of non-cooperation, as 'the great prize'.[30] Nothing was to stand in the way of winning it. When Eisenhower reassured Macmillan and showed him his draft directive authorizing the resumption of technical talks about nuclear collaboration at the White House on 24 October 1957, he 'could hardly believe [his] ears'.[31] There was probably a flurry of covert anxiety concealed by his overt pleasure – or, two anxieties, to be precise.

Firstly, 'the entrance fee', which required the British government to demonstrate its own home-grown capacity to produce a hydrogen bomb, had still not been met in full. The first thermonuclear test in the South Pacific on 15 May 1957 had produced a yield of 300 kilotons, just 30 per cent of the megaton standard[32] (though the world was told Britain was now an H-bomb power[33]). A bigger bang on 31 May (between 700 and 800 kilotons) was produced by an enhanced fission weapon, not a fusion (or thermonuclear) device.[34] The first true British thermonuclear bomb was not detonated until 8 November 1957 off Christmas Island (codenamed Grapple X, it achieved 1.8 megatons – seventy-five times more powerful than the British atomic device detonated off Australia just over five years earlier[35]) two weeks *after* Eisenhower had delighted Macmillan in the White House with his draft proposal for restored collaboration.

There was another concern in Macmillan's mind that day in Washington. On Thursday 10 October 1957 the graphite core in plutonium pile no. 1 at Windscale in Cumberland had caught fire.[36] I shall never forget Lord Plowden, Chairman of the Atomic Energy Authority, reliving for me the decision that had to be taken the following day about extinguishing the fire, raging at over 400 degrees centigrade.[37] Dousing the pile with water risked triggering a vast explosion scattering highly toxic and immensely persistent contamination that would have made the Lake District a hazardous wasteland well into this century.[38] But there was no other option. The hoses worked. The following day pile no. 1 was cold 'and an environmental catastrophe had been averted'.[39]

It was, nevertheless, a serious incident, and not without repercussions. I can remember watching cinema newsreels of milk pouring from churns into drains in Cumberland and Westmorland for fear that it had become contaminated with radioactive iodine.[40] An inquiry was inevitable. The hugely experienced Sir William Penney was summoned and he worked fast. His committee made severe criticisms of technical, organizational and managerial failings at Windscale.[41]

The Penney Report reached Macmillan on 28 October 1957, the day after he returned from his talks with Eisenhower in Washington. He was alarmed. There was a clamour in Parliament, not least from Hugh Gaitskell, for Penney to be published in full.[42] Plowden and the Atomic Energy Authority lobbied similarly.[43] However, Macmillan was not persuaded. He wrote in his diary for 30 October 1957:

Edwin Plowden (Atomic Energy Authority) called – in a state of great emotion – about the report on the accident at Windscale. He wants to offer his resignation. I dissuaded him as best I cd. But the problem remains – how are we to deal with Sir W. Penny's [sic] report? It has, of course, been prepared with scrupulous honesty and even ruthlessness. It is just such a report as the board of a company might expect to get. But to publish to the world (esp. to the Americans) is another thing. The publication of the report, as it stands, might put in jeopardy our chance of getting Congress to agree to the President's proposal [for the restoration of US–UK nuclear collaboration].[44]

In the event, the government published a White Paper in November 1957 with the Penney Report, shorn of nearly half its paragraphs, among its conclusions and recommendations.[45]

Renewed transatlantic co-operation had not, in the event, been jeopardized by Windscale. Grapple X in November reassured ministers that the Churchill Cabinet's decision of July 1954 had been implemented. On 30 June 1958 Congress approved changes to the US Atomic Energy Act which permitted Anglo-American nuclear co-operation once more.[46] Two months later British and American weaponeers began serious discussions.[47] Designs were shared; techniques pooled. Edward Teller, the great brooding intellect behind the US hydrogen bomb, told his British opposite numbers that, after twelve years of separation, it was obvious that the laws of physics operated on both sides of the Atlantic.[48]

Yet a majority of those at Chequers on 7 June would have appreciated the very real problems that continued to afflict the UK's nuclear weapons programme despite the 'great prize' of restored collaboration now resting on Macmillan's mantelpiece. For example, it would not have been lost on them that the huge effort required to get from the Cabinet decision of July 1954 to Christmas Island in November 1957 had been expended largely for naught, since the British design which yielded 1.8 megatons that day had been abandoned in favour of the better-engineered American Mark 28 weapon once the British scientists had fully absorbed the characteristics of the US kit after getting access to it.[49] (A British version of it – codenamed 'Red Snow' – was later used in the UK free-fall H-bombs and in the warheads of the Royal Navy's Polaris system.)[50]

Plowden, Brook and the Chiefs of Staff, as well as Powell from the Ministry of Defence and Makins from the Treasury, would have been aware of the growing doubts about the viability of the liquid-fuelled Blue Streak as a successor system to the V-bombers (its costs were rising and it took far longer to make ready for flight than the solid-fuelled missiles being developed by the Americans and the Russians, making it very vulnerable to pre-emptive strikes[51]). Keeping Ernie Bevin's 'bloody Union Jack on top of it' was going to be tough and costly, even with the help of the Americans' nuclear weapons laboratories.

These anxieties were candidly encapsulated in a Foreign Office paper prepared in October–November 1959 as part of the *Future Policy Study* ahead of a special session of its steering committee on nuclear deterrent policy scheduled for early December. It suggested that from the latest work on weapons systems underway in Whitehall, it 'seems likely to emerge that an effective independent UK deterrent could probably be achieved *in 1970* by airborne or sea-borne launched missiles, and that a nuclear force composed of land-based missiles [such as Blue Streak] could not then be relied upon to deter a Russian attack'.[52] In fact, within months, in March/April 1960, the British-made Blue Streak rocket was abandoned on grounds of cost and vulnerability in favour of the stand-off Skybolt missile the US was developing, which could be fitted to the RAF's V-bombers.

Keeping the Union Jack on it would, the Foreign Office warned, probably be even harder in the last quarter of the twentieth century:

Looking beyond 1970, it is perhaps worth noting that, because of the rapidity of technological advance, it can by no means be certain that a deterrent force which was effective in 1970 would still be effective in 1975 or 1980. In particular, it seems highly probable that, by 1980, the Russians will have greatly improved their ABM [anti-ballistic missile] defences. It seems therefore equally probable that, in order to maintain an effective deterrent over the years, the UK would have to spend increasingly vast sums, presumably at the expense of our other activities in defence and even of the Welfare State at home.[53]

So, could it be a choice, by the end of the twentieth century, between Beveridge and the bomb?

What to advise Macmillan and his ministers in the final report? Was this the moment to pull out of the business? Were the hard realities of Britain's economic and technical positions about to make nuclear disarmers of them all? When Norman Brook's meeting of military chiefs and permanent secretaries sat down on the morning of 4 December 1959 to ponder Britain's atomic future, the CND option was dealt with swiftly and easily, partly because the old 1945 dream of international control of the bomb was even less feasible than when Attlee's GEN 75 Cabinet Committee had considered it: 'There was general agreement on the disadvantages of a policy of unilateral British nuclear disarmament and that we should retain our position as a nuclear power. It was noted that new processes had been found for the manufacture of fissile material which would make any system of international control much more difficult to operate.'[54]

Plainly the crown servants in and out of uniform could not envisage the UK playing a significant role in the world without a nuclear weapons capacity of some kind. But how much British kit was required to *deter* the Soviet Union? And how much was needed to *influence* the United States? On these points, the biggest disagreement of the future policy exercise arose.

As in 1940, the Royal Air Force stood alone. Sir Dermot Boyle, the Chief of the Air Staff (the man who thought Eden had 'gone bananas' over Suez), was the only participant to make the case for large-scale deterrence. Peter Ramsbotham, the senior diplomat whose Foreign Office team provided a substantial input into the study, recalled that at the 4 December meeting 'Boyle was wrapped up in the Union Jack',[55] and his minute recording the discussion captures Boyle's Bevin-like insistence that the bomb should indeed continue to have a Union Jack on top of it:

SIR DERMOT BOYLE said that he felt our influence in the world would be greater if we maintained an independent nuclear deterrent, capable through the next ten years of inflicting unacceptable damage on Russia, than if we merely provided a contribution to the Western deterrent. In any event it was essential that we should have complete positive control and not merely a right of veto over the use of our nuclear forces. He did not accept that the independent deterrent need cost more than a contribution . . .[56]

His peers were not so bullish or so sanguine about the 'Union Jack' option. Norman Brook caught the dominant mood in his characteristically polished summing up, declaring,

there was unanimous agreement that, while we should not adopt a policy of unilateral nuclear disarmament, we could not hope to have strategic nuclear forces sufficient to take on Russia on our own. The Chief of the Air Staff thought that we could, on our own, maintain without undue cost a deterrent that would deter the Russians from attacking us and that in this way we could exercise the greatest influence in world affairs.

But the Steering Committee as a whole took the view that in the world-wide economic and military struggle over the next ten years, no one country, not even the United States, could on its own prevent the position of the Free World being eroded by the Russians, and later by the Chinese as well. Therefore we must think increasingly in terms of alliances in all our efforts, military as well as political and economic, and we must use our nuclear skill and capacity in the way best calculated to contribute [to] the West's containment of the threat. We should consider what the size and nature of the deterrent should be in order to perpetuate the position of equipoise.[57]

Boyle sustained his solo flight till the end. The Cabinet paper containing the final report stated in its concluding section dealing with 'The Strategic Nuclear Deterrent' that: 'Our purpose should be to maintain a strategic nuclear force which is accepted by the Americans, and by the Alliance as a whole, as a significant contribution to the Western deterrent . . . This would not mean (except in the view of one of those associated with this study) that we were aiming to provide a force capable by itself of deterring Russia.'[58]

Brook explained his use of the word 'equipoise' in his elegant dismissal of the Boyle case in the final report, referring to the 'position of nuclear equipoise [which] will shortly be reached between the Americans and the Russians when each side can destroy the other and when no real purpose would be served by adding to the striking power of the opposing forces'.[59] The UK seeking to maximize its influence in a world of menacing equipoise was perhaps a delusion that deformed the whole exercise.*

The opening section of the final document (it was completed at the end of February 1960) rubbed in the price Britain and the other European powers had paid for their civil war of 1939–41 which triggered the world war of 1941–5. Pre-eminence had gone, probably for ever, to the two great global powers. In the UK's case, its residual Empire and its growing Commonwealth would do nothing to rectify the imbalance. In fact,

The United States and the USSR will increase their already formidable lead over the rest of the world; the United Kingdom and Western Europe will continue to grow, though more slowly; by contrast, the under-developed countries with their rapidly expanding populations and relatively inert economies, will be hard put to it to advance at all, and some may fall still further behind than they are now. Economic growth in our colonies may, however, continue at a slightly higher rate than that at which the population increases. None of the under-developed countries, with the possible exceptions of China and India, are likely to develop a significant industrial base.[60]

For a country, and a Prime Minister, used to 'top table' status (not least at the Paris summit due in ten weeks' time) the wider picture was sombre.

The narrower one of the UK and its European neighbours and comparators was little better: 'The European Economic Community is of immense potential importance. Their aggregate industrial power is probably greater than that of the USSR and if they continue to grow at their recent pace they will approach and perhaps reach the present United States level by 1970. If, therefore, the "Six" achieve a real measure of integration a new world power will have come on the scene.'[61]

Though the report did not spell it out, the message of that paragraph was in neon: the Commonwealth/Empire was now no longer serviceable as a magnifier of Britain's relative power in the world; a leading role inside a coming world power just across the Channel could be. The following paragraph

---

* Even Macmillan, who commissioned what we would now call the 'reality check' which the 1959–60 study represented, was, in Peter Ramsbotham's view when I interviewed him in June 2005, vulnerable here. 'Macmillan', he said, 'was a dreamer. He dreamt positively – one day we will recover!'

rammed the point home: 'Even if the United Kingdom's economy expands at the rate required to "double the national income in 25 years" (2.8 per cent per annum), we shall fall still further behind the other groups. Though in absolute terms our economic resources should grow significantly, our relative position *vis-à-vis* both the United States and Western Europe will nevertheless decline.'[62]

The framers of the *Future Policy Study*, like their readers, were well aware that the size of a country's economy was but part of the story; a key question was how much of the nation's wealth governments, parliaments and people (where all three mattered, not just the government) were prepared to see converted into the instruments of international influence.

To supplement the report, the Treasury produced a table detailing, year by year, the proportion of its wealth Britain had spent since 1948 in support of its 'overseas policies' in 'aggregate' (i.e. 'defence, economic aid, diplomatic expenditure, the overseas information and cultural services, civil defence, etc.'[63]). It showed, in so far as any set of figures can, the price of sustaining a serious place in the world at a time of Cold War plus imperial retreat with between 7.7 and 12.3 per cent of the national product flowing into its sustenance (see table overleaf).[64]

Even if, the Whitehall crystal-gazers warned, the UK was willing to continue pouring such a high proportion of its resources into its defence and overseas efforts in the 1960s, relative decline by 1970 was assured:

The economic, military and political pull which a state can exert in the world in peacetime should be measured not so much by its total resources as by that part of them which its Government and people are prepared to use for defence and other international purposes. Viewed in these terms, only the United States (because of her enormous resources) and the USSR (because although her resources are smaller a greater proportion of them are at the Government's disposal) have the strength to provide and sustain a complete power apparatus.[65]

Macmillan would almost certainly have known that Part II of the *Future Policy Study* dealing with 'The Resources of the United Kingdom' would have been minted by his least favourite department, HM Treasury. In fact, the driving force behind it was Otto Clarke.[66] Even allowing for the Treasury's habitual pessimism, Macmillan and his ministerial colleagues would have found this section compounded the growing gloom. It did recognize a dash of 'having it so good', however, before resuming its customary Treasury Cassandra role:

THE 'AGGREGATE', 1948–59 (£M)

	1948	1949	1950	1951	1952	1953	1954	1955	1956	1957	1958	1959
Defence [a]	805	765	805	1,080	1,440	1,535	1,555	1,500	1,570	1,525	1,515	1,550
Economic aid	59	51	60	83	62	57	73	98	67	87	94	131
Other [b]	46	44	35	222	223	173	122	82	73	63	71	69
Total	910	860	900	1,385	1,725	1,765	1,750	1,680	1,710	1,675	1,680	1,750
Proportion of gross national product at factor cost	8.7	7.7	7.7	10.8	12.3	11.8	11.0	9.9	9.4	8.7	8.3	8.4

[a] Precise figures on the latest Defence Budget definitions are not available before 1959; the figures shown in the table for earlier years are those for the Defence Budget on the old definitions, increased proportionally to the difference between new and old definitions in 1959–60.

[b] Includes home defence and strategic stock-piling, as well as overseas claims such as diplomatic expenditure, information and cultural services.

The national economy has recovered well since the war. Our industrial and techno-logical resources are stronger and better attuned to world demand than for a very long time – perhaps even since the early years of the century. The prospects for economic growth in the next decade provide a fair expectation that the gross national product in 1970 will be significantly higher than in 1959.[67]

Now came the rub:

There are internal risks as well as external – the United Kingdom cannot claim to have solved the problem of combining full employment and rapid economic growth with internal price stability. In order to earn our living as a relatively smaller power, subject to the danger that capital and skilled resources will be attracted to the greater agglom-erations of economic resources, we have to show greater adaptability and readiness to change our traditional practices than in the past.[68]

How easy would it be to wrest what one might call a place-in-the-world dividend from a less than world-class domestic economy in the 1960s? The 'resources' section of the *Future Policy Study* saw overload and difficulty immediately ahead:

In the next five years . . . there are no declining public programmes to make room for the expanding ones. The defence and overseas claims are expanding; public investment is expanding; education and health and public services generally are expanding. These are all good claims, and recently there has been a succession of new ones, such as a greatly expanded road programme . . .* [and] if the defence and aid programmes were carried out without the necessary moderation in private and public spending, the impact would fall on the balance of payments and on sterling. This is invariably the consequence of overloading the economy with large and inflexible commitments.[69]

In the Cabinet Office committee rooms, where the *Future Policy Study* was pieced together, the British New Deal was creaking audibly a mere decade and a half after its creation.

Macmillan's Cabinet (which was entirely male in 1960) had all come to their formation during one or both of the world wars and the economic slump which disfigured many of the years between the conflicts. Standing alone in 1940–41 and victory in 1945 were memories both powerful and relatively recent. None of them was minded to contemplate a Scandinavian or Netherlandic future for

---

* The first motorway programme was underway. Macmillan had opened a tiny section of the M6, the Preston by-pass, in December 1958. A substantial stretch of the M1 from near Watford to west of Coventry opened in November 1959.

his country. The eleven 'general conclusions' of the report spared their feelings to a degree noticeably out of line with the relative rigour of the analysis which had preceded it. Bullets remained unbitten, not least on Europe.

Churchillian geometry constructed the mental framework of the eleven men who put their signature to the document on 24 February 1960:

> The core of our policy is the Atlantic Alliance. Our main task in the next decade will be to maintain and make more intimate the association between North America, the United Kingdom and the continental countries of Western Europe. We must therefore work to ensure continuation of the United States presence in Europe, effective co-operation between ourselves and the continental countries, and the development of a wide economic and political community of interests embracing both the United States and Western Europe.
>
> ... We must do all we can to strengthen the Commonwealth, which can be a valuable instrument for maintaining our influence as a Power with world-wide interests and for propagating our ideas and ideals, and can form a bridge between the Western world and the developing countries of Asia and Africa.[70]

The sustenance of such a world role, however, would depend on many people at home and abroad being persuaded to see things the way the British political, administrative and military classes did – a huge proviso.[71]

Firstly, the Queen's subjects and taxpayers would have to be prepared to see '8$^1/_2$ per cent of the Gross National Product now devoted to defence, aid and other overseas activities' continue to be deployed on those purposes. The British public, too, would have to restrain its appetites for public and private spending to heed the 'call for restraint' from ministers. Abroad, the UK 'must work increasingly with and through our friends and allies' as the 'ability of the United Kingdom to play its full part in meeting the commitments of the West over the next decade will largely depend on the co-operation of our friends and allies ... Most of them are doing less than their fair share and we must make them realise this and do more.'[72]

The final section of the *Future Policy Study* – part Pollyanna, part old-style public school housemaster – simply did not do justice to the paragraphs which preceded it. Yet it was those passages of tough reality which seem to have struck ministers when they finally received the document rather than the mixture of reassurance and wishful thinking in its peroration.

Lord Hailsham, whom Macmillan had appointed Lord Privy Seal and Minister for Science and Technology after the 1959 general election, took characteristically ebullient exception to its pessimism. Hailsham had plainly

46. Dismissing the political crisis over spending as 'little local difficulties', Macmillan prepares to leave Heathrow for a Commonwealth tour, 7 January 1958.

47–9. The 'local difficulties' in person: Treasury resigners Peter Thorneycroft (*bottom left*), Enoch Powell (*bottom right*) and Nigel Birch (*above*).

61. Parisian gloom, 18 May 1960: De Gaulle, Macmillan and Eisenhower after Krushchev breaks up the summit which 'has blown up, like a volcano! It is ignominious; it is tragic; it is almost incredible,' Macmillan wrote.

46. Dismissing the political crisis over spending as 'little local difficulties', Macmillan prepares to leave Heathrow for a Commonwealth tour, 7 January 1958.

47–9. The 'local difficulties' in person: Treasury resigners Peter Thorneycroft (*bottom left*), Enoch Powell (*bottom right*) and Nigel Birch (*above*).

50. 'When I got back six weeks later I found a quite different atmosphere': an exuberant Macmillan returns to Downing Street from his Commonwealth trip, 14 February 1958.

51. Harold on Rab: he 'had the ambition but not the will . . . a sort of vague ambition – like saying it would be nice to be Archbishop of Canterbury'.

52. Macmillan and Derick Heathcoat Amory: 'Chancellor of the Exchequer, this is a *very bad paper*. Indeed, a disgraceful paper. It might have been written by Mr Neville Chamberlain's ghost.'

53. The Mac and Ike show: Macmillan and President Dwight D. Eisenhower pass down Fleet Street in a renumbered Rolls-Royce borrowed from Douglas Fairbanks Jr, 31 August 1959.

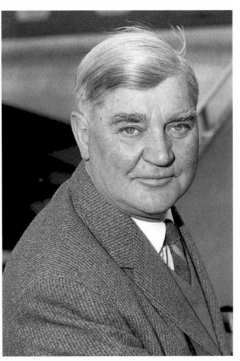

54. Hugh Gaitskell: 'Reckless honesty' pitted against Supermac's 'flamboyance'.

55. Nye Bevan and the Bomb, never the same after denouncing unilateral nuclear disarmament as an 'emotional spasm'.

56. Macmillan and Lady Dorothy having it so good in Clapham en route to a 100-seat majority, September 1959.

57. Changing of the guard in Africa? Macmillan reviews the First King's African Rifles, Lusaka, Northern Rhodesia, 22 January 1960.

58. The Welenskys welcome the Macmillans to Southern Rhodesia, January 1960: in Salisbury he talked 'gravely ... of the ebb and flow of civilizations, especially those which have touched the African continent ... It was the effortless superiority of the Balliol man being displayed before an audience which every moment became more helpless'.

59. General Charles de Gaulle praises British democracy and its lack of
'meticulously worked out constitutional texts' when addressing both Houses of
Parliament in Westminster Hall, 7 April 1960.

60. General de Gaulle and the Queen ride through the streets of London, 6 April 1960: 'In
that station to which God has called you, be who you are, Madam!'

61. Parisian gloom, 18 May 1960: De Gaulle, Macmillan and Eisenhower after Krushchev breaks up the summit which 'has blown up, like a volcano! It is ignominious; it is tragic; it is almost incredible,' Macmillan wrote.

got hold of the document in draft before its circulation as a Cabinet paper. On 19 February 1960 he minuted Macmillan personally that he found 'some aspects of the Future Policy Study 1960–70 somewhat disappointing and depressing'. He thought the analysis lacked 'an appraisal of the economic effects of past and future developments in science and technology' and failed to appreciate the possibility that scientific investment in the 1950s might feed through as higher productivity in the 1960s plus the fact that it was 'well known that new techniques of computation and automation will be increasingly applied'.[73]

Heathcoat Amory, to whom Hailsham's minute was copied, sent a Treasury-drafted rejoinder rightly pointing out that Hailsham's equation of science plus technology plus investment equals eventual productivity increases and improved economic growth was excessively simple. He agreed that with a 'higher volume of industrial investment, and a more favourable attitude by industry to technological change, there could certainly be a basis for faster growth. But a large part of the working population is in service activities which are not susceptible to increased productivity in any ordinary sense.' Amory also stressed the need 'to bear in mind that a large part of our scientific and technological effort is engaged upon defence and similar projects which are not intended to yield an economic return . . .'[74]

With hindsight, Hailsham was right about the eventual impact of the electronic revolution which, a quarter of a century later, began to have a profound transforming effect on the productivity of many service industries. In the rejoinder to Amory which Hailsham sent Macmillan, the Minister for Science and Technology had a sense of this. 'At the moment', he told the Prime Minister and the Chancellor of the Exchequer, 'it is an unpleasant fact that in [sic] this field of civil industry is being dragged forward, as it were by its hair by our research expenditure on our defence Budget. I look forward to the day when much larger sums of public money are spent on developing technologies which have a primarily or directly civil interest. At present we are only beginning to think on these lines. It is for this reason that I have returned to intervene in the discussion.'[75]

I doubt if Hailsham was fully briefed in February 1960 on the latest electronic R & D in the USA. Nor does he seem to have appreciated that both America and the EEC nations could expect to achieve significant technological advances themselves in the 1960s which would decrease the chances of a relative improvement in the UK's position. But, in terms of the nature and scope of the UK's and the advanced world's service industries, the transforming moment was 12 September 1958 in the Texas Instruments' laboratory in Dallas. That day a 34-year-old obsessed by the miniaturization of electronic components called Jack Kilby 'first demonstrated that an integrated circuit worked' – the silicon chip was about to usurp the age of the transistor just as the transistor had made obsolete the radio valve in the years after 1947.[76]

The bumping and grinding between Hailsham and Amory may be part of the explanation of a mystery which still clings to the *Future Policy Study* Cabinet paper. As Dean briefed Selwyn Lloyd on 15 March 1960, the plan was for the full Cabinet to discuss it over two meetings on 23 and 25 March.[77] For some reason Macmillan pulled it from the Cabinet's agenda over the following week. The paper went instead to an ad hoc 'Meeting of Ministers', coded F.P. (for 'Future Policy') by the Cabinet Office, which met on the late afternoon of 23 March 1960 in the Prime Minister's Room at the House of Commons. It consisted of Macmillan and five other ministers (Butler, Home Secretary; Lloyd; Amory; Home, Commonwealth Relations; and Watkinson, Minister of Defence).[78] Perhaps significantly, Hailsham was not a member of the group.

Macmillan gives no clue in his diary as to why he decided the *Future Policy Study* would be taken by a smaller, special group. The puzzle particularly intrigued Field Marshal Lord Carver, who as Brigadier Michael Carver had been the War Office's military representative at the working level of the *Future Policy Study*. He had been posted elsewhere before it was completed,[79] but spent a great deal of time in the early 1990s trying to get the whole report published[80] and investigating why it did not go to Cabinet.[81]

In his 1992 study of British defence policy since 1945, Carver suggested that the report's realistic attitude to the Commonwealth might have disturbed several Conservative ministers as it 'was not and never would be comparable as a source of power with the USA or Western Europe. With the right policies and some luck, it could be useful to us, but sentimentality must not blind us to the facts, and that, in some respects it could become more of a liability than an asset.'[82]

Macmillan, in fact, recognized the Carver point in his opening remarks summarizing the study at the meeting of ministers on 23 March 1960: 'At the same time we should try to strengthen the Commonwealth, the future of which should not be incompatible with our place in the Atlantic Community. But we must recognise that all other groups in the last resort were subsidiary to the Atlantic Alliance – to developing a wide economic and political community of interests that embraced both the United States and Western Europe.'[83]

The only clue as to one of the reasons the study had been kept from the whole Cabinet came in Macmillan's very first words that evening to his FP group: 'THE PRIME MINISTER said that the Report should provide a valuable background for consideration of oversea [sic] policy questions; it did not, however, attempt to provide answers to all the problems which it raised and these, when specific decisions were required, would come forward in the ordinary course to the Cabinet or the appropriate Cabinet Committee.'[84] In fact, Macmillan was in his *longue durée* mode – broody, thinking in grand sweeps above and beyond the immediate irritations, of Britain's waning material power amid Cold War and European economic anxieties.

It was almost as if he was taking the line of that most perceptive of Anglophile French observers, Raymond Aron, who in a lecture in London at much the same time caught the paradox of the moment of decline amidst prosperity: 'The whole of Western Europe, including Britain, has lost its colonies, its power and its diplomatic prestige, yet it has never before reached such levels of production and productivity.'[85]

In a later passage in the same lecture, Aron unknowingly cued in the short burst of consoling philosophy with which Macmillan opened the discussion of the wider significance of the *Future Policy Study*. 'Greatness', Aron told his listeners, 'is no longer indissolubly linked to military force, because the superpowers can no longer use their weapons without causing their own destruction by way of reprisal, and because no society need rule over others in order to give its children a decent life.'[86] Macmillan, as we saw at the very beginning of this chapter, decided to stress the enduring genius of his country which had preceded its great-powerdom and which would outlast it.[87] But not everyone round the Prime Minister's table was so sanguine – or so sensible.

Alec Home, the Commonwealth presence in the room, thought his patch was underplayed by the *Future Policy Study*: 'Without the USA we should be defenceless, without Western Europe we should be poorer, but without the Commonwealth our position in the world would rapidly decline. This latter consideration deserved greater emphasis.'[88] Watkinson, the Minister of Defence, backed him up: 'Part I seemed to be more pessimistic than the rest of the paper regarding the international role we could play. By working through our alliances and with the Commonwealth we could directly exert leadership in many fields where the Free World was in need of direction.'[89]

The Chancellor of the Exchequer, Amory, would have none of these consoling lullabies. Part I of the *Future Policy Study* 'was not defeatist; indeed in some respects it was too optimistic'. He 'could not see how we could continue to carry our present commitments overseas, even with the help of our friends and allies'. And could these friends and allies really be persuaded to see things Britain's way? For example, 'it was difficult to see at present how we could enter Europe in order to exercise greater leadership there: the attitudes of the EEC countries and of the United States were not encouraging'.[90]

But the most bizarre contribution was made by the number two figure in the government. Butler may have been a vacillator/sceptic over Suez, but, less than four years later, he now wanted to biff Johnny Foreigner into line: 'THE HOME SECRETARY thought the trend of Part I too defeatist. It did not sufficiently bring out the possibilities of development of the Commonwealth and Colonial system. Why should we assume that we had to follow an inevitable course in granting independence to our colonial territories and thus create trouble for ourselves in the United Nations?'

As if this parody of Lord Curzon were not enough, the same Butler who had found the agenda of the Messina talks so boring five years earlier now wanted to bring Europe into line as well: 'The forecasts of the growing strength of France and Germany and of the EEC Group in Western Europe . . . carried serious implications for the United Kingdom. Should we not "invade" Europe and take the lead before it was too late, thus forestalling the possibility of France adopting isolationist policies with the consequent risk of collapse of West European unity?'[91] Quite how the UK should do this, or what instruments lay at hand for the British government to so steer Europe, the minutes do not record Butler as divulging.

The stress of adjusting to straitened circumstances understandably produced moments of private petulance among ministers. And the *Future Policy Study* was much tougher on their psyches than the post-Suez reviews of 1957–8 had been. As we have seen, Macmillan could exhibit a mixture of pessimism and resentment at moments when irritation with allies, anxieties about the Cold War and a sense of waning British power afflicted him. The 1959–60 review discussion took place against the backdrop of a renewed Berlin crisis with Khrushchev pushing his running demand, first articulated in November 1958, that the 1945 victors sign a peace treaty recognizing two separate Germanys, end their military occupation of Berlin and turn it into a 'free city'. His initial six-month deadline had turned out to be moveable.[92] But, as we have seen, Macmillan lived in fear that the rolling Berlin crisis might trigger a thermonuclear Third World War.[93]* This continued to be his chief motivation for pressing on both the American and Soviet leaderships the need for a summit.

About the time he was setting up the *Future Policy Study*, Macmillan, secretly and quite separately from its options, was also confronting his worst fear – the consequences of nuclear war. Brook, naturally, was involved, but not a whisper of the doomsday planning reached the calibrators of future policy. On Friday 5 June 1959, the day before he set off for Chequers and the weekend that launched the FPS, Macmillan presided over a mixed Cabinet Committee in No. 10, GEN 684, which reviewed the readiness of the single most secret Cold War installation in the UK, the 'emergency Government headquarters in war'. Codenamed 'Stockwell' at this stage, it had been authorized by Eden in September 1955[94] (and given the apt cover-name of 'Subterfuge') in the aftermath of the Strath inquiry into the effect of ten 10-megaton Soviet hydrogen bombs dropped on the UK.[95] But in June 1959 it was still in the process of construction beneath Box Hill on the Wiltshire–Somerset border.[96] Macmillan's immensely secret group that summer afternoon had to ponder 'the extent to which the Headquarters could be used if an emergency arose in the near future'.[97]

In fact, one of the last post-Suez reappraisals to reach the public domain was a 'crash' review of emergency readiness for a Third World War undertaken by two young officials in the Home Office, Tony Brennan and Dennis Trevelyan, in the very week in November 1956 that the Suez crisis boiled over. They found inadequacy all round.[98] And the civil and home defence position was still worrisome in the summer of 1959. Macmillan's GEN 684 group was the first general review by ministers of the machinery of government during and after a global war since Eden had commissioned the building of 'Subterfuge'/'Stockwell' deep inside the old Bath stone quarry.

Macmillan was told that building work should be completed on 'Stockwell' by the autumn of 1960 and full communications installed in 1961–2. If an emergency occurred in the meantime, the 'headquarters could be manned on a limited basis in the near future' (there would be room for about 1,500 of

---

* A view shared, interestingly, by the 'father' of the first atomic bombs, Robert Oppenheimer, who also said in 1961, in an article titled 'A Time of Sorrow and Renewal', that those responsible for the command and control of nuclear weapons 'have added chance to anger as another cause of disaster' (*Encounter*, February 1961, p. 70).

the planned 4,000 officials, military and communications staff to accompany Macmillan and his Third World War Cabinet should Berlin trigger global conflict in the meantime).[99]

GEN 684 agreed that the constructing of 'Stockwell' should proceed as planned; 'that no provision need be made in advance for the continued functioning of Parliament after nuclear attack'; and that the

security of STOCKWELL should be most carefully safeguarded and no visits should be made by Ministers or others whose presence might draw attention to the site. The present cover story that a last war site was being tidied up would not satisfactorily explain constructional and other developments later in the year. A new cover story was being prepared and would be promulgated as soon as possible.[100]

It was.

After several refinements and help from MI5 and the Directorate of Forward Plans, the Ministry of Defence's deception organization, the inquisitive, whether natives of Whitehall or the West Country curious about the building work visible on the surface, were from May 1960 to be told that the 'site is primarily one of a number of Post Office centres for internal and overseas communications in war. Part of the remaining accommodation is being developed as a Standby Regional Headquarters while any space left over will be used for storage by Government Departments.'[101] It had taken eleven months to work this up – three months longer than it took to complete the *Future Policy Study*.

But neither the Cold War nor the decay of the remaining British Empire nor the European question stood still while the planners planned and the deception experts deceived. Over thirty years later Sir John Coles, when Head of the Diplomatic Service, sent for the FPS files and was struck by the difficulty his predecessors had in knowing quite what to do with it. 'This', he wrote, 'was strategic and long-term planning at the highest level, for Macmillan had clearly intended intensive Cabinet discussion at a later stage. The struggle to define clear aims for overseas policy continued but the problem of choice apparently remained intractable for the authors of this document.'[102]

The world was simply too molten and British power too diminished in 1960 for the 'opposition of events' (as Macmillan liked to put it to distinguish them from the parliamentary Opposition facing him across the floor of the House of Commons[103]) to be malleable, however powerful the ministerial and official grey cells devoted to coping with them. It is to Macmillan's credit, however, that for all his proneness to gloom, he did not cease to seek ways, as he expressed it in the 'Note' to Cabinet colleagues he attached to the final FPS report, 'to formulate policies for the intervening years [1960–70] which would allow us to continue to play a significant part in world affairs'.[104]

In fact, he was in Africa in the throes of just such an enterprise as the final touches were being put to the FPS by its framers. The trip was intended to be the sequel to his Commonwealth tour of January–February 1958 through India, Pakistan, the Far East and Australia. But a great deal had happened within the residual territorial Empire in the meantime: 1959 was the moment when the rush to decolonize over the next five years (between 1960 and 1964 seventeen British colonies – mostly in Africa – gained independence) could be fully sensed in Whitehall for the first time.[105]

Macmillan was a natural wooer of middle opinion. Part of his brain was filled with a finely tuned electoral calculator (a piece of human technology of which Lord Hailsham would undoubtedly have approved). The African factor worried him, especially the impact of the atrocities at the Hola Camp in Kenya where Mau Mau suspects were detained. During a riot on 3 March 1959, eleven inmates were beaten to death by warders.

Imperial questions (rather like the European question in the 1990s) also had a considerable capacity to split intra-Conservative opinion. With his Colonial Secretary Alan Lennox-Boyd considering resignation over the Kenyan authorities' handling of the Hola atrocity,[106] Macmillan spent a great deal of June–July 1959 on Africa in general and stiffening Lennox-Boyd in particular. On 4 June he noted in his diary:

A most unfortunate incident in one of the Mau Mau camps (only the 'hard core' rebels and fanatics remain) has put us in difficulties in Parl and we now have to face a vote of censure. The Scottish Church is getting worked up about Nyasaland. We shall probably get a bad report from Mr Justice Devlin and his ctee. I have set up an 'African Ctee' – wh will meet every week, to try to work out a policy and give us a grip on the situation.[107]

Macmillan was, for all his other, feline qualities, prone to coarseness and snobbery when it came to men he disliked or regarded as humbugs. In that same diary entry for 4 June 1959, he wrote:

Gaitskell, Griffiths [Deputy Leader of the Labour Party] and Callaghan – the three musketeers, a Professor, a Professional Preacher and an Irish Corner Boy [in fact, James Callaghan was a Hampshire boy who represented a Welsh constituency] came to see us this afternoon. We have been in negotiations for a 'bipartisan approach' to African problems. This was the third meeting. As I expected, their position had hardened. Seeing nothing else to clutch at – full employment has been restored and the economy is stable – they cannot resist trying to exploit the African situation.[108]

Yet Macmillan reserved one of his ripest pieces of abuse for the most eloquent critic of his colonial policies on his own Conservative benches – Enoch Powell. On 24 July, the day the Devlin Report on disturbances in Nyasaland was published dismissing the colonial authorities' claim that Dr Hastings Banda's Congress Party had been planning murder and assassination and describing the colony as 'no doubt temporarily – a police state',[109] Powell succeeded in really getting up his leader's nostrils. In his diary Macmillan described him as 'a sort of Fakir'.[110] But on Hola, the Fakir was to prove much more troublesome.

The brutality which led to the death of eleven Kenyan African detainees had been triggered by their refusal to undertake compulsory work in the camp. The Conservative Whips tried to minimize the embarrassing consequences of the resulting White Paper by timing the debate late at night on 27 July 1959 on the eve of the summer recess.[111] Powell was determined that there should be no double standards anywhere in the Queen's realms, colonies and territories when it came to coercive powers over her subjects.

Powell's 'explosive speech' in the Commons (perhaps the best that he ever delivered) 'was much more damaging to the Government's case than the furious attacks launched from the Opposition benches'.[112] His magnificent peroration came during the small hours of the morning of 28 July 1959 (he rose to his feet at 1.15 a.m.):

Finally it is argued that this is Africa, that things are different there. Of course they are. The question is whether the difference between things there and here is such that the taking of responsibility there and here should be upon different principles. We claim that it is our object – and this is something which unites both sides of the House – to leave representative institutions behind us wherever we give up our rule. I cannot imagine that it is a way to plant representative institutions to be seen to shirk the acceptance and the assignment of responsibility which is the very essence of responsible government.

Nor can we ourselves pick and choose where and in what parts of the world we shall use this or that kind of standard. We cannot say, 'We will have African standards in Africa, Asian standards in Asia and perhaps British standards here at home.' We have not that choice to make. We must be consistent with ourselves everywhere. All Government, all influence of man upon man, rests upon opinion. What we can do in Africa, where we still govern and where we no longer govern, depends upon the opinion which is entertained of the way in which this country acts and the way in which Englishmen act. We cannot, we dare not, in Africa of all places, fall below our own high standards in the acceptance of responsibility.[113]*

Some historians of Empire are convinced that the 'Fakir' had an influence on the way Macmillan's thinking on Africa developed during the summer and autumn of 1959. 'By the beginning of November 1959', writes imperial historian Larry Butler, 'Macmillan had decided to make a visit to Africa. Among the factors influencing his decision were the criticism of government policy made by the former Conservative minister, Enoch Powell, and Macmillan's growing concern about his government's apparent failure to get its message across to the young.'[114] On 1 November Macmillan told Brook of his plan to visit Africa early in the new year – 'young people of all Parties are uneasy about our moral basis. Something must be done to lift Africa on to a more national plane, as a problem to the solution of which we must all contribute not out of spite . . . but by some really imaginative effort.'[115]

No Whig sceptic in this instance, he drafted this letter on a particularly broody Sunday at Chequers – perhaps suffering from post-election *tristesse* rather than euphoria, as he implied to his diary on 1 November 1959:

Today I shall *not* go to Church, but continue the cure [his doctor had suggested a few days' rest at Chequers] till after luncheon, when I shall go to Eton and hope to see my 3 grandsons.

I feel *much* better, tho' still without much vigour. Perh I shall not recover it, but shall just be an old gentleman from now on. (One can make quite a normal P.M. on this basis. Perh less dangerous than with too much intellectual energy – a sort of Attlee.)[116]

Yet on the imperial front, Macmillan had just appointed the youthful Iain Macleod, brimming with intellectual energy, to succeed Lennox-Boyd at the Colonial Office.

The 45-year-old Macleod was very much a young(ish) man in a hurry when Macmillan gave him 'the worst job of all'[117] in the post-election reshuffle. There is no doubt that he wanted a vigorous new Colonial Secretary.[118] There is equally no doubt that Macleod's celerity in unscrambling much of British tropical Africa took the older man's breath away. Seven years later – with the

---

* When Rob Shepherd and I interviewed Powell almost thirty-four years later to the day for *What Has Become of Us?* we asked him what happened next. 'I remember sitting down and crying.' And then? 'Peter Thorneycroft got up and walked over and sat down beside me,' Mr Powell recalled on 29 July 1993 – and promptly burst into tears again!

disentanglement largely complete apart from the enduringly knotty Rhodesia – Macleod was very candid about his differences with his patron and fellow Highlander (as Macmillan liked to regard the two of them[119]):

I think the difficulty with Harold Macmillan in relation to Africa was that he had all the right instincts, as his 'Winds of Change' speech showed quite clearly. He was more than prepared for a rapid move to independence – as his appointment of myself showed. But from time to time he wanted, as I dare say we all do, the best of all worlds, he didn't want to fall out with his good friends either at home or in Central or East Africa as the case may be. Whereas, I took the brutal, but I think practical view that this was an omelette that you couldn't make without breaking eggs and one couldn't be friends with everybody however much one wanted to do it, while one was pursuing such a policy.[120]

Macmillan's ambivalence was reflected in perhaps the best examples of his gift for ambiguity in what for ever will be remembered as the 'Wind of Change' tour in January–February 1960 to which Macleod referred. Every line of every remark he made in public was scrutinized for ripples of meaning, especially in the Central African Federation – Northern and Southern Rhodesia and Nyasaland (now Zambia, Zimbabwe and Malawi) – as Macmillan attempted to find a middle way between settler and nationalist aspirations with gradually growing political representations for Africans. Roy Welensky, the Federation's bull of a premier (ex-railway engine driver and prize fighter), treated his dealings with Macmillan and Macleod as if he were wrestling with eels. The only British minister he did trust was Alec Home, who, as Commonwealth Secretary, had responsibility for the semi-autonomous Southern Rhodesia while Macleod had it for the other two legs of the Federation's tripod.

Welensky suspected that Macmillan, despite his protestations to the contrary, would envisage the break-up of the Federation if the Commission pondering its future currently sitting under his old friend from Oxford, Walter Monckton, so recommended.[121] In a moment of probably studied indiscretion while talking to journalists on the second leg of his tour in Nigeria, Macmillan 'was asked by a group of reporters . . . whether it was conceivable that the commission could recommend the break-up' of the Federation. He 'shrugged his shoulders and said: "Well, I suppose if they all agreed that nothing could be done, they might have to say so. It would be like that rhyme from Belloc:

> They answered as they took their fees
> 'There is no cure for this disease.'"'[122]

Welensky was furious. When he arrived in Salisbury, Southern Rhodesia (the Federation's capital), Macmillan told him his Lagos statement had been misreported, 'which', noted Anthony Sampson, one of the journalists to whom Macmillan's remarks had been addressed, 'it had not'.[123]

The private chats, as opposed to the public statements, of Macmillan on his African tour are very revealing. Sampson quotes him as saying of Africa that for so long it had seemed secondary to Asia and cut off from the rest of the world before suddenly erupting on the world scene (Macmillan had never visited sub-Saharan Africa before) rather 'like a sleeping hippo in a pool, suddenly it gets a prod from the white man and wakes up; and it won't go to sleep again'.[124]

In old age Macmillan talked of one particular white man who had influenced him in Nigeria (itself a few months away from independence). He was Sir James Robertson, a Colonial Service veteran about to retire as Governor General in Lagos. After 'attending some meeting of the so-called cabinet, or council', with Robertson, Macmillan inquired,

'Are these people fit for self-government?' and he said, 'No of course not.' I said, 'When will they be ready?' He said 'Twenty years, twenty-five years.' Then I said, 'What do you recommend me to do?' He said, 'I recommend you to give it to them at once.' I said, 'Why that seems strange.' 'Well,' he said, 'if they were twenty years well spent, if they would be learning administration, if they were getting experience, I would say wait, but what will happen? All the most intelligent people, all the ones I've been training on [sic] will all become rebels. I shall have to put them in prison. There will be violence, bitterness and hatred. They won't spend the twenty years learning. We shall simply have us twenty years of repression, and therefore, in my view, they'd better start learning [to rule themselves] at once.' I thought that was very sensible.[125]

Robertson's view was similar to that of Macleod (who did not accompany Macmillan on the African trip). Macleod later recalled, 'It has been said that after I became Colonial Secretary there was a deliberate speeding-up of the movement towards independence. I agree. There was. And in my view any other policy would have led to terrible bloodshed in Africa. This is the heart of the argument.'[126]

Macmillan was plainly susceptible to Robertson's reasoning. Towards the end of the first leg of the tour in Ghana, Peregrine Worsthorne, covering it for the *Daily Telegraph*, was summoned for an evening drink with the Prime Minister and Lady Dorothy in Accra. He received a classic gownsman/swordsman performance laced with world-weary irony:

he struck a mournful note which was one of his favourites. How sad it was, he said, that Britain was giving up her African Empire just at the time when technology and resources had made it possible for us to transform the continent. During the thirties, he went on, Britain could do very little for Africa. Even if we had the money, the technology was not there. We had the political power, but not the physical means to put it to good effect. Now, just at the very moment when imperialism had the means to translate its high-sounding paternalistic words into actions, to do all the good it had promised, it was coming to an end.[127]

What did the future hold? Very little for imperialists and imperialized alike:

Foreign aid, he said, was no substitute. Nor was there much hope that black Africa would be able to modernise itself on its own. Fate was cruel. Freedom was coming to Africa at the wrong time. Having had all the humiliation of being bossed around by whites, the blacks, poor innocents, were bent on kicking us out just when they ought to be begging us to stay.[128]

Macmillan, the old classicist, was plainly in his grand-sweep-of-history mode that night.

He was again, to even greater effect, in public and in infinitely trickier circumstances at a meeting in Southern Rhodesia on the penultimate stage of the tour. This time it was that connoisseur among Macmillan watchers, Henry Fairlie, who caught the moment for the readers of *Encounter*:

The white population of Salisbury was angry, even bewildered, and was certainly not in a mood to treat him kindly. When Mr Macmillan rose to address a huge meeting – all white – anything might have happened. Sir Roy Welensky, in introducing him, had made it quite plain he was not pleased with the Lagos declaration. But Mr Macmillan had his own methods: within a minute he was talking gravely to his audience of the ebb and flow of civilisations, especially those which have touched the African continent; there was even time for a word about the Phoenicians of the Mediterranean world. For perhaps a quarter of an hour this cultivated discourse went on. It was the effortless superiority of the Balliol man being displayed before an audience which every moment became more helpless. By the time he reached the 20th century – and the Lagos declaration – they were ready to believe anything.[129]

For all that extraordinary public poise and *sang froid*, Macmillan was irritable and tetchy for the bulk of the tour and remained so until he had delivered *the* speech in Cape Town on the final leg in early February 1960.[130] The press, as Sampson later told Macmillan's official biographer, had been the recipients right across Africa of hints from Tim Bligh, the Prime Minister's Principal Private Secretary, that 'something was cooking which would astonish and satisfy us all'.[131]

Macmillan's fifty-minute version of what Fairlie called his 'ebb and flow of civilisations' theme in the old Cape Colony House of Assembly building on 3 February 1960 was, as Anthony Sampson (who was listening from the balcony) put it, 'probably the finest of Macmillan's career ... a speech of masterly construction and phrasing, beautifully spoken, combining a sweep of history with unambiguous political points'.[132] It did, and it has suitably impressed the compilers of great political speeches ever since.[133] Yet far from his Cape Town speech being the crowning example of Balliol-generated 'effortless superiority'[134] on Macmillan's part, for all the poise of his eventual delivery of it, he was physically sick with anxiety in the hours before it.[135]

In its classically constructed paragraphs we can detect the baby-hippo echoes of the regret-tinged performance he had laid on for Perry Worsthorne in Accra and the Mediterranean lost world that so mesmerized the ill-disposed white settlerdom he faced in Salisbury. All that was lacking was the impromptu morris dance he had skipped earlier in Pretoria to show 'that the English also have their tribal dances ...'[136]

'Ever since the break-up of the Roman Empire,' he began, timelessly attired in his Savile Row chalkstriped suit and, as usual, his Old Etonian tie,[137]

one of the constant facts of political life in Europe has been the emergence of independent nations. They have come into existence over the centuries in different forms, with different kinds of Government, but all have been inspired by a deep, keen feeling of nationalism, which has grown as the nations have grown.

In the twentieth century, and especially since the end of the war, the processes which gave birth to the nation states of Europe have been repeated all over the world. We have seen the awakening of national consciousness in peoples who have for centuries lived in dependence upon some other power. Fifteen years ago this movement spread through Asia. Many countries there of different races and civilizations pressed their claim to an independent national life.[138]

Then, before this most resistant of white-settler audiences with Dr Hendrik Verwoerd, the South African Prime Minister and incarnation of unflinching apartheid, beside him, Macmillan preached reality and delivered the phrase which was to gust round the world:

Today the same thing is happening in Africa, and the most striking of all the impressions I have formed is of the strength of this African national consciousness. In different places it takes different forms, but it is happening everywhere. The wind of change is blowing through this continent, and whether we like it or not, this growth of national consciousness* is a political fact. We must all accept it as a fact, and our national policies must take account of it.[139]

The phrase 'wind of change' was minted by David Hunt, the Commonwealth Relations Office official accompanying Macmillan on the tour[140] (though others have claimed a hand in it[141]).

What is generally forgotten about this remarkable *tour de force* is its Cold War element. 'As I see it,' Macmillan explained, 'the great issue in this second half of the twentieth century is whether the uncommitted peoples of Asia and Africa will swing to the East or to the West. Will they be drawn into the Communist camp? Or will the great experiments in self-government that are now being made in Asia and Africa, especially within the Commonwealth, prove so successful, and by their example so compelling, that the balance will come down in favour of freedom and order and justice?'[142]

And in a passage strongly evocative of Enoch Powell's closing remarks on Hola that night in the House of Commons just over six months earlier, Macmillan declared: 'The struggle is joined, and it is a struggle for the minds of men. What is now on trial is much more than our military strength or our diplomatic and administrative skill. It is our way of life. The uncommitted nations want to see before they choose.'[143]

Macmillan's speech was, as so often with him, accompanied by a whiff of ambiguity. Was it a plea for swift imperial retreat, as Macleod was urging? Or was it an appeal for a more measured withdrawal – not least with Cold War repercussions in mind – of the kind favoured by Alec Home? Home himself sensed this element when recalling the Cape Town speech:

When I was in the Commonwealth Office and Macleod was in the Colonial Office, he was always for galloping along with independence as fast as he could. I took the view that every year gained gave the countries a better chance when they became independent to be viable. There was something to be said for both points of view.

When one looks at some of the African countries, one realises that another five years of tuition wouldn't have done them any harm. But Macmillan was beginning to think that our destiny lay really in Europe, so I think he leaned rather towards the faster pro-

---

*On 'growth of national consciousness' he banged the lectern for effect; this is clearly audible in the archive recording.

gramme than the slower. If you want to put it in a nutshell, I think that Macmillan was a wind of change man and Macleod was a gale of change man.[144]

Home, as we have seen, thought the *Future Policy Study* was too gloomy on Commonwealth matters. He was right to mix, retrospectively, the undeniable imperial sunset with the possible European dawn for Britain. This very much represented Macmillan's frame of mind in the early weeks of 1960.

There was a third element swirling around in that classically formed mind of the occupant of 10 Downing Street. It had the unmistakable profile of General Charles de Gaulle. Both were gownsmen/swordsmen; both quite naturally thought geopolitically; both had a certain idea of how their countries' pasts spoke to their present and could hint heavily about their future. Both were proud and impressive political performers and their two nations had much in common: both anciently occupied the same patches of Europe; both were considerable extenders of their territory overseas; and de Gaulle had just partially caught up militarily with the testing of an atomic device in the Algerian Sahara in February.[145] On 14 February Macmillan noted wryly in his diary, 'De Gaulle has exploded his atomic bomb, and now claims equal partnership with Britain. Yet another problem!'[146]

Macmillan was preoccupied by de Gaulle. In a letter to the Queen at the end of 1959 he told her, 'in the present state of Europe, if we are to reach agreements helpful to this country, so long as de Gaulle remains in power the French are the key'.[147] Yet if Macmillan felt he was the prisoner of 'events' and de Gaulle very often their initiator or shaper, he was succumbing to both gloom and exaggeration. For Macmillan's 'events' read de Gaulle's 'torrent'; as the French President wrote to Raymond Aron in May 1959: 'I both admire and envy your ability to make instant judgements on the events that we are living [sic] and the torrent that is sweeping us along.'[148] The difference between them perhaps was the degree to which de Gaulle 'loved catastrophe . . . because out of catastrophe would come regeneration'.[149]

Certainly the drafters of the *Future Policy Study* saw de Gaulle around many a crucial corner in the coming decade. For them, 'the future of Western Europe, and of NATO as a whole, depends chiefly upon two unpredictable factors – the policy of France and the future of Germany. For France there are two main possibilities. The first is that de Gaulle or his successors will decide to push ahead with the economic (and consequently political) integration of the "Six". If this happens, [a] . . . new world Power . . . will emerge, probably with its own "European" nuclear deterrent.'[150]

The planners could – perhaps should – also have mentioned the degree to which the pace of French decolonization might affect the rate at which the UK shed its remaining territories in Africa especially. Certainly this was one of the themes Macmillan intended to raise with de Gaulle on his trip to Paris over 12 and 13 March 1960. In the words of No. 10's pre-briefing note: 'How does he [de Gaulle] see the development of Africa and the French [overseas] community generally?'[151]

Macmillan's aide Philip de Zulueta's record of the 'Points discussed with General de Gaulle at Rambouillet on March 12 and 13, 1960'[152] is fascinating on several levels – not least because, without mentioning it, naturally, Macmillan seems to have tried out several of the key themes of the *Future Policy Study* (eleven days before his own ministerial group met to discuss it) on the French President. On 'Africa generally' the report notes that:

General de Gaulle said that the various states of the French community would gradually demand independence and he would not object. Some of them might not really exist in any effective way, but they would no doubt manage somehow. He was worried about the position in Guinea and the help which Mr Nkrumah was giving to Mr Sekou-Toure, who was slipping into the Communist camp. It was very important to have continuing Anglo-French contacts about Africa.[153]

That last sentence is intriguing, not least because such 'contacts' had been few and occasional over the previous two years.

Perhaps this was unsurprising. For there was no pattern of co-operation between Europe's imperial powers (Suez briefly excepted in the case of the UK and France) even when rising nationalism in Africa and Asia threatened all of them.[154] The decisions of de Gaulle and his immediate predecessors had not helped the school of thought still prevalent in Whitehall in 1957–8, if not 1959–60, which believed that, apart from Ghana and Nigeria, if things went well the rest of British Africa could expect their flag-down/flag-up moment somewhere between 1970 and 1980:

In 1956 the French Fourth Republic, grappling with insurrection in Algeria, tried to rally the loyalty of its other African territories by an extension of representative government. Two years later the Republic itself was overthrown as a direct consequence of the Algerian rebellion. The new constitution framed by De Gaulle offered French Africa self-government within a French Community and then, as the struggle in Algeria intensified, full independence inside or outside the Community.[155]

Largely as a response to French developments the 'political geography of colonial Africa' had changed within two years. The sudden decision of the Belgians in January 1960 to pull out of the Congo during the summer was the most dramatic consequence but, in 1960, sixteen new African countries (mainly Francophile) joined the United Nations.[156]

Macmillan made a strong pitch for real Anglo-French co-operation in his talks with de Gaulle at Rambouillet and tried to use the scramble out of imperialism as a kind of European entry card: 'We had no Empires left – and therefore no rivalries. All these days were past. I think I did something to convince him of our real desire to work closely together, not only in Europe, but everywhere.'[157] Macmillan felt the 'talks were intimate' and said of the General, 'Now that he is old (69) and mellowed, his charm is great. He speaks beautiful, rather old-fashioned French. He seemed quite impersonal and disinterested.'[158] The old statesmen had but one aide each in the room (de Zulueta with Macmillan; de Courcel with de Gaulle[159]) and Macmillan 'felt tired from the strain of talking nothing but French ... and trying not to fall into any major error of judgement'.[160]

There are certain passages in de Zulueta's note of the exchanges which do suggest a genuine intimacy, not least when de Gaulle made a pitch for British help in building up his nuclear weapons capacity. If there was no general nuclear disarmament, the British record reports de Gaulle as saying,

and he doubted if the Russians for reasons of prestige really wanted this, then France would continue to try to obtain a nuclear armament. The Americans had refused to give any help. He would be glad if it was possible for the United Kingdom to assist even with means of delivery only. The Prime Minister explained the complications of the [1958] United Kingdom arrangement with the United States. General de Gaulle understood this.[161]

The General might have 'understood', but he didn't approve of the wider geopolitics that made such an 'arrangement' possible.

Under the heading 'Anglo-French Relations' de Zulueta recorded, 'General de Gaulle said that he thought the United Kingdom was always unwilling to choose between being part of Europe and having a special connection with the United States. The Prime Minister explained the special position of the United Kingdom, which France in many ways shared. The United Kingdom would like to see a renascent Europe led by France'[162] – a fair degree of high-level flim-flam there.

In his diary Macmillan left a rather fuller account of de Gaulle's rawness on this probably greatest area of contention between them:

I had fortunately read the last volume of his memoirs, and I asked de G why he continually harped on the theme of the 'Anglo-Saxons'. Apart from a general feeling that he is left out of Anglo-American talks, and jealousy of my close association with this particular President [Eisenhower], it clearly all stems from the war.

He resented – rather absurdly in the setting of Vichy and all that – the Roosevelt–Churchill hegemony. He goes back too – in his retentive mind – to all the rows about Syria; about D-Day; about the position of the French Army in the final stages of the war; about Yalta (and the betrayal of Europe) and all the rest.[163]

Regarding other troubling areas, however, Macmillan left Paris somewhat encouraged. On that substantial cause of concern to the FPS planners – the possible economic superpowerdom of the EEC 'Six' by 1970 – de Zulueta's note contained other surprises, especially the revelation that had de Gaulle been France's head of government in 1957 he would not have signed the Treaty of Rome:

The Prime Minister explained the dangers which he saw in a division of Europe between the [EEC] Six and the [European Free Trade Area] Seven, and in particular urged that the programme of the Six should not be accelerated because this would increase the measure of discrimination. General de Gaulle said that he regarded the Six as a commercial treaty; he would not have signed it but he accepted it. It had had certain good effects, particularly on French industry which had been forced to make itself more competitive. As it was a commercial arrangement it should be possible to make a commercial bargain between the Six and the Seven. He did not commit himself about accelerating the Six's programme.[164]

A future symbol of Anglo-French accord, the Channel Tunnel, even had its brief moment on the Rambouillet agenda. 'There was', de Zulueta recorded, 'some desultory discussion about this. President de Gaulle said that it would be a fine thing. The Prime Minister said that it would be better if it did not need trains. President de Gaulle did not seem to attach any urgency to the Tunnel idea.'[165]

The most urgent single matter sculling about the château over those two days was the forthcoming four-power summit, the diplomatic prize for which Macmillan had long been striving – made all the more pressing by the running crisis over Berlin. Here de Gaulle and Macmillan were closer than Macmillan and Eisenhower. A year earlier Macmillan had flown to Paris to brief de Gaulle on his talks in Moscow, and, to the Prime Minister's pleasure, the President agreed that a cap-badge at the checkpoints on the Autobahn to Berlin if the East Germans replaced the Russians was not worth a Third World War. When they met at the Elysée on 10 March 1959 Macmillan recorded that: 'De Gaulle rather put out of countenance his team, by admitting right away that one cd not have a nuclear war in Europe on the question of who signed the pass to go along the autobahn or the railway to W. Berlin – a USSR sergeant or a DDR [East German] sergeant. In his view the only question which wd justify war wd be an actual physical blockade.'[166]

A year later at Rambouillet, as de Zulueta noted, both Macmillan and de Gaulle hoped the Paris summit two months ahead would take the venom out of the Berlin crisis: 'General de Gaulle agreed that it was desirable to reach some agreement at the summit; he felt that Mr Khrushchev would also want this. On Berlin he thought that some provisional arrangements might perhaps be made to last for a limited number of years, leaving the *status quo* more or less unaltered.' De Gaulle and Macmillan also 'agreed that the final decision on Berlin could probably only be taken at the very end of the summit meeting and that meanwhile the West should appear very firm'.[167]

On returning to London Macmillan penned one of his most amusing letters to the Queen, briefing her on what had happened in Paris and what might transpire when the de Gaulles arrived in London for their state visit in early April: '... Madame de Gaulle is very shy and speaks practically no English. She is a woman of considerable character: I have even heard it said that she is the only human being of whom the General stands mildly in awe – but I can scarcely believe this ...'[168]

In fact, it turned out to be one of the most stylish state visits of the post-war years. In the opinion of Macmillan's official biographer it stood out 'as the most magnificent reception accorded a visiting ruler in the post-war era. It would not have escaped de Gaulle's eye that it was considerably more lavish than that even bestowed on Macmillan's beloved Ike the previous summer ... Huge Crosses of Lorraine, lit by a myriad of fireworks, illuminated the front of Buckingham Palace. After a fanfare by the massed trumpeters of the Household Cavalry, de Gaulle was accorded the signal honour of addressing the Lords and Commons jointly assembled in Westminster Hall.'[169]

There was a little spasm of mutual emotion when de Gaulle caught Churchill's eye just before he spoke.[170] And how the General rose to the occasion! He delivered a marvellous eulogy upon the British genius for government and the mystical (in fact, non-existent) constitution which captured it. He talked of Britain's 'outstanding role in the midst of the storm' of the Second World War, linking it to 'the legitimacy and authority of the state', continuing in a similar vein:

Although since 1940 you have undergone the hardest vicissitudes in your history, only four statesmen, my friends Sir Winston Churchill, Lord Attlee, Sir Anthony Eden and Mr Harold Macmillan, have guided your affairs over these extraordinary years. Thus, lacking meticulously worked out constitutional texts, but by virtue of an unchallengeable general consent, you find the means on each occasion to ensure the efficient functioning of democracy without incurring the excessive criticism of the ambitious, or the punctilious blame of the purists.[171]

All this was delivered in French without a note in front of him, as Macmillan noticed with admiration.[172]

Two days earlier, shortly after his grand arrival at Victoria station and his progression in a landau through the streets of London beside the Queen, de Gaulle told Macmillan he was optimistic about the forthcoming summit, though he was worried about the Americans: 'De G thinks that K[hrushchev] *does* want a "détente" – *does* want disarmament, but that (except perhaps for Eisenhower) the Americans want neither.'[173]

Neither of them could have foreseen the May Day event that would doom the summit due within days. Espionage is meant to be an aid to diplomacy, not its destroyer. But on 1 May 1960 a Soviet surface-to-air missile brought down an American U-2 reconnaissance aircraft and its CIA pilot, Gary Powers, over Russian airspace. Eisenhower had authorized the flight, 'Operation Grand Slam', so called because 'it was the longest and most daring U-2 mission yet attempted, traversing the whole of the Soviet Union from Peshawar in Pakistan to Bodo in Norway'.[174] Bad weather had delayed it. And, it being the May Day holiday in Russia, there 'was almost no military traffic over the Soviet Union and so the U-2 was easy to track . . . [The Russians] had fired 14 SAM missiles [at 70,000 feet, the Americans had believed their U-2s to be invulnerable], destroying one of their own MiGs that was in hot pursuit. One missile damaged the control surfaces of the flimsy U-2. With the aircraft in a flat spin, caused by the U-2's large wingspan, Powers struggled even to get the canopy open and was unable to activate the self-destruct mechanism before bailing out. The flat spin also ensured that the Soviets retrieved the aircraft all but intact.'[175]

Macmillan lived in blissful ignorance of this ruinous event for six days, until the news was brought to him as he sat worrying in the country about the huge rows at the Commonwealth Prime Ministers' Conference between South Africa and the rest (on 21 March, sixty-seven Africans had died with a further 180 wounded when police fired on demonstrators in the Sharpeville township[176]):

7 May: Chequers. A glorious day – warm and sunny. The Americans have committed a great folly. There have been going on for some time photographic flights at very high altitudes over Russia. We actually have done some very successful ones (with airplanes wh the Americans gave us). We call the exercise 'Oldster'. But, with the summit negotiations coming on, all ours have been cancelled by my orders. The Americans were to do the same, but made their ending date the end of April. Now one of their machines has been shot down by a rocket (it is said, a few hundred miles from Moscow) . . .

The Russians have got the machine; the cameras; a lot of the photographs – and the pilot. God knows what he will say when tortured! I don't know (but I greatly fear) how far he knows about what we have done. The President, State Dept, and Pentagon have all told separate and conflicting stories, and are clearly in a state of panic. Khrushchev has made two very amusing and effective speeches, attacking the Americans for spying incompetently and lying incompetently too. He may declare the summit off. Or the Americans may be stung into doing so.

With a touch of the *comédie noire*, a frequent consolation, Macmillan concluded: 'Quite a pleasant Saturday – the Commonwealth in pieces and the summit doomed.'[177]

So it proved. The four leaders met in Paris on 14–17 May. Khrushchev postured. Eisenhower refused to offer apologies or assurances that reconnaissance flights over Soviet airspace would not recur. Macmillan tried to act the honest broker, telling Khrushchev that 'espionage was a fact of life, and a disagreeable one'.[178] De Gaulle did his best, too, observing, as Alistair Horne put it, 'with his usual lofty irony' that: 'At the present time, anyway, a Soviet satellite passes each day over the sky of France. It flies over at an altitude much higher than an airplane, but it still flies over it.'[179] All to no avail.

No disarmament. No Berlin settlement. Nothing. Macmillan came home on the afternoon of 19 May. That morning, dog tired and 'with much pain in the region of the heart. Is it thrombosis or indigestion?', he found he could scarcely read or write.[180] He reached Downing Street to find a cheering message from the Queen. He immediately wrote to thank her (these letters were another form of consolation – or certainly they read that way):

I hope I may say how heartened I was on my return to 10, Downing Street to receive the message which Sir Michael Adeane [the Queen's Private Secretary] had transmitted on your behalf. It is indeed sad to have returned without anything to show for our work of the last few years and I shall not conceal from Your Majesty the shock and disappointment which I have sustained.

Then, over eight pages, the tired old man gave the Queen a full account of his futile efforts to salvage a little from the wreckage and speculated, erroneously as it turned out, that possibly 'there has been some internal change in the balance of power in Russia which has caused Mr Khrushchev to retreat from his policy of détente . . . It may be, therefore, that the Russian Government used the American aircraft incident as a convenient excuse . . .'[181]

He cheered up a little the following day, Friday, after he had a good reception for his statement on the summit in the House of Commons and his doctor told him he had not had a heart attack, 'but that the symptoms of extreme exhaustion are not dissimilar'. He turned to Dickens (*Dombey and Son*) for respite.[182] By Saturday morning gloom struck him powerfully once more as he lay in bed at Birch Grove and started to write up his diary: 'The *Summit* – on wh I had set high hopes and for which I worked for over 2 years – has blown up, like a volcano! It is ignominious; it is tragic; it is almost incredible.'[183] It was unquestionably one of the greatest disappointments of his life.

It is easy, looking back, to claim that Macmillan was overplaying his and Britain's hand as the great summit maker. It did not seem so hubristic at the time – and not just to the Prime Minister himself. It is intriguing, for example, to find the admittedly Anglophile Raymond Aron writing in 1955 (perhaps significantly, pre-Suez) that 'Great Britain was never much liked at the time when she dominated the world. British diplomacy has regained some prestige since the end of the Second World War; now that she no longer takes the major decisions and has adopted the role of critic, adviser and referee . . .'[184]

Paris in May 1960 was the time and the place, however, when the lack of relative British power really caught up with its would-be sustainer and deployer. Macmillan sensed it – as did those closest to him, such as Philip de Zulueta: 'I never saw him more depressed. He was really cast down and glum after it. Apart from all the effort he had personally put into it, this was the moment he suddenly realised that Britain counted for nothing; he couldn't move Ike to make a gesture towards Khrushchev, and de Gaulle was simply not interested. I think this represented a real watershed in his life . . .'[185] Could salvation lie on the other side of that mountain of disappointment? It might. And if it did, it would come with a label marked 'Europe'.

De Zulueta was the man best placed to pick up Macmillan's geopolitical thought on a daily basis. After the débâcle in Paris had worked its way through that tired but finely tuned mind of Macmillan's, de Zulueta believed 'the failure of the 1960 summit was really crucial in the development of his concept of Europe, because at that summit it became apparent that he really couldn't, by himself, bring irreconcilable American and Russian positions closer. General de Gaulle just washed his hands of it and said the whole thing had been decided in advance in Moscow anyway, and there was no point in arguing and [he] really wasn't intensely worried on the subject.'[186] Not so for Macmillan:

I think this led him to think very much again about what the British position was in the world. The colonial empire was, if not gone, rapidly going, the Commonwealth obviously not being really strong enough, coherent enough as an economic force. So what does Britain do? How does she play a part in the world? . . .

I don't think there was a day on which he suddenly decided, you know, Europe is the thing. But certainly he moved, from then onwards, really rather fast in the direction of feeling that this was the right road for Britain to follow, and that Europe was going to be united, and that without being a part of it Britain would neither be important on its own nor play a part in a wider grouping.[187]

Somewhere in the twelve days between the Thursday afternoon of 19 May 1960, when he sat down in No. 10 to draft his letter to the Queen about the ruined summit, and 1 June 1960 Macmillan seems to have crossed the mental threshold described by Philip de Zulueta. For on that day he circulated a list of questions to his top officials on the pros and cons of British entry to the EEC. The exercise possessed a bite and an urgency lacking in the Europe-related sections of the *Future Policy Study* just over three months earlier. It carried a Macmillanesque title – 'The Six and the Seven: The Long-Term Objective'[188] – and it was led by one of the most remarkable Whitehall officials of the postwar years, Sir Frank Lee, whom we have already encountered as a rarity in 1955–6 in believing Britain should have taken the road from the Messina talks to the Treaty of Rome.

By early 1960 it was evident to both Lee and Macmillan that the British-designed European Free Trade Area (the old Plan G applied to non-EEC western Europe) would not hold as a permanent or dynamic trading arrangement for the UK. The final EFTA agreement had been concluded in November 1959. EFTA came into operation on 1 January 1960, embracing Britain, Sweden, Norway, Denmark, Switzerland, Austria and Portugal. But from the start, it was 'ineffective as a lever on the Six to make them change their commercial policy. For one thing, it was not a big enough market. For another, important political differences between EFTA member states made them act less coherently than the EEC. In a period when high rates of growth of foreign trade were believed to be making a major contribution to high rates of growth of GNP', its EFTA partners 'could not do as much for British exports as the EEC did for the exports of its member-states'.[189]

It must be remembered, too, that as Whitehall wrestled with the 'sixes and sevens' question in May–July 1960, 'Europe' for the British was not a shining collective goal in itself but a means of sustaining *British* power; as a concept, therefore, it was *instrumental* rather than *inspirational*. As Raymond Aron put it in 1962, 'those for whom Europe is to be a fatherland cannot avoid recognizing that in British eyes (except for a small minority), it will never be anything but a means for something else'.[190]

The historian of Britain and Europe, in Chris Patten's words, whatever the period under examination, is dealing with a 'psychodrama'.[191] François Mitterrand when President of France is said to have remarked that the great divide within the European Community was between those who treated it as a wall and those who saw it as a cathedral.[192] Margaret Thatcher, Mitterrand's political contemporary, declared in the autumn of 1999, 'In my lifetime all our problems have come from mainland Europe and all the solutions have come from the English-speaking nations of the world.'[193] 'Psychodrama' really *is* the word.

Macmillan's European instincts were profoundly different from Thatcher's. It was significant that the leading politician in the Cabinet and the top economic permanent secretary of the day now breathed largely as one on Europe. Eric Roll, who represented the Ministry of Agriculture, Fisheries and Food on the Lee Committee, always believed that Lee and Macmillan thought this was where Britain's future lay even before the exercise began. 'Frank', Lord Roll told me in 1991, 'held a tremendous position' in the Whitehall of 1960. He reached his decisions 'on a sober calculation of the facts. That is why when he came down in favour of Europe it had a tremendous impact. His word counted for a great deal. Harold Macmillan had reached that conclusion anyway.'[194]

The answer to Macmillan's Question 22 in *The Six and the Seven* report captures the essence of the Prime Minister's and Lee's thinking and what they sensed as special about the circumstances now facing the UK:

QUESTION 22

What has changed in the situation since Ministers decided on the basis of a full review in 1956 and again in 1959 against joining the Common Market?

ANSWER

There have been five main changes in the situation:

(i) Earlier on it seemed very doubtful if the European Economic Community would ever see the light of day owing to the inability of a weak France to withstand increased competition from her future partners, especially from Germany.

(ii) We thought that, even if the Common Market did come off, we should be able to make our own terms for associating with it. The Free Trade Area negotiations proved us wrong.

(iii) France – and Western Europe generally – is no longer weak. The Common Market is becoming a powerful and dynamic force, economically and politically.

(iv) In 1956 we thought that joining the Common Market would weaken our special relationship with the United States. The position has now changed and the United States are attaching increasing importance to the views of the Community. It is by no means clear, therefore, that the best way of retaining our influence with the United States would be by staying outside the Community, rather than by becoming a leading member of the group with a powerful influence on their policies.

(v) In so far as our previous attitude was influenced by our desire to do nothing which might prejudice the Commonwealth relationship, this consideration is now matched by the fear that the growing power and influence of the Six will seriously affect our position in the world – if we remain outside – and this itself will be damaging to our relationship with the Commonwealth.[195]

In the fuller answer to Macmillan's Question 22, which was appended as an annex to the main report of the Lee group, the threat to Britain's place in the world is even more bluntly expressed – 'They [the Six] may become a *bloc* comparable in influence with the United States and the USSR, and if that happens and if we remain outside, our relative position in the world is bound to decline . . .'[196]

As with the *Future Policy Study*, and the Prime Minister's own mind after the failure of the May summit, the motor driving *The Six and the Seven* was the need to sustain Britain's power in international affairs. The working papers of the Lee group, whose full title (as an official Cabinet Office body) was the Economic Steering (Europe) Committee, show this plainly. On 27 June, a draft circulated which, under the heading 'Foreign Policy Considerations', stated that: 'In the first place, it emerges that there are very strong reasons of foreign policy for our joining the Six; indeed, the arguments of foreign policy are perhaps even stronger than the arguments of economic policy.'[197]

The final report did not quite give this degree of primacy to the great-power impulse over economic factors, but in answer to Macmillan's Question 7 – '*How will the development of the Six affect our relationship with the United States and our influence in the rest of the world?*' it did say that, were Britain to remain 'aloof from the Six, the relative decline in our status would reduce our influence in the Commonwealth and with the uncommitted countries. We should run the risk of losing political influence and of ceasing to be able to exercise any claim to be a World Power.'[198]

The 'great power' impulse was the element within *The Six and the Seven* likely to have most favourable impact upon the ministers round Macmillan's Cabinet table. But what about their equally instinctive anxiety about the loss of British sovereignty implicit in joining the EEC?

Macmillan had posed this in his Question 19 – '*To what extent would joining the Six require us to give up sovereignty, i.e. to give up such control as we still have over our domestic economic policies including agriculture and our social policies?*' The Lee Committee was soothing, even in the face of looming federalism:

ANSWER

Between now and 1970 there would be some progressive loss of sovereignty in a number of matters affecting domestic policy, of which agriculture is likely to be an important example. It is difficult to say how much would be involved in any single field. The terms of application of the generally imprecise provisions of the Rome Treaty affecting the issues other than tariffs have still to be agreed between the Six in many cases. If we were to join the EEC at an early date we could take part in the formulation of these provisions, and influence the extent to which they affected freedom in domestic policy. The effects of any eventual loss of sovereignty would be mitigated:

(i) by our participation in majority voting in the Council of Ministers and by our being able to influence the Commission's preparatory work;

(ii) if resistance to Federalism on the part of some of the Governments continues, which our membership might be expected to encourage.[199]

A dash of wishful thinking there and a trace of a British tendency – which endured – *not* to believe what the Treaty of Rome had to say about ever closer union in its opening paragraphs on the grounds that only French mystics such as Monnet and his followers could possibly subscribe to it.

Where *The Six and the Seven* really did rub ministers' noses in reality was in its passage on the weaknesses of the British economy that had to be remedied if the UK were to be competitive inside *or* outside the EEC. After a paean to the benefits of joining 'a single market of over 200 million people' in terms of 'more specialisation, larger-scale production, higher efficiency through greater competition and a more rapid spread of technical skills and new developments', the report warned that,

> [w]hether we join the Six or not, we shall have to reduce the proportion of our output devoted to consumption, and increase the proportion which is invested or exported. If we join the Six and seek to secure the benefits of association with the Community, we shall have to be fully competitive with them and this may involve changes in our industrial structure which may be both more rapid and of a different character than would be the case if we stayed outside. While these changes were taking place, there would be greater need for mobility of labour in the United Kingdom, and some social hardship might be involved.[200]

But entry could lead to economic expansion and changes in the pattern of industry would be easier to handle in such circumstances. 'If, on the other hand, we decide to stay out of the Common Market, we shall not be faced with these particular, short-term problems, at any rate in the same form. But neither will United Kingdom industry have the advantages of our association with the Six, and this may lead to stagnation and the country as a whole being the poorer for it.'[201]

As part of its own deliberations the Lee group did think about the psychodramatic elements implicit in the Six/Seven question. But their conclusions did not find a place in the final report, perhaps because of a traditional Whitehall belief that it was not for civil servants to tell ministers how to manage public opinion. (That was a skill the political class was, and is, expected to possess.) Yet the 27 June 1960 draft contains a section on 'Public Opinion in the United Kingdom' that still has extraordinary resonance today:

> It is to be expected that, if we were to join the Six, there would be considerable opposition from some sections of public opinion in this country which would find expression in Parliament and in some newspapers . . . We should have to contend with the ordinary Englishman's almost innate dislike and suspicion of 'Europeans'.

This opposition would require careful handling; intensive re-education would be needed to bring this section of the public to realise that in the modern world even the United Kingdom cannot stand alone, and that if we are excluded from the powerful European Community our influence and standing in the world at large – including the Commonwealth and the uncommitted countries – would be bound to diminish.[202]

What a chilling, decidedly *un*-English word 're-education' is.

None the less, the Cabinet – or a substantial section of it – was apparently in need of just such 're-education' themselves when they met on 13 July 1960 to consider *The Six and the Seven* document. The minutes do not reveal who made the most effective case against. Norman Brook, however, put the resistance together in a composite paragraph:

In further discussion it was suggested that the advantages of joining the Community and the dangers of staying outside had been exaggerated. Many other parts of the world besides Europe were expanding rapidly; and as a country with world-wide trading connections we were in a good position to exploit these wider opportunities. To become a member of the EEC could be positively harmful to our position in the world, since some of the political and economic policies of the EEC countries did not inspire respect. France and Belgium had colonial difficulties, Germany was following an ungenerous credit policy, and the EEC countries generally were seeking to expand their production of primary commodities at the expense of the less-developed countries. In trying to negotiate a settlement with the Community we might run grave risks of impairing the unity of the Commonwealth and undermining the confidence of its other members in the United Kingdom, with serious financial and economic consequences to ourselves.[203]

In the UK/European psychodrama, Act I, Scene i took place in 1950 when Monnet and Schuman carried the plan for a Coal and Steel Community to London, Scene ii was Eden and Messina and Scene iii Macmillan and Plan G. Perhaps the Cabinet Room on 13 July 1960 was the setting for Scene i of Act II.

It may have been that, but for Cabinet disagreements about the Lee report, the first British application to join the EEC would have come before July 1961.[204] The tone of the minutes of the 13 July meeting do suggest that – especially the bridging position taken by both Alec Home (still Commonwealth Secretary) and Macmillan himself.

Home's views were attributed in Brook's minute, and they took on an even greater significance within a few days when, as part of his ministerial reshuffle, Macmillan made him Foreign Secretary. For Home on 13 July,

from the point of view of our future political influence in the Atlantic Community there were strong arguments for joining the EEC. We might hope eventually to achieve leadership of it and we could use our influence in it to keep West Germany independent of the Soviet *bloc*. On the other hand our wider interests and influence throughout the world depended to a considerable extent on our links with the Commonwealth; and if by joining the EEC, we did fatal damage to these we should lose our power to exert our influence on a world scale. An association short of membership would not secure for us enough influence in the Community to make the price worth paying. We should therefore consider full membership, but seek special terms to meet our fundamental interests and those of the Commonwealth.[205]

Macmillan summed up in a similar fashion. Parliament should be told 'that there were insuperable difficulties in the way of our accepting membership of the Community under the existing provisions of the Treaty of Rome, especially in relation to our responsibilities to the Commonwealth; but that we fully accepted the establishment of the Community and, with our partners in EFTA, would continue to seek for a mutually satisfactory arrangement between the EEC and EFTA'.[206]

As Eric Roll recalled, Whitehall had already sensed the tilt towards Europe; the Lee Committee became its fulcrum.[207] The best-informed journalists had sensed it too. On 5 July 1960 Don Cook, after talking discreetly to Patrick Dean and others,[208] ran a finely crafted article in the *New York Herald Tribune* which pulled together the strands linking the *Future Policy Study* with the 'Europe Questions' facing Macmillan and his Cabinet: 'the senior civil servants have now advised the Prime Minister in a special report on trends of British foreign policy that a basic aim of the future must be a solution of British relations with Europe. Though carefully worded, as befits advisers to the government, the report invites the conclusion that entry into the European Economic Community should be the logical objective.'[209]*

Macmillan, still brooding post-summit (he recalled in his memoirs that 'my

---

* Peter Ramsbotham, who had no idea of the identity of Cook's informants, minuted Dean himself on 7 July 1960, saying, 'There have been odd leaks before about the Future Policy Report, but Don Cook has this time clearly got more information about it ... it is just possible that the attention of the Prime Minister or of some other Minister will be drawn to this article. So many officials and Ministers have read the Report that any post-mortem would be useless.' Dean initialled and ticked Ramsbotham's minute on 8 July.

mind was still turning more and more to the dangers of Britain remaining outside a community which controlled a central position in what was left of free Europe'[210]), placed a particularly evocative entry in his diary for 9 July 1960 as he prepared to put the Lee report before his Cabinet:

Shall we be caught between a hostile (or at least less friendly) America and a boastful, powerful 'Empire of Charlemagne' – now under French but later bound to become under German control. Is this the real reason for 'joining' the Common Market (if we are acceptable) and for abandoning (a) the Seven (b) British agriculture (c) the Commonwealth? It's a grim choice.[211]

This was Macmillan's own personal manifestation of the 'psychodrama'. The facts, as Churchill might have put it, glared upon him.[212] The geometric conceit had turned into an asymmetric nightmare for Macmillan, his government and his country. Over a mere fifteen years since 1945, Britain had gone from the peacemaker and reconstructor of Europe to its awkward supplicant. The view from No. 10 and those Cabinet Office committee rooms suggested the road to 1970 might prove even rockier.

Was it a moment that marked a change of period in British history? The rims of epochs, whether great or small, are very difficult to define. It is tempting for a British historian to use the dates of general elections for such purposes. Often this is justified: 1945, 1951, 1979 and 1997 unarguably fit the bill. But even though there was no change of government or even Prime Minister that year, 1960 is, in my judgement, such a moment. The 'Wind of Change', the failed summit, the turning of the European question, the abandonment of the attempt to stand alone as a nuclear power – all crammed into the first six months of 1960 – combine to illustrate a proud old political society on a tilt. This is not the same thing as a sclerotic society on the slide. Much was still to be played for in the world. The appetite for the game was still there, even if it was now shaped by interlocking worries about domestic economic performance and overseas influence. But early 1960 did present a new geometry and it marks the end of the 'short post-war'.

Certainly illusions remained to be shed in 1960 from senior Cabinet ministers to those of the Queen's subjects tasting affluence for the first time and assuming that full employment and steadily rising consumption was as much a given as fear of unemployment and privation had been just a generation earlier. Similar strictures can be applied, with hindsight, to those policy-makers who believed that such a benign cycle was sustainable thanks to the combination of ideas and instruments bequeathed to the postwar generation by William Beveridge and Maynard Keynes.

But this, in the words of Edward Thompson, amounts to an example of 'the enormous condescension of posterity'.[213] Thompson was a man of the left writing in the 1960s about the eighteenth and nineteenth centuries, and intellectually, on this point at least, he had a curious ally in a celebrated man of the right, the late-nineteenth and early-twentieth-century Conservative Prime Minister, the third Marquess of Salisbury. For Salisbury, the 'axioms of the last age are the fallacies of the present, the principles which save one generation may be the ruin of the next'.[214]

In 1960 the tough and the soft-minded alike could, with reason, have regarded the mixed-economy welfare state model as a generally successful banisher of the domestic and economic ills of 1930s Britain. Homes and jobs had been available for returning wartime heroes and their families, fulfilling post-1945 Lloyd George's vain boast to the Tommies of the Great War in 1918.[215]

There is much to be said for 'a better yesterday' as a politico-economic and social motivator. But, of itself, it is not enough. Societies and economies need to be stimulated, not just to right past wrongs but to face future difficulties and developments, many of which, as the Lee report to ministers showed, were certainly foreseeable as the decades turned. Yet, as the increasing personal consumption of the Fifties put flesh on the austere bones of the late Forties, only the most abstemious and mean-spirited curmudgeon could fail to give at least two cheers. Britain, unlike most of its western European competitors, was not in 1960 completing the first fifteen of 'thirty glorious years' (as the French came to call them[216]) of high and sustained economic growth. But Britain in the Fifties was flecked – even if it wasn't plated – with gold.

The country should have felt a greater sense of urgency about its relative economic performance, its place in Europe and the wider world. But comfortable societies can be very difficult to invigorate. Much of the Sixties were to be marked by competition between the political parties as to who could most effectively 'modernize' the ancient polity that had become the world's first industrial society, which will be a theme of my next volume.

But in early 1960, in Shakespearean metaphor, the blood was not summoned up any more than the sinews were stiffened. The British people were not girding themselves for a decade of struggle in Europe's or the world's markets. The politics of affluence rather than anxiety (the bomb apart) were making the weather. Despite Suez and a cluster of vexing colonial wars and retreats, the still-vivid memory of a brave, heroic, energetic and world-saving Forties continued to envelop Fifties Britain like a comfort blanket.

In April 1960, during the state visit of Charles de Gaulle, the Queen, as one head of state to another, had asked him what he thought should be her role amid the uncertainties that faced her country. The General replied, perhaps as only he could, by saying: 'In that station to which God has called you, be who you are, Madam!'[217] She did so; so did her ministers and so did her country. Perhaps her people, like Her Majesty, could do no other.

Chronology

1951

October	25	General election: Conservatives win but with a smaller percentage of the votes cast than Labour (48.0 per cent to 48.8 per cent); Conservatives, 321 seats; Labour, 295; Liberals, 6; others, 3. Conservative majority of 17. Turnout 82.5 per cent.
	26	Churchill becomes Prime Minister.
	30	Butler announced as Chancellor of the Exchequer, Eden as Foreign Secretary, Maxwell Fyfe as Home Secretary.
	31	Butler drafts Cabinet paper warning of a parlous and deteriorating economic position.
November	7	Butler announces rise in Bank rate from 2 to 2 per cent. Labour's planned increases in defence spending rephased over four years instead of three.
	21	Churchill briefed on Attlee governments' work on the atomic bomb.
	23	UN and North Korean negotiators agree 'in principle' to a truce line along the 38th parallel.
	29	Churchill's 'United Europe' Cabinet paper makes plain that he never contemplated Britain actually joining the European Coal and Steel Community.
December	12	Churchill briefed on how Attlee governments concealed cost of the atomic bomb from Parliament.
	14	Churchill authorizes bomb test in Australia.

1952

January	5	Churchill arrives in Washington for talks with President Truman.
	11	Eden tells a New York audience that joining a federated western Europe 'is something which we know, in our bones, we cannot do'.
	29	Butler announces austerity measures including extra NHS charges.
February	6	King George VI dies.
	8	Princess Elizabeth is proclaimed Queen on her return home from Kenya.
	18	Churchill announces that the UK will test an atomic bomb in Australia later in the year.
	21	Wartime identity cards abolished.
	28	Plan ROBOT for floating the pound sprung on a surprised Cabinet.
	29	Cabinet meets twice on ROBOT. Plan shelved after Churchill withdraws support from Butler.
March	5	Churchill tells the House of Commons that 30,000 men had enlisted for the revived Home Guard.
	11	Butler introduces Budget. Raises Bank rate to 4 per cent.
	17	Government ends utility clothing scheme.
	25	20,000 NHS doctors win pay rise of £500 a year back-dated to 1948.
	27	Cheese ration reduced to an ounce a week.
	28	Churchill briefed on Soviet capacity to smuggle an atom bomb into a UK harbour in a Russian freighter.
April	12	Eisenhower indicates a willingness to resign from the US Army and to run for President.
	21	Stafford Cripps dies.
May	2	World's first scheduled jet airliner flight. BOAC Comet leaves Heathrow for Johannesburg with thirty-six people on board.
	7	Macleod appointed Minister of Health.
	8	Renewed UN air attacks on North Korea.
June	4	Churchill briefed on damage Russian atomic bombs could inflict on the UK.

| | 16 | France, Germany, Italy and Benelux ratify Schuman Plan for a European Coal and Steel Community. |

16 France, Germany, Italy and Benelux ratify Schuman Plan for a European Coal and Steel Community.

18 Eden circulates to the Cabinet his review of 'British Obligations Overseas'.

23 UN planes bomb North Korean hydroelectric plants.

July 5 Last London tram runs from Woolwich to New Cross.

11 Eisenhower wins Republican nomination. Richard Nixon Vice-Presidential nominee.

August 10 European Coal and Steel Community comes into being.

14 Eden marries Clarissa Churchill, the Prime Minister's niece.

19 Disastrous flash flood in Lynmouth, North Devon, kills over thirty people.

24 Curfew in three districts outside Nairobi in response to Mau Mau attacks.

28 The Vulcan bomber makes its first flight.

September 1 UN air raids on North Korea close to Soviet border.

October 3 First British atomic bomb detonated in the Monte Bello Islands off north-west Australia.

6 Tea rationing ends.

16 In Iran, Mossadegh severs relations with the UK.

19 Troops sent to Kenya to curb Mau Mau.

21 Kenyatta arrested.

23 Churchill praises Attlee in the House of Commons for initiating the UK atomic bomb programme.

November 1 US tests first hydrogen bomb at Eniwetok. At 10.4 megatons, its power is twice that of all the explosives used in the Second World War.

5 Eisenhower wins US presidency in a landslide.

20 Eisenhower chooses John Foster Dulles as his Secretary of State.

25 Agatha Christie's *The Mousetrap* begins an as yet unfinished run in London.

December 5–9 Severe smog descends on London. Mortality rate rises by 120 per cent.

8 Queen gives permission for the Coronation to be televised.

11 Derek Bentley sentenced to hang for the murder of a policeman.

1953

January	3	Churchill sails to Washington for talks with Eisenhower.
	20	Eisenhower inaugurated as President.
	28	Bentley hanged in Wandsworth Prison.
February	3	Storm-force winds and a high spring tide cause devastation along Britain's east coast. Over 120 drowned and 500 missing on Canvey Island in the Thames Estuary.
	5	Creation of a Central African Federation of Northern and Southern Rhodesia and Nyasaland announced. Sweet rationing ends.
	19	Thorneycroft, President of the Board of Trade, puts a paper to Cabinet questioning the desirability of sustaining an Empire trading system in the long term.
March	5	Stalin dies in Moscow.
	6	Malenkov becomes First Secretary of the Communist Party of the Soviet Union.
	14	Khrushchev replaces Malenkov.
April	6	UN and North Korean delegations open talks at Panmunjom on exchange of prisoners of war.
	8	Kenyatta sentenced to seven years for Mau Mau activities.
	12	Eden undergoes surgery for a biliary tract condition – the operation goes seriously wrong.
	13	Ian Fleming's *Casino Royale* published.
	14	Butler introduces Budget. Income tax cut by sixpence (2½p) in the pound.
	17	One thousand Mau Mau suspects rounded up.
	20	Sick and wounded prisoners of war swapped in Korea.
	25	Watson and Crick unveil the structure of DNA in Cambridge.
	27	UK and Egypt open talks on the future of Britain's Suez Canal Zone base.
	29	Eden close to death during second operation.
May	2	38-year-old Stanley Matthews inspires Blackpool to a dramatic last-minute 4–3 win over Bolton Wanderers in the FA Cup Final.
	29	Everest climbed by a Commonwealth expedition led by

Colonel John Hunt. Edmund Hillary, a New Zealander, and Tenzing, a Sherpa, are the first men to reach the summit.

31 Dulles warns that if the Viet Minh drive the French out of Vietnam the rest of South-East Asia could fall to communism like a 'row of dominoes'.

June 2 Queen Elizabeth crowned in Westminster Abbey. The ceremony was televised and watched eventually by 277 million people across the world.

15 Chinese troops launch a surprise attack ahead of an expected armistice in Korea.

17 Workers' uprising in East Berlin suppressed by Soviet forces.

23 Churchill suffers a stroke. Its severity is not made public.

24 The Queen reviews the Scottish royal regalia in St Giles' Cathedral, Edinburgh. Her handbag causes a row.

July 16 Hillary and Hunt knighted. Tenzing receives the George Medal.

27 Armistice is signed in Panmunjom ending the Korean War, which had begun in June 1950.

August 12 Soviet Union tests an H-bomb. (It was, in fact, a hybrid device, not a true thermonuclear explosion.)

19 England win the Ashes for the first time since 1932–3 after an eight-wicket victory over Australia at the Oval.

22 The Shah returns to Iran following the fall of the Mossadegh government.

September 3 Churchill reshuffles Cabinet. 'Overlords' experiment ended. Florence Horsburgh becomes the first ever female Conservative Cabinet member.

October 9 Commercial television to be established in the UK.

31 A record of 30,031 new homes built during October.

November 5 All rationing to end in 1954.

7 First Blue Danube atomic bomb arrives from Aldermaston at RAF Wittering.

13 Government publishes Television White Paper.

25 England lose 6–3 to Hungary at Wembley.

December 1 Macmillan tells the Commons that 301,000 new houses were built during the Conservative government's second year in office.

5 Churchill, in Bermuda for talks, is deeply alarmed by Eisenhower's suggestion that the US might use the atomic bomb if North Korea broke the truce talks.

10 Churchill wins Nobel Prize for Literature.

1954

January 11 BOAC Comets are grounded following a crash off Elba in the Mediterranean.

February 5 Kingsley Amis's *Lucky Jim* published.

17 Government announces meat rationing to end in July.

28 Nasser emerges as dominant figure in Cairo Revolutionary Council.

March 1 US explodes a 15-megaton H-bomb at Bikini Atoll.

5 Television Bill introduced in Parliament.

22 *Lucky Dragon* returns to Japan with its fishermen crew suffering from radiation sickness.

April 5 Commons debates H-bomb. Churchill causes uproar by accusing the Attlee government of abandoning the veto over the use of atomic weapons he had negotiated with Roosevelt.

6 Butler delivers first ever Budget Day broadcast by a Chancellor of the Exchequer.

13 Churchill tells ministers on the GEN 464 Cabinet Committee he would like the full Cabinet to authorize the manufacture of a British H-bomb.

14 Vladimir Petrov defects from the KGB to the West in Australia.

26 Churchill refuses to commit British troops to Vietnam to fight the Viet Minh communists.

May 6 Roger Bannister runs the first ever sub-4-minute mile at Oxford (3 minutes 59.4 seconds).

8 The French fortress of Dien Bien Phu falls to the Viet Minh in Vietnam after a 55-day siege.

29 Butler says UK could double its standard of living in twenty years if inflation avoided.

June 1 Chiefs of Staff brief Churchill and members of his Defence Policy Committee on the danger of the USA starting a 'forestalling' war against the Soviet Union. They also claim that a UK armed with its own H-bomb could 'be on terms with the United States and Russia'.

16　Churchill's Defence Policy Committee authorizes an H-bomb programme.

25　Churchill arrives in Washington for talks with Eisenhower. Eisenhower agrees to Churchill's proposal for a meeting with the Russian leadership.

July　1–4　Churchill conducts personal diplomacy with the Russians from on board the *Queen Elizabeth*, to Eden's fury.

3　With meat decontrolled, all rationing ends after fourteen years.

5　Churchill and Eden land at Southampton.

7　Cabinet breaks up in disarray after discussing proposed talks with the Russians and the making of a British H-bomb. Some ministers complain at lack of consultation.

8　Cabinet discusses morality and cost of an H-bomb.

9　Cabinet discusses summit proposal. Salisbury threatens to resign over Churchill's failure to consult his Cabinet before making it.

21　Agreement reached in Geneva on French withdrawal from Indo-China and the division of the country at the 17th parallel into a communist North and a non-communist South Vietnam.

23　Eden outburst at Cabinet regarding Churchill's refusal to listen to him while returning across the Atlantic.

26　Cabinet agrees to the manufacture of a British H-bomb. Soviets propose a conference involving all European governments rather than a great-power summit.

30　Television Bill becomes law.
Lennox-Boyd replaces Lyttelton as Colonial Secretary.

August　4　Independent Television Authority established.

September　14　Kidbrooke School opens; the first comprehensive in London.

October　2　West Germany admitted to NATO.

18　Eccles becomes Minister of Education.

19　Eden secures agreement with Egypt for withdrawal of British troops from the Suez Canal Zone by June 1956.

November	17	Nasser removes President Neguib in Egypt.
December	2	Senator Joseph McCarthy censured by the US Senate for excesses in his search for communists in American public services, armed forces and professions.
	7	Eccles announces plans to expand technical education.
	18	Rioters in Cyprus demand union with Greece.

1955

January	13	Joint Intelligence Committee states that the only warning of an H-bomb attack on the UK will probably be the presence of Russian bombers on RAF and Allied radar screens.
	19	Governor of Kenya announces amnesty for Mau Mau.
	25	Railway modernization plan published.
February	2	Government announces £212m for road improvements, including the first motorways.
	3	Government announces 347,605 new houses were built in 1954.
	8	London Transport announces plans for a new underground line from Victoria to Walthamstow.
	15	Government announces plans to build twelve civil nuclear power stations over ten years.
	17	Defence White Paper reveals government is to make the H-bomb.
	20	Eden and Nasser dine in Cairo. Seeds of future mistrust sown.
	24	Baghdad Pact of mutual cooperation between Iraq, Turkey, the UK, Pakistan and Iran signed.
March	1	Churchill warns of 'hideous epoch' of the H-bomb and tells the country, 'never despair'.
	8	Secret Strath report on H-bomb fall-out circulated to the Cabinet.
	26	National newspaper strike begins (blotting out coverage of Churchill's pending resignation).
April	4	Churchill tells Colville, 'I don't believe Anthony [Eden] can do it [the job of Prime Minister].'
	5	Churchill resigns as Prime Minister. The Queen sends for Eden.

	7	Macmillan to be Foreign Secretary; Butler stays at the Treasury.
	19	Butler's Budget reduces income tax by sixpence (2½p) in the pound.
	22	Eden asks the Queen for a dissolution of Parliament. General election to be held on 26 May.
May	14	Soviet bloc countries form Warsaw Pact as counterpoise to NATO.
	15	Treaty signed ending occupation of Austria by the USA, UK, France and the Soviet Union.
	26	General election. Conservatives increase majority to 59, taking 49.7 per cent of votes cast. Conservatives, 345 seats (including Speaker); Labour, 277; Liberals, 6; others, 2. Turnout 76.8 per cent.
June	1–2	Talks on a possible European Common Market open at Messina in Sicily.
	10	Mau Mau amnesty ended.
	21	Ruth Ellis sentenced to death.
	30	Arms seized in Cyprus in raids on EOKA hideouts after bomb attacks and riots.
July	13	Ruth Ellis hanged in Holloway Prison.
	18	'Big Four' summit opens in Geneva.
	23	Geneva summit ends. Eisenhower and Khrushchev agree that a nuclear war could destroy the Northern Hemisphere.
	25	Butler raises hire-purchase charges to cool the economy.
	28	Clean Air Bill published.
August	24	Tension rises between Israel and Egypt over Gaza Strip; Egypt suspends talks.
September	3	Israel accepts UN cease-fire over Gaza.
	15	EOKA declared illegal in Cyprus.
	18	Burgess and Maclean surface in Moscow at a press conference. Foreign Office confirms they were long-term Soviet agents.
	22	Commercial Independent Television begins with Associated Rediffusion broadcast to the London area.
	26	*Double Your Money*, presented by Hughie Green, begins on ITV.

| | 27 | Czech arms deal with Egypt announced. |

October   26   Butler introduces autumn measures. Extra purchase tax on utensils; hence the 'pots and pans Budget'.

November   3   Cabinet discusses immigration and rejects controls.

            11   Philby denies he is the 'third man' in the Burgess and Maclean affair.

Cabinet's Economic Policy Committee decides that it is 'against the interests of the United Kingdom to join a European Common Market'.

            17   Housing Minister Sandys tells House of Commons that high-rise-flat building will be encouraged.

            20   Talks open in Washington on a Western loan to finance the Aswan Dam in Egypt.

            22   Riots in Cyprus.

Soviet Union tests its first true H-bomb. Yield 1.6 megatons.

            28   State of emergency declared in Cyprus.

December   6   British Ambassador to the OEEC announces in Paris that Britain cannot join the proposed Common Market.

             7   Attlee announces he will resign as Labour leader.

            14   Gaitskell elected Labour leader, winning 157 votes to 70 for Bevan and 30 for Morrison in a ballot of the Parliamentary Labour Party.

            19   Eccles circulates memorandum on technical education to the Cabinet.

            20   Eden reshuffles Cabinet. Macmillan becomes Chancellor of the Exchequer; Butler, Lord Privy Seal; Lloyd to the Foreign Office.

1956

January   2   Eden circulates Cherwell's paper to Cabinet ministers on the need to transform scientific and technical education in the UK. Later Eden, speaking in Bradford, says in future the 'prizes' will go to those countries with the 'best systems of education'.

             4   Ramsey becomes Archbishop of York.

	6	Macmillan warns Cabinet of the precariousness of the UK's gold and dollar reserves.
	16	Nasser assumes full executive powers in Egypt.
February	3	Macmillan urges wage restraint.
	11	Macmillan threatens resignation if Cabinet will not back him on cuts to bread and milk subsidies.
	16	MPs vote in favour of abolishing the death penalty.
	18	ITV begins broadcasting in the Midlands.
	29	Eisenhower to seek re-election as President.
March	1	King Hussein dismisses Glubb as commander of the Arab Legion.
		Eden tells Nutting he wants Nasser 'destroyed'.
	3	*Daily Telegraph* criticizes Eden for lacking the 'smack of firm government'.
	18	News breaks that Khrushchev has denounced Stalin during a party speech in February.
	22	Treasury publishes White Paper on *The Economic Implications of Full Employment*.
April	4	Joint Intelligence Committee does not believe Nasser has become 'an instrument of Soviet policy. He probably still believes he can steer a middle course . . .'
	17	Macmillan's Budget introduces Premium Bonds.
	18	Khrushchev and Bulganin arrive on the cruiser *Ordjonikidze* in Portsmouth to begin official visit to the UK.
	19	Commander Buster Crabb dives in Portsmouth harbour on a secret mission to examine the rudder and propellors of the *Ordjonikidze*. Fails to return.
	25	Eden warns Khrushchev and Bulganin that Britain would be prepared to fight for its oil if Middle East supplies were cut off.
May	4	Eden told of Crabb's disappearance.
	10	Osborne's *Look Back in Anger* opens at the Royal Court.
	11	Independence to be granted to the Gold Coast (Ghana) in 1957.
	14	Government admits that a navy frogman, Commander Crabb, was diving near the *Ordjonikidze* and is presumed drowned.

June	1	Macmillan warns Eden of financial collapse if the country refuses to face the inflationary consequences of full employment and excessive defence spending and overseas commitments are not curbed.
	13	British troops leave Suez Canal Zone.
	23	Nasser is elected unopposed to Egyptian presidency.
July	5	Clean Air Act passed.
	10	House of Lords votes against the abolition of capital punishment 238 to 95.
	11	Cabinet rejects immigration controls once more.
	19–21	US and UK pull out of financing the Aswan Dam.
	26	Nasser nationalizes the Suez Canal Company.
	27	Cabinet agrees that if diplomacy fails the Suez Canal should be retaken by force, even though the legal case for this is 'weak'. Boyle, Chief of the Air Staff, tells his officials Eden 'has gone bananas'. At Old Trafford Jim Laker takes 19 Australian wickets for 90 runs.
August	1	Foreign Office Legal Adviser, Fitzmaurice, warns Attorney General, Manningham-Buller, of the UK's weak legal case for using force against Egypt.
	3	Joint Intelligence Committee warns that if early military action to retake Suez is not possible, 'the international consequences … might give rise to extreme embarrassment and cannot be forecast'.
	10	Treasury warns Macmillan action to protect the pound might be necessary in the autumn even if Britain did not go to war.
	18	International conference opens in London on future of Suez Canal.
	29	Government announces French troops to join British build-up in Cyprus.
September	3	Eisenhower warns Eden privately not to use force against Egypt.
	5	Israel condemns Nasser's seizure of the Suez Canal.
	7	Treasury warns Macmillan the pound may have to be devalued if Britain goes to war without American and Commonwealth support.

9	Nasser rejects US plan for international control of the Canal.
11	Showings of *Rock Around the Clock* cause disturbances in British cinemas.
21	Second London conference agrees to establish a Suez Canal Users' Association.
	Elvis Presley's 'Hound Dog' reaches no. 2 in the charts.

October 5 Eden taken ill; kept overnight at University College Hospital.

14 French envoys travel to Chequers to unveil to Eden the possibility of a secret Anglo-French-Israeli agreement to attack Egypt and topple Nasser.

16 Lloyd returns from New York (on Eden's instructions) believing he could settle the crisis in negotiations with the Egyptian Foreign Minister at UN talks.

17 Queen opens Calder Hall, the first UK civil nuclear power station, in Cumberland.

20 Anglo-French task force sails from Malta for Port Said. US Sixth Fleet later harasses it.

22–24 Clandestine conversations at Sèvres, near Paris, in which British, French and Israeli representatives agree a secret protocol whereby Israel will attack Egypt first before Britain and France invade as peacekeepers to separate the combatants.

23 Eden tells full Cabinet of 'secret conversations' in Paris, 'with representatives of the Israeli Government', which now make it appear 'that the Israelis would not alone launch a full-scale attack against Egypt'.

Demonstrators in Hungary demand independence and withdrawal of Soviet troops.

24 Chiefs of Staff advisers warn of planning gap for post-invasion Egypt.

25 Eden tells Heath that only he, Lloyd, Macmillan and Butler are to know in full the Anglo-French-Israeli secret plan. Eden describes it as 'the highest form of statesmanship'.

Eden warns Cabinet of 'risk that we should be accused of collusion with Israel'.

26   Armed uprising in Hungary. New Prime Minister, Nagy, calls for withdrawal of Soviet forces.

29   Israeli troops enter Egypt and sweep through Sinai to within twenty miles of the Suez Canal.

      The pound begins to trade very close to its lower limit against the US dollar.

30   Anglo-French ultimatum to Egypt and Israel to withdraw from the Suez Canal inside twelve hours. Eisenhower sends a furious telegram to Eden criticizing Anglo-French-Israeli actions and warning of Soviet intervention in the Middle East.

31   RAF bombers leave Cyprus to attack Egyptian targets.

November   1   Manningham-Buller tells Eden and Lloyd that UN charter does not allow Britain and France legally to intervene to stop Israelis and Egyptians fighting.

2   Nagy says Hungary will leave Warsaw Pact and seek neutrality.

      Senior Foreign Office diplomats sign 'round-robin' condemning Anglo-French action.

      Mountbatten, Chief of the Naval Staff, writes to Eden offering his resignation over Suez.

3   Eden makes his 'man of peace' broadcast.

      Nutting resigns from the Foreign Office.

4   Large anti-war demonstrations in London.

      Red Army launches attack on Budapest.

      United Nations votes for a UN force to be sent to Middle East.

5   Macmillan warns heavy Bank of England support needed for the pound as reserves continue to fall.

      Red Army crushes Hungarian uprising.

      Hailsham, First Lord of the Admiralty, orders Mountbatten to stay at his post.

      Bulganin threatens to use rockets on Britain and France.

6   British troops land in Port Said.

      Macmillan warned by US Treasury that only a cease-fire will secure US support for the pound.

      Cabinet agrees to stop Suez invasion. British troops halt twenty-three miles down the Suez Canal.

Eisenhower re-elected President.

7 UN votes for Anglo-French withdrawal from Egypt.

9 UN votes for Soviet withdrawal from Hungary.

12 Eden tells Mollet that 'history will prove we acted rightly over Suez'.

13 Resignations from the British Communist Party in protest at Soviet actions in Hungary.

20 Cabinet agrees to pursue 'Plan G' for a free trade area in Europe as an alternative to a Common Market.

21 Britain to make way for the UN in Egypt.

22 Macmillan tries to rally Conservative backbenchers, telling them Britain must be the Greece to America's Rome.

23 Eden flies to Jamaica to rest.

26 European free trade area proposal outlined in House of Commons and wins Labour backing.

29 Churchill tells Colville Suez was the most ill-conceived and ill-executed operation imaginable.

December 3 Lloyd tells House of Commons British troops are to leave Egypt without delay.

7 Britain and France start Suez withdrawal.

10 IMF authorizes $1.3 billion loan to the UK.

14 Eden returns to London.

18 Eden tells Conservative backbenchers he will 'never apologise for what we did' at Suez.

20 Eden denies colluding with Israel over Suez invasion during his last appearance in the House of Commons.

27 Eden at Chequers asks Kilmuir if, given his poor health, he should resign.

27–28 Eden drafts 'Thoughts . . . after Suez'.

1957

January 5 Eden sees his doctors and accepts their advice that he should resign.

8 Eden visits the Queen at Sandringham and tells her she will need to find a new Prime Minister.

9 Eden resigns.

	10	The Queen appoints Macmillan Prime Minister.
	13	Thorneycroft becomes Chancellor of the Exchequer; Butler, Home Secretary; Sandys, Minister of Defence; Hailsham, Minister of Education.
	28	Macmillan commissions cost–benefit analysis of the British Empire.
February	7	Bill Haley and his Comets arrive at Southampton on the *Queen Elizabeth* to an enthusiastic reception.
	22	Vulcan bomber undergoes trials with the RAF.
March	6	The Gold Coast becomes independent as Ghana.
	20–24	Macmillan and Eisenhower confer in Bermuda. They agree to station US Thor missiles in eastern England under joint US/UK control.
	25	France, Germany, Italy, Belgium, the Netherlands and Luxembourg sign the Treaty of Rome agreeing to create a European Economic Community or 'Common Market'.
	29	Lord Salisbury resigns from the government.
April	3	Tom Finney voted Footballer of the Year.
	4	Sandys' Defence White Paper published stressing primacy of nuclear deterrence and foreshadowing the end of National Service.
	11	Singapore becomes self-governing.
May	15	UK tests a hybrid bomb at Christmas Island. Widely (but erroneously) reported as Britain's first H-bomb.
June	26	Commander Crabb's headless body found in the sea near Chichester Harbour.
July	20	Macmillan delivers his 'most of our people have never had it so good' speech in Bedford.
August	9	State of emergency ends in Cyprus.
	30	Malaya becomes independent.
September	4	Wolfenden Report recommends homosexual acts between consenting adults in private should be legalized.
	6	Review of Empire's future completed.
	13	Agatha Christie's *Mousetrap* becomes Britain's longest-running play.
	19	Bank rate rises from 5 to 7 per cent.
October	3	Bevan heckled at Labour Party conference for arguing this is not the time for Britain to renounce the H-bomb.

4 Soviet Union launches SPUTNIK-I into orbit; the world's first satellite.

10 Windscale nuclear plant suffers a fire in one of its plutonium piles.

11 Decision taken to douse the fire with water. It works.

24 Eisenhower agrees to amend the McMahon Act prohibiting the exchange of nuclear weapons technology during talks in Washington with Macmillan.

28 Penney Report on Windscale presented to Macmillan.

November 3 Soviet Union puts a dog, Laika, into orbit.

8 Britain's first 'true' H-bomb explodes off Christmas Island yielding 1.8 megatons.

White Paper on Windscale fire published but omits full details of Penney Report.

December 4 Government refuses to implement Wolfenden recommendations on homosexuality.

23 Serious row erupts in public spending Cabinet Committee over Treasury's proposed welfare cuts.

1958

January 1 European Economic Community comes into existence.

5 Cabinet in crisis discussions on public expenditure.

6 Thorneycroft and his junior Treasury ministers, Powell and Birch, announce their resignations.

7 Macmillan leaves for Commonwealth tour referring to 'little local difficulties'.

15 Meeting at Canon Collins' home near St Paul's Cathedral sees birth of Campaign for Nuclear Disarmament (CND).

23 Thorneycroft's resignation speech warns of a 'road to ruin' unless spending levels are curbed.

February 6 BEA Ambassador crashes in Munich killing or injuring many Manchester United players.

7 Perry Como's 'Magic Moments' reaches no. 1 in the charts.

17 Campaign for Nuclear Disarmament holds its first meeting in Westminster Central Hall.

March	12	Macmillan speech on the twentieth anniversary of his *The Middle Way* pledges 'never to allow ... [the] ... shadow' of unemployment 'to fall again' upon the UK.
	27	In Moscow Bulganin goes. Khrushchev adds prime ministership to his Party First Secretary post.
April	4	4,000 protestors leave Trafalgar Square for the Atomic Weapons Research Establishment at Aldermaston.
	7	They arrive.
	15	Heathcoat Amory's first Budget cuts purchase tax.
May	13	Uprising by French settlers in Algeria.
	22	Bank rate reduced to 5½ per cent.
	29	General de Gaulle agrees to become Prime Minister of France if National Assembly approves his wish to remake the Constitution.
June	1	De Gaulle becomes Prime Minister of France.
	5	*Position of the United Kingdom in World Affairs* report presented to Macmillan.
	19	Bank rate reduced to 5 per cent.
	30	Congress approves repeal of those sections of the McMahon Act that prevented nuclear weapons collaboration with the UK.
July	1	Cabinet discusses report on rising Commonwealth immigration. Decides on administrative curbs rather than legislation.
	3	Amory announces ending of credit squeeze.
	10	First parking meters operational in Mayfair.
	31	Macmillan persuades Cabinet to boost public spending on housing, hospitals and roads.
August	14	Bank rate reduced to 4½ per cent.
	23	Racial disturbances in Nottingham.
	31	Rioting begins in Notting Hill, west London.
September	1–6	Rioting continues in Notting Hill.
	8	Cabinet discusses riots. Butler blames white/black competition for housing and work and 'disputes about women'.
	19	First Thor missiles delivered to RAF bases in eastern England.
October	27	Macmillan denigrates (in private) Amory's call for tighter Treasury control over spending and long-term investment.

November   6   French Foreign Minister tells British government France could not sustain competition from both EEC countries and proposed UK-designed free trade area.

          7   Macmillan urges de Gaulle to think again on free trade area.

        14   De Gaulle's Minister of Information announces France will have no part in free trade area.

        20   Bank Rate cut from $4\frac{1}{2}$ to 4 per cent.

        24   Butler tells the House of Commons that public opinion is not yet ready for the legalization of homosexual acts between consenting adult males.

        27   Soviet note announces Khrushchev's intention to transfer responsibility for Berlin to East German government. Threatens unilateral action if Western powers do not negotiate their withdrawal from the city within six months.

December   5   Britain's first motorway, the 8-mile M6 Preston by-pass, is opened by Macmillan.

      6–7   Ministry of Defence police attempt to disperse CND demonstrators at the Thor missile base near Swaffham in Norfolk.

1959

January   2   Britain recognizes the new Castro government in Cuba.

          8   General de Gaulle inaugurated in Paris as first President of the Fifth Republic.

        22   BBC announces television ownership has risen from 19m to 24.5m since January 1957.

February   4   Treasury drops controls on borrowing.

        20   Rioting in Nyasaland.

        21   Macmillan arrives in Moscow at start of an official visit to the Soviet Union.

        23   Cyprus to be independent inside a year.

March   3   Macmillan returns from Moscow.

              Eleven detainees killed at the Hola Camp in Kenya during a riot.

        18   Patrick Devlin delivers his 'Morals and the Criminal Law' lecture at the British Academy.

	19	Macmillan in Washington for talks on Berlin crisis.
April	7	Budget cuts income tax by ninepence (3.75p) in the pound.
May	6	Britain protests to Iceland about coastguard harassment of UK trawlers in international waters.
	11	Foreign Ministers meet in Geneva on future of Germany.
June	5	Macmillan chairs secret Cabinet Committee on plans for a War Cabinet to operate from a bunker beneath the Cotswolds in the event of a Third World War.
	7	Macmillan confers with a secret group of officials and military at Chequers and commissions a *Future Policy Study* on UK prospects 1960–70.
	23	Fuchs freed from prison; leaves for East Germany.
July	27–28	Heated parliamentary debate on Hola Camp killings in Kenya. Powell denounces conduct of the authorities.
	30	Herbert Hart's 'Immorality and Treason' broadcast rebuts Devlin lecture.
August	18	British Motor Corporation launches the Mini.
	27	Eisenhower arrives in London for talks with Macmillan.
	31	Eisenhower and Macmillan make pre-dinner television broadcast from 10 Downing Street.
September	7	Monckton to lead inquiry into future of the Rhodesias and Nyasaland.
	8	Queen agrees to a dissolution of Parliament; general election announced for 8 October.
	28	Gaitskell pledges Labour will not raise the rate of income tax as long as peacetime conditions prevail.
October	1	Labour Party promises to remove purchase tax from certain essential items if elected. Macmillan replies, 'If this is an auction, I am not in it!'
	8	Macmillan triumphs at the polls, taking 49.4 per cent of votes cast. Conservatives, 365 seats; Labour, 258; Liberals, 6; other, 1. Conservative majority of 100. Turnout 78.7 per cent. Margaret Thatcher elected MP for Finchley.
	14	Heath appointed Minister of Labour; Macleod Colonial Secretary.
November	2	Macmillan opens the first section of the M1.
	20	In Stockholm, Britain, Austria, Denmark, Sweden, Nor-

way, Switzerland and Portugal sign agreement to create a seven-nation European Free Trade Area (EFTA).

December 14 Makarios becomes President of Cyprus.

1960

January	1	EFTA comes into existence.
	4	BBC survey shows half the UK population watches television at peak time.
	31	Kennedy announces his intention to run for the Democratic nomination for the Presidency.
February	3	Macmillan delivers 'Wind of Change' speech in Cape Town.
	13	In the Sahara, France tests its first atomic bomb.
	24	*Future Policy Study* completed.
March	12–13	Macmillan in talks with de Gaulle at Rambouillet.
	23	Cabinet Committee meets to discuss *Future Policy Study*.
April	4	Profits tax and tobacco duties raised in the Budget.
	7	De Gaulle on a state visit to London addresses both Houses of Parliament.
	13	Government announces abandonment of the Blue Streak missile.
May	1	Soviets shoot down US U-2 spy plane; pilot Gary Powers survives.
	11	In Washington Eisenhower refuses to apologize for the U-2 flight.
	14	Summit opens in Paris.
	17	Summit breaks up in disarray after Khrushchev walks out over the U-2 incident.
	19–31	Macmillan privately accepts that Britain must join the EEC in order to maintain its influence in Europe and the world.
June	1	Macmillan circulates a list of questions on the pros and cons of UK membership of the EEC to a group of top officials.
	29	House of Commons votes against the legalization of homosexual acts.

July 6 Bevan dies of cancer at the age of sixty-two.
Top officials complete *The Six and the Seven* report replying to Macmillan's UK/EEC questions.

13 Cabinet meets to discuss *The Six and the Seven* report.
Agrees to 'seek ... a mutually satisfactory arrangement
between the EEC and EFTA'.

Notes

Prelude

1 George Orwell, *The English People* (Collins, 1947). Orwell wrote the book in 1943–4 but it was not published for three years. See Peter Davison (ed.), *Orwell's England* (Penguin, 2001), pp. 290–333. This quote is at p. 292.

2 Jonathan Miller interviewed by Joan Bakewell for her *My Generation* series broadcast on BBC2 4, 11 and 18 June 2000.

3 Ian Aitken (ed.), *The Documentary Film Movement: An Anthology* (Edinburgh University Press, 1998), pp. 112, 149, 164.

4 *Holiday*, first shown in 1957, was reissued as a part of *An Invitation to Travel: The British Transport Films Collection, Volume Three* by the British Film Institute in 1998.

5 John Benson, *The Rise of Consumer Society in Britain, 1880–1980* (Longman, 1994), p. 103.

6 James Walvin, *Beside the Seaside* (Allen Lane, 1978), p. 124.

7 This was in October 1973 when I was the 'gossip' columnist of the *Times Higher Education Supplement* and Rhodes, though not yet an MP, was already famous in education circles as the outspoken headmaster of Highbury Grove comprehensive school in Islington.

8 In the late 1940s, the decoration of the Compton scalp brought him £1,500 a year, a substantial sum for those times. Derek Birley, *A Social History of Cricket* (Aurum, 1999), p. 279.

9 Richard Hoggart, *Promises to Keep: Thoughts in Old Age* (Continuum, 2005), p. 126.

10 A phrase Lord Dahrendorf once used in a conversation with the author to describe the electoral programme of the Social Democrat Party in the mid-1980s.

11 Jonathan Miller interviewed by Joan Bakewell, *My Generation*.

Overture

1 Harold Macmillan, *Riding the Storm, 1956–1959* (Macmillan, 1971), p. 350.

2 National Archives, Public Record Office, PREM 11/3480, 'Letters from Prime Minister to HM The Queen, 1958 and 1959', Harold Macmillan to the Queen, 10 October 1959.

3 Peter Laslett, 'On Being an Englishman in 1950', *Cambridge Journal*, vol. 3 (1949–50), p. 494.

4 Howard Mallinson, 'The Lost Childhood?', January 2001. Mr Mallinson, whom I came to know through his work on urban regeneration with Michael Heseltine in the 1980s, hosted a dinner on 8 January 2001 in Brown's restaurant in Mayfair at which a group of 'children of the 1940s' (largely but not wholly beneficiaries of the 1944 Education Act) pooled memories and judgements. Out of this evening came Mr Mallinson's memoir which he sent me on 26 January 2001.

5 Mark Connelly, *We Can Take It! Britain and the Memory of the Second World War* (Pearson Longman, 2004), p. 296.

6 Ibid., p. 2.

7 Phil Hardy and Dave Laing, *The Faber Companion to 20th-Century Popular Music* (Faber, 1990), p. 164.

8 For a taste of the scholarly debate, see Dennis Kavanagh and Peter Morris, *Consensus Politics from Attlee to Thatcher* (Blackwell, 1989); Harriet Jones and Michael Kandiah (eds.), *The Myth of Consensus: New Views on British History* (Macmillan/ICBH, 1996).

9 Iain Dale (ed.), *Labour Party General Election Manifestos, 1900–1997* (Routledge/Politico's, 2000), pp. 49–60.

10 Lord Young of Dartington interviewed for the Widevision Productions/Channel 4 series, *What Has Become of Us?*, 24 March 1994.

11 In his *The Case for Conservatism* (Pelican, 1947), p. 31, Hogg claimed that the 1945 general election showed that '[o]ver 80% of the field of politics the great mass of decent opinion of all parties was agreed as to the best practicable course to take. Never before perhaps at a General Election did the intentions of the principal protagonists more closely resemble one another.' Lord Healey delivered his judgement in a conversation with the author on 17 July 2002.

12 Bob Morris addressing the 'Hidden Wiring' seminar of the MA in Twentieth-Century History programme at Queen Mary, University of London, 22 March 2006.

1 The British New Deal and the Essentials of Life

1 A. H. Halsey, *No Discouragement: An Autobiography* (Macmillan, 1996), p. 40

2 Richard Eyre, *Utopia and Other Places* (Bloomsbury Classics, 1996), pp. 4–5.

3 Martin Wiener, *English Culture and the Decline of the Industrial Spirit* (Cambridge University Press, 1981), p. 3.

4 Felipe Fernández-Armesto, *Food, A History* (Pan, 2002), p. xiii.

5 The phrase is Arthur Koestler's: *The Yogi and the Commissar and other Essays* (Cape, 1945), p. 256.

6 Ross McKibbin, *Classes and Cultures: England 1918–1951* (Oxford University Press, 1998), p. 536.

7 Ibid., p. 534.

8 George Orwell, *The Lion and the Unicorn: Socialism and the English Genius*, first published by Secker and Warburg in 1941 and reproduced in Peter Davison (ed.), *Orwell's England* (Penguin, 2001), p. 264.

9 Raymond Aron, *On War: Atomic Weapons and Global Diplomacy* (Secker and Warburg, 1958), p. 107. Aron wrote this essay originally in August 1956 under the title *De La Guerre*. Ibid., p. 5.

10 Ina Zweiniger-Bargielowska, *Austerity in Britain: Rationing, Controls and Consumption, 1939–1955* (Oxford University Press, 2000), p. 35.

11 Ibid., pp. 35, 83.

12 Ibid., p. 2

13 Ibid., p. 37, table 1.2.

14 Ibid., p. 231.

15 Christopher Driver, *The British at Table, 1940–1980* (Chatto and Windus, 1983), p. 59.

16 Ibid., p. 60.

17 Roy Fitzpatrick and Tarani Chandola, 'Health', in A. H. Halsey and Josephine Webb (eds.), *British Social Trends* (Macmillan, 2000), p. 110.

18 Ibid., p. 118.

19 Zweiniger-Bargielowska, *Austerity in Britain*, p. 2.

20 David Butler, *British General Elections since 1945* (Blackwell, 1989), pp. 60–66.

21 Driver, *The British at Table*, p. 43.

22 Elizabeth David, *French Country Cooking* (Penguin, 1951), pp. viii–ix, 21–2.

23 Driver, *The British at Table*, p. 60.

24 I owe the point about the halting and resumption of 1930s retailing to the late Derek Rayner, who, as Lord Rayner, was Chairman of Marks and Spencer. See also Peter Pagnamenta and Richard Overy, *All Our Working Lives* (BBC, 1984), pp. 116–17.

25 Driver, *The British at Table*, pp. 73–4.

26 Ibid., p. 79.

27 Ibid., p. 75.

28 Harry Hopkins, *The New Look: A Social History of the Forties and Fifties in Britain* (Secker and Warburg, 1963), p. 44.

29 Ibid., p. 351.

30 Driver, *The British at Table*, p. 74.

31 Ibid., p. 77.

32 David Hillman and David Gibbs, *Century Makers* (Weidenfeld & Nicolson, 1998), p. 109.

33 Raymond Postgate writing in the preface to *The Good Food Guide 1959–60* (n.p., 1959); Garrett Anderson, *'Hang Your Halo in the Hall!' A History of the Savile Club* (Savile Club, 1993), pp. 106–8.

34 Driver, *The British at Table*, p. 63.

35 Richard Hoggart, *The Uses of Literacy: Aspects of Working-Class Life with Special Reference to Publications and Entertainments* (Chatto and Windus, 1957; Pelican, 1958), Pelican edition, pp. 9–10; Richard Hoggart, *A Sort of Clowning: Life and Times*, vol. II: *1940–1959* (Chatto and Windus, 1990), pp. 140–5.

36 Richard Hoggart, *An Imagined Life: Life and Times*, vol. III: *1959–91* (Chatto, 1992), pp. 4–5.

37 Hoggart, *The Uses of Literacy*, Pelican edition, pp. 247–8.

38 Ibid., p. 248.

39 Chris Patten, *Not Quite the Diplomat: Home Truths about World Affairs* (Allen Lane, 2005), p. 94.

40 A phrase attributed to the publisher and US diplomat Clare Booth Luce.

41 Hoggart, *The Uses of Literacy*, Pelican edition, p. 248.

42 Eyre, *Utopia and other Places*, p. 226.

43 Hillman and Gibbs, *Century Makers*, pp. 17–18.

44 Hoggart, *The Uses of Literacy*, Pelican edition, p. 37.

45 Ibid., p. 38.

46 Ibid.

47 Hillman and Gibbs, *Century Makers*, pp. 137–8.

48 Stephen Constantine, *Buy and Build: The Advertising Posters of the Empire Marketing Board* (HMSO, 1986).

49 Driver, *The British at Table*, pp. 75–6.

50 Ibid., p. 76.

51 Ibid., p. 73.

52 Conversation between Kathleen Tobin, Terry Walter, Maureen Smith and the author, 7 June 2003.

53 Jane Ashelford, 'Utility Fashion', in *CC41: Utility Furniture and Fashion 1941–1951* (ILEA, 1974), p. 33.

54 Ibid., pp. 33–4.

55 Ibid., p. 34.

56 Ibid., p. 33.

57 Ibid., p. 35.

58 Ibid., p. 33.

59 Ibid., p. 35.

60 Quoted in Marcus Sieff, *Don't Ask the Price* (Fontana, 1988), p. 233.

61 Ibid., p. 234.

62 Hopkins, *The New Look*, p. 315.

63 Ibid.

64 Marty Wilde speaking in *What Has Become of Us?*, programme 3, 'The Last Roar', Wide-Vision/Channel 4 Television, first broadcast 11 December 1994.

65 Hopkins, *The New Look*, p. 315.

66 Ibid.

67 Peter Catterall (ed.), *The Macmillan Diaries: The Cabinet Years, 1950–1957* (Macmillan, 2003), p. 186, diary entry for 27 September 1952.

68 Ibid.

69 Ibid.

70 See especially his Cabinet paper of 22 January 1953, 'Houses – Old and New', National Archives, Public Record Office [NA, PRO], CAB 129/58 C (53) 24.

71 NA, PRO, CAB 129/55. 'Investment in 1953: Reconstruction of Blitzed City Centres', C (52) 350, 20 October 1952.

72 He cited this at the Conservative Party meeting which confirmed him as its leader on 22 January 1957. Alistair Horne, *Macmillan, 1957–1986* (Macmillan, 1989), p. 17.

73 NA, PRO, CAB 129/55, C (53) 24, 22 January 1953.

74 As Patrick Nuttgens has pointed out, in 1953 '77 per cent of public dwellings approvals were houses, 20 per cent low-rise flats and 3 per cent high-rise flats'. Nuttgens, *The Home Front* (BBC Books, 1989), p. 67.

75 NA, PRO, CAB 129/56, 'Housing', C (52) 396, 7 November 1952.

76 Harold Macmillan in conversation with Ludovic Kennedy, *Reflections*, BBC2, 20 October 1983.

77 Harold Macmillan, *The Middle Way: A Study of the Problem of Economic and Social Progress in a Free and Democratic Society* (Papermac, 1966), p. 23.

78 Peter Hennessy, *Never Again: Britain, 1945–1951* (Cape, 1992), p. 454.

79 Anne Digby, *British Welfare Policy* (Faber, 1989).

80 Rodney Lowe, *The Welfare State in Britain since 1945* (1993 and 1999).

81 Nicholas Timmins, *The Five Giants: A Biography of the Welfare State* (HarperCollins, 1995, second edition, 2001).

82 *Social Insurance and Allied Services*, Cmd. 6404 (HMSO, 1942), p. 6.

83 Halsey, *No Discouragement*, pp. 49–50.

84 T. H. Marshall, *Citizenship and Social Class and other Essays* (Cambridge University Press, 1950).

85 Quoted in Peter Hennessy, *Muddling Through: Power, Politics and the Quality of Government in Postwar Britain* (Gollancz, 1996), pp. 171–2.

86 Quoted in Martin Gilbert, *Winston. S. Churchill*, vol. VII: *Road to Victory, 1941–1945* (Heinemann, 1986), p. 292.

87 Quoted in Martin Gilbert, *Winston S. Churchill*, vol. VIII: *Never Despair, 1945–1965* (Heinemann, 1988), pp. 275–6.

88 Noel Annan, *Our Age: Portrait of a Generation* (Weidenfeld & Nicolson, 1990), p. 3.

89 Ibid., p. 217.

90 Ibid., p. 218.

91 Michael Foot, *Aneurin Bevan, A Biography*, vol. II: *1945–1960* (Davis Poynter, 1973), p. 105.

92 Annan, *Our Age*, p. 219.

93 Lord Bancroft, 'The Art of Management', Three Cantor Lectures, II, 'Whitehall and Management: A Retrospect', Royal Society of Arts, 30 January 1984.

94 Quoted in Peter Hennessy and Caroline Anstey, 'From Clogs to Clogs? Britain's Relative Economic Decline since 1851', Strathclyde Analysis Paper no. 3, Department of Government, University of Strathclyde, 1991, p. 21.

95 Correlli Barnett, *The Collapse of British Power* (Eyre Methuen, 1972); *The Audit of War* (Macmillan, 1986); *The Lost Victory* (Macmillan, 1995); *The Verdict of Peace* (Macmillan, 2001).

96 Alan S. Milward, *The Reconstruction of Western Europe, 1945–51* (Methuen, 1984), p. 51.

97 Ibid.

98 Ibid., pp. 477–8.

99 Hennessy, *Muddling Through*, p. 172.

100 For a classic survey of this great debate see Professor Barry Supple's Presidential Address delivered to the Economic History Society at the University of Hull on 2 April 1993 – 'Fear of Failing: Economic History and the Decline of Britain'. It is reproduced in Peter Clarke and Clive Trebilcock (eds.), *Understanding Decline: Perceptions and Realities of British Economic Performance* (Cambridge University Press, 1997), pp. 9–31.

101 David. S. Landes, *The Unbound Prometheus: Technological Change and Industrial Development in Western Europe from 1750 to the Present* (Cambridge University Press, 1969), p. 528.

102 Ibid., p. 535.

103 Bernard Donoghue and G. W. Jones, *Herbert Morrison: Portrait of a Politician* (Phoenix Press, 2001), pp. 400–25; Peter Clarke, *The Cripps Version: The Life of Sir Stafford Cripps* (Allen Lane, 2002), pp. 479–538.

104 NA, PRO, PREM 8/1415, Part 1; CP (49) 159. 'The Economic Situation. Memorandum by the Lord President of the Council', 21 July 1949.

105 Ibid.

106 Ibid.

107 I heard Lord Jenkins use it more than once.

108 NA, PRO, PREM 8/1415, Part 1; CP (49) 159.

109 Anthony King, 'Overload: Problems of Governing in the 1970s', *Political Studies*, vol. 22, nos. 2–3 (June–September 1975).

110 Roy Jenkins, *A Life at the Centre* (Macmillan, 1991), pp. 147–8. Gaitskell's death in January 1963 left him feeling that the 'savour of politics had been destroyed for me . . . I have not seen his like [since]'.

111 NA, PRO, CAB 129/48, 'The Economic Position: Analysis and Remedies. Memorandum by the Chancellor of the Exchequer', C (51) 1, 31 October 1951.

112 Philip M. Williams (ed.), *The Diary of Hugh Gaitskell, 1945–1956* (Cape, 1983), p. 268, entry for 10 August 1951.

113 See Hennessy, *Never Again*, pp. 413–16.

114 NA, PRO, PREM 8/1415, Part 4, EPC (51) 65, 'Economic Policy. Memorandum by the Chancellor of the Exchequer', 22 June 1951.

115 Ibid.

116 Ibid.

117 Hennessy, *Never Again*, pp. 382–3, 421, 466.

118 NA, PRO, PREM 8/1415, Part 4, EPC (51) 65.

119 Lord Butler, *The Art of the Possible* (Penguin, 1973), pp. 17–18.

120 Ibid., p. 158.

121 Ibid.

122 Williams, *The Diary of Hugh Gaitskell*, p. 305, entry for 23 November 1951.

123 Butler, *The Art of the Possible*, p. 159.

124 Alec Cairncross (ed.), *The Robert Hall Diaries, 1947–1953* (Unwin Hyman, 1989), p. 177, entry for 31 October 1951.

125 Butler, *The Art of the Possible*, p. 159.

126 NA, PRO, CAB 129/48, C (51) 1, 31 October 1951.

127 Ibid.

128 Ibid.

129 Gilbert, *Never Despair*, p. 644.

130 Butler, *The Art of the Possible*, p. 159.

131 Cairncross, *The Robert Hall Diaries, 1947–1953*, p. 179, entry for 8 November 1951.

132 Hennessy, *Never Again*, pp. 222–3.

133 NA, PRO, CAB 66/65, WP (45) 301.

134 Bernard Alford, '1945–1951: Years of Recovery or a Stage in Economic Decline?', in Clarke and Trebilcock, *Understanding Decline*, p. 189.

135 Cairncross, *The Robert Hall Diaries, 1947–1953*, p. 161, entry for 20 July 1951.

136 In Hennessy and Anstey, 'From Clogs to Clogs?', p. 21.

137 NA, PRO, CAB 129/53, C (52) 202, 'British Overseas Obligations. Memorandum by the Secretary of State for Foreign Affairs', 18 June 1952.

138 Ibid.

139 Ibid.

140 Ibid.

141 Michael Howard, *The Continental Commitment: The Dilemma of British Defence Policy in the Era of the Two World Wars* (Ashfield Press, 1989), p. 10.

142 NA, PRO, CAB 129/53, C (52) 202.

143 Peter Laslett, 'On Being an Englishman in 1950', *Cambridge Journal*, vol. 3 (1949–50), p. 494.

144 NA, PRO, CAB 129/53, C (52) 202.

145 Andrew Shonfield, *British Economic Policy since the War* (Penguin, 1958).

146 NA, PRO, CAB 129/53, C (52) 202.

147 Shonfield, *British Economic Policy since the War*, p. 122.

148 Michael Shanks, *The Stagnant Society* (Penguin, 1961). For the impact of Shonfield and Shanks in particular and the 'Penguin Specials' in general, see Matthew Grant, 'Historians, the Penguin Specials and the "State-of-the-Nation" Literature, 1958–64', *Contemporary British History*, vol. 17, no 3 (Autumn 2003), pp. 29–54.

149 Mancur Olson, *The Rise and Decline of Nations: Economic Growth, Stagflation and Social Rigidities* (Yale University Press, 1982), p. 6.

150 Keir Thorpe, '"The Missing Pillar", Economic Planning and the Machinery of Government during the Labour Administration of 1945–51', unpublished PhD thesis, Queen Mary and Westfield, University of London, 1998.

151 Ibid.

152 Alec Cairncross (ed.), *The Wilson Years: Treasury Diary, 1964–1968* (Historians' Press, 1997), p. 52, entry for 22 May 1965.

153 Peter Hennessy, *Whitehall* (Pimlico, 2001), p. 395.

154 Hennessy, *Never Again*, p. 415.

155 Peter Hennessy, *The Prime Minister: The Office and Its Holders since 1945* (Allen Lane, 2000), p. 304.

156 I kept this exchange private until Lord Croham gave me permission to attribute it during a conversation on 8 September 2003. Nearly thirty years after Lord Croham delivered this relative solace, it turned out not to be quite true. The Office of National Statistics, as the old Central Statistical Office was known, published in the autumn of 2003 a recalculation of UK economic growth figures for gross domestic product right back to 1949 based on a more sophisticated 'chain-linked' calculation which, year-by-year, took closer account of the content of goods and services traded and changes therein. For the period covered by this volume, the figures were altered only slightly, usually in a downward direction:

UK GDP ANNUAL GROWTH 1949–64

	OLD FIGURE	REVISED FIGURE
	%	%
1949	3.5	3.3
1950	3.1	2.9
1951	2.8	3.0
1952	0.4	0.2
1953	3.9	3.7
1954	4.3	4.1
1955	3.1	3.1
1956	1.0	1.0
1957	1.8	1.7
1958	0.4	0.4
1959	4.4	4.4
1960	5.4	5.5
1961	2.5	2.5
1962	1.3	1.2
1963	5.0	5.1
1964	5.4	5.6

Source: 'Chain-linking GDP: New Calculation for Estimation of Economic Growth', Office of National Statistics, 2003.

157 Professor King wrote them down and initialled and dated them on the back of the menu for the Governor's Dining Room at the Bank of England on 13 August 2003.
158 Tom Finney, *My Autobiography* (Headline, 2003), pp. 190–2.
159 Ibid., p. 193.
160 For an excellent survey of competing arguments see Andrew Gamble, 'Theories and Explanations of British Decline', in Richard English and Michael Kenny (eds.), *Rethinking British Decline* (Macmillan, 2000), pp. 1–22.
161 Milward, *The Reconstruction of Western Europe*, p. 477.
162 Ibid., p. 489.
163 Ibid.
164 Gamble, 'Theories and Explanations of British Decline', p. 19.
165 H. C. G. Matthew, 'The Liberal Age', in Kenneth O. Morgan (ed.), *The Oxford Illustrated History of Britain* (Oxford University Press, 1984), pp. 463–4; Hennessy and Anstey, 'From Clogs to Clogs?', p. 4.
166 Gamble, 'Theories and Explanations of British Decline', pp. 19–20.
167 Ibid., p. 20.
168 Milward, *The Reconstruction of Western Europe*, p. 489.
169 Shonfield, *British Economic Policy since the War*, pp. 251–80.
170 Shanks, *The Stagnant Society*, pp. 103, 221–31.
171 Landes, *The Unbound Prometheus*, p. 506.
172 Ibid., p. 536.
173 Ibid., p. 506.
174 Charles H. Feinstein, 'The End of Empire and the Golden Age', in Clarke and Trebilcock, *Understanding Decline*, p. 228.
175 Geoffrey Owen, *From Empire to Europe: The Decline and Revival of British Industry since the Second World War* (HarperCollins, 1999), p. 29.
176 Milward, *The Reconstruction of Western Europe*, p. 488.

177 Hennessy, *Never Again*, pp. 399–402; François Duchêne, *Jean Monnet: The First Statesman of Independence* (Norton, 1994), pp. 147–80.

178 Milward, *The Reconstruction of Western Europe*, p. 406.

179 Ibid., p. 489.

180 Feinstein, 'The End of Empire and the Golden Age', pp. 228–9.

181 For his varied career within Whitehall, the universities and international economic institutions see Alec Cairncross, *Living With the Century* (iynx, 1998).

182 Alec Cairncross, *The British Economy since 1945* (Blackwell, 1992), p. 14.

183 Jim Tomlinson, 'The Failure of the Anglo-American Council on Productivity', *Business History*, 33 (1991), pp. 82–92.

184 Jim Tomlinson, *Democratic Socialism and Economic Policy: The Attlee Years, 1945–1951* (Cambridge University Press, 1997), p. 72.

185 H. J. Habbakuk, *American and British Technology in the Nineteenth Century* (Cambridge University Press, 1962).

186 S. N. Broadberry, *The Productivity Race: British Manufacturing in International Perspective* (Cambridge University Press, 1997), pp. 1–16; Owen, *From Empire to Europe*, pp. 14–17.

187 Owen, *From Empire to Europe*, pp. 9–29.

188 Broadberry, *The Productivity Race*, p. 3.

189 Ibid., p. 397.

190 Ibid., p. 398.

191 Ernest Gellner, *Plough, Sword and Book: The Structure of Human History* (Collins Harvill, 1988).

192 Ernest Gellner, *Nations and Nationalism* (Blackwell, 1983), p. 22.

193 Geoffrey Searle, *The Quest for National Efficiency* (Oxford University Press, 1971); Martin Wiener, *English Culture and the Decline of the Industrial Spirit* (Cambridge University Press, 1981); Hennessy, *Never Again*, pp. 146–58.

194 Owen, *From Empire to Europe*, p. 16.

195 Hennessy, *Never Again*, pp. 156–7.

196 A. H. Halsey, *Change in British Society* (Oxford University Press, 1987), p. 31.

197 NA, PRO, CAB 129/102 part 1, C(60) 107, 'The Six and the Seven: The Long-Term Objective. Answers to the Prime Minister's Questions', 6 July 1960.

198 Gellner, *Nations and Nationalism*, p. 23.

199 Ernest Gellner, *Conditions of Liberty: Civil Society and Its Rivals* (Hamish Hamilton, 1994), p. 91.

200 Cairncross, *The British Economy since 1945*, p. 276.

201 For these techniques see Robert Skidelsky, *John Maynard Keynes: Fighting for Britain, 1937–1946* (Macmillan, 2000), pp. 138–58.

202 A. J. P. Taylor, *English History, 1914–1945* (Oxford University Press, 1965), p. 511.

203 English and Kenny (eds.), *Rethinking British Decline*, pp. 68–9.

204 W. D. Rubinstein, *Capitalism, Culture and Decline in Britain, 1750–1990* (Routledge, 1993), p. 82.

205 See Evelyn Waugh, *Brideshead Revisited* (Penguin, 2003), pp. 21–2, for his evocation through his hero, Charles Ryder, of encountering Brideshead in its wartime garb.

206 Rubinstein, *Capitalism, Culture and Decline in Britain*, p. 82.

207 NA, PRO, PREM 8/1415, Part 1, CP (49) 159.

208 Ibid.; for Morrison's sense of 'Middle Britain' see Donoghue and Jones, *Herbert Morrison*, p. 441.

209 NA, PRO, CAB 134/856, EACE (51) 13.

210 Martin Daunton, *Just Taxes; The Politics of Taxation in Britain, 1914–1979* (Cambridge University Press, 2002), pp. 221–2.

211 J. M. Keynes, *The General Theory of Employment, Interest and Money* (Macmillan, 1936).

212 Skidelsky, *John Maynard Keynes: Fighting for Britain*, p. 499.

213 Conversation with Lord Croham, 7 August 2003.

214 John Saville, *Memoirs from the Left* (Merlin Press, 2003), p. 76.

215 Ibid.

216 I have written about this at some length in chapters 3 and 4 of my *Whitehall* (Pimlico, 2001), pp. 88–168.

217 NA, PRO, T 273/9, 'Civil Service Organization', Cooper to Attlee, 12 February 1946.

218 Ibid. Bridges' letters dated 26 February 1946.

219 Lord Franks interviewed for the London Weekend Television *Whitehall* programme, 17 March 1987.

220 NA, PRO, T 273/9.

221 Ibid.

222 Olson, *The Rise and Decline of Nations*, pp. 84–7.

223 Jon Davis, 'Prime Ministers and the Reform of British Central Government, 1960–74', unpublished PhD thesis, Queen Mary, University of London, 2006.

224 Hennessy, *Whitehall*, pp. 589–627.

225 Hennessy, *The Prime Minister*, pp. 533–8.

226 David Marquand, *The Unprincipled Society: New Demands and Old Politics* (Cape, 1988), pp. 13, 102–7.

227 Julian Jackson, *The Fall of France: The Nazi Invasion of 1940* (Oxford University Press, 2003), p. 244; General Charles de Gaulle, *War Memoirs: Salvation 1944–1946* (Weidenfeld & Nicolson, 1959), pp. 100–101, 271.

228 Duchêne, *Jean Monnet: The First Statesman of Interdependence*, pp. 147–80.

229 Hennessy and Anstey, 'From Clogs to Clogs?', p. 27.

230 Hennessy, *Never Again*, p. 424.

231 Owen, *From Empire to Europe*, pp. 32–40.

232 Alford, '1945–1951: Recovery or Economic Decline?', p. 200; Owen, *From Empire to Europe*, p. 50.

233 Owen, *From Empire to Europe*, p. 421; Tomlinson, *Democratic Socialism and Economic Policy*, p. 70.

234 Conversation with Dick Olver, 3 June 2003.

2 Society, Pleasure and the Imponderables

1 R. H. Tawney, 'The War and Social Policy', originally published in 1950 and reproduced in R. H. Tawney, *The Attack and Other Papers* (Allen and Unwin, 1953), p. 147.

2 Ernest Gellner, *Language and Solitude: Wittgenstein, Malinowski and the Habsburg Dilemma* (Cambridge University Press, 1998), p. 6.

3 Michael Young and Peter Willmott, *Family and Kinship in East London* (Pelican, 1962), pp. 11–12.

4 David Cannadine, *Class in Britain* (Pelican, 2000), p. ix.

5 Tawney's 'Some Reflections of a Soldier' first appeared in October 1916 in the *Nation*. The essay is reproduced in Tawney, *The Attack*, pp. 21–8. The 'other England' quote is on p. 21.

6 I am grateful to Professor Ben Roberts (who himself once beat out a Tawney fire at a meeting of the LSE's Economic History Society) for reconstructing this charming and alarming scene.

7 Tawney, *The Attack*, p. 181.

8 Ibid.

9 Ibid.

10 Ross McKibbin, *Classes and Cultures: England, 1918–1951* (Oxford University Press, 1998), pp. 160–61.

11 Ernest Gellner, *Nations and Nationalism* (Blackwell, 1983), p. 63.

12 Ibid.

13 Ibid.

14 Ibid.

15 Ibid., pp. 63–4.

16 Harold Perkin, *The Origins of Modern English Society* (second edn, Routledge, 2002), p. 375.

17 Hugh Dalton, *High Tide and After* (Muller, 1962).

18 National Archives, Public Record Office [NA, PRO], CAB 118/21, WP (43) 199, 11 May 1943.

19 Gellner, *Nations and Nationalism*, p. 69.

20 Ibid., pp. 63–4.

21 This phrase was used by Professor Alison Richard on becoming Vice-Chancellor of Cambridge University in the autumn of 2003.

22 Michael Young, 'Down with Meritocracy', *Guardian*, 29 June 2001.

23 'Tony Blair's First Keynote Speech of the Campaign', Labour Party, 13 May 2001.

24 Peter Hennessy, *Never Again: Britain, 1945–51* (Cape, 1992), pp. 144–62.

25 Michael Barber, *The Making of the 1944 Education Act* (Cassell Education, 1994).

26 Ibid., pp. 107–22.

27 Michael Barber, *The Learning Game: Arguments for an Education Revolution* (Indigo, 1997), pp. 160–61.

28 Ibid., p. 162.

29 A. H. Halsey and Josephine Webb (eds.), *Twentieth-Century British Social Trends* (Macmillan, 2000), p. 288.

30 Conversation with Professor Michael Barber, 24 September 2003. See also Peter Hennessy, 'Letter from Whitehall: The Ties that Bind', *The Tablet*, 27 March 2004.

31 Gellner, *Nations and Nationalism*, p. 63.

32 Perkin, *The Origins of Modern English Society*, p. 434.

33 Barber, *The Making of the 1944 Education Act*, p. 117.

34 Conversation with Gillian Shephard, 28 October 2003.

35 Correlli Barnett, *The Audit of War: The Illusion and Reality of Britain as a Great Nation* (Macmillan, 1986), p. 283.

36 Barber, *The Making of the 1944 Education Act*, p. 119.

37 Bernard Alford, '1945–1951: Years of Recovery or a Stage in Economic Decline?', in Peter Clarke and Clive Trebilcock (eds.), *Understanding Decline: Perceptions and Realities of British Economic Performance* (Cambridge University Press, 1997), p. 206.

38 McKibbin, *Classes and Cultures,* pp. 225–6.

39 Ibid., p. 225.

40 Ibid., pp. 226–7.

41 Ibid., pp. 260–61.

42 Ibid., p. 233.

43 Ibid., pp. 261–2.

44 Ibid., pp. 263–4. See also Richard Hoggart, *The Uses of Literacy* (Penguin, 1992), pp. 291–304.

45 Conversation with Professor George Steiner, 25 October 1991. His thoughts were included in the BBC Radio 4 *Analysis* programme broadcast on 31 October 1991.

46 McKibbin, *Classes and Cultures*, p. 254.

47 Daniel Snowman, *The Hitler Emigrés: The Cultural Impact on Britain of Refugees from Nazism* (Chatto and Windus, 2002).

48 James T. Paterson, *Great Expectations: The United States 1945–1974* (Oxford University Press, 1996), pp. 8, 68; McKibbin, *Classes and Cultures*, p. 270.

49 A. H. Halsey, *No Discouragement: An Autobiography* (Macmillan, 1996), p. 36.

50 McKibbin, *Classes and Cultures*, pp. 248–59.

51 Joan Bakewell, *The Centre of the Bed: An Autobiography* (Hodder, 2003), pp. 83–8.

52 Ibid., p. 85.

53 McKibbin, *Classes and Cultures*, p. 262.

54 Halsey and Webb, *Twentieth-Century British Social Trends*, p. 226.

55 Fred Hirsch, *Social Limits to Growth* (Routledge, 1977), p. 27.

56 Harold Perkin, *The Rise of Professional Society: England since 1880* (Routledge, 1989), p. 451.

57 Trevor Royle, *The Best Years of Their Lives: The National Service Experience 1945–63* (Coronet, 1988), p. xiii.

58 For the making of post-1945 National Service see L. V. Scott, *Conscription and the Attlee Governments: The Politics and Policy of National Service, 1945–1951* (Oxford University Press, 1993).

59 B. S. Johnson (ed.), *All Bull: The National Servicemen* (Quartet, 1973), pp. 1–2.

60 Scott, *Conscription and the Attlee Governments*, p. 200.

61 Michael Dockrill, *British Defence since 1945* (Blackwell, 1988), p. 36.

62 Johnson, *All Bull*, p. 2.

63 Royle, *The Best Years of Their Lives*, p. 27.

64 Scott, *Conscription and the Attlee Governments*, pp. 25–6, 33, 38.

65 Johnson, *All Bull*, p. 1.

66 Ibid., p. 41.

67 Royle, *The Best Years of Their Lives*, p. 40.

68 Johnson, *All Bull*, p. 3.

69 Royle, *The Best Years of Their Lives*, p. 44.

70 Johnson, *All Bull*, p. 14.

71 Royle, *The Best Years of Their Lives*, p. xiii.

72 Ibid., p. 30.

73 Ibid.

74 Johnson, *All Bull*, p. 15.

75 Ibid., p. 3.

76 Royle, *The Best Years of Their Lives*, p. 35.

77 Johnson, *All Bull*, p. 4.

78 Ibid., p. 5.

79 Alan Bennett, *Telling Tales* (BBC Books, 2001), p. 82.

80 Royle, *The Best Years of Their Lives*, pp. 71–2.

81 Ibid., pp. 101–12.

82 Ibid., p. 101.

83 Ibid., p. 102.

84 Michael Frayn, *The Russian Interpreter* (Penguin, 1967); Alexander Games, *Backing into the Limelight: The Biography of Alan Bennett* (Headline, 2001), pp. 24–5. See also Geoffrey Elliot and Harold Shukman, *Secret Classrooms: A Memoir of the Cold War* (St Ermin's Press, 2002).

85 Royle, *The Best Years of Their Lives*, p. 72.

86 Ibid., p. 74.

87 Conversation with Eric Pankhurst, 6 April 2002.

88 Humphrey Carpenter, *That Was Satire That Was: The Satire Boom of the 1960s* (Gollancz, 2000), pp. 216–19.

89 Royle, *The Best Years of Their Lives*, p. 311.

90 Mark Garnett and Ian Aitken, *Splendid! Splendid! The Authorized Biography of Willie Whitelaw* (Cape, 2002), pp. 234, 246, 275.

91 Terence Morris, *Crime and Criminal Justice since 1945* (Blackwell, 1989), p. 4.

92 Ibid., pp. 14–21, 90–91.

93 Ibid., p. 16.

94 Ibid., pp. 16–17.

95 The phrase is Ernest Gellner's. Gellner, *Nations and Nationalism* (Blackwell, 1983), p. 12.

96 Harry Hopkins, *The New Look: A Social History of the Forties and Fifties in Britain* (Secker and Warburg, 1963), pp. 206–9.

97 Ibid., pp. 427–9, 433.

98 NA, PRO, PREM 11/858, 'Proposed Legislation to Prevent Sale and Publication of Horror Comics. Includes Examples of US Publications 1944–1955'; CAB 128/27, CC (54) 82, 6 December 1954.

99 George Orwell, *The English People*, in Peter Davison (ed.), *Orwell's England* (Penguin, 2001), pp. 296–7.

100 George Orwell, 'A Hanging', *The Adelphi*, 1931; reproduced in Peter Davison (ed.), *Orwell and Politics* (Penguin, 2001), pp. 9–14.

101 Hennessy, *Never Again*, p. 447.

102 Morris, *Crime and Criminal Justice since 1945*, pp. 80–81.

103 George Orwell, *The Lion and the Unicorn*, in Davison, *Orwell's England*, pp. 257–8.

104 Morris, *Crime and Criminal Justice since 1945*, pp. 179–80.

105 Ibid., pp. 174–5.

106 Orwell, *The Lion and the Unicorn*, p. 255.

107 McKibbin, *Classes and Cultures*, pp. 371–2.

108 Ibid., p. 372.

109 Ibid.

110 Ibid., pp. 373–4.

111 Ibid., p. 374. See also Hoggart, *The Uses of Literacy*, pp. 137–40.

112 Orwell, *The English People*, p. 296.

113 Bakewell, *The Centre of the Bed*, p. xiii.

114 Richard Holt, *Sport and the British* (Oxford University Press, 1990), pp. 83–6.

115 Clifford Geertz, *The Interpretation of Cultures* (Basic Books, 1973), pp. 412–54.

116 McKibbin, *Classes and Cultures*, p. 384.

117 Ibid., p. 332.

118 David Rayvern Allen, *Arlott: The Authorised Biography* (HarperCollins, 1996), pp. 59–60.

119 John Arlott, *Test Match Diary, 1953* (The Sportsman's Book Club, 1954); *Basingstoke Boy: An Autobiography* (Fontana, 1992), pp. 126, 166.

120 Neville Cardus, *Close of Play* (Collins, 1956), p. 47.

121 Neville Cardus, *Cardus in the Covers* (Queen Anne Press, 1990), pp. 37–8.

122 Max Weber, as cited by Clifford Geertz in *The Interpretation of Cultures*, p. 5.

123 Cardus wrote these words in 1930. They are reproduced in Christopher Martin-Jenkins, *The Spirit of Cricket: A Personal Anthology* (Faber, 1994), p. 5.

124 The phrase is Clifford Geertz's. See his *Available Light: Anthropological Reflections on Philosophical Topics* (Princeton, 2001), p. 119.

125 Cardus, *Cardus in the Covers*, p. 104.

126 Ibid., p. 106.

127 Ibid., pp. 105–6.

128 G. M. Trevelyan, *English Social History* (Longmans, 1944), p. 408. For the Nazis and cricket see Derek Birley, *A Social History of Cricket* (Aurum, 1999), p. 261.

129 Harold Perkin, 'Teaching the Nations How to Play: Sport and Society in the British Empire and Commonwealth', *International Journal of the History of Sport*, vol. 6, no. 2 (1989), p. 151.

130 Arlott, *Basingstoke Boy*, p. 198.

131 Perkin, 'Teaching the Nations How to Play', p. 153.

132 Holt, *Sport and the British*, pp. 291–2.

133 Arlott, *Test Match Diary, 1953*, pp. 193–5.

134 Cardus, *Cardus in the Covers*, pp. 106–7.

135 Roger Opie, *The 1950s Scrapbook* (New Cavendish Books, 1988), p. 22.

136 David Crystal, *The Cambridge Biographical Encyclopaedia* (Cambridge University Press, 1994), p. 22.

137 McKibbin, *Classes and Cultures*, p. 340.

138 Tom Finney, *Tom Finney* (Headline, 2003), pp. 1–2.

139 Ibid., p. 3.

140 Jimmy Hill, *The Jimmy Hill Story* (Hodder, 1999), p. 64.

141 Ibid., pp. 60–82.

142 Ibid., pp. 36–7.

143 Ibid., p. 37.

144 Finney, *Tom Finney*, p. 271.

145 Ibid. Front cover.

146 Sean Magee (ed.), *Runners and Riders: An Anthology of Writing on Racing* (Methuen, 1993), p. 30. For Gordon Richards see Crystal, *The Cambridge Biographical Encyclopaedia*, p. 797.

147 McKibbin, *Classes and Cultures*, p. 363.

148 Ibid., p. 362.

149 Ibid., p. 365.

150 Ibid., p. 367.

151 Joe Brown, *The Hard Years* (Phoenix, 2001), p. 54.

152 Ibid., p. 56.

153 Ibid., pp. 37–8.

154 For Lewis see Julian Symons (ed.), *The Essential Wyndham Lewis* (Vintage, 1991).

155 Orwell, *The English People*, p. 296.

156 Ibid., p. 319.

157 John Le Carré, *The Tailor of Panama* (Coronet, 1996), pp. 30–31.

158 Orwell, *The English People*, p. 326. For the 'Estuary English' phenomenon see David Crystal, *The Cambridge Encyclopaedia of the English Language*, second edition (Cambridge University Press, 2003), p. 327.

159 Nancy Mitford, 'The English Aristocracy', *Encounter*, later republished in her *Noblesse Oblige: An Enquiry into the Identifiable Characteristics of the English Aristocracy* (Weidenfeld & Nicolson, 1956).

160 Hopkins, *The New Look*, p. 354.

161 The insert belongs to the editor of the Waugh letters, Mark Amory (see next note).

162 Mark Amory (ed.), *The Letters of Evelyn Waugh* (Penguin, 1982), Evelyn Waugh to Nancy Mitford, 1 September 1955.

163 Ibid.

164 McKibbin, *Classes and Cultures*, p. 531.

165 Quoted ibid., p. 386.

166 Ibid., pp. 485–6; see also Jeremy Lewis, *Penguin Special: The Life and Times of Allen Lane* (Allen Lane, 2005).

167 Tawney's article, 'A National College of All Souls', appeared in the *TES* on 22 February 1917. It is reproduced in Tawney, *The Attack*, pp. 29–34. This quotation is from p. 30.

168 Tawney, 'Some Reflections of a Soldier', ibid., p. 22.

169 Tawney, 'A National College of All Souls', ibid., p. 34.

170 Hoggart, *The Uses of Literacy*, pp. 320–21.

171 See his conversation with John Carver in the appendix to the 1992 Penguin edition of *The Uses of Literacy*, p. 387.

172 Ibid., p. 332.

173 Hennessy, *Never Again*, p. 313.

174 Hoggart, *The Uses of Literacy*, p. 193.

175 Ibid., pp. 322–3.

176 Ibid., p. 292.

177 Ibid.

178 Ibid.

179 Ibid., p. 296.

180 Ibid.

181 Ibid., p. 293.

182 Colin Seymour-Ure, *The British Press and Broadcasting since 1945* (Blackwell, 1991), p. 16.

183 Ibid., p. 17.

184 Ibid., p. 16.

185 It was Mrs Thatcher's first government that finally abolished all exchange controls in 1979.

186 Seymour-Ure, *The British Press and Broadcasting since 1945*, p. 16.

187 Ibid., p. 1.

188 McKibbin, *Classes and Cultures*, p. 503.

189 Ibid., pp. 503–4.

190 Ibid., p. 419.

191 Seymour-Ure, *The British Press and Broadcasting since 1945*, p. 76.

192 Ibid., p. 136.

193 McKibbin, *Classes and Cultures*, pp. 419, 421.

194 Seymour-Ure, *The British Press and Broadcasting since 1945*, p. 1.

195 McKibbin, *Classes and Cultures*, p. 468.

196 All the theme tunes I have mentioned (and more) were collected together in 1982 and published as a long-playing record by the BBC as part of their sixtieth anniversary celebrations. *On the Air: 60 Years of BBC Theme Music*, BBC Records, REP 454 MONO/STEREO (BBC Enterprises, 1982).

197 McKibbin, *Classes and Cultures*, p. 411.

198 *The Greatest Fifties Collection* (EMI Records, 2001).

199 Jo Rice, Tim Rice, Paul Gambaccini and Mike Reid, *The Guinness Book of British Hit Singles* (Guinness Superlative, 1983), p. 289.

200 McKibbin, *Classes and Cultures*, p. 457.

201 Humphrey Carpenter, *The Envy of the World: Fifty Years of the BBC Third Programme and Radio 3* (Weidenfeld & Nicolson, 1996), p. 134.

202 Ibid., p. 26.

203 John Freeman, *Face to Face* (BBC Books, 1989), p. 131.

204 Ibid., p. 126.

205 McKibbin, *Classes and Cultures*, p. 402.

206 Carpenter, *The Envy of the World*, pp. 8–9.

207 Asa Briggs, *The Golden Age of Wireless* (Macmillan, 1965), p. 55.

208 Charles Stuart (ed.), *The Reith Diaries* (Collins, 1975), p. 475, entry for 18 April 1951.

209 Quoted in Carpenter, *The Envy of the World*, p. 9. Drawn from an interview with Haley conducted by Frank Gillard in 1978.

210 'The Head of His Profession', *New Statesman and Nation*, 6 February 1954. It is reproduced in *New Statesman Profiles* (Readers' Union, 1958), pp. 35–41.

211 Carpenter, *The Envy of the World*, p. 109.

212 Seymour-Ure, *The British Press and Broadcasting since 1945*, p. 164.

213 Ibid., p. 76.

214 Peter Lewis, *The Fifties* (Heinemann, 1978), p. 208.

215 Seymour-Ure, *The British Press and Broadcasting since 1945*, p. 164.

216 Ibid., p. 166.

217 David Butler, *British General Elections since 1945* (Blackwell, 1989), p. 2.

218 Seymour-Ure, *The British Press and Broadcasting since 1945*, pp. 166–7.

219 Michael Cockerell, *Live from Number 10: The Inside Story of Prime Ministers and Television* (Faber, 1988), pp. 11–13; Seymour-Ure, *The British Press and Broadcasting since 1945*, p. 166.

220 'The Goons', *Observer*, 23 December 1956, reproduced in Robert Low (ed.), *The Observer Book of Profiles* (W. H. Allen, 1991), pp. 322–4.

221 'Tony Hancock', *Observer*, 30 March 1960, reproduced ibid., pp. 333–6; Chris Bumstead, *Hancock's Half Hour* (BBC Books, 1987), p. 13.

222 For a taste of the scripts and short biographies of the main characters see Spike Milligan, *The Goon Show Scripts* (Sphere, 1973); see also Carpenter, *That Was Satire That Was*, p. 54.

223 Davison, *Orwell's England*, p. 254.

224 Hoggart, *The Uses of Literacy*, p. 327.

225 Charles Quest-Ritson, *The English Garden: A Social History* (Viking, 2001), p. 256.

226 Ibid., p. 241.

227 Ibid., p. 253.

228 Ibid., p. 256.

229 Hilary Kingsley and Geoff Tibballs, *Box of Delights: The Golden Years of Television* (Macmillan, 1989), p. 59.

230 Walter Bagehot, *The English Constitution* (Kegan Paul, Trench, Trubner, 1891 [1867]), p. 38.

231 Opie, *The 1950s Scrapbook*, pp. 12–13.

232 Kingsley and Tibballs, *Box of Delights*, p. 36; for the foundation of *Do It Yourself* magazine, ibid.

233 Asa Briggs, *Michael Young, Social Entrepreneur* (Palgrave, 2001), pp. 149–51.

234 B. W. Clapp, *An Environmental History of Britain since the Industrial Revolution* (Longman, 1994), p. 17.

235 Ibid., p. 18.

236 Halsey, *No Discouragement*, pp. 153–4.

237 In many a conversation over the past quarter of a century.

238 Graham Harvey, *The Killing of the Countryside* (Vintage, 1998), p. 22.

239 Ibid., p. 245.

240 Rachel Carson, *Silent Spring* (Houghton Mifflin, 1962).

241 Letter from Brian O'Leary, 30 November 2001.

242 Ibid.

243 Clapp, *An Environmental History of Britain*, p. 43.

244 For Monet see Peter Ackroyd, *London: The Biography* (Vintage, 2001), p. 436; for the Hurd quote in the footnote see Douglas Hurd, *Memoirs* (Little, Brown, 2003), p. 91.

245 Clapp, *An Environmental History of Britain*, p. 44.

246 Ibid.

247 Ackroyd, *London*, p. 434.

248 Clapp, *An Environmental History of Britain*, pp. 44–5.

249 Ibid., p. 244.

250 Ibid., pp. 50–51.

251 Nicholas Whittaker, *Platform Souls: The Trainspotter as Twentieth-Century Hero* (Gollancz, 1995).

252 The Departmental Committee on Air Pollution, *Interim Report* (HMSO, 1953), p. 25.

253 *A Plan for the Modernisation and Re-equipment of British Railways* (British Transport Commission, 1955).

254 O. S. Nock, *The Last Years of British Railways Steam: Reflections, Ten Years After* (David and Charles, 1978), p. 13.

255 House of Commons Official Report, 3 February 1955, col. 1328.

256 E. C. Loft, 'One Big Row: Government and the Railways, 1951–64', unpublished PhD thesis, Queen Mary and Westfield, University of London, 1999. See the extended version of Dr Loft's thesis *Government, Railways and the Modernization of Britain* (Routledge, 2006).

257 'Millions for Cinderella', *The Economist*, 29 January 1955.

258 Walter C. Patterson, *Nuclear Power* (Penguin, 1976), pp. 218–33.

259 Jane Lewis, *Women in Britain since 1945* (Blackwell, 1992), pp. 78–80.

260 Ben Pimlott, *The Queen: Elizabeth II and the Monarchy*, Golden Jubilee Edition (Harper-Collins, 2001), pp. 175–81.

261 *Social Insurance and Allied Services. Report by Sir William Beveridge* (HMSO, 1942), p. 53.

262 Lewis, *Women in Britain since 1945*, p. 21.

263 Grace Davie, *Religion in Britain since 1945: Believing Without Belonging* (Blackwell, 1994).

264 Peter Brierley, 'Religion', in Halsey and Webb, *Twentieth-Century British Social Trends*, pp. 650–51.

265 Ronald A. Knox, *Caliban in Grub Street* (Sheed and Ward, 1930), pp. 2–3.
266 Ibid., p. 3.
267 Brierley, 'Religion', p. 657.
268 Ibid., pp. 654–5.
269 'Christianity and Education', in Michael Ramsey, *Durham Essays and Addresses* (SPCK, 1956), pp. 49–50.
270 Ibid., p. 53.
271 Dennis Sewell, *Catholics: Britain's Largest Minority* (Penguin, 2002), p. 2. See also the special report on 'Britain's Top 100 Lay Catholics' in *The Tablet*, 18 March 2006, pp. 25–32.
272 McKibbin, *Classes and Cultures*, pp. 281–2.
273 Ibid., p. 282.
274 E. P. Thompson, *The Making of the English Working Class* (Vintage, 1966), pp. 350–74.
275 Philip Ziegler, *Wilson, The Authorised Life* (Weidenfeld & Nicolson, 1993), pp. 2–3.
276 Kenneth O. Morgan, *Callaghan: A Life* (Oxford University Press, 1997), p. 11.
277 Kenneth Harris, *Attlee* (Weidenfeld & Nicolson, 1982), p. 564.
278 For Melbourne see *The Oxford Dictionary of Quotations*, second edition (Oxford University Press, 1953), p. 335. For Churchill on death see Mark Pottle (ed.), *Daring to Hope: The Diaries and Letters of Violet Bonham Carter* (Weidenfeld & Nicolson, 2000), pp. 230, 298.
279 McKibbin, *Classes and Cultures*, pp. 356–7.
280 Alun Chalfont, *Montgomery of Alamein* (Weidenfeld & Nicolson, 1976), p. 111. He used the phrase in what became a notorious memo, dated 15 November 1939, about the problem of venereal disease among the British Expeditionary Force in northern France.
281 Geoffrey Gorer, *Exploring English Character* (Cresset, 1955), pp. 1–11.
282 Ibid., p. 96.
283 Ibid., p. 95.
284 Ibid.
285 Ibid., p. 105.
286 McKibbin, *Classes and Cultures*, pp. 302–3.
287 David Coleman, 'Population and Family', in Halsey and Webb, *Twentieth-Century British Social Trends*, pp. 62–3.
288 I am very grateful to Professor Pat Thane for her emphasis on this neglected theme in conversation.
289 I am very grateful to my colleague at Queen Mary, Dr Dan Todman, for bringing Dr Main's paper to my attention: T. F. Main, 'Clinical Problems of Repatriates', *Journal of Mental Science*, vol. 92 (April 1947), pp. 354–63.
290 Ibid., p. 354.
291 Ibid.
292 Richard Overy, *Why the Allies Won* (Pimlico, 1996).
293 Tawney, *The Attack*, p. 180.
294 Melvyn Bragg, *Crossing the Lines* (Sceptre, 2003), p. 16.
295 The lunch took place in Victoria in what were then the magazine's offices on 30 November 2000. It was presided over by the *New Statesman*'s proprietor, Geoffrey Robinson MP.
296 R. H. Tawney, *The Radical Tradition* (Allen and Unwin, 1964), p. 172.
297 M. M. Postan, *Fact and Relevance: Essays on Historical Method* (Cambridge University Press, 1971), p. 170. Professor Postan writes that Gaitskell and he 'were prepared to sit and listen' to Tawney, 'to us the greatest living Englishman. The views he held happened to be very near to those to which Hugh was moving . . .'
298 Ross Terrill, *R. H. Tawney and His Times: Socialism as Fellowship* (Harvard University Press, 1973), p. 117.
299 Ramsey, *Durham Essays and Addresses*, p. 41.
300 Ibid., pp. 41–2.

3 The Shadow of the Bomb

1 National Archives, Public Record Office [NA, PRO], PREM 11/163 'Possible Line of Attack by Soviet Union in Europe in War', Prime Minister's Personal Minute, M.30 (c)/51, 12 November 1951.

2 Michael Caine, *What's It All About?* (Arrow, 1993), p. 78. The modern equivalent of four shillings is 20p.

3 Professor Eric Hobsbawm in conversation with Peter Hennessy, The Purcell Room, South Bank, London, 16 October 2002.

4 NA, PRO, CAB 134/940, HDC (55) 3, Cabinet Home Defence Committee, 'Fall-Out: Report of a Working Group', 8 March 1955.

5 NA, PRO, CAB 134/808, DP (54) 6, 'United Kingdom Defence Policy. Memorandum by the Chiefs of Staff,' 1 June 1954.

6 Peter Hennessy, *The Prime Minister: The Office and Its Holders since 1945* (Allen Lane, 2000), p. 204.

7 Ibid., pp. 188–95.

8 NA, PRO, PREM 5/225, 'Ministerial Appointments. Ministry of Sir Winston Churchill (Conservative). Part 3', Churchill to Woolton, 2 September 1953.

9 Max Hastings, *The Korean War* (Pan, 1988), pp. 401–4.

10 Christopher Andrew, *Secret Service: The Making of the British Intelligence Community* (Heinemann, 1985), p. 448.

11 NA, PRO, CAB 158/1, JIC (47) 7/2, 'Soviet Interests, Intentions and Capabilities – General', 6 August 1947.

12 NA, PRO, PREM 11/163, Churchill to General Kenneth McLean, Prime Minister's Personal Minute M109 c/51, 29 November 1951.

13 NA, PRO, CAB 158/11 Part I, JIC (50) 77 (Revise), 'The Likelihood of War with the Soviet Union and the Date by which the Soviet Leaders might be Prepared to Risk It', 18 August 1950.

14 NA, PRO, PREM 8/1547, 'Clandestine Use of Atomic Weapons'; see especially the identically titled brief from the Cabinet Secretary, Sir Norman Brook, 12 July 1951.

15 NA, PRO, AVIA 65/2055, 'Clandestine Introduction of Weapons into the UK: Import Research Committee', IR (50) Final, 'Ministry of Defence. Imports Research Committee. Report to the Chiefs of Staff', 2 November 1950.

16 NA, PRO, PREM 11/560, 'Clandestine Use of Atomic Weapons', Brook to Churchill, 28 March 1952.

17 NA, PRO, CAB 21/1647, 'Structure of a War Cabinet', see especially Brook's 'Note for the Record' of 14 February 1951 and 'Machinery of Supreme Control in the Event of War. Draft of a submission to be Made to the Prime Minister in Precautionary Stage if not Earlier', undated.

18 Ibid., Attlee to Shinwell (the then Minister of Defence), 12 March 1951.

19 Peter Hennessy, *Never Again: Britain, 1945–1951* (Cape, 1992), chapter 7 and pp. 245–72, 350–58, 384–90, 404–16.

20 NA, PRO, CAB 130/2, GEN 75/1, 'The Atomic Bomb. Memorandum by the Prime Minister', 28 August 1945.

21 Ibid.

22 Ibid.

23 NA, PRO, FO 800/476, 'Middle East', ME /47/1, Attlee to Bevin, 5 January 1947.

24 Ibid.

25 NA, PRO, CAB 130/2, GEN 75/1.

26 Christopher Andrew and Vasili Mitrokhin, *The Mitrokhin Archive: The KGB in Europe and the West* (Allen Lane, 1999), pp. 180–81.

27 Christopher Andrew, 'The Venona Secret', in K. G. Robertson (ed.), *War, Resistance and Intelligence: Essays in Honour of M. R. D. Foot* (Pen and Sword, 1999), p. 213.

28 Andrew and Mitrokhin, *The Mitrokhin Archive*, p. 155; Lorna Arnold, *Britain and the H-Bomb* (Palgrave, 2001), p. 23.

29 David Holloway, *Stalin and the Bomb: The Soviet Union and Atomic Energy* (Yale University Press, 1994), pp. 213–19.

30 NA, PRO, CAB 130/2, GEN 75/1.

31 Ibid.

32 NA, PRO, CAB 130/16, GEN 163, 1st Meeting, 8 January 1947, 'Confidential Annex Minute 1. Research in Atomic Weapons'.

33 Brian Cathcart, *Test of Greatness: Britain's Struggle for the Atomic Bomb* (John Murray, 1994), pp. 236–60.

34 Peter Hennessy, *What the Papers Never Said* (Politics Association, 1985), pp. 19–23.

35 The Earl of Birkenhead, *The Prof in Two Worlds: The Official Life of Professor F. A. Lindemann, Viscount Cherwell* (Collins, 1961), pp. 211–68; John Colville, *The Churchillians* (Weidenfeld & Nicolson, 1981), pp. 31, 37, 40.

36 NA, PRO, PREM 11/292, 'Atomic Bomb test on Monte Bello', Cherwell to Churchill, 21 November 1951.

37 Ibid., Cherwell, 'Atomic Energy. Summary', 21 November 1951.

38 NA, PRO, PREM 11/297, 'Prime Minister's concern that Parliament had not been informed about atomic research funding', Prime Minister's Personal Minute, M140 c/51, Churchill to Bridges, 8 December 1951.

39 Ibid., Bridges, 'Atomic Energy Expenditure', Annex A, 'Total (Net) Expenditure on Atomic Energy', Bridges to Churchill, 12 December 1951.

40 Ibid., Annex C, 'Disclosures of Information about Atomic Energy'.

41 Ibid., 'Atomic Energy Expenditure'.

42 Ibid., Annex A, 'Total (Net) Expenditure on Atomic Energy' and Annex B, 'Ministry of Supply. Estimate 1951/2. As Revised December 1951'.

43 Ibid., 'Atomic Energy Expenditure'.

44 Ibid., Cherwell to Churchill, 21 December 1951.

45 Ibid.

46 NA, PRO, PREM 11/292, Prime Minister's Personal Minute, M47 c51, Churchill to Cherwell, 15 November 1951.

47 For the Fulton speech, its making and its delivery see John Ramsden, *Man of the Century: Winston Churchill and His Legend since 1945* (HarperCollins, 2002), pp. 158–65.

48 Ibid., p. 81.

49 Ibid., p. 162.

50 NA, PRO, PREM 11/292, Churchill to Cherwell, 15 November 1951.

51 Margaret Gowing, *Independence and Deterrence: Britain and Atomic Energy 1945–1952*, vol. I: *Policy Making* (Macmillan, 1974), pp. 1–2.

52 NA, PRO, PREM 11/292, Churchill to Cherwell, 15 November 1951.

53 The Quebec Agreement is reproduced as Appendix 4 and the Hyde Park aide-memoire as Appendix 8 in Margaret Gowing, *Britain and Atomic Energy, 1939–1945* (Macmillan, 1964), pp. 439–47. For Senator Brian McMahon's ignorance of these documents see Gowing, *Independence and Deterrence*, vol. I, pp. 107–8.

54 NA, PRO, PREM 11/292, Cherwell to Churchill, 21 November 1951.

55 Ibid., 'Atomic Energy Summary'.

56 Ibid.

57 NA, PRO, PREM 11/565, 'Record of Events Leading to Dropping of Bombs on Hiroshima and Nagasaki', Cherwell to Churchill, 28 January 1953. Churchill had asked Cherwell to prepare a note on, in Cherwell's words, 'the principal events leading up to the dropping of the atomic bombs at Hiroshima and Nagasaki'.

58 NA, PRO, PREM 11/292, 'Atomic Energy. Relations with America'.

59 Ibid.

60 Cathcart, *Test of Greatness*, p. 109.

61 Ibid., pp. 98–107.

62 NA, PRO, PREM 11/292, 'Atomic Energy. Relations with America'.

63 Ibid.

64 Ibid., 'Production in the U.K.'.

65 NA, PRO, CAB 130/2, GEN 75, 15th Meeting, 25 October 1946.

66 NA, PRO, PREM 11/292, 'Production in the U.K.'.

67 Ibid.

68 Ibid., Churchill to Cherwell, 15 November 1951.

69 'Testing the First Bomb', Cherwell to Churchill, 21 November 1951.

70 House of Commons Official Report, 23 October 1952, col. 1268.

71 NA, PRO, PREM 11/292, 'Testing the First Bomb'.

72 Ibid., Cherwell to Churchill, 14 December 1951.

73 Alec Guinness, *Positively Final Appearance: A Journal, 1996–1998* (Hamish Hamilton, 1999), pp. 183–4.

74 *Peace News*, 10 August 1945, quoted in Christopher Driver, *The Disarmers: A Study in Protest* (Hodder and Stoughton, 1964), p. 17.

75 Driver, *The Disarmers*, p. 16.

76 George Orwell, 'London Letter', *Partisan Review*, Fall 1945, reproduced in Sonia Orwell and Ian Angus (eds.), *The Collected Essays, Journalism and Letters of George Orwell*, vol. III: *As I Please, 1943–1945* (Penguin, 1970), p. 452. I am grateful to my research student Matthew Grant for bringing this passage to my attention.

77 Driver, *The Disarmers*, p. 17.

78 For his most fluent observations, see Ronald Knox, *God and the Atom* (Sheed and Ward, 1945), pp. 9, 17, 57–8, 86–7, 142–3. For Knox's disappointment with its reception, see Evelyn Waugh, *Ronald Knox* (Chapman and Hall, 1959), pp. 303–4.

79 For the PN Committee see NA, PRO, CAB 134/3120 and Peter Hennessy, *The Secret State: Whitehall and the Cold War* (Penguin, 2003), pp. 72–4.

80 Cathcart, *Test of Greatness*, pp. 26–47.

81 Andrew Boyle, *No Passing Glory: The Full and Authentic Biography of Group Captain Cheshire, VC, DSO, DFC* (Collins, 1955), p. 261.

82 Tony Benn, *Years of Hope: Diaries, Papers and Letters, 1940–1962*, edited by Ruth Winstone (Hutchinson, 1994), pp. 97–8.

83 Ibid., p. 98.

84 Richard Hoggart, *A Sort of Clowning: Life and Times*, vol. II: *1940–1959* (Chatto and Windus, 1990), p. 195.

85 Driver, *The Disarmers*, p. 18.

86 Hennessy, *What the Papers Never Said*, pp. 23–7.

87 Hennessy, *The Secret State*, pp. 25–6.

88 NA, PRO, CAB 158/4, JIC (48) 26 (0), 'Russian Interests, Intentions and Capabilities', 23 July 1948.

89 House of Lords Official Report, 9 November 1949, col. 427.

90 NA, PRO, CAB 21/8719, 'Consultation with Leaders of the Parliamentary Opposition (Policy)', 'Memorandum on Defence by Mr Churchill', 10 May 1949. The minutes and memoranda of GEN 293, the Cabinet Committee on Defence Discussions, are preserved in CAB 130/47.

91 Francis Williams, *A Prime Minister Remembers* (Heinemann, 1961), p. 172.

92 NA, PRO, CAB 158/4, JIC (48) 26 (0). See also the briefing given to the Chiefs of Staff by General Sir Brian Robertson, the Military Governor and Commander-in-Chief of the British Armed Forces in Germany, on 12 July 1948 (NA, PRO, DEFE 4/14, COS (48), 97th Meeting).

93 Williams, *A Prime Minister Remembers*, p. 173.

94 Percy Cradock, *Know Your Enemy: How the Joint Intelligence Committee Saw the World* (John Murray, 2002), pp. 79–80.

95 NA, PRO, CAB 130/38, GEN 241, 4th Meeting, 22 July 1948.

96 NA, PRO, CAB 175/1, 'Government War Book, November 1948'.

97 As the Civil Defence Act 1948 it remained Whitehall's legal basis for over fifty years until, in 2002–3, new Civil Contingencies legislation was drafted. See Hennessy, *The Secret State*, 'Epilogue: The Safety of the Realm: Retrospect and Prospect', pp. 211–23.

98 Ibid., pp. 101, 126. See also NA, PRO, AIR 20/11367, 'Air Ministry. Notice to Directors and Heads of Division. Routine War Planning'. Extract from the minutes of the Defence Transition Committee Meeting, 5 January 1949. The full DTC minutes have yet to be declassified.

99 NA, PRO, CAB 21/1885, 'Situation in Berlin (June–July 1948)', Brook to Attlee, 29 June 1948.

100 Hennessy, *The Secret State*, pp. 83–97; NA, PRO, CAB 120/30, PV (50) 11, 'Committee on Positive Vetting. Report', 27 October 1950.

101 NA, PRO, PREM 8/1405, Part 1, 'Main File: Korea', confidential annex on 'Situation in Korea' from the Chiefs of Staff Meeting, COS (50) 96th Meeting of 27 June 1950.

102 NA, PRO, PREM 8/1355, Part 2, 'Civil Defence Expenditure', 1948–1951, Chuter Ede to Attlee, 4 July 1950.

103 Ibid., 'Civil Defence', 3 July 1950.

104 NA, PRO, CAB 130/2, GEN 75/1, 'The Atomic Bomb. Memorandum by the Prime Minister', 28 August 1945.

105 NA, PRO, PREM 8/1355, Part 2, 'Civil Defence', 3 July 1950.

106 Cradock, *Know Your Enemy*, p. 92.

107 Colin Seymour-Ure, 'British "War Cabinets" in Limited Wars: Korea, Suez and the Falklands', *Public Administration*, vol. 62 (summer 1984), pp. 181–200.

108 NA, PRO, PREM 8/1405, Part 1, DO (50), 12th Meeting, 6 July 1950.

109 Hennessy, *The Secret State*, pp. 91–6.

110 Ibid., p. 97.

111 Andrew and Mitrokhin, *The Mitrokhin Archive*, p. 188.

112 PRO, CAB 120/30, PV (50) 11; Andrew, 'The Venona Secret'.

113 Thomas Powers, *Intelligence Wars* (New York Review of Books, 2004), pp. 110–13.

114 PRO, CAB 130/20, GEN 183, 6th Meeting, 13 November 1950.

115 Hennessy, *The Secret State*, pp. 93, 98.

116 Chapman Pincher, *Inside Story* (Sidgwick and Jackson, 1978).

117 Stephen Guy, '"Someone Presses a Button and it's Goodbye Sally": *Seven Days to Noon* and the Threat of the Atomic Bomb', in Alan Burton, Tim O'Sullivan and Paul Weller (eds.), *The Family Way: The Boulting Brothers and British Film Culture* (Flicks Books, 2000), pp. 143–54.

118 Stephen Guy, '"High Treason" (1951): Britain's Cold War Fifth Column', *Historical Journal of Film, Radio and Television*, vol. 13, no. 1 (1993), pp. 35–47.

119 Guy, '"Someone Presses a Button . . .", p. 143.

120 Ibid., p. 147.

121 NA, PRO, CAB 130/41, GEN 253, 1st Meeting, 1 October 1948.

122 NA, PRO, PREM 11/294, 'Possible Effect of Atomic Bombing', Maxwell Fyfe to Churchill, 4 June 1952.

123 Ibid., Prime Minister's Personal Minute, M.312/52, Churchill to Cherwell, 8 June 1952.

124 Ibid., Churchill to Private Office, 3 July 1952.

125 NA, PRO, PREM 11/294.

126 Ibid. Maxwell Fyfe mentions the chief scientist's involvement in his covering note to the Prime Minister.

127 Ibid.

128 Ibid.

129 Ibid.

130 Ibid.

131 Ibid.

132 Ibid., Churchill to Cherwell, 8 June 1952.

133 Cathcart, *Test of Greatness*, p. 39.

134 Arnold, *Britain and the H-Bomb*, p. 234.

135 NA, PRO, PREM 11/294, Cherwell to Churchill, 1 July 1952.

136 Ibid.

137 Arnold, *Britain and the H-Bomb*, p. 17.

138 Hennessy, *The Secret State*, pp. 131–46.

139 NA, PRO, CAB 134/942 HDC (53) 5 (Revise), Home Defence Committee Working Party, 'Estimates of Casualties and House Damage. Note by the Home Office', May 1953.

140 Hennessy, *Never Again*, p. 99.

141 See Hennessy, *The Secret State*, p. 138.

142 Alec Cairncross (ed.), *The Robert Hall Diaries, 1954–1961* (Unwin Hyman, 1991), entry for 20 January 1955.

143 House of Commons Official Report, 5 April 1954, cols. 46–7.

144 Arnold, *Britain and the H-Bomb*, pp. 19–20.

145 For an audit of CND's effectiveness on civil defence see Matthew Grant, 'The Impact of CND on Civil and Home Defence Planning, 1948–66', unpublished MA dissertation, Department of History, Queen Mary, University of London, September 2002.

146 Andrew Lycett, *Ian Fleming* (Phoenix, 1996), pp. 222, 398. For Godfrey's gifts see Cradock, *Know Your Enemy*, pp. 13–14.

147 Jeremy Black, *The Politics of James Bond: From Fleming's Novels to the Big Screen* (Praeger, 2001).

148 Ian Fleming, *Casino Royale* (Cape, 1953).

149 Mark Amory (ed.), *The Letters of Ann Fleming* (Collins Harvill, 1985), p. 108; Lycett, *Ian Fleming*, pp. 216–19.

150 Philip Knightley, *Philby: The Life and Views of the KGB Masterspy* (André Deutsch, 1988), pp. 179–218.

151 George Blake, *No other Choice: An Autobiography* (Cape, 1990), pp. 121–49.

152 NA, PRO, CAB 158/1, JIC (47) 7/2, Final, 'Soviet Interests, Intentions and Capabilities – General', 6 August 1947.

153 Fleming, *Casino Royale*, p. 10

154 NA, PRO, CAB 158/1, JIC (47) 7/2, Final, 'Soviet Interests, Intentions and Capabilities – General', 6 August 1947. See also Klaus Dodds, 'Licensed to Stereotype: James Bond, Popular Geopolitics and the Spectre of Balkanism', *Geopolitics*, vol. 8, no. 2 (2003), pp. 125–54.

155 Ian Fleming, *From Russia With Love* (Cape, 1957).

156 David Cannadine, *In Churchill's Shadow: Confronting the Past in Modern Britain* (Allen Lane, 2002), pp. 279–80.

157 Ian Fleming, *Dr No* (Cape, 1957); Lycett, *Ian Fleming*, pp. 315–17, 412, 430–1, 446.

158 Peter Clarke, *Hope and Glory: Britain 1900–1990* (Allen Lane, 1996), pp. 274–5; Richard Weight, *Patriots: National Identity in Britain 1940–2000* (Macmillan, 2002), pp. 396–7; Nick Yapp, *1960s. The Hulton Getty Picture Collection* (Konemann, 1998), p. 153.

159 Black, *The Politics of James Bond*, p. xiii; see also Klaus Dodds, 'Screening Geopolitics: James Bond and the Early Cold War Films (1962–1967)', *Geopolitics*, vol. 10 (2005), pp. 266–89.

160 Private information.

161 Private information.

162 A phrase I used when I wrote *The Times'* first leader in the edition of 21 March 1983 to mark the burial of Donald Maclean in English soil in Buckinghamshire. (I did not know, at that stage, that John Cairncross, a Scot, was the 'Fifth Man'.)

163 See pp. 159–60.

164 NA, PRO, CAB 175/1, 'Government War Book, November 1948'.

165 NA, PRO, KV4/245, 'Policy; Setting up of Detention Camps in the UK for the Detention

of British Subjects and the Internment of Aliens in the Event of an Emergency, 1948–1954', 'Internment Camps in War. Summary of Agreed Plans as of 9 February 1954'.

166 NA, PRO, CAB 130/37, 'The Communist Party. Its Strengths and Activities: Its Penetration of Government Organisations and of the Trade Unions', attached as an appendix to a report prepared by a working party on 'Security Measures against Encroachments by Communists or Fascists in the United Kingdom' for ministers on GEN 226, the Cabinet Committee on European Policy, and circulated to them on 26 May 1948.

167 Ibid.

168 NA, PRO, HO 45/25577, 25578, 25579, 'Disturbances: Communist Party of Great Britain: Reports on Aims, Policy, Activities and Meetings, 1948–1954'. See especially the Metropolitan Police Special Branch fortnightly summaries for the Home Office and MI5.

169 NA, PRO, CAB 130/37, 'The Communist Party'.

170 Ibid. For an example of a revealing personal file see NA, PRO KV 2/1759, 'Dobb, Maurice Herbert', 1951–4.

171 NA, PRO, CAB 130/37, 'The Communist Party'.

172 David Caute, The Great Fear (Weidenfeld & Nicolson, 1978); Richard Rovere, Senator Joe McCarthy (Meridian, 1960); Paul Rogin, The Intellectuals and McCarthy (MIT Press, 1966).

173 Peter Hennessy and Gail Brownfeld, 'Britain's Cold War Security Purge: The Origins of Positive Vetting', Historical Journal, vol. 25, no. 4 (1982), pp. 965–73.

174 Walter Goodman, The Committee: The Extraordinary Career of the House Committee on Un-American Activities (Secker and Warburg, 1969).

175 Hennessy and Brownfeld, 'Britain's Cold War Security Purge', p. 965.

176 Edward Shils, The Torment of Secrecy (Heinemann, 1956), pp. 48–9.

177 Christopher Andrew and Oleg Gordievsky, KGB: The Inside Story of Its Foreign Operations from Lenin to Gorbachev (Hodder, 1990), p. 360.

178 House of Commons Official Report, 25 October 1955, cols. 2029–30.

179 Andrew and Gordievsky, KGB, p. 361.

180 NA, PRO, CAB 129/78, CP (55) 161, 'Disappearance of Two Foreign Office Officials, Burgess and Maclean', 19 October 1955.

181 NA, PRO, CAB 128/29, CM (55) 36, 20 October 1955. See also Peter Hennessy and Kathleen Townsend, 'The Documentary Spoor of Burgess and Maclean', Intelligence and National Security, vol. 2, no. 2 (April 1987), pp. 291–301.

182 Peter Hennessy, Whitehall (Heinemann, 1989), p. 543; Hennessy, The Secret State, p. 98.

183 Colville is quoted in Andrew Boyle, The Climate of Treason (Hodder and Stoughton, 1980), p. 422; see also Colville, The Churchillians, p. 60.

184 Rovere, Senator Joe McCarthy, p. 10.

185 Martin Gilbert, Winston S. Churchill, vol. VIII: Never Despair, 1945–1965 (Heinemann, 1988), p. 836.

186 Quoted in Hennessy and Brownfeld, 'Britain's Cold War Security Purge', p. 972.

187 House of Commons Official Report, 12 May 1949, col. 29.

188 John Mahon, Harry Pollitt: A Biography (Lawrence and Wishart, 1976), pp. 314–15.

189 Gilbert, Never Despair, p. 403.

190 'Pollitt tells Russians his campaign plan', Daily Express, 10 October 1952.

191 NA, PRO, PREM 11/24, 'Speech by Harry Pollitt, Leader of UK Communist Party, on Infiltration of Trade Unions'.

192 Andrew and Gordievsky, KGB, pp. xxiv, 243.

193 The British Road to Socialism (CPGB, 1951).

194 NA, PRO, PREM 11/24, Liddell to Montague Browne, 27 October 1952.

195 Ibid.

196 For a vivid account by one of the beneficiaries of this swing of fortunes see Janet Morgan (ed.), The Backbench Diaries of Richard Crossman (Hamish Hamilton/Cape, 1981), entries for 26 September to 3 October 1952, pp. 139–54.

197 NA, PRO, PREM 11/24, Liddell to Montague Browne, 27 October 1952.
198 NA, PRO, CAB 130/37, 'The Communist Party'.
199 NA, PRO, PREM 11/1238, 'Communist Influence in Industry and Trades Unions', Brook to Eden, 28 April 1956.
200 NA, PRO, PREM 11/372, 'Defence of UK from Risk of Airborne Attack', 'Possibility of Airborne Attack on the United Kingdom'. Memorandum by the Chiefs of Staff for the Prime Minister, 10 April 1953.
201 NA, PRO, PREM 11/760, 'Soviet Apparatus for Listening to Conversations in Room without Wire Connection', Cherwell to Churchill, 8 October 1952; Churchill to Alexander, 9 October 1952.
202 Ibid., 'Russian Eavesdropping', Alexander to Churchill, 15 July 1954.
203 Peter Hennessy, *Cabinet* (Blackwell, 1986), p. 51.
204 Conversation with Lord Home, 6 February 1985.
205 Gilbert, *Never Despair*, p. 598.
206 Hennessy, *Never Again*, pp. 409–16.
207 Cairncross, *The Robert Hall Diaries, 1947–1953*, entry for 7 November 1951.
208 Hennessy, *The Secret State*, pp. 12–34.
209 House of Commons Official Report, 5 March 1952, col. 435.
210 Minute 5 of the Cabinet Defence Committee meeting of D (53), 4th Meeting, 6 March 1953, in NA, PRO, PREM 11/372.
211 Ibid., 'Possibility of Airborne Attack on the United Kingdom' Memorandum by the Chiefs of Staff for the Prime Minister, 10 April 1953.
212 Ibid.
213 Shils, *The Torment of Secrecy*, p. 67.
214 John Colville, *The Fringes of Power: Downing Street Diaries, 1939–1955* (Hodder, 1985), p. 673, entry for 31 July to 4 August 1953.
215 House of Commons Official Report, 25 February 1954, col. 587.
216 House of Commons Official Report, 5 April 1954, col. 60.
217 Geoffrey Best, *Churchill: A Study in Greatness* (Hambledon and London, 2001), p. 290.
218 Driver, *The Disarmers*, p. 21.
219 NA, PRO, PREM 11/292; Churchill initialled the draft on 16 February 1952.
220 Ibid., 'Deception in Support of Operation "Hurricane"', Alexander to Churchill, 9 April 1952.
221 Ibid.
222 Roger Hesketh, *Fortitude: The D-Day Deception Campaign* (St Ermin's Press, 1999); for the general history of Second World War deception see Michael Howard, *British Intelligence in the Second World War*, vol. V: *Strategic Deception* (HMSO, 1990).
223 NA, PRO, PREM 11/292, Alexander to Churchill, 9 April 1952.
224 Ibid.
225 Ibid., 'Deception in Support of Operation "Hurricane"', Alexander to Churchill, 6 June 1952.
226 Ibid., Alexander to Churchill, 6 June 1952.
227 Ibid., Churchill to Jacob, 8 June 1952.
228 Ibid., Jacob to Churchill, 9 June 1952.
229 Lord Moran, *Winston Churchill: The Struggle for Survival, 1940–1965* (Constable, 1966), p. 366, diary entry for 22 February 1952.
230 NA, PRO, PREM 11/292, Drew to Colville, 15 August 1952.
231 Ibid., Prime Minister's Personal Minute, M.439/52, Churchill to Brook, 16 August 1952.
232 Ibid.
233 John L. Garbutt, 'Tactical Atom Bomb Exercise Planned', *Sunday Express*, 17 August 1952. For details of the assembly of the bomb in Australia see Cathcart, *Test of Greatness*, pp. 202–35.
234 NA, PRO, PREM 11/292, '"APEX" COMMITTEE', Brook to Churchill, 8 April 1952.
235 Ibid., Brook to Churchill, 18 August 1952.

236 A phrase she used in conversation with Tam Dalyell, MP, when she agreed to see him during the Falklands War of 1982. Mr Dalyell told me.
237 NA, PRO, PREM 11/292, 'House of Commons. 27 May 1952. Adjournment Debate on the Atomic Bomb Test in Australia', Ministry of Supply Brief, undated, but reached the Prime Minister on 26 May 1952.
238 House of Commons Official Report, 27 May 1952, col. 1326.
239 NA, PRO, PREM 11/292, Ministry of Supply Brief.
240 House of Commons Official Report, 28 March 1950, col. 201.
241 House of Commons Official Report, 27 May 1952, col. 1325.
242 NA, PRO, CAB 134/942, HDC (53) 5 (Revise), Home Defence Committee Working Party, 'Estimates of Casualties and House Damage. Note by the Home Office', May 1953.
243 NA, PRO, PREM 11/292, Ministry of Supply Brief.
244 Quoted as the frontispiece in Cathcart, *Test of Greatness*.
245 PRO, PREM 11/292, 'Hurricane', Cherwell to Churchill, 17 September 1952.
246 Ibid. Churchill's response is scrawled beneath Cherwell's minute and dated 20 September.
247 Margaret Gowing, *Independence and Deterrence*, vol. II: *Policy Execution* (Macmillan, 1974), pp. 494–5.
248 See the map of the Monte Bello islands in Cathcart, *Test of Greatness*, p. xiv.
249 Ibid., p. 261.
250 Anthony Montague Browne, *Long Sunset: Memoirs of Winston Churchill's Last Private Secretary* (Cassell, 1995).
251 Quoted in Gilbert, *Never Despair*, p. 764.
252 Cathcart, *Test of Greatness*, p. 258.
253 Ibid., p. 270. See also, for comparative purposes, the 'Summary of Nuclear Weapons Tests, 1945–58', in Arnold, *Britain and the H-Bomb*, pp. 234–6.
254 House of Commons Official Report, 23 October 1952, col. 1269.
255 Ibid.
256 Cathcart, *Test of Greatness*, p. 265.
257 NA, PRO, AIR 8/2309, 'Operation Hurricane, Director's Report'.
258 Cathcart, *Test of Greatness*, p. 265.
259 NA, PRO, DEFE 21/62, 'USSR: Atomic Energy', Soviet Atomic Capabilities. Appreciation for SACEUR, 14 November 1952.
260 Ibid., 'Atomic Energy Intelligence', Turney to the Secretary of the JIC, 23 July 1952.
261 Cathcart, *Test of Greatness*, p. 273; Humphrey Winn, *The RAF Strategic Nuclear Deterrent Forces: The Origins, Roles and Deployment, 1946–69 – A Documentary History* (HMSO, 1994), p. 92.
262 House of Commons Official Report, 23 October 1952, col. 1269.

4 The Natural Coalitionist

1 John Colville, *The Fringes of Power: Downing Street Diaries, 1939–1955* (Hodder, 1985), p. 647.
2 Mark Amory (ed.), *The Letters of Evelyn Waugh* (Penguin, 1982), p. 538.
3 Martin Gilbert, *Winston S. Churchill*, vol. VIII: *Never Despair, 1945–1965* (Heinemann, 1988), p. 744.
4 Ibid., p. 1002.
5 Peter Quennell, *The Wanton Chase: An Autobiography from 1939* (Collins, 1980), p. 108. Churchill addressed this remark to Quennell while staying with Lord Beaverbrook at Cap d'Ail in the South of France.
6 Gilbert, *Never Despair*, p. 779.
7 Ibid., p. 809, and Randolph S. Churchill (ed.), *The Unwritten Alliance* (Cassell, 1961), pp. 24–5.

8 House of Commons Official Report, 11 February 1952, col. 962.

9 Gilbert, *Never Despair*, p. 733.

10 Ibid., p. 816.

11 Colville, *The Fringes of Power*, entry for 31 July to 4 August 1953.

12 Lord Moran, *Winston Churchill: The Struggle for Survival, 1940–1965* (Constable, 1966), p. 444, diary entry for 25 July 1953.

13 Colin Seymour-Ure, *The British Press and Broadcasting since 1945* (Blackwell, 1991), p. 28.

14 *Daily Mirror*, 25 October 1951.

15 David Butler, *British General Elections since 1945* (Blackwell, 1989), p. 11.

16 Gilbert, *Never Despair*, p. 648.

17 Paul Addison, *Churchill on the Home Front, 1900–1955* (Cape, 1992), pp. 387, 439.

18 Gilbert, *Never Despair*, p. 510.

19 bid., p. 643.

20 Ibid., p. 648.

21 Addison, *Churchill on the Home Front*, p. 406; for Mossadegh and Anglo-Iranian see James Bamberg, *British Petroleum and Global Oil, 1950–1975: The Challenge of Nationalism* (Cambridge University Press, 2000), pp. 20–21.

22 Addison, *Churchill on the Home Front*, p. 398.

23 Ibid., p. 403.

24 Mark Pottle (ed.), *Daring to Hope: The Diaries and Letters of Violet Bonham Carter, 1946–1969* (Weidenfeld & Nicolson, 2000), p. 101, letter from Violet Bonham Carter to Winston Churchill, 18 October 1951.

25 Ibid., diary entry for 15 October 1951.

26 Gilbert, *Never Despair*, p. 646.

27 Addison, *Churchill on the Home Front*, pp. 403–4.

28 Ibid., p. 434.

29 Gilbert, *Never Despair*, p. 646.

30 Pottle, *Daring to Hope*, p. 100, entry for 15 October 1951.

31 House of Commons Official Report, 23 February 1955, col. 1277. For Churchill and trains see Roy Jenkins, *Churchill* (Macmillan, 2001), p. 794. Plate 66 shows Churchill 'working on his famous wartime train'.

32 Pottle, *Daring to Hope*, p. 101, entry for 15 October 1951.

33 Ibid., p. 103.

34 Ibid.

35 Ibid., p. 105, entry for 7 December 1951.

36 Gilbert, *Never Despair*, p. 655; Peter Barberis, *Liberal Lion: Jo Grimond – A Political Life* (I. B. Tauris, 2005), p. 52.

37 Pottle, *Daring to Hope*, p. 105. Pottle describes this only as a 'late November' entry.

38 Colin Clifford, *The Asquiths* (John Murray, 2003), p. 477.

39 Addison, *Churchill on the Home Front*, p. 433.

40 Butler, *British General Elections since 1945*, pp. 11–12.

41 Addison, *Churchill on the Home Front*, p. 407; Kenneth O. Morgan, *Labour in Power, 1945–1951* (Oxford University Press, 1984), p. 486.

42 Ina Zweiniger-Bargielowska, *Austerity in Britain: Rationing, Controls and Consumption, 1939–1955* (Oxford University Press, 2000), p. 255.

43 Colville, *The Fringes of Power*, p. 644, entry for 22–23 March 1952.

44 Ibid.

45 Andrew Roberts, *Eminent Churchillians* (Weidenfeld & Nicolson, 1994). See especially his chapter on Walter Monckton, pp. 243–86.

46 Addison, *Churchill on the Home Front*, p. 407.

47 Butler, *British General Elections since 1945*, p. 13.

48 Ibid.

49 Peter Hennessy, *The Prime Minister: The Office and Its Holders since 1945* (Allen Lane, 2000), pp. 187, 193.

50 John W. Wheeler-Bennett, *John Anderson, Viscount Waverley* (Macmillan, 1962), p. 352.

51 Lord Woolton, *The Memoirs of the Rt. Hon the Earl of Woolton* (Cassell, 1959), pp. 328–30; John Ramsden, *An Appetite for Power: A History of the Conservative Party since 1830* (Harper-Collins, 1998), p. 335.

52 For the internal 'overlords debate' of 1951–3 see Hennessy, *The Prime Minister*, pp. 189–95.

53 National Archives, Public Record Office [NA, PRO], PREM 5/225, 'Ministerial Appointments, Ministry of Sir Winston Churchill (Conservative)', part 3, Churchill to Bridges and Brook, 9 August 1953.

54 Iain Dale (ed.), *Conservative Party General Election Manifestos, 1900–1997* (Routledge/Politicos, 2000), pp. 93–100.

55 Ramsden, *An Appetite for Power*, p. 345.

56 *The Industrial Charter. A Statement of Conservative Industrial Policy* (Conservative and Unionist Central Office, 1947), p. 345.

57 For Lyttelton's reflections on this period see Lord Chandos, *The Memoirs of Lord Chandos* (Bodley Head, 1964), pp. 338–42.

58 John Ramsden, *The Making of Conservative Party Policy* (Longman, 1980), p. 114.

59 Ramsden, *An Appetite for Power*, p. 345.

60 Lord Chandos, *The Memoirs of Lord Chandos*, p. 343.

61 Ibid., p. 344.

62 Ibid., p. 339.

63 Ibid., p. 342.

64 Quoted in Addison, *Churchill on the Home Front*, p. 397. Dr Addison discovered Lyttelton's letter to Churchill of 26 August 1947 in the Chandos Papers at the Churchill Archives Centre in Cambridge.

65 John Boyd-Carpenter, *Way of Life* (Sidgwick and Jackson, 1980), p. 87.

66 Lord Butler, *The Art of the Possible* (Penguin, 1973), p. 158.

67 Ibid., pp. 157–8.

68 Ibid., p. 158.

69 Lord Chandos, *The Memoirs of Lord Chandos*, p. 342.

70 Alec Cairncross (ed.), *The Robert Hall Diaries, 1947–1953* (Unwin Hyman, 1989), entry for 5 November 1951.

71 Butler, *The Art of the Possible*, p. 158.

72 Gilbert, *Never Despair*, p. 656.

73 Janet Morgan (ed.), *The Backbench Diaries of Richard Crossman* (Hamish Hamilton and Jonathan Cape, 1981), entry for 31 October 1951.

74 Roberts, *Eminent Churchillians*, p. 258.

75 Lord Butler, *The Art of Memory: Friends in Perspective* (Hodder, 1982), p. 141.

76 Ibid., p. 137.

77 Ibid., p. 136.

78 Ibid.

79 Robert Neild, 'At the Treasury', in Ann Gold (ed.), *Edward Boyle: His Life by His Friends* (Macmillan, 1991), p. 86.

80 Edmund Dell, *The Chancellors: A History of the Chancellors of the Exchequer, 1945–90* (HarperCollins, 1996), p. 166.

81 See Edmund Dell, *A Hard Pounding: Politics and Economic Crisis, 1974–76* (Oxford University Press, 1991).

82 Dell, *The Chancellors*, p. 194.

83 Kenneth O. Morgan, *The People's Peace: British History, 1945–1989* (Oxford University Press, 1990), pp. 126–7.

84 Dell, *The Chancellors*, p. 154.

85 Roy Jenkins, Foreword to Edwin Plowden, *An Industrialist in the Treasury: The Post-War Years* (André Deutsch, 1989), p. ix.

86 For a brief account of Clarke see Peter Hennessy, *Whitehall* (Pimlico, 2001), pp. 175–80.

87 Butler, *The Art of the Possible*, pp. 160–6; see also Plowden, *An Industrialist in the Treasury*, p. 143.

88 Peter Catterall (ed.), *The Macmillan Diaries: The Cabinet Years, 1950–1957* (Macmillan, 2003), entry for 29 February 1952.

89 Ibid., entry for 1 March 1952.

90 Alan Milward, *The European Rescue of the Nation-State* (Routledge, 1992), p. 354.

91 Arthur Salter, *Slave of the Lamp: A Public Servant's Notebook* (Weidenfeld & Nicolson, 1967), p. 222.

92 Scott Newton, *The Global Economy, 1944–2000: The Limits of Ideology* (Arnold, 2004), pp. 27–54.

93 Alec Cairncross, *The British Economy since 1945* (Blackwell, 1992), p. 122.

94 Alec Cairncross, *Years of Recovery: British Economic Policy, 1945–1951* (Methuen, 1985), pp. 254–5.

95 NA, PRO, T 236/3240, 'Sterling Convertibility: OPERATION ROBOT', R. W. B. Clarke, 'Convertibility', 25 January 1952.

96 NA, PRO, T 236/3245, 'Sir Robert Hall's (director of Cabinet Office economic section) Papers', R. W. B. Clarke to Robert Hall, 24 February 1952.

97 Dell, *The Chancellors*, p. 192.

98 Cairncross, *Years of Recovery*, p. 240.

99 Dell, *The Chancellors*, p. 167.

100 Cairncross, *Years of Recovery*, p. 245.

101 Dell, *The Chancellors*, p. 168.

102 Cairncross, *Years of Recovery*, p. 248.

103 Ibid., p. 249.

104 Cairncross, *The Robert Hall Diaries, 1947–1953*, entry for 27 March 1952.

105 Ibid., entry for 28 March 1952.

106 NA, PRO, T 236/3240, Bridges to Plowden, 22 February 1952, quoted in Plowden, *An Industrialist in the Treasury*.

107 Hall to Plowden, 22 February 1952, from the same archive quoted ibid.

108 Ibid., p. 147.

109 NA, PRO, PREM 11/138, 'Financial Situation and Particulars of the Proposals in the Forthcoming Budget', Churchill to Eden, 22 February 1952.

110 Ibid., Eden to Churchill, 23 February 1952.

111 Plowden, *An Industrialist in the Treasury*, pp. 147–8.

112 Quoted in D. R. Thorpe, *Eden: The Life and Times of Anthony Eden, First Earl of Avon, 1897–1977* (Chatto and Windus, 2003), pp. 373–4.

113 Plowden, *An Industrialist in the Treasury*, p. 156.

114 Thorpe, *Eden*, p. 374.

115 Butler, *The Art of the Possible*, p. 162.

116 Catterall, *The Macmillan Diaries: The Cabinet Years, 1950–1957*, entry for 29 February 1952.

117 Dell, *The Chancellors*, p. 180.

118 Ibid., pp. 178–9.

119 NA, PRO, T 236/3240, Hall to Plowden, 22 February 1952.

120 NA, PRO, T 236/3241, 'Sterling Convertibility: OPERATION ROBOT', R. W. B. Clarke, 26 February 1952.

121 Catterall, *The Macmillan Diaries: The Cabinet Years, 1950–1957*, entry for 29 February 1952.

122 Ibid.

123 Ibid.
124 Ibid., entry for 1 March 1952.
125 Ibid.
126 Philip M. Williams, *The Diary of Hugh Gaitskell, 1945–1956* (Cape, 1983), entry for 9 November 1954.
127 NA, PRO, T 236/3242, 'Sterling Convertibility: OPERATION ROBOT'.
128 Henry Pelling, *Churchill's Peacetime Ministry, 1951–55* (Macmillan, 1997), p. 35.
129 Butler, *The Art of the Possible*, p. 162.
130 *Economist* articles were – and are – anonymous. But it has long been known this was Macrae's work.
131 Butler, *The Art of the Possible*, pp. 162–3.
132 Scott Kelly, *The Myth of Mr Butskell: The Politics of British Economic Policy, 1950–55* (Ashgate, 2002), p. 1.
133 Norman Macrae, *Sunshades in October: An Analysis of the Main Mistakes in British Economic Policy since the mid Nineteen-fifties* (Allen and Unwin, 1963), see especially chapter 3, 'What Mr Butler Saw', pp. 28–41.
134 Kelly, *The Myth of Mr Butskell*, pp. 226–8.
135 'Diverse Reminiscences Ending with Suez', 18 April 1957. Papers of R. A. Butler, G 31, 88, Trinity College Cambridge.
136 Butler, *The Art of the Possible*, p. 202.
137 Salter, *Slave of the Lamp*, p. 224.
138 Plowden, *An Industrialist in the Treasury*, p. 157.
139 Butler, *The Art of the Possible*, pp. 160–61.
140 Ibid., p. 159.
141 Ibid., p. 163.
142 Cairncross, *The Robert Hall Diaries, 1947–1953*, entry for 21 March 1952.
143 NA, PRO, PREM, 11/137, 'Memorandum from Lord Cherwell, Paymaster General, to the Prime Minister on "Setting the Pound Free"', 'Setting the Pound Free', Cherwell to Churchill, 18 March 1952.
144 Ibid., Churchill to Butler, 20 March 1952.
145 Moran, *Churchill: The Struggle for Survival*, diary entry for 30 July 1952.
146 House of Commons Official Report, 30 July 1952, cols. 1508–9.
147 Cairncross, *Years of Recovery*, p. 256.
148 Ibid., pp. 254–5.
149 Cairncross, *The British Economy since 1945*, pp. 123–6.
150 Cairncross, *Years of Recovery*, p. 256.
151 Cairncross, *The British Economy since 1945*, p. 102; Michael Dockrill, *British Defence since 1945* (Blackwell, 1988), p. 151.
152 Peter Clarke, *Hope and Glory: Britain 1900–1990* (Allen Lane, 1996), p. 244.
153 Alan Thompson, *The Day Before Yesterday: An Illustrated History of Britain from Attlee to Macmillan* (Sidgwick and Jackson/Thames Television, 1971), p. 94.
154 Ibid.
155 As reported by his friend Eric Roll in *Where Did We Go Wrong? From the Gold Standard to Europe* (Faber, 1995), p. 27. Clarke died in 1975.
156 Ibid.
157 He used this phrase more than once over lunch with the author in the mid to late 1970s.
158 Dell, *The Chancellors*, p. 180.
159 Nicholas Timmins, *The Five Giants: A Biography of the Welfare State*, revised edn (HarperCollins, 2001), p. 197.
160 Gilbert, *Never Despair*, p. 880, footnote 1.
161 Timmins, *The Five Giants*, p. 198.
162 John Colville, *The Churchillians* (Weidenfeld & Nicolson, 1981), p. 122.
163 Addison, *Churchill on the Home Front*, pp. 414–15.

164 Moran, *Churchill: The Struggle for Survival*, diary entry for 24 February 1953.

165 Fred Blackburn, *George Tomlinson* (Heinemann, 1954), p. 202.

166 Timmins, *The Five Giants*, p. 198.

167 Martin Gilbert, *Winston S. Churchill*, vol. VII: *Road to Victory, 1941–1945* (Heinemann, 1986), p. 292.

168 Peter Hennessy, *Muddling Through: Power, Politics and the Quality of Government in Postwar Britain* (Gollancz, 1996), p. 200.

169 These ministerial exchanges took place in early 1953. Charles Webster, *The Health Services since the War*, vol. I: *Problems of Health Care: The National Health Service before 1957* (HMSO, 1988), p. 204.

170 Timmins, *The Five Giants*, p. 192.

171 Peter Hennessy, *Never Again: Britain, 1945–1951* (Cape, 1992), p. 416.

172 Webster, *Problems of Health Care*, p. 157.

173 Ibid., pp. 166–78.

174 Ben Pimlott, *Harold Wilson* (HarperCollins, 1992), pp. 158–60.

175 Powell used the phrase when speaking to his biographer, Simon Heffer; author's conversation with Simon Heffer, 26 April 2006.

176 Howard Glennerster, *British Social Policy since 1945* (Blackwell, 1995), p. 75.

177 Robert Shephard, *Iain Macleod* (Hutchinson, 1994), pp. 73–8.

178 Webster, *Problems of Health Care*, p. 185.

179 House of Commons Official Report, 27 March 1952, cols. 841–56.

180 Timmins, *The Five Giants*, p. 204.

181 Ibid., p. 205.

182 Ibid.

183 Ibid., pp. 205–6; Webster, *Problems of Health Care*, p. 208.

184 Ibid., p. 209.

185 Ibid., p. 233.

186 Ibid., pp. 234–5.

187 Ibid., p. 235.

188 NA, PRO, CAB 128/19, CM (51) 15, 12 February 1951; Hennessy, *Never Again*, pp. 441–3. For the papers of the Cabinet Committee, GEN 325, see NA, PRO, CAB 130/61.

189 Hennessy, *Never Again*, p. 442.

190 Mel Risebrow, 'An Analysis of the Responses of British Government to Coloured Colonial Immigration during the Period 1945–51', unpublished undergraduate thesis, University of East Anglia, 1983.

191 Peter Hennessy, *What the Papers Never Said* (Politics Association, 1985), p. 108.

192 Randall Hansen, *Citizenship and Immigration in Post-war Britain* (Oxford University Press, 2000), p. 58.

193 Philip Williams, *Hugh Gaitskell* (Cape, 1979), pp. 677–8.

194 Hansen, *Citizenship and Immigration in Post-war Britain*, pp. 74–5.

195 Ibid.

196 Ibid., p. 78.

197 Hennessy, *Never Again*, pp. 439–42.

198 Hansen, *Citizenship and Immigration in Post-war Britain*, p. 64.

199 Ibid., pp. 78–9.

200 Zig Layton-Henry, *The Politics of Immigration* (Blackwell, 1992), p. 13.

201 Quoted in Roberts, *Eminent Churchillians*, p. 230. The letter is preserved in the Chandos Papers at the Churchill Archives Centre.

202 NA, PRO, DO 35/5216, 'Coloured People: Control of Entry into and Employment in UK', Salisbury to Lyttelton, 19 March 1954.

203 Catterall, *The Macmillan Diaries: The Cabinet Years, 1950–1957*, p. 382.

204 Hansen, *Citizenship and Immigration in Post-war Britain*, p. 74.

205 Ian Gilmour, *Inside Right* (Hutchinson, 1977), p. 134.

206 Nicholas Deakin, 'The Immigration Issue in British Politics (1948–1964)', unpublished D.Phil. thesis, University of Sussex, 1972, p. 13; Paul Foot, Hugh's son, told me he was Deakin's source and described his father's distaste for Churchill's words. (Paul had gone to Chequers with his father.) Paul explained all of this over dinner on 3 February 2004 after he and Richard Ingrams had delivered the 2004 Bagehot lecture on 'The Historical Impact of *Private Eye*' at Queen Mary.

207 Roberts, *Eminent Churchillians*, p. 238.

208 Kenneth O. Morgan, *The People's Peace: British History, 1945–1989*, p. 33; Layton-Henry, *The Politics of Immigration*, pp. 1–2; Clarke, *Hope and Glory*, p. 321.

209 Dale, *Conservative Party General Election Manifestos*, pp. 95–9.

210 Pelling, *Churchill's Peacetime Ministry*, p. 73.

211 Hennessy, *Never Again*, p. 337.

212 NA, PRO, CAB 128/23, CC (51) 1, 30 October 1951; CC (51) 2, 1 November 1951; CC (51) 3, 2 November 1951. See also Kathleen Burk, *The First Privatisation: The Politicians, the City and the Denationalisation of Steel* (Historians' Press, 1988), pp. 41–2.

213 Pelling, *Churchill's Peacetime Ministry*, p. 78.

214 NA, PRO, CAB 128/25, CC (52) 65, 3 July 1952.

215 Hennessy, *The Prime Minister*, p. 178. Old Sarum was the name of the mound of earth outside Salisbury in Wiltshire which was one of the most notorious of the pre-1832 'rotten boroughs'.

216 Burk, *The First Privatisation*, p. 68, n.69. Professor Burk found Salisbury's note in the Swinton Papers.

217 NA, PRO, CAB 128/25, CC (52) 68, 14 July 1952.

218 Pelling, *Churchill's Peacetime Ministry*, p. 79.

219 NA, PRO, CAB 128/25, CC (52) 69, 15 July 1952.

220 House of Commons Official Report, 27 November 1952, col. 266.

221 Pelling, *Churchill's Peacetime Ministry*, p. 80.

222 Burk, *The First Privatisation*, p. 142.

223 Ibid.

224 E. C. Loft, 'One Big Row: Government and the Railways, 1951–64', unpublished PhD thesis, Department of History, Queen Mary and Westfield College, University of London, 1999, pp. 31–52.

225 NA, PRO, CAB 134/1180, T (52) 4, 28 January 1952.

226 Hennessy, *The Prime Minister*, p. 193.

227 NA, PRO, CAB 128/25, CC (52) 91, 29 October 1952.

228 Pelling, *Churchill's Peacetime Ministry*, p. 77.

229 Part of the 1953 legislation was amended by the Transport (Disposal of Road Haulage Property) Act, 1956.

230 Hilary Kingsley and Geoff Tibballs, *Box of Delights: The Golden Years of Television* (Macmillan, 1989), p. 24.

231 Ibid.

232 Brian Palmer speaking on the WideVision Productions/Channel 4 series *What Has Become of Us?*, programme 4, 'Having It So Good', first broadcast 18 December 1994.

233 D. R. Thorpe, *Selwyn Lloyd* (Cape, 1989), pp. 1–101.

234 Ibid., p. 116.

235 Ibid., p. 115.

236 NA, PRO, HO 254/8, 'Minutes and Secretary's Notes: Nos 241–290'.

237 Thorpe, *Selwyn Lloyd*, p. 143.

238 Ibid., p. 124.

239 It's reproduced in full as an appendix ibid., pp. 446–57.

240 House of Commons Official Report, 19 July 1951, cols. 1423–98.

241 Thorpe, *Selwyn Lloyd*, p. 137.

242 Asa Briggs, *The BBC: The First Fifty Years* (Oxford University Press, 1979), p. 264.

243 'Broadcasting: Memorandum on the Report of the Broadcasting Committee 1949', Cmd. 8291 (HMSO, 1951).

244 Thorpe, *Selwyn Lloyd*, pp. 134–5, 152–5.

245 Seymour-Ure, *The British Press and Broadcasting since 1945*, p. 80.

246 Quoted in Thompson, *The Day Before Yesterday*, p. 101.

247 Lord Woolton, *The Memoirs of the Rt. Hon the Earl of Woolton*, pp. 387–8; Thorpe, Selwyn Lloyd, p. 137.

248 Thompson, *The Day Before Yesterday*, p. 101.

249 Conversation with Jack Profumo, December 2003; for Churchill and television see Michael Cockerell, *Live from Number 10: The Inside Story of Prime Ministers and Television* (Faber, 1988), pp. 15–16, 21, 24–6.

250 Ibid., pp. 23–4.

251 Ibid., p. 14.

252 Thorpe, *Eden*, pp. 384–6.

253 Pottle, *Daring to Hope*, pp. 127–8, entry for 6 August 1953.

254 Thorpe, *Selwyn Lloyd*, p. 140.

255 Cockerell, *Live from Number 10*, pp. 25–6.

256 Pelling, *Churchill's Peacetime Ministry*, p. 86.

257 *Broadcasting: Memorandum on Television Policy* (HMSO, 1953).

258 House of Lords Official Report, 25–26 November 1953, cols. 511–748.

259 Pelling, *Churchill's Peacetime Ministry*, p. 87.

260 House of Commons Official Report, 25 March 1954, cols. 1440–1554.

261 Gilbert, *Never Despair*, p. 1132.

262 NA, PRO, PREM 11/385, 'Cuts in Expenditure on Adult Education', Churchill to Horsbrugh, 9 February 1953.

263 Henry Pelling, *Winston Churchill* (Macmillan, 1974), p. 603.

264 Butler, *British General Elections since 1945*, pp. 13–14.

265 Colville, *The Churchillians*, p. 121.

266 Ibid.

267 William Shawcross, *Queen and Country* (BBC Books, 2002), p. 62.

268 Colville, *The Fringes of Power*, pp. 658–9, diary entry for 3 January 1953.

5 Coronation, Kingdom and Empire

1 Ben Pimlott, *The Queen: Elizabeth II and the Monarchy* (Golden Jubilee Edition, HarperCollins, 2001), pp. 446–7.

2 Ibid., p. 450.

3 George Orwell, *The English People*, in Peter Davison (ed.), *Orwell's England* (Penguin, 2001), p. 297.

4 National Archives, Public Record Office [NA, PRO], CAB 128/28, CC (55) 28, 5 April 1955.

5 'The Crowning Glory – Everest Conquered', *Daily Mail*, 2 June 1953.

6 Jan Morris, *A Writer's World: Travels 1950–2000* (Faber, 2003), pp. 3–6.

7 Ibid., p. 6.

8 Sir Edmund Hillary, *View from the Summit* (Corgi, 2000), pp. 342–3.

9 Walter Bagehot, *The English Constitution* (Kegan Paul, Trench and Trubner, 1891 [1867]), p. 38.

10 Lord Charteris was speaking on the WideVision Productions/Channel 4 series, *What Has Become of Us?*, programme 3, 'The Last Roar', first broadcast 11 December 1994.

11 Ibid.

12 Edward Shils and Michael Young, 'The Meaning of the Coronation', *Sociological Review* (new series), vol. 1, no. 2 (December 1953), pp. 67–8.

13 Walter Bagehot, *Physics and Politics* (Henry King, 1872), p. 27.

14 The essay, in a slightly modified form, is reproduced in Edward Shils, *The Intellectuals and the Powers and Other Essays* (University of Chicago Press, 1972), pp. 135–53. This quotation is taken from p. 136.

15 Ibid., p. 137.

16 Asa Briggs, *Michael Young, Social Entrepreneur* (Palgrave, 2001), p. 42.

17 Michael Young, *Small Man, Big World* (Labour Party, 1948), pp. 13–14.

18 Shils and Young, 'The Meaning of the Coronation', p. 65. For the 'moral economy' see E. P. Thompson, *Customs in Common* (Merlin Press, 1991), pp. 188–9.

19 Shils and Young, 'The Meaning of the Coronation', p. 65.

20 Ibid., p. 67.

21 Ibid., p. 77.

22 Owen Chadwick, *Michael Ramsey: A Life* (Oxford University Press, 1990), p. 81.

23 Ibid., p. 354. Conversation with Professor Eamon Duffy, 9 February 2004.

24 William Shawcross, *Queen and Country* (BBC Books, 2002), pp. 50–51.

25 Ibid., p. 51.

26 Shils and Young, 'The Meaning of the Coronation', pp. 68–9.

27 Ibid., p. 69.

28 Ibid.

29 Ibid., p. 70.

30 Ibid., p. 73.

31 Shawcross, *Queen and Country*, p. 54.

32 Ibid., p. 50.

33 Ibid.

34 'Elizabethan Express (1954)', *The British Transport Films Collection*, vol. I (British Film Institute, 2001).

35 Philip Gibbs, *The New Elizabethans* (Hutchinson, 1953).

36 Michael Young, *The Rise of the Meritocracy* (Penguin, 1961), p. 131.

37 Ibid., p. 27.

38 Richard Ollard (ed.), *The Diaries of A. L. Rowse* (Allen Lane, 2003), p. 426, entry for 17 March 1968.

39 Richard Weight, *Patriots: National Identity in Britain 1940–2000* (Macmillan, 2002), p. 232.

40 When we conversed in the Library of Windsor Castle for the *What Has Become of Us?* television series on 6 June 1994.

41 Ibid.

42 Pimlott, *The Queen*, pp. 190–91.

43 NA, PRO, PREM 11/34, 'Question of Television inside Westminster Abbey at the Coronation', Colville to Churchill, 7 July 1952.

44 NA, PRO, CAB 128/25, CC (52), 67th Conclusions, 10 July 1952.

45 Pimlott, *The Queen*, p. 205; Michael Cockerell, *Live from Number 10: The Inside Story of Prime Ministers and Television* (Faber, 1988), p. 19.

46 Pimlott, *The Queen*, p. 206. (There are no minutes taken of the PM/Monarch weekly audience.)

47 The Earl of Swinton (with James Margach), *Sixty Years of Power: Some Memories of the Men who Wielded It* (Hutchinson, 1966), pp. 138–9.

48 Ibid., p. 139.

49 Ibid., pp. 139–40.

50 Peter Catterall (ed.), *The Macmillan Diaries: The Cabinet Years, 1950–1957* (Macmillan, 2003), p. 191. See also NA, PRO, CAB 128/25, CC (52), 90th Conclusions, 28 October 1952.

51 Catterall, *The Macmillan Diaries: The Cabinet Years*, p. 142, entry for 11 February 1952.

52 Ibid.

53 D. R. Thorpe, *Selwyn Lloyd* (Cape, 1989), pp. 117–18.

54 Hilary Kingsley and Geoff Tibballs, *Box of Delights: The Golden Years of Television* (Macmillan, 1989), p. 10.

55 Jonathan Dimbleby, *Richard Dimbleby: A Biography* (Hodder, 1975), p. 324.

56 Kingsley and Tibballs, *Box of Delights*, p. 10.

57 Colin Seymour-Ure, *The British Press and Broadcasting since 1945* (Blackwell, 1991), p. 9.

58 Kingsley and Tibballs, *Box of Delights*, p. 10.

59 Weight, *Patriots*, p. 214.

60 Quoted ibid.

61 Peter Hennessy, *The Prime Minister: The Office and Its Holders since 1945* (Penguin, 2001), p. 266.

62 Gibbs, *The New Elizabethans*, p. 216.

63 Brian Palmer speaking on the WideVision Productions/Channel 4 series *What Has Become of Us?*, programme 4, 'Having It So Good', first broadcast on 18 December 1994.

64 Fernand Braudel, *A History of Civilizations* (Penguin, 1995), p. 31.

65 Christopher Harvie, *No Gods and Precious Few Heroes: Scotland since 1914* (Arnold, 1981), pp. 90, 109; James Stuart, *Within the Fringe* (Bodley Head, 1967), pp. 160–62; D. R. Thorpe, *Alec Douglas-Home* (Sinclair-Stevenson, 1996), pp. 140–45.

66 Arnold Kemp, *The Hollow Drum: Scotland since the War* (Mainstream, 1993), p. 87; Weight, *Patriots*, pp. 131–4.

67 Ibid., p. 222.

68 Catterall, *The Macmillan Diaries: The Cabinet Years, 1950–1957*, p. 142.

69 Kemp, *The Hollow Drum*, p. 92; Harvie, *No Gods and Precious Few Heroes*, p. 108.

70 Martin Gilbert, *Winston S. Churchill*, vol. VIII: *Never Despair, 1945–1965* (Heinemann, 1988), p. 510.

71 Kemp, *The Hollow Drum*, p. 87.

72 Thorpe, *Alec Douglas-Home*, p. 151.

73 Kemp, *The Hollow Drum*, p. 87.

74 Philip Ziegler, *Crown and People* (Collins, 1978), p. 124.

75 Thorpe, *Alec Douglas-Home*, p. 150.

76 Charles L. Warr, *The Glimmering Landscape* (Hodder and Stoughton, 1960), p. 289.

77 Thorpe, *Alec Douglas-Home*, p. 150.

78 Kemp, *The Hollow Drum*, p. 90.

79 Ibid., Thorpe, *Alec Douglas-Home*, p. 151.

80 Ibid., p. 142.

81 Stuart, *Within the Fringe*, p. 57.

82 Ibid., p. 17.

83 Ibid., p. 7.

84 Sarah Bradford, *King George VI* (Weidenfeld & Nicolson, 1989), p. 101.

85 Private information.

86 Thorpe, *Alec Douglas-Home*, p. 141.

87 For Stuart's influence on Whitelaw see Mark Garnett and Ian Aitken, *Splendid! Splendid! The Authorized Biography of Willie Whitelaw* (Cape, 2002), pp. 36, 39, 46–7.

88 Alistair Horne, *Macmillan, 1894–1956* (Macmillan, 1988), p. 67.

89 Catterall, *The Macmillan Diaries: The Cabinet Years, 1950–1957*, entry for 29 February 1952.

90 Ibid., entry for 29 August 1951.

91 Stuart, *Within the Fringe*, pp. 155–6.

92 Ibid., p. 164.

93 Harvie, *No Gods and Precious Few Heroes*, p. 54.

94 Arthur Marwick, *A History of the Modern British Isles, 1914–1999* (Blackwell, 2000), p. 125.

95   Harvie, *No Gods and Precious Few Heroes*, p. 108.
96   Kemp, *The Hollow Drum*, p. 107.
97   Thorpe, *Alec Douglas-Home*, p. 55.
98   Ibid., p. 141.
99   Ibid., p. 144.
100 bid.
101 Harvie, *No Gods and Precious Few Heroes*, p. 109.
102 Kemp, *The Hollow Drum*, pp. 91–2.
103 *Royal Commission on Scottish Affairs Report*, Cmd. 9212 (HMSO, 1954), p. 12.
104 Thorpe, *Alec Douglas-Home*, p. 152.
105 Ibid., p. 144.
106 Harvie, *No Gods and Precious Few Heroes*, pp. 3–5; Peter Pagnamenta and Richard Overy, *All Our Working Lives* (BBC Books, 1984), pp. 124–30.
107 Ian Jack, *Before the Oil Ran Out: Britain, 1977–86* (Secker and Warburg, 1987), p. 15.
108 Ibid., pp. 40–41.
109 Alec Cairncross (ed.), *The Scottish Economy* (Cambridge University Press, 1953), p. 4.
110 Fernand Braudel, *The Mediterranean in the Ancient World* (Penguin, 2001), p. 15.
111 Quoted in Michael Fry, *The Scottish Empire* (Birlinn, 2002), p. 1.
112 Jack, *Before the Oil Ran Out*, p. 6.
113 Eamon Duffy, *The Stripping of the Altars: Traditional Religion in England, 1400–1580* (Yale University Press, 1992), p. 4.
114 Grace Davie, *Religion in Britain since 1945* (Blackwell, 1994), p. 17.
115 Ibid., p. 95.
116 T. M. Devine, *The Scottish Nation, 1700–2000* (Penguin, 2000), p. 583.
117 Davie, *Religion in Britain since 1945*, p. 96.
118 R. F. Mackenzie, *A Search for Scotland* (Collins, 1989), p. 258.
119 Fry, *The Scottish Empire*, p. 155.
120 Lord Macaulay, *The History of England* (Penguin, 1986), p. 51.
121 Ibid., pp. 359, 361–2.
122 Thorpe, *Alec Douglas-Home*, p. 15.
123 *Lord Macaulay's Essays and Lays of Ancient Rome* (Longmans, Green, 1889), p. 565.
124 Thorpe, *Alec Douglas-Home*, p. 20.
125 Harvie, *No Gods and Precious Few Heroes*, p. 4.
126 Devine, *The Scottish Nation*, p. 570.
127 Geoffrey Owen, *From Empire to Europe: The Decline and Revival of British Industry since the Second World War* (HarperCollins, 1999), p. 185.
128 Mark Pottle (ed.), *Daring to Hope: The Diaries and Letters of Violet Bonham Carter, 1946–1969* (Weidenfeld & Nicolson, 2000), entry for 24 February 1950.
129 Ibid., p. 86. See also Peter Barberis, *Liberal Lion: Jo Grimond, a Political Life* (I. B. Tauris, 2005), pp. 30–32.
130 Devine, *The Scottish Nation*, p. 325.
131 Ibid., p. 565.
132 Ibid., p. 566.
133 Ibid.
134 Ibid., p. 567.
135 Andrew Marr, *The Battle for Scotland* (Penguin, 1992), p. 97.
136 Devine, *The Scottish Nation*, p. 567.
137 Neal Ascherson, *Stone Voices: The Search for Scotland* (Granta, 2002), p. viii.
138 Ibid., p. 232.
139 Ibid., p. 86.
140 Ibid., p. 84.
141 Ibid., p. 84–5.
142 Ibid., p. 85.

143 Ibid., p. 298.

144 Jan Morris, *The Matter of Wales: Epic Views of a Small Country* (Oxford University Press, 1984), p. 382.

145 Gwyn A. Williams, *When Was Wales? A History of the Welsh* (Penguin, 1985), p. 296.

146 Morris, *The Matter of Wales*, pp. 382–3.

147 Ibid., p. 412.

148 Kenneth O. Morgan, *Rebirth of a Nation: Wales, 1880–1980* (Oxford University Press/ University of Wales Press, 1982), p. 298; House of Commons Official Report, 17 October 1944, col. 2312.

149 Morgan, *Rebirth of a Nation*, pp. 134–5.

150 J. M. Keynes, *Essays in Biography* (Royal Economic Society/Macmillan, 1972), pp. 22–3.

151 Morgan, *Rebirth of a Nation*, p. 135.

152 Ibid., p. 134.

153 Michael Foot, *Aneurin Bevan, A Biography*, vol. I: *1897–1945* (Four Square, 1966), p. 11.

154 Ibid., p. 23.

155 He told the story first in the House of Commons in 1943, before he had ministerial experience; Foot, *Aneurin Bevan*, I, pp. 71–2. Later he elaborated it to his friend, to include the Cabinet experience, while adding the 'coat-tails' image; conversation with Geoffrey Goodman, 29 April 2006.

156 Morgan, *Rebirth of a Nation*, p. 206.

157 Ibid., p. 206.

158 Ibid., p. 377.

159 Ibid., p. 378.

160 House of Commons Official Report, 26 January 1948, col. 693.

161 Williams, *When Was Wales?*, p. 291.

162 John Ramsden, *An Appetite for Power: A History of the Conservative Party since 1830* (HarperCollins, 1998), p. 318.

163 Morgan, *Rebirth of a Nation*, p. 379.

164 Williams, *When Was Wales?*, p. 291.

165 Michael Foot, *Aneurin Bevan, A Biography*, vol. II: *1945–60* (Davis Poynter, 1973).

166 John Campbell, *Nye Bevan and the Mirage of British Socialism* (Weidenfeld & Nicolson, 1987).

167 Foot, *Aneurin Bevan*, I, p. 53.

168 Williams, *When Was Wales?*, p. 280.

169 'John Charles', *The Times*, 23 February 2004.

170 Dervla Murphy, *A Place Apart* (Penguin, 1979).

171 F. S. L. Lyons' 1981 Rankin Lecture delivered in Belfast and reprinted in Ciaran Brady (ed.), *Interpreting Irish History: The Debate on Historical Revisionism* (Irish Academic, 1994).

172 R. F. Foster, *The Irish Story: Telling Tales and Making It Up in Ireland* (Allen Lane, 2001), p. 38.

173 Private information.

174 Private information.

175 Conversation with James Molyneaux, 29 June 1976.

176 J. J. Lee, *Ireland 1912–1985: Politics and Society* (Cambridge University Press, 1989), pp. 411–12.

177 Paul Arthur and Keith Jeffrey, *Northern Ireland since 1968* (Blackwell, 1988), p. 21.

178 R. F. Foster, *Modern Ireland, 1600–1972* (Penguin, 1989), p. 582.

179 Arthur and Jeffrey, *Northern Ireland since 1968*, pp. 24–5.

180 Lee, *Ireland, 1912–1985*, p. 412.

181 Ibid.

182 Ibid., p. 430.

183 F. S. L. Lyons, *Ireland since the Famine* (Fontana, 1973), p. 741.

184 John Darwin, *Britain and Decolonisation: The Retreat from Empire in the Post-War World* (Macmillan, 1988), pp. 167–221.

185 Two very good and vivid surveys of the emergencies of various kinds in the postwar British Empire are Brian Lapping, *End of Empire* (Granada/Channel 4, 1985), and Christopher Bayly and Tim Harper, *Forgotten Wars* (Allen Lane, forthcoming January 2007).

186 Anthony Montague Browne, *Long Sunset: Memoirs of Winston Churchill's Last Private Secretary* (Cassell, 1995), p. 162.

187 NA, PRO, CAB 128/28, CC (55) 28, 5 April 1955.

188 James Morris, *Farewell the Trumpets: An Imperial Retreat* (Penguin, 1979), pp. 498–9.

189 Conversation with Lord Charteris, 13 March 1989.

190 Pimlott, *The Queen*, p. 117.

191 *The Coronation of Her Majesty Queen Elizabeth II: Approved Souvenir Programme* (King George's Jubilee Trust, 1953), p. 1.

192 Anil Seal, 'Preface' to John Gallagher, *The Decline, Revival and Fall of the British Empire*, ed. Anil Seal (Cambridge University Press, 1982), p. xi.

193 Peter Hennessy, *Whitehall* (Secker and Warburg, 1989), pp. 565–8.

194 Peter Hennessy, 'The Eternal Fireman who Always Answers the Call to Duty', *The Times*, 30 January 1976.

195 Hennessy, *Whitehall*, p. 567.

196 'Mountstuart Elphinstone' was delivered as the Romanes Lecture at Oxford University on 25 May 1962 and is reproduced in Lord Radcliffe, *Not in Feather Beds* (Hamish Hamilton, 1968), pp. 183–210.

197 The broadcast is reproduced ibid., pp. 1–6.

198 David Watt's metaphor emerged in our conversations about the study of the Milner 'Kindergarten' on which he was engaged at the time of his death.

199 Radcliffe, *Not in Feather Beds*, p. 5.

200 Ibid., p. 206.

201 Elizabeth Knowles (ed.), *The Oxford English Dictionary of 20th Century Quotations* (Oxford University Press, 1998), p. 1.

202 'The Dissolving Society', Annual LSE Oration delivered on 10 December 1965 and reproduced in Radcliffe, *Not in Feather Beds*, pp. 229–46.

203 Ibid., pp. 233–4.

204 Ronald Robinson and John Gallagher with Alice Denny, *Africa and the Victorians: The Official Mind of Imperialism* (Papermac, 1965).

205 John M. Mackenzie, *Propaganda and Empire: The Manipulation of British Public Opinion 1880–1960* (Manchester University Press, 1984), p. 1.

206 David Cannadine, *Ornamentalism: How the British Saw their Empire* (Allen Lane, 2001), pp. 181–99.

207 Daniel J. Boorstin, *The Image or what Happened to the American Dream* (Atheneum, 1962), pp. 45–9.

208 WideVision Productions/Channel 4, *What Has Become of Us?*, programme 3, 'The Last Roar', first broadcast 11 December 1994.

209 Ibid.

210 *Daily Express*, 7 May 1954.

211 'The Last Roar'.

212 Adrian Thrills, *You're Not Singing Anymore* (Ebury Press, 1998), p. 15. I am grateful to Dr Richard Weight for drawing my attention to this gem.

213 Pottle, *Daring to Hope*, pp. 118–19, entry for 3 April 1953.

214 Conversation with Mel Cappe, 17 March 2004.

6 The Geometric Conceit

1 Evelyn Shuckburgh, *Descent to Suez: Diaries, 1951–56* (Weidenfeld & Nicolson, 1986), p. 32.

2 Michael Charlton, *The Price of Victory* (BBC Books, 1983), p. 137.

3 Sir Frank was speaking on the WideVision Productions/Channel 4 Television series, *What Has Become of Us?*, programme 3, 'The Last Roar', first broadcast 11 December 1994.

4 Charlton, *The Price of Victory*, p. 58.

5 As recalled by his foreign affairs private secretary, Sir Anthony Montague Browne, in Peter Hennessy, *Muddling Through: Power, Politics and the Quality of Government in Postwar Britain* (Gollancz, 1996), p. 202.

6 Ibid.

7 David Reynolds, *Britannia Overruled: British Policy and World Power in the 20th Century* (Longman, 1991), p. 202.

8 Hennessy, *Muddling Through*, p. 202.

9 Charles de Gaulle, *War Memoirs*, vol. II: *Unity, 1942–1944* (Weidenfeld & Nicolson, 1956), p. 227.

10 John Gallagher, *The Decline, Revival and Fall of the British Empire,* ed. Anil Seal (Cambridge University Press, 1982), p. 146.

11 Peter Hennessy, *Never Again: Britain, 1945–1951* (Cape, 1992), pp. 295–6.

12 Edmund Dell, *The Chancellors: A History of the Chancellors of the Exchequer, 1945–90* (HarperCollins, 1996).

13 Edmund Dell and Lord Hunt of Tanworth, 'The Failings of Cabinet Government in mid to late 1970s', *Contemporary Record*, vol. 8, no. 3 (winter 1994), pp. 453–72.

14 Edmund Dell, *The Schuman Plan and the British Abdication of Leadership in Europe* (Oxford University Press, 1995).

15 Ibid., pp. 289–90.

16 Ibid., p. 302.

17 Ibid., p. 303.

18 Ibid., p. 232.

19 Ibid., pp. 299–300.

20 Ibid., p. 300.

21 Ibid.

22 Alan S. Milward, *The Rise and Fall of a National Strategy, 1945–1963: The United Kingdom and the European Community*, vol. I (Frank Cass, 2002), p. 52, fn. 11.

23 Dell, *The Schuman Plan and the British Abdication of Leadership in Europe*, p. vii.

24 Hennessy, *Never Again*, pp. 360–62.

25 Robert Marjolin, *Architect of European Unity: Memoirs, 1911–1986* (Weidenfeld & Nicolson, 1989), p. 271.

26 Quoted in Charlton, *The Price of Victory*, p. 157.

27 Quoted in Nora Beloff, *The General Says No: Britain's Exclusion from Europe* (Penguin, 1963), p. 60.

28 Ibid.

29 John W. Young, 'The Schuman Plan and British Association', in John W. Young (ed.), *The Foreign Policy of Churchill's Peacetime Administration 1951–1955* (Leicester University Press, 1988), pp. 111–12.

30 Beloff, *The General Says No*, p. 59.

31 Ibid., pp. 58–9.

32 Peter Catterall (ed.), *The Macmillan Diaries: The Cabinet Years, 1950–1957* (Macmillan, 2003), entry for 22–24 November 1950.

33 Robert Cooper, *The Breaking of Nations: Order and Chaos in the Twenty-First Century* (Atlantic Books, 2003), p. 94.

34 Charlton, *The Price of Victory*, p. 310.

35 Ibid., p. 307.

36 National Archives, Public Record Office [NA, PRO], CAB 129/48, C(51) 32, 'United Europe: Note by the Prime Minister and Minister of Defence', 29 November 1951.

37 Catterall, *The Macmillan Diaries: The Cabinet Years, 1950–1957*, entry for 4 December 1951.

38 Ibid., entry for 5 April 1952.

39 Alistair Horne, *Macmillan, 1894–1956* (Macmillan, 1988), p. 351.

40 Peter Hennessy, *The Prime Minister: The Office and Its Holders since 1945* (Penguin, 2001), pp. 189–94.

41 Catterall, *The Macmillan Diaries: The Cabinet Years, 1950–1957*, p. 162.

42 John Colville, *The Fringes of Power: Downing Street Diaries, 1939–1955* (Hodder, 1985), entry for 13–15 June 1952.

43 Ibid., p. 651.

44 Catterall, *The Macmillan Diaries: The Cabinet Years, 1950–1957*, p. 144.

45 Colville, *The Fringes of Power*, entry for 30 May 1952.

46 NA, PRO, CAB 129/48, C (51) 32.

47 Alan S. Milward, *The European Rescue of the Nation-State* (Routledge, 1992), p. 131.

48 Ibid., p. 177.

49 Milward, *The Rise and Fall of a National Strategy*, p. 273.

50 See also Milward, *The European Rescue of the Nation-State*, p. 393.

51 Peter Hennessy and Caroline Anstey, 'From Clogs to Clogs? Britain's Relative Economic Decline since 1851', Strathclyde Analysis Paper no. 3, Department of Government, University of
Strathclyde, 1991, p. 29.

52 Milward, *The European Rescue of the Nation-State*, pp. 393–4.

53 Ibid., p. 393.

54 Anthony Sampson, *Anatomy of Britain* (Hodder, 1962), p. 273.

55 Robert Skidelsky, *John Maynard Keynes: Fighting for Britain, 1937–1946* (Macmillan, 2000), p. 339.

56 F. G. Lee, 'The International Negotiator', in Milo Keynes (ed.), *Essays on John Maynard Keynes* (Cambridge University Press, 1975), p. 220.

57 Letter from Lord Wilson of Dinton, 5 May 2004. For Lee and Europe see Samuel Brittan, *The Treasury under the Tories* (Pelican, 1964), pp. 213–14.

58 Peter Hennessy, *Whitehall* (Secker and Warburg, 1989), p. 160. See also Thorneycroft's Cabinet paper on 'Commercial Policy in Europe', NA, PRO, CAB 129/59, CC (53) 70, 19 February 1953. I am grateful to my colleague Dr James Ellison for drawing my attention to the significance of this paper.

59 Charles H. Feinstein, 'The End of Empire and the Golden Age', in Peter Clarke and Clive Trebilcock (eds.), *Understanding Decline: Perceptions and Realities of British Economic Performance* (Cambridge University Press, 1997), p. 228.

60 Conversation with Lord Thorneycroft, 29 July 1993.

61 Oliver S. Franks, *Britain and the Tide of World Affairs, The BBC Reith Lectures 1954* (Oxford University Press, 1955), pp. 23–4.

62 Ibid., p. 52.

63 Ibid., p. 37.

64 Young, 'The Schuman Plan and British Association', p. 109.

65 D. R. Thorpe, *Eden: The Life and Times of Anthony Eden, First Earl of Avon, 1897–1977* (Chatto, 2003), p. 368.

66 Charlton, *The Price of Victory*, p. 160.

67 NA, PRO, CAB 129/48, C (51) 32, 'United Europe'.

68 Charlton, *The Price of Victory*, p. 160.

69 Ibid.

70 Peter Hennessy and Caroline Anstey, 'Moneybags and Brains: The Anglo-American "Special Relationship" since 1945', Strathclyde Analysis Paper no. 1, Department of Government, University of Strathclyde, 1990, p. 8.

71 David Goodall, 'The World as a Danger Zone', *The Tablet*, 17 April 2004.

72 Franks, *Britain and the Tide of World Affairs*, p. 38.

73 Ibid., pp. 37–8.

74 Charlton, *The Price of Victory*, p. 151.

75 John W. Young, 'German Rearmament and the European Defence Community', in Young, *The Foreign Policy of Churchill's Peacetime Administration*, pp. 81–107.

76 Ibid., p. 98.

77 Franks, *Britain and the Tide of World Affairs*, p. 46.

78 Ibid.

79 Ibid., pp. 46–7.

80 Ibid., p. 47.

81 Young, 'The Schuman Plan and British Association', pp. 129–30.

82 Franks, *Britain and the Tide of World Affairs*, p. 12.

83 I am very grateful for a conversation in the Captain Kidd public house, Wapping, with Jon Davis and Oliver Tebbit on 1 May 2004 for clearing my thoughts a little on this.

84 NA, PRO, CAB 129/48, C (51) 32.

85 L. J. Butler, *Britain and Empire: Adjusting to a Post-Imperial World* (I. B. Tauris, 2002), p. 113.

86 Ernest Gellner, *Anthropology and Politics: Revolutions in the Sacred Grove* (Blackwell, 1995), pp. 11–13.

87 Ibid., p. 246.

88 Private information.

89 Peter Hennessy, 'The Itch after the Amputation? The Purposes of British Intelligence as the Century Turns: An Historical Perspective and a Forward Look', in K. G. Robertson (ed.), *War, Resistance and Intelligence: Essays in Honour of M. R. D. Foot* (Leo Cooper, 1999), p. 228.

90 Ibid.

91 John Darwin, *Britain and Decolonisation: The Retreat from Empire in the Post-War World* (Macmillan, 1998), p. 167.

92 Sir Michael had the postwar Air Ministry in mind as he was writing the entry on Sir Frank Cooper for the *Dictionary of National Biography*.

93 John Lonsdale, 'British Colonial Officials and the Kikuyu People', in John Smith (ed.), *Administering Empire: The British Colonial Service in Retrospect* (University of London Press, 1999), p. 96.

94 Hilaire Belloc, 'Introduction' to *Week-End Wodehouse* (first published by Herbert Jenkins, 1939) (Pimlico, 1991), p. 9.

95 Butler, *Britain and Empire*, pp. 34–5, 50.

96 Ibid., p. 83.

97 Ralph Furse, *Aucuparius: Recollections of a Recruiting Officer* (Oxford University Press, 1962), chart attached to p. 314.

98 Ibid., p. 283.

99 Butler, *Britain and Empire*, p. 186.

100 Brian Lapping, *End of Empire* (Granada/Channel 4 Television, 1985), p. 404.

101 Ibid., p. 370.

102 Darwin, *Britain and Decolonisation*, p. 177.

103 Butler, *Britain and Empire*, p. 110.

104 Lapping, *End of Empire*, pp. 446–535.

105 Darwin, *Britain and Decolonisation*, p. 187. See also Caroline Elkins, *Britain's Gulag: The End of Empire in Kenya* (Cape, 2005); David Anderson, *Histories of the Hanged: Britain's Dirty War in Kenya and the End of the Empire* (Weidenfeld & Nicolson, 2005).

106 Lapping, *End of Empire*, pp. 317–49.

107 Lord Chandos, *The Memoirs of Lord Chandos* (Bodley Head, 1964), pp. 394–5.

108 Lapping, *End of Empire*, p. 409.

109 Lonsdale, 'British Colonial Officials and the Kikuyu People', p. 95.

110 Ibid., pp. 100–101.

111 Ibid.

112 Darwin, *Britain and Decolonisation*, p. 187.

113 Lapping, *End of Empire*, pp. 415–19.

114 Ibid., p. 429.

115 Darwin, *Britain and Decolonisation*, p. 187.

116 Lapping, *End of Empire*, p. 370.

117 Lord Chandos, *The Memoirs of Lord Chandos*, p. 418.

118 Hennessy, *Whitehall*, pp. 409–10.

119 Butler, *Britain and Empire*, p. 117.

120 Ibid.

121 Lord Chandos, *The Memoirs of Lord Chandos*, p. 362.

122 Ibid., p. 359.

123 Ibid., p. 371.

124 Lapping, *End of Empire*, pp. 160–61, 182–4.

125 Ibid., pp. 169–75.

126 Darwin, *Britain and Decolonisation*, p. 202.

127 Anthony Adamthwaite, 'The Foreign Office and Policy-making', in Young, *The Foreign Policy of Churchill's Peacetime Administration*, p. 21.

128 Ibid., p. 20.

129 Thorpe, *Eden*, pp. 384–7.

130 Adamthwaite, 'The Foreign Office and Policy-making', p. 13.

131 Fernand Braudel, *A History of Civilizations* (Penguin, 1995), p. xxxvii.

132 Malcolm Muggeridge, *Tread Softly for You Tread on My Jokes* (Collins, 1967), p. 147.

133 Thorpe, *Eden*, p. 410.

134 Ibid., p. 412.

135 Eden to Salisbury, 17 July 1954, quoted in Thorpe, *Eden*, p. 411.

136 Robert Hinde and Joseph Rotblat, *War no More: Eliminating Conflict in the Nuclear Age* (Pluto, 2003), p. 40.

137 Thorpe, *Eden*, p. 412.

138 Peter Lowe, 'The Settlement of the Korean War', in Young, *The Foreign Policy of Churchill's Peacetime Administration*, pp. 207–32.

139 Ibid., pp. 223–4.

140 Butler, *Britain and Empire*, pp. 76–7; Lapping, *End of Empire*, pp. 246–57.

141 Shuckburgh, *Descent to Suez*, entry for 20 January 1953.

142 Thorpe, *Eden*, p. 420.

143 NA, PRO, CAB 128/27, CC (54) 37, 2 June 1954. See also Ritchie Ovendale, 'Egypt and the Suez Base Agreement', in Young, *The Foreign Policy of Churchill's Peacetime Administration*, pp. 135–55.

144 Ibid., p. 151.

145 Lapping, *End of Empire*, pp. 258–9.

146 Sampson, *Anatomy of Britain*, p. 298.

147 Mohammed H. Heikal, *Cutting the Lion's Tail: Suez through Egyptian Eyes* (André Deutsch, 1986), p. 65.

148 Ibid., p. 257; Thorpe, *Eden*, p. 426.

149 Quoted in Lapping, *End of Empire*, pp. 257–8.

150 Ibid., p. 258.

151 Robert Rhodes James, *Anthony Eden* (Weidenfeld & Nicolson, 1986), p. 556.

152 Zbigniew Brzezinski, *The Grand Chessboard: American Primacy and its Geostrategic Imperatives* (Basic Books, 1997).

153 Conversation with Chris Patten, 9 May 2004.

154 Michael Howard, *Captain Professor: A Life in War and Peace* (Continuum, 2006), pp. 142–3.

155 Thorpe, *Eden*, p. 45.

7 The H-Bomb and the Search for Peace

1 Quoted in Gerard De Groot, *The Bomb: A Life* (Cape, 2004), p. 12. Professor Weisskopf's remark appeared originally in the *Los Angeles Times*, 27 April 2002.

2 National Archives, Public Record Office [NA, PRO], CAB 134/940, HDC (55) 3, Cabinet Home Defence Committee, 'Fall-Out: Report of a Working Group', 8 March 1955.

3 NA, PRO, CAB 158/20, JIC (55) 12, 'The H-Bomb Threat To The United Kingdom In The Event of a General War', 13 January 1955.

4 Conversation with Sir John Willis, 7 May 2004. Sir John was talking after a National Archives colloquium on the bomb, part of its 'Secret State' Exhibition.

5 House of Commons Official Report, 1 March 1955, col. 1905.

6 Martin Gilbert, *Winston S. Churchill*, Vol. III: *Never Despair, 1945–1965* (Heinemann, 1988), p. 1097.

7 House of Commons Official Report, 1 March 1955, col. 1895.

8 Sir David was on the platform at the National Archives, Kew, with the author to launch the exhibition on 31 March 2004.

9 George Steiner, *Grammars of Creation* (Faber, 2001), p. 2.

10 Sir John mentioned this during a conversation with Sir Michael Quinlan, the former Permanent Secretary at the Ministry of Defence, at the National Archives on 7 May 2004.

11 Elizabeth Knowles (ed.), *The Oxford Dictionary of Twentieth-Century Quotations* (Oxford University Press, 1998), p. 66.

12 Michael Herman, 'The Role of Military Intelligence since 1945', paper delivered to the Twentieth-Century British Politics and Administration Seminar at the Institute of Historical Research, University of London, 24 May 1989.

13 Michael Herman, 'The Cold War: Did Intelligence Make a Difference?', paper produced for the Royal Institute of International Affairs/BBC Conference 'Cold War: Heroes, Villains and Spies', and reproduced in Michael Herman, *Intelligence Services in the Information Age: Theory and Practice* (Frank Cass, 2001), pp. 159–63.

14 Ibid.

15 Peter Hennessy, *The Prime Minister: The Office and Its Holders since 1945* (Penguin, 2001), p. 451.

16 For example, item 11 on the 1962 JIC 'Red List' reads as follows: 'Arrival of Soviet army specialist units in forward areas (especially missile, medical and interrogation units) and military personnel wearing rocket insignia', NA, PRO, CAB 158/45, JIC (62) 21, 'Indications of Sino-Soviet Bloc Preparations for Early War', 26 February 1962.

17 NA, PRO, CAB 158/26, JIC (56) 105 (Final), 'Indicators of Soviet Preparations for Early War', 5 December 1956.

18 Ibid.

19 NA, PRO, CAB 158/20, JIC (55) 12.

20 For Walpole's taking the grand weekend to new heights see J. H. Plumb, *Sir Robert Walpole: The King's Minister* (Cresset Press, 1960), pp. 84–8.

21 NA, PRO, CAB 158/32, JIC (58) 50 (Final), 'Warning of Soviet Attack on the West in Global War up to the End of 1959', 20 June 1958. I am grateful to my research student Alban Webb for drawing this paper to my attention.

22 See Peter Hennessy, *The Secret State: Whitehall and the Cold War* (Penguin, 2003), chapter 1, pp. 1–43.

23 NA, PRO, CAB 158/24, JIC (56) 21 (Final), 'Likelihood of Global War and Warning of Attack', 1 May 1956.

24 Ibid.

25 Ibid.

26 Ibid.

27 Ibid.

28 Ibid.

29 Private information.

30 For the scare stories, see Anatoli Golitsyn, *New Lies for Old: The Communist Strategy of Deception and Disinformation* (Bodley Head, 1984); Tom Mangold, *Cold Warrior: James Jesus Angleton, the CIA's Master Spyhunter* (Simon and Schuster, 1991); for their refutation: Christopher Andrew and Vasili Mitrokhin, *The Mitrokhin Archive: The KGB in Europe and the West* (Allen Lane, 1999).

31 Private information.

32 Private information.

33 Private information. See also George Blake, *No other Choice: An Autobiography* (Cape, 1990), pp. 196–200. In 1961 SIS was sufficiently confident to assess the approaches of Colonel Oleg Penkovsky, the Russian military intelligence officer and missile expert, and to take him on and run him (jointly with the CIA) for eighteen months until he was captured days before the Cuban missile crisis began in earnest in 1962; see Oleg Penkovsky, *The Penkovsky Papers* (Collins, 1965); Jerrold S. Schecter and Peter S. Deriabin, *The Spy Who Saved the World* (Brassey's, 1992).

34 Richard J. Aldrich, *The Hidden Hand: Britain, America and Cold War Secret Intelligence* (John Murray, 2001), p. 233.

35 Ibid., pp. 398, 401–2. See also Alexander Craig, 'The Joint Intelligence Committee and British Intelligence Assessments, 1945–1956', unpublished PhD thesis, Faculty of History, University of Cambridge, 1999, pp. 109–10.

36 Aldrich, *The Hidden Hand*, pp. 254–5.

37 NA, PRO, CAB 158/24, JIC (56) 21 (Final).

38 Lord Moran, *Churchill: The Struggle for Survival, 1940–65* (Constable, 1966), p. 530, diary entry for 26 March 1954.

39 NA, PRO, PREM 11/294, 'Possible Effect of Atomic Bombing', Maxwell Fyfe to Churchill, 4 June 1952.

40 De Groot, *The Bomb*, p. 177. Lorna Arnold, *Britain and the H-Bomb* (Palgrave, 2001), p. 234.

41 Gilbert, *Never Despair*, p. 837.

42 NA, PRO, CAB 134/940, HDC (55) 3.

43 Gilbert, *Never Despair*, chapter 45, pp. 846–57.

44 Moran, *Churchill: The Struggle for Survival*, p. 451, diary entry for 16 August 1953.

45 Ibid., p. 494, diary entry for 25 July 1953.

46 John Colville, *The Fringes of Power: Downing Street Diaries, 1939–1955* (Hodder, 1985), pp. 667–80.

47 D. R. Thorpe, *Eden: The Life and Times of Anthony Eden, First Earl of Avon, 1897–1977* (Chatto, 2003), p. 389.

48 Gilbert, *Never Despair*, pp. 827–45.

49 Arnold, *Britain and the H-Bomb*, p. 41.

50 Ibid., pp. 27–8.

51 Ibid., pp. 29–30.

52 Brian Cathcart, *Test of Greatness: Britain's Struggle for the Atom Bomb* (John Murray, 1994), p. 273, Humphrey Winn, *The RAF Strategic Nuclear Deterrent Forces: The Origins, Roles and Deployment, 1946–69 – A Documentary History* (HMSO, 1994), p. 92.

53 Arnold, *Britain and the H-Bomb*, p. 18.

54 Peter Catterall (ed.), *The Macmillan Diaries: The Cabinet Years, 1950–1957* (Macmillan, 2003), entry for 31 March 1954.

55 Gilbert, *Never Despair*, p. 952.

56 Ibid.

57 Arnold, *Britain and the H-Bomb*, p. 19.

58 Ibid., p. 18.

59 Ibid., p. 19.

60 Ibid., p. 111.

61 House of Commons Official Report, 12 July 1954, col. 34.
62 Ibid.
63 Gilbert, *Never Despair*, p. 959.
64 Ibid.
65 NA, PRO, CAB 130/101, GEN 465 (1st), 12 March 1954.
66 Ibid.
67 Arnold, *Britain and the H-Bomb*, p. 40.
68 NA, PRO, CAB 130/101, GEN 465 (1st).
69 Gilbert, *Never Despair*, p. 959. For the details of the Strath Report see Hennessy, *Secret State*, chapter 4.
70 Ibid.
71 Arnold, *Britain and the H–Bomb*, p. 20.
72 Ibid.
73 William L. Lawrence, 'Vast Power Bared: March 1 Explosion Was Equivalent to Millions of Tons of TNT', *New York Times*, 1 April 1954. It is reproduced in Arleen Keylin (ed.), *The Fabulous Fifties: As Reported by the New York Times* (Arno Press, 1978), p. 118.
74 Ibid.
75 NA, PRO, CAB 130/101, GEN 465 (1st).
76 Compare NA, PRO, CAB 130/101, GEN 465 (1st) with Arnold, *Britain and the H–Bomb*, p. 234.
77 Compare NA, PRO, CAB 130/101, GEN 465 (1st) with Arnold, *Britain and the H-Bomb*, p. 235.
78 NA, PRO, CAB 130/101, GEN 465 (1st).
79 Arnold, *Britain and the H-Bomb*, p. 41.
80 NA, PRO, CAB 130/101, GEN 465 (1st).
81 Ibid.
82 Ibid.
83 Ibid.
84 Gilbert, *Never Despair*, p. 960.
85 NA, PRO, CAB 130/101, GEN 465 (1st).
86 NA, PRO, CAB 130/100, GEN 458/1, 'Atomic Energy Estimates. Note by the Minister of Supply', 3 March 1954.
87 Ibid.
88 Ibid., GEN 458/1st meeting, 4 March 1954.
89 Peter Hennessy, *Cabinet* (Blackwell, 1986), pp. 153–4.
90 Robert Cooper, *The Breaking of Nations: Order and Chaos in the Twenty-First Century* (Atlantic Books, 2003), p. 129.
91 Sir Michael Quinlan in conversation with Sir John Willis and the author, the National Archives, Kew, 6 May 2004.
92 Ibid.
93 Ibid.
94 John W. Young, 'Cold War and Détente with Moscow', in John W. Young (ed.), *The Foreign Policy of Churchill's Peacetime Administration, 1951–1955* (Leicester University Press, 1988), p. 55.
95 Conversation at the National Archives, 6 May 2004.
96 Hennessy, *The Secret State*, pp. 49–58.
97 Arnold, *Britain and the H-Bomb*, p. 84.
98 Peter Hennessy, *Muddling Through: Power, Politics and the Quality of Government in Postwar Britain* (Gollancz, 1996), pp. 105–6. Lord Plowden described this classic vignette of Churchillian decision-reaching (as opposed to making, which Cabinet and Cabinet Committees did) when interviewed for the BBC Radio 4 programme *A Bloody Union Jack on Top of It*, which was broadcast in two parts on 5 and 12 May 1988.
99 Moran, *Churchill: The Struggle for Survival*, p. 504, diary entry for 3 December 1953.

100 Colville, *The Fringes of Power*, entry for 3 December 1953.

101 Moran, *Churchill: The Struggle for Survival*, p. 504, diary entry for 3 December 1953.

102 Martin Gilbert found the record of this exchange on 5 December 1953 at Bermuda in the Eisenhower papers and reproduced it in *Never Despair*, p. 924.

103 NA, PRO, PREM 11/418, 'Tripartite Meeting between the United Kingdom, the United States and France, held in Bermuda, December 1953', Note ('Summary of the Prime Minister's Remarks'), JRC, 5 December 1953. See also Gilbert, *Never Despair*, p. 928.

104 Colville, *The Fringes of Power*, entry for 6 December 1953.

105 Ibid.

106 Moran, *Churchill: The Struggle for Survival*, p. 508, diary entry for 7 December 1953.

107 Ibid.

108 Evelyn Shuckburgh, *Descent to Suez: Diaries, 1951–56* (Weidenfeld & Nicolson, 1986), entry for 24 April 1954.

109 Ibid.

110 NA, PRO, PREM 11/645, 'Franco-Vietnamese Negotiations: Consideration Given to the Extent of British US Assistance and Possible Defence of South-East Asia and Western Pacific', Record of a conversation at dinner at Chequers, Monday, April 26, 1954.

111 Janet Morgan (ed.), *The Backbench Diaries of Richard Crossman* (Hamish Hamilton/Cape, 1981), entry for 6 April 1954.

112 Ruth Winstone (ed.), *Tony Benn, Years of Hope: Diaries, Papers and Letters 1940–1962* (Hutchinson, 1994), p. 178.

113 Kenneth Harris, *Attlee* (Weidenfeld & Nicolson, 1982), p. 411.

114 Morgan, *The Backbench Diaries of Richard Crossman*, entry for 6 April 1954.

115 Ibid.

116 House of Commons Official Report, 5 April 1954, cols. 51–2.

117 Gilbert, *Never Despair*, p. 970.

118 Shuckburgh, *Descent to Suez: Diaries, 1951–56*, entry for 5 April 1954.

119 Ibid.

120 Gilbert, *Never Despair*, p. 966.

121 Ibid. House of Commons Official Report, 5 April 1954, col. 50.

122 'HORROR BOMBS: A Policy for Survival', *Sunday Pictorial*, 28 March 1954.

123 Catterall, *The Macmillan Diaries: The Cabinet Years, 1950–1957*, entry for 6 April 1954.

124 Harris, *Attlee*, p. 517.

125 Robert Rhodes James, *Bob Boothby: A Portrait* (John Curtis/Hodder, 1991), pp. 113–23, 126–9.

126 Catterall, *The Macmillan Diaries: The Cabinet Years, 1950–1957*, entry for 6 April 1954.

127 Rhodes James, *Bob Boothby*, p. 373.

128 Catterall, *The Macmillan Diaries: The Cabinet Years, 1950–1957*, entry for 6 April 1954.

129 Roy Jenkins, *Churchill* (Macmillan, 2001), p. 502.

130 Macmillan's diary (in the original) has a charming vignette from early 1955 of Churchill's budgerigar, Toby, perching on Macmillan's shoulder and kissing his neck 'while the sonorous "Gibbonesque" sentences were rolling out of the maestro's mouth on the most terrible and destructive engine of mass warfare yet known to mankind'. (Macmillan was, by this time, Minister of Defence.) The Macmillan Diary, Department of Western Manuscripts, Bodleian Library, University of Oxford, file d. 19, entry for 26 January 1955.

131 Moran, *Churchill: The Struggle for Survival*, p. 536, diary entry for 5 April 1954.

132 Gilbert, *Never Despair*, p. 969.

133 Moran, *Churchill: The Struggle for Survival*, p. 538, diary entry for 6 April 1954.

134 NA, PRO, CAB 130/101, GEN 464, 1st meeting, 'Atomic Energy Development', 13 April 1954.

135 Ibid.

136 NA, PRO, PREM 11/666, 'Prime Minister's Visit to Washington, June 1954'.

137 Gilbert, *Never Despair*, p. 973, fn. 1.

138 Ibid., p. 997.

139 Moran, *Churchill: The Struggle for Survival*, p. 560, diary entry for 25 June 1954.

140 Gilbert, *Never Despair*, p. 997.

141 Ibid., p. 995.

142 NA, PRO, CAB 134/808, DP (54) 6, 'United Kingdom Defence Policy. Memorandum by the Chiefs of Staff', 1 June 1954.

143 NA, PRO, CAB 129/69, C (54) 249, 'United Kingdom Defence Policy', 23 July 1954.

144 NA, PRO, CAB 134/808, DP (54) 6, 'Annex. Report by the Working Party on the Operational Use of Atomic Weapons: Hydrogen Bomb Research and Production in the United Kingdom'.

145 Ibid.

146 Ibid.

147 NA, PRO, CAB 158/5, JIC (48) 116 (Final), JP (49) 80 (Final), 'The Use of Atomic Weapons in a War against the Soviet Union. Report by the Joint Intelligence Committee and the Joint Planning Staff', 4 August 1949. I am grateful to Dr Stephen Twigge of the National Archives for bringing this document to my attention.

148 NA, PRO, CAB 134/808, DP (54) 6, 'Annex. Report by the Working Party on the Operational Use of Atomic Weapons: Hydrogen Bomb Research and Production in the United Kingdom'.

149 Moran, *Churchill: The Struggle for Survival*, p. 634, diary entry for 1 March 1955.

150 Ibid.

151 NA, PRO, CAB 134/808, DP (54) 6.

152 Ibid.

153 Ibid.

154 Raymond Aron, *On War: Atomic Weapons and Global Diplomacy* (1956; published in Britain by Secker and Warburg, 1958), p. 46.

155 Ibid., p. 87.

156 NA, PRO, CAB 134/808, DP (54), 2nd meeting, 19 May 1954.

157 Ibid., 3rd meeting, 'Atomic Weapons Programme', 16 June 1954, confidential annex.

158 Ibid.

159 Colville, *The Fringes of Power*, entry for 25 June 1954.

160 Ibid.

161 Moran, *Churchill: The Struggle for Survival*, p. 561, diary entry for 25 June 1954.

162 Ibid.

163 Ibid., p. 563, diary entry for 26 June 1954.

164 Ibid. Gilbert, *Never Despair*, p. 997.

165 Moran, *Churchill: The Struggle for Survival*, p. 563, diary entry for 26 June 1954.

166 Ibid.

167 Ibid.

168 Ibid.

169 Martin Gilbert makes rich use of it in his *Never Despair*, pp. 1001–3.

170 Ibid., p. 1007.

171 Colville, *The Fringes of Power*, p. 693.

172 Gilbert, *Never Despair*, p. 1007.

173 Colville, *The Fringes of Power*, entry for 27 June 1954.

174 Catterall, *The Macmillan Diaries: The Cabinet Years, 1950–1957*, entry for 6 July 1954.

175 Harold Macmillan, *Riding the Storm, 1956–59* (Macmillan, 1971), p. 324.

176 Arnold, *Britain and the H-Bomb*, p. 197.

177 Ibid., pp. 197–8.

178 Cmnd. 537 (HMSO, 1958).

179 Arnold, *Britain and the H-Bomb*, pp. 198–220.

180 NA, PRO, CAB 128/27, CC (54) 47, 7 July 1954.

181 http://data2.collectionscanada.ca/e/e034/e00832103/gif/. I am very grateful to the Canadian High Commissioner in London, Mel Cappe, for sending this minute to me on 21 April 2004.

182 Colville, *The Fringes of Power*, entry for 29 June 1954.

183 Arnold, *Britain and the H-Bomb*, p. 54. As an official historian Mrs Arnold had access to still-classified minutes and memoranda.

184 Ibid., pp. 54–5.

185 Moran, *Churchill: The Struggle for Survival*, p. 571, diary entry for 1 July 1954.

186 Colville, *The Fringes of Power*, entry for 2 July 1954.

187 Ibid.

188 Ibid.

189 Thorpe, *Eden*, p. 443.

190 Colville, *The Fringes of Power*, entry for 2 July 1954.

191 Ibid.

192 Ibid.

193 Ibid.

194 Moran, *Churchill: The Struggle for Survival*, p. 576, diary entry for 4 July 1954.

195 Ibid., p. 577, diary entry for 5 July 1954.

196 Ibid., p. 578.

197 Ibid.

198 Catterall, *The Macmillan Diaries: The Cabinet Years, 1950–1957*, entry for 6 July 1954.

199 Ibid.

200 Ibid.

201 Ibid., entry for 10 July 1954.

202 Ibid., entry for 31 July 1954.

203 Ibid.

204 Ibid., diary entry for 7 July 1954.

205 Simon Ball, *The Guardsmen: Harold Macmillan, Three Friends and the World They Made* (HarperCollins, 2004).

206 Peregrine Worsthorne, 'The Race of the Thoroughbreds', *The Spectator*, 22 May 2004.

207 Ball, *The Guardsmen*, p. 232.

208 Ibid., p. 233.

209 Catterall, *The Macmillan Diaries: The Cabinet Years, 1950–1957*, entry for 7 July 1954; NA, PRO, CAB 128/27, 'Confidential Annex', CC (54), 47th Conclusions, Minute 4, 7 July 1954.

210 NA, PRO, CAB 128/27, 'Confidential Annex', CC (54), 47th Conclusions, Minute 4, 7 July 1954.

211 Catterall, *The Macmillan Diaries: The Cabinet Years, 1950–1957*, entry for 7 July 1954.

212 NA, PRO, CAB 128/27, CC (54), 47th Conclusions, 7 July 1954.

213 Catterall, *The Macmillan Diaries: The Cabinet Years, 1950–1957*, entry for 7 July 1954.

214 Ibid., entry for 8 July 1954; NA, PRO, CAB 128/27, CC (54), 48th Conclusions, 8 July 1954.

215 Catterall, *The Macmillan Diaries: The Cabinet Years, 1950–1957*, entry for 9 July 1954.

216 NA, PRO, CAB 128/27, 'Confidential Annex', CC (54), 49th Conclusions, Minute 1, 9 July 1954.

217 Catterall, *The Macmillan Diaries: The Cabinet Years, 1950–1957*, entry for 9 July 1954.

218 Ibid.

219 Ball, *The Guardsmen*, p. xix.

220 Catterall, *The Macmillan Diaries: The Cabinet Years, 1950–1957*, entry for 9 July 1954.

221 Ibid., entry for 16 July 1954.

222 Colville, *The Fringes of Power*, entry for 16 July 1954.

223 Catterall, *The Macmillan Diaries: The Cabinet Years, 1950–1957*, entry for 18 July 1954.

224 Ibid., entry for 23 July 1954.

225 Ibid.

226 Ibid.

227 NA, PRO, CAB 128/27, 'Confidential Annex', CC (54), 52nd Conclusions, Minute 3, 23 July 1954.

228 W. C. Sellar and R. J. Yeatman, *1066 and All That: A Memorable History of England* (Macmillan, 1930), p. 52.

229 Catterall, *The Macmillan Diaries: The Cabinet Years, 1950–1957*, entry for 23 July 1954.

230 Ibid.

231 NA, PRO, CAB 128/27, 'Confidential Annex', CC (54), 52nd Conclusions, Minute 3, 23 July 1954.

232 Ibid., 53rd Conclusions, Minute 2, 26 July 1954.

233 Ibid., Minute 3, 26 July 1954.

234 Winn, *RAF Strategic Nuclear Deterrent Forces*, p. 205, fn. 2.

235 Private information.

236 Colville, *The Fringes of Power*, entry for 16 July 1954.

237 Jenkins, *Churchill*, p. xv.

238 Lord Home, *The Way the Wind Blows* (Collins, 1976), p. 217.

239 James Margach, *The Abuse of Power* (W. H. Allen, 1978), p. 105.

240 Ibid., pp. 105–6.

241 Colville, *The Fringes of Power*, entry for 4 April 1955.

242 Catterall, *The Macmillan Diaries: The Cabinet Years, 1950–1957*, entry for 6 April 1955.

243 The first was Robert Rhodes James, whose *Anthony Eden* was published by Weidenfeld & Nicolson in 1986.

8 Out of the Stalls

1 Macmillan in conversation with Richard Thorpe, 23 April 1975 and quoted in D. R. Thorpe, *Eden: The Life and Times of Anthony Eden, First Earl of Avon, 1897–1977* (Chatto, 2003), p. 430.

2 Philip M. Williams (ed.), *The Diary of Hugh Gaitskell, 1945–1956* (Cape, 1983), entry for 9 January 1956.

3 Roy Jenkins' *Observer* review of Robert Rhodes James, *Anthony Eden* (Weidenfeld & Nicolson, 1986) is reproduced in Roy Jenkins, *Gallery of 20th-Century Portraits* (David and Charles, 1988), pp. 76–9.

4 Ben Pimlott (ed.), *The Political Diary of Hugh Dalton, 1918–1940, 1945–60* (Cape, 1986), pp. 657–8.

5 David Butler, *British General Elections since 1945* (Blackwell, 1989), pp. 13–16.

6 Thorpe, *Eden*, p. 438.

7 Peter Catterall (ed.), *The Macmillan Diaries: The Cabinet Years, 1950–1957* (Macmillan, 2003), entry for 5 May 1955.

8 James Margach, *The Abuse of Power* (W. H. Allen, 1978), p. 106.

9 Janet Morgan (ed.), *The Backbench Diaries of Richard Crossman* (Hamish Hamilton/Cape, 1981) entry for 3 May 1955.

10 John Boyd-Carpenter, *Way of Life* (Sidgwick and Jackson, 1980), p. 123.

11 Peter Hennessy, *Muddling Through: Power, Politics and the Quality of Government in Postwar Britain* (Gollancz, 1996), p. 201.

12 Butler, *British General Elections since 1945*, p. 18.

13 *United for Peace and Progress* (Conservative Party, 1955) is reproduced in Iain Dale (ed.), *Conservative Party General Election Manifestos, 1900–1997* (Routledge/Politicos, 2000), pp. 101–26.

14 Thorpe, *Eden*, p. 439.

15 Ibid.

16 Ibid., p. 441.

17 Ibid., p. 440.

18 See plate 2 of the photographs between pp. 130 and 131 in Peter Hennessy, *The Prime Minister: The Office and Its Holders since 1945* (Penguin, 2001).

19 Catterall, *The Macmillan Diaries: The Cabinet Years, 1950–1957*, entry for 28 October 1951.

20 John Ramsden, *An Appetite for Power: A History of the Conservative Party since 1830* (HarperCollins, 1998), p. 352.

21 Ibid.

22 Ibid., p. 354. For the footnote: letter from Bernard Black to Peter Hennessy, 27 August 2002.

23 Hennessy, *The Prime Minister*, pp. 213–14.

24 National Archives, Public Record Office [NA, PRO], PREM 11/948, 'Request by Prime Minister for Notes from Ministers on Main Problems in Their Departments so as to Review General Situation', sent on 10 April 1955.

25 Ibid., Macleod to Eden, 13 April 1955.

26 Rhodes James, *Anthony Eden*, p. 625.

27 Lord Moran, *Churchill: The Struggle for Survival 1940–65* (Constable, 1966), p. 579, diary entry for 5 July 1954.

28 NA, PRO, CAB 129/17, CP (56) 1, 'Technological Education. Memorandum by the Prime Minister', 2 January 1956.

29 Ibid. 'Note by Lord Cherwell', 28 December 1955.

30 Ibid.

31 Keith Kyle, *Suez* (Weidenfeld & Nicolson, 1991), p. 155.

32 Harold Macmillan, *Riding the Storm, 1956–1959* (Macmillan, 1971), p. 105.

33 NA, PRO, CAB 129/78, CP (55) 205, 'Technical Education. Memorandum by the Minister of Education', 19 December 1955.

34 *Technical Education*, Cmnd. 9703 (HMSO, 1956).

35 NA, PRO, CP (55) 205

36 Peter Hennessy, *Whitehall* (Pimlico, 2001), p. 37.

37 Noel Annan, *Our Age: Portrait of a Generation* (Weidenfeld & Nicolson, 1990), p. 407.

38 Ibid., p. 362.

39 Nicholas Timmins, *The Five Giants: A Biography of the Welfare State*, revised edn (HarperCollins, 2001), p. 198.

40 NA, PRO, CAB 129/78, CP (55) 205, 'Technical Education. Memorandum by the Minister of Education', 19 December 1955.

41 Ibid.

42 Ibid.

43 NA, PRO, CAB 129/79, CP (56) 1.

44 Ibid.

45 Catterall, *The Macmillan Diaries: The Cabinet Years, 1950–1957*, entry for 20 January 1956.

46 Timmins, *The Five Giants*, p. 199.

47 NA, PRO, PREM 11/1138, 'Thoughts on the General Position after Suez', Bishop to Laskey, 28 December 1956.

48 Ibid.

49 Timmins, *The Five Giants*, pp. 202–3; *Higher Education*, Cmnd. 2154 (HMSO, 1963).

50 Geoffrey Owen, *From Empire to Europe: The Decline and Revival of British Industry since the Second World War* (HarperCollins, 1999), pp. 32–40.

51 Andrew Roberts, *Eminent Churchillians* (Weidenfeld & Nicolson, 1994), p. 274.

52 Ibid., pp. 239–40.

53 Ibid., p. 284.

54 Ibid., p. 241.

55 Macmillan, *Riding the Storm*, pp. 4–6.

56 For an excellent account of the spectrum of Whitehall ministerial and official views on the Messina talks of the Six and the resultant Spaak Committee see James Ellison's 'Malicious Conception' chapter in his *Threatening Europe: Britain and the Creation of the European Community, 1955–58* (Macmillan/Institute of Contemporary British History, 2000), pp. 13–36.

57 Alan S. Milward, *The Rise and Fall of a National Strategy, 1945–1963: The United Kingdom and the European Community*, vol. I (Frank Cass, 2002), p. 178.

58 Ibid.

59 Macmillan, *Riding the Storm*, p. 5.

60 Zig Layton-Henry, *The Politics of Immigration: 'Race' and 'Race' Relations in Postwar Britain* (Blackwell, 1992), p. 33. For the 1953 report see NA, PRO, DO 35/5216, 'Report of the Working Party on Coloured People Seeking Employment in the United Kingdom', December 1953.

61 NA, PRO, CAB 129/77, 'Report of the Committee on the Social and Economic Problems arising from the Growing Influx into the United Kingdom of Coloured Workers from other Commonwealth Countries', Appendix 2, 3 August 1955.

62 NA, PRO, CAB 129/81, 'Colonial Immigrants. Report of the Committee of Ministers', 22 June 1956.

63 Randall Hansen, *Citizenship and Immigration in Post-war Britain: The Institutional Origins of a Multicultural Nation* (Oxford University Press, 2000), pp. 73–4; Layton-Henry, *The Politics of Immigration*, pp. 32–6; House of Commons Official Report, 10 November 1955, cols. 2005–6.

64 NA, PRO, CAB 128/27, Part II, CM (54), 82nd Conclusions, 6 December 1954.

65 Hansen, *Citizenship and Immigration in Post-war Britain*, pp. 74–5.

66 NA, PRO, CAB 129/78, 'Colonial Immigrants. Memorandum by the Secretary of State for the Colonies', 1 November 1955.

67 Hansen, *Citizenship and Immigration in Post-war Britain*, p. 77; NA, PRO, CAB 128/29, CM (55), 39th Conclusions, 3 November 1955.

68 NA, PRO, PREM 11/2920, 'Consideration of Question of Taking Powers to Control Commonwealth Immigration', Brook to Eden, 10 November 1955.

69 NA, PRO, DO 35/5217, 'Control of Entry of British Subjects into the United Kingdom', 13 April 1955.

70 NA, PRO, CAB 129/77, CP (55) 113, 'Colonial Immigrants. Memorandum by the Secretary of State for Commonwealth Relations', 2 September 1955.

71 NA, PRO, CAB 129/81, 'Coloured Immigrants: Report of the Committee of Ministers', 22 June 1956.

72 NA, PRO, CAB 128/30, Part II, CM (56), 48th Conclusions, 11 July 1956.

73 Hansen, *Citizenship and Immigration in Post-war Britain*, p. 78.

74 Richard Lamb, *The Failure of the Eden Government* (Sidgwick and Jackson, 1987), p. 23.

75 Ibid., p. 24.

76 Ibid., p. 28.

77 Robert Taylor, *The Trade Union Question in British Politics: Government and Unions since 1945* (Blackwell, 1993), p. 93.

78 Ibid., p. 101; Geoffrey Goodman, *The Awkward Warrior Frank Cousins: His Life and Times* (Davis Poynter, 1979), p. 135.

79 Taylor, *The Trade Union Question in British Politics*, p. 101.

80 NA, PRO, CAB 134/1273.

81 NA, PRO, PREM 11/1238, 'Communist Influence in Industry and Trade Unions', Brook to Eden, 28 April 1956.

82 Lamb, *The Failure of the Eden Government*, p. 27.

83 Thorpe, *Eden*, p. 442.

84 Rhodes James, *Anthony Eden*, p. 409.

85 NA, PRO, PREM 11/1029, 'Lord Nuffield's Views on Trades Union and Recent Strikes'.

86 Rhodes James, *Anthony Eden*, p. 416.

87 Taylor, *The Trade Union Question in British Politics*, p. 29.
88 Macmillan, *Riding the Storm*, p. 5.
89 Ibid., p. 6.
90 Ibid., p. 4.
91 Catterall, *The Macmillan Diaries: The Cabinet Years, 1950–1957*, p. 464.
92 Lord Butler, *The Art of the Possible: The Memoirs of Lord Butler* (Hamish Hamilton, 1971), p. 176.
93 Sidney Pollard, *The Wasting of the British Economy*, second edn (Croom Helm, 1984), p. 38.
94 Edmund Dell, *The Chancellors: A History of the Chancellors of the Exchequer, 1945–90* (HarperCollins, 1996), p. 201.
95 Ibid., p. 201.
96 Lord Lawson of Blaby, R. A. Butler Memorial Lecture to the Coningsby Club delivered at the Carlton Club, 23 June 2004.
97 Ibid.
98 Dell, *The Chancellors*, p. 200.
99 Harold Macmillan, *Tides of Fortune, 1945–1955* (Macmillan, 1969), p. 696.
100 Alistair Horne, *Macmillan, 1894–1956* (Macmillan, 1988), p. 374.
101 Ibid., p. 375.
102 Thorpe, *Eden*, p. 564.
103 Rhodes James, *Anthony Eden*, p. 423.
104 Thorpe, *Eden*, p. 456.
105 Dell, *The Chancellors*, p. 1.
106 Victor Rothwell, *Anthony Eden: A Political Biography, 1931–57* (Manchester University Press, 1992), p. 165.
107 Thorpe, *Eden*, p. 449.
108 Harold Wilson, *A Prime Minister on Prime Ministers* (Weidenfeld & Nicolson/Michael Joseph, 1977), p. 297.
109 Hennessy, *The Prime Minister*, p. 160.
110 Macmillan, *Riding the Storm*, p. 4.
111 Ibid., p. 6.
112 Ibid., p. 5. For the footnote, see Timmins, *The Five Giants*, p. 207; Peter Hennessy, *Cabinet* (Blackwell, 1986), p. 53.
113 Ibid., p. 6.
114 Catterall, *The Macmillan Diaries: The Cabinet Years, 1950–1957*, p. 481.
115 Horne, *Macmillan, 1894–1956*, pp. 371–2.
116 Conversation with Sir Michael Quinlan, 9 August 2004.
117 Catterall, *The Macmillan Diaries: The Cabinet Years, 1950–1957*, entry for 8 October 1955.
118 NA, PRO, PREM 5/228, 'Ministerial Appointments. Ministry of Sir Anthony Eden (Conservative) Part I', Macmillan to Eden, 24 October 1955.
119 Thorpe, *Eden*, p. 456.
120 Ibid., p. 450.
121 Alec Cairncross (ed.), *The Robert Hall Diaries, 1954–1961* (Unwin Hyman, 1991), entry for 24 November 1955.
122 Ibid., entry for 21 December 1955.
123 Horne, *Macmillan, 1894–1956*, p. 63. For Keynes and Macmillan in 1940 see Robert Skidelsky, *John Maynard Keynes: Fighting for Britain, 1937–1946* (Macmillan, 2000), pp. 61–4. J. M. Keynes, *How to Pay for the War* (Macmillan, 1940).
124 Catterall, *The Macmillan Diaries: The Cabinet Years, 1950–1957*, entry for 25 August 1950.
125 J. M. Keynes, *The General Theory of Employment, Interest and Money* (Macmillan, 1936), p. 383.

126 Ibid., pp. 383–4.
127 Macmillan, *Riding the Storm*, p. 2.
128 Ibid.
129 Letter from Dr Stephen Twigge of the National Archives, 16 August 2004.
130 Catterall, *The Macmillan Diaries: The Cabinet Years, 1950–1957*, p. 520.
131 Ibid., entry for 16 January 1956.
132 Ibid., entry for 30 December 1955.
133 Dell, *The Chancellors*, p. 209.
134 Ibid., p. 196; Hennessy, *The Prime Minister*, p. 318; Dell, *The Chancellors*, pp. 437–8.
135 Dell, *The Chancellors*, p. 196.
136 Ibid.
137 NA, PRO, T 230/405, 'General Economic Situation', Macmillan to Petch, 2 January 1956. I am grateful to Dr Stephen Twigge of the National Archives for finding this memo and for drawing it to my attention.
138 NA, PRO, CAB 129/79, CP (56) 7, 'The Economic Situation. Memorandum by the Chancellor of the Exchequer', 6 January 1956.
139 Ibid.
140 NA, PRO, PREM 11/414, 'Cabinet, 1951–63', 'Economic Policy Committee', Brook to Eden, 29 May 1956. Eden scribbled this request on Brook's minute.
141 NA, PRO, CAB 129/79, CP (56) 7.
142 NA, PRO, T 172/2135, 'Minutes to Ministers', Macmillan to Eden, 2 January 1956.
143 Ibid., Macmillan to Eden, 2 July 1956 (referring back to the figure for the end of May).
144 Ibid.
145 Ibid., Macmillan to Eden, 16 July 1956.
146 Dell, *The Chancellors*, p. 172.
147 Macmillan, *Riding the Storm*, pp. 7–8.
148 NA, PRO, CAB 129/79, CP (56) 7.
149 Cairncross, *The Robert Hall Diaries, 1954–1961*, entry for 15 May 1956.
150 Ibid., entry for 19 January 1956.
151 Catterall, *The Macmillan Diaries: The Cabinet Years, 1950–1957*, entry for 12 January 1956.
152 Cairncross, *The Robert Hall Diaries, 1954–1961*, entry for 15 May 1956.
153 *The Economic Implications of Full Employment*, Cmd. 9725 (HMSO, 1956).
154 Catterall, *The Macmillan Diaries: The Cabinet Years, 1950–1957*, entry for 22 March 1956.
155 NA, PRO, CAB 129/79, CP (56) 17, 'The Economic Situation. Memorandum by the Chancellor of the Exchequer', 21 January 1956.
156 Ibid.
157 Catterall, *The Macmillan Diaries: The Cabinet Years, 1950–1957*, entry for 20 January 1956.
158 NA, PRO, CAB 129/79, CP (56) 17.
159 Catterall, *The Macmillan Diaries: The Cabinet Years, 1950–1957*, entry for 20 January 1956.
160 Ibid., entry for 11 February 1956.
161 Ibid.
162 Ibid., entry for 15 February 1956.
163 Ibid.
164 Dell, *The Chancellors*, p. 210.
165 House of Commons Official Report, 17 April 1956, col. 867.
166 Catterall, *The Macmillan Diaries: The Cabinet Years, 1950–1957*, entry for 24 April 1956.
167 Dell, *The Chancellors*, p. 196.
168 Ibid., pp. 284–5.
169 Catterall, *The Macmillan Diaries: The Cabinet Years, 1950–1957*, entry for 24 April 1956.
170 NA, PRO, PREM 11/1325, 'UK Economic Situation', 'Half-Time', Macmillan to Eden, 1 June

1956; Alec Cairncross, *The British Economy since 1945* (Blackwell, 1992), p. 105.

171 NA, PRO, PREM 11/1325.

172 Ibid.

173 Ibid.

174 Ibid. For the figures quoted in the footnote see Michael Dockrill, *British Defence since 1945* (Blackwell, 1988), p. 151.

175 NA, PRO, PREM 11/1325.

176 Catterall, *The Macmillan Diaries: The Cabinet Years, 1950–1957*, entry for 21 July 1956.

177 Timothy Garton Ash, *Free World* (Allen Lane, 2004), p. 28.

178 He did so, for example, after his ninetieth birthday dinner at his old college, Balliol, in 1984. Conversation with Sir Anthony Kenny, 30 September 2003.

179 Horne, *Macmillan, 1894–1956*, p. 49.

180 Conversation with his grandson, the Earl of Stockton, 8 May 2003. See also Horne, *Macmillan, 1894–1956*, p. 445.

181 Edward Heath, *The Course of My Life* (Hodder, 1998), p. 184.

182 Milward, *The Rise and Fall of a National Strategy*, p. 229.

183 Ibid., pp. 229–30.

184 Michael Charlton, *The Price of Victory* (BBC Books, 1983), p. 195.

185 I am grateful to Roy Jenkins for this image as he used it of Fifties British politicians when speaking at the Cabinet Office launch of Professor Alan Milward's *The Rise and Fall of a National Strategy*, on 8 July 2002.

186 Catterall, *The Macmillan Diaries: The Cabinet Years, 1950–1957*, p. 517.

187 Milward, *The Rise and Fall of a National Strategy*, p. 231; Ellison, *Threatening Europe*, pp. 25–7.

188 Catterall, *The Macmillan Diaries: The Cabinet Years, 1950–1957*, entry for 14 December 1955.

189 NA, PRO, T 232/433, 'European Economic Integration: Discussions Arising out of Messina Conference June 1955 and Brussels Conference July 1955', Bridges to Butler, 20 September 1955.

190 NA, PRO, T 234/100, 'Working Group under R. W. B. Clarke: Memoranda, Minutes and Correspondence', Macmillan to Bridges, 1 February 1956.

191 Milward, *The Rise and Fall of a National Strategy*, p. 229.

192 NA, PRO, CAB 134/1044, 'Mutual Aid Committee: Working Party on a European Common Market', Bretherton to Turnbull, 4 August 1955.

193 NA, PRO, BT 11/5715, 'European Free Trade Area: Papers Relating to Early Stages of Negotiations', R. F. Bretherton, 'Brussels Conference', 29 October 1955.

194 Patrick O'Brien, 'Security of the Realm and Economic Growth', in Peter Clarke and Clive Trebilcock (eds.), *Understanding Decline: Perceptions and Realities of British Economic Performance* (Cambridge University Press, 1997), p. 70.

195 David Cannadine, 'Apocalypse When?', ibid., pp. 267–8.

196 Ellison, *Threatening Europe*, pp. 134–5.

197 Hugo Young, *This Blessed Plot: Britain and Europe from Churchill to Blair* (Macmillan, 1998), p. 338.

198 Ellison, *Threatening Europe*, p. 135.

199 Miriam Camps, *Britain and the European Community, 1955–1963* (Princeton University Press, 1964), p. 169.

200 David Reynolds, *Britannia Overruled: British Policy and World Power in the 20th Century* (Longman, 1991), p. 218.

201 Milward, *The Rise and Fall of a National Strategy*, p. 215.

202 NA, PRO, CAB 134/1226, EP (55), 11th Meeting; Ellison, *Threatening Europe*, pp. 25–6.

203 For the genesis of MAC see Hennessy, *The Prime Minister*, p. 187.

204 NA, PRO, CAB 134/1026, MAC (55), 45th Meeting.

205 Preserved in NA, PRO, PREM 11/1333, 'Messina Conference', Petch to Cairncross,

16 November 1955. For Macmillan's conversation with Hare the following day: Catterall, *The Macmillan Diaries: The Cabinet Years, 1950–1957*, entry for 21 November 1955.

206 Charlton, *The Price of Victory*, p. 190.

207 Milward, *The Rise and Fall of a National Strategy*, pp. 182–4, 186–7.

208 NA, PRO, PREM 11/1333, 'European Integration'.

209 Ibid.

210 Milward, *The Rise and Fall of a National Strategy*, p. 183.

211 Ibid.

212 NA, PRO, PREM 11/1333, 'European Integration'.

213 Milward, *The Rise and Fall of a National Strategy*, pp. 302–3.

214 NA, PRO, PREM 11/1333, 'European Integration', Thorneycroft to Eden, 20 January 1956.

215 Lord Thorneycroft interviewed for the WideVision Productions/Channel 4 Television series, *What Has Become of Us?*, 29 July 1993.

216 NA, PRO, PREM 11/1333, Cairncross to Eden, 18 November 1955.

217 Ibid., 'European Integration'.

218 Ibid.

219 Ellison, *Threatening Europe*, p. 34; NA, PRO, T 232/433, Watts to Hall, 14 October 1955.

220 Ellison, *Threatening Europe*, p. 25; NA, PRO, CAB 134/889, ES (55), 8th Meeting.

221 NA, PRO, PREM 11/1333, 'European Integration'.

222 Ellison, *Threatening Europe*, p. 21.

223 For the flavour of Clarke see Hennessy, *Whitehall*, pp. 175–8.

224 Ellison, *Threatening Europe*, p. 31.

225 NA, PRO, T 234/100, 10 February 1956.

226 Ibid., Macmillan to Bridges, 1 February 1956.

227 Ibid., 24 February 1956.

228 NA, PRO, BT 11/5715, 'Working Group on a United Kingdom Initiative in Europe. Report', 20 April 1956.

229 Milward, *The Rise and Fall of a National Strategy*, p. 237.

230 NA, PRO, T 234/183, 'European Economic Integration: General Policy', 16 May 1956.

231 Milward, *The Rise and Fall of a National Strategy*, p. 246. The meeting in Macmillan's office took place on 31 May 1956.

232 John Lewis Gaddis, *We Now Know: Rethinking Cold War History* (Oxford University Press, 1997), p. 207.

233 Catterall, *The Macmillan Diaries: The Cabinet Years, 1950–1957*, p. 428, diary entry for 14 May 1955.

234 Gaddis, *We Now Know*, p. 207.

235 Lord Moran, *Churchill: The Struggle for Survival, 1940–65* (Constable, 1966), p. 655, diary entry for 11 May 1955.

236 Catterall, *The Macmillan Diaries: The Cabinet Years, 1950–1957*, entry for 18 July 1955.

237 Thorpe, *Eden*, p. 446.

238 André Fontaine, *History of the Cold War: From the Korean War to the Present* (Secker and Warburg, 1970), p. 130.

239 Dwight D. Eisenhower, *Mandate for Change: The White House Years, 1953–1959* (Doubleday, 1963), p. 521.

240 Catterall, *The Macmillan Diaries: The Cabinet Years, 1950–1957*, entry for 19 July 1955.

241 Ibid., entry for 22 July 1955.

242 Gaddis, *We Now Know*, p. 229.

243 Rhodes James, *Anthony Eden*, pp. 436–8; Christopher Andrew, *Secret Service: The Making of the British Intelligence Community* (Heinemann, 1985), pp. 495–6. At the time of writing, the Bridges report on the Crabb affair has yet to reach the National Archives. When it does it will be found in NA, PRO, PREM 11/2077, 'Commander Crabb'.

244 Thorpe, *Eden*, p. 470.

245 Ibid., p. 471.
246 Ibid.
247 Ibid.
248 Catterall, *The Macmillan Diaries: The Cabinet Years, 1950–1957*, pp. 553–4, entry for 26 April 1956.

9 To the Canal and Back

1 Peter Hennessy, *The Prime Minister: The Office and Its Holders since 1945* (Penguin, 2001), p. 247.
2 D. R. Thorpe, *Eden: The Life and Times of Anthony Eden, First Earl of Avon, 1897–1977* (Chatto, 2003), p. 528.
3 National Archives, Public Record Office [NA, PRO], FO 800/747, 'Legal Advisers: Nationalisation of Suez Canal Company', Fitzmaurice to Coldstream (and Kilmuir), 6 September 1956. I am grateful to Geoffrey Marston for bringing this memo to my attention in his 'Armed Intervention in the 1956 Suez Canal Crisis: The Legal Advice Tendered to the British Government', *International and Comparative Law Quarterly*, vol. 37 (October 1988), pp. 786–7.
4 Marc Bloch, *Feudal Society*, first published in 1940 (Routledge, 1961), p. 72.
5 Thorpe, *Eden*, p. 533. Mr Thorpe found this letter in Mollet's papers.
6 Victor Rothwell, *Anthony Eden: A Political Biography, 1931–57* (Manchester University Press, 1992), p. 255.
7 Ibid., p. 204.
8 Reflected jovially in the nickname of 'Big Q' given to Sir Michael by two of his protégés who later succeeded him as Permanent Secretary at MOD. Private information.
9 Michael Quinlan, 'Britain's Wars since 1945', paper presented to a conference on 'Just War', Wolfson College, Oxford, June 2003. I am grateful to Sir Michael for sending it to me.
10 Peter Hennessy, 'The Lightning Flash on the Road to Baghdad: Issues of Evidence', in W. G. Runciman (ed.), *Hutton and Butler: Lifting the Lid on the Workings of Power* (British Academy/Oxford University Press, 2004), p. 80.
11 Robert Cooper, *The Breaking of Nations: Order and Chaos in the Twenty-First Century* (Atlantic, 2003), pp. 5–6.
12 J. M. Keynes, *The General Theory of Employment, Interest and Money* (Macmillan, 1936), p. 383.
13 Sir Frank Cooper interviewed for the WideVision Productions/Channel 4 series *What Has Become of Us?*, 28 March 1994.
14 Evelyn Shuckburgh, *Descent to Suez: Diaries, 1951–56* (Weidenfeld & Nicolson, 1986), entry for 1 November 1956.
15 John W. Braasch, 'Anthony Eden's (Lord Avon) Biliary Tract Saga', *Annals of Surgery*, vol. 238, no. 5 (November 2003), pp. 772–5. I am very grateful to a surgeon who treated me, Mr J. M. Wellwood, for bringing this article to my attention.
16 Thorpe, *Eden*, p. 384.
17 Ibid.
18 Ibid., p. 385.
19 Ibid.
20 Ibid.
21 Ibid., p. 387.
22 Rhodes James, *Anthony Eden*, p. 597.
23 The Earl of Avon, *The Eden Memoirs: Full Circle* (Cassell, 1960), p. 419.
24 Rhodes James, *Anthony Eden*, p. 453.
25 Thorpe, *Eden*, p. 511.
26 D. R. Thorpe, *Selwyn Lloyd* (Cape, 1989), p. 227.
27 Rhodes James, *Anthony Eden*, p. 523.

28 Ibid., pp. 523–4.

29 Hugh L'Etang, *Fit to Lead?* (Heinemann Medical, 1980), p. 7; *The Pathology of Leadership* (Heinemann Medical, 1969), p. 165.

30 Percy Cradock, *Know Your Enemy: How the Joint Intelligence Committee Saw the World* (John Murray, 2002), p. 111.

31 Sir Anthony was speaking on *A Canal Too Far*, first broadcast on BBC Radio 3 in January 1987. The text of the programme is reproduced in Peter Hennessy, *Muddling Through: Power, Politics and the Quality of Government in Postwar Britain* (Gollancz, 1996). Nutting is quoted on pp. 131–2.

32 Shuckburgh, *Descent to Suez*, pp. 340–41.

33 Ibid., entry for 4 March 1956.

34 Ibid., entry for 3 March 1956.

35 Anthony Sampson, *Anatomy of Britain* (Hodder and Stoughton, 1962), p. 298.

36 Kevin Ruane and James Ellison, 'Managing the Americans: Anthony Eden, Harold Macmillan and the Pursuit of "Power by Proxy"', in Gaynor Johnson (ed.), special edition of *Contemporary British History*, vol. 18, no. 3 (Autumn 2004), p. 154.

37 The phrase was coined by David Reynolds in *Britannia Overruled: British Policy and World Power in the 20th Century* (Longman, 1991), pp. 177–8.

38 NA, PRO, CAB 129/53, C (52) 202, 'Britain's Overseas Obligations. Memorandum by the Foreign Secretary', 18 June 1952.

39 Ruane and Ellison, 'Managing the Americans', pp. 133–5.

40 Ibid., p. 137.

41 Ibid.

42 Keith Kyle, *Suez* (Weidenfeld & Nicolson, 1991), p. 56.

43 Peter Catterall (ed.), *The Macmillan Diaries: The Cabinet Years, 1950–1957* (Macmillan, 2003), entry for 14 July 1955.

44 Kyle, *Suez*, pp. 72–6; Cradock, *Know Your Enemy*, pp. 113–15.

45 John Lewis Gaddis, *We Now Know: Rethinking Cold War History* (Oxford University Press, 1997), p. 171.

46 Ibid.

47 Cradock, *Know Your Enemy*, p. 117; W. Scott Lucas, *Divided We Stand: Britain, the US and the Suez Crisis* (Hodder, 1991), pp. 111–27.

48 Cradock, *Know Your Enemy*, p. 110.

49 Kyle, *Suez*, p. 77.

50 Cradock, *Know Your Enemy*, pp. 114–15.

51 Chester L. Cooper, *The Lion's Last Roar* (Harper and Row, 1978), p. 170.

52 NA, PRO, CAB 158/23, JIC (56) 20, (Final), 4 April 1956, 'Factors Affecting Egypt's Policy in the Middle East and North Africa'.

53 Cradock, *Know Your Enemy*, pp. 115–16.

54 Shuckburgh, *Descent to Suez*, p. 345.

55 Cradock, *Know Your Enemy*, p. 109.

56 Shuckburgh, *Descent to Suez*, p. 354, diary entry for 24 September 1956.

57 Ibid., entry for 20 April 1956.

58 Kyle, *Suez*, p. 85.

59 Ibid., pp. 124–5.

60 Cradock, *Know Your Enemy*, p. 116.

61 Kyle, *Suez*, p. 129.

62 Ibid., pp. 133–4.

63 Ibid., pp. 125–6; NA, PRO, FO 371/11905, Johnston to Phillips, 6 June 1956.

64 Kyle, *Suez*, p. 130.

65 Thorpe, *Eden*, pp. 475–8.

66 Ibid., pp. 477–8.

67 Lord Sherfield speaking on *A Canal Too Far*.

68 Alistair Horne, *Macmillan, 1894–1956* (Macmillan, 1988), p. 438.

69 Hennessy, *The Prime Minister*, pp. 108, 221–2, 235, 239–42.

70 Catterall, *The Macmillan Diaries: The Cabinet Years, 1950–1957*, pp. 579–80.

71 NA, PRO, CAB 128/30, CM (56) 54, 27 July 1956.

72 Cradock, *Know Your Enemy*, p. 133; for its consideration by Scarlett and Dearlove see Hennessy, 'The Lightning Flash on the Road to Baghdad: Issues of Evidence', p. 74.

73 Cradock, *Know Your Enemy*, p. 133.

74 Private information.

75 Hennessy, 'The Lightning Flash on the Road to Baghdad: Issues of Evidence', p. 70.

76 *Review of Intelligence on Weapons of Mass Destruction. Report of a Committee of Privy Counsellors*, HC 898 (Stationery Office, 14 July 2004), pp. 153–5.

77 Cradock, *Know Your Enemy*, p. 133.

78 NA, PRO, CAB 158/25, JIC (56) 80 (Final) (Revise), 'Egyptian Nationalization of the Suez Canal Company', 3 August 1956.

79 Ibid.

80 Ibid.

81 Ibid.

82 NA, PRO, PREM 11/1152, 'Complaint by Cabinet Ministers that They Were not Sufficiently Informed of Decisions Made by the Suez Committee [sic] on Military Operations and Personal Letters to the Prime Minister Concerning Discussions in Cabinet on Suez Policy', Home to Eden, 24 August 1956.

83 NA, PRO, CAB 158/25, JIC (56) 80 (Final) (Revise).

84 Macmillan delivered this no doubt carefully considered line at a press conference on 24 July 1955 on returning to London from the Geneva Conference; Thorpe, *Eden*, p. 446.

85 Gaddis, *We Now Know*, p. 207.

86 Cradock, *Know Your Enemy*, p. 122.

87 NA, PRO, PREM, 11/1177, 'Exchange of Personal Messages between the Prime Minister, Sir Anthony Eden, and President Eisenhower', Eisenhower to Eden, 3 September 1956.

88 Shuckburgh, *Descent to Suez*, entry for 3 March 1956.

89 NA, PRO, PREM, 11/1177, Eisenhower to Eden, 3 September 1956.

90 NA, PRO, T 236/4188, 'Measures Introduced to Protect Sterling during the Suez Crisis', Bridges to Macmillan, 8 August 1956.

91 NA, PRO, T 172/2135, 'Minutes to Ministers', Macmillan to Eden, 16 July 1956.

92 Ibid., Macmillan to Eden, 27 August 1956.

93 Peter Hennessy, *Whitehall* (Pimlico, 2001), p. 145.

94 NA, PRO, T 172/2135, Bridges to Macmillan, 7 September 1956.

95 Ibid.

96 Ibid.

97 Catterall, *The Macmillan Diaries: The Cabinet Years, 1950–1957*, p. 596.

98 Ibid., entry for 25 September 1956.

99 Horne, *Macmillan, 1894–1956*, p. 422. Makins' note of the Eisenhower/Macmillan conversation of 25 September 1956 had still to reach the National Archives at the time of writing. When it does it will be found in NA, PRO, PREM 11/1102, 'Setting up of an organisation called the Co-operative Association of Suez Canal Users (CASU) and dispute with Egypt taken to the UN, 1956'.

100 Ibid., p. 603.

101 NA, PRO, T 172/2135, Rowan to Macmillan, 21 September 1956.

102 Ibid.

103 NA, PRO, T 172/2135.

104 Kyle, *Suez*, pp. 411–13. For Horne's comment in the footnote, see Peter Hennessy and Mark Laity, 'Suez – What the Papers Say'. *Contemporary Record*, vol. 1, no. 1 (Spring 1987), p. 8.

105 NA, PRO, T 172/2135, Macmillan to Eden, 29 October 1956.

106 Ibid., Macmillan to Eden, 5 November 1956.

107 Ibid.

108 Ibid., 'Gold and Dollar and EPU. Position. Report for the Week Ending 22nd December 1956'.

109 In the section that follows, I am deeply indebted to Geoffrey Marston's meticulous reconstruction of the ebb and flow of the legal debate over the Suez affair and the use of force; Marston, 'Armed Intervention in the 1956 Suez Canal Crisis', pp. 773–817.

110 NA, PRO, CAB 128/30, CM (56) 54, 27 July 1956.

111 Lord Kilmuir, *Political Adventure: The Memoirs of the Earl of Kilmuir* (Weidenfeld & Nicolson, 1964), p. 268.

112 Marston, 'Armed Intervention in the 1956 Suez Canal Crisis', pp, 778–9.

113 Ibid., pp. 779–91.

114 Ibid., p. 775.

115 NA, PRO, FO 800/747, Fitzmaurice to Manningham-Buller, 1 August 1956.

116 Anthony Nutting, *No End of a Lesson: The Story of Suez* (Constable, 1967), p. 95.

117 Edward Heath, *The Course of My Life* (Hodder, 1998), p. 169.

118 NA, PRO, PREM 11/1129, 'Lord Chancellor's memorandum on the use of force and question of consultation with the Law Officers'.

119 NA, PRO, FO 800/749, Manningham-Buller to Lloyd,' 1 November 1956.

120 Ibid.

121 NA, PRO, FO 371/119164, 'Suez Canal Nationalization; Legal Opinion from Lord Chancellor, Law Officers and Legal Adviser FO', Fitzmaurice to Kirkpatrick, 31 October 1956.

122 Ibid.

123 NA, PRO, FO 371/119728, 'Political Relations between Libya and UK', Fitzmaurice to Beeley, 10 August 1956.

124 Hennessy, *Muddling Through*, p. 142. At the time of writing, Macmillan's 24 August 1956 note to Eden has yet to reach the National Archives. When it does it will be found in NA, PRO, PREM 11/1100, 'Military action in the event of a breakdown of the Suez Canal Conference: question of referring to NATO and UN'.

125 Kyle, *Suez*, p. 288; Hennessy, *The Prime Minister*, pp. 245–6.

126 Hennessy, *Muddling Through*, p. 142.

127 Shuckburgh, *Descent to Suez*, p. 363.

128 Gore-Booth, Ms, Bodleian Library, Department of Western Manuscripts. I am grateful to Helen Langley of the Department for providing me with a copy.

129 Hennessy, *Muddling Through*, p. 142.

130 Shuckburgh, *Descent to Suez*, entry for 2 March 1956.

131 Hennessy, *Muddling Through*, p. 138.

132 Kyle, *Suez*, p. 92.

133 Hennessy, *Muddling Through*, pp. 138–9.

134 Ibid., p. 139.

135 Cradock, *Know Your Enemy*, p. 126.

136 Hennessy, *Muddling Through*, p. 138.

137 NA, PRO, DEFE 4/91, Annex to JP (56) 160 (Final), 'Military Implications of Mounting Operation Musketeer', 24 October 1956.

138 Ibid.

139 NA, PRO, WO 32/16731, 'Lessons from Operation Musketeer', Sir Dudley Ward, Deputy Chief of the Imperial General Staff, to the Army Council, April 1957.

140 NA, PRO, DEFE 4/91, 'Military Implications of Mounting Operation Musketeer'.

141 Avi Shlaim, 'The Protocol of Sèvres 1956: Anatomy of a War Plot', *International Affairs*, vol. 3, no. 73 (1997), p. 516.

142 Catterall, *The Macmillan Diaries: The Cabinet Years, 1950–1957*, p. 607.

143 Kyle, *Suez*, pp. 296–7.

144 Hennessy, *Muddling Through*, p. 139.

145 Shlaim, 'The Protocol of Sèvres 1956', p. 516.

146 Hennessy, *Muddling Through*, p. 140.
147 Ibid.
148 Shlaim, 'The Protocol of Sèvres 1956', p. 526. The first English translation of the Sèvres Protocol was published in Kyle, *Suez*, pp. 565–7. For Eden's order to destroy it, see Heath, *The Course of My Life*, p. 177.
149 Heath, *The Course of My Life*, p. 169.
150 Cradock, *Know Your Enemy*, p. 125.
151 Peter Hennessy, 'No End of an Argument', *Contemporary Record*, vol. 1, no. 1 (Spring 1987), pp. 12–13.
152 NA, PRO, CAB 128/30, CM (56) 72, Confidential Annex, 23 October 1956.
153 Hennessy, *The Prime Minister*, p. 222.
154 Thorpe, *Eden*, fn. to p. 517.
155 *Review of Intelligence on Weapons of Mass Destruction*, pp. 147–8; Hennessy, 'The Lightning Flash on the Road to Baghdad', p. 75. See also Peter Hennessy, 'Informality and Circumspection: The Blair Style of Government in War and Peace', *Political Quarterly*, vol. 70, no. 1 (January–March 2005), pp. 3–11.
156 NA, PRO, CAB 128/30, CM (56) 72, Confidential Annex.
157 Ibid., CM (56) 74, 25 October 1956.
158 Ibid., CM (56) 74, 25 October 1956 and CM (56) 75, 30 October 1956; Hennessy, *The Prime Minister*, pp. 224–5.
159 Sir Frank Cooper, 'Suez: Air Aspects', *RAF Historical Society Proceedings*, no. 3 (January 1988), p. 20.
160 Sir Frank Cooper addressing the 'Hidden Wiring' seminar at the Queen Mary and Westfield College MA in Contemporary British History programme, 10 February 1999.
161 Hennessy, *Muddling Through*, p. 143.
162 Ibid.
163 Cradock, *Know Your Enemy*, p. 125.
164 NA, PRO, DEFE 4/91, COS (56) 108, 1 November 1956.
165 NA, PRO, PREM 11/1090, 'Lord Mountbatten, First Sea Lord, Writes to the Prime Minister Expressing His Doubts About the Operation in Egypt', Mountbatten to Eden, 2 November 1956; Mountbatten to Hailsham, 4 November 1956; Hailsham to Mountbatten, 5 November 1956; Hailsham to Eden, 5 November 1956; Eden to Hailsham, 5 November 1956. See also Philip Ziegler, *Mountbatten* (Fontana/Collins, 1985), pp. 537–47.
166 Thorpe, *Eden*, pp. 586–9.
167 Lord Charteris interviewed for *What Has Become of Us?*, 6 June 1994.
168 Thorpe, *Eden*, p. 586.
169 NA, PRO, PREM 11/1163, '1956 The Queen'; Hennessy, *The Prime Minister*, p. 218.
170 Shuckburgh, *Descent to Suez*, p. 363.
171 At the time of writing, this particular message from Eden to Eisenhower had yet to reach the National Archives. When it does it will be found in NA, PRO, PREM 11/1105, 'Joint Communication (France–UK) to the Governments of Israel and Egypt, 1956)', Eden to Eisenhower, 30 October 1956.
172 NA, PRO, PREM, 11/1177, 'Exchange of Personal Messages between the Prime Minister, Sir Anthony Eden, and President Eisenhower', Eisenhower to Eden, 30 October 1956.
173 Ibid.
174 Dennis Greenhill, *More by Accident* (Wilton 65, 1992), p. 85.
175 NA, PRO, PREM, 11/1177, Eisenhower to Eden, 30 October 1956.
176 Ibid.
177 Cradock, *Know Your Enemy*, p. 124.
178 NA, PRO, CAB 158/25, JIC (56) 98 (Final), 4 October 1956.
179 Ibid.
180 Ibid.
181 Gaddis, *We Now Know*, p. 211.

182 NA, PRO, PREM 11/1105, 'Joint Communication (France–UK) to the Governments of Israel and Egypt', UK Del New York, telegram no. 1071 to Foreign Office, Sir P. Dixon, 5 November 1956.

183 Douglas Hurd, *Memoirs* (Little, Brown, 2003), pp. 138–9.

184 Kyle, *Suez*, pp. 456–7.

185 Gaddis, *We Now Know*, p. 236.

186 Ibid. For Eisenhower's address see Kyle, *Suez*, p. 386.

187 Hennessy, *The Prime Minister*, p. 209.

188 NA, PRO, AIR 8/1940, 'Operation Musketeer General Papers 1956–1958', DH Message 41329, 6 November 1956.

189 NA, PRO, CAB 159/25, 'Joint Intelligence Committee Minutes, October–December 1956', JIC (56), 101st Meeting, 8 November 1956, item 5, 'Daily Intelligence Estimates'.

190 'Sino-Soviet Intentions in the Suez Crisis: The Estimate', 6 November 1956, reproduced in Scott A. Koch (ed.), *CIA Cold War Records: Selected Estimates on the Soviet Union, 1950–1959* (CIA, 1993), pp. 145–6; Tom Bower, *The Perfect English Spy: Sir Dick White and the Secret War, 1939–90* (Heinemann, 1995), pp. 199–200.

191 Thorpe, *Eden*, p. 502.

192 Ibid., p. 528. For the Cabinet minutes see NA, PRO, CAB 128/30 CM (56).

193 Rhodes James, *Anthony Eden*, p. 574.

194 NA, PRO, CAB 128/30, CM (56), 80th Conclusions, 6 November 1956.

195 Horne, *Macmillan, 1894–1956*, p. 442.

196 Ibid., p. 440.

197 Ibid., p. 439.

198 NA, PRO, CAB 128/30, CM (56) 80.

199 Ibid.

200 Iverach McDonald, *A Man of The Times* (Hamish Hamilton, 1976), p. 153.

201 Ibid.

202 Ibid.

203 Ibid.

204 Ibid.

205 NA, PRO, CAB 128/30 Part 2, CM (56), 89th Conclusions, 27 November 1954.

206 Ibid., Part II, CM (56), 89th Conclusions, 27 November 1956.

207 Alec Cairncross (ed.), *The Robert Hall Diaries, 1954–1961* (Unwin Hyman, 1991), entry for 29 November 1956.

208 Horne, *Macmillan, 1894–1956*, pp. 441–2.

209 Hennessy, *Muddling Through*, p. 146.

210 Ibid.

211 NA, PRO, AIR 8/1940, 'Ministry of Defence to Allied Force Headquarters; Chiefs of Staff to General Keightley', 6 November 1956.

212 Hennessy, *Muddling Through*, p. 146.

213 Conversation with Sir Christopher Hogg, 25 July 1999.

214 Hennessy, *Muddling Through*, p. 149.

215 House of Commons Official Report, 3 December 1956, cols. 887–96.

216 Kyle, *Suez*, p. 514.

217 Shuckburgh, *Descent to Suez*, p. 366.

218 Denis Healey, *The Time of My Life* (Michael Joseph, 1989), p. 169.

219 Ibid.

220 House of Commons Official Report, 20 December 1956, col. 1493.

221 Ibid., col. 1518.

222 Thorpe, *Eden*, p. 545.

223 Heath, *The Course of My Life*, pp. 176–7.

224 Hennessy, *Whitehall*, p. 167.

225 Thorpe, *Eden*, p. 545.

226 Ibid., pp. 534–5.

227 Ibid., p. 538.

228 Ibid.

229 Peter Catterall (ed.), *The Macmillan Diaries: Prime Minister and After* (Macmillan, forthcoming), entry for 3 February 1957.

230 Horne, *Macmillan, 1894–1956*, p. 447.

231 Ibid., p. 455.

232 Thorpe, *Eden*, p. 539.

233 Heath, *The Course of My Life*, p. 176.

234 Philip Goodhart, *The 1922: The Story of the 1922 Committee* (Macmillan, 1973), p. 175.

235 Anthony Sampson, *Macmillan: A Study in Ambiguity* (Allen Lane, 1967), p. 124.

236 Horne, *Macmillan, 1894–1956*, p. 457.

237 Nigel Nicolson, *Long Life* (Weidenfeld & Nicolson, 1997), pp. 158–76.

238 Horne, *Macmillan, 1894–1956*, p. 457.

239 Lord Butler, *The Art of the Possible* (Hamish Hamilton, 1971), p. 194.

240 Horne, *Macmillan, 1894–1956*, p. 457.

241 Ibid., p. 458.

242 Shuckburgh, *Descent to Suez*, p. 366.

243 Thorpe, *Eden*, p. 544.

244 Ibid.

245 Lord Kilmuir, *Political Adventure*, pp. 283–4.

246 Thorpe, *Eden*, p. 546.

247 Rhodes James, *Anthony Eden*, p. 597.

248 Thorpe, *Eden*, p. 549.

249 Ibid., pp. 547–8.

250 Rudyard Kipling, *A Book of Words* (Macmillan, 1928), p. 26.

251 Peter Laslett, 'On Being an Englishman in 1950', *Cambridge Journal*, vol. 3 (1949–50), p. 494.

252 Cradock, *Know Your Enemy*, p. 134.

253 Michael Howard, *Captain Professor: A Life in War and Peace* (Continuum, 2006), p. 155.

10 Lightning Flash

1 Quoted in Peter Hennessy and Caroline Anstey, 'Moneybags and Brains: The Anglo-American "Special Relationship" since 1945', Strathclyde Analysis Paper no. 1, Department of Government, University of Strathclyde, p. 10.

2 Lord Hunt speaking on the WideVision Productions/Channel 4 series *What Has Become of Us?*, programme 3, 'The Last Roar', first broadcast 11 December 1994.

3 Conversation with Sir Christopher Mallaby, 8 December 2002.

4 Percy Cradock, *In Pursuit of British Interests: Reflections on Foreign Policy under Margaret Thatcher and John Major* (John Murray, 1997), p. 134.

5 Jean Monnet, *Memoirs* (Collins, 1978), p. 306.

6 Ibid., p. 452.

7 James Callaghan, *Time and Chance* (Collins, 1987), p. 341.

8 Margaret Thatcher, *The Path to Power* (HarperCollins, 1995), p. 88.

9 Ibid.

10 Anthony Montague Browne, *Long Sunset: Memoirs of Winston Churchill's Last Private Secretary* (Cassell, 1995), p. 210.

11 Ibid., p. 213.

12 John Colville, *The Fringes of Power: Downing Street Diaries, 1939–1955* (Hodder, 1985), p. 721.

13 Montague Browne, *Long Sunset*, p. 215.

14 National Archives, Public Record Office [NA, PRO], PREM 11/1138, 'Thoughts on the General Position after Suez', Bishop to Laskey, 28 December 1956.

15 Ibid.

16 Ibid.

17 Ibid.

18 Anthony Howard, *RAB: The Life of R. A. Butler* (Cape, 1987), p. 233.

19 Terence Price, *Political Physicist* (The Book Guild, 2004), p. 136.

20 NA, PRO, PREM 11/1138.

21 Sir Richard Powell, Permanent Secretary at the Ministry of Defence, made this point strongly in the BBC Radio 3 programme *A Canal Too Far*, first broadcast January 1987; see Peter Hennessy, *Muddling Through: Power, Politics and the Quality of Government in Postwar Britain* (Gollancz, 1996), p. 133.

22 Ibid.

23 Ibid., p. 134.

24 NA, PRO, PREM 11/1138.

25 Ibid. The missing section finally came to light in January 2006 when the No. 10 file dealing with Eden's requests to the Cabinet Office for papers needed for background to his memoirs was declassified at the National Archives: NA, PRO, PREM 16/424, 'Request from Lord Avon (Anthony Eden) for Cabinet Papers Relating to His Period as Prime Minister and His Concern about the Proposed Release in 1972 of the "Cream" of Second World War Records', Lord Avon to Trend, 2 June 1970.

26 Ibid.

27 Ibid.

28 Jean Lacouture, *De Gaulle, the Ruler: 1945–1970* (Harvill, 1991), pp. 174–8.

29 Ibid., p. 435.

30 Ibid., p. 164.

31 NA, PRO, CAB 129/84, CP (56) 256, 'A Mutual Free Trade Area with Europe. Memorandum by the Chancellor of the Exchequer and the President of the Board of Trade', 6 November 1956.

32 Alan S. Milward, *The Rise and Fall of a National Strategy, 1945–1963: The United Kingdom and the European Community*, vol. I (Frank Cass, 2002), p. 262.

33 Keith Kyle, *Suez* (Weidenfeld & Nicolson, 1991), p. 267.

34 NA, PRO, CAB 128/30, CM (56), 83rd Meeting.

35 Ibid., CM (56), 85th Meeting, 20 November 1956.

36 James Ellison, *Threatening Europe: Britain and the Creation of the European Community, 1955–58* (Macmillan/Institute of Contemporary British History, 2000), p. 86.

37 House of Commons Official Report, 26 November 1956, col. 108.

38 Alistair Horne, *Macmillan, 1957–1986* (Macmillan, 1989), p. 45.

39 Ibid., p. 49.

40 *Defence: Outline of Future Policy, 1957*, Cmnd. 124 (HMSO, 1957).

41 Ibid.

42 Anthony Sampson, *Macmillan: A Study in Ambiguity* (Allen Lane, 1967), p. 132.

43 Conversation with Lord Home, 13 February 1985.

44 Horne, *Macmillan, 1957–1986*, p. 48.

45 Ibid., pp. 45–7.

46 Ibid., p. 48.

47 Peter Catterall (ed.), *The Macmillan Diaries: The Cabinet Years, 1950–1957* (Macmillan, 2003), entry for 3 February 1957.

48 Peter Hennessy, *The Prime Minister: The Office and Its Holders since 1945* (Penguin, 2001), pp. 69–70, 75–6.

49 Catterall, *The Macmillan Diaries: The Cabinet Years, 1950–1957*, p. 614.

50 Private information. See also Michael Carver, *Tightrope Walking: British Defence Policy since 1945* (Hutchinson, 1992), p. 48.

51 Horne, *Macmillan, 1957–1986*, p. 51.
52 Carver, *Tightrope Walking*, p. 44.
53 Ibid., p. 43.
54 Peter Catterall (ed.), *The Macmillan Diaries: Prime Minister and After, 1957–1966* (Macmillan, forthcoming).
55 Ibid., entry for 25 February 1957.
56 *Defence: Outline of Future Policy*. Cmnd. 124.
57 Horne, *Macmillan, 1957–1986*, p. 50.
58 Sampson, *Macmillan*, p. 132.
59 Horne, *Macmillan, 1957–1986*, p. 49.
60 Christopher Driver, *The Disarmers: A Study in Protest* (Hodder, 1964), p. 74.
61 NA, PRO, PREM, 11/4285, 'The Development of the Nuclear Disarmament Movement'.
62 *Defence: Outline of Future Policy*, Cmnd. 124.
63 Ibid.
64 Ibid.
65 House of Commons Official Report, 4 June 1957, col. 1080.
66 Catterall, *The Macmillan Diaries: Prime Minister and After, 1957–1966*, entry for 4 June 1957.
67 Ibid., entry for 5 June 1957.
68 Ibid., entry for 10 November 1957.
69 *Defence: Outline of Future Policy*, Cmnd. 124.
70 NA, PRO, AIR 8/2400, 'Medium Bomber Force: Size and Composition', Defence Board, 'The V-Bomber Force and the Powered Bomb. Memorandum by the Secretary of State for Air', DB (58) 10, 29 October 1958.
71 Peter Hennessy, *The Secret State: Whitehall and the Cold War* (Penguin, 2003), see especially pp. 44–76.
72 'Why Is Blair in Bush's Gang?', William Keegan in conversation with J. K. Galbraith, *Observer*, 10 October 2004.
73 Lord Hurd and the author have talked of it more than once.
74 NA, PRO, AIR 8/1940, COS (57) 220, 11 October 1957, 'Part II of General Sir Charles Keightley's Despatch on Operations in the Eastern Mediterranean November–December, 1956'.
75 Ibid.
76 Ibid.
77 Ibid.
78 Ibid.
79 Ibid.
80 Ibid.
81 Ibid.
82 Ibid.
83 *How to Be Prime Minister*, BBC2 Television, 17 September 1996.
84 Catterall, *The Macmillan Diaries: Prime Minister and After, 1957–1966*, entry for 20 March 1957.
85 Michael Dockrill, *British Defence since 1945* (Blackwell, 1988), p. 71.
86 See Wide Vision Productions/Channel 4 Television series *What Has Become of Us?*, programme 4, 'Having It So Good', first broadcast 18 December 1994, for footage of the CND march from Swaffham to the Thor base in North Pickenham, Norfolk, in 1959; for the Thor deployment see Jacob Neufeld, 'The Thor IRBM', *Royal Air Force Historical Society Journal*, no. 32 (2004), pp. 72–82.
87 Lorna Arnold, *Britain and the H-Bomb* (Palgrave, 2001), p. 198.
88 Ibid., pp. 201–2.
89 Catterall, *The Macmillan Diaries: Prime Minister and After, 1957–1966*, entry for 24 October 1958.
90 NA, PRO, AIR 8/1940, COS (57) 220.

91 Horne, *Macmillan, 1957–1986*, pp. 36–9.

92 NA, PRO, CAB 134/1555, Macmillan to Salisbury, 28 January 1957.

93 NA, PRO, PREM 11/2321, 'Arrangement by Cabinet Secretary for Small Group of Officials to Carry Out Re-assessment of UK Interests Abroad', Brook to Macmillan, 5 June 1958.

94 NA, PRO, CAB 134/1555, Macmillan to Salisbury, 28 January 1957.

95 Hennessy, *The Prime Minister*, p. 257.

96 NA, PRO, CAB 134/1555, Lennox-Boyd to Salisbury, 15 February 1957.

97 Ibid., CPC (57) 30 (Revise), 'Future Constitutional Development in the Colonies. Report by the Chairman of the Official Committee on Colonial Policy', 6 September 1957.

98 Harold Macmillan, *Riding the Storm, 1956–1959* (Macmillan, 1971), p. 251.

99 Ibid., pp. 251–2.

100 Ibid., p. 252.

101 Ibid., pp. 252–3.

102 Catterall, *The Macmillan Diaries: Prime Minister and After, 1957–1966*, entry for 21 March 1957.

103 Lord Hunt speaking on *What Has Become of Us?*, 'The Last Roar'.

104 NA, PRO, CAB 134/1555, Macmillan to Salisbury, 28 January 1957.

105 Ibid.

106 Ibid.

107 Macmillan, *Riding the Storm*, p. 200.

108 NA, PRO, CAB 134/1555, Macmillan to Salisbury, 28 January 1957.

109 Tony Hopkins, 'Macmillan's Audit of Empire, 1957', in Peter Clarke and Clive Trebilcock (eds.), *Understanding Decline: Perceptions and Realities of British Economic Performance* (Cambridge University Press, 1997), p. 240.

110 NA, PRO, CAB 134/1555, Lennox-Boyd to Salisbury, 15 February 1957.

111 Ibid.

112 Hopkins, 'Macmillan's Audit of Empire, 1957', pp. 246–58.

113 NA, PRO, CAB 134/1555, CPC (57) 30 (Revise).

114 Ibid.

115 Ibid.

116 Ibid.

117 Ibid.

118 Ibid.

119 Ibid.

120 Ibid.

121 Ibid.

122 Hopkins, 'Macmillan's Audit of Empire, 1957', p. 252.

123 NA, PRO, PREM 11/2321, 'The Position of the United Kingdom in World Affairs. Report by Officials', undated but forwarded to Macmillan on 5 June 1958.

124 Ibid.

125 Ibid.

126 NA, PRO, CAB 134/1555, CPC (57) 30 (Revise).

127 NA, PRO, PREM 11/2321, 'The Position of the United Kingdom in World Affairs. Report by Officials'.

128 Ibid.

129 Ibid.

130 Ibid.

131 Ibid.

132 Ibid.

133 For the full story see Ellison, *Threatening Europe*, pp. 198–200.

134 Milward, *The Rise and Fall of a National Strategy*, p. 290.

135 NA, PRO, PREM 11/2532, 'Negotiations on Free Trade Area', Macmillan to de Gaulle, 7 November 1958.

136 Ellison, *Threatening Europe*, p. 212.

137 NA, PRO, PREM 13/2688, 'Reorganisation of Central Machinery for Politico-Military Planning and Intelligence, 1967–1968', Trend to Wilson, 13 March 1967.

138 NA, PRO, FO 371/135610, 'Meetings of Steering Committee and Planning Papers', SC (58) 6, Overseas Planning Committee and Political Intelligence Group, Steering Committee, undated (probably May 1958).

139 Ibid.

140 NA, PRO, CAB 158/30, JIC (57) 101, 'Terms of Reference for the Joint Intelligence Committee', P. H. Dean, 1 October 1957.

141 Percy Cradock, *Know Your Enemy: How the Joint Intelligence Committee Saw the World* (John Murray, 2002), p. 262.

142 NA, PRO, PREM 11/2418, 'Middle East 1957–58', Brook to Macmillan, 6 December 1957.

143 Private information.

144 NA, PRO, PREM 11/2082, 'Printing of Weekly CX Reports and Discontinuation of Weekly CX Summary', Dean to Bishop, 10 August 1957.

145 Ibid., and de Zulueta to Dean, 14 August 1957.

146 Ibid., and de Zulueta to Bishop, 13 September 1957.

147 Horne, *Macmillan, 1957–1986*, p. 453.

11 Dam Bursts

1 Dennis Potter, *The Glittering Coffin* (Gollancz, 1960). The book was written, however, in 1959 and 'would have been out much sooner were it not for the printing strike ...' (p. i.).

2 Arthur Marwick, *The Sixties: Cultural Revolution in Britain, France, Italy and the United States, c. 1958–1974* (Oxford University Press, 1998), p. 37.

3 Ernest Gellner, *Nations and Nationalism* (Blackwell, 1983), p. 12.

4 John Le Carré, *Call for the Dead*, first published 1961 (Coronet, 1992), p. 9.

5 Perry Anderson, 'Origins of the Present Crisis', *New Left Review*, 23 (January–February 1964), reproduced in Perry Anderson, *English Questions* (Verso, 1992), pp. 15–47.

6 Anderson, *English Questions*, p. 2.

7 Matthew Grant, 'Historians, the Penguin Specials and the 'State-of-the-Nation' Literature, 1958–64', *Contemporary British History*, vol. 17, no. 3 (Autumn 2003), pp. 29–54.

8 Walter Bagehot, *Physics and Politics* (Henry King, 1872), p. 27.

9 Conversation with Eric Hobsbawm, 22 May 2002.

10 Conversation with Gillian Shephard, 13 February 2001.

11 Sue Harper and Vincent Porter, *British Cinema of the 1950s: The Decline of Deference* (Oxford University Press, 2003), p. 261.

12 Phil Hardy and Dave Laing, *The Faber Companion to 20th-Century Popular Music* (Faber, 1990), p. 330.

13 Ibid., p. 638.

14 Ibid., p. 639.

15 Ray Gosling, *Personal Copy: A Memoir of the Sixties* (Faber, 1980), p. 35.

16 Harper and Porter, *British Cinema of the 1950s*, p. 261.

17 Marwick, *The Sixties*, p. 806.

18 Le Carré, *Call for the Dead*, p. 157.

19 *Report of the Departmental Committee on Homosexual Offences and Prostitution*, Cmnd. 247 (HMSO, 1957).

20 Lord Wolfenden, *Turning Points* (Bodley Head, 1976), pp. 142–3; Andrew Holden, *Makers and Manners: Politics and Morality in Postwar Britain* (Politico's, 2003), pp. 65–7, 82–7.

21 Holden, *Makers and Manners*, pp. 68–73.

22 Ministry of Education, *The Youth Service in England and Wales*, Cmnd. 929 (HMSO, 1960).

23 National Archives, Public Record Office [NA, PRO], CAB 128/32, CC (58) 69th Conclusions, 8 September 1958; CC (58) 71st Conclusions, 11 September 1958.

24 Patrick Nuttgens, *The Home Front: Housing the People, 1840–1990* (BBC Books, 1989), pp. 68–77.

25 Michael Young and Peter Willmott, *Family and Kinship in East London*, first published in 1957 (Pelican, 1962), p. 186.

26 House of Commons Official Report, 17 November 1955, cols. 796–7.

27 Nicholas Timmins, *The Five Giants: A Biography of the Welfare State*, new edn (Harper-Collins, 2001), p. 185.

28 Lord Young of Dartington interviewed for the WideVision Productions/Channel 4 Television series *What Has Become of Us?*, broadcast 24 March 1994.

29 Nuttgens, *The Home Front*, pp. 68–9.

30 Ibid., p. 68.

31 Ibid., p. 70.

32 Ibid., pp. 69–70.

33 Professor Peter Townsend speaking on *Michael Young: The Quiet Crusader*, BBC 4 Television, 2 September 2003.

34 Ibid.

35 Julia Parker and Catriona Mirrlees, 'Housing', in A. H. Halsey (ed.), *British Social Trends since 1900* (Macmillan, 1988), pp. 374, 377.

36 Roy Porter, *London: A Social History* (Penguin, 2000), p. xiii.

37 Ibid.

38 Ibid., pp. xiii–xiv.

39 Ibid., p. xv.

40 Ibid.

41 Ibid., pp. xv–xvi.

42 NA, PRO, CAB 129/93, C (58) 129, 'Commonwealth Immigrants. Memorandum by the Lord President of the Council', 20 June 1958. For Salisbury's resignation see Alistair Horne, *Macmillan, 1957–1986* (Macmillan, 1989), pp. 37–8.

43 NA, PRO, CAB 129/93, C (58) 129 (Annex A).

44 Ibid. (Annex C).

45 Ibid.

46 Ibid. Butler put in a Cabinet paper of his own supporting the Hailsham line and adding detail about the complications involved in legislating to curb: C (58) 132, 'Commonwealth Immigrants. Memorandum by the Secretary of State for the Home Department and Lord Privy Seal', 25 June 1958.

47 NA, PRO, CAB 128/32, CC (58) 51, 1 July 1958.

48 Edward Heath, *The Course of My Life* (Hodder, 1998), p. 455.

49 Harry Hopkins, *The New Look: A Social History of the Forties and Fifties in Britain* (Secker and Warburg, 1963), p. 467.

50 Randall Hansen, *Citizenship and Immigration in Post-war Britain* (Oxford University Press, 2000), pp. 80–81.

51 Peter Ackroyd, *London: The Biography* (Vintage, 2001), p. 525.

52 WideVision Productions/Channel 4 Television, *What Has Become of Us?*, programme 4, 'Having It So Good', first broadcast 18 December 1994.

53 Ackroyd, *London*, p. 398.

54 *What Has Become of Us?*, 'Having It So Good'.

55 Ruth Winstone (ed.), *Tony Benn: Years of Hope. Diaries, Papers and Letters 1940–1962* (Hutchinson, 1994), p. 286.

56 Ackroyd, *London*, p. 399.

57 Peter Catterall (ed.), *The Macmillan Diaries: Prime Minister and After, 1957–1966* (Macmillan, forthcoming), entries for 9 September and 12 September 1958.

58 Macmillan diaries (unpublished), Western Manuscripts Department, Bodleian Library, University of Oxford, entry for 8 September 1958.

59 Catterall, *The Macmillan Diaries: Prime Minister and After, 1957–1966*, entry for 6 September 1958.

60 Horne, *Macmillan, 1957–1986*, p. 423.

61 These extracts were screened in *What Has Become of Us?*, 'Having It So Good'.

62 NA, PRO, CAB 128/32, CC (58) 69th Conclusions, 8 September 1958.

63 Ibid.

64 Catterall, *The Macmillan Diaries: Prime Minister and After, 1957–1966*, entry for 12 September 1958.

65 Lord Butler, *The Art of the Possible* (Hamish Hamilton, 1971), p. 206; footnote: for Powell's expulsion see Heath, *The Course of My Life*, pp. 293–4, and for his comment to me, *What Has Become of Us?*, 'Having It So Good'.

66 Ackroyd, *London*, p. 399.

67 *What Has Become of Us?*, 'Having It So Good'.

68 Butler, *The Art of the Possible*, p. 204.

69 Lord Allen of Abbeydale interviewed for *What Has Become of Us?*, 31 May 1994. See also Wolfenden, *Turning Points*, pp. 129–46.

70 Anthony Howard, *RAB: The Life of R. A. Butler* (Cape, 1987), p. 265.

71 House of Commons Official Report, 24 November 1958, cols. 366–7; Wolfenden, *Turning Points*, pp. 144–5.

72 Catterall, *The Macmillan Diaries: Prime Minister and After, 1957–1966*, entry for 8 February 1957.

73 Horne, *Macmillan, 1957–1986*, p. 485.

74 Colin Wilson, *The Outsider* (Gollancz, 1956).

75 Colin Wilson, *Dreaming to Some Purpose, An Autobiography* (Century, 2004), pp. 117–59.

76 Wilson, *The Outsider*, p. 281.

77 Wilson, *Dreaming to Some Purpose*, p. 136.

78 Noel Annan, *Our Age: Portrait of a Generation* (Weidenfeld & Nicolson, 1990), p. 299.

79 Ibid., p. 360.

80 Wilson, *Dreaming to Some Purpose*, p. 138; see also Robert Hewison, *In Anger: Culture in the Cold War 1945–60* (Weidenfeld & Nicolson, 1981), p. 130.

81 Wilson, *Dreaming to Some Purpose*, p. 138.

82 Ibid., p. 139.

83 John Osborne, *Look Back in Anger* (Penguin, 1982).

84 Ibid.

85 Hewison, *In Anger*, pp. 130–35.

86 Kingsley Amis, *Lucky Jim* (Gollancz, 1954), p. 62.

87 See p. 77; Joan Bakewell, *The Centre of the Bed: An Autobiography* (Hodder, 2003), p. 85.

88 Amis, *Lucky Jim*, p. 88.

89 Ibid., p. 231.

90 Hewison, *In Anger*, p. 132.

91 Len Deighton, *Blood, Tears and Folly: An Objective Look at World War II* (Pimlico, 1995), p. xvii.

92 Nicola Lacey, *A Life of H. L. A. Hart: The Nightmare and the Noble Dream* (Oxford University Press, 2004), p. 2.

93 Holden, *Makers and Manners*, pp. 27–8, 33, 36.

94 The lecture is reproduced in Patrick Devlin, *The Enforcement of Morals* (Oxford University Press, 1965), pp. 1–25. See also R. F. V. Heuson, 'Patrick Arthur Devlin, 1905–1992', in *Proceedings of the British Academy*, vol. 84 (1992), pp. 247–62.

95 Mr Blair's speech is reproduced in Holden, *Makers and Manners*, pp. 2–3.

96 Heuson, 'Patrick Arthur Devlin', p. 252.

97 Ibid.

98 A comment in the *Guardian* on 11 August 1992 cited Ibid., p. 257.

99 Macmillan diaries (unpublished), Western Manuscripts Department, Bodleian Library, University of Oxford, entry for 13 July 1959.

100 *Report of the Nyasaland Commission of Inquiry*, Cmnd. 814 (HMSO, 1959).

101 Lacey, *A Life of H. L. A. Hart*, p. 1; see also Tony Honore, 'Herbert Lionel Adolphus Hart 1907–1992', in *Proceedings of the British Academy*, vol. 84 (1992), pp. 295–321. For Hart's service in MI5 see Nigel West (ed.), *The Guy Liddell Diaries*, vol. I: *1939–1942* (Routledge, 2005).

102 Lacey, *A Life of H. L. A. Hart*, p. 270.

103 Ibid., p. 271.

104 Ibid., pp. 147–8.

105 Ibid., pp. 1–2.

106 Annan, *Our Age*, p. 306.

107 Devlin, *The Enforcement of Morals*, p. 1.

108 Ibid., pp. 13–14.

109 Ibid., p. 15.

110 Ibid., p. 18.

111 Ibid., p. 25.

112 Ibid., p. 13.

113 H. L. A. Hart, 'Immorality and Treason', *The Listener*, 30 July 1959.

114 Lacey, *A Life of H. L. A. Hart*, pp. 61–2, 73–9, 203–5.

115 H. L. A. Hart, *Law, Liberty and Morality* (Oxford University Press, 1963), pp. 61–2.

116 Ibid., p. 79.

117 Ibid.

118 Marwick, *The Sixties*, p. 19.

119 Herbert Marcuse, *Towards a Critical Theory of Society* (Routledge, 2001), p. 177.

120 Marwick, *The Sixties*, p. 19.

121 Horne, *Macmillan, 1957–1986*, p. 81.

122 Catterall, *The Macmillan Diaries: Prime Minister and After, 1957–1966*, entry for 30 June 1960.

123 Horne, *Macmillan, 1957–1986*, p. 81.

124 Hart, *Law, Liberty and Morality*, 'Preface', unpaginated.

125 I am grateful to Mark Jarvis for bringing Macmillan's memo and Butler's reply to my attention. Mark Jarvis, *Conservative Governments, Morality and Social Change in Affluent Britain, 1957–64* (Manchester University Press, 2005), p. 95. The original can be found in NA, PRO, PREM 11/3241, 'Discussions on Act to Amend Law Relating to Suicide', Macmillan to Butler, 24 June 1961.

126 NA, PRO, HO 291/141, 'Suicide and Attempted Suicide: Proposals to Amend Law', Draft for Butler's reply to Macmillan.

127 For Macmillan's boredom see Jarvis, *Conservative Governments*, p. 96. Dr Jarvis found this comment in an entry in the Butler diary for 24 October 1961; for Powell on mental hospitals see Timmins, *The Five Giants*, p. 211.

128 Henry Fairlie, *The Life of Politics* (Methuen, 1968), p. 16; for Macmillan's view expressed in the footnote, Macmillan diaries (unpublished), Western Manuscripts Department, Bodleian Library, University of Oxford, entry for 31 December 1958.

129 Fairlie, *The Life of Politics*, p. 57fn.

130 Jarvis, *Conservative Governments*, p. 161.

131 Catterall, *The Macmillan Diaries: Prime Minister and After, 1957–1966*, entry for 10 June 1960.

132 William F. Buckley, Jr. in his *Firing Line* programme in New York on 20 November 1980. Quoted in Horne, *Macmillan, 1957–1986*, p. 612.

133 Jarvis, *Conservative Governments*, p. 65.

134 Ibid., pp. 6–7.

135 Ibid., p. 1.

136 Ibid., p. 115.

137 Roy Jenkins, *A Life at the Centre* (Macmillan, 1991), pp. 98, 175–6.

138 *Report from the Select Committee on Obscene Publications*, HC 123 (HMSO, 1958).

139 Marwick, *The Sixties*, p. 146.

140 Ibid.; see also Richard Hoggart, *An Imagined Life: Life and Times, 1959–91* (Chatto and Windus, 1992), pp. 47–59. For the success of *Lady Chatterley* see Marwick, *The Sixties*, p. 146; Jeremy Lewis, *Penguin Special: The Life and Times of Allen Lane* (Allen Lane, 2005), pp. 315–33.

141 *The Next Five Years*, reproduced in Iain Dale (ed.), *Conservative Party General Election Manifestos, 1900–1997* (Routledge/Politico's, 2000), pp. 127–40.

142 Jarvis, *Conservative Governments*, p. 67.

143 Ibid., p. 79.

144 Antony Jay (ed.), *The Oxford Dictionary of Political Quotations* (Oxford University Press, 1996), p. 46.

145 Butler, *The Art of the Possible*, p. 202.

146 Ibid., p. 201.

147 Ibid., p. 202.

148 For the fluctuating views of Butler on capital punishment see Howard, *RAB: The Life of R. A. Butler*, pp. 225–7, 253–4, 271–2, 286.

149 House of Commons Official Report, 15 February 1956, cols 2536–656. Terence Morris, *Crime and Criminal Justice since 1945* (Blackwell, 1989), p. 84.

150 D. R. Thorpe, *Eden: The Life and Times of Anthony Eden, First Earl of Avon, 1897–1977* (Chatto and Windus, 2003), p. 454.

151 Jarvis, *Conservative Governments*, p. 51.

152 Peter Catterall (ed.), *The Macmillan Diaries: The Cabinet Years, 1950–1957* (Macmillan, 2003), entry for 21 July 1956.

153 Ibid., entry for 16 February 1956.

154 Holden, *Makers and Manners*, p. 70.

155 Morris, *Crime and Criminal Justice since 1945*, p. 93.

156 David Butler, *British General Elections since 1945* (Blackwell, 1989), p. 18.

157 Jarvis, *Conservative Governments*, p. 167.

158 Morris, *Crime and Criminal Justice since 1945*, p. 91.

159 Ibid., p. 96.

160 Ibid., pp. 97–8.

161 Peter Brierley, 'Religion', in A. H. Halsey (ed.), *British Social Trends since 1900: A Guide to the Changing Social Structure of Britain* (Macmillan, 1988), pp. 519–20.

162 Ibid., p. 524.

163 *The Problem of Homosexuality* (Church Information Board, 1952); Holden, *Makers and Manners*, p. 65.

164 Catterall, *The Macmillan Diaries: The Cabinet Years, 1950–1957*, entry for 21 July 1956.

165 Ibid., entry for 13 September 1956.

166 Richard Weight, *Patriots: National Identity in Britain, 1940–2000* (Macmillan, 2002), p. 442; Owen Chadwick, *Michael Ramsey: A Life* (Oxford University Press, 1990), pp. 145–76.

167 Kenneth Harris, *Conversations* (Hodder, 1967), pp. 84–5.

168 The Earl of Swinton (with James Margach), *Sixty Years of Power* (Hutchinson, 1966), p. 182.

169 Ibid., p. 187.

170 Macmillan diaries (unpublished), Western Manuscripts Department, Bodleian Library, University of Oxford.

171 Fred Hirsch, *Social Limits to Growth* (Routledge, 1977), p. 1.

172 Peter Clarke, *Hope and Glory: Britain, 1900–1990* (Allen Lane, 1996), pp. 254–5.

173 Hirsch, *Social Limits to Growth*, p. 33.

174 Meryle Secrest, *Kenneth Clark: A Biography* (Weidenfeld & Nicolson, 1984).

175 Kenneth Clark, *The Other Half: A Self-Portrait* (John Murray, 1977), p. 217.

176 J. K. Galbraith, *The Affluent Society* (Hamish Hamilton, 1958), p. 240.

177 During a talk on the BBC Third Programme quoted on the dust cover of the British hardback edition of Galbraith, *The Affluent Society.*

178 C. A. R. Crosland, *The Future of Socialism* (Cape, 1956), p. 281.

179 Ibid., pp. 521–2.

180 Ibid., p. 523.

181 Ibid., p. 527.

182 Susan Crosland, *Tony Crosland* (Cape, 1982), pp. 256–7.

183 Alec Cairncross, *The British Economy since 1945* (Blackwell, 1992), pp. 98–9, 277–8.

184 It (and 'Supermac') is reproduced in Butler, *British General Elections since 1945*, p. 17.

185 Halsey, *British Social Trends*, p. 150. The figures are Charles Feinstein's cited in Andrew Dilnot, 'The Economic Environment', ibid., pp. 135–61.

186 *Britain Belongs to You*, reproduced in Iain Dale (ed.), *Labour Party General Election Manifestos, 1900–1997* (Routledge/Politico's, 2000), pp. 89–102.

187 The poster is reproduced in D. E. Butler and Richard Rose, *The British General Election of 1959* (Macmillan, 1960), between pages 136 and 137; Philip M. Williams, *Hugh Gaitskell: A Political Biography* (Cape, 1979), p. 525. For Butler's claim see *The Times*, 30 May 1954.

188 Williams, *Hugh Gaitskell*, pp. 30–59; Brian Brivati, *Hugh Gaitskell* (Richard Cohen Books, 1996), pp. 25–42.

189 Ibid., pp. 248–83.

190 Roy Jenkins, *Nine Men of Power* (Hamish Hamilton, 1974), p. 180.

191 Ibid.

192 Ibid., p. 176.

193 *Britain Belongs to You*, in Dale, *Labour Party General Election Manifestos*, p. 101.

194 Jay, *The Oxford English Dictionary of Political Quotations*, p. 390. The occasion was the Labour Party conference on 1 October 1962.

195 Roy Jenkins, *The Labour Case* (Penguin, 1959), pp. 135–46.

196 Michael Howard, *War and the Liberal Conscience* (Temple Smith, 1978), p. 77; Christopher Driver, *The Disarmers: A Study in Protest* (Hodder, 1964), p. 14; Bertrand Russell, *Autobiography* (Routledge, 1991), pp. 238–325.

197 Catterall, *The Macmillan Diaries: Prime Minister and After, 1957–1966*, entry for 1 December 1957.

198 Ibid.

199 Horne, *Macmillan, 1957–1986*, p. 52.

200 Edward Hyams, *The New Statesman: The History of the First Fifty Years, 1913–1963* (Longmans, 1963), p. 287.

201 Michael Foot, *Aneurin Bevan: A Biography*, vol. II: *1945–1960* (Davis Poynter, 1973), p. 574.

202 Ibid., p. 575. Much of the speech is reproduced in Brian MacArthur (ed.), *The Penguin Book of Twentieth-Century Speeches* (Viking, 1992), pp. 278–80.

203 Foot, *Aneurin Bevan*, II, p. 575.

204 John Mortimer, *In Character* (Penguin, 1984), p. 127. His interview with Butler, 'Remember Compassion!', is reproduced pp. 126–30.

205 Foot, *Aneurin Bevan*, II, p. 577.

206 J. B. Priestley, 'Britain and the Nuclear Bomb', *New Statesman*, 1 November 1957. The article is reproduced in full in Edward Hyams, *New Statesmanship, An Anthology* (Longman, 1963), pp. 236–44.

207 Ibid.

208 Hyams, *The New Statesman*, p. 216.

209 Driver, *The Disarmers*, p. 39.

210 *Defence: Outline of Future Policy*, Cmnd. 124 (HMSO, 1957); NA, PRO, PREM 11/4285, 'Development of Nuclear Disarmament: Memorandum by the Home Office ...', 'The

Development of the Nuclear Disarmament Movement'; Driver, *The Disarmers*, p. 34; Peter Hennessy, *The Secret State: Whitehall and the Cold War* (Penguin, 2003), p. 104.

211 George F. Kennan, *Memoirs 1950–1963* (Hutchinson, 1973), p. 230.

212 Ibid., p. 229.

213 Ibid., p. 230.

214 Ibid., p. 240.

215 Ibid.

216 Ibid., p. 244.

217 Ibid.

218 Ibid., p. 250.

219 Driver, *The Disarmers*, p. 42.

220 Denis Healey, *The Time of My Life* (Michael Joseph, 1989), p. 240.

221 Peggy Duff, *Left, Left, Left: A Personal Account of Six Protest Campaigns, 1945–65* (Allison and Busby, 1971), pp. 113–25.

222 Diana Collins, *Partners in Protest* (Gollancz, 1992), pp. 231–2; Driver, *The Disarmers*, pp. 43–6.

223 A. J. P. Taylor, *A Personal History* (Hamish Hamilton, 1983), p. 226.

224 The lectures were published as A. J. P. Taylor, *The Troublemakers: Dissent over British Foreign Policy, 1792–1939* (Hamish Hamilton, 1957).

225 Kathleen Burk, *Troublemaker: The Life and History of A. J. P. Taylor* (Yale University Press, 2000), pp. 203–4.

226 Adam Sisman, *A. J. P. Taylor: A Biography* (Sinclair-Stevenson, 1994), p. 277.

227 Ibid., p. 274.

228 Ibid., p. 275.

229 Macmillan diaries (unpublished), Western Manuscripts Department, Bodleian Library, University of Oxford, entry for 17 February 1958.

230 Horne, *Macmillan, 1957–1986*, p. 268.

231 Burk, *Troublemaker*, pp. 208–9.

232 Williams, *Hugh Gaitskell*, p. 605.

233 Ibid., pp. 610–14.

234 Ibid., p. 605.

235 Ibid., p. 575.

236 Russell, *Autobiography*, p. 597.

237 Driver, *The Disarmers*, pp. 54–5.

238 Ibid., p. 36.

239 Ibid., p. 48.

240 Ibid., p. 51.

241 Ibid., p. 55.

242 Ibid.

243 *Daily Mail*, 8 April 1958.

244 Quoted in Hewison, *In Anger*, p. 165.

245 NA, PRO, PREM 11/4285, 'The Development of the Nuclear Disarmament Movement'.

246 Quoted in Hewison, *In Anger*, p. 165.

247 Driver, *The Disarmers*, p. 58.

248 Ibid.

249 Pat Arrowsmith was speaking on *What Has Become of Us?*, programme 4, 'Having It So Good', first broadcast on Channel 4 Television 18 December 1994.

250 Driver, *The Disarmers*, p. 59.

251 Willie Thompson, *The Good Old Cause: British Communism, 1920–1991* (Pluto Press, 1992), p. 116.

252 Ibid., pp. 116–17.

253 Palme Dutt delivered this denunciation of the CND in *Labour Monthly*, January 1958 after the original CND meeting in Canon Collins' house.

254 Francis Beckett, *Enemy Within: The Rise and Fall of the British Communist Party* (John Murray, 1995), pp. 146–9. For party membership figures see Henry Pelling, *The British Communist Party: A Historical Profile* (A&C Black, 1975), p. 193.

255 John Saville, *Memoirs from the Left* (Merlin Press, 2003), pp. 105, 109, 115–16, 123; Michael Newman, *Ralph Miliband and the Politics of the New Left* (Merlin Press, 2002), p. 64.

256 Mortimer, *In Character*, p. 101. His interview with Thompson, 'The Guru and the Radioactive Frog', is reproduced between pages 99 and 105.

257 From the *New Reasoner*, summer 1959, quoted in Driver, *The Disarmers*, p. 60.

258 Humphrey Carpenter, *That Was Satire That Was: The Satire Boom of the 1960s* (Gollancz, 2000), pp. 95–126.

259 Richard Ingrams (ed.), *The Life and Times of Private Eye* (Penguin, 1971).

260 Driver, *The Disarmers*, p. 61.

261 Potter, *The Glittering Coffin*, p. 5.

262 Ibid., pp. 28–9.

263 Ibid., p. 28.

264 Anthony Hartley, *A State of England* (Hutchinson, 1963), pp. 89–90.

265 Ibid., p. 90.

266 Taylor, *A Personal History*, p. 227.

267 Grant, 'Historians, the Penguin Specials and the "State-of-the-Nation" Literature, 1958–64'.

268 Potter, *The Glittering Coffin*, p. 33.

269 Ibid.

270 Ibid., p. 41.

271 Ibid.

272 Ibid., p. 159.

273 Ibid., p. 158.

274 Macmillan, *Riding the Storm*, p. 350.

275 Ibid.

276 Ibid., pp. 350–51.

277 Ibid., p. 351.

278 Cyril Connolly, 'This Gale-swept Chip', *Encounter*, July 1963, p. 15.

279 Hilary Kingsley and Geoff Tibballs, *A Box of Delights: The Golden Years of Television* (Macmillan, 1989), p. 55.

280 Ibid.

281 Ibid.

282 Ibid., pp. 200–201.

283 Ibid., pp. 219–20.

284 Sir Dennis Foreman speaking on *What Has Become of Us?*, programme 4, 'Having It So Good'.

285 Asa Briggs, *The BBC: The First Fifty Years* (Oxford University Press, 1985), p. 299.

286 Ibid., p. 308; Clarke, *Hope and Glory*, pp. 250–52.

287 Holden, *Makers and Manners*, p. 59.

288 Ibid., pp. 87–96.

289 Harper and Porter, *British Cinema of the 1950s*, p. 220.

290 Ibid., p. 239.

291 Alan Sillitoe, *Saturday Night and Sunday Morning* (W. H. Allen, 1958); Marwick, *The Sixties*, pp. 129–31.

292 Harper and Porter, *British Cinema of the 1950s*, p. 239.

293 Richard Hoggart was speaking on *What Has Become of Us?*, programme 4, 'Having It So Good'.

294 Kingsley and Tibballs, *Box of Delights*, p. 24.

295 Sir Dennis Foreman speaking on *What Has Become of Us?*, programme 4, 'Having It So Good'.

296 J. M. Keynes, *Essays in Persuasion* (Rupert Hart-Davis, 1952), p. 368.

297 James Margach, *The Abuse of Power* (W. H. Allen, 1978), p. 121.

298 Fairlie, *The Life of Politics*, p. 250.

299 *Financial Times*, 16 June 1959.

300 Piers Brendon, *Thomas Cook: 150 Years of Popular Tourism* (Secker and Warburg, 1991), pp. 286–7.

301 Anthony Sampson, *Who Runs this Place? The Anatomy of Britain in the 21st Century* (John Murray, 2004), p. 575.

302 Brian Palmer speaking on *What Has Become of Us?*, programme 4, 'Having It So Good'.

303 Conversation with David Kingsley, 19 January 2005.

304 Brian Palmer speaking on 'Having It So Good'.

305 Marwick, *The Sixties*, pp. 16–20.

306 Ibid., p. 56.

307 I am grateful to Joan Bakewell for the transcript of this interview.

308 Kingsley and Tibballs, *Box of Delights*, p. 24.

309 Richard Holt, *Sport and the British* (Oxford University Press, 1989), p. 318.

310 Ted Fenton, *At Home with the Hammers* (Nicholas Kaye, 1960), pp. 21–7. I am grateful to my friend Andy Dalton, lifelong 'Hammer', for giving me the Fenton memoir.

311 'Some Recollections of the Fifties', Clive Priestley to Peter Hennessy, 19 May 2004.

312 Kingsley and Tibballs, *Box of Delights*, p. 34.

313 Priestley, 'Some Recollections of the Fifties'.

314 The book was published by Cape in 1964; the film went on release in 1966.

315 Conversation with Sir John Willis, 14 September 2004.

12 Supermac

1 Michael Oakeshott, 'Learning and Teaching', reproduced in Timothy Fuller (ed.), *The Voice of Liberal Learning: Michael Oakeshott on Education* (Yale University Press, 1989), p. 56.

2 Lord Hailsham interviewed for the Brook Productions/Channel 4 Television series *All the Prime Minister's Men*, first broadcast 1 July 1986.

3 Bernard Levin, *The Pendulum Years: Britain and the Sixties* (Pan, 1972), p. 391.

4 Alistair Horne, *Macmillan, 1894–1956* (Macmillan, 1988), p. xi.

5 Anthony Sampson, *Macmillan: A Study in Ambiguity* (Allen Lane, 1967).

6 Harold Macmillan, *The Past Masters: Politics and Politicians, 1906–1939* (Macmillan, 1975), pp. 26–8.

7 Peter Catterall (ed.), *The Macmillan Diaries: The Cabinet Years, 1950–1957* (Macmillan, 2003), entry for 13 October 1954.

8 Macmillan, *The Past Masters*, p. 197.

9 Ibid., p. 28.

10 Michael Oakeshott, *The Politics of Faith and the Politics of Scepticism* (probably written in the early 1950s but discovered only after his death, edited by Timothy Fuller and published by Yale University Press in 1996).

11 Ibid., p. 32.

12 Sampson, *Macmillan*, illustrations section; caption to a photograph of Macmillan in top hat and tails, seated smoking a cigar at Ascot.

13 Anthony Sampson, 'The Pleasures and Pains of Writing Contemporary British History and Anatomising Britain', Mile End Group, Queen Mary, University of London, 21 October 2004.

14 Robin Denniston, 'Anthony Sampson: Author of "Anatomy of Britain" and Biographer of Mandela', *The Independent*, 21 December 2004.

15 Anthony Sampson, *Anatomy of Britain* (Hodder, 1962), p. 322.

16 Alistair Horne, *Macmillan, 1957–1986* (Macmillan, 1989), p. 153.

17 Lord Home, *The Way the Wind Blows* (Collins, 1976), p. 192.

18 George Hutchinson, *The Last Edwardian at Number 10: An Impression of Harold Macmillan* (Quartet, 1980).

19 Enoch Powell, 'Super Whig?', *The Spectator*, 1 March 1980, reproduced in Rex Collings (ed.), *Reflections of a Statesman: The Writings and Speeches of Enoch Powell* (Bellew, 1991), p. 318.
20 Ibid., p. 39.
21 Peter Catterall (ed.), *The Macmillan Diaries: Prime Minister and After, 1957–1966* (Macmillan, forthcoming), entry for 6 January 1958.
22 Macmillan diaries (unpublished), Western Manuscripts Department, Bodleian Library, University of Oxford.
23 Catterall, *The Macmillan Diaries: Prime Minister and After, 1957–1966*, entry for 31 January 1958.
24 Edward Heath, *The Course of My Life* (Hodder, 1998), p. 186.
25 Enoch Powell, 'Winds of Change', a 1973 review of volume 1 of Macmillan's memoirs, in the *Glasgow Herald*, reproduced in Collings, *Reflections of a Statesman*, pp. 321–4.
26 John Ramsden, *The Winds of Change: Macmillan to Heath, 1957–1975* (Longman, 1996), pp. 34–5.
27 Margaret Thatcher, *The Path to Power* (HarperCollins, 1995), p. 92. The footnoted remarks are from a seminar at Mile End Group, Queen Mary, University of London, 26 January 2005, and Nigel Lawson, *The View from No. 11: Memoirs of a Tory Radical* (Bantam, 1992), p. 33.
28 Conversation with Lord Thorneycroft for WideVision/Channel 4 Television series *What Has Become of Us?*, 29 July 1993.
29 Norman St John-Stevas (ed.), *The Collected Works of Walter Bagehot*, vol. XV: *Miscellany* (The Economist, 1986), p. 222.
30 Harold Macmillan, *Riding the Storm, 1956–59* (Macmillan, 1971), p. 372.
31 Rodney Lowe, *The Welfare State in Britain since 1945*, third edn (Palgrave, 2005), p. 94.
32 John Turner, *Macmillan* (Longman, 1994), p. 238.
33 Enoch Powell, 'Winds of Change', reproduced in Collings, *Reflections of a Statesman*, pp. 321–2.
34 National Archives, Public Record Office [NA, PRO], PREM 11/3480, 'Letters from Prime Minister to HM the Queen, 1958 and 1959', Macmillan to the Queen, 29 May 1959.
35 NA, PRO, CAB 128/32, CC (58) 3rd Conclusions, 5 January 1958; Catterall, *The Macmillan Diaries: Prime Minister and After, 1957–1966*, entry for 6 January 1958.
36 NA, PRO, CAB 128/32, CC (58) 3rd Conclusions.
37 Ibid.
38 House of Commons Official Report, 23 January 1958, cols. 1295–6.
39 Edmund Dell, *The Chancellors: A History of the Chancellors of the Exchequer, 1945–90* (HarperCollins, 1996), p. 232.
40 Alec Cairncross, *The British Economy since 1945* (Blackwell, 1992), p. 276; Michael Dockrill, *British Defence since 1945* (Blackwell, 1988), p. 151.
41 Dell, *The Chancellors*, pp. 233–8.
42 Ibid., pp. 233–7.
43 J. M. Keynes, *The General Theory of Employment, Interest and Money* (Macmillan, 1936), p. 383.
44 House of Commons Official Report, 23 January 1958, col. 1295.
45 Robert Shepherd, *Iain Macleod: A Biography* (Hutchinson, 1994), pp. 132–3.
46 NA, PRO, CAB 130/139, GEN 625/2nd Meeting, 23 December 1957.
47 Horne, *Macmillan, 1957–1986*, p. 77.
48 NA, PRO, PREM 11/3510, 'Letters from the Prime Minister to HM the Queen, 1960 and 1961', Macmillan to the Queen, 30 July 1960.
49 Catterall, *The Macmillan Diaries: Prime Minister and After, 1957–1960*, entry for 7 January 1958.
50 Macmillan diaries (unpublished), Western Manuscripts Department, Bodleian Library, University of Oxford, entry for 7 January 1958.

51 Macmillan, *Riding the Storm*, p. 373.

52 NA, PRO, PREM 11/2421, 'Position of Conservative Party after Resignation of Mr Thorneycroft: Message to Ministers from Prime Minister', Telegraph No. 24, 7 January 1958, Bishop to Cairncross.

53 Ibid., Allan to Butler, 8 January 1958.

54 Ibid., Macmillan to Heath, 12 January 1958.

55 Ibid., Hailsham to Macmillan, 13 January 1958.

56 'Mr Thorneycroft Rejects "Mere £50m" Argument', *The Times*, 15 January 1958.

57 NA, PRO, PREM 11/2421, Hailsham to Macmillan, 16 January 1958.

58 Catterall, *The Macmillan Diaries: Prime Minister and After, 1957–1966*, entry for 14 February 1958.

59 John Ramsden, *The Winds of Change: Macmillan to Heath, 1957–1975* (Longman, 1996), p. 36.

60 Catterall, *The Macmillan Diaries: Prime Minister and After, 1957–1966*, entry for 14 February 1958.

61 Sampson, *Macmillan*, p. 136.

62 Ibid.

63 Ibid., p. 137.

64 Ibid.

65 Ibid.

66 Ibid., p. 138.

67 Ibid., between pp. 262 and 263. (See also plate 50 of the illustrations in this book.)

68 Ibid., p. 160.

69 Macmillan diaries (unpublished), Western Manuscripts Department, Bodleian Library, University of Oxford, entry for 12 March 1958.

70 Ibid., entry for 13 March 1958 (as written up on 15 March).

71 The whole speech is reproduced as 'The Middle Way: 20 Years After', in Harold Macmillan, *The Middle Way: A Study of the Problem of Economic and Social Progress in a Free and Democratic Society* (Macmillan, 1966), pp. xiii–xxix. This particular passage is at pp. xiv–xv.

72 Ibid., p. xx.

73 Ibid., p. xxi.

74 Ibid.

75 Ibid., pp. xxii–xxiii.

76 Thatcher, *The Path to Power*, pp. 93–7.

77 Macmillan, 'The Middle Way: 20 Years After', p. xxiv.

78 James Margach, *The Abuse of Power* (W. H. Allen, 1978), pp. 116–17.

79 Ibid., p. 117.

80 Ibid., pp. 117–18.

81 Catterall, *The Macmillan Diaries: Prime Minister and After, 1957–1966*, entry for 15 March 1958.

82 Ibid., entry for 25 June 1961.

83 Ramsden, *The Winds of Change*, p. 44.

84 Dell, *The Chancellors*, p. 243.

85 Ibid.

86 Catterall, *The Macmillan Diaries: Prime Minister and After, 1957–1966*, entries as stated.

87 Horne, *Macmillan, 1957–1986*, p. 140.

88 Ibid., pp. 140–41.

89 NA, PRO, PREM 11/2311, 'Discussions on Future Economic Prospects Following Recession', 'Public Investment and Reflation', 23 October 1958.

90 Catterall, *The Macmillan Diaries: Prime Minister and After, 1957–1966*, entry for 27 October 1958.

91 NA, PRO, PREM 11/2311, 'Public Investment and Reflation'.

92 Ibid. Macmillan does not date his reply.

93 Alec Cairncross (ed.), *The Robert Hall Diaries, 1954–1961* (Unwin Hyman, 1991), entry for 20 November 1958.

94 Ibid.

95 Ibid.

96 Dell, *The Chancellors*, p. 252.

97 Cairncross, *The British Economy since 1945*, p. 112; Peter Clarke, *Hope and Glory: Britain 1900–1990* (Allen Lane, 1998), p. 277.

98 Cairncross, *The Robert Hall Diaries, 1954–1961*, p. 196, entry for 7 May 1959.

99 Catterall, *The Macmillan Diaries: Prime Minister and After, 1957–1966*, entry for 9 April 1959.

100 This was the title of his chapter 17 covering the period 1957–9. Philip Williams, *Hugh Gaitskell* (Cape, 1979), pp. 459–91.

101 Ibid., p. 488.

102 Brian Brivati, *Hugh Gaitskell* (Richard Cohen Books, 1996), p. 308.

103 Denis Healey, *The Time of My Life* (Michael Joseph, 1989), p. 154.

104 Ibid.

105 Roy Jenkins, *Nine Men of Power* (Hamish Hamilton, 1974), p. 161.

106 Healey, *The Time of My Life*, p. 154.

107 Roy Jenkins in W. T. Rodgers (ed.), *Hugh Gaitskell 1906–1963* (Thames and Hudson, 1964), p. 124.

108 Jenkins, *Nine Men of Power*, p. 175.

109 Quoted in D. E. Butler and Richard Rose, *The British General Election of 1959* (Macmillan, 1960), pp. 32–3.

110 Quoted in Horne, *Macmillan, 1957–1986*, p. 154.

111 Harold Macmillan, *The Past Masters* (Macmillan, 1975), pp. 57–8.

112 Ibid., p. 58.

113 Brivati, *Hugh Gaitskell*, p. 349.

114 Ibid., p. 414.

115 Horne, *Macmillan, 1957–1986*, p. 156.

116 Catterall, *The Macmillan Diaries: Prime Minister and After, 1957–1966*, entry for 5 October 1957.

117 Geoffrey Goodman, *The Awkward Warrior. Frank Cousins: His Life and Times* (Davis Poynter, 1979), p. 177.

118 Macmillan, *Riding the Storm*, p. 714.

119 Goodman, *The Awkward Warrior*, pp. 179–80.

120 Macmillan, *Riding the Storm*, p. 714.

121 Williams, *Hugh Gaitskell*, p. 463.

122 Ibid.

123 Ibid., p. 464.

124 Macmillan, *Riding the Storm*, p. 718.

125 Ibid., pp. 718–19.

126 Ibid., p. 719.

127 Horne's words in *Macmillan, 1957–1986*, p. 146.

128 His grandson, Alexander Stockton, speaking on Michael Cockerell's documentary *Hotline to the President*, first shown on BBC2 8 September 2002; he revealed the name of the Rolls-Royce's owner to me in conversation, 14 May 2006.

129 Ramsden, *The Winds of Change*, pp. 62–3.

130 Ibid., p. 62.

131 Butler and Rose, *The British General Election of 1959*, p. 86.

132 Williams, *Hugh Gaitskell*, p. 524.

133 There is a particularly good sequence of pictures of Macmillan, beside a behatted and beaming Lady Dorothy, in action in Clapham in this mode in Alan Thompson, *The Day Before*

Yesterday: An Illustrated History of Britain from Attlee to Macmillan (Thames Television, 1971), pp. 174–5. (See plate 56 of the illustrations in this book.)

134 Catterall, *The Macmillan Diaries: Prime Minister and After, 1957–1966*, entry for 22 September 1959.

135 Peter Hennessy, *The Prime Minister: The Office and Its Holders since 1945* (Allen Lane, 2000), p. 251.

136 Macmillan, *Riding the Storm*, p. 197.

137 Williams, *Hugh Gaitskell*, p. 525.

138 Catterall, *The Macmillan Diaries: Prime Minister and After, 1957–1966*, entry for 13 November 1960.

139 Williams, *Hugh Gaitskell*, p. 93.

140 Jenkins, *Nine Men of Power*, p. 176.

141 Ibid.

142 Williams, *Hugh Gaitskell*, p. 525.

143 Ibid., p. 910, fn. 24.

144 Ibid., p. 526.

145 Butler and Rose, *The British General Election of 1959*, p. 59.

146 David Butler, *British General Elections since 1945* (Blackwell, 1989), p. 18.

147 Butler and Rose, *The British General Election of 1959*, p. 60.

148 Ibid., p. 59.

149 Ramsden, *The Winds of Change*, p. 65.

150 Horne, *Macmillan, 1957–1986*, p. 151.

151 Ibid.

152 Ramsden, *The Winds of Change*, p. 65.

153 Harold Macmillan, *Pointing the Way, 1959–1961* (Macmillan, 1972), p. 12.

154 Ibid.

155 Macmillan, *Pointing the Way*, p. 13.

156 Geoffrey Goodman, *From Bevan to Blair: Fifty Years' Reporting from the Political Front Line* (Pluto Press, 2003), p. 84.

157 Ibid.

158 Conversation with Geoffrey Goodman, 31 May 2005.

159 Butler, *British General Elections since 1945*, pp. 14–19.

160 Catterall, *The Macmillan Diaries: Prime Minister and After, 1957–1966*, entry for 11 October 1959.

161 Ibid., entry for 7 June 1959.

162 Butler and Rose, *The British General Election of 1959*, p. 198.

163 Ibid., p. 72 (the only reference to the EEC in Butler and Rose's 201 pages).

13 Wealth, Power and Influence

1 National Archives, Public Record Office [NA, PRO], CAB 134/1929, 'Study of Future Policy 1960/70', FP (60), 1st Meeting, 23 March 1960. I am grateful to my former student Nahdia Khan, who discovered this minute while preparing her undergraduate research project at the Queen Mary and Westfield College Department of History on 'Harold Macmillan and Foreign Policy Rethinks, 1957–60'.

2 James Margach, *The Abuse of Power* (W. H. Allen, 1978), p. 121.

3 Quoted in Peter Hennessy and Caroline Anstey, 'Moneybags and Brains: The Anglo-American "Special Relationship" since 1945', Strathclyde Analysis paper no. 1, Department of Government, University of Strathclyde, 1990, p. 6.

4 P. G. Wodehouse, *The Clicking of Cuthbert*, first published by Herbert Jenkins, 1922 (Vintage, 1992), p. 11.

5 Fernand Braudel, *A History of Civilizations* (Penguin, 1995), p. 412.

6 NA, PRO, T 234/203, 'Initiative in Europe (Plan G), Correspondence and General Papers', Prime Minister's Personal Minute, no. M 210/58, Macmillan to Lloyd and Amory, 24 June 1958.

7 Ibid.

8 Alistair Horne, *Macmillan, 1957–1986* (Macmillan, 1989), p. 148.

9 Peter Catterall (ed.), *The Macmillan Diaries: Prime Minister and After, 1957–1966* (Macmillan, forthcoming), entry for 26 July 1959.

10 Peter Hennessy, *The Prime Minister: The Office and Its Holders since 1945* (Allen Lane, 2000), p. 251.

11 NA, PRO, CAB 129/100, C (60) 35, 'Future Policy Study, 1960–70'. Note by the Prime Minister, 29 February 1960.

12 NA, PRO, FO 371/143702, 'UK Study on Future Planning Policy 1960–1970', Brook to Dean, 29 May 1959.

13 Ibid.

14 Private information.

15 Macmillan diaries (unpublished), Western Manuscripts Department, Bodleian Library, University of Oxford, entry for 7 June 1959.

16 NA, PRO, FO 371/143702, Prime Minister's Personal Minute, M.202/59, Macmillan to Lloyd, 10 June 1959.

17 Ibid., Dean to Gore-Booth and others, 23 June 1959.

18 Ibid.

19 NA, PRO, CAB 134/1929, 'Study of Future Policy. Record of a Meeting held at Chequers on 7 June 1959'.

20 Letter from Don Cook to the author, 18 February 1991. Don Cook, 'Macmillan Confronted by European Questions: Entry into Economic Community Seems to be Civil Servants' Goal', *New York Herald Tribune*, 5 July 1960.

21 NA, PRO, CAB 134/1929, 'Study of Future Policy. Record of a Meeting held at Chequers on 7 June 1959', Annex A.

22 Ibid.

23 Ibid.

24 Ibid.

25 NA, PRO, CAB 134/1934, FP (B) (59) 11, 'Study of Future Policy for 1960–70 Working Group. Economic Strength', 20 July 1959.

26 NA, PRO, CAB 134/1929, 'Study of Future Policy. Record of a Meeting held at Chequers on 7 June 1959'.

27 Ibid.

28 Ibid.

29 Gerard De Groot, *The Bomb: A Life* (Cape, 2004), p. 235.

30 Alistair Horne, *Macmillan, 1957–1986* (Macmillan, 1989), p. 36.

31 Catterall, *The Macmillan Diaries: Prime Minister and After, 1957–1966*, entry for 24 October 1957.

32 Lorna Arnold, *Britain and the H-Bomb*, (Palgrave, 2001), p. 145.

33 Horne, *Macmillan, 1957–1986* p. 45; *Britain's Cold War Super Weapons*, Blakeway Productions/Channel 4 Television, 24 April 2005.

34 Arnold, *Britain and the H-Bomb*, p. 147.

35 Ibid., pp. 159–62.

36 Lorna Arnold, *Windscale 1957: Anatomy of a Nuclear Accident* (St Martin's Press, 1992), pp. 47–50.

37 Ibid., p. 48.

38 Conversation with Lord Plowden.

39 Arnold, *Windscale 1957*, p. 52.

40 Ibid., p. 63.

41 Ibid., p. 79.

42 Ibid., pp. 80–81.

43 Ibid., pp. 81–2.

44 Catterall, *The Macmillan Diaries: Prime Minister and After, 1957–1966*, entry for 30 October 1957.

45 *Accident at Windscale No. 1 Pile on 10 October 1957*, Cmnd. 302 (HMSO, November 1957); Arnold, *Windscale 1957*, pp. 85–6.

46 Arnold, *Britain and the H-Bomb*, p. 201.

47 Ibid., pp. 201–10.

48 As reported to me by Victor Macklen, a member of the UK delegation to the Washington talks in August 1958. Peter Hennessy, *Muddling Through: Power, Politics and the Quality of Government in Postwar Britain* (Gollancz, 1996), p. 108.

49 Arnold, *Britain and the H-Bomb*, p. 209; *Britain's Cold War Super Weapons*.

50 Arnold, *Britain and the H-Bomb*, pp. 209, 214–15.

51 Hennessy, *Muddling Through*, p. 109.

52 NA, PRO, CAB 134/1936, 'United Kingdom Deterrent Policy in 1970', Foreign Office paper circulated to the 'Study of Future Policy for 1960/1970 Working Group' on 7 November 1959.

53 Ibid.

54 NA, PRO, CAB 134/1930, FP (A) (59), 7th Meeting, 4 December 1959.

55 Conversation with Sir Peter Ramsbotham, 28 June 2005.

56 NA, PRO, CAB 134/1930, FP (A) (59), 7th Meeting, 4 December 1959.

57 Ibid.

58 NA, PRO, CAB 129/100 C (60) 35.

59 Ibid.

60 NA, PRO, CAB 129/100, FP (60) 1, 24 February 1960, 'Future Policy Study 1960–70'.

61 Ibid.

62 Ibid.

63 Ibid.

64 Ibid.

65 Ibid.

66 Conversation with Sir Peter Ramsbotham, 28 June 2005.

67 NA, PRO, CAB 129/100, FP (60) 1.

68 Ibid.

69 Ibid. For Britain's fledgling motorway network see Sir Peter Baldwin and Robert Baldwin (eds.), *The Motorway Achievement* (Thomas Telford Publications, 2004), pp. 146–9.

70 NA, PRO, CAB 129/100, FP (60) 1.

71 Both Sir Peter Ramsbotham and my Queen Mary colleague Dr James Ellison made this point during our conversation on 28 June 2005 and I am grateful to them.

72 NA, PRO, CAB 129/100, FP (60) 1.

73 NA, PRO, FO 371/152131, 'Future UK Foreign Policy', Hailsham to Macmillan, 19 February 1960.

74 Ibid., 'Future Policy Study – Economic Growth', attached to Heathcoat Amory to Macmillan, 24 February 1960.

75 Ibid., Hailsham to Macmillan, 26 February 1960.

76 'Jack Kilby', *The Times*, 23 June 2005.

77 NA, PRO, FO 371/152133, 'Future UK Foreign Policy', 'Future Policy Study, 1960–70', Dean to Lloyd, 15 March 1960.

78 NA, PRO, CAB 134/1929, FP (60), 1st Meeting. I am grateful to my former student Nahdia Khan, for first discovering this minute.

79 Michael Carver, *Out of Step: The Memoirs of Field Marshal Lord Carver* (Hutchinson, 1989), pp. 288–9.

80 Letter from Lord Carver to the author, 6 March 1991.

81 Letter from Lord Carver to the author, 16 January 1991.

82 Michael Carver, *Tightrope Walking: British Defence Policy since 1945* (Hutchinson, 1992), pp. 63–4.

83 NA, PRO, CAB 134/1929, FP (60), 1st Meeting.

84 Ibid.

85 Raymond Aron, 'The Dawn of Universal History', reproduced in Yair Reiner (ed.), *Raymond Aron: The Dawn of Universal History. Selected Essays from a Witness of the Twentieth Century* (Basic Books, 2002), p. 480.

86 Ibid., p. 486.

87 NA, PRO, CAB 134/1929, FP (60), 1st Meeting.

88 Ibid.

89 Ibid.

90 Ibid.

91 Ibid.

92 Jeremy Isaacs and Taylor Downing, *Cold War* (Bantam, 1998), pp. 165–72.

93 Macmillan diaries (unpublished), Western Manuscripts Department, Bodleian Library, University of Oxford, entry for 25 June 1961.

94 NA, PRO, CAB 134/940, HDC (55) 7 (Revise), 'Home Defence Committee. Submission to Ministers on the Machinery of Government in War', 6 July 1955; ibid., HDC (MG) (55) 8, 'Home Defence Committee. Working Party on Machinery of Government in War', 'Machinery of Government in War. Note by the Secretary', 15 September 1955.

95 NA, PRO, CAB 134/1616, GEN 684, 1st Meeting; for the Strath Report see CAB 134/940, HDC (55) 3, 'The Defence Implications of a Fall-Out from a Hydrogen Bomb: Report by a Group of Officials', 8 March 1955.

96 Peter Hennessy, *The Secret State: Whitehall and the Cold War* (Penguin, 2003), pp. 186–205.

97 NA, PRO, CAB 134/1616, GEN 684, 'Machinery of Government in War', 1st Meeting, 5 June 1959.

98 NA, PRO, HO 322/206, 'War Planning', note by A. J. F. Brennan and D. J. Trevelyan, 16 November 1956. I am grateful to Matthew Grant for drawing this to my attention.

99 NA, PRO, CAB 134/1616, GEN 684, 1st Meeting; DH (o) (MG) (59) 8, 'Home Defence Committee Sub-committee on Machinery of Government in War', 'STOCKWELL: Report to the Prime Minister', 14 May 1959.

100 NA, PRO, CAB 134/1616, GEN 684, 1st Meeting.

101 NA, PRO, CAB 134/1618, DH (o) (MG) (60) 17, 'Stockwell: Dissemination of Cover Story. Note by the Secretaries. Annex', 30 May 1960.

102 John Coles, *Making Foreign Policy: A Certain Idea of Britain* (John Murray, 2000), pp. 69–70.

103 Peter Hennessy, *The Hidden Wiring: Unearthing the British Constitution* (Gollancz, 1995), p. 165.

104 NA, PRO, CAB 129/100, C (60) 35, 29 February 1960: 'Future Policy Study, 1960–70. Note by the Prime Minister', 24 February 1960.

105 L. J. Butler, *Britain and Empire: Adjusting to a Post-Imperial World* (I. B. Tauris, 2002), p. 148.

106 Horne, *Macmillan 1957–1986*, pp. 174–6; NA, PRO, PREM 5/232, 'Ministerial Appointments. Ministry of Harold Macmillan (Conservative), Part 3', Macmillan to Lennox-Boyd, 23 June 1959.

107 Catterall, *The Macmillan Diaries: Prime Minister and After, 1957–1966*, entry for 4 June 1959.

108 Ibid.

109 *Report of the Nyasaland Commission of Inquiry*, Cmnd. 814 (HMSO, 1959).

110 Catterall, *The Macmillan Diaries: Prime Minister and After, 1957–1966*, entry for 24 July 1959.

111 Robert Shepherd, *Enoch Powell: A Biography* (Hutchinson, 1996), p. 195.

112 Ibid.

113 House of Commons Official Report, 27 July 1959, cols. 234–7; the speech is reproduced in Rex Collings (ed.), *Reflections of a Statesman: The Writings and Speeches of Enoch Powell* (Bellew, 1991), pp. 203–7; Powell's footnoted comment can be found in Shepherd, *Enoch Powell*, p. 197 (we interviewed him in the magnificent Victorian office of the Keeper of the Public Records in Chancery Lane).

114 Butler, *Britain and Empire*, p. 151.

115 Horne, *Macmillan, 1957–1986*, p. 185.

116 Catterall, *The Macmillan Diaries: Prime Minister and After, 1957–1966*, entry for 1 November 1959.

117 Horne, *Macmillan, 1957–1986*, p. 183.

118 Ibid.

119 Ibid., p. 184.

120 Robert Shepherd, *Iain Macleod* (Hutchinson, 1994), p. 199.

121 Butler, *Britain and Empire*, pp. 161–3; Horne, *Macmillan, 1957–1986*, pp. 208–11.

122 Anthony Sampson, *Macmillan: A Study in Ambiguity* (Allen Lane, 1967), pp. 184–5.

123 Ibid., p. 184.

124 Ibid., p. 181.

125 Horne, *Macmillan, 1957–1986*, p. 190.

126 Shepherd, *Iain Macleod*, p. 162.

127 Peregrine Worsthorne, *Tricks of Memory: An Autobiography* (Weidenfeld & Nicolson, 1993), p. 190.

128 Ibid.

129 Henry Fairlie, 'London Commentary: From Walpole to Macmillan', *Encounter*, February 1961, p. 60.

130 Horne, *Macmillan, 1957–1986*, p. 198.

131 Ibid., p. 195.

132 Sampson, *Macmillan*, p. 188.

133 Brian MacArthur (ed.), *The Penguin Book of Twentieth-Century Speeches* (Viking, 1992), pp. 288–93.

134 Anthony Sampson, *Anatomy of Britain* (Hodder, 1962), p. 202.

135 Horne, *Macmillan, 1957–1986*, p. 195.

136 Harold Evans, *Downing Street Diary: The Macmillan Years, 1957–1963* (Hodder, 1981), pp. 102–3.

137 See the photographs opposite page 152 in Harold Macmillan, *Pointing the Way, 1959–1961* (Macmillan, 1972).

138 MacArthur, *The Penguin Book of Twentieth-Century Speeches*, p. 289.

139 Ibid.

140 Sir David Hunt speaking on the WideVision/Channel 4 Television series *What Has Become of Us?*, programme 4, 'Having It So Good', first broadcast 18 December 1994.

141 Horne, *Macmillan, 1957–1986*, pp. 194–5.

142 MacArthur, *The Penguin Book of Twentieth-Century Speeches*, p. 290.

143 Ibid.

144 Brian Lapping, *End of Empire* (Granada/Channel 4, 1985), p. 484.

145 De Groot, *The Bomb: A Life*, p. 235.

146 Catterall, *The Macmillan Diaries: Prime Minister and After, 1957–1966*, entry for 14 February 1960.

147 Horne, *Macmillan, 1957–1986*, pp. 221–2.

148 Robert Colquhoun, *Raymond Aron*, vol. II: *The Sociologist in Society, 1955–1983* (Sage, 1986), p. 399.

149 Professor Julian Jackson speaking at the Institut Français in London on 18 June 2003 on the occasion of his *De Gaulle* (Haus) being launched.

150 NA, PRO, CAB 129/100 FP (60) 1.
151 NA, PRO, PREM 11/2985, 'UK Relations with Rest of Europe: Effect of EEC on Future Policy', 'Notes for the Prime Minister's Conversations with President de Gaulle on March 12 and 13, 1960', 29 February 1960.
152 NA, PRO, PREM 11/2998, 'Meeting between Prime Minister and President de Gaulle, Rambouillet, 12 and 13 March 1960'. The note is undated.
153 Ibid.
154 John Darwin, *Britain and Decolonisation: The Retreat from Empire in the Post-War World* (Macmillan, 1988), p. 251.
155 Ibid.
156 Ibid.
157 Macmillan diaries (unpublished), Western Manuscripts Department, Bodleian Library, University of Oxford, entry for 13 March 1960.
158 Ibid.
159 Ibid., entry for 12 March 1960.
160 Ibid., entry for 13 March 1960.
161 NA, PRO, PREM 11/2998, 'Points Discussed with General de Gaulle at Rambouillet on March 12 and 13, 1960'.
162 Ibid.
163 Catterall, *The Macmillan Diaries: Prime Minister and After, 1957–1966*, entry for 13 March 1960.
164 NA, PRO, PREM 11/2998, 'Points Discussed with General de Gaulle at Rambouillet on March 12 and 13, 1960'.
165 Ibid.
166 Catterall, *The Macmillan Diaries: Prime Minister and After, 1957–1966*, entry for 10 March 1959.
167 NA, PRO, PREM 11/2998, 'Points Discussed with General de Gaulle at Rambouillet on March 12 and 13, 1960'.
168 NA, PRO, PREM 11/3510, 'Letters from Prime Minister to HM the Queen, 1960 and 1961', Macmillan to the Queen, 14 March 1960.
169 Horne, *Macmillan, 1957–1986*, p. 223.
170 Ibid.
171 Jean Lacouture, *De Gaulle: The Ruler, 1947–1970* (Collins Harvill, 1991), p. 352.
172 Macmillan diaries (unpublished), Western Manuscripts Department, Bodleian Library, University of Oxford, entry for 7 April 1960.
173 Ibid., entry for 5 April 1960.
174 Richard J. Aldrich, *The Hidden Hand: Britain, America and Cold War Secret Intelligence* (John Murray, 2001), p. 535.
175 Ibid.
176 Butler, *Britain and Empire*, p. 137.
177 Catterall, *The Macmillan Diaries: Prime Minister and After, 1957–1966*, entry for 7 May 1960.
178 Horne, *Macmillan, 1957–1986*, p. 228.
179 Ibid., p. 229.
180 Catterall, *The Macmillan Diaries: Prime Minister and After, 1957–1966*, entry for 19 May 1960.
181 NA, PRO, PREM 11/3510, Macmillan to the Queen, 19 May 1960.
182 Macmillan diaries (unpublished), Western Manuscripts Department, Bodleian Library, University of Oxford, entry for 20 May 1960.
183 Catterall, *The Macmillan Diaries: Prime Minister and After, 1957–1966*, entry for 21 Mary 1960.
184 Raymond Aron, *The Opium of the Intellectuals*, originally published in Paris in 1955 and in English translation by Secker and Warburg in 1957, p. 222.

185 Horne, *Macmillan, 1957–1986*, p. 231.

186 Michael Charlton, *The Price of Victory* (BBC Books, 1983), p. 237.

187 Ibid.

188 NA, PRO, CAB 129/102, Part 1, C (60) 107, 6 July 1960, 'The Six and the Seven: The Long-Term Objective. Covering Note to the Answers to the Prime Minister's List of Questions'.

189 Alan S. Milward, *The United Kingdom and the European Community*, vol. 1: *The Rise and Fall of a National Strategy, 1945–1963* (Frank Cass, 2002), p. 316.

190 Raymond Aron, *Memoirs: Fifty Years of Political Reflection* (Holmes and Meier, 1990), p. 288.

191 Lord Patten characterized it thus at Peter and Avril Riddell's wedding anniversary party on 9 May 2004 and gave me permission to quote it as he prepared to deliver the annual Ditchley Foundation Lecture on 8 July 2005 as I wished to cite it in my vote of thanks.

192 Though the phrase is widely attributed to Mitterrand, I have been unable to locate a definitive source.

193 *The Times*, 6 October 1999.

194 Conversation with Lord Roll of Ipsden, 3 January 1991.

195 NA, PRO, CAB 129/102, Part I, C (60) 107, 'The Six and the Seven: The Long-Term Objective', 6 July 1960.

196 Ibid., 'Annex G'.

197 NA, PRO, CAB 134/1853, ES (E) (60) 14, 'The Six and the Seven: The Long-Term Objective – Draft Covering Note to the Prime Minister's Questions. Note by the Secretaries', 27 June 1960.

198 NA, PRO, CAB 129/102, Part I, C (60) 107.

199 Ibid.

200 Ibid.

201 Ibid.

202 NA, PRO, CAB 134/1853, ES (E) (60) 14.

203 NA, PRO, CAB 128/34, CC (60), 41st Conclusions, 13 July 1960.

204 James R. V. Ellison, 'Accepting the Inevitable: Britain and European Integration', in Wolfram Kaiser and Gillian Staerck (eds.), *British Foreign Policy, 1955–64* (Macmillan, 2000), p. 181.

205 NA, PRO, CAB 128/34, CC (60) 41st Conclusions.

206 Ibid.

207 Conversation with Lord Roll of Ipsden, 3 January 1991.

208 Letter from Don Cook to the author, 18 February 1991.

209 Don Cook, 'Macmillan Confronted by European Questions. Entry into Economic Community Seems to be Civil Servants' Goal', *New York Herald Tribune*, 5 July 1960. For the footnote: conversation with Sir Peter Ramsbotham, 28 June 2005 and NA, PRO, FO 371/152133, Ramsbotham to Dean, 7 July 1960.

210 Macmillan, *Pointing the Way*, p. 316.

211 Catterall, *The Macmillan Diaries: Prime Minister and After, 1957–1966*, entry for 9 July 1960.

212 Hennessy, *Muddling Through*, p. 202.

213 E. P. Thompson, *The Making of the English Working Class* (Vintage, 1966), p. 12.

214 Andrew Roberts, *Salisbury, Victorian Titan* (Weidenfeld & Nicolson, 1999), p. 63.

215 In a speech in Wolverhampton on 23 November 1918. Antony Jay (ed.), *Oxford Dictionary of Political Quotations* (Oxford University Press, 2006), p. 239.

216 The term is taken from the title of a work by economist Jean Fourastié: *Les trente glorieuses: ou La Révolution invisible de 1946 à 1975* (Fayard, 1979).

217 Jean Lacouture, *De Gaulle: The Ruler*, p. 352.

Index